THE DROPANCHOR CHRONICLE:
A SAT VOCABULARY NOVEL

by Stephen D. Ring

"The Dropanchor Chronicle: a SAT Vocabulary Novel," by Stephen D. Ring. ISBN 1-58939-627-8.

Published 2004 by Virtualbookworm.com Publishing Inc., P.O. Box 9949, College Station, TX 77842, US. © 2004, Stephen D. Ring. All rights reserved. No part of this publication may be reproduced, stored in a retrieval system, or transmitted in any form or by any means, electronic, mechanical, recording or otherwise, without the prior written permission of Stephen D. Ring.

Manufactured in the United States of America.

TABLE OF CONTENTS

INTRODUCTION

The new SAT adds an essay—the author being you—and in this way it invites you to show the vocabulary skills of a writer and not just of a reader. There is a difference. In many cases a reader is adequately equipped in the vocabulary department if he grasps the general meaning of a word, if he knows that "fallow"—in general—means "not in use," that "taciturn"—in general—means "keeping quiet." A writer, though, needs to know her words in more detail, in order to use them pointedly, and to avoid unintentionally comic lines, such as "Stupid laundry room—never a fallow washer!" or "The teacher gave us five seconds to be taciturn."

Does all this mean by any chance that *The Dropanchor Chronicle* is your book? Could be. It's a word book, a story with definitions, and the definitions get taken pretty seriously. Many of them are fairly detailed and explanatory, trying to catch the special twist of a word, so that you are ready to use it with confidence, if the need arises, when you write your SAT essay. And ready as well when eventually you take up the writing challenges that come with college and career.

Where does this leave you, though, as a reader? Sitting pretty, to tell the truth. If you gain a writer's mastery of the words defined in *Dropanchor*, you have certainly gained a reader's mastery of them also, and you are prepared to meet them with assurance when they show up on the SAT or in any other reading you pursue.

One last point. *Dropanchor* defines a lot of words—1,491, give or take a couple. The universe of challenging words, though, is of course considerably bigger than that. Again, *Dropanchor* as a general rule defines only one meaning for a word, the meaning that is operative in the story. Yet it goes without saying that some words carry two meanings or more, often stubbornly distinct from one another. All those additional meanings and additional words are out there, and nothing says they can't find their way onto the SAT. Thus—read widely, as time permits. Stay friends with your dictionary. Circle back through your material, since repetition is the mother of learning. And good luck.

ACKNOWLEDGEMENT

To all of you who furnished encouragement—thank you.

ABOUT THE AUTHOR

Stephen D. Ring is a retired attorney living in Houston. Exactly how he became a vocabulary guy is unclear, but some of the credit belongs to the many years of turning out legal prose, and some to the enduring influence of the Latin, Greek and philosophy that he studied—and liked—in his university days.

Chapter 1: THE LAST OF THE UNCONVENTIONALS

There are better things to hate than the number seventeen. Too bad, thought Ricky, that's what I hate. He was sitting at a long desk, alone in his attic room. There was just one window and, though he scarcely noticed, the pane was growing crimson with light.

> **luminous:** giving off light, whether a reflected light or a light originating from within
> **embark:** to set out, as upon a journey, career, etc.
> **insipid:** flat, uninspired and without taste; not having enough freshness or appeal to capture your interest

It was an evening in early September, and the sun was slipping toward the sea. In its blaze everything was **luminous**, all the scene that lay beyond the window—the winding streets of Dropanchor, the wooden docks, the capes which north and south enclosed the little town. The capes especially—by some magic the streaming light relieved them of their mass, and they were, at that hour, ships **embarking**.

"Sorry to ignore the beauty," Ricky murmured to no one in particular, "but frankly, the sunsets are **insipid**. And those floating capes—well, sorry for the second time, but there's no enchantment, not for me. How can I get excited about such things when I ... I test positive for seventeen?"

Seventeen was his age. "What a dumb age," he muttered. "Awkward and threadbare. And way less than twenty-seven—huh, Sallie—insanely beautiful twenty-seven-year-old Sallie."

> **accessories:** little items of clothing and other personal gear which, though not absolutely essential, do serve to leave you completely and stylishly prepared for some activity
> **unconventional:** departing from the ordinary, established way of thinking or acting
> **dearth:** a shortage in supply, often severe enough to leave people worried

He switched on a small TV. An image formed, although scarcely the image of a Sallie, insanely beautiful or otherwise. A stout man was on the screen, squeezed behind the wheel of a Jeep. He wore a wide hat and a handsome cape, and he had the air of one who likes his work. "I'm risking my neck," he boomed, "and my fancy **accessories**"—he beckoned to the hat and cape—"in the high Rockies, on the road to Nameless, Colorado. This is Uncle Reggie. You're watching *The Last of the Unconventionals*. Beside me is my niece, Sallie Driven. Twenty-seven years old, and she's already met more of the nation's weirdos than you or I ever will."

A tart voice interrupted: "Uncle Reggie, are you looking for a problem?" The camera turned from the driver to the passenger, a slender young woman, delicate of features, but with a glint in the dark eyes and a stubborn set in the chin. "The persons on my show are not weirdos. Call them **unconventional**— that's the better term. They do things differently—eating dessert first, throwing lentils at weddings. They have six seasons, they build houses without front doors, they charge a fine if you return your books too soon. Not many of them are left. I would say there's a **dearth**. They are a critical resource, and we're running short. The few who remain we call the Last of the Unconventionals. But we don't call them weirdos."

> **enthrall**: to hold in a state of almost hypnotized fascination
> **majority**: the age at which you are granted the full rights of an adult
> **censure** (noun): a judgment that you have done wrong, usually delivered in a sharp tone and often by someone in authority

Ricky was **enthralled**. His words had a hollow, vanishing quality as he said, "Whatever you say to call 'em, it's OK with me." His pulse had fallen well below normal, and his breathing was growing slower and slower as Sallie arrived in Nameless, Colorado.

Nameless was one of those mountain towns where the highway becomes the main street, and most of the stores and restaurants are lined along the sides of it. While the Jeep went cruising slowly through this corridor, Sallie looked over to her uncle. "You know when to stop, right?"

"When we see the word Waffles on the big neon sign."

"Uncle! You go from bad to worse. You ..." Her attention was distracted by the sight of a woman pushing a stroller. "There! Look! You almost drove right by."

The Jeep stopped and Sallie greeted the woman. "Ma'am, good evening. I'm Sallie Driven, from *The Last of the Unconventionals*. Please, what are the names of those beautiful, slobbering baby boys in the stroller?"

In the attic room Ricky murmured, "Ricky and Ricky."

The woman smiled. "The little twins are called Primo and Segundo. But those aren't permanent. Here in Nameless we don't name the babies once and for all. When they reach **majority** they choose their own names. I suppose we're ... what's the word?"

Uncle Reggie muttered a word, but not quietly enough to escape **censure**. Sallie blazed, "Stop right now, dear Uncle—the humor is out of place. 'Wacko'

2

is not the word she's looking for. It's 'unconventional.' She is the Last of the Unconventionals."

As Sallie spoke with the mother and twins, Reggie began getting ready for something. He spread his cape over the hood of the Jeep and on top of it he placed a telephone and a strange object with a long tail. It was a ceramic lizard, battery-operated. It had light-bulb eyes, and one of them was shining red at the moment.

> **timorous**: frightened and anxious, even about little challenges and problems
> **dally**: to let time slip by while you amuse yourself or chat idly

Seeing this, Ricky also made some quick preparations. He stooped and unplugged a cord from the wall. Then, returning to his chair, he pulled an old speaker phone close to him, and waited. A weak smile crossed his face as he said to himself, "How to tell the **timorous** lover—he unplugs the phone and then calls his beloved."

Sallie said good-by to the slobbering twins and their mother. As she came over to the Jeep she was checking her watch and frowning. "We're running out of time, Uncle, and it must be your fault somehow. So don't **dally**. Give the instructions quickly."

> **pandemonium**: the wild, noisy confusion of a crowd that has gone out of control
> **dexterity**: (1) a quickness and skillfulness in moving the hands through the motions required by some complicated task; (2) more generally, a quick and expert skillfulness in carrying through some task
> **colleague**: a companion in a profession or line of work

Reggie tugged at his hat. "You know the rules, America. When the lizard shows a green eye our phone line is open. Then it's nationwide **pandemonium** as millions of viewers shout and scream and try to be the first to dial our special thirty-seven-digit number. **Dexterity** is your only hope: skillful hands and nimble fingers dancing on the telephone keys. The person who dials first tonight talks to Sallie. Tell her about your oddball neighbors, your weirdo **colleagues** down at the office. Anyway, phone. Maybe we'll come see you."

> **poignant:** touching your feelings deeply
> **concert:** the deliberate coordination of actions to achieve some unified effect
> **entreat:** to beg very seriously for some favor

"Dexterity we have," said Ricky to himself, wriggling his fingers. "Supreme self-confidence—that we're short on." With a sigh he looked toward the fish tank at the far end of his table. "That's where I belong, with the rest of the guppies. But I'm out here, an imitation boy destined to love a real girl. A **poignant** story, actually, a touching piece of drama. Whoops, we're on!"

In Nameless, Colorado Uncle Reggie threw a switch. The red eye of the ceramic lizard went out, and its green one was suddenly lit. Ricky's fingers came alive, falling in a swift precision upon the keys of his speaker phone. Wrist and forearm worked in **concert** with the marching fingers. In a matter of seconds the thirty-seven digits were tapped in, and Ricky leaned back.

"You are good," he said to himself, "the fastest in the land. And how do we know who's second fastest? That's who will talk to Sallie tonight."

Abruptly, a female voice interrupted his reflections. His eyes widened, and a sweat began breaking out across his forehead. In a moment, though, the tension dissolved, as someone small and familiar came pushing in through his open door. It was Rachel, his seven-year-old sister, with her spelling cards. She asked him again, "Which one do you want me to spell—'love' or 'stupid'? Those are the choices."

He groaned. "Spell 'dexterity,' completely useless dexterity."

Suddenly, her little mouth dropped open. "What's that?"

"Rachel," he **entreated**, "I beg you—just let me be."

The plea bounced off her without effect. "They need their bubbly things!" Her tone was growing urgent. Without warning she dodged around him and ran to the fish tank. "They need their bubblies or they'll die!"

> **implausibility**: some claim or explanation that is so inconsistent with known facts and accepted understandings that you are not able to believe it
> **rife**: having lots of something; characterized by an uncontrolled abundance or overabundance of something

Ricky gulped. The tank was dark, and nothing was emerging from the air hose. He looked with horror to the side of his room, to the baseboard and the outlets. "Oh no, I unplugged the tank and not ..."

Someone was saying Hello in a calm, musical voice, a beautiful voice. It came from his speaker phone. "Hello, this is Sallie Driven. Is anyone there?"

AUTHOR: Well, we're launched. Great first chapter.

READER: Great, if you like **implausibilities**. It's **rife** with them—every other line.

AUTHOR: That's the nature of fiction. Still—an example, perhaps.

READER: That thirty-seven-digit phone number. The phone company would never ... I mean, it'll never happen.

AUTHOR: You realize, of course, that with everybody getting their own phone these days—even second-graders—thirty-seven digits may not be enough.

READER: You realize, of course, that with just sixteen digits—not much longer than what we have now—we could generate about a quadrillion phone numbers.

AUTHOR: Are you aware how many second-graders there are? We have to stuff 'em in T-shacks. And in a short time each one of them will grow up and have more second-graders. It's geometric.

READER: Can we please go on to the next chapter?

Chapter 2: IDIOSYNCRATIC CITY

Ricky stared in **consternation** at the phone. "This is absolutely not happening," he groaned.

But it was. Again the beautiful sound came from the speaker: "Hello, is anyone there?"

He staggered to his feet—why he couldn't have told you—and clutched the receiver. "Hello, how are you, Sallie?" His words came in a gasp, and he felt Rachel jump as they played back instantly from the television.

> **consternation**: a condition of being so dismayed and upset that you have trouble thinking or taking a decision
> **diffidence**: a shy, hesitating manner which results from a low opinion of yourself and your capabilities
> **cryptic**: mysterious and difficult to make any sense of; expressed in riddles

On the screen Sallie's perplexity was apparent. "All is well here in the Rockies. But whatever is happening at your end?"

Ricky choked out one word. "**Diffidence**."

A moment went by as Sallie thought. "Diffidence. You mean like feeling shy, personal net worth zero, that sort of thing?"

"Yormp. Sorry. Yes. Over soon."

"Mr. Yormp," said Sallie, "less **cryptic**, if you please. Less mystery. What's over soon? My program?"

"Normp," blurted Ricky. "Not the program. The diffidence, my ... It's over soon."

"Oh dear. Just relax, Mr. Yormp. I think you're somewhere between diffidence and anxiety attack. Start by telling me where you are calling from."

> **obtuse**: dull of mind and perception; slow to comprehend things
> **ostracize**: to force someone to leave your group or social circle and remain outside it, enjoying no further interaction with it
> **disparage**: to talk about, or otherwise react to, something in a way suggesting that it is of low status or inferior worth

Ricky labored. "That's a geography question. And I am such a blockhead at geography, seriously **obtuse**. Remember those lines that somebody drew, Marco Polo I think, like around the Earth—latitude, longitude, that sort of thing. Well, I can never keep 'em straight. And then trying to spell 'tsunami' and ... Oh well, it should be over soon—the diffidence, I mean."

6

Sallie tried again. "Here's an easy one, home-run material. Are you with some of your friends?"

"With friends, ma'am? Nice try. People generally like me until they meet me, and then—well, they circle the wagons and put up the No Admittance signs. I'm turned out, ma'am, and **ostracized**. There's something about my style."

Sallie scolded, "You need to join the Mr. Yormp fan club, and stop being so **disparaging** about yourself. Where did you get such a negative image?"

"It's diffidence," murmured Ricky, "or the little anxiety thing. Mercifully, whatever it is, it passes, and my true, moderately warped personality emerges. In fact ..."

His voice was swiftly transforming itself, growing deeper, calmer. "In fact—whew! It's happening. Yeah—feeling better about myself. Open to questions. Maybe you'd like to ask me why I'm calling."

> **brashness**: an assertive, high-energy style that pushes forward without worry about offending others
> **grandiose**: done on a very large scale, often with elements of exaggeration and show designed to impress some audience
> **composure**: the state of being calm, collected and in control of your words and actions

Now it was Sally who faltered for a moment. "Well ... well, why are you calling?"

Brashness was assuming control in Ricky. "To learn your pleasure in weddings, ma'am: private, public; modest, **grandiose**. I'm flexible."

Proposals of marriage were an everyday affair for Sallie, but this one caught her unprepared. "My pleasure in weddings!"

"That's right, ma'am. And when may we expect you in Dropanchor? It's very unconventional, very ... shall we say ..."

The little pause gave Sallie, a veteran of many odd conversations, all that she needed—a moment to regain her **composure**. "I don't even know your first name, Mr. Yormp."

"You don't even know my last name." He hesitated. "I am ... yes, definitely ... I am Foster Farbugle. Ow!"

> **alias**: a fake name
> **skeptical**: tending to receive the statements of others with doubt, and sometimes with sharp questions as well
> **notwithstanding**: in spite of (often used to show that one thing has failed to prevent another thing; and sometimes placed after its object, as in "the game was played, bad weather notwithstanding")

There was a sharp stamp on his foot, which said clearly—Rachel was unhappy with the **alias**. A moment later, though, and the stamp was forgotten as Sallie delivered a sharper blow: "So, Foster, how old are you, and when did your folks get you a private line?"

All America heard Ricky draw in a long breath, before answering, "At least twenty-seven, ma'am, at the very least. Don't live with folks. No way."

A **skeptical** reply: "Foster, are we fudging?"

Sheer momentum carried him forward. "At least twenty-seven, ma'am, youthful voice **notwithstanding**."

Sallie let the subject drop. "Very well then. Can you tell me, Mr. Farbugle, is there anything unconventional about Dropanchor—besides an undue haste in matrimony—or any reason to do a show there?"

Ricky's face lit up. He looked out his window at the sweep of fire in the sky to the west. "Of all the unusual things which the sun saw today as it crossed the world, at least seventy-five percent were in Dropanchor. Listen. The most beautiful girl in town, not to mention the Milky Way Galaxy, is a high school sophomore named Merci. And she knows it. Rich besides. But she carries a pencil behind her ear, and reads books about welding. Her gift list, like for her birthday, included a cordless drill and a road grader."

Uncle Reggie adjusted his hat. "Somewhat weird, I must admit."

> **loquacity**: a tendency to talk on and on, beyond what is appropriate
> **unconventional**: departing from the ordinary, established way of thinking or acting
> **idiosyncratic**: unique to the thought or behavior of one individual person or community, often to the point of being viewed as peculiar and odd

Ricky went on. "When the town council has a meeting they hold it on the beach, at the line of low tide and the hour of low tide, to discourage **loquacity**. If the speakers ramble, the tide turns and before long everybody is squeezing out their socks. Another wild place is the public library. The fines are serious. The first day overdue is a penny, but each day after that is the double of the day before. The mayor forgot a book in his briefcase for a month one time and wound up owing over a million dollars."

Reggie looked to Sallie. "Real grabber of a show, at least for library freaks and math majors. Listen, Niece. We need to get beyond the merely **unconventional**. We need stranger stuff—people incorporating toasters into their hairdos, leaving fortunes to geckos, that sort of thing. It's time for the wildly **idiosyncratic**."

Ricky still had the solution. "Not a problem—this place is Idiosyncratic City—one-of-a-kind personalities expressing themselves through strange, gotta-be-me behavior. You could start with the Martians."

Sallie laughed. "You have Martians, Mr. Farbugle?"

"No, ma'am, we have the Farnum boys. They're twins, juniors in high school. They publish a catalog, over fifty items, complete with prices. And they are taking orders. But they don't know what they're selling. The catalog has no descriptions or photos, because the items come from Mars and the Farnums haven't found the Martian sales rep yet. They're convinced that he, she or it has landed, but they're still trying to make contact."

> **terrestrial**: having to do with the Earth (as opposed to other planets) or with dry land (as opposed to water)
> **tectonic**: relating to the crust of a planet and the forces which shape that crust
> **palpable**: readily perceived by the senses, especially the sense of touch

Uncle Reggie was gazing out toward the high ridge that lifted above Nameless. He looked distracted. "Maybe they have a Martian waffle maker. My **terrestrial** one sticks a lot, especially when I do that recipe with the ..."

Sallie broke in menacingly. "Uncle, if we could stay focused ..."

"To be sure," he said, returning to business. "Mr. Farbugle, I am not won over yet. The Farnums are weird, I admit, but they're juniors, and one expects a good bit of weirdness from juniors. How about older people, the so-called grown-ups? How are you fixed for odd grown-ups?"

Ricky knew where to start. "Principal Ironbane, now there's a strange one."

"May I assume this is the principal of the high school," asked Sallie innocently, "where you graduated ten years ago?"

"That's exactly it," said Ricky with a slight air of discomfort. "And anyway he has this thing about the **tectonic** plates—you know—in the earth's crust. He can feel them moving—not earthquakes, but all the time—inching along day and night. He gets this funny look and says, 'There! Another slip—tiny but quite **palpable**. We are another millimeter closer to Japan.' Mr. Ironbane is OK. But then there's also the not-so-nice lady who actually owns the high school, Ms. Framley."

"The idiosyncratic Ms. Framley, I suppose," said Sallie.

> **prerogative**: some particular privilege or right which you enjoy because of your status or rank
> **succumb**: to give in to some force, usually because the strength necessary for any further resistance to it has been lost

9

whimsy: something fanciful that you conceive when you give free play to your imagination and feelings

"Absolutely. She has a spoon hanging from her right ear—it's solid gold. She says it's the **prerogative** of royalty, to wear a gold spoon. And she uses the thing to take these awful looking vitamin syrups, at inappropriate times."

Uncle Reggie was beginning to **succumb**. "You are right, Mr. Farbugle, you have a lot of peculiar behavior out there, maybe enough to deserve the name Idiosyncratic City. But you're far, very far. Do you have any really big-time strange ducks, to make the long trip worthwhile?"

READER: There's this kid at school who can feel the tectonic plates also. Actually, it's my friend Larry and …

AUTHOR: I sort of tossed in that line about the plates as a bit of **whimsy**, not to be taken …

READER: No, no—it's real for Larry. And not just the plates either. You know how the Earth doesn't do a perfect circle around the sun, how it makes a slight ellipse, so now it's a little closer, now a little farther?

AUTHOR: Umm, why …?

READER: Well, Larry—he can feel when the Earth reaches the farthest point from the sun, when it swings through the tight part of the ellipse.

AUTHOR: There's no chance that he's the type who …?

READER: Oh no—he's not faking it. He can feel this crack-the-whip effect. His whole face distorts, like a jet pilot. You couldn't fake that.

AUTHOR: We really need to move on.

Chapter 3: THE MEGALOMANIAC BULLFROG

As Reggie and Sallie waited, Ricky made a series of little noises—*hrrrggmm* and the like—that showed he was thinking. The process ended abruptly with another stamp on the foot from Rachel. He had been slowly twisting a knot in her hair—unconsciously—and she wasn't grateful.

"On the topic of big-time strange ducks," he said at last into the phone, "we've got this guy who's so ... I mean ... so ... Like what did they put in his formula anyway?"

> **minute** (adjective): extremely small and insignificant; at the level of tiny details
> **megalomaniac**: a person obsessed with accomplishing things on a giant scale; a person who believes he is one of the great ones of the earth
> **ineffable**: beyond the power of words to express

"Facts if you don't mind, Mr. Farbugle," said Sallie in a clinical tone. "Obviously, we're not asking for the **minute** details. Brand of toothpaste, mother's maiden name—those you can spare us. But at least the basic biographical facts."

"Check, OK—facts. Well—he's in his late forties, whiny, and quite large—a doorblocker to be honest. He's got an acre of stomach, which he knows how to pull up into his chest to look grand and puffed out. He has big eyeballs, that never blink. And this wide, wide mouth that swings open like along the entire length of the jawbone."

"Sounds like a bullfrog," tossed in Reggie.

A smile crossed Sallie's face. "Sounds very much like you, dear Uncle."

Ricky protested, "No, no—any comparison between your uncle and our guy should be avoided. Your uncle isn't working to rename the world Planet Reggie."

"And your guy is?" asked Sallie with interest.

"I'll bet he is," Ricky answered. "He's that kind of **megalomaniac**. Planet Bamalford—he'd love it. That's his name—Bamalford, and he lives to see it in big letters. The largest structure in town is the exhibition hall—and it's called the Bamalford Dome. And our newspaper is *Bamalford's Beacon*, or something like that."

11

"So—the Megalomaniac Bullfrog," said Reggie. "Maybe. But look. What is the chance he's just a modest guy and these honors are being forced on him?"

"Normp!" returned Ricky, with a wild sweep of his arms that made Rachel feel trapped in a windmill. "Normp and normp. No one forced him to put a statue on top of the exhibition dome—a bronze statue of himself, forty feet tall, with an inscription that reads: P. Bamalford—Words Fail before the **Ineffable** Splendor. And no one called the newspaper *Bamalford's Beacon* against his will. He's the editor, and the owner—he named it. And it's the mouthpiece of his vanity. The page-one photo today was this shot of Bamalford the man gazing on Bamalford the statue, with great contentment."

"So he thinks he's something of a ... figure," ventured Sallie.

> **simile**: an imaginative or poetic comparison expressed directly through use of the word "as" or "like"
>
> **vacillate**: to swing back and forth between alternate choices without being able to decide on one or the other with finality

"To use the standard **simile** in such matters," said Ricky, "he is like the peacock with feathers fanned. We expect that any day he will do what the Roman emperors did and declare himself divine. It hasn't happened yet because he's still **vacillating** between being called Jupiter and being called Zeus. And that's just the ..."

Sallie cut him off, with a sudden note of concern in her voice. "Foster, do you suppose that your Mr. P. Bamalford ever watches my show? I shouldn't have let you get so ... descriptive."

Alarm flashed for a moment in Ricky's brown eyes, and then was gone. "No, ma'am. He watches his statue, he watches his mirror—those are his programs. So I wouldn't ..."

A tugging at his cuff interrupted him. It was Rachel, demanding his attention, whispering sharply, "I was just over there by your window, Ricky, and something's wrong ... like with the air."

> **idiosyncratic**: unique to the thought or behavior of one individual person or community, often to the point of being viewed as peculiar and odd
>
> **primordial**: having the raw force or stark simplicity that characterize a primitive situation
>
> **monogram** (verb): to mark your belongings with an identifying symbol, often the initials of your name

He whispered back, "Call me Foster. And what is wrong with the air?"

"It's got this noise, like killer bees."

Ricky apologized. "Excuse me, Sallie, Reggie, the American People, something **idiosyncratic** is starting to happen." At the window he heard what Rachel had heard, a harsh, repeated cry, ringing in the twilight air. It was human speech, though barely, for the words seemed to ride on something more **primordial** than language, a fierce stream of rage and frustration. Ricky strained to catch them, and wished he hadn't, for the voice was roaring over and over, "Foster Farbugle! Foster Farbugle!"

Letting out his breath slowly, he returned to the phone. "I'd better go. It's not easy to be Foster Farbugle these days, especially when you shoot your mouth off on national television. But I'll worry about that. All you need to worry about, Sallie, is to be here soon. And if you get any luggage **monogrammed**, don't forget the F."

> **effrontery**: speech or action that is in bold disregard of the courteous treatment that people expect
> **germane**: having something to do with the topic you're interested in at the moment; having a significant connection to some subject matter
> **ambulatory**: walking; accomplished while you are walking; having some connection to walking
> **queue** (verb): to form a line, waiting for your turn to do something (for example, to buy a ticket)

She widened her eyes and struggled not to smile. "Such **effrontery**!"

Reggie's looming figure advanced to the camera. "We've run out of time. So let me say, as I always say at this moment—Hang in there, America." The closing credits began drifting across the screen.

Rachel was tugging again at Ricky's cuff. "Where, Ricky? Hang in where?"

Ricky pushed his fingers through his hair. "Aargh! Mt. Rushmore, Old Faithful, I don't know. I need a walk."

Rachel took his hand. "But the killer bees. My teacher said never go outside when ..."

"Ricky," came a call from below, "Rachel, time for supper."

Ricky groaned. "Food? Now? It's just not **germane**."

READER: Fulano uses "vacillate" too, and he gives a great example—"Little Gabriella was vacillating between growing older or getting bigger, after her brother told her she could do one but not both."

AUTHOR: Exactly who is Fulano?

READER: Roland Fulano, of course, the author of a vocabulary book called *How to Become an **Ambulatory** Dictionary*.

AUTHOR: A walking dictionary! It sounds grotesque. Maybe this Fulano guy…
READER: Careful. He's the competition. People are **queuing** up to buy his book.
AUTHOR: Well, they're stampeding to buy mine!
READER: Touchy, touchy.

Chapter 4: A GRATUITOUS LESSON IN CRIMINAL LAW

Ricky ate supper that night in a trance. At the far edge of his consciousness the angry voice was still calling, "Foster Farbugle." It was cause for worry, he knew, but at the moment there was just no room for worry. His thoughts were filled with the image of Sallie and the smile she couldn't repress after his nonsense about the monogramming.

"I shall walk once more by the sea," he said dreamily when dessert was over.

Rachel knew a bad idea when she heard one. "You are not going, Ricky. That noise might still be out there."

He only smiled. "Then we'll just have to ... I don't know ... digitize it, commercialize it, anesthetize it—something along those lines."

> **bravado**: bold, exaggerated speech and gestures adopted to give the appearance of courage
> **protrude**: to stick out from something, sometimes in a conspicuous way

With this piece of **bravado**, he passed quickly out of the house and into the gathering dusk. The way was a short one, through the winding streets and down a low bluff by an earthen stair, down to the beach which ran from a harbor on the south to the high, blocky cape on the north. He noticed Rachel following him, a stubborn little shadow, but he did not mind.

The beach was complicated. The winter storms had thrown a maze of drift along it, a crisscross of massive logs, crowding back near the line of the bluff, beyond the usual surge of the tide. And where the tides did reach in their everyday course, there was a gallery of forms—stacks and benches and hollows—carved in the granite and basalt which **protruded** in great outcrops from the sand.

Ricky surveyed this landscape of stone and timber, pale under the half-moon emerging in the darkening sky. "Great bone yard and stone yard," he cried, "Sallie is coming! At least, she didn't say she wasn't, which means ... Anyway, if I can think it, she can do it."

> **femur**: the thighbone of a human being or other creature
> **mutation**: a change in the very nature of something
> **oblivious**: without any awareness of something; not paying any attention to something

15

With that he fell silent—it was enough just to be a walker in the coolness of that evening. Enough for a while anyway—he could not contain himself indefinitely. After some minutes he became once again the talker, the messenger, the bringer of good news. "And when she's here, my friends, everything will change. For the better. This huge log, if that's what it is and not a dinosaur **femur**, will become—who knows—snapdragons, a long, blooming row of them. And I—to take another example—I will also undergo a **mutation**, probably turning into a supernova, radiating a happiness so intense and sickening that no one will be able to stand me."

He felt a familiar yank on his sleeve. "Ricky, don't spin out. She didn't say she was coming. And besides she's way older."

There was sense in what Rachel said, but Ricky was **oblivious** to it. "I know what you mean, Rach. It's like she has a magic wand. Poof! Some magic here, some magic there. Maybe it'll be Poof Rachel! and in one instant you'll know how to spell 'love' and 'stupid' and the other fourteen million words in the English language."

That didn't do much for his little sister. "It's not like you thought it up," she scolded. "Half of my books have magic wands, turning stuff into other stuff. And they all say Poof!"

> **hackneyed**: overused to the point of being stale (often applied to phrases, slogans and other verbal expressions)
> **alleged**: asserted but not yet proved
> **specious**: capable of deceiving you because of having the appearance, but only the appearance, of something genuine, valuable, respected, etc.

Ricky put up no defense. "Guilty as charged—using **hackneyed** images. But that's just the point—with Sallie around everything that's worn out and stale will get a new life. I mean, take this ridiculously huge rock, for example."

Rachel had already scrambled onto the rock, a squarish expanse of granite near the low-tide line, only four or five feet high, but stretching seaward like a vast stage or platform. "Leave my rock alone," she warned. "It's just fine."

"No, no, no, Rach," he answered tolerantly. "It's not fine. It needs a crop of sunflowers, tall and waving in the breeze, confusing the sea gulls. And Sallie can handle that. She'll sprinkle on the star dust and ... Hey, very cold!"

A splash of salt water broke into his fancies. The tide was turning. He retreated toward the upper beach, shivering, but with no reduction in rpm's, telling every object in his path what it could expect from Sallie's magic. "Sad little clam shells, she will turn you into those orangish-red geraniums with reddish-orange overtones. And you, yes, the dumb looking kelp, unattractive in spite of your **alleged** nutritional value, her wand will go Splack! on your green little nubs and you will be transformed into—what's another flower?—daffodils! And you, sir, you will make a fine oleander or crepe myrtle, though certainly not a pansy."

There was another yank on his sleeve, a desperate one. "Ricky! Tune in! There's a man ..."

Rachel was right. There was a man, very near, barrel-chested, looming like a tree in the darkness. He stood for a moment, huge and silent, and then— "Halt!" The command was spoken with a lot of breath, and once it was spoken the great but **specious** chest dropped and became an equally great stomach.

"Mr. Bamalford," stammered Ricky.

"Yes, Peerless Bamalford, and not a pansy as you said just now. A tiger. A puma. An eagle—with a score to settle. Have you seen that slime-covered amoeba, Foster Farbugle?"

> **refractory**: reacting with a stiff-necked resistance to the attempts of people to guide or govern you
> **fetid**: having a smell that is rotten, stale or otherwise foul
> **callow**: noticeably young and unfinished; not yet possessing the emotional and judgmental maturity of a grown-up

Rachel was the first to find her tongue. "Haven't seen any slimy guys at all."

Bamalford pointed to Ricky. "What's his name?"

"He's my brother—big brother."

Bamalford let out a snort of impatience. "Don't be **refractory**, kid. Defy your parents, defy your teachers, but don't get stubborn with Bamalford. What's his name? I said."

Ricky was over the first shock now, and able to answer for himself. "Ricky Snoozer—sometimes known as big brother."

"Big mouthy brother, it sounds like," muttered Bamalford. "Well, let me show you something." With a look of disgust, and a trace—it almost seemed— of apprehension, he picked up a mass of seaweed from the sand. "This is Dropanchor. All tangled and twisted together—everybody knows everybody. And too long in the sun besides. Phew! **Fetid**."

He threw down the ripening clump. "Everybody knows everybody around here, Ricky Sicky. I think you know Foster. You're in high school, right. Well, I think Farbugle is too. He's no twenty-seven. He's got **callow** written all over him. Still wet behind the ears. But he'll be smarter after he's learned a lesson from me—no question!"

> **gratuitous**: (1) given without any demand for payment; (2) given, although not asked for, not wanted and not justified by the situation (as in "gratuitous advice")

recede: to pull back gradually from a point of farthest advance

Ricky started to object, but Bamalford, pulling a slip of paper from his coat pocket, cut him short. "Take this to Foster. A coupon, that's all. Good for a lesson in criminal law. Completely free. No charge. **Gratuitous**."

Something like a tank maneuver took place there in the darkness. The figure of Bamalford drew closer and then **receded**, and Ricky found the coupon in his hand, though he could scarcely say that he wanted it. And he found himself listening to a lecture about criminal law, although he scarcely wanted that either. Gratuitous says it all, he thought—unrequested and uncalled for.

> **misdemeanor**: a lesser crime, for which you usually won't be sentenced to prison
> **felony**: a more serious crime, usually within a justice system that draws a sharp distinction between a category consisting of more serious crimes and a category consisting of less serious crimes
> **slander** (verb): deliberately to damage a person's good name by making statements, generally false, that lay him open to scorn and contempt

"Every criminal code," Bamalford was proclaiming, "distinguishes **misdemeanors** from **felonies**. You jaywalk—that's a misdemeanor. The bad stuff, knocking off a bank, that's a felony. And one of the most vicious felonies in the eyes of the law is to **slander** an editor. If editors are held up to public contempt, nothing is sacred. Tell that to Foster."

> **peremptory**: arrogantly cutting short all questions and objections, often because of your supreme certainty of the correctness of your position
> **tirade**: a long, angry speech, often marked by shouting and the exaggerated statement of grievances and criticism

Ricky's attempt to break in was dismissed by a **peremptory** wave of Bamalford's hand. "Zip it, OK. There's nothing you can add to this conversation. Your only job is to listen. Now, the things I just taught you, they're only the beginning. You tell young Foster that a person convicted of slandering an editor can count on at least 260 years in the big house, with no chance of parole."

Bamalford's voice was rising to a shout. The huge jawbone was swinging open and shut, and the great eyes were popping and starting, as the lesson degenerated into a **tirade** against Foster Farbugle.

By the time it was over Foster stood arm in arm with the worst wretches of human history. And Bamalford was exhausted. He had to take a moment to catch his breath, and as he did so he seemed to be gazing steadily at something which lay to the south.

"I am gazing toward the south," he said in a solemn tone, as though civilizations rose and fell depending on which way he looked, "far to the south, toward Los Angeles, where my brother Fearless is a lawyer. It was he who taught me these truths which I have repackaged into a lesson for our sick, sick friend, Foster—a Gratuitous Lesson in Criminal Law. But enough. I shall go."

His huge figure began to retreat up the beach. After a few steps, though, he paused. The rumble of his voice reached out one last time to catch at Ricky and Rachel. "Look there—what a beautiful vision!"

> **eminence**: (1) generally, the condition of standing out from what is average or normal; (2) a point where the land pushes upward to form an isolated hill or rise
> **minatory**: threatening you with harm; having a menacing aspect

Lifting a heavy arm, he beckoned toward the cape at the northern end of the beach. It was a high ridge of moonlight and shadow, running out to a point where it swept up in one final **eminence** and then dropped in steps and terraces to the sea. On the upsweep stood the dome that Ricky had told Sallie about, and the dome in turn was the base of the enormous bronze statue of Bamalford himself.

Something was not right about the statue—that was what everyone thought. They said it was too commanding or too straight like a spike, too big or maybe just too there. And some of them—noting the vague air of menace that hung around it—said that it was rather too **minatory** for their taste.

> **vagabond**: one who drifts about from place to place, with no ties or responsibilities, commonly dependent on begging to get the necessities of life
> **inebriate** (noun): a person who gets drunk on a regular basis
> **exude**: to give off a softly flowing stream of some substance (such as a sweat, a vapor, a fragrance) or some quality (such as self-assurance or cheerfulness)
> **vernacular**: the everyday form of a language spoken by ordinary people, rather than a literary or academic form

Whatever the reason, something was not right about it, and yet when Bamalford said "What a beautiful vision," it was the statue he was referring to. "They have no excuse," he continued, "the young mothers of Dropanchor, if their children grow up to be **vagabonds** and **inebriates**. They could have brought the little gummers here, in full sight of the statue, and let them soak up its influence. It **exudes** virtue, it gives off an air of responsibility and self-control. Take this young imp, for example"—he was addressing Rachel now—"could you go off and wander like a tramp after coming under the influence of this statue? Could you turn into a drunk?"

19

Rachel made one of the internationally recognized throwing-up signs to show what she could do under the influence of the statue. Fortunately, Bamalford didn't notice—he was moving off again, losing shape and detail in the darkness until at last his great bulk was absorbed by the night airs.

Ricky suddenly felt a protective urge toward his sister—she had suffered a long exposure to the foul humor of the man, and hopefully no lasting harm had been done. He took her hand and they made their way back home.

––––––––––––––––––

AUTHOR: I assume you noticed there near the beginning how naturally I worked in the word "Splack."

READER: Yeah—why did you have to do that?

AUTHOR: It's part of the **vernacular**. It's the sort of everyday word used on the street. And a book that speaks English the way ordinary folks do—well, it earns big rewards at the cash register.

READER: Hold on—we can check sales right now. Just splack the keyboard a couple times and—OK, so far this book has sold twenty-seven copies.

AUTHOR: Twenty-seven copies! Obviously, there are a few zeros missing on that number. It's like saying the Earth is ninety-three miles from the sun.

READER: Nice try.

Chapter 5: THE SEISMOLOGIC BEAUTY

Ricky always dreamed of giants, laboring giants, building the huge mountain that towered to the north of Dropanchor. Tonight was no exception. During his heaviest sleep the great **titans** carved a stairway in a granite slope. Sallie was at the top. Ricky started to climb toward her, but each stairstep was as big as a house, and to his horror the number of them was increasing, until at last there were 260. He woke with the **disconcerting** realization that Bamalford's anger about Foster Farbugle could be serious. Two hundred and sixty years in the slammer—would Sallie wait that long? He was beginning to feel anxious.

> **titan**: a person who is giant in size, forcefulness or achievement
> **disconcerting**: troubling; throwing you off stride by making you anxious about something
> **immoderate**: observing no limits; doing something to excess
> **perverse**: set squarely in opposition to what is good and right
> **virtually**: (1) almost; (2) in possession of what it basically takes to be "X" and yet not officially able to bear the name "X" because some formal or technical requirement has not been met (for example, "He's virtually a doctor," as said of someone who has long experience in treating wounds and illnesses, but who lacks a medical degree)

His anxiety was increasing as he collected his books and began climbing the long hill to school. And it would have increased more rapidly if he had known that higher on that same hill, higher even than the ridge where the school sat, a large woman in her mid-fifties was smiling at the thought of Foster Farbugle serving time. The early sun glinted on her lips, red and waxy from the **immoderate** use of lipstick. Her wrists and ankles were heavy with jewelry, and a golden spoon dangled from one ear. She stood on the porch of a white marble house, almost a temple, which rose in a high clearing. She was Ms. Victoria Framley, and by a piece of **perverse** bad luck she—with her utter indifference to the value of a good education—was **virtually** the owner of the school where Ricky was heading.

> **epiphany**: the act of a god or goddess making himself or herself visible to human eyes; more generally, the emergence of a truth or meaning so dramatically that all at once you behold and comprehend it
> **flair**: an instinctive appreciation for something; a natural talent for spotting, creatively using or promoting something

21

evanescent: having only a fragile hold on existence; vanishing away like smoke

Some thirty-five or forty years earlier, as a teenage girl, she had possessed a momentary beauty. It drew compliments, and one of them was especially extravagant. She had been coming down from the marble house when she was spied through the binoculars of a Greek sailor, who exclaimed in very good English, "An **epiphany**! A goddess! It is young Athena, descending from Olympus, appearing among us." She never met the man, but she learned of his compliment and remarked that Greek sailors have a **flair** for picking superior binoculars.

Some years passed, very few really, but they were enough to show how **evanescent** Ms. Framley's beauty was. Long before she reached thirty the bloom was gone. That was evident to everyone—except to her, for the sailor's compliment had become one of the organizing themes of her life, and she clung to it blindly.

> **acquiesce**: to remain silent and raise no objection, and in this manner to let some proposed activity go forward or some statement stand as correct
>
> **meddle**: to stick your nose into matters which are (or which are said to be) none of your business
>
> **tantamount**: fundamentally the same as something else in meaning or impact, although differing in form

Then after many more years Bamalford arrived in Dropanchor and became editor of the town paper. He saw Victoria Framley, now in her early fifties, a tyrant at Dropanchor High School, often pulling an old document from her handbag, waving it about, and threatening to rip it up if people didn't **acquiesce** in her demands. And most people did—swallowing their objections and holding their silence, while she had her way.

Bamalford learned that what Ms. Framley took from her purse on those occasions was a one-hundred-and-ninety-nine-year lease. It was from her historic ancestor, Abner, to the mayor of Dropanchor. It covered 4.6 acres on a ridge above town, and by its terms the mayor and his successors could use that land as the site for a high school.

The lease was a strange document, rambling and oppressive, giving Abner—and Ms. Framley as his heir—extensive rights to **meddle** in the affairs of the school. Bamalford saw clearly that the lease meant power. It gave Ms. Framley the whip hand. It let her say without exaggeration that her ownership of the land where the school sat was **tantamount** to owning the school itself— that was how she gloated each time teachers and principals had to bow to her wishes.

opportunistic: seizing full advantage of the opportunities that present themselves, even at the expense of honesty, loyalty or morality
denizen: one of the people who live in a place or region
seismologic: having to do with earthquakes and the study of earthquakes

Something about the woman—the constancy of her foul humor, the ruin of her beauty, perhaps her petty tyranny over the high school—something about her awoke Bamalford's interest. He decided to take up where the Greek sailor left off.

When an old photo came into his hands, showing Victoria Framley at age nineteen, beautiful and pouting on the porch of the marble house, he saw his chance. By this time the newspaper was his, to use as he pleased, so he published the photo, **opportunistically** labeling it a "recent likeness." In the article he wrote to go with the photo, he called Ms. Framley a **denizen** of Mount Olympus—for where else should one so fair live except with the classical gods and goddesses? That was weird enough, but he went on to ask—if Jove scorches the earth with his lightning bolts, doesn't she shake it with her beauty? "For she has," the article concluded, "a **Seismologic** Beauty, turning men's hearts into earthquake zones."

It was so shameless and calculating that it should have failed miserably. Yet Ms. Framley showed no displeasure—far from it. After she read the article she hurried out to buy a hundred extra copies and to tell everyone that "at last we have a real newspaper in this town." And from that day forward her loyalty belonged to Bamalford.

coalesce: to grow together into a single mass or into a tightly knit unity
ponderous: heavy, bulky and without gracefulness

Now as Ricky crossed the ravine in front of the school—shuffling over the wooden bridge, throwing down some coins from his lunch money—the Seismologic Beauty was about to make an appearance. Stepping back for a moment into the shadow of the marble porch she watched him and the other students joining him: Joannie, Allen the Snoop, Tedesco the exchange student from Brazil, Calvin, Meagan, François, and Lumps, the hulking joker whom she hated dearly. When they had drifted off the bridge and around to the seniors' entrance at the back of the school, and had **coalesced** into a little knot, she let out a blood-chilling shriek: "It shall not be!"

They heard it as if she were next to them. For a moment there was nothing to be seen, though they looked wildly around, and then, abruptly, the big woman marched out from the shadow of the porch and into the early sun. "The

23

Fram," gasped Ricky to his companions, staring up the long slope that led to the marble house. "The Fram—in a grind-your-bones sort of mood."

Crying again, "It shall not be!" Ms. Framley came stamping **ponderously** down the slope toward them.

READER: How many Greek sailors did you interview before you wrote that chapter?

AUTHOR: Exactly zero.

READER: I thought so. Then how do you know that forty years ago Greek sailors carried binoculars?

AUTHOR: It seemed like a reasonable assumption.

READER: This would have never happened in Fulano's book.

Chapter 6: THE ASYLUM OF VIRTUE

The seniors let their conversations collapse into silence as Ms. Framley smoked down the mountainside through the chill morning air. They saw that she was heading directly toward the wooden bridge that crossed the gully between her slope and the schoolyard. Some of them swore later that the ground shook under her feet. Others felt this bordered on **hyperbole**. But all of them agreed that the bridge itself wobbled like a thing made from matchsticks as she stormed across it.

> **hyperbole**: dramatically exaggerated description
> **analogy**: a similarity observed in the general structure of two things, in the general pattern of two events, etc., even though physically the two things, events, etc., may be quite distinct from one another
> **banter** (noun): light-hearted conversation, with quick, witty exchanges, and often a good deal of teasing

"Bridge closed to vehicular traffic," muttered Lumps, the only one in the crowd who could think of anything—dumb or otherwise—to say.

A moment later several thousand dollars worth of jewelry, including a solid-gold spoon, was jumping before his eyes. Ms. Framley had pulled to a shaky stop directly in front of him. She was starved for oxygen, but managed to shriek again, "It shall not be, Foster!"

Lumps seemed unmoved. "The name is Constantin, Ms. Framley, which for some reason my father shortened to Nople when I was still very small, and"—now his voice faltered, though just for a moment—"and there was no time to ask him why. Then in first grade my little friends worked on Nople until it became Nomple, Omple, Oplem. In the second grade too—it went from Oplem to Oplems, and then on to Plems, Plums, Plumps, until finally the process arrived at Lumps. A lot of names, ma'am, but Foster was never one of them."

Ricky, at any rate, thought it was an excellent story, well told, noncontroversial, capable of defusing the tense confrontation with Ms. Framley. He was so relieved that he blurted, "There's a perfect **analogy** between your name getting transformed like that, Lumps, and this toy I had a few years ago. It started out as a ballet shoe and changed into a bedroom slipper, and then a loafer, a tie shoe, a tennis shoe, and finally wound up as a roller skate."

One of the girls in the group—a tall girl, athletic in her manner—was smiling more and more widely as Ricky went on. This was Meagan, and she was starting to ask if Ricky had been wearing the shoe during the changes, and if it had hurt, when suddenly Ms. Framley—at last recovering her breath—broke in. The last thing she wanted was for the situation to lose its tension and slip back into the normal **banter** of a circle of students waiting for the bell. "Stop jabbering," she cried, "and listen to what I say." Her voice was rising once more to a screech. "It shall not be! Do you hear me? It shall not be!"

> **calumny**: the act of making false statements about someone in a deliberate attempt to hurt his reputation
> **detraction**: the act of making negative statements that have the effect of tearing away at the reputation of someone
> **inscrutable**: revealing nothing to the searching eye or the inquiring mind; remaining beyond comprehension

Lumps at this point was genuinely perplexed, and he asked, "What shall not be, Ms. Framley?"

"It," she screamed, "it, the foulest act of **calumny** yet: a flaky teenager lies his head off on national TV and shreds the reputation of our Mr. Bamalford. That's what shall not be, got it, Foster?"

Lumps blinked. "OK, glad I asked."

Ricky spoke up. "Lumps can't be Foster. He's only eighteen and Foster is twenty-seven."

"Ha!" said Ms. Framley with a snort. "Foster's no twenty-seven. He's a foulmouthed teenager, with a gift for **detraction**. Sound like anyone we know?" There was another wicked glance at Lumps. "But it shall not be: if the cuffs aren't slapped on that sniper in seventy-two hours, and a gag put on that spiteful mouth, this gets torn up." She pulled a thick and yellowed document from her purse.

At this point a look of vast confusion was materializing on the face of a boy at the edge of the group. He was Tedesco, the student from Brazil, and the face manifesting the confusion was ever so slightly roundish, with good width in the mouth, a solid, straight nose, a wealth of eyebrow. His perplexity had grown as he saw Ms. Framley charging down the hillside, crying the strange "shall not" against them, pulling the heavy old document from her purse. For all his efforts to comprehend what the behavior of this woman meant, it remained **inscrutable** to him.

Near Tedesco in the group of seniors there was a girl named Joannie, trimly made, with hair the color of straw. She leaned toward him now, explaining in a whisper how Ms. Framley was the landlady of the school, and how the bulky document drawn from her purse was the lease.

Tedesco whispered in return, "You have grand documents—no, I mean big documents—here in America." A spark of humor flashed in his dark, patient eyes.

> **dogmatic**: asserting opinions as if they were absolutely true and not open to debate
> **induce**: to persuade someone to take an action because of some benefit that you have associated with it

Joannie mirrored it back, as the worry on her features relaxed, though only for a moment, into a pretty smile. Then she went on, still in a hushed voice. "It's a horrible thing. The lease proper is just a page or two. The rest, all the rest, is a list of these fussy conditions. The lease can be canceled if the people don't bathe twice a week, if the ladies swear, if the children eat with their fingers. But the tone is the worst—preachy, totally sure of being right. Like—here's how it is, and no questions will be entertained. Yech! We call it the **Dogmatic** Lease, and I hate dogmatic stuff—unless of course it's me being dogmatic."

"Uh, uh, uh," came a clucking sound, as though from a giant fowl. Ms. Framley had spied the conversation between Joannie and Tedesco. "The lease is out—you all know there shouldn't be any talking when the lease is out. It's more than a century old, and it was written by a Framley, Abner Framley. As a very young man he had sailed with that more or less ridiculous Farnum Expedition that came to establish a trading settlement here. He was a lad of great moral virtue and many rare talents, all of which, of course, have passed down the Framley line to me."

She paused, as though giving everyone a brief opportunity to admire the rare talents, and then continued eagerly. "Was it any surprise that Captain Farnum, a man of unimpressive gifts, grew insanely jealous of Abner? Or any surprise that the pack of moral misfits serving as crew hated him? At last, to **induce** Abner to leave the ship entirely the desperate captain offered him a grant of the best land in the new town, all the land from the high saddle where my house now is down to 'the leaping brook,' the stream called the Bad Pony. Which—in case some of you have never noticed—is the stream that flows through the ravine in front of the school."

> **asylum**: a place where someone is sheltered, and often is given protection from persecution
> **frugality**: the habit of spending only as necessary, and of stretching your money and other resources as far as they will go
> **ingrate**: a person who shows no thanks for favors received

She toyed with the golden spoon that dangled from her ear. Not even her red-hot indignation over Foster could displace the pleasure of returning again to the familiar pages of the Abner story. "Abner took the land," she resumed, "and he gave it a beautiful name, the **Asylum** of Virtue, because it would be a refuge for him from all those he had met on his sea voyaging who were hostile to his righteousness. Soon he built the marble house. He had saved almost every penny that ever came into his hands—**frugality** is part of virtue, you know—and with those pennies he built the marble house."

Lumps started asking some misguided question about whether Abner kept the pennies in a jar, but Meagan—to preserve the peace—pulled out a sweatshirt and pushed it in his mouth before he could finish. Ms. Framley seared them both with a fierce look, and menaced them as well with a guillotine-like motion of her hand. Then she went on. "From the marble porch Abner looked down and saw how the people of Dropanchor wallowed in ignorance. Maybe they weren't as nasty as the sailors but they were every bit as dumb, morally dumb, unable to tell right from wrong. He tried to teach them, in every way, but they never so much as said thank you for his efforts, because then as now they were a band of **ingrates**."

There was a low mutter and she swung sharply toward Lumps. "What was that, funny boy?"

"Just a sec," he answered, "let me stop eating this sweatshirt. There. What I said was—*merci*, Abner. A little late perhaps, but—*merci*. That's French for 'thank you.' I learned it here, French class most likely."

> **sedulous**: sticking to a task; dedicating the time and attention necessary to push a project forward, to master an area of learning, etc.
> **precept**: a rule of conduct handed down by an established authority to govern some particular area of human activity

"Don't tell me about French," she snapped. "Paris was mine for the asking. I could have rocked it with the same beauty that jolted that poor sailor and his binoculars. Now hold your foul tongue and let me finish the Abner story. Abner, of course, would not give up. The people needed to know right from wrong, and he was going to teach them. He stuck to the task. Dear, **sedulous** Abner. When the town council came to him begging for a lease of school land, he saw his opportunity. He wrote the lease himself, and into it he poured a wealth of ethical wisdom, hundreds of moral **precepts** for the people of Dropanchor. And each of these rules was accompanied by a simple, encouraging message—obey this or the Framleys will hurt you, they will cancel the lease and take back your school. A simple message. And simple messages are always best."

> **derogatory**: openly expressing a negative opinion, often bordering on contempt

28

maladroit: bumbling, clumsy; doing or saying the wrong thing in social situations
brandish: to display a weapon and make threatening motions with it

A heavy sigh escaped from her. "So much labor, Abner, teaching these moral midgets the difference between right and wrong."

"How about right from left?" growled Lumps, stung by the **derogatory** tone Ms. Framley always used when talking about the people of Dropanchor. "How about rope from sail? I heard that what really earned Abner an invitation to leave the ship was his nearly perfect incompetence. He didn't know how to do anything. He was apparently so clumsy, bumbling, **maladroit** ..."

Lumps could get no further than that, as a strong blast of outrage broke across him. "Filthy ape," Ms. Framley shrieked. "I've got one for you!" She **brandished** the lease in his face as though driving back a wild animal, then pulled it away and opened it eagerly. "One of Abner's first rules, all about respect for the Framleys, let me just read page seven ... let me ..."

malevolent: having an intense desire that someone suffer harm
profuse: present or pouring forth in abundant quantities
illiterate: not able to read and write at all, or not able to read and write at the level appropriate to your age

A look of **malevolent** pleasure was suddenly awakening in her face. "Ha. No—I won't read page seven. You will! The day gets better!"

She thrust the opened lease toward Lumps. "Why don't you read page seven for us, Lumps"—her voice became gentle and coaxing—"you know, see the letters on the page and tell us what words they are forming."

It was a horrible moment for Lumps. As he stared at the page before his eyes, and saw the letters jumping, a **profuse** sweat began streaming out from his close-cropped hair. It streaked down his wide face and chilled at once— shadow still lingered in the schoolyard—but he made no attempt to wipe it away. All he could manage in his distress was to stammer, "You know that ... I can't ..."

"Ms. Framley," came the pleasant, hopeful voice of Meagan, "Lumps is a person who struggles with a special challenge. He's as smart as can be, but he has ... some difficulty with ..."

"Are you referring to his total and complete inability to read, sweetums, is that it?" There was not a trace of pity in Ms. Framley's pale eyes, as she drove the lance home. "I'd say he was challenged, OK, I'd say he's like a hundred percent **illiterate**, and he can no more read page seven for me than ... than old baldie up there can." She motioned toward a huge, reddish boulder, thirty or forty feet high, that stood like a guardian at the top of a long meadow rising out to the east from the school.

parry: to turn aside a sword-thrust or other blow before it does you harm

facade: the outer surface or face of something, determining its appearance, but often inconsistent with the inner core or nature of the thing

Meagan winced. She knew that on almost any other topic Lumps would have easily **parried** the clumsy insults—he had a sharp wit, lying in wait behind a rough **facade** of clownishness. But when it came to his strange reading problem he refused to defend himself, almost as though it were a point of honor to take whatever abuse the disability brought upon him.

She winced again as she looked around her—hoping for what, she couldn't have told you—and caught sight of Calvin. You never knew with Calvin anymore—he was talented and good-looking, but in recent months an air of boredom and mockery had been gradually twisting the fine proportion of his features. Now his head was thrown back, and his lips had the curl of someone about to make an ugly remark. Meagan felt the chilling suspicion that he was on the verge of sharing in the sport—Ms. Framley's sport—by calling out some taunt against Lumps.

speculation: the act of turning a question over in your thoughts and arriving at possible conclusions about it, although you lack knowledge of facts which would permit definite conclusions

savor (verb): to enjoy the taste of; to take a slow, deliberate delight in something

avocation: an interest pursued seriously on your own time

Meagan wasn't alone in her fear. Joannie, the one who knew Calvin best, had been watching him also, and now as she saw him on the point of speaking, she raised one hand, palm outward, as though to turn back anything brutish that came from his mouth.

What Calvin was about to say, though, remained forever a matter of **speculation**. His words, and anyone's words, were cut off by a loud snarl from Ms. Framley. Having **savored** her revenge upon Lumps, she was returning to business with a foul-tempered outburst. "Ironbane! Where is Ironbane? Did I hire a principal or a bum? Where are you, Ironbane? I need you now—we must assemble the students. Bamalford is coming to speak to them."

Again it was Meagan who made the response, trying to explain to Ms. Framley where the school principal, Mr. Ironbane, might be. "Maybe up there," she said brightly, with a sweep of her arm toward the north, toward the mountain heights towering up behind Ms. Framley's hillside. "That's his **avocation**. Every minute that's left over from his work as principal he spends up there, hiking about, doing his research."

30

> **reproach** (verb): to point out to someone his fault, often in a tone more expressive of disappointment than of sharp anger
> **oxymoron**: a brief phrase in which the sense of one word is contrary to the sense of the other word or words (for example, "a well-organized chaos")
> **riddle** (verb): to penetrate a flat object with many holes, or a solid object with many tunnels

"Research!" snorted Ms. Framley. "He's trying to look through my windows. Just like that sailor."

Meagan **reproached** her gently. "No, no, no, Ms. Framley. That's not fair. The only thing on his mind is the mountain"—she motioned again to the north—"and proving his theory about it. It's hollow, he says, or—sorry for the **oxymoron**—filled with hollows. Maybe **riddled** with hollows is better, or ..."

Ms. Framley glared at her. "Oops," stammered Meagan. "Sorry. We mustn't diddle. Anyway, down below the mountain two of those plate things in the Earth's crust are grinding away at each other. That's Mr. Ironbane's theory. I think for many years they have been grinding at him too, and wearing at him with questions. Like—where's the smoke, where's the fire? Why don't the plates trigger volcanic activity? I don't know all his theory, but I guess he thinks the plates under Dropanchor are secondary ones. They don't cause huge eruptions, but they do generate some magma. And they do spawn some tremors too, even though ..."

"But of course," responded Ms. Framley with a ghastly toss of the head, "where I am, earthquakes will follow."

> **demography**: the science that counts populations, analyzes their makeup, and tracks their movements
> **conjure up**: through magic, imagination or inventiveness to cause something—a presence, an image, etc.—to take shape before you
> **exculpation**: the act of establishing, on the basis of some excuse or explanation, that a person is not to blame for something of which he has been accused

"No doubt, Ms. Framley, no doubt," said Meagan, not wanting to debate the point. "But at least you can see how all this is very important to Mr. Ironbane. It's almost a question of **demography**—he counts the number of people in Dropanchor, around Dropanchor, and for him that's the number of reasons to know all he can about the mountain—just in case. And any news is big news. He told us yesterday that he had spotted a wisp rising like a pale column over one of the summits, and—just perhaps—it was smoke from the deep fires, passing up through the hollows, coming out through a crack in the stonework. But it was the faintest whiff, and he was worried maybe it wasn't

really there, just something **conjured up** in his imagination, or a tiny imper-
fection in the lenses—he was using his binoculars, you see, when he ..."

"Oh yes!" exclaimed Ms. Framley, as though the subject were only too familiar. "Oh yes! And the sailor was too. So no more **exculpations**, honey.
Ironbane is on my guilty list—for not being here when he should, and for trying to peek through my windows. And nothing you've said in all your long
blabber gets him off. In fact ..."

> **forgo**: to hold yourself back from the use or enjoyment of something
> **encroach**: to extend or lap over into the property or domain of some-
> one else; to commit trespass bit by bit
> **celerity**: swiftness; quickness in the performance of a work or motion

Meagan's attention, though, was drawn away at this moment by the sight of
one of her companions staring intently up the mountainside. It was Allen,
known to his friends as Allen the Snoop, a boy of average height, and rather
pudgy through the waist and arms and neck, as though **forgoing** exercise had
gotten to be a habit. Pudgy was not the way you would describe the face, however. The mouth had that defined, ready-to-speak-on-any-subject look that you
see sometimes on the veteran newscasters. The eyes were attentive. The dark
hair was wiry, high-voltage, generally resistant to grooming.

Meagan called to him now, "That's what I thought too, that Ironbane
would go up there this morning. Have you spotted him?"

"Uh, uh," Ms. Framley blazed before Allen could respond. "Let's get one
thing straight. Even if everything you—the girl—say about Ironbane and what
he does up there is true, still his mountain-man hobby had better not **encroach**
on the time he owes me. He's my hired help, my thug. He's responsible for en-
forcing the Framley code of education for boys and girls, right here at this institution. And if anything else in his little life spills over into the time required
for that basic responsibility, nice Victoria Framley is going to be peeved."

Ignoring Ms. Framley's outburst completely, Allen responded to Meagan's
question. "There's someone up there, a small human speck, marching along
very rapidly, trying to stay warm maybe. And yet in spite of its **celerity**, the
impression it gives is of a man much older than Ironbane."

> **acuteness**: sharpness of perception; the ability to pick up even mini-
> mal occurrences of light, sound, odor, etc.
> **expository**: presenting an orderly, point-by-point explanation of a
> complex subject matter
> **plausible**: believable, at least for the time being, by reason of appear-
> ing to be consistent with known facts and accepted understandings

Meagan was straining to catch sight of the human speck, but she lacked Allen's extraordinary **acuteness** of vision and could see only the face of the

mountain itself, a complex study of crags and slopes, meadowland and patch-work forest. "Who else could it be," she asked, "if it's not Ironbane?"

She had no idea what a cruel opportunity her question put in the hands of Ms. Framley. The big woman let out the yip of a dog running down its prey and exclaimed, "Who else could it be? Maybe Mad Yuri looking for his brains."

Lumps cried out in pain. Yuri was his father, and Yuri had disappeared on the mountain many years ago. Before Lumps could speak, though, another voice imposed itself. "Wrong, Victoria, I'm afraid you've gotten it quite wrong!"

"Mr. Ironbane!" gasped Joannie. "You're not up there."

A tall man in his forties met her remark with a generous smile. It remained on his lean features for only an instant, however. As he turned away from her his face again darkened with anger. "No, I'm not up there, but"—he was look-ing directly at Ms. Framley now—"I was up there. Got that, Victoria? I was up there, in the days after Yuri was caught in the storm, and ..."

He paused, and let out a long breath, which seemed to carry off some of his emotion. "OK, start again, start again. I will be ... **expository**. I will take you through it point by point, Victoria, so that you can understand. I was up there, so many of us were up there. The mayor held some back, but so many of us went up, and it was all on foot, until at last after more than two weeks of searching without a trace we had to tell this young man"—he motioned toward Lumps—"who was then a very young man of three, by the name of Constan-tin, that his father probably wasn't coming down again."

Lumps was looking at the ground, shaking his head so slowly you could hardly tell, as Ironbane continued. "The reaction of the boy to the news more or less blew us away. He explained to us that everything was OK, it was just a question of a hat. Yuri had apparently lost his hat on the mountain, and he was looking for it, and once he found it he would come down. When the boy fin-ished we just stood there for a minute with nothing to say. Finally, Mayor Povano babbled that it was a very **plausible** explanation, that Yuri's hat was an excellent hat, that ... He didn't know what he was saying."

> **rancor**: a festering hatefulness that you bear toward someone
> **conjunction**: the being together of two or more things, often with sufficient union of their forces to produce a combined effect
> **malignancy**: some condition or influence which over time will bring harm or death to the organism, system, community, etc., on which it is operating
> **retort** (noun): a stinging reply, sometimes throwing back on the original speaker the accusation or insult that was carried by his state-ment

Ironbane could not help a faint smile as he thought of his friend Povano. "Of course, for the Mayor that's just a day's work. And Yuri would agree with that if … Anyway, in the weeks that followed, the story got around—Yuri was looking for his hat. And as the years began to pass by, the Yuri of the story became Old Yuri, or even Old Man Yuri. But never Mad Yuri, Victoria, and never anything about looking for his brains. Just the hat, the very elusive hat. So … that's all and … and I hope it makes more sense now."

By the end Ironbane's voice had become gentle, and free of **rancor**. The early sunlight was angling down now from the range to the east, undoing knots of mist and chill with the first warmth of a September morning. And the sound of distant water was spilling faint and clear into the stillness—the race of the Bad Pony, the throw of the surf far below on the beach. It was a momentary **conjunction** of influences, and perhaps it had the power to cure—to make well even the **malignancy** of hatefulness that had rooted like a last illness in Ms. Framley's life. But she shrugged off the possibility as though it were an irritant. She had thought of a good **retort** to Ironbane's preachings and had no desire to waste it. "If Yuri," she said, "had ever found his brains, he wouldn't have lost his hat! Ha-uck! Ha-uck!"

The laugh was like a large engine turning over. It was horrible on the silence that met it, and it went on for an indecently long time until at last—abruptly—Ms. Framley remembered again the business that had brought her thrashing down the mountain. "Ironbane," she snapped, "the auditorium, we must get every one to the auditorium, the freshmen, the seniors, and everyone in between. Bamalford is coming."

> **conducive**: possessing qualities or influences which promote the occurrence of a certain outcome
> **equivocation**: a statement which seems to affirm "X" but which contains some double meaning or tricky grammar allowing the speaker to claim later on that what the statement really meant was different from "X"

An expression of pain and weariness appeared on the principal's face. "This is a place of learning, Victoria, and I assume Bamalford is coming to say something or show something that is **conducive** to learning."

She looked at him sharply. "No fear, Mr. Ironbane, he comes to teach the children a lesson."

"OK, work with me, Victoria. I'm sure your little **equivocation** was unintended, but do you mean an improve-your-mind sort of lesson or a humiliating-punishment sort of lesson?"

> **advocate** (noun): someone who speaks out, often on a regular basis, to promote and make a case for some position, cause or practice

34

demote: to remove someone from a higher position in an organization and place him in a lower one

bizarre: so strange and outside the normal course of things as to be rather shocking

allegory: a story in which the characters represent moral qualities, social values, etc., and in which the plot, besides presenting the basic chain of events, develops some point about those qualities and values

With that she blew. "What gives you, a hired hand, the right to interrogate me?" She was screaming. "Am I not, for all practical purposes, the owner of this school? Mr. Bamalford is a gentleman. He has a fine eye for beauty, and he is an **advocate** of ... of the right things, the things that need to be spoken out for, like long terms in the penitentiary for those who trespass, even accidentally, on private property. But above all he is my guest. He may pursue whatever agenda he pleases with the students, including the Farbugle agenda. And any more frivolous objections on your part Mr. Ironbane and your days as principal are over. I'll have you **demoted** down to assistant to the late-slip lady. Now for the thirteenth millionth time, get the little JD's to the auditorium."

READER: Larry—who does not always watch his mouth—Larry made this joke that Lumps shouldn't feel bad about being illiterate—at least he doesn't have to read *The Scarlet Letter*.

AUTHOR: Larry didn't like *The Scarlet Letter*?

READER: Not enough explosions—a common criticism, by the way. But the problem is that Larry—who does not always watch his mouth—Larry made his joke in front of his father, Mr. 1600.

AUTHOR: I've heard that number somewhere.

READER: Larry's dad says the lowest acceptable SAT score in their house is a 1600.

AUTHOR: Whoa! And the man was not pleased with his son's little joke about illiteracy, and there was some sort of a **bizarre** reaction.

READER: Correct. Now Larry has to read *The Scarlet Letter*, *War and Peace*, *Don Quixote* and *Moby Dick*, and write a seventy-page essay showing how each of them is an **allegory** for the importance of a college education.

AUTHOR: Buried alive.

Chapter 7: THE JOY OF EXPUNGING

It was not an especially good moment as Ms. Framley, very much like a lava flow, began using her great bulk to push the students in the direction of their meeting with Bamalford. Yet a smile widened on Tedesco's face as he turned, along with the rest of the pack, and headed toward the school building.

> **obfuscate**: to cover something with darkness or confusion, leaving it difficult to see or comprehend
> **precipitation**: the event of water falling in the form of rain, snow or hail upon the earth
> **impeccable**: made, done or performed perfectly and without flaw

The cause of his pleasure was the building itself. It was a comforting structure, blockish and enormously solid, four stories tall, made of brick from top to bottom. The morning sun was upon it now, showing as always that its builders had merrily disregarded the rule—buy all your bricks at once. There was a ragged line, and the sun revealed it, just above the second story, where a lower zone of tomato-red brick met an upper zone of cranberry-red brick. It was a collision of colors, not easily overlooked. Tedesco loved it, now as much as when he had first seen it some days before, and his reaction was a charitable one—"Everything will look great when it starts to get dark." A questionable compliment, but at least a true one, for in the **obfuscating** dimness of late evening or the early dawn—and only then—the tomato red and the cranberry red went together well.

The building would have been a perfect cube except for one architectural oddity—a long wing, narrow and just one story high, that came pushing out from the front and disappeared into the gully where the waters of the Bad Pony ran. The wing fell sharply down the near slope of the gully, down to a large, irregular structure wedged at the bottom, the school auditorium.

This had pleased Tedesco from the moment he first saw it—placing the auditorium in such an improbable setting. But it had also stirred some perplexity in his mind, so now as he passed through the wing, in the growing band of students being herded along by Ms. Framley, he was looking around for Joannie. She was some ways ahead, and when he caught up with her he began to ask her questions, in his rapidly improving English, about annual **precipitation** levels in Dropanchor, the maximum rainfall or snowfall in twenty-four hours, and things of that nature.

At that moment Joannie was walking with her friend François. Although she—François—was a quiet girl with a vague air of refinement that came from somewhere—the delicacy of her features, the **impeccable** cut of her clothing, it was hard to say—still she was the one whose eyes flashed with mischief when Tedesco asked his questions. "Shouldn't you talk to someone who's been around longer, someone older,"—she made sure that Ms. Framley was not within hearing—"someone like our friend Ricky Snoozer, who's got about nine years on the rest of us?"

> **vie**: to engage in a hard-fought competition for some privilege or award
> **mandate** (verb): to lay something down as an obligation or requirement
> **unwarranted**: lacking a justifying basis or explanation

Ricky, a few steps behind them, also looked around to see where Ms. Framley was, before firing back, "And shouldn't you put an 'e' on your name so people will know you are a girl? Besides, what's wrong with a twenty-seven-year-old senior? Anyway, though, Tedesco's questions are really about floods, and the one to answer them should be the mayor. He can tell you how much they worried about floods when the auditorium was built. I know there were two firms—architectural firms—**vying** for the contract. According to one of them, the latest thinking on flood control **mandated** that the stream go under the auditorium. The other firm swore the stream had to go around. Finally the mayor decided on through—or at least partly through. It was an inspired compromise, as you can see."

They were well into the ravine now, two-thirds of the way or so down the slope, and passing from the long wing into the auditorium. The seating, twenty rows of simple stone benches, followed the natural line of the slope, dropping steeply. The stage was stone as well, a wide ledge of stone, carved in place in the ravine's opposite side. The interval of space between the stage and the seating brimmed with a reflected light, and into it Ricky tossed another coin from his lunch money. There was a little *kerplunk* and the coin was carried off by the torrent of the Bad Pony. Part of the stream ran there, flowing swiftly across the width of the auditorium through a blue tile-work shallows.

Tedesco stopped in his tracks and gazed on the sight. Joannie, fearing he was about to say Wow, warned him, "Calvin will make fun of you. You're supposed to be bored with everything. But right now there's a look of admiration on your face that is completely unrestrained and ..."

"And completely **unwarranted**," came the harsh voice of Ms. Framley. She pointed impatiently to the stream. "There's nothing here to admire, just a long, open sewer, done in blue. So let's get the lead out. Mr. Bamalford will arrive in a few moments."

> **prerogative**: some particular privilege or right which you enjoy because of your status or rank
> **resonant**: (said of voices and other sounds) full, richly toned, echoing, easily carrying a long way
> **partial**: inclined to give more favorable treatment to one person than to another, even though on the merits the second person may be more deserving

With an indignant look at the old scourge François ushered Tedesco to a seat in the front row, only a small distance from the leaping waters of the stream. She explained to him how the first several rows were reserved for the seniors.

"Great **prerogative**," muttered Joannie, "it just puts us closer to Bamalford."

At the mention of that name Ricky shuddered. "This is going to be so bad—unless he does a no-show. Maybe he got lost. Maybe he's in custody. Maybe … that's him."

From the far aisle came the **resonant** boom of a voice Ricky knew only too well. It easily reached every corner of the auditorium. Everyone could hear Bamalford going on at length, telling Ms. Framley that in his treatment of Foster there would be nothing **partial**. Even if Foster turned out to be Bamalford's own son—which was unlikely since Bamalford was without children—there would be no favoritism. Justice demanded—and here the voice boomed even louder—260 years in the slammer for the little criminal, no matter whose kid he was.

Ricky groaned, slumped down in his seat, and closed his eyes. He heard a heavy, ringing tread—Bamalford and Ms. Framley were on the wooden bridge that led over the stream and to the stage. He heard François murmur indignantly, "Filthy man. Go spit your gum somewhere else."

> **aversion**: an attitude of turning away from something in disgust and dislike
> **histrionic**: performed to have maximum theatrical effect
> **prostrate**: stretched out flat on the floor, often without strength to get up

Then, unexpectedly, another sound—François again, but gasping. "I hate it!"

"The gum?" asked Ricky, quickly opening his eyes. He knew at once it wasn't the gum. François had a strong **aversion** to the dark, and the auditorium lights had just been cut, plunging the windowless hall into darkness.

There was no time, however, to reflect on this strange development, for from the front of the auditorium a cry of suffering rang forth, warbling, drawn out, **histrionic**, just the sort of cry you hear in the early rehearsals of a tragic drama. It was followed by a heavy thud. The lighting was restored, and there at center stage lay Bamalford with a dagger in his chest.

Ms. Framley ran and stood near him. She made a gesture—a grand sweep of the arms—toward the immense heap of his fallen figure, as though to cover the one-in-a-million chance that someone had failed to notice it. Then with a swinging turn that almost pitched her into the seating, she confronted the audience and howled, "Feeling good, Foster, now that your work is done? Why just wound 'em when you have the option of giving 'em a one-way ...?"

A muffled cough came from the direction of Bamalford, muffled but insistent, and Allen, blessed with hearing as keen as his eyesight, swore later that he heard something like "Pssst, Seismo!" Whatever was the case, Ms. Framley interrupted her attack on Foster and bent her head toward the **prostrate** hero. After a pause of a minute or more she again swung around to face the students, launching at once into a complex agenda.

> **sanction** (verb): to give your approval to some activity, or to let it go ahead without objection, often in a situation where your authority would be sufficient to forbid the activity if you so chose
> **aura**: the mood or feeling or air that a person or object gives off
> **despicable**: so low or foul as to be worthy of contempt

"First, a message for Foster Farbugle. We know you're here in this auditorium, with a worried look on your criminal face. Well, Foster dear, yes—there is a slammer in your future. If you don't serve time, people will think that smearing the good name of a person like Mr. Bamalford is OK, that it's a form of recreation, **sanctioned** by the authorities. And we don't want that. Therefore—in the next day or two, you need to get the packing list—what to take to the big house, what to leave at home. So let's be heads up, OK. And, Foster— we're gonna miss ya, you little sicko. For sure. No doubt. Now ... let's see, what else?"

She paused, and let her gaze rake across the student body, slow and searching. Under that gaze, Ricky was sure that he felt the letters FF starting to grow in thick, fleshy ridges on his forehead—"thick, fleshy, neon-pink ridges," he would tell his friends later. He had no doubt that from the stage Ms. Framley had spied the weird and telltale sign. Why else would she be reaching in her purse to get ...? His heart was racing, and when all she pulled out was a small notebook, bound in violet-colored leather, he felt it race again, for the book had a definite **aura** of menace.

"What else?" she repeated. "What else should we talk about?" Ricky blinked in astonishment, for her voice was suddenly sweet and airy. "Here's an idea," she went on. "Let's see who's got their name in the book, who's in trouble."

She was thumbing through the violet notebook now, giving it hard use, doubling back its spine with her heavy fingers. Yet for a few seconds more the tone in which she spoke was a softened one, in violent contrast to the oppressive hands. "Look, children. Here's a page with Foster's name, Foster Farbugle. That's no surprise, is it?"

Then without warning the sweetness fell away, the voice was grim and lashing. "After all, for an action as **despicable** as slaughtering a good man's reputation—you get your name in the book, don't you? Don't you?"

The snarl had followed so quickly on the sweetness, and was so fierce, that one of the freshman boys cracked under the pressure. There was an answer to the angry Don't you?—a little yes that came squeaking out from the back rows of the auditorium.

> **culpable**: worthy of blame for having done something wrong
> **expound**: to explain something, often in a detailed, orderly fashion, and often with a self-assurance that comes with being a master of the subject matter involved
> **espouse**: to adopt some position or theory and, often, to support and promote it

That was a welcome sign, and for a moment Ms. Framley was calmer as she tapped her fingertips together in a gesture of satisfaction. Then she was off again, continuing her review of the violet notebook, turning heavily through the pages. "Just an initial!" she cried suddenly, holding up a page with a large D. "Somebody got their initial in the book. Maybe Dave, maybe Doug, or maybe, just maybe, do you think—Dropanchor? Because you know, after all, on further reflection—Dropanchor is **culpable** too. A slasher like Farbugle didn't just happen—he learned his moves in a school like Dropanchor. So share the blame, little town on the coast. There's something not right in your homes, some bad mistake in your little teddy bear families. The wrong stuff is going in the baby bottles, or ... "

She had to stop, for there was a noise like the last part of the hibernation movie, when the bear is waking up in the springtime. Bamalford was getting up. Snorting and grunting, the big man was struggling to his feet. The dagger fell away from his chest, bounced once off his stomach and landed on the floor—all handle, and no blade.

Even before he reached the front of the stage and took his place beside Ms. Framley, he was **expounding** in an academic tone. "That's an excellent ques-

40

tion, Ms. Framley—what have they done in the little houses of Dropanchor to produce obscenities like Foster? The explanation begins—I am quite sure—with the First Amendment of the United States Constitution. That amendment was written for the limited purpose of helping me—and other editors, of course—in our work, by giving us the right of free speech. But what have the biological mothers and fathers of Dropanchor done? Some of them have **espoused** that theory which pops up every few years, the very wrong theory, Ms. Framley, that the First Amendment applies in the home. And they have convinced the others. The result is that here in Dropanchor the children have free speech rights. Which, of course, they abuse terribly, turning into little dragonmouths."

> **differentiate**: to take note of, or take into account, the differences between two things—often essential and defining differences
> **expunge**: to scratch out or otherwise erase some mark; more generally, to wipe something out or reduce its effect to zero
> **naive**: ignorant of the way things really are in some area of life such as politics, class differences, human reproduction, etc.; holding childish beliefs about such an area

Bamalford's temperature was rising, and his professorial tone was dropping away. "Does it at least remain in the home? Does the free speech child at least **differentiate** between trashing mom and dad—they asked for it—and trashing perfect strangers? I'm afraid not—we're all in the cross hairs of the little gunners. And that's how we got a Foster."

He paused to draw a long breath, and suck the great stomach up into his chest. "That's how we got a Foster. Dropanchor hatched him, spawned him, encouraged him. So it was not an error that Dropanchor got its name in Ms. Framley's book, was it?" A short silence, and then sternly, with rising volume, "Was it?"

"No!" Again, the little squeak from the freshman rows.

"Good," said Bamalford, pacing the stage now, his voice falling quickly to a confidential hush. "Look—we all know that one of the worst things is getting your name in the book. When that happens, all you can think about is—**expunging**, right? Getting your name out of the book, erasing it, scratching it out. At that moment you desperately want what the big-time shrinks refer to as the Joy of Expunging, and until you get it, there's only the pain. That's where Foster is right now, clutching his belly in pain, aching to remove his name from the book. Well, jerk! Clutch away, because ... "

Bamalford shook himself, like a man trying to stick to business. "OK, to keep it simple, Mr. Farbugle will not be experiencing the Joy of Expunging for a long time—260 years or so. But for Dropanchor there's still a chance. Kids, listen, your mamas, your pops—they are Dropanchor, and they too are clutching their bellies in pain—or they're gonna be! They're desperate to have Dropanchor's name removed from the book. Maybe some of them think it will just happen—time cures all wounds, happy endings are automatic, and so forth. But that's **naive**. They'd better learn how the game is played. Getting Dropanchor's name out of the book means putting the smile back on this handsome mug"—he lifted his chin—"and that is not a simple matter. Do you want to know what it will take? Anybody?"

Bamalford let his question hang in the air. The tension built quickly, weighing most heavily, as before, on the unknown freshman in the back row. And it was from that direction that before long Bamalford heard what he was waiting for, a little squeak of a What?

> **delineate**: to describe an object or situation carefully, tracing out its basic structure, dimensions and features
> **placate**: to cause someone's anger to lessen by giving him presents, honors or privileges
> **autocratic**: holding absolute authority, and exercising it harshly

"Alright, then, I'll tell you what it will take. A present. To me from Dropanchor. Merry Christmas, Peerless, and happy birthday, from your town. Kids, take this message home to the parents. When Bamalford gets a very nice present, Dropanchor gets its name scratched out of the book, and not before. And, yes, they will ask questions about what Bamalford wants. Tell them that very soon now I will ... **delineate** everything that's involved in giving this present—what it is, how big it is, when it must be given, where it must be given. And some of them, kids, your own mothers and fathers, may grow rude and ask if the present is expensive. There's never a shortage of fools! Just tell them that a **placated** Bamalford is worth any price."

After repeating this closing line two or three times Bamalford stepped back and allowed Ms. Framley once again to occupy the front of the stage. She stared out at the students, a scowl darkening on her face. "Still there, Squeaky," she asked at last, "with your little friends, in the back row? I know exactly what you're thinking. Who's Bamalford, right? Why be nice to Bamalford, right?" Her tone was becoming more and more **autocratic**. "I could have you expelled for thinking such things, couldn't I, Squeaky?"

> **conciliatory**: said or done in a pleasing and considerate way, to make peace
> **incriminate**: (1) to present evidence which justifies accusing someone of a crime or other wrongdoing; (2) (as said of circumstances, appearances, clues, unguarded statements, etc.) to be such evidence

"Y-yes," came a nervous response from the freshman rows.

"But I won't," said Ms. Framley, suddenly **conciliatory**, and with the steeliness gone from her voice. "Let's try to be friends, you and I. And let's watch a little documentary film that shows why Dropanchor can never do too much for Mr. Bamalford."

READER: Larry focused on the accuser letters.

AUTHOR: The ... ? Oh, the neon-pink letter F's that formed on Ricky's forehead. They were a little weird, I must admit.

READER: No, no. Larry thinks it really happens.—when you do something wrong there are signs which the body produces to **incriminate** you.

AUTHOR: I should just start the next chapter, but, uh ... has Larry had some strange personal experience along that line?

READER: Check. One day his English teacher was asking who replaced her chalk with cheese sticks, when completely against his will his mouth slowly formed the words, "Why don't you ask Larry?" He sounded like a robot, but everybody heard what he said.

AUTHOR: So that cooked his goose.

READER: No. Larry's quick. He couldn't stop his mouth, but he could make it say more, like "Why don't you ask Larry ... the difference between gerunds and participles?"

AUTHOR: Quick indeed!

Chapter 8: THE BELLICOSE PARAGRAPH

Slowly the lights dimmed in the auditorium, a screen descended from above the stage, and a film began to play. The title was *Bamalford at War*, and the accompanying music was **martial** in tone. Evidently Bamalford's war was a naval one, for the opening scene, shot from several angles, was set at Dropanchor's harbor, a corner of the bay protected with a long breakwater. People of every age and description were lined up on the beach, silent and watching. Halfway out on the dock Mayor Povano and his council members had gathered, silent and watching as well. Every face in the mayor's circle and in the crowd at large—with the possible exception of Rachel's, which wore a **pondering** look—registered anxiety, and there was no mistaking the object.

> **martial**: bearing some relation to war and the military forces responsible for conducting war
> **ponder**: to examine or go over something at length in your thoughts, with a careful weighing of all its elements
> **belligerence**: a hostile defiance and aggressiveness in the way you treat people
> **hue**: a color; a shade or variation of a color
> **formidable**: so large, powerful, numerous, extreme, etc., as to inspire fear and awe

Not far from shore, its motor idling noiselessly, a U.S. patrol boat held position. Dancing a strange, troubled dance on its oaken deck was a man of forty-five or so, with a massive forehead. Rather than life or love or any of the other common reasons for dancing, rage was the theme and the motive here, for the dance was an angry stomping of feet, a furious flinging of arms. In one fist the man was waving an empty beer can, in the other a maroon-colored book, and both items looked like weapons, so great was his **belligerence**.

"Number nineteen," said Rachel all at once to Ricky, speaking quietly, but pulling at his cuff, obviously proud of her accomplishment.

"Good, Rach," he answered, squatting down so that he could talk to the little girl in a low voice. "You read the boat. You're some kind of infant marvel." His words were barely audible on the sound track. "Nineteen it is—but I don't think nineteen will be our favorite number when that madman is through."

The boat was marked Bureau of Ecology Patrol Vessel 19. It had the length of a yacht, but was cut more sleekly and bristled with antennas and signal dishes. Even more equipment seemed to be hidden away under canvases.

Everything—the boat and its gear—was painted in a gleaming purple. The one exception, contrasting sharply, was the dragon crouching at the bow. It was sculptured from an orangy **hue** of agate, and it blazed brightly—orange and orange-red—under the midday sun. Its function, probably, was to inspire fear, but there it failed—it was too much a piece of art. The crouch was carefully posed, the long tail was carved upon with an intricate scrollwork.

If the dragon figurehead, however, was not especially **formidable**, the dragon captain was. His name was Draco, and his wide forehead was twisting into shadows now as he screamed at the people on shore. "Look at me, garbage lovers. Look at what I'm holding."

> **infraction**: the breaking of a rule
> **confiscate**: under authority of law, to seize the property of someone
> **breach** (noun): the failure to do, or to hold back from doing, some particular action that you have the obligation to do or not do

He was waving the can. "When this is full and sitting on the grocery shelf, it's beer. But when it's empty and floating in the public waters of the United States, it's pollution. And that's where my equipment detected it—floating in your bay. And don't tell me it drifted up from California either. Look at the label—Terebinth Beer. I ran a check on it. Dropanchor is the only place where they make the wretched stuff, and the only place where they drink it. So listen carefully, slobs of every generation. Dropanchor now has offender status. There has been an **infraction**. What Title 51 forbids, Dropanchor has done."

He had lifted the maroon book high for everyone to see. His voice, as from the beginning, seemed to be straining with hostility. "*United States Code*, Title 51, the Clean Water title. Bad news for polluters. It says I can bankrupt you with fines, **confiscate** your boats, your vehicles, eventually your homes. Too harsh? Come on, let me hear the whining. It was only a beer can, right? What about the quality of mercy, right? Well listen, piggies, what about the solemn obligation you have to keep America clean? A beer can, one beer can, tossed in the public waters is a **breach** of that obligation. And the violation is not a trivial one. It's your contribution to a dead, toxic planet. So start squealing, piggies, because Dropanchor is looking at penalties a lot nastier than just a ..."

> **diatribe**: a speech or writing, sour and harsh in tone, which goes on at length criticizing or attacking
> **imperious**: proud, cold and commanding; ordering people about as though they were servants and you were royalty
> **bellicose**: liking war; inclined to start quarrels, and to respond to problems by going to war

He stopped in mid-sentence, staring at something. The camera swung about to show a figure striding across the beach, portly and confrontational. "That's quite enough of your **diatribe**, Inspector Draco," the figure declared.

"And who might you be?" demanded Draco. His tone was **imperious**, and he seemed confident that without much trouble the stranger could be reduced to silence and obedience.

"The name is Peerless Bamalford," replied the newcomer, in a voice that reached easily across the interval of quiet water between the sand and the purple boat. "Accent on the second syllable. Hit the "mal," hit the "malf"—ba-MALF-ord. Yeah. P. Bamalford, editor. There's a little daily we publish here in town, and I'm the editor. And I wrote an editorial for you today. It starts off calmly enough, but at the end there is some business you won't like, a **Bellicose** Paragraph. We might call it a declaration of war."

Draco looked in the direction of Mayor Povano. "Next time why don't you just offer me lunch and forget the clown program?"

> **noisome**: repugnant to the senses; foul smelling
> **blanch**: to turn suddenly pale, often under the influence of shock or fear
> **vexation**: a petty torment; a persistent bother or affliction

Bamalford was unperturbed. He pulled a clipping from his pocket and began reading. "'Dear inspector—man is master of the planet. The Earth is his. As he chooses he may drain her wetlands, level her forests, cage her creatures, and leave her meadows **noisome** with his garbage. And yes, Draco, because man is lord of land and sea he may, if it pleases him, launch his empty beer cans upon the waters.'"

After listening to a few more sentences in the same vein, Draco interrupted. "A trillion pardons, Spearless, but are we there yet?"

Bamalford ignored the question and read on for several minutes more. Pausing at last, he gazed severely at the inspector, who by this time, bored and unimpressed, was leaning idly against his dragon.

"Ah," said Draco, "a brief staring contest. Maybe it means that now we are there—the Bellicose Paragraph."

"Precisely," answered Bamalford, "the declaration of war." He resumed reading. "'More than one Bamalford is watching you, Draco. I, Peerless Bamalford, editor, promoter of civic enterprises, I watch you, close at hand, prepared to strike as may be necessary. But from far away another Bamalford watches you, also ready for the strike—my older brother, the famous attorney, Fearless Bamalford.'"

Draco's large head jerked up. His mouth dropped open, and the color was gone in an instant from his cheeks. "Fearless Bamalford is your brother, that attorney from Los Angeles who … I mean … they say he grinds his teeth when he cross-examines."

Bamalford nodded grimly. "Yes, Inspector—**blanching** Inspector—and they are sharp teeth. Now—the rest of it. Please listen. Quoting again: 'Fearless Bamalford has had enough. Dropanchor may not be his biggest client, or his richest, but as long as his younger brother lives there it is a client he feels very protective about. So hands off Dropanchor, or Fearless is coming after you, Draco, with every **vexation** available in the Anglo-American system of law. You will be subpoenaed, indicted, arraigned, deposed and, of course, cross-examined mercilessly. Garnishments will dry up your income, liens will cling to your property, restraining orders will dog your steps. The fun is over, Draco, the war has begun.'"

> **aegis**: (1) the shield used by one of the Greek gods, such as Zeus or Athena; (2) the shielding effect of some authority, law, established institution, etc., under whose protection or sponsorship you carry on some activity
>
> **tumultuous**: marked by the roar and wild stir or movement of a disorderly crowd
>
> **ensue**: to occur after some event, and often as a natural development or consequence of it

Bamalford folded the clipping and returned it to his pocket. He slowly lifted his arm and extended his index finger in the direction of Draco. There was a dreadful silence; the inspector had shrunk a bit. "That," said Bamalford at last, "was the Bellicose Paragraph." He gave a slight flick with his finger. "Perhaps you and your purple pirate vessel, and your fiery dragon, should be going now, Draco. And perhaps in the future you'll be more careful about overstepping your authority. Because if ever again I learn that your enforcement activity is not being carried on squarely under the **aegis** of the law … Well, you get the idea, don't you, Inspector? It won't be pleasant."

A shadow of rage and frustration creased the wide forehead, but after an instant it was gone and in a hollow voice, addressed to no one in particular, Draco said, "Yes—I should be going. I have a … very busy schedule."

A minute later and Bureau of Ecology Patrol Vessel 19 was slipping out of the harbor, to cross the bay and disappear on the open sea. A **tumultuous** cheer went up from the beach, and a wild celebration **ensued**, dance and triumph, almost a riot. For the moment, Dropanchor and her people belonged to Bamalford.

READER: That was a nice touch, saying that Fearless Bamalford grinds his teeth when he cross-examines.

AUTHOR: Oh, well, thanks.

READER: Fulano, of course tells us the technical name for teeth-grinding—bruxism.

AUTHOR: Bruxism! I knew it, of course, but do you think it will ever show up on the entrance exams?

READER: Could be. It's very common, especially from tension. You should be there during finals in the AP classes—sounds like a flour mill.

AUTHOR: Next chapter!

Chapter 9: THE SUPERCILIOUS EYEBROWS

Ms. Framley switched off the film. "There you are, Squeaky. That's why Dropanchor can never do too much for Mr. Bamalford. He saved our hide. Questions?"

> **zealot**: a person who is dedicated energetically and absolutely to a cause, sometimes to the point of losing sight of other values
> **ascendancy**: a commanding influence, often based on some superiority of strength or advantage and not merely on high rank within a power structure
> **complacence**: an untroubled satisfaction with your situation, often to the point of overlooking problems and shortcomings

In the nervous silence which followed, Joannie's remark to François, although muttered in a low voice, was distinctly audible. "It looks too easy. One nasty editorial and Draco wilts. One minute he's this very believable **zealot**, defender of ultra-clean oceans no matter what the human cost, and the next he's mush."

Bamalford pounced. "There's a spiteful question—I heard it, and I will answer it directly. You saw the part in the movie where I pointed my index finger at Draco. You saw it, but obviously you missed what it was about. At that moment all of my superiority—moral, intellectual, physical—was concentrated in the tip of that finger. The net result, the only possible result— Bamalford rules, the inspector obeys."

"It's called **ascendancy**," said Ms. Framley in a solemn tone. "A controlling influence over one's fellow men. It often accompanies greatness." She looked admiringly at Bamalford. "And beauty," she added with a smile of **complacence**.

> **intractable**: firmly resisting the attempts of others to guide, manage or instruct you
> **austere**: severely simple; marked by a self-discipline which holds back from pleasure and ornamentation
> **immune**: unaffected by some force or influence which in most people does produce effects, often negative ones

"Thank you, my dear Seismo," answered Bamalford. "The unworried satisfaction you take in your appearance could not be more justified. As for me I have yet to find man or beast who can resist the concentrated force of my ascendancy. Man or beast. But why take my word for it? Ms. Framley, of all the students at Dropanchor High, who is the most stiff-necked, stubborn, **intractable** and difficult to govern?"

A spark flashed in Ms. Framley's eyes, like a flaring from the coals of a deep hostility. Without hesitation she approached Bamalford and whispered something to him, going on for some while. At last he growled in return, "And besides all that, she's rude, you say?"

He turned to the students. "Sophomores—yes, I'm looking at you, sophomores. Many of you are stubborn, and many of you are rude, but among you is one who is exceptional in both categories, a rude girl, a rebellious girl. Yes you, Merci Dubois. Stand, I say."

A slender girl rose from her seat. Her clothing was **austere**—a khaki work shirt, a pair of jeans without ornamentation—but she possessed an exceptional beauty. Even in the subdued light of the auditorium the exquisite measure in the lines and angles of her face, from the slight arch of the brows to the fine parting of the lips, could not be mistaken.

Bamalford extended his arm toward her, with the forefinger raised. "Wild creature, Merci Dubois, always refusing, always defying, you have no power to resist the force now concentrated in this one lifted finger. You can only obey. Hold your hands in front of you."

The girl raised her hands in front of her.

"Ha!" cried Bamalford. "And you thought maybe you were **immune**. No one is immune, my dear, to Bamalford's overwhelming mastery. Now cup your hands and place them as though you were wrapping them around a stovepipe."

> **languor**: a sometimes deliberate attitude of fatigue, weakness and avoidance of exertion
> **throttling**: the act of choking someone
> **premonition**: a feeling, not fully supported by objective evidence, that something is going to happen

In a trance, Merci obeyed.

Bamalford let his arm droop a bit and allowed a hint of **languor** into his voice, as though showing how effortless his control over Merci was. "If you please, Ms. Dubois, imagine that your hands are wrapped not around a stovepipe but around the neck of Foster Farbugle." Then with a lazy flick of his wrist he commanded: "Give Foster a good **throttling**!"

Slowly Merci's hands began to move. They disengaged from one another and rejoined, palm to palm, and with small motions rose and fell several times. It wasn't a throttling. "A handshake!" cried Squeaky.

"Shut it, Squeakface!" roared Ms. Framley in an instant. Even as the eyes of Bamalford bugged with rage, Merci's right hand lifted itself to shoulder height and gave several friendly pats upon the air. Then rising on her toes and turning towards the face of the imaginary Foster, she placed a kiss.

Bamalford looked like a boiler explosion. "Mock me, will you, goblin child! Give Foster a kiss, will you? Wait until you see what I give him. Ms. Framley—all students to their homerooms. We will visit the classes, one by one. We will find that maggot, and when we do, it ..." With his threat hanging unfinished in the air, he left the stage and took up a furious watch on the little bridge over the Bad Pony, flinging his gum once more into the stream, and waiting to see that his orders were obeyed.

Ms. Framley lost no time. She knew how to make people jump, and now with a snarl here, a scowling there, she quickly brought the students to their feet and sent them hurrying on a forced march through the long wing, returning to the main block of the school.

The seniors went first. From her position near the front of the pack François kept glancing back over her shoulder, trying without success to catch sight of Merci. The two were sisters, and François was anxious. She had a strong **premonition** that when Bamalford and Ms. Framley reached the sophomore homeroom, the first object of their attention would be Merci.

> **pernicious**: gradually having a destructive, often deadly, effect
> **mettle**: an underlying strength of character by which you stand up to difficult situations with spirit, courage and resourcefulness

The seaward side of the school building was entirely occupied by the homerooms. They were large and comfortable, with a spacious view to the north, south and west. Because they were stacked one on top of another and because on this particular day the windows were open to admit the late summer breezes, the seniors on the fourth floor could hear the freshmen being interrogated on the first. It was ugly but brief, as Squeaky was badgered by Ms. Framley into agreeing that Foster was an agent of destruction, a **pernicious** misfit, who should be squashed as soon as possible.

That was enough for the freshman class. Now the manhunt began an upward sweep. Ricky and the other seniors could hear the heavy thudding of boots ascending to the second floor, and the opening and closing of the large oak door of the sophomore classroom. François groaned, "Poor Merci, she's in for it."

"She's tough," answered Meagan, trying to console her friend. "A brat on occasions, but she has ... **mettle**. Look how she defied the big people there in the auditorium."

"I know," said François, "but sometimes that mettle collapses, and all of a sudden she's just a little kid. Some things spook her—strangely, not the direct head-ons with nasty people but more subtle things like disciplinary systems, monitoring networks, the recording of violations. I'll bet she didn't like that violet notebook with the names in it one bit."

> **ruminate**: to think something over slowly, bit by bit
> **supercilious**: haughty and proud; giving the sense of being above everyone else
> **disdain** (noun): the feeling that someone is far inferior to you, or the scornful manner in which that feeling is expressed

François was right that her sister would be singled out. After a horrible silence—you could feel a sick brooding, as though Ms. Framley were **ruminating** on wrongs received and insults suffered—the big woman at last burst out, "But you are the worst, you stuck-up little snip in your khaki shirt. Miss Dubois, the beauty, cool and proud, finer stuff than the rest of us. Look at those eyebrows, everyone, look how she lifts them, arches them, as a sign that she's better. Haughty creature! Drop them. Drop those **Supercilious** Eyebrows at once! This is America, snot child. No royalty here, no duchesses, czarinas or princesses. So drop them!"

There was a soft, lengthy reply, and Allen, sitting near the window, let out a low whistle and reported, "Her mettle is fine, François. She admits that she is a brat, although because of her extraordinary beauty everyone forgives her. But she objects to the phrase Supercilious Eyebrows. It is not haughtiness which lifts her eyebrows, but natural arch."

The windowpanes trembled with Ms. Framley's reply. "Supercilious Eyebrows! Period. The expression of your cool **disdain**. Lower them, or I'll call the State Patrol."

Merci was not intimidated. Her response was firm, louder than before, easily audible in the senior homeroom: "Thirty feet straight up, Ms. Framley, that's where the senior boys are; they're devoted to my extraordinary beauty, and they would tell you that I'm not supercilious."

> **innate**: forming part of your character right from birth
> **despot**: someone ruling with unlimited authority, often in an oppressive manner
> **suffrage**: the right to cast a vote in the election of public officials and in the decision of issues referred to the people

Bamalford broke in. "You don't know boys any better than you know distances. If that's thirty feet, so is my mother. And senior boys aren't devoted to anything but their stomachs."

Merci flared. "I know distances, Mr. Bamalford. I have an **innate** sense of distances. I got the gene." There was a metallic click. "Shall we check with my tape measure? It's got thirty feet on it."

52

In Room 401 Allen looked like a stout version of Sherlock Holmes. "Ah! The scraping of a chair, the quick sound of footsteps. She's gone to the window."

He raised his hand. "Requesting permission to stick head out the window, ma'am." He didn't know what to expect. The senior class had a new teacher, Ms. Jensen, a trim woman in her early thirties. With her hair pulled back into a single braid, and the gray of her eyes repeated by the silver-gray of wire-rimmed glasses, she looked efficient and stern. Yet Allen's question drew a faint smile, and she said, "**Despots** must be resisted, must they not?"

Allen took that as a yes and poked his round head out the window. Almost at once he fished in something yellow and metallic, the end of Merci's measuring tape. With his free hand he pulled a pen and a pad of sticky notes from his supplies. On the pad he wrote in large letters, Ballot of the Senior Boys.

"OK, guys," he said, "the right to vote—you've all got it. Universal **suffrage**. Ready? First choice—natural arch." There was a forest of hands. "Second choice—Supercilious Eyebrows." François smiled as though she knew something about the subject, but no hands went up.

> **abet**: to encourage and assist a person to accomplish an objective, often one that is criminal or contrary to accepted morality
> **redundancy**: an expression that is unnecessary because it repeats an idea that you have already communicated

On the sticky note Allen recorded the results: natural arch—too many to count, Supercilious Eyebrows—zero. He wrapped the note around the tape measure at the one-inch mark and then gave a little tug. The tape slid from view as Merci let it retract.

Her exclamation came in a silvery, childlike voice. "They sent me a sticky note!"

She read it aloud, and the reaction was immediate. "The clowns!" cried Ms. Framley. "You just can't give clowns the right to vote—they get confused, they get it all wrong. But we'll straighten their heads out—those nice senior boys—we'll fix their wiring. Every one of them gets the treatment—and also that four-eyed teacher who aided and **abetted** them."

READER: Fulano's book says that "supercilious" comes from the Latin word for eyebrow.

AUTHOR: Actually—we're not sure there was a Latin word for eyebrow.

READER: Like you were there! Anyway, though, if Fulano's right, the title of this chapter is a **redundancy**—The Eyebrow Eyebrow.

AUTHOR: It's too late now to change it—we've already shipped. But if you'd feel better, perhaps the bookstore people could paste an advisory on the cover—May Contain Redundant Material, something like that.

READER: I'd feel a lot better. It could go right under the warning about not driving or operating machinery after reading this book.

AUTHOR: OK—fine, but we don't need to keep bringing that up, do we? How would you feel?

Chapter 10: THE DECADENT VITAMINS

The seniors listened grimly as the interrogators pounded up the stairs to the juniors' homeroom. Allen commented quietly to Ricky, "The Farnums, I'll bet."

> **strident**: sounding loud and harsh, often with the intensity of a screech
>
> **progeny**: the children, grandchildren and further descendants of someone
>
> **impudence**: a show of disrespect or defiance, often bold and direct and marked by some degree of cleverness or smartness

Ricky answered, "Yeah, the Farnums. She hates the Farnums."

They flinched as a **strident** accusation shot up from the third floor. "The Farnums! Of course, the Farnum twins, **progeny** of the foul-tongued Captain Farnum. Answer me this, you two: did just one of you do the Farbugle thing, or was it both of you?"

A simple Neither would have been a very good answer, but the twins had a well-known gift for complicating things, and Ricky and the others waited to see what they would come up with.

"Yormp!" came the voice of Henry Farnum. "Normp!" volleyed Andrew. Then for several rounds it was Yormp and Normp until suddenly the two voices joined, in a harmony that was spooky it sounded so much like Ricky, and asked, "So when may we expect you in Dropanchor, Sallie?"

Ms. Framley pounced eagerly. "So—is this a confession?"

Andrew began to explain. "No, ma'am, just a passing **impudence**, just ..."

Henry hushed his brother severely, and said to Ms. Framley, "He's very disrespectful. But anyway, it's unthinkable that we could be Foster. Remember what Foster did. He invited Sallie Driven to Dropanchor. We would never do that, ma'am. She's the competition. We would sooner invite the killer bees."

> **hypothesis**: a theory which serves as a possible explanation for facts you have observed, and which is to be tested to see if it proves true or not
>
> **heretical**: having the character of a heresy, namely, an opinion that stands in opposition to the official belief of a religion or other institution

Andrew took over. "Why does Sallie Driven drive all over the USA looking for oddball people? Why does she ask so many questions? We have a **hypothesis**, ma'am, which explains these facts. May we share it with you?"

"You may be sharing 260 years with a penal institution," snarled Ms. Framley. "But go ahead."

Henry began. "We call it the Martian hypothesis, ma'am, because it has to do with Mars. Maybe you weren't aware, but the shopping is much better on Mars."

Andrew slipped in. "That sounds **heretical**, we know, because there's this ... this universal belief that the best shopping is on Earth. It's like an article of faith. And yet on Mars the products are better, truly world-class, because—help me with it, Henry—because the designs are wilder."

"The colors are more subtle."

"The metals are lighter and stronger."

"The plastics are more ... more textured."

"The batteries are semi-eternal."

"The ..."

"And all this has what to do with that Sallie Driven creature?" growled Ms. Framley.

> **extraterrestrial**: originating in, or having something to do with, some part of the universe lying beyond the planet Earth
>
> **solicit**: to use arguments, pleas, the offer of benefits, etc., to persuade someone to furnish something to you
>
> **plutocracy**: a class of wealthy people who through their wealth control a nation or society

"She's looking for the rep," answered Henry smartly.

"The sales rep," added Andrew.

"The Martian sales rep—a genuinely **extraterrestrial** rep. And so are we."

"You're extraterrestrial too?" asked Ms. Framley, frowning with distaste.

"No—we're looking for the rep too." It was Andrew who answered. "We think a sales rep from Mars landed about three years ago, to study the market. We think he's working on his own, not **soliciting** any help. Whoever finds him and forms a marketing alliance with him, well, your cash flow problems are history, I mean—you're into the **plutocracy**, you're the world's first trillionaire. And why not us, I mean we? After all, we have a catalog already prepared—just needs some product descriptions. But Henry, you talk—why should I have to do it all?"

Henry took over willingly. "Returning where we started, ma'am—why does Sallie seek out strange humans? Because that's her best shot to find the Martian rep—not a bad hypothesis, huh? There's no question he's adopted a human form—when in Rome, look like the Romans, right? And there's little question that in his human form the rep must be a strange piece of work. I mean, think ma'am, if you for example were a Martian, accustomed to your own graceful kind of body, and if you came to Earth and had to ... had to"—he was gesturing dramatically toward Ms. Framley's substantial person—"had to restate yourself as a big, clunky human body, well, you might act strange too."

> **implication**: something which is not said in so many words but which can be understood from what has actually been said
> **propriety**: the conformity of what we say or do to the standards of decency and courtesy which are generally accepted in our society
> **diminutive**: small; scaled down to a size below normal

She didn't like the tone of this. "If there is any **implication**, little beast, in what you say that I'm a Martian, or that I'm looking for Martians, or that Martians would not find me attractive, well, your last twenty test grades just went to zero. And for your information I hate hypotheses—they're just so much rain on the roof, so much sweat off a duck's rump, so ..."

"Ma'am," broke in Henry, "before there's any more offense against **propriety** and good breeding let me say that what you hate are bad hypotheses. Good hypotheses—and that's what Andrew and I deal in—include a prediction, and if the prediction comes true the hypothesis is proven. We predict that if Sallie is searching for the Martian rep, well—eventually she will find him. And we predict that he will give her the chance to show her stuff, to display her marketing skills. Slowly at first, a couple of products, like ... like ... What's that one, Andrew, that you thought of?"

"The little toaster!" said Andrew. "The very little toaster, it's so **diminutive** you can hang it on your key chain like any other trinket. But it functions, and when the toast pops up it's normal size toast."

> **axiom**: a proposition which is considered to state a fundamental and evident truth and which often serves as the basis on which some area of learning is built
> **shackle** (verb): (1) to restrain a person by locking his ankle or wrist into a metal ring or cuff attached to an immovable object; (2) more generally, to hold a person back from growth or progress

Bamalford was wagging his finger, and shaking his head furiously. Andrew took it in stride. "The usual reaction. You obviously buy the **axiom** that the inside of a thing cannot be bigger than its outside, the toast can't be bigger than the toaster. But for the Martians that's no axiom at all, just an outdated opinion which they refuse to be **shackled** by."

"Just like the theory," added Henry, "that it's impossible to construct a perpetual motion machine. The Martians do it constantly, and we expect that our

Martian catalog will include items like a cute little perpetual-motion scarecrow for suburban gardens. It will flap its arms to chase off the birds, and it will flap them until the end of time."

> **Armageddon**: a huge, once-and-for-all battle between good and evil taking place at the end of time
> **inane**: silly, without weight or depth, empty of significance

Bamalford's mouth pulled down at the sides, in a look of repugnance. "I see little hope for our nation, Ms. Framley, if this is where our future leaders are coming from. Toasters on key chains, scarecrows flapping their arms until the **Armageddon**—enough! Think, Seismo, if a monkey runs up and makes an obscene gesture, I am not insulted—for it is just a silly mammal, many steps down the ladder from me. And if the Farnums are Farbugle, then let them say what they choose, I am not dishonored. Who cares about the **inane** babblings of creatures ten steps down from the monkeys? Enough, enough! Onward to the fourth floor—better hunting awaits us there!"

> **perfunctory**: performed with minimal effort and enthusiasm, often to satisfy—although in a mechanical way—some requirement
> **baleful**: heavy with the menace of evil to come
> **feign**: to make a false showing of something; often, to pretend to be in such and such a condition or emotional state

Again there was the thudding of footsteps on the stairs, as horrible as before, although the pace was slower. Then a **perfunctory** knock, brief, without effort, the minimum necessary to satisfy the demands of courtesy. Before Ms. Jensen was two steps from her desk a voice growled, "Well, we tried the good manners route," and the door flew open, to reveal a perspiring Bamalford and a panting Ms. Framley. Still at the threshold, they stared **balefully** at the seniors, like two fiery hounds pausing for a moment but showing by every sign that soon they will be on the attack.

Ms. Jensen was in the path of the intruders, and she watched them a second or two. Then with a sweetness that was obviously **feigned**, she asked, "Won't you come in?"

Casting a steely look at her Ms. Framley observed to Bamalford, "It's an exhausting work ... fighting juvenile crime ... and dealing with the four-eyed misfits we get for teachers."

> **sluggard**: a person whose laziness has gotten control of him, causing him to avoid any activity requiring much effort
> **vial**: a little jar, able to be closed tightly, and used for holding a liquid
> **confide**: to tell something that is delicate or sensitive, with the expectation that the hearer will keep it secret

"You're no **sluggard**, Seismo," said Bamalford, a note of concern in his voice. "Far from it—you crackle with energy like a power transformer. But ... but the stairs in this building—they're like one of those climbing walls, and I can see they've tired you." He was still catching his own breath, and had to finish choppily. "A spoon ... or two ... no harm ... no harm at all."

"A spoon or two," she repeated gratefully, unfastening the golden spoon that dangled from her ear. Out of her purse she took a glass **vial**, studded with tiny sapphires, and containing a mocha-colored liquid. As she uncapped the little jar, her voice fell toward a whisper, and she **confided** to Bamalford that what was inside was called Brandy Harbor Vitamin Elixir.

"Still more quiet, Seismo," he counseled. "You mustn't give away any of your beauty secrets. This crowd looks pretty desperate."

> **viscous**: (said of liquids) thick, sticky and slow-flowing
> **decadent**: (1) in a state of moral or cultural decline, often from being too absorbed in pleasures, especially those exhibiting an exaggerated and pampering refinement; (2) marked by the exaggerated and pampering refinement just mentioned
> **puritanical**: very severe in your life-style; condemning or sharply limiting most forms of physical pleasure or enjoyment

So in an even softer voice, which most of the seniors could still hear, she continued. "The base of the elixir is a mix of chocolate cream, almond paste and brandy. Look how thick it is." She poured a **viscous** liqueur into the spoon. "The potency of the B vitamins, in particular the thiamine, is boosted by adding jasmine honey in its crystalline form, at the time of administration." A fistful of amber flakes, taken from a side pocket of her purse, came sprinkling down on the spoon, and on the oaken floor as well.

The preliminaries were over, and with a deep grunt of satisfaction Ms. Framley let the elixir run slowly down her throat. "We all need them so much," she sighed, pouring out another spoonful, "our fortifying vitamins."

"Our **Decadent** Vitamins, that's what I would say," murmured Joannie to Meagan.

Calvin heard. "Don't be so **puritanical**," he murmured in return. "Refined pleasures are a sign of progress."

Joannie shook her head violently. "Not always. And not this vitamin elixir, at least not the way she snorts it down. It's just one more self-indulgence, and one more factor, I'm afraid, leading to the decay of the lady's moral fiber!"

> **reiterate**: to make a point over and over again
> **debilitate**: to make something feeble; to reduce to a state of weakness
> **lackluster**: dull, flat, average; having nothing extraordinary or sparkling to call your attention

"Alright, Mother Joannie," whispered Calvin, "condemn the world. But at least the stuff is profitable. Somebody's making a bundle on it."

"Decadent Vitamins," **reiterated** Joannie, forgetting to whisper. "I don't care if somebody is getting rich as kings."

Ms. Framley looked up sharply. "Decadent Vitamins—my Brandy Harbor syrup? Foolish child! The few great humans remaining on this Earth, my dear, can absorb vast pleasures without being **debilitated**. Indeed, I'm stronger for it."

Her eyes slowly scanned the students. "Much stronger for it, and ready now to weed the garden, to pluck out Foster Farbugle like an unwanted thistle."

Licking the last drops of vitamin liqueur from her lips, and returning the spoon—smeared now with traces of chocolate—to her ear, she strode to the window and shouted, "Squeaky, what's your favorite number?"

"Thirty-three," answered a nervous voice from three stories below.

"Thank you, Squeaky. It's a **lackluster** number—nothing very hot about thirty-three—but it'll do."

> **extraneous**: not belonging to the native material or makeup of something; showing up from the outside
> **diversion**: some entertainment or leisure activity that gives you a break from more serious matters
> **virulent**: marked by an intense and forceful hostility

Returning to the front of the room, she stood near the chalkboard. Bamalford took a position beside her. "Here is the game, children," she said grimly. "Mr. Bamalford and I will face the blackboard until we have counted to a certain number. When we turn back around, Foster Farbugle had better be—standing. And ready to travel. As for the number we count to, there is nothing in the rules of this game that says it should be this or that, twenty or eighty-nine or whatever. So I got it from an **extraneous** source named Squeaky. We will count to thirty-three."

She swung around toward the chalkboard. Bamalford did the same. They were as horrible turned away as turned toward you, and Ricky felt a nasty dread tugging at him as he gazed on the hunching backs and clenching fingers of the two avengers, and heard the graveyard tone in which Ms. Framley called off the numbers.

"Twenty-seven, twenty-eight, twenty-nine." A mix of hysteria and menace was growing in her voice as she drew near the end. When she intoned thirty, however, there was the loud scraping of a chair upon the floor, and her tension visibly eased. "Ah," she crowed, "the fun begins. This will be a **diversion**.

Thirty-one, thirty-two, thirty-three. Now let's see the little criminal, our own junior felon."

She turned, stared and shrieked in rage. Ricky was standing, but so were Allen, François, Meagan and Joannie.

"I call this an obstruction of justice," stormed Ms. Framley. As she saw how Ms. Jensen could hardly keep from smiling, her voice grew even more **virulent**. "Sandwich, four eyes?" She shook a hammy fist at the teacher. "If it's not an obstruction of justice, what do you call it?"

> **plethora**: an excessive number or amount of something
> **winnow**: after wheat has been cut and beaten, to toss it a little ways in the air so that the wind will carry off the unwanted part (the chaff) and leave only the grain
> **diction**: the manner of your speech, referring both to your selection and arrangement of words and to the crispness, accent, pace, etc., of your actual speaking
> **misconstrue**: to be mistaken in the interpretation or reading you put on something

Without a word, and apparently untroubled by the waves of hostility radiating toward her, Ms. Jensen walked to the blackboard and wrote: A **Plethora** of Felons.

"That's very cute," roared Ms. Framley, "but there are ways to handle a plethora. I'll prune it like a bush, I'll smelt it like ore. I'll **winnow** these jerks like wheat, until I get my hands on the true Farbugle. You cannot hide, maggot."

The first to answer was François. Her calm, perfect **diction** was civilization itself against the raging bellow of Ms. Framley. "You **misconstrue** my action completely. I stand neither to hide nor to help anyone else to do so. I am standing to take my punishment, for changing my name, and changing my voice, and saying what I did on national television last night."

Ricky broke in, Meagan, Allen and Joannie broke in, each claiming to be Foster, each ready for punishment.

"I'm very inspired," sneered Ms. Framley. "Five heroes. That's quite a lot." She looked around the room. "Any other heroes? Last call. Lumps? Reading skills not required you know."

> **quotidian**: part of the normal, unexciting everyday routine we follow
> **umbrage**: the displeasure and indignation you feel when you are the object of speech or conduct which you believe is insulting
> **unorthodox**: outside of the established mainstream of acceptable opinion and conduct; running against the official teaching about how something should be or should be done

She caught sight of the enormous senior class aquarium, at the back of the room. "Why not?" she cried. "Why not fish as heroes? Oh guppies and darters and ... whatever—rise above your **quotidian** worries, your search for algae and bonemeal day after day—and be heroes!"

Near the aquarium was a lemon tree, sickly and without fruit. Its leaves were a dull yellow, and they hung limply, obscuring the enormous turquoise urn where it was planted. Miss Framley, who had a taste for scenes of ruin, was attracted to this one. "I have to ask this, OK dying tree, so don't take **umbrage**—are you Foster? I mean—it's a good match on the IQ. Why don't you just come up to the front, that would be very heroic, in fact ..."

She jumped back a step or two, paused—and jumped again as she heard a loud clunk behind her. That was Bamalford, retreating rapidly until the chalkboard brought him up short.

"S-Seismo," he stammered, "there's a sound coming out of the lemon tree."

"The direct result," she replied in a shaken but indignant voice, "of allowing teenagers in our high schools. I'm sure there's a connection."

"S-Seismo," he stammered again, "It sounds like ... talking, almost like English. That's what I hate about this place—it's so **unorthodox**. Go anywhere else—Spokane, Chicago, Denver—I don't care—the trees don't talk, the people do, just like it's supposed to be. But Dropanchor could care less for the standard practice. Listen."

> **foliage**: leaves on the stem; the cluster of leaves growing on a plant or group of plants
> **injudicious**: failing to weigh carefully the competing considerations in a complex situation, and thus often making regrettable decisions

Out of the drooping arc of the lemon tree's **foliage** a steady stream of speech was flowing, and as Bamalford had suggested it was English, though not entirely free of irregularities. "The my father says don't get a girlfriend, don't get a job, and don't get with some trouble. But ... but this Sallie leaves me crazy and I am phoning to her on the television and I call the Senhor Bamalford of a big frog, and ..."

A boy came crawling out from the shelter of the lemon tree. His motions were nimble and rubbery, and though it's not wrong to say that he was crawling, there were some little hops that didn't seem one hundred percent necessary, and after the hops some little plops, and on the whole a slight impression ...

"No, no, no," François murmured silently to herself. "Tedesco would never be so **injudicious**. He's a heads-up boy. He knows that you don't make hair-loss jokes in front of the balding emperor, and that in front of a man who's wrathful about being called a bullfrog, you don't go hop and plop as though you were a ..." Still, she couldn't help laughing.

> **admonish**: to give someone a warning, criticism or other piece of advice, usually in a gentle way and in order to help him
> **debase**: to cause something to fall in status or worth; to cheapen
> **ideological**: related to an ideology (an ideology is a theory of—and often a plan for—human society and the role of government, culture and individual persons within society)

Luckily, however, it was Tedesco's accent and not his movements that caught Bamalford's attention. A light kindled in the staring eyes. "The foreign boy!" he exclaimed with triumph. "It's him, look how he talks. I **admonished** Ironbane about foreign boys. I took him aside. I said, 'No foreign boys, Ironbane, it is not wise.' But he would not listen. Harrrumph—now he will!"

Bamalford rubbed his big hands together. "Ha! I can see it. Here's Ironbane at the airport, waving at the jet as it disappears to the southeast, and mumbling over and over, 'Good-by, foreign boy, safe trip to São Paulo. I hope you enjoyed your ... your nineteen days as an exchange student at my school.'"

READER: You're fully responsible.

AUTHOR: No doubt. But for what?

READER: My friend Larry has been **debased** by this chapter—he's a moral wreck.

AUTHOR: I was afraid of that. Ms. Framley's theory, wasn't it—how great humans can absorb vast pleasures?

READER: Exactly. It gave Larry the **ideological** basis for a chocolate binge. He bought the eighty-five-pound box, each piece individually wrapped.

AUTHOR: And he's eating them two or three pieces per day, right?

READER: He's wolfing them two or three pounds per hour. He's totally lost his ability to delay gratification. He hasn't even got time to mess with the wrappers.

AUTHOR: We probably need to get this on video.

Chapter 11: THE GREEN AFFINITY

Bamalford's **animosity** toward the "foreign boy" invigorated Ms. Framley as much as the Decadent Vitamins had done. She joined in willingly. "Peerless Bamalford seems to have taken a strong dislike to you, boy. Can you feel it? You're a hair in his soup, an insect on his windshield. So how's your anxiety level? Are you worrying that he will send you home, get you out of his sight? Well, good news—on that point nice Victoria Framley, always an angel of consolation, can **assuage** your distress. Because—you won't be going home for 260 years!" With a jangle of gold she tossed back her head and laughed.

> **animosity**: a sentiment of bad will toward someone, deeply felt, and ready—in many cases—to express itself through hostile behavior
> **assuage**: to lessen a pain or anguish; to bring some calmness to a troubled person or situation
> **fecund**: giving birth to many children; yielding harvests in abundance; bringing forth many creative ideas

"Excuse me, Ma'am," protested Joannie, "but the most **fecund** imagination in the world could not dream that Tedesco is Foster Farbugle. There is zero evidence."

> **moribund**: drawing near to death; showing the weakness and decline of one close to death
> **chronology**: an ordering of events according to date of occurrence, or according to which came before and which came after
> **blight** (verb): to cause something to stop growing, waste away and often to die off

The ornaments jangled again, and the golden spoon with its chocolate smears swung out like a tetherball as Ms. Framley turned her head abruptly toward Joannie. "Look at that tree, that **moribund** lemon tree. If that's not evidence, then you tell me what to call it. Observe the **chronology** of events. First—much earlier this morning, the tree is starting another day of good health and prosperity. Later—the foreign boy returns from our chat in the auditorium and sits close to it. Then, promptly—it begins to die, it makes good progress at dying, it's on the doorstep. Doesn't all that tell you something? Only a feverish criminal mind—melting down, vaporizing, throwing off deadly fumes—could **blight** a plant so fast."

Joannie was growing indignant. "Ma'am, the lemon tree was dying before Tedesco ever got close to it! The fact is—he's there to help. If he sits by it for a

64

while—without disturbance—he begins to sense what's wrong. He's got a gift, a talent—the comprehension of growing things. He picks up their signals. It's almost like he can ... hear what they're saying."

> **mores** (used only as a plural noun): the habits which structure and govern the behavior of a group or community, especially as regards more serious matters
> **condescension**: the act of treating someone with an exaggerated carefulness which suggests that he is of inferior intelligence or rank and that you are graciously stooping for a moment from a position of superiority
> **proximity**: the condition of being very close (in space or time) to something

Bamalford smacked his palms violently together. "He listens to plants! He chats with biomass! Ironbane! Where are you now, Ironbane? I told you—no foreign boys! They will introduce strange customs, they will observe barbarous **mores**. That's what I said, and you gazed on me with **condescension**, as though to say—there, there, my little Bamalford, thank you for your effort at understanding the complicated dynamics of foreign exchange programs. Well, have a look now, Ironbane. Your foreign boy talks with plants. They whine in his ear, and he mispronounces English in theirs."

Before Joannie could resume the defense, Tedesco rose and took hold of a small branch that had fallen that morning from the tree. It was nothing really, a little stick with three or four leaves, but he carried it over to Bamalford. "Can you hear anything?" he asked, holding out the stick. "Well—neither me, I do not hear anything either. Because the plants—they are not speaking my Portuguese or your English, or making some big sounds. But they give many tiny signals, and those are what I pick up. Maybe that is my gift. And maybe you have it too—I'm not the only one. Maybe I can teach ..."

With the motion of a falling ax Bamalford struck the branch from Tedesco's hand, and then stared at him, making no effort to hide his revulsion. "Ms. Framley, quick now! Am I turning yellow and pale like the tree? The mere **proximity** of this loony, this little strep virus, makes me feel unwell."

"Away from him, boy!" cried Ms. Framley. "You're a carrier, it's plain to see. Yellow fever, malaria, river madness for sure, and what else?"

Tedesco bent calmly to retrieve the branch, and then turned to Ms. Jensen. "I try to explain to them, but they still think I am the crazy one."

> **dissipate**: to cause something gradually to lose mass and density and become thinner and thinner to the point of vanishing
> **propensity**: a compelling tendency (often part of your basic makeup) toward some particular activity
> **penury**: bitter poverty

From somewhere in the middle of the room came a low, taunting voice. "Well?"

Joannie snapped furiously, "Calvin, keep your idiot remarks to yourself."

"Just a little joke, Mother Joannie," said Calvin in a very unapologetic tone. "To help people relax a bit, to **dissipate** the tension we're all feeling."

"Ha-uck, ha-uck, ha-uck!" The sound was like a large diesel engine, first turning over on a cold morning. "That's the way I laugh," shrieked Ms. Framley to Ms. Jensen. "So stop staring. I thought Calvin's joke was funny, so I laughed. Don't I have the right to laugh, four eyes?"

"Does anyone have the right," returned Ms. Jensen quietly, "to cheapen himself—or herself—by abusive behavior?"

At this point Tedesco broke in. "Please, not to fight. Everything is legal … no, I mean, everything is OK. Please—I will tell you this little story, when I was a boy. It will explain a lot."

Bamalford whispered loudly to Ms. Framley, "Let him babble. Career criminals often have this **propensity** for getting autobiographical. Gotta tell my life story! And life stories are loaded with confessions."

"When I was two years, three years, I don't know," began Tedesco, "we were very bad in what you call I think the **penury**, OK. We didn't have a house then, or any land, just this little shack with a dusty garden on a hillside of *mangueiras*—the mango trees. It was a big farm where my father worked picking the mangos. And higher up on this same hill were the coffee bushes, and my father worked there too, gathering in the coffee beans. And in those days I could not sleep—it was hot, it was dusty, and my father's worry about the money and about no rain, I didn't understand, of course, but I could feel how it sat on him. I couldn't sleep. So one night my mother takes my cradle and hangs it in the lower branches of a mango tree."

"And during the night you picked all the mangos and made your daddy a rich man!" interposed Calvin.

> **callous** (adjective): insensitive to the emotions which others are experiencing or the suffering through which they are passing
> **durability**: a ruggedness which makes someone or something resistant to wear and tear and battering forces
> **salutary**: bringing good health of body or spirit, or promoting some other worthwhile effect

Joannie tried to shut him down. "You **callous** hog, Calvin, why show off the fact that you're short on normal human feelings?"

Tedesco was OK, though. He had an impressive **durability**, and Calvin's rudeness bounced off him without effect. "I fell asleep," he went on, "just like a stone, and the cradle was swinging, and there was the little breeze that comes when the sun goes down. But later on, when the night grew deep, something began, and I awoke. There was this glad thing, such a glad feeling—just wait a little more, only a little more. It was in the leaves—not anything I can say, not a whisper, not a breath, not some quiet, green fire—but it was in the leaves. Twenty minutes passed by, maybe thirty—and then the first fall of the rain! What a **salutary** rain!—that is right, I think. The rain came at last to the hillside, quietly, with little splashes, falling like it will not stop for hours."

"And Baby Tedesco got all wet on his soft spot! Ha, ha!" It was Calvin again.

Tedesco rubbed the crown of his head for a moment. "Anyway—it is dry now, huh. But I did not get very wet that night—my older brother came and carried me inside. He saw—I don't know how—that something had happened. And he never forgot. As I turned older he was asking me what I remembered about the night in the mango tree. So I told him what I am telling you, and he said that I have this *afinidade*, which in English would be ..."

> **affinity**: a deep orientation of interest and affection which you have toward something, and which often brings you to insightful understandings of it
>
> **sardonic**: conveying scorn, bitterness or disillusionment, often through words and expressions marked with something of wit or cleverness

Meagan ventured, "An **affinity**."

"Yes, of course. An affinity. My brother tells me that I have this affinity with the mango trees, probably with all trees, maybe with other things growing. It is a Green Affinity—that is what he calls it. And then he says he knows the explanation. I must be a plant—some cabbage maybe—which has learned to make human noises and play soccer and all of that."

"How nice," said Ms. Framley in a **sardonic** tone. "We don't have to take your word about this special ... oneness with plants. We have the testimony of your big brother—a perfect witness I'm sure, smart like the rest of the family, and completely impartial!"

"Yes," answered Tedesco, missing the sarcasm or riding over it. "And each day since the school opens I am here early—that is what my father says—and I see Miss Jensen, how she is sad and often looking at this lemon tree. But it just gets worse, and she does not know why. So I think—why not help her know why? I will start sitting close to the tree, trying to hear what is wrong. But I wonder—can I still do this, or is the Green Affinity like ... like the asthma, going away when you grow older?"

> **decry**: to voice the strong opinion that something is wrong, inadequate, worthy of rejection, etc.

digression: the act of getting off the point, of wandering away from the main subject matter in a speech, essay or conversation

"Ha!" cried François, waving an inhaler, "that theory about asthma going away ..."

Two or three other students were beginning to **decry** the theory as well, when a low reverberation filled the room. Bamalford was pushing into the conversation. "Seismo, if you please, squash this little **digression** about asthma, and keep the foreign boy on track. Ask him what he has learned with his Green Affinity. What is the problem with the sickly tree?"

Tedesco did not look at Bamalford, or at Ms. Framley. Turning instead to Ms. Jensen, he said, "I am sitting for a long time by your tree, and at last I know what it is trying to tell—it is sick of the ocean."

"Gotcha!" cried Bamalford, his big face widening with triumph. "Gotcha, liar boy! Sick of the ocean? Ha! Why not sick of the planet Jupiter, sick of the Great Smoky Mountains? You made it up. It's just a lie."

holistic: explaining things in terms of whole and complete systems rather than analyzing things part by part
reprehensible: deserving sharp disapproval or blame
ludicrous: so bumbling, silly or out of touch with reality as to deserve to be laughed at

He turned to Ms. Framley. "You may slap the cuffs on the liar boy, Seismo. I take a very **holistic** approach to crime, you know. If a person is evil in one part of his conduct, he's evil in all of it. If the foreign boy is capable of shameless lies, then he's capable of the whole range of criminal behavior— looting, arson, counterfeiting, treason, and most **reprehensible** of all— trashing editors on nationwide TV."

Ms. Jensen stared at him. "You're joking, right? Poor Tedesco with his laboring English—improving every day, but still laboring—you really suspect that he is Foster? That's **ludicrous**."

Bamalford, though, stared right back. "His accent is a disgrace, but the child uses some very big words, haven't you noticed?"

"I've seen this before," said Ms. Jensen stubbornly. "In some foreign students the vocabulary gets way out in front, even while the syntax and grammar are still iffy. So I repeat—you may think Tedesco is Farbugle, and Tedesco for his own honorable reasons may claim to be Farbugle, but he is not!"

peer (noun): a person who is your equal in rank, competence, social standing, etc.
indict: to accuse someone of wrongdoing, usually after a review of the evidence available to support such an accusation

Saying nothing, Bamalford surveyed the room for a long moment, smiling at last as though he had spied something which pleased him. "My dear Ms. Jensen," he resumed, "there is no need to become emotional. Let us put the matter to the foreign boy's **peers**, his fellow students. If they do not **indict** him, neither will I."

Turning to the class he said softly, "What do you think of the little foreign boy whom Ironbane let in? Who would like to share their ideas on this topic?"

A tense silence followed, broken finally by Bamalford's murmured "Aha!" Ms. Jensen watched with horror as he made his way down the far aisle and stopped at Calvin's desk. "Calvin, my lad," he **exulted**, "we have something very interesting here, don't we?"

He held up a drawing which Calvin had dashed out in the last ten minutes. It was an advertising poster, showing a cradle in the branches of a tree. In the cradle was a baby, with the face of Tedesco, holding out a large, smooth-skinned fruit, obviously a mango. Big letters spelled out the message: Rock-a-bye Baby, in the Treetop, Try a Fine Mango, from Farbugle's Crop.

Bamalford was in ecstasy. "At last," he rejoiced, "some honesty about Foster Foreign Boy. How can I ever thank you?"

Calvin took up the question as though he had been waiting for it. "Let me work for your paper, sir, drawing advertisements. I draw very well, and I like selling things."

"Oh, that's for sure," came a voice, choking and furious. "You're a peddler from head to toe."

"Tender, high-strung, highly moralistic Joannie," answered Calvin **derisively**. "Don't you recall—peddlers brought pots and pans to frontier mothers."

"You're not that kind of peddler," Joannie shot back. "You're the kind who peddles what he shouldn't, his friends, his soul. And Calvin—you do it good, you're the **epitome**. All the little beginner peddlers look to you, because you're the real thing, the full-blown example, the peddler's peddler."

Calvin was **unabashed**. "Joannie, hon, I hate to say it but, on the subject of epitomes, you've become the epitome of a shrew."

READER: My friend Larry liked the part where Calvin talks about Baby Tedesco's soft spot.

AUTHOR: Larry's tastes are nicely **honed**. He picks out the most refined passages.

READER: His tastes weren't so finely honed in his recent chocolate binge. He went whole hog. He put on weight, broke out, needs dental work, and has about fifty cents left to his name.

AUTHOR: The usual **upshot** of that sort of thing. But he learned his lesson, I'm sure, and won't be buying any eighty-five-pound boxes of chocolate for a while.

READER: Not for a while. As I said, he has about fifty cents to his name.

Chapter 12: CAPE SCURRILITY

Bamalford was beaming, shifting from foot to foot in a **rudimentary** victory dance, hooking his thumbs through imaginary suspenders. "All in all, a good morning's work. Let us go as we came, Ms. Framley, quiet as pumas, ruthlessly efficient as pumas. And please advise your staff member—I refer of course to Ms. Jensen—that the foreign boy is left in her charge until arrangements are made for the arrest. Let her not fail in this."

> **rudimentary**: very basic; of the simplest sort; not yet developed into a state of higher complexity or sophistication
> **remiss**: not paying enough attention to your duties, and thus leaving them unperformed or poorly performed
> **derivative** (adjective): (1) drawing validity, importance, character, etc., from something else; (2) happening or being done only as a consequence of something else happening or being done

Ms. Framley made a strange shoulder-rolling, fist-rubbing gesture toward Ms. Jensen which said as clearly as words that the young teacher had better not be **remiss** in this duty.

"And those other five, Seismo, the ones who stood up, they shouldn't go anywhere either. They may have some **derivative** liability. They didn't say the bad stuff on TV, but they obviously gave support, and the support draws guilt from the guilt of Foster."

> **viable**: (1) capable of existing or surviving in a self-sustaining way, without any sort of special outside support; (2) able to be carried into practice successfully
> **inquisitor**: one who carries out a long questioning or investigation, often under authority of law, and often in a harsh, oppressive manner
> **patent** (adjective): open and obvious; perceived without difficulty

That sort of news always heartened Ms. Framley. "A good morning's work indeed," she said, "a good cast of the net. Maybe we can see about some derivative liability for that dreadful Merci snot on the second floor."

"That may be a **viable** proposal, Seismo," answered Bamalford with enthusiasm. "It could definitely work. And she's a very disrespectful girl."

His last words went to Calvin. "Come by this afternoon, lad. An hour after school or so. We'll talk jobs. And bring the mango poster—gotta see that thing again!"

With a slam of the door and a heavy thudding of boots the two **inquisitors** were gone. Although visibly upset, Ms. Jensen said no more than, "Absurd! **Patently** absurd. A four-year-old could see how absurd it is." She returned at once to the morning's study—it was already third period, the hour for reading. "My felons," she vowed, "will at least know some Homer and Twain and Tolkien."

> **maelstrom**: a strong, wild whirlpool; a violent, spinning turmoil
> **xenophobia**: fear and mistrust of people from foreign countries, and hostility toward them
> **convoluted**: complicated and hard to follow because of being all twisted about, wound around, folded in and out, etc.

Ricky liked the course—they were tracking some of the great journeys of world literature—but after the events of the morning he was unable to follow the lesson, catching only snatches of it. When he heard Ms. Jensen ask what a **maelstrom** was, and how many of their literary wanderers had to face one, he murmured under his breath, "The mess in my head right now—that's a maelstrom." That was fair—his thoughts were spinning, his mind was turbulent and anxious. Maybe Tedesco would be sent back to Brazil. Maybe calling people a Megalomaniac Bullfrog really was a crime. For that matter, he doubted that his own father—the town judge—would see it as something all that innocent.

When the lunch hour came and Room 401 was emptying out, Ricky caught Tedesco by the arm. "If you're not too exhausted—I mean, from being hammered by the Bamalford brand of **xenophobia** and the Framley brand of xenophobia—come for a walk. We'll hike out to the cape. It's a tiny bit of exercise, but ... well, even cabbage needs exercise, right?"

Tedesco's face lit up. "So you are not worried about getting the river madness?" he asked.

Ricky laughed. "Does a beaver worry about getting the dreaded Rocky Mountain Flat-Tail Disease?"

Tedesco knew it was funny, but had no idea what it meant. "There are some of the words ..."

"C'mon, I'll explain as we go. And it's not just the words. My ideas get rather **convoluted** sometimes—I'm well known for losing myself and friends in the tangle."

They caught a trail that ran out from the school toward the sea. It followed the crest line of the ridge, cutting through a sparse grove of pine and myrtle. The grove itself, Ricky informed Tedesco, was as good as you could wish, because after some ways it screened off any further sight of the school, but it never seriously blocked their view of the Bad Pony tumbling in a fine rush through the ravine on their left.

The ravine was descending sharply, carrying the stream down to the sea. And along the other side of the ridge, the north side, the dry gully that ran there was falling as well. But the ridge itself described a long horizontal through the checkered sunlight of the trees, never dropping, standing ever higher above the stream. "And here it even starts to rise a little," Tedesco announced, as he and Ricky emerged at last from the grove.

> **tenacious**: holding tightly and stubbornly to some position or value
> **precipitous**: (1) falling steeply like a cliff; (2) acting abruptly and without forethought
> **scurrility**: speech which uses coarse humor or vulgar references, often to ridicule or offend someone

From that point the ridge did begin to climb, though gently, through what little remained of its push to the sea. It became an ascent of granite steps and terraces, and sandy patches where the sea grass held **tenaciously** against the gales. Crossing this windswept yard, Ricky brought Tedesco to a promontory high above the shoreline. This overlook was the farthest limit of the ridge, and from there the land fell sharply, and at many points **precipitously**, to the beach.

The walk had calmed Ricky, and the vast realm of sunshine which was all about them had driven much of the storminess from his thoughts. He looked over to Tedesco and gave a quick, beckoning toss of his head, as though to point out the fine perch they had arrived at and to ask "Whad'ya think?" Tedesco put on a serious face and inquired, "Didn't you say that there was a cape?"

"It was always here before," replied Ricky, equally serious. "Maybe it sailed away, I don't know. But listen, Cabbage, it gets stranger. This is a beautiful cape, right—high and majestic. But it has a low-life name—we call it Cape **Scurrility**. And here I must tell you part of the history of Dropanchor, which—by the way—I studied in the second grade, the fifth grade, once in junior high and twice more during high school!"

> **sate**: to satisfy an appetite to the point of weariness and disgust
> **satire**: the clever use of the tools of humor (exaggeration, ridicule, saying one thing but meaning another, etc.) to hold up the faults of someone to criticism
> **denigration**: criticism in a mean, destructive vein, often denying any measure of worth in the target being criticized

"So you are full up to your eyes with Dropanchor history, and pretty sick of it, huh?"

"**Sated** you mean?" asked Ricky. "On the contrary, it is my unspeakable privilege that Dropanchor has a history, that it is in large part a history suitable for tender ears, and that the school district lets me study it—repeatedly. That, anyway, is what the mighty ones tell me. But—putting aside the professional **satire**—this story about the cape really is kind of interesting. A hundred and eighty years ago, maybe a little more, Captain Jack Farnum and his merchant ship, out of Boston, sailed into this bay and dropped anchor in the most sheltered corner, there to the south, where now we see the harbor."

"The captain was coming to do some ... some commerce about the flat-tailed animal?" asked Tedesco. He was in the process of making a comfortable seat for himself in a little rounding of granite, several steps back from the brow of the cape.

"To trade for beaver," Ricky translated. "Yes—to trade for beaver. To get fresh water, fruit, meat. To start a settlement—there's a minor little piece of business. But mainly to solve a problem with the cook. The ship's cook was a large, gloomy man of fifty or so, and he and his helper, the two of them, had fallen into a rotten mood that wouldn't go away—maybe for having nothing but beans to cook with, who knows? And in this mood they were carrying on the art of **denigration**, the foulmouthed version thereof—that was how Captain Farnum described it in his log. They were saying nasty things about everyone on board—the officers, the crew, the homesteaders. And everyone not on board—the Bostonians, Argentineans, Californians."

"You do not mention any nasty things against the Brazilians," said Tedesco, turning over in his fingers a stalk of sea grass, dried and golden, that he had caught out of the wind. "So the story may continue."

> **ephemeral**: lasting for only a short time, and then passing away
> **mundane**: related to ordinary day-to-day, down-to-earth matters

"Thank you, senhor," responded Ricky. "You are what I would call a tough audience. Anyway, when the ship was anchored in what is now our harbor Captain Farnum told the cook and his helper that they needed to work it out, that they should go some place where he could see them but not hear them, and work it out. They came up here, and for an hour they shouted vulgarities and obscenities, coarse humor, offensive one-liners—all of it directed against the many people on their bad list. It hung in the air, an unlovely bit of freight. Unlovely but **ephemeral**—and as the two angry voices weakened, the wind carried off the last of the ravings before anyone had to hear it. After that, though, only one name seemed right for this cape—Cape Scurrility."

By this time there was a broad smile on Tedesco's face. "You liked my story that much then?" asked Ricky, with a touch of hesitation.

"I like this place," said Tedesco. "This is where I will come if some morning I wake up and my wings have been attached. The light is at work here in such a good way, Ricky. It gives such a good *trabalho*, marking the far-off

74

boundaries of the water, and making all this open ... blue where maybe we could fly. But the story too—it is a great story. And it helps me a lot. My brother told me—don't just send letters about what is **mundane**, about what I had for dinner, about whether my locker is big enough. He wants exciting news, funny news. So I will write to him that my school sits on a cape called Cape Scurrility, and he will laugh."

> **prologue**: an opening part (of a book, drama, speech, etc.) that serves in some way to prepare the listener or reader for what follows
> **interminable**: going on to exhausting lengths; not coming to an end

Ricky was flagging him down. "Your letter will need a short **prologue**, I'm afraid, informing the reader that in Dropanchor people are generally very nice but on questions of geography they argue fiercely, and **interminably**. The argument never really finishes—it always resurfaces. Then, Tedesco, after that very helpful introduction, you should inform your brother that one such never ending argument is about Cape Scurrility. Some very respected people around here say it is no cape at all, because it stops at the beach and doesn't jut out into the sea. Another group says Fie, of course it's a cape, it leans out over the beach, doesn't it? But it's only a cape, they say, back to the point where this open stretch of granite we're on now meets the grove of pine and myrtle trees. Beyond that point it's just a nameless ridge."

> **tactful**: perceptive of the feelings of others, and handling delicate matters in a way that does not bruise those feelings
> **acknowledge**: to give a clear indication that you agree that certain facts are true, or that certain rights, claims or obligations are valid
> **faction**: a loosely organized group that struggles for power against other such groups, usually within the framework of some institution or political system

Tedesco frowned. "They are wrecking my letter."

"Fear not," said Ricky. "There's a third group, which includes the mayor. He does not say Fie, he's very **tactful**, he thanks his opponents for their sincerity, he **acknowledges** the merits of their case—but to his mind this is a cape, Cape Scurrility. And it's Cape Scurrility all the way back to the school and beyond, up the long strip of meadow rising to the east, all the way up to East Bridge and that huge standing boulder of reddish granite that many people call the Giuseppe Stone. That's where Cape Scurrility finishes, he says, because only there does the ridge fuse into the mountain."

On a little swelling of stone, some yards back from the hollow where Tedesco was presently installed, a stingy ration of soil had collected over the years in some cracks and crevices, and three pines—tough and bent from the wind—had taken root there. In the small circumference of their shadow, Ricky now spread out his lunch, an unexciting pair of cheese sandwiches, a plastic container with a questionable mixture of smashed banana, mayonnaise and hot sauce, and—lastly—his water bottle. "We must drink this stuff," he murmured to himself.

Tedesco came and joined him. "The letter," he said after a moment, "will be OK. I will alarm my brother, and the whole family, by saying I am part of the mayor's **faction**, and that we defend the rights of Cape Scurrility—from here all the way to the big stone with the name of my uncle who stayed in Calabria."

> **flagrant**: offending strikingly against law, morality or some other rule, in a way that is extreme, conspicuous, and often contemptuous of authority
> **predilection**: the special, sometimes blind, affection you have for someone or something that is your favorite

"Ah, that blasted stone." Ricky was laughing. "I'm afraid its name refers to Povano's uncle who stayed in Calabria. You see—Bamalford wanted that stone carved into a forty-foot statue of ... Bamalford. This was in the days after he had chased off Draco, as you saw in the film. The people were intensely grateful, and he was milking their gratitude in the most **flagrant** manner. Almost every day he was asking for some new gift, and getting most of what he asked for—including eventually the exhibition dome, to take a small example. But when he pointed up the hillside to the red granite stone and described the statue to be carved from it—a weary, storm-tossed forty-foot Bamalford, one hand raised forever to his brow, gazing out to sea—Povano said no."

"He is on my list of heroes," said Tedesco with emotion.

"Well, Povano's the sort—and maybe you are too, Cabbage—who has strong feelings about such things. That reddish stone is dear to him. 'It's the object of my **predilection**,' that's what he tells us sometimes."

> **amorphous**: lacking any definite shape or recognizable form
> **nondescript**: lacking traits or features that are sharp enough to permit positive identification or classification
> **rebuff** (noun): a sharp rejection of someone's proposal or invitation
> **tactical**: related to the moves and maneuvers you make to win a game, or defeat an enemy or competitor

"All this I can understand," said Tedesco simply.

Ricky smiled. "I was afraid of that. At any rate—Povano said no. He told Bamalford, 'You can't make a statue out of that stone, it already is a statue, a perfect likeness of my uncle Giuseppe.' When Bamalford cried foul, claiming that the stone was just an **amorphous** mass, as formless now as the day it came out of the oven, Povano answered indignantly that his uncle was a formless, **nondescript** man, that the stone was indeed a faithful likeness, and that no further sculpting would be permitted. It was a **rebuff** for Bamalford, but an opportunity as well. If he played it right it would strengthen his hand when he asked for other things. So he pouted for a while, but you could see the struggle inside him between the urge to keep pouting and the desire to get back in the game and squeeze whatever **tactical** advantage he could from Povano's refusal. Finally he got control of his hurt feelings, stopped pouting and ..."

"And convinced the town to approve a different statue," broke in Tedesco, "also of forty feet. At least, that's my guess." As he said this he was looking to the north, toward Cape Stairstep, where the bronze likeness of Bamalford, astride the dome, was huge and fiery under the sun.

"Whoa," said Ricky, freezing halfway through a stretch to grab his water bottle, "that is exactly what happened. We look on the Cabbage with new respect. Behind the round face and tolerant smile—you are a strategy whiz!"

"Usually," answered Tedesco, "that is not me, and not the way I think. But I am thinking like that today because—all those threats of Mr. Bamalford this morning, all that noise—I have to figure out what it means."

> **desiccated**: (1) dried out, often to the point of being withered and parched; (2) dry as dust and incapable of stirring interest
> **prophetic**: stating what will happen in the future and usually stating it on the basis of mystical insight or revelation from a divine source
> **retract**: to take something back (such as a statement or an offer), often as a way of showing that you no longer support or sponsor it

"Oof!" groaned Ricky. "We need to talk about that. Let me just take some water. I never drink enough—lack of thirst apparently—and I go around seriously **desiccated**. Especially under a sun like today." He took a long pull, and then returned the bottle to his pack. "I'm getting very worried that Bamalford might actually deliver on his threat to send you home."

Tedesco was working on something that was not a sandwich, a little pocket of dough, fried briefly in oil, and filled with small tomato chunks, cheese stringers, and slices of an unknown whitish vegetable. "Why am I eating this thing so *tranquilo*," he asked, "and not with any fear that I will have to go home? Because it is clear to me that tomorrow or on the after tomorrow Mr. Bamalford will come back, or maybe Ms. Framley, to say that the foreign boy is not the one, that he is not Farbugle. So, Ricky, I am telling you the future, but I am not **prophetic**. I am only reaching conclusions from the big mistake of Bamalford this morning."

Ricky was squirming a little. "I would love to believe that he is going to **retract** his accusation of you, but he didn't look to me this morning like someone making a mistake. He seemed to be having quite a good time."

immoderate: observing no limits; doing something to excess
perspicacious: sharp and perceptive in your understanding of complicated situations
traverse (verb): to pass across from one side to the other

"Yes, he seemed this way," granted Tedesco, "but right now, I am betting with you, he's angry at himself about it. There was so much pleasure to be rough on the foreign boy—that he let it go outside of control. He was **immoderate**, he was like some person who cannot put the cork in the bottle again. And that wrecked his plan. His real plan, don't you think, is the big present, however that may be. Today was the day for him to create fear, to make the mothers and fathers believe that one of their kids is going to the jail, and leave them so scared that they will give him—Mr. Bamalford I mean—whatever present he asks. But see the mistake—he became focused on me, and he didn't stop with just roughing me around a bit for the fun, he went to the end and accused me of being Foster. Me, Ricky, a foreign boy who nobody knows, with parents who are far away and poor. Who will give a big present to save a boy like this? Nobody! Right now as we are talking Bamalford is starting to see this, and I think he is not so happy."

"Well," said Ricky with a grin, "they told us there at the common border that they were sending across a very **perspicacious** boy, and they were correct. Your reading on what it was all about this morning may be right on."

Tedesco tilted his head to one side and looked at his friend. "Ricky, you understand that between your country and my country there is no ... Oh well, it's only a detail."

READER: Larry says don't be so sure that the cook's scurrilities were never heard.
AUTHOR: Was he there or something?
READER: He believes that sound waves travel forever through space, **traversing** the voids between the stars. Someday the scurrility waves will come to a planet with intelligent life, and will be heard and understood.
AUTHOR: Well, we'd better hope they don't take it personally.

Chapter 13: THE HARBINGER DUCK

Ricky felt an enormous relief, the lifting of a burden. All at once he was more in touch with the **dominant** themes of the cape—the clean, scoured spaces, the abundance of sunlight, the free passage of the winds. And it was all because of what Tedesco had just said.

> **dominant**: being above all others or most others in power, importance, number, conspicuousness, etc.
> **cohesive**: holding or sticking together well; made up of parts that go together well, harmoniously and without conflict
> **demise**: the act or process of something finishing up and passing out of existence (sometimes used as a polite term for death)

Tedesco had stated the case that he was in no real danger of deportation, and had done so convincingly. The different elements of the analysis held together well. Ricky told him, "It's **cohesive**, Cabbage. It may be right on. And what a relief for me if it is. Perhaps at least I haven't wrecked your time in America. Which is good, because I've started looking like a wrecker and a plague—don't get near Ricky, anybody, unless you're ready to check out. Take the poor lemon tree, for example. As you know too well, it's not far from its tragic **demise**—even though I do question whether that one is really my fault."

> **horticultural**: related to the activity or the science of gardening
> **pedestrian** (adjective): dull, flat, plodding; possessing a dreary ordinariness; not touched by any grace or inspiration
> **allay**: to cause the sharpness or sting of something (such as pain, anxiety, suspicion, etc.) to be reduced or grow quiet

Tedesco, who had been watching his friend eat large spoonfuls of the strange banana mash, lifted his head suddenly. "You are like the lemon tree man?"

Ricky laughed. "I don't strike you as the **horticultural** type? Maybe I'm not. But my father, Judge Snoozer, says—Ricky, once in a while at least, down from the clouds and the enchanted realms, OK, down to this **pedestrian** world where dishes need to be washed and gardens weeded and petty squabbles worked out. So when Ms. Jensen was looking for someone to water the lemon tree, I thought—that's pretty pedestrian, hauling water for a plant everyday. And I volunteered. But I guess I'm having too much fun."

Tedesco's dark eyes showed a trace of worry. "This 'too much fun,' Ricky, it is like ...?"

"Well—I'm supposed to be hauling water, OK, but I found a better way."

The mention of a better way did little to **allay** Tedesco's awakening suspicion. "And it is sort of top secret?"

"No, no," answered Ricky. "In fact, in a few minutes I will show you. I water the tree during lunch hour. We'll go and do it now together. Just let me choke down the rest of my dessert."

As Tedesco stared again at the banana mixture that Ricky was eating, and at the streaky blotches where the mayonnaise and the hot sauce had not been adequately stirred in, he couldn't help asking, "This is crazy, I know, but you don't give that to the lemon tree, do you?"

> **discriminating**: perceiving the subtle differences between things through the careful exercise of the senses or of judgment
> **rent**: a hole or gash made in something when it is torn
> **improvisation**: something put together through a creative use of whatever materials happen to be at hand; some arrangement or solution that you come up with on the spot

Ricky thought for a second. "Not yet. And probably not ever. The tree isn't equipped. This is quite a refined dish, and as you move through it there are subtle changes in flavor. Without a **discriminating** sense of taste you lose them. Does Ricky have it? We believe so. Does the lemon tree? Sorry."

He was closing the plastic container now, taking a last gulp of water, checking his watch. "Oh boy, Cabbage, what I don't have is a discriminating sense of time—we're on the edge of running late."

They set out at a quick pace and soon were passing again through the grove of pine and myrtle. Moving in this direction, progressing farther and farther inland, they were returning into the attraction of the great mountain on whose roots Dropanchor lay. Wherever there was a **rent** in the screening of branches that stretched over them, they saw its heights lifting toward the sun, and occupying all the north. At these moments Ricky noted Tedesco's face. "That's how Joannie looks sometimes around this mountain," he said, "and Ms. Jensen too. Don't worry, you'll get up there—I'm sure the mountain is in your future."

Their march along the trail was swift and unbroken. In spite of Ricky's worries they reached the school with several minutes to spare. "Just time to do the watering," he said, as they scrambled up the stairs and into Room 401. "Let no man claim that this lemon tree is dying for lack of water! C'mon—I'll show you my **improvisation**. You know—it's not like there's a manual on how to water lemon trees in fourth-floor classrooms—I had to make it up as I went along."

> **copious**: enough and more than enough; presenting an abundant supply of something

impetuous: acting or reacting in a quick and sometimes dramatic way, in the inspiration or feeling of the moment

Tedesco watched him keenly as he went over by the drooping plant and took a large jam jar from a nearby cabinet. "This is the vessel," he explained. "Humble but efficient, scrounged from the cafeteria. Now—where does the water come from? Does Ricky make repeated trips down the hall to the mop closet, where the nearest faucet is? Or does the resourceful Ricky draw his water from a supply near at hand? A **copious** supply, by the way, with enough water for fifty lemon trees."

His reference was clear—the enormous senior aquarium sat just steps from the tree. It was a reservoir in its own right, and would hardly miss a few jam jars of water. "Pardon me, guppies," said Ricky, as he filled the jar and, turning round, poured its contents over the base of the lemon tree. Tedesco observed the process intently, hesitated, and then—even as Ricky was refilling the jar—gave his opinion. "It's not happy with that water, Ricky, I can feel it."

"The tree, you mean, Cabbage? The tree has to be happy with this water. Look." He held the jar in front of him. "It's great water, it's been through the aquarium filtration system, it's enriched with little half-eaten flakes of fish food, it's ... Hey! Manners, young lady!"

A wadded up brown-paper lunch bag had just come flying through the air and beaned him on the back of his head.

"She's like an **impetuous** girl sometimes?" asked Tedesco.

"Joannie," answered Ricky, "is usually a very serious, rational, level-headed and thoughtful girl. Today, however ..."

tout: to praise something loudly and insistently, often to attract customers or supporters for it

hypochondriac (noun): a person so over-anxious about his health that he constantly thinks he's getting, or is being exposed to, some serious disease

begrudge: (1) to give or furnish something in a regretful, resentful way; (2) to hold it against someone that he has certain possessions or enjoyments

Joannie fired a second missile, the crumpled front page of the school paper. "Ricky, we've just come in this instant"—Meagan and François were with her—"and obviously there are some questions we need to ask you. Would you drink that water yourself, Ricky? You **tout** it like you wanted to join Calvin in the advertising business—it's filtered, it's enriched. But would you drink it yourself? Answer me good."

"No, ma'am," replied Ricky. "It's a little matter of guppy saliva, ma'am. In this water there is guppy saliva—I mean, just for starters. I'm no **hypochon-**

driac—I sleep without mosquito netting, I don't leave the theater when some-one coughs. But guppy saliva worries me—it could give you some bad stuff. It ..."

"Ricky," broke in Joannie sternly, "do you water every day?"

"Yormp—every day. But in the middle of the lunch hour, not at the end like today."

"Thank you, Ricky. That's why we haven't seen you watering before. And each day, using a jam jar, you draw the necessary ration of water from the fish tank?"

"That's what I do—yes, ma'am."

"And the ... the guppies don't **begrudge** the water that you draw?"

"On the contrary, they're always happy to have my business. The real flat, round one there in the corner, for example, he does this little ripply thing when he sees the jar."

"Speaking of the flat, round one, Ricky, there's no question whatsoever in your mind that it's a guppy?" Joannie's gaze was severe.

> **infallible**: not capable of making a mistake; beyond error; always right
> **fabrication**: a false story or report, invented to deceive someone
> **temerity**: an excess of self-assurance and boldness leading you to scorn dangers that should be taken more seriously

Ricky looked more closely at the fish, more closely than he had ever looked before. His eyes widened slightly, and there was a catch in his breath. After a moment, though, he squared his shoulders bravely and responded, "Well, ma'am, no claim to be **infallible** in matters of fish, I could be wrong, but I would still say—yes, it's a guppy, apparently one that has suffered a bad case of the dreaded Rocky Mountain Flat-Tail Disease."

Tedesco slapped a hand to his forehead. "Without shame! This Ricky is without shame."

Joannie continued. "The fish near the bottom there, hovering over the sunken lighthouse. See how it resembles a little pony with a little rider. Is that a guppy? And think carefully—you are in danger." She was holding another ball of tightly crumpled newspaper. Meagan and François were similarly armed.

Ricky answered in the low voice of someone with little hope of finding any sympathy in his audience. "Well, ma'am, since you ask—yes, that too is a guppy. Obviously, though, it has suffered cruelly from the dreaded Rocky Mountain Palomino Disease—the one that makes you look like a horse."

"A shameless **fabrication**," cried Joannie, launching the paper wad in her hand. "Your **temerity** in the face of certain destruction is remarkable. Fire away, Meagan and François."

> **deduce**: to start with the known facts of a particular case, to consider them in light of general principles, and through a process of reasoning to arrive at new conclusions about the case
> **cryptic**: mysterious, and difficult to make any sense of; expressed in riddles
> **vindicate**: to show that some opinion or action is right after all, in spite of people having criticized or rejected it

She watched two more direct hits, and then continued. "Why won't you admit that Fish A is a flounder and Fish B is a sea horse?"

"Because then," groaned Ricky, "you will make me also admit that these are ocean fishes. And then, in your nicest voice, you will ask, 'And now, Ricky, is there anything we can **deduce** from the fact that the creatures in this tank are sea creatures?' And I will have to answer, 'Yes, Mrs. Snergglebottom, from this fact we conclude that the water in this tank must be seawater.'"

By this point everyone was yelling at once. Ricky remembered François laughing and shaking her finger at him and crying out, "The big brain in trigonometry, the big brain in chemistry—and he waters the tree with salt water until it's ..."

"Until it's sick of the ocean," shouted Meagan. "Sick of the ocean. Remember Tedesco's **cryptic** diagnosis—no one was sure what he meant. There he is! Hey, Tedesco, I think your Green Affinity is **vindicated** and then some."

> **lot**: the basic package of good and bad fortune which life seems to deal out to you as your destiny
> **acclaim**: to praise someone, often loudly and publicly

Ricky was not seriously disgraced by the episode; his friends knew that strange mishaps were his **lot**. But Tedesco was **acclaimed**. Even Ms. Jensen joined in the praise, declaring that for every thousand people who say what sounds true but is really babble, there is only one who says what sounds like babble but is really true. And Tedesco was the one.

Allen saw a good story in the making, for the school paper. He started to interview Tedesco. "You're famous. They love you. What else can you tell me about your Green Affinity?"

Tedesco, though, hesitated. "Probably I have said too much about it already. Maybe the more I talk about it, the less I will have it. Some things are like that. Can you see ...?"

> **reticence**: strong reluctance to discuss a matter in any detail

garrulous: inclined to talk and chatter at great length

Allen wasn't called Allen the Snoop for nothing, and he was disappointed by Tedesco's **reticence**. But he respected it. "With the Green Affinity, I can understand," he said. "That's a rare gift, and you don't want to talk a gift like that to death. But I hope Ricky is feeling more **garrulous** on the subject of his special gift of botching things up. Because he's my next interview."

> **candor**: full and honest disclosure, even of personal sentiments and delicate information
> **notorious**: known far and wide for something that is questionable or shameful
> **monologue**: a drawn-out statement or speech by one person, often inflicted on others who are forced into silence until it is over

Ricky was ready to talk. In fact, it was going to be difficult to shut him up. "Allen, forget the little tiptoe introductory questions, and let's speak with great **candor**. We both know what it is you want to ask—how could anyone be so dumb? It's unkind of you to put it with such bluntness, but because of my usual sick desire for attention I am prepared to answer. It all comes down to practical details. The whole world knows my approach to practical details—I ignore them, I'm **notorious** for ignoring them. They make me nervous. There's some evidence that if you look at too many practical details you'll go blind, or turn into a grown-up—I forget which. And the grown-up thing, Allen, think—you get to wear itchy clothes and pay property taxes all the time, you ..."

Allen, fearing a runaway **monologue**, broke in. "And the most recent practical detail to be ignored, I suppose, is the little distinction between fresh water and salt water. Well, after all ... that's not a bad story."

> **lurid**: boldly emphasizing gory, grotesque or outrageous details
> **parody**: the mocking imitation of something spoken or written, recreating its unique features with a mix of skill and distortion in order to hold them up to ridicule

Ricky heard the wistful note. He knew that Allen, a seeker of scandals and hair-raising accounts, had been hoping for something more **lurid**. "You know," he offered, "we could make it a tad more shocking, if you liked. First, I strangle you a bit, for being so nosy, then I make you listen to some pulp. See if you recognize this. Ricky is master of the planet. The Earth is his. As he chooses he may drain her wetlands, level her forests, cage her creatures, and give several jars of salt water per day to her lemon trees."

"Ugh!" said François, giving Allen no chance to react. "Ugh—Bamalford's speech to Draco. It gave me the creeps to hear him say it live four years ago,

84

and to hear it again in the film. And it gives me the creeps now, Ricky, hearing you do a **parody** of it."

Joannie tapped her forehead, like someone just remembering something. "It gives me the creeps too, but that part about caging her creatures reminds me, I need to go and pay a visit."

> **hypothetical**: not really existing, but assumed to exist for the sake of discussion
> **quibble** (verb): (1) to build an argument on a strained interpretation of a phrase, on a picky point of procedure, or on some other unworthy basis of that sort; (2) to make arguments about small, insignificant points
> **dispassionate**: calm and businesslike; not under the influence of strong emotion or strong likes and dislikes

Tedesco was suddenly attentive. "A visit to … the caged creature? The caged creature is not just … **hypothetical**?"

Joannie shook her head. "It was hypothetical when Bamalford gave the speech, a little let's-suppose sort of thing that he tossed in to help make his point. But later on, I'm afraid, it became all too real. A real creature. And a real cage, an awful thing, shaped from bending a single long bar of metal. The creature itself … is a bird. A duck for that matter. There are sea ducks, you know, and this is one of them. Exactly what species, we're unsure. But when you hear its quack and its quock—like very loud and brassy—you won't **quibble** about some remote chance that it's actually a pelican, a gull, maybe an egret. It's a duck, with amber feathers and maroon eyes—a beautiful duck."

"And such a good duck is in a cage?" asked Tedesco. "How does this make sense?"

Joannie had struggled—successfully—to keep her voice informational and **dispassionate**. As François took over the narrative, however, the emotion was more obvious in hers. "It's not a story that makes a lot of sense. Joannie and I saw it, we were part of it, but it's one of those sad, dumb stories we could all live without. It happened one morning three springtimes ago. We were at the tip of Cape Scurrility, standing watch. The whales were coming."

"You will see," interrupted Meagan, speaking to Tedesco, "that the whales rule around here. The rest of us, of course, we matter—we measure the tides, we turn the pages on the calendar—but the whales rule."

"Except that in one strange respect," said François, resuming her story, "the whales follow. Who knows why, but year after year the ducks with the amber feathers come before and the whales come after. The ducks fly through here, on their way north, and then three days later, maybe two, the first wave of the whale migration appears."

harbinger: something that comes in advance of a future event and serves as a sign foretelling it
congenial: in tune with your preferences and dispositions, and thus pleasant for you and welcome

Tedesco nodded slowly, as though such connections in the realm of nature were familiar to him.

"It's as though the ducks," continued François, "carry a sign—Whales to Follow. That's where their name comes from—we call them **Harbinger Ducks**. And as you can now see, watching for the whales, as Joannie and I were doing that morning, really means watching for the Harbinger Ducks. It is thrilling beyond words to be the first to spy the ducks. And that morning we were the first. A line of them came into view, working up the coast from the south. It was twenty Harbingers or so—not a lot, but in this whole world there are not a lot of them. At that hour the tide was low but rising, and it was splashing over that huge stone table that lies north from Cape Scurrility. I'm sure that's a **congenial** sight if you're a sea duck—surf running and retreating across a large face of stone. So the little Harbinger flock landed there, out by the seaward edge, and ..."

benign: kindly and well-wishing; subtly influencing things to turn out well; causing no serious harm
exacting: demanding your closest attention and most careful performance

"And I hate the next part of this story," said Meagan. "I wasn't even there, but I hate it."

"So do I," said François, "but Tedesco probably needs to hear it. The ducks were feeding, when all of a sudden things turned bad. Which is so strange—because that stone has always been such a **benign** place. But a big wave leaned up over it and broke with great force, sending out a race of water. Not a problem in itself—the ducks rode the flood easily. But one of them caught its dangling foot in a crack and was stuck, wedged, just like that. It was scared, obviously, and there was a quack or a quock that we heard even up on the promontory."

Joannie smiled faintly. "They do not suffer in silence."

"No," agreed François, "it got our attention. We were on our way at once. There is a path down the north side of the cape, steep and irregular, and ordinarily descending it is an **exacting** work. You have to plant your foot just right, step after step. That morning, though, we flew down it like never again, slipping, scrabbling, down into the dry gully. The path meets the bottom where it is sandy and flat, so at that point nothing could hold us back. We came tearing out of the gully mouth and shot along the beach. Joannie is a faster sprinter

86

and she was out in front. As she got closer to the near edge of the stone table she shouted back something like—'We lost the race.'"

> **offspring**: children; or as applied more generally to the animal kingdom, the creatures born of a mother
>
> **appropriate** (verb): to take possession of something (sometimes a thing which has previously been for common use and had no particular owner) and make it yours

François shook her head, remembering the confusion. "I couldn't get it straight. At first I thought—you didn't lose the race, Joannie, you won by fifty yards. Then the darker meaning hit me—the race against time, the poor creature in its panic had already thrashed itself to death. Yet it wasn't that either, for as I scrambled onto the stone I saw in the first instant how the duck was free, hopping about. In the next instant, though, it all came clear. The trapped duck was still trapped, the one I saw free was smaller, maybe **offspring**. And the race was the race against—Bamalford. He had seen the accident from the Dome, and for his own reasons had hurried to the spot. For him it was a ride, an elevator ride, a ride on the fat-tired thing. He beat us, and now his hand was around the neck of the trapped duck, trying to jerk it free from the stone. Joannie was screaming at him, but in another moment the duck was yanked free, and now she yelled again, that he should let it go before it hurt itself struggling in his hands. But ..."

Joannie told the final part of the story. "So big surprise—the last thing on Bamalford's mind was letting the duck go. Under all the unwritten laws by which men **appropriate** wild things from the earth, he told us, the duck was now his. He kept repeating that he'd like to appropriate another one. And this wasn't just chatter, because all of a sudden he made a lunge for the second duck. But there his luck failed, barely—right at that moment a heavy wave was breaking onto the stone, and the little duck fled into the surge. Even so, it was in Bamalford's grasp for a second—and it left him with a handful of feathers."

> **lucrative**: yielding attractive profits
>
> **synergy**: the coordination of two or more resources, systems, etc., in a way that enables each to have a greater effect or reach a more efficient outcome than if it were acting separately
>
> **arbitrary**: done or said without a rational basis and simply as the free and unrestricted expression of will or fancy

Without realizing it, she was illustrating her story now, holding up a closed hand as though she were Bamalford with his feathers. "He shook them at us. There was a crazy look coming into his eyes, and he raved some words like, 'Under the amber feathers, the amber down! And people pay a lot for down, and a lot more for amber down. These brown buzzards could be very **lucrative**. If I could catch a few more of them ..."'

"I am thinking Foster was too nice with this man," growled Tedesco.

Joannie wore a grim look. "We asked what gave him the right to terrorize a harmless creature, and he pulled out this yellow card that said Press, and asked if we had heard about the freedom of the press. He held the card over the eyes of the duck in his grasp and said, 'Quack if you support a free press!' Very funny, right? But it made him laugh wildly. He flashed the card at the other duck, which was still there, a few yards off. He flashed it at us. And then he left, carrying his prize."

AUTHOR: Tough chapter. I was going to have Ricky say that leaves from the tree fall into the fish tank, and that the fish eat them. That way there would have been a **synergy**, with the tank providing water for the tree and the tree furnishing a food supply for the tank. But I was afraid of 450,000 peevish E-mails, pointing out that fish don't eat lemon leaves.

READER: Make that twenty-seven peevish E-mails! And why are you telling me all this?

AUTHOR: We need to work in "synergy." That word is really hot, and you can't say you're a twenty-first-century vocab book without it.

READER: That's rather **arbitrary**, just pull one word out of the air and make it like the touchstone for what's a twenty-first-century vocab book and what isn't.

AUTHOR: Well, does Fulano use "synergy"?

READER: Are you ready? He's in about the twenty-fifth century. He uses "synergy," "synergism," "synergistic," and "synergize."

AUTHOR: He's a maniac.

Chapter 14: THE AMBIVALENCE DOME

As Joannie and François finished the story of the Harbinger Duck, Ricky was picking up the paper wads that had been thrown at him and was handing them to Tedesco. "If I act in bad taste again," he said, "then you bonk me with these. Because my little spin on Bamalford's cage-her-creatures speech—that was in bad taste, I think. There are some strong feelings involved here. So you will be my **mentor**, Cabbage. With word and example and paper wads you will educate me to be a person of good taste, like yourself. A person of good timing, of ..."

> **mentor**: a person who teaches and guides you, often someone in whom you place a special trust
> **dubious**: hesitating to accept something as true, legitimate, well-founded, etc.
> **surreptitious**: using sly tricks and concealments to avoid being noticed or detected

Joannie was eyeing him **dubiously**. "One doubts whether this radical change in style, this turnaround, this ... Let's just say, Ricky, that you're something of a fraud. Lovable, but something of a fraud. Now if you would like to help, you can join me this afternoon when I go to the Dome and visit the poor duck in its cage. Bamalford always gives me some dirty looks—so today you take half and I take half."

"Dirty looks?" asked Allen. "You enter right under his eyes? I had this idea of you going in **surreptitiously**, sneaky as a field mouse. Or at least going at a time when he was over at his newspaper."

"Well, remember," explained Joannie, "Bamalford doesn't own the Bamalford Dome. He acts like he does, but he doesn't. It's a public place. And, Tedesco, you put that arm down"—she had seen him start to lift his hand, his usual signal before asking a question—"because, no, I don't really know who owns it. The bondholders, the corporate backers, the State—I don't know. It's ridiculously complicated."

> **commendable**: deserving to be praised or pointed out with approval
> **hew** (verb; the past participle can be either "hewed" or "hewn"): to cut (and possibly shape) something by striking at it with an ax or other heavy blade
> **impregnable**: not able to be stormed and captured

89

Joannie was not surprised, nor was Ricky, when Tedesco joined them after school, saying that he would like to see the prisoner duck. The group soon became six, as Meagan, François and Allen attached themselves also. What made Joannie think seven might be even better she could never say, but when Calvin crossed the schoolyard she asked if he wanted to come along. It was a terrible mistake. He told her in a sarcastic tone that her duck visit was highly **commendable**, an item she could add to the community-service section of her college applications, but that he for his part had some real business to take care of—his job interview with Bamalford.

So it was six of them who followed the path out through the grove of pine and myrtle, heading seaward along the high back of Cape Scurrility. At the far edge of the grove, they turned off, catching the side path which fell in a zigzag down the north flank of the cape, into the dry gully. It was the path which François had described to the others only a few hours before and, as she had said, it was primitive, at places just a gash **hewn** into the slope.

This was not to Allen's liking, threading his way down the steep descent. He said nothing on the trail itself, but when they finally reached the sandy bottom of the gully and began the short trek to its mouth, he could be heard murmuring, "Much better, my friends!"

Joannie gave him an elbow in the ribs. "The trail we just came down," she told him, "is called the Anxious-Boy Trail. You'll like the next one too. It's called the Exhausted-Boy Trail. There—it's coming into view."

They were emerging from the dry gully, passing round a last shoulder of stone on their right, and moving onto the open beach. The sands were ivory and pale yellow, and they ran to the north a mile or so, and met the immense wall of storm-battered rock known as Cape Stairstep. Its proudest point—a final crest before it fell in a series of terraces to the water—was the site where the Dome rose up, solid and sea-green and crowned in its own turn with the massive statue of Bamalford.

"Whew!" Allen exclaimed, "I'm glad we're just trying to visit it, not capture it. It looks like the twenty-first-century version of the **impregnable** fortress, parked on that impossible cape. And thank heaven for the elevators."

> **presumptuous**: assuming without good reason—and often through an exaggerated sense of your importance—that certain rights, privileges, favors, affections, etc., belong to you or are at your disposal
> **anarchy**: the chaos resulting from the absence of effective law and governing authority
> **procrastinator**: someone who keeps putting off things that he knows deserve attention right away

Two large elevator cars, done in the same sea green as the dome itself, were scaling the cape on bright rails. Joannie looked to them, and then back to Allen. "**Presumptuous** child," she said to him, shaking her head. "You're confident those elevators are just waiting to give you a ride. Sorry, Jack, but to think that way you either have to be a paying guest or a load of freight. We go up like goats, I'm afraid."

It was hard for Allen to let go of his elevator idea, even more so after he had made the hike north to the base of Cape Stairstep and had actually begun the ascent. "They're modern elevators," he was grumbling, already starting to draw his breath in gulps, "and I'm sure they're not attended. Would it be so wrong just to sneak on, ride up, sneak off? Would our society, Joannie, slip into a hundred years of **anarchy** and chaos because we bent the rules one smidge and rode for free?"

"The time I tried it," replied Joannie in a dry voice, from the rear of the column of marchers, "the elevators were attended. You're right, Allen, they're modern equipment and don't need operators. But Bamalford keeps an attendant there anyway, at the base, to enforce the restriction about paying guests only. Lookies—and that's who we are in his estimation—lookies take the trail. At least it's got a wooden railing."

Allen should have saved his breath for the climb, but he had been struck with another brilliant idea. "Plan B," he wheezed out. "We stop here, camp, pass the night, and go on tomorrow when we're … rested."

"You're as bad as Ricky," cried François with a short laugh.

"Hey!" Ricky yelled. "I get stuff done right away. I don't camp and save it for tomorrow. I'm not a **procrastinator**."

"No, but you're out of your mind," explained François sweetly. "Sorry if I wasn't as clear as …"

> **terminology**: the words and phrases which have a specific, often technical, meaning within some particular field of activity or study
> **affluent**: quite well off financially; possessing significant wealth
> **vulnerable**: exposed in some special degree to harm, often for lack of ordinary defenses, but also sometimes because of being positioned squarely in harm's way

Allen broke in. "I did not come up here to be compared to Ricky, nor to die. I don't know the exact **terminology** for this sort of thing, but why don't we take all our money and go offer it to the elevator attendant as a little … token of our affection—and then he lets us ride. Maybe he's someone nice."

"Every time you open your mouth," answered Joannie, "it gets worse. Besides, the person there at the elevators the time I tried to use them wasn't all that nice—it was Bezzle."

Allen's plodding figure straightened in a sudden show of curiosity. "Bez! What's Bezzle doing here at the Dome, I mean, working for Bamalford?"

"Money, probably," suggested Joannie. "You don't become **affluent** on the wages of the town librarian. I'm not sure you even pay the rent. So he took a second job as a … a …"

"Maybe as a second Ms. Framley," said Meagan. She wore a thoughtful air as she joined the conversation. "That's what bothers me. Bamalford has this way of winning over damaged people. He knows where they are needy and hurt—and most **vulnerable** to his lies. Because that's his trick—he tells you the lie you want to hear, and then he wins you for his service. What did he tell to Bezzle? I won't even guess, since I don't really know how the man has been hurt. But beneath all the grouchiness, there's no question—he carries a wound."

> **traumatic**: (said of blows, shocks, misfortunes, etc.) falling with such force, physically or psychologically, as to cause significant injury
> **proliferate**: to reproduce in large numbers and, often, to spread over a large extent
> **pragmatic**: mainly concerned with achieving practical, down-to-earth goals in an efficient manner

François, who was the lead marcher on the steeply ascending trail, turned about for a moment to face the others. "It's like this cliff," she said, slapping her palm against the vast face of rock they were scaling. "We touch its surface with our hand, that's easy, but stretching away from my hand, in and away, are immense … whatever, depths of stone, and they are hidden from us. That is how people are, and their hurts. So what this wound really was that Bezzle suffered, I don't know either. But when it happened—that I have heard. My mother says Maurice Bezzle came here seventeen or eighteen years ago, full of plans, introducing himself to everyone—and as Maurice. But after two or three years in Dropanchor something **traumatic** took place, and the injury it caused inside him has never healed. And we are left with … Bezzle. Bezzle of the big fines."

Time always sped by when they were together, probably because they talked so much. And it was no different on the trail twisting up Cape Stairstep. As Allen looked down to measure their progress, he gasped. "Hey—we've been at it for a while!"

The complicated sweep of Dropanchor's shoreline was far below now—the yellow fairway of sand, the driftwood piles, the pillars and benches and other shapes of emergent stone.

Joannie looked down too and saw all this, and for her the feature of greatest interest was the one with the saddest story, the immense square of stone extending from the sand out into the tide, the rough table where the Harbinger Duck had been captured. At that hour it was glinting, all across its expanse, with the bottle greens and sullen oranges that the falling, half-obscured sun awoke. And it was thriving, she knew, at that hour or any hour, with the anemones and starfish that **proliferated** in its little pools.

Meagan, for her part, checked their progress by looking up, out of a **pragmatic** urge to see how much of the climb remained. An image of great simplicity met her eyes—the cliff wall still reared high above them and across its tawny summit the sky, fiercely blue, was streaming. For a moment she forgot the practical question—how far did they still have to go?—and just took in the elementary splendor. Elementary—and suddenly broken when a face came thrusting into view, peering down at them from far above.

> **irascibility**: a tendency to lose your temper quickly
> **arduous**: hard to do; requiring much toil and exertion
> **garish**: so intense and overdone (often in the choice of colors but sometimes in the choice of other artistic and dramatic effects as well) as to confer a shock or offend good taste

She couldn't make out the features clearly—the distance was too great—but the overall impression given by the line and shadow of that face was one of **irascibility**, and she guessed that it was Bamalford. He's always mad, she thought, or on the verge. I'm afraid that's him.

Twenty **arduous** minutes were needed for the rest of the climb, and the marchers were in varying degrees of exhaustion as they stepped onto the long brick plaza stretching from the cape's edge to the entryway of the Dome. As Meagan had feared, Bamalford was there waiting for them, at the wheel of one of the runabouts that served to ferry around the guests and their luggage. He was an alarming figure both in his sheer bulk and in the **garish** suit of scarlet that he wore.

"They say the walk down is easier than the walk up," he snapped at them, "so you might as well get started."

> **bourgeois** (adjective): supporting the values often associated with a well-to-do class of merchants and shop owners—values such as private property, orderly and respectable behavior, and the accumulation of wealth through your own enterprise
> **cower**: to wait helplessly—often crouching, shrinking back, covering your head—while something frightening approaches or is at hand
> **despondent**: feeling very low and depressed, often because you've judged that there is little or no hope of things getting better

Joannie pulled in a long breath. "This is a public place," she protested.

"And six of you at once like this," returned Bamalford, "are a public menace. The guests will be terrified. They know what's entertaining for a pack of six teenagers—property destruction and wildness—just the contrary of the solid **bourgeois** values we stand for here."

François, standing at Joannie's side, had to smile at that one. She feared sometimes that the future planned for her, after she had become Françoise, was all too bourgeois—a small, respectable business of her own, a comfortable house, the quiet increase of wealth. But she said nothing, Joannie said nothing, and it was Allen, still catching his breath, who responded. "Sir—I have the very thing that will calm your guests."

From his shirt pocket he drew a yellow card. It bore the word Press, in large letters over some smaller script.

"Press!" howled Bamalford. "What's your paper—the *Amoeba Daily*? Ha, ha!"

"No, sir," answered Allen, "the *Dropanchor High School Trumpet*. And if I show my *Trumpet* press card, sir, and my five friends stay close to me, your terrified guests will know we're reporters, not a vandal horde, and they can stop **cowering** against the walls."

"You think I'm turning six amoeba reporters loose in the B-Dome, one of whom is a foreign boy and one of whom is almost certainly Foster Farbugle?" Bamalford's face was still gleaming with an intense eagerness to throw the rabble out.

François wondered if Allen had any other tricks that he could try. She saw him cast a swift glance toward the main entry of the Dome. There, across the long expanse of the red brick plaza, she saw three women emerging. They were all in their forties, and all sipping at mugs of hot coffee and talking in the bright tone of people turned loose on a new and curious place. She couldn't see what was written on the identical sweatshirts they wore. But she murmured to Joannie, "I think it says Allen's Last Chance."

Allen saw his chance, and played for time. "I don't know, sir, how you find reporting work, but for me it's very depressing, it gets me down, I become **despondent** sometimes."

"Ha!" sneered Bamalford. "I would be despondent also, working for an amoeba rag like you do."

> **unimpeachable**: so proper in conduct and truthful in speech as to be above all accusation
> **ferret** (verb): to dig and scratch all about, in order to bring some information to light
> **transmutation**: the change of a thing of one nature into a different, sometimes higher, nature

"Oh no, it's not that," clarified Allen, watching the progress of the three ladies. "It's the local news part. People are so perfect around here, their conduct is so **unimpeachable**, there's never any scandal. But that's what I live for—to blow open some big scandal. You know—Mayor Prints Twenties and Fifties in Spare Time; Cafeteria Places Large Order with Foam-Rubber Factory. That sort of thing."

"So that's your agenda," roared Bamalford, "poking around, trying to **ferret** out some scandal here at the Dome. I have every reason to be insulted. And on behalf of my guests I am insulted. End of the discussion, end of the visit! I want the six little amoeboid journalists back on the trail before I ..."

"Oh, Mr. Bamalfy," came a nice voice—nice but free of any hesitation or submissiveness. "Does that young man have a yellow card in his hand, a yellow press card?"

It was one of the three ladies. They had approached to within a few steps now. Bamalford had his back to them, and he let one black scowl pass quickly across his face, and one oath fall silently from his lips, before turning and undergoing an instantaneous **transmutation** into Mr. Bamalfy. "Ladies—how pleasant—I bow deeply. And yes, my young friend is with a journal, and his young friends as well."

There were introductions all around. The three women were with a cosmetics company—A Thousand Ships. The one who had first spoken—a Mrs. Amanda Cook—now asked Bamalford in the same sweet but self-sure tone, "Would anything in the whole world be more sensible, Mr. Bamalfy, than for the young people to come sit with me and my two friends, at those tables by the entry, and do an interview?"

> **dissemble**: to hide what you really feel or think through the expression of a false emotion, preference or opinion
>
> **dilatory**: habitually or intentionally letting things remain undone beyond the time when they should be done; engaging in delay

Bamalford not only agreed but—master of **dissembling** that he was—put on a show of great enthusiasm. "Perfect idea! Get comfortable, do a warm-up on the coffee, and tell the young journalists here about A Thousand Ships. Just be sure lad"—he was speaking for a moment to Allen—"that the yellow card is on display at all times, at every second. And yes, ladies, I should be along in a few minutes. You'll know it's me by the conservative business suit. Just have to make one call first." He took a cell phone from his blazing red coat.

Allen saw a snooping opportunity, and when his companions began crossing the long patio, he hung back. With his sharp hearing he was able to catch Bamalford's end of the telephone call. It was a call to Bezzle, and there was a carefulness in Bamalford's tone, a treading lightly, as though he were making an effort not to give offense. "Say—listen, Bez, on your way back, I mean please on your way back to the library, could you stop by the paper? That artist boy will be there, Calvin, from the high school. Very useful qualifications, and definitely the right attitude. Please let him know that I'll be late. And as always, Bez, let's manage the optics. It's not that Mr. Bamalford has a **dilatory** streak. No, no. Mr. Bamalford is late because some pesky business requiring his attention has come up at the Dome. And you know which pesky business I'm referring to, I'm sure you do. Thank you, Bez."

> **elite** (adjective): related to a small, select group of persons, often of superior ability or believing themselves superior, who enjoy special privilege and influence
> **reciprocal**: having the nature of a two-way relation in which one side receives something from the other and returns a rough equivalent

Allen moved off quickly as the call finished. Now that is enlightening, he thought. Bezzle really does belong to some kind of **elite** team, a special little inner circle attached to the person of Bamalford; and Calvin, apparently, is about to be offered membership.

The interview with Amanda Cook and her friends was more interesting than Allen had expected, and more **reciprocal**. Amanda was editor of a little newsletter within A Thousand Ships, and after she had told some action stories from the cosmetics industry—bidding wars, ferocious battles over scents and shades—she asked some questions of her own. "This dome with the inspired name", she said, pointing to a wide marble ledger over the entry, chiseled with the words The Bamalford Dome, "what has it meant for a little coastal town like Dropanchor?"

> **ambivalence**: the mental state of both liking and disliking something; both believing it is true and suspecting it is false; or having other conflicting sentiments toward it
> **cosmopolitan**: having a wide and often sophisticated familiarity with the various cultures of the world
> **provincial**: having the narrow outlook, quaint customs and unsophisticated manner sometimes associated with out-of-the-way places

The six friends looked at one another for a moment, and then Meagan spoke for them all, saying, "The name you see there above the doors—that's not what we call it. For us six, and for most of the people in town, this is the **Ambivalence** Dome. We love it, you see—it means jobs, and our young people don't have to seek work in the big cities and become misfits—we can stay here and be misfits. But we hate it too—it means traffic snarls and lines and those shuttles with fat tires zipping along the beach. Still, we love it—lots of **cosmopolitan** guests, people with three or four million frequent-flyer miles, telling us about things in Rio and Madrid and all such places. And yes, we hate it—lots of strangers smirking at our small-town customs, referring to us as **provincial**. So for us it could only have one name, and we call it the Ambivalence Dome."

It was an easy telling of a serious story, and Amanda Cook was won over. "Don't worry about us, Meagan, we aren't smirking at your customs. I could fall in love with this place. I just hope your Mr. Bamalfy doesn't put his stamp too heavily on it."

> **altruistic**: done out of a concern for the welfare of other human beings, without regard for your own gain
> **heedless**: not aware of or not taking notice of certain facts, often facts which deserve your attention
> **slothful**: preferring a heavy, sluggish inactivity, and avoiding work and other energetic action

"The forty-foot Bamalfy," said one of the other women, glancing up on a sharp angle over the entryway, trying to see the huge sculpture. Her name was Hadley. "Oh! Can't even see it from here—it's blocked by the big name ledger. That's OK—what an offensive hunk of bronze that statue is. I'm positive, though, that Bamalfy put it up with an **altruistic** motive—maybe as an aid to navigation."

She took a long sip from her coffee. "Be careful of that man, children. There's something not very nice about him. And you—you're Allen, right— you be especially careful right now. I think he set you up when he said to display the yellow card at all times. That way, if he finds you not displaying it, he has an excuse to storm for a while and then kick you out."

"Oops!" Allen fumbled in his shirt pocket. "I put it away **heedlessly**. I should pay more attention. You probably saved my life, Hadley."

With a pin borrowed from François, he fixed the card to the outside of the pocket. Beneath the word Press it said in smaller letters, *Dropanchor High School Trumpet*.

Ricky smiled. "Better known as the *Amoeba Daily*."

READER: Larry felt a pang at the beginning, when Calvin mentioned college applications, and listing your community services on them.

AUTHOR: Umm—Larry has nothing to list?

READER: Well, actually … there is one thing. Last Fourth of July, a day when everyone travels of course, he offered free coffee by the side of the road, to help drivers stay alert.

AUTHOR: I think that's excellent. And this was like at some busy rest stop on the freeway, I suppose.

READER: No. He said it's a lot of work, dragging all the stuff to a rest stop. And Larry—even when performing community service—is, I won't say lazy, he is a bit … **slothful**. So he set up the free coffee operation in his front yard, at the curb.

AUTHOR: Well, hey, that's OK. I assume he lives on a busy street.

READER: No. He lives on a cul-de-sac.

AUTHOR: I should not ask so many questions.

Chapter 15: THE CHIMERICAL MEGA-DUCK

As Hadley lifted her coffee for another sip, she spied the dust devil. It was swirling at the far edge of the brick plaza, graceful in its dance of nods and bows and darting half-circles. She watched it for a long moment, and at last said, "Beautiful **choreography**. If that were on stage it could cost you seventy-five dollars."

> **choreography**: the design or plan of a dance; the arrangement of steps and turns and other motions that make up a dance
> **dogmatic**: asserting opinions as if they were absolutely true and not open to debate
> **adage**: a compact and often poetic expression about human affairs which has been repeated so often as to become a standard saying

"So I am seeing my first tornado?" asked Tedesco.

Joannie had to laugh. "No, but get ready for a late-summer storm. The wind is rising." She looked up. The sky was still clear for the most part, but gray tatters of cloud were driving across it, riding in from the sea.

"Up, Ricky!" she said. "Up, Allen! We should conduct our business and get on home. A storm is coming."

Ricky raised a protest, pointing at the long sweeps of blue that still remained in the sky, but Joannie would tolerate no objection. "Ricky, you're bringing out my **dogmatic** streak. Joannie knows weather, OK, and she is not often wrong. You saw that whirlwind. And you've heard the old saying— Afternoon spinner, storm by dinner. It says all that needs to be said, don't you think? So, up!"

Ricky grumbled something about rude girls who make up **adages**, but Joannie had her way. The six of them said good-by to Amanda Cook and her friends, and passed in through the entry. A wide corridor went bending out to their left. "It curves around a long ways," Joannie told Tedesco, "out and back, and finally opens onto the main exhibition hall. A little before that point we will come to the cage."

> **incongruity**: a striking inconsistency or lack of proportion between two things
> **agitation**: a condition in which your feelings are stirred up and troubled
> **discern**: to catch sight of and recognize an object, often one that is hard to see, such as one that is distant or set against a confused or indistinguishable background

Tedesco recalled what he had been told of the cage—how a single rod of steel was bent back and forth to form it, how a small door with a huge lock and titanium hinges was fitted into one of its sides. But only when he saw it in the long corridor did he perceive its utter **incongruity**. It was a million times too strong in comparison to its occupant. For there before them was the Harbinger Duck, not large, not mighty—and penned within a cube of steel that could have contained an atomic blast.

Joannie went ahead, coming to the cage before the others, and she slipped a hand between the bars to stroke the duck lightly along its golden back. It let her do this, and its eyes, a soft maroon in the half-light of the corridor, were calm in her familiar presence. But they sparked with a sudden **agitation** as the others drew near, and even as Joannie whispered quickly, "They won't hurt you," a volley of quacks and quocks rang out, frightened and angry.

"Maybe it's our sheer numbers," said François in confusion.

"Or hearing our strange voices," said Meagan, as the outcry continued.

It was Ricky who first **discerned** what was really going on. "Allen," he cried, "the yellow press card! Remember—Bamalford stuck his press card over the eyes of the duck that day when he captured her. Get it out of sight!"

> **equanimity**: a steady calmness in mind and feeling
> **protocol**: a set of actions and formalities dictated by a code of courtesy
> **affront** (noun): a direct insult or challenge to someone's dignity

Allen tore the card from his shirt pocket and buried it deep in his wallet. The duck fell silent at once, and within two or three minutes was regaining **equanimity**—only in time to lose it again at the sight of Bamalford pounding toward them. From a hundred feet away, the booming voice reached out. "Mr. Snoop. Foul! I call foul. You've broken the rule about the press card, haven't you?"

He came thrashing up the corridor, and its entire width was filled—or so it seemed—with his great, lurching bulk. Coming to a sudden stop in front of Allen, he steadied himself by clutching the top of the cage.

"So!" he let loose, "displaying the card was a formality, you thought, to be ignored as you chose. It was a piece of dispensable **protocol**, right? Well, it may be protocol, but here at the Bamalford Dome it's not dispensable. I'm afraid, Mr. Snoop, that you've just written your own exit visa. And no use looking around for Amanda Cook and company. She's in the auditorium way at the other side. The panel from the E.U. is on now, and she wouldn't miss that ... Ow!"

Suddenly Bamalford was hopping around and wailing, "It bit me! Me!"

100

He got very little sympathy from his fellow humans. "No one ever died of duck bite," muttered Joannie.

"It's not the pain," he raged. "Bamalford laughs at pain. It's the **affront** to my … my position. And it will not be overlooked."

He squeezed a meaty hand through the bars as though to catch the duck by its throat. The effort was abandoned abruptly, however, when he nearly received a second bite.

> **novice**: one who is just beginning to learn some profession or way of life
>
> **audacity**: the bold and self-assured disregard of, or challenge to, some authority figure or some custom or rule

"You're not getting off scot-free," he swore. He began to rummage madly through the pocket of his scarlet coat, muttering all the while. "I know it's there—a free sample, a weird product. These Thousand Ships people—they're insane. They hire inexperienced kids, **novices**, and tell 'em to invent the next wave of cosmetics. What's the result? There it is—spray-on lipstick! And the three aunties like it!"

He pulled a silver canister from the pocket and, wasting no time, positioned it between two bars at the top of the cage. "I'll put it to good use!" he snarled, pressing down on a small firing pin. The canister at once delivered a long spray that left the duck with a waxy stripe of fluorescent pink across its bill.

Tedesco was jarred by the aggression, and reacted at once. He shot forward to the cage and in only a few seconds wiped the bill clean with a handkerchief. He ignored completely Bamalford's furious blast—"For that **audacity**, boy, you'll walk back to South America"—and spoke instead to the trembling duck. "We are too small, that is our mistake. It is very sad, little duck, but to stop the big ones from doing these things, maybe we need to be big also."

> **oblique**: not head-on; having an indirect meaning or impact
>
> **chimerical**: too monster-like, magical, idealistic or otherwise extreme, to be real; conceived by a wild flight of imagination

"Or have big friends," added François, staring sharply at Bamalford. She was furious with his abuse of the duck, and at that moment she felt no fear of him.

He met her look with a pouncing contempt. "Surely that's not an **oblique** reference, Ms. Dubois, to the **Chimerical** Mega-Duck, of all comic ducks the most comical of all?"

"Call it chimerical at your own risk," she fired back. "Maybe it's not merely a creation of fancy. Maybe it does live up there, a strange creature on a strange mountain. And maybe, Mr. Bamalford, it really is bigger than all big editors, big as a horse, never sleeping … and, as the story goes, waiting for you to make a mistake."

> **infinitesimal**: too small even to be measured; small to the point of vanishing
> **intermittent**: occurring for a while, stopping for a while, occurring again, and so forth
> **provisional**: serving only for the time being until something more permanent or more conclusive is put in place

For an **infinitesimally** brief moment Bamalford's huge white eyeballs rolled in the direction of the mountain heights. Then he was master of himself again, and he turned at once to the task of throwing Allen and the others out of the Dome for failure to display the press card.

The descent from Cape Stairstep was a hurried one. As Joannie had foreseen, stormy weather was at hand. A dark front of clouds was moving in from the west, and the wind was fitful, building **intermittently** to flurries that pushed against the marchers and left them thankful for the cedar railing along the path.

"It's just **provisional**, Cabbage," Ricky told his friend. "A permanent aluminum railing is on the mayor's list. And could be on his list for years to come. That's why, provisional or not, they built this one pretty sturdy."

> **conjecture** (noun): guesswork, often the sort in which you do your best to arrive at conclusions from inadequate evidence
> **gamut**: the whole lineup or range of possibilities, sometimes ranked between extremes, as from least to greatest, simplest to most complex, etc.
> **proclivity**: a deep-seated tendency toward some object or activity

"Thank you," said Tedesco in a casual tone, "and since …"

"The answer is no," answered Ricky, "no, normp and not a chance."

"Why do you say no, when you didn't hear my question?"

"Well, Cabbage, listen to my **conjecture** and try to tell me I got it wrong." Without taking his eyes from the falling pathway, Ricky pointed straight over his head. "Up there, and not long ago, François made a passing reference to a duck which never sleeps and stands as tall as a horse. My guess is that you are at the point of asking to hear the full story. So—right on or what?"

"You are right on," Tedesco admitted. "But remember the obligations which I have. When I go back home someday, my group—it is waiting to ask one million questions about Dropanchor. So I must learn everything, since A to Z."

"The whole **gamut**," smiled Ricky, "from our table manners to our monsters. I don't blame you, Cabbage. You need to hear about the Chimerical Mega-Duck—definitely. But it's Allen's story. It's all about Allen. And if I tell it, you might think it was invented. What if I ham it up? You know my **proclivity** in that direction. But it's too good of a story for that. Telling it needs to be for Allen."

> **propitious**: favoring and "smiling upon" some plan or work, and creating conditions for its success
> **ominous**: indicating, though not directly declaring, that forces are at work to bring about some evil
> **fatuous**: empty-headed and silly; said or conceived without consideration of the way things really are

"And he will tell it," broke in Allen himself, "in the near future, but in more **propitious** circumstances if you please. This"—he made a vague circular gesture—"this is not the right setting for telling stories. At least not for Allen the non-wilderness boy. I would be completely incomprehensible."

The storm front was pushing in steadily from the ocean, darkening the air, bringing a premature evening. The scene was **ominous**, and the zigzag pattern of the trail made it worse. "It's like all these unwelcome news updates," said Meagan. "The trail does a hairpin and suddenly you're facing the ocean again—and the heart of the storm is blacker, closer. Then another hairpin, and you're looking inland, and that's bad news too—the last patch of blue, the one you had your hopes on, has already been lost."

Ricky felt that some sort of response was required, so he announced gravely, "I can add nothing to what Meagan just said."

"Then march," ordered Joannie.

The rain, at least, waited a few minutes more, even as the air became heavy with the expectation of it. It waited while the marchers reached the bottom of the trail and hastened along the beach, past the great stone table, past the jutting shadow of Cape Scurrility, toward the road which joined the harbor to the center of the town. And only when they were on that road and Ricky was making some **fatuous** remark about outrunning the rain gods did the rain at last begin to fall, pouring down in splattering drops and giving everyone a good soaking on their way to supper.

———————————

READER: Larry wants you to remember that today's teenagers grew up on a steady diet of monsters.

AUTHOR: That's what I understand

READER: So a horse-high duck, whether real, mythological, chimerical or whatever, could be quite a yawner.

AUTHOR: Tell him that before we're done he'll be sleeping with his lights on.

READER: I think he does anyway, but I'll tell him.

Chapter 16: DESULTORY WARM-UPS

The senior floor was not the top floor of the school. Above it, under the high rafters, there was a **garret** out of which a spacious office had been carved for Ms. Framley. She came there often, and was rarely quiet, so the seniors heard her rummagings and mutterings. Early on the morning after the supper-time storm, she was already there, and was more disturbing than usual. Allen was at the front of Room 401, setting up his cassette player, and Ms. Jensen and the students were waiting more or less patiently, when a heavy scraping sound came from overhead, from Ms. Framley's roost.

> **garret**: the often rough and unfinished area of a building just below the roof; an attic
>
> **ascribe**: to explain something by pointing out its cause or what is thought to be its cause
>
> **predatory**: regularly meeting the need for food by stalking and devouring some other creature; habitually getting what you need by seizing it from others or by taking advantage of them, often forcefully or with the threat of force

Allen gave a gray smile. "With a little imagination," he said quietly, "I'm sure we could **ascribe** that sound to something perfectly innocent."

"I'd love that," answered Joannie, also in a quiet voice, "but I feel like the Three Little Pigs when they hear the huffing and puffing. There is no innocent explanation."

Meagan agreed. "What I always feel like is the zebra at the water hole when the lion shows up. There's something **predatory** about that woman."

As the scraping sound came again, more strongly, and with some splintering of the attic floorboards, François murmured to herself, "I could think of better ways to use that attic, oh yes."

She leaned her head back and closed her eyes. "Better ways," she repeated to herself, a little dreamily. "Much better ways."

And now she heard a different voice floating down from above—the voice of a man in his thirties or forties. It was good-humored, not too serious. The man was answering a phone. "Hello, yes, this is R&T's Socially Responsible Brickwork Company, doing business for nineteen years under the school roof—a better way to use the attic. Ricky speaking."

With her eyes still shut, François smiled. Just like you, Ricky, she thought. And if the R is you, I wonder if the T is ...

homogeneous: quite similar in texture, quality, appearance, etc., all across some expanse or range; not marked by significant variation between any one point and another
vulgar: sharing the opinions and preferences of the common mass of people; rough, earthy, without refinement or grace
sweltering: very hot, often without breezes, and to the point of making you sweat and grow faint

The phone conversation went on. "Oh no—not again! Lady, I know you would pay us well to re-brick the four walls, so that for the first time in its history the school building would be **homogeneous**, the same style of brick, the same shade of red, from top to bottom. But lady, we aren't going to do it. First off, it wouldn't be socially responsible. Well—it just wouldn't be. Society needs its odd-looking buildings. Besides, my partner and me, we like it. We lack your refined taste, we're just the common, **vulgar** clay, ordinary Joes with faded salad dressing stains on the front of our shirts. Yeah—me and the T, we like it—cranberry red meets tomato red—that's cool. So—sorry, lady, didn't wanna wreck your day."

François smiled again, wondering if the lady of the conversation was named Françoise, wondering ... Abruptly, the brickwork company disappeared into the remote future, and François sat bolt upright, as Ms. Framley finished her business overhead. There was a last, loud scrape and then a hellish racket as something enormously heavy tumbled down the stairs and into the fourth-floor hall.

"She's gone crazy," said Ricky softly, "from the **sweltering** heat in the attic."

"But there is no sweltering heat in the attic," responded Allen, still at the front of the room. "She bugged poor Ironbane until he approved a very fancy A.C. system. It was almost a scandal."

antagonist: one whose role is to be an opposing force in some struggle
abdicate: to surrender a position of authority and the responsibilities that go with it

Now there was a second pounding on the stairs, and in a moment the door of Room 401 flew open and the doorway was filled with the massive figure of Ms. Framley. She stood there silently, a huge opposing force, and Ms. Jensen took the opportunity to observe, in the politest voice, "I see the frown, the disapproval, the readiness for battle. Excuse me, but ... you look like all the **antagonists** of world literature rolled into one. Is there ... anything we can do?"

106

"And you look like someone who has **abdicated** her responsibility to teach," fired back Ms. Framley, "and surrendered her classroom to a riffraff truant." She gestured contemptuously toward Allen.

> **succinct**: stated in tightly knit expressions, with no more words than are necessary
> **desultory**: jumping about from one subject to another in your conversation, or from one approach to another in your action; not holding steady in the pursuit of a plan or theme

Ms. Jensen, a very responsible teacher, was stung by the charge of casting off her duties. She could have defended herself at some length but, resisting the urge, she kept her reply **succinct** and to the point. "For the first twenty minutes of each day I permit the seniors to engage in an exercise called **Desultory** Warm-ups." She said no more.

Ms. Framley caught up the phrase. "Desultory Warm-ups! How about it class"—her eyes were scanning the students now—"are we having a nice Desultory Warm-up today?"

"You know, Ms. Framley," said François somewhat sharply, "it's really just a conversation. But a very good one—maybe because it is desultory. It jumps all over. Ricky started today with one of those dreams of his about the giants. That reminded Meagan of Jack and the Beanstalk. Just a kids' story, true—but she heard an alternate ending, and she told it to us. Then Lumps goes 'Wait a minute!' and we get a not-too-serious report on the green-bean crop of his grandfather. That, in turn, was Allen's opening—the old-timers of Dropanchor—and he went up to the front to play back this interview he did. It was with the hermit, about the possibility of happiness, and ..."

> **banal**: too unoriginal, uninspired or shallow to absorb your deeper interest
> **felicity**: a condition of deep happiness, often grounded in favoring circumstances
> **querulous**: griping and complaining all the time

"The usual **banal** topics," groaned Ms. Framley. "Old men raising beans, hermits blabbing about the road to **felicity**, dreams with really big giants in them. Have we been here before, children? Must I die of weariness?"

Meagan objected. "That's really unfair treatment, Ms. Framley, and ..."

"Uh, uh, uh," warned the visitor, still standing in the doorway, and still blocking any view of whatever it was that had fallen so heavily down the stairs. "No whining or complaining on my property. There's certainly a page about **querulous** children in the Dogmatic Lease, probably right after the one about slack-off teachers."

At this point Room 401 was beaten into a temporary silence. Ms. Framley surveyed her conquest, with obvious pleasure.

> **pseudo** (often combined with the word it modifies, as in "pseudovolcano"): false; not genuine; looking very much like X, and yet lacking some fundamental quality that it is necessary to have in order to be X
> **cantankerous**: grouchy, touchy, quick to get in quarrels or give people a piece of your mind
> **censorious**: disposed to tell people, in a severe and condemning way, that they have done wrong

Oh no, thought Ricky, here comes that **pseudo**-sweetness again.

In just the voice he was afraid of—gentle and coaxing—Ms. Framley said, "Children, I don't mean to be **cantankerous**. I get a little upset with teachers who don't teach—that's all."

Casting a pointed look at Ms. Jensen, she continued. "Maybe some of you heard—there was a little item that preceded me down the stairs. I have something to show you."

She stepped into the hall, bent over, and then with the loud groan of a weight lifter stood straight again and stumbled back into the classroom. In her hands was a length of steel rail, two feet or so, the sort used for train tracks.

It was a strange, dramatic entry, and everyone of course was staring at her with a Who-is-this-woman? sort of expression. But it was Ms. Jensen she lashed out at. "Don't you dare look at me with that **censorious** eye—like I'm some offender. And don't you dare blame Abner for anything either. This was his, you know. Abner was a great investor in his later years, he invested heavily in the railroads. And they treated him right—they gave him free rides, with other investors, across the prairie. And the riders brought their rifles, and the rides turned into buffalo hunts, just poppin' away from the caboose, thinning the herds."

> **grimace** (noun): a facial expression in which the features pull or twist to show some emotion, such as repugnance or dismay
> **euphemism**: an indirect and inoffensive phrase used in place of one that too frankly or bluntly names some disturbing reality
> **obesity**: the condition of being seriously overweight

She saw the **grimace** appearing on Joannie's face at the description of the hunt, and decided it was highly disrespectful. "Ragged little beast-lover! And smart-mouthed to boot. Don't try suggesting that thinning the herds is a **euphemism** for wiping them out. That wasn't Abner's fault. Got it? Now I was saying … Oh, yes. The railroads treated him right. They even gave him this piece of track, with his name engraved on it and his number of shares."

She was still holding the track. "It's very heavy," she said, and that at least seemed true, for her arms were beginning to tremble. "But why should you have to take my word for it? Let's see, let's see ..."

She fixed her gaze on the unfortunate Allen, who had not left his position at the front of the classroom. "You—yes, you, the pudgy one, flirting with **obesity**, you're the journalistic boy, aren't you—a writer of articles."

"Photographer too, ma'am," said Allen, trying to turn the conversation away from the rail and from Ms. Framley's apparent desire to park it.

> **detachment**: a steady, impartial calmness that results from not letting your emotions and biases get involved in a situation
> **subside**: to settle down and become less intense or forceful

"Photographer too, ma'am," mimicked Ms. Framley. "Yes, that is interesting. A camera person. A respected role, but it has some problems, doesn't it? You're always on one side of the camera, and the story's on the other. The story streams with emotion, but you remain untouched. No doubt you have this professional **detachment**—cool, efficient, impartial. Well, camera boy, now's your chance to be part of the story! To be touched ... to feel the pain. Here!"

Suddenly Allen was holding the track, as Ms. Framley pushed it into his hands. His knees buckled under the weight, and he gave several lurching steps to keep his balance. The trembling which began to **subside** almost at once in Ms. Framley's arms started to appear in his.

> **abstinence**: the act of deliberately holding back and not participating in some pleasant activity
> **advocate** (verb): openly to promote and make a case for some position, cause or practice
> **specificity**: the quality of naming or describing something with sufficient detail to allow for a clear identification of it

At such a moment he was in no condition to listen to a fitness sermon, and yet that was what Ms. Framley gave him. "There, boy, more sit-ups, more chin-ups. And at the dinner table, a little **abstinence** now and then—push away from the gravies, the casseroles, the cakes and tarts. But above all, remember your vitamins." She was tapping the golden spoon that hung from her ear. "It is impossible to **advocate** too strongly, boy, a daily program of vitamins."

There was a solid *clunkk* as Allen set down the length of track. He was desperate at the way it seemed to be doubling in weight every ten seconds. Where he set it was the corner of Ms. Jensen's desk, and although the rail was a good piece of steelwork, perfectly flat along the bottom, it appeared to rest unevenly there. Suddenly he realized why. "Umm, ma'am, like Ms. Jensen—the M, I think I squashed the M."

The M was an odd little three-dimensional figurine, in the shape of an M, which had an honored place on Ms. Jensen's desk. Not rigid like ceramic, not floppy like cloth, painted along its base, and otherwise finished with an irregular pattern of sequin work and inlay, the M defied you to say with any **specificity** what it was made out of. But whatever the materials, they hadn't stood up very well to the railroad track. As Allen raised one end of the track, the object which Ms. Jensen retrieved from under it, though still in one piece, was squashed flat.

Allen groaned, but Ms. Jensen gave him an encouraging smile. "I'm sure it will snap back," she said. "And it's not really your fault. You were working on the railroad and they say it's very tough work, not to ..."

> **ennobling**: tending to lift your thoughts to high truths and your desires to honorable objects
> **deplete**: to take from some supply until it is gone or severely reduced
> **chronic**: not going away; continuing indefinitely to be a problem and, often, proving resistant to attempted remedies or solutions

"Well, thank you, four eyes," interrupted Ms. Framley, "for the lead-in. Railroad work is what I came to talk about. It's the reason I carried down this piece of track which journalism boy put to such good use. Let me say at the beginning—since many of you have never worked a day in your life!—that, yes, physical labor can be **ennobling**, improving the character, lifting up the thoughts. Oh my, yes. But, children, don't choose railroad work for that reason alone. Because it's ... very physical, very mean. You start at dawn, by ten your supply of energy is **depleted**, and for the rest of the day you run on zero. For the first few weeks the back pain goes away now and then, and you think you can beat it, but after that it's **chronic**. You ask for help lifting a two-foot piece of track like this, and they send you to carry a twenty-foot one—alone. One in each hand for that matter."

The little part of Allen's brain that was still functioning through it all suspected gross exaggeration, but his body was believing every word of the bleak description. His eyes grew larger, apparently at the unwelcome image of carrying around twenty-foot lengths of rail. Ms. Framley noticed, but let it pass for the moment. She seemed to have a clear idea where she was heading.

> **encompass**: to include within the sphere of activities and topics that belong to some profession, program, undertaking, etc.
> **pondering** (noun): the mental examination of something at length, with a careful weighing of all of its elements
> **autochthonous**: not coming to a place from the outside; native; having originated in the place where now encountered

110

"So," she went on, "Foster is scheduled for two hundred and sixty years in the pen. Have you thought what that **encompasses**? Far more, I'm afraid, than just publishing his memoirs. A prison career for Foster means work, physical work—yes, children—railroad work. Bamalford will see to it. Two hundred and sixty years of railroad work."

"Then you should take me now, so I can become started." It was Tedesco. "I will just put my things in the backpack, OK." He was beginning to gather up his stuff.

"Not so fast," snapped Ms. Framley. "Listen, every one of you. Bamalford has thought it all through at great length. And I am authorized to tell you where his **ponderings** have come out. He now sees that the foreign boy, pronouncing his English the way he does, like a toucan with its mouth full, could not be Foster. There are other reasons to deport him, of course—failure to show his passport at the Bamalford Dome, to name but one—and Mr. Bamalford warmly recommends that he be kept under house arrest. But it was not the foreign boy who did the dirty business on that Sallie Driven show two nights ago. No, class, Foster Farbugle is homegrown, Bamalford is sure of that now. We seek an **autochthonous** criminal."

"What you seek," said Ms. Jensen indignantly, "is a poor teenager with a disabling crush on a newswoman, who blurted out whatever came into his mind in order to attract her to our town. I don't say it was right, but it's an issue that in the first place should be worked out in his family."

> **anachronism**: something which fits in with an earlier age, but seems odd and out of place in today's world
>
> **pedantic**: overly academic; emphasizing fine points and narrow distinctions of the sort usually found in scholarly books, sometimes with the intention of showing off how learned you are
>
> **peruse**: to read through something, usually in a careful, searching manner; to give something a careful looking through

Ms. Framley gave a loud snort. "With those views you belong in another century. You are really quite an **anachronism**, four eyes. Family!—how cute! In the twenty-first century the criminal justice system is where we work things out."

"That may be all too true," shot back Ms. Jensen, "but I have read some psychology and sociology and ..."

"I don't believe this," cried Ms. Framley, flinging up her hands. "How **pedantic**! So you read some books with big footnotes, and you filled up some file cards **perusing** scholarly articles. And now you want us to hold still while you impress us with long words and hairsplitting distinctions. Well—I'll have none of it!"

solicitous: anxious about the condition of someone or something, and eager to find some way to help

relent: to back off from a hostile attitude or plan of action that you adopted in a time of anger

converse (noun): a relation between two situations, propositions, etc., such that the key elements of the second are basically the reverse of the key elements of the first (for example: "Then I was poor but in good health. Now my situation is the converse—I am rich but my health has failed.")

The offended woman paused to gulp in a long breath, and then went on. "There's just one reason why you can be in the mood to show off your educational accomplishments at a moment like this. You don't have children at risk. If you, four eyes, were a mother, you would be **solicitous** for one thing only—how do I keep my kid from going off to the clink for two hundred and sixty years? Or, to put it another way—you would be desperate to know what is the big present that will make Bamalford **relent**."

"And if you were a mother," answered back Ms. Jensen, staying calm with great effort, "you might have learned a bit of human kindness, you might have found better things to do this morning than tumble train tracks down attic stairs, you ..."

"Oh my," said Ms. Framley with fatigue, "you look ready to go on for a while. If I were a mother I probably wouldn't say this—but I'm feeling bored. It may be about time for me to go."

She took the piece of rail slowly from the desk, letting out a low groan as the weight pulled against her arms once more. François closed her eyes gratefully, thinking—when I open them again, she'll be gone. But she wasn't. Apparently there was still one last piece of business.

Straining and moaning, Ms. Framley hefted the track up to shoulder height. "Can you do what I'm about to do, children—AP railroad work?"

With a horrible snorting she lifted the rail above her head, and held it there. "Because if you can't do this, or can't do it for ten hours straight, or simply don't like the way it makes you look"—her face was turning a violent red, the eyes were bulging—"then you should talk with Dad and Mom, real seriously, about a rather nice present for Mr. Bamalford."

READER: Larry says that today the situation is the **converse** of Abner's day.
AUTHOR: I like it. And I'll probably like it even more after I get it.
READER: Well, he says that in Abner's day most people had enough time, but space was the problem, spaces were too big, too far.

AUTHOR: And today somehow it's the other way around?

READER: Yeah. Today space is OK—we get from here to there pretty easily. But time is the problem. No one has enough of it.

AUTHOR: Well, the railroad was the answer for the space problem. Does Larry have a solution for the time problem?

READER: Yes, and it's a Larry solution—time candles. You light a time candle, say the thirty-minute size, and you get an extra half an hour right then and there.

AUTHOR: That could really fly! But I'll bet manufacturing those things is tricky.

READER: No—Larry's already made some. He's wrestling with the legal issues now—I mean, what if by mistake a customer puts sixteen time candles on a birthday cake?

AUTHOR: Could be a long party. But I think we'd better move on.

Chapter 17: THE *VOCIFEROUS BEACON*

It was a **daunting** sight—the stout arms of Ms. Framley straining to keep the rail above her head—and it **occasioned** some odd behavior on Ricky's part. He began squirming around at his desk, fumbling in his pack, all with a now-or-never sort of urgency. Ms. Jensen watched him apprehensively, fearing that he had cracked, that he was loading his things as a **prelude** to coming forward and asking to be handcuffed.

> **daunting**: so impressive or forceful as to shake your courage
> **occasion** (verb): to give rise to some effect, often not as the sole cause of that effect, but rather as the motive or material that calls other causal forces into play
> **prelude**: an event of relatively minor proportions that introduces and sometimes foreshadows some main event
> **exult**: to express great joy about some outcome or situation, often through outbursts of triumph and satisfaction
> **covet**: to want very badly what belongs to another, often to the point that you would consider using improper means to get it

In fact, however, he was pulling things out of his pack, not putting them in, and the ninth or tenth article appeared to be what he was after—a small camera. Half concealing it behind the bushiness of Joannie's straw-colored hair, and **exulting** in a low voice that "Sallie will have to come when she sees this!" he lined up a shot.

"The flash!" whispered Joannie.

"Not with all this light," he whispered back. "There's not a chance it will flash." He pressed the button.

The camera flashed, Ricky gave a loud Oops! and in moments Ms. Framley had set down the rail and come marching up the aisle toward his seat near the back of the room. She was in full stride, and starting to lean forward to snatch the camera, when by chance the line of her gaze passed through the south windows. She saw something disagreeable there, and her face, which was already stormy, darkened with a fiercer indignation.

The camera was forgotten. She rushed to the windows and poked her head through to bawl out a warning. "You!" she cried. "Yes, you, the three fossils with your anti-pronation tennis shoes, going for a walk on the mountain are you? Following the Bad Pony up the valley? Well, don't even think about setting foot on the west side of the stream. That is the property—the very private property—of our Ms. Framley. Don't look at it. Don't breathe in its direction. And don't **covet** anything on it—because you'll never get it!"

> **verbosity**: the quality of being stated with a lot more words than are necessary
> **anthology**: a selection (often between the covers of a single book) of the best or most representative pieces of some art form such as poetry, short stories, photos, etc.

Her scolding was a lengthy version of No Trespassing, and its **verbosity** worked against her. When she turned back from the window, the camera was gone, spirited away. Ricky expected a fiery reaction, but—rather abruptly— Ms. Framley seemed to be of a different mind about the picture that he had snapped. "Most of the classic photos," she murmured, "the ones that find their way into the end-of-the-century **anthologies**, are stolen shots. Beauty surprised, beauty captured, for all time. No doubt journalism boy could confirm that fact."

She threw a last withering glance at Allen, hoisted the rail, and was out the door. Almost at once there was a shuddering crash, and then the heavy tread of steps ascending to the attic.

Allen gave a quick look through the doorway and reported, "We now have a railroad track in our corridor. Ms. Framley dropped it off, you could say."

"Sounded like the whole locomotive," said Ms. Jensen, returning to the front of the classroom, and speaking in a low voice that wouldn't carry up to the attic. "The woman herself is a locomotive, to tell the truth. And yet—how funny—I feel just a little bad. Maybe I should be trying harder to listen to her, to seek common ground. I mean—back on the train thing—she likes trains, I like trains, Tedesco told me once that he's very much into them. You know— common ground."

> **pluralistic**: allowing a variety of outlooks, religions, cultures, lifestyles, etc., to maintain their identity and to find open expression within a single society or group
> **caustic**: speaking or writing in a cutting, acid-like style, often with a sharp, biting humor
> **berate**: to give someone a sharp scolding or subject him to a stream of bitter criticism

There was an uncomfortable stir among her students, but Ms. Jensen pushed ahead with the idea. "I know—violent motion sickness. But being **pluralistic**—isn't that the great need today? Certainly it's one of our goals in Desultory Warm-ups. And maybe giving equal airtime even to a Ms. Framley is part of pluralism. No one said it was easy, being open to other styles and value systems." She gave a faint smile. "What a tongue, though—**caustic** and caustic. I have little acid burns all over. But you"—she was looking now at Allen—"you got the worst of it."

He shrugged and mumbled something about the M actually getting the worst of it. "And I guess," he continued, "that we should put this away for the time being." He was packing up his tape player.

"If we could carry over the secret of life until tomorrow morning," answered Ms. Jensen with a smile, "that would help. One thing, though—any of you. Who were the people she was **berating** from the window?"

> **paradoxical**: embodying what appears to be a self-contradiction or a crazy union of opposites
> **cavalier**: dismissing serious concerns with a wave of the hand, as though you are too high and sophisticated to trouble with such things
> **melancholy** (adjective): marked by a depression or sadness that is often brooding and given over to thought

François didn't need any time to think. "I am sure," she volunteered, "that one of them was a lady Ms. Framley should be careful about—a peppery old widow, Grandma Dubois. Grandma lives with us, and for several days now she has been planning a hike on the mountain. She keeps an eye on some special briars that grow up there. They are close to her heart, they'll probably inherit her money. But they aren't doing well this year. So she's a bit anxious, even though usually she's not the anxious type. As for her companions—one is probably Peter Oakum. He was an engineer at a power company for many years, and then a manager, and finally he retired and came here so that, **paradoxically**, he could work even harder. And I'll bet the other one is Mayor Povano."

"Oh, the mayor," exclaimed Ms. Jensen with pleasure. She had interviewed with the mayor before being hired on as a teacher, and she had liked his unpretentious style. She turned toward Allen. "There's your scandal, journalism boy—the mayor goes off to the mountain, on frolics, on picnics, in **cavalier** disregard of the official business of Dropanchor."

"If only it were true," groaned Allen with a **melancholy** smile. "Sadly, though, the briars that he went to see *are* the official business of Dropanchor. And is Povano cavalier? We could only wish—but he takes everything pretty seriously. Where else does a new teacher interview with the mayor?"

> **inherent**: showing up as a natural, inescapable part of a situation; bound up with the very essence or structure of something
> **jaundiced**: marked or colored, as it were, with bias and deep-rooted dislike
> **intransigence**: the state of stubbornly clinging to an opinion or position, and being dead set against any compromise

"Good point. That was a surprise. Well, anyway, don't be down—one day your scandal will come slouching over the horizon. Who knows—maybe I'm the Martian rep!" She did a quick imitation of a tentacled creature. "Seriously, though, you'll see your share of it. Wherever there are people, eventually there will be scandal. It's almost **inherent** in our nature. And now—if we don't get this school day started, that will be a scandal of its own!"

Within minutes books were out and Ms. Jensen was leading her students through an intricate passage of the *Odyssey*. Her hopes lifted—the day might yet be salvaged.

Unfortunately, it just wasn't that sort of a day. In a short while Ms. Framley started a telephone conversation with Bamalford, one that was so loud and unguarded that it came spilling down from the attic and through the open windows of 401. Allen swore he could almost hear Bamalford's end of it. Certainly, no one had much trouble hearing Ms. Framley's, as she gave a thoroughly **jaundiced** report of her visit to Ms. Jensen and the seniors.

"It all sums up," she was saying, "with one word, sir, **intransigence**. I have been among mules, that is how stubborn they are. They're dead set against the big present, I can feel it. And the parents will be the same—because the kids mirror the parents."

> **approbation**: approval, often an official approval by a person or group responsible for upholding certain standards
> **vehement**: (1) intense; marked by forceful, highly charged emotion; (2) marked by an intense, concentrated hostility
> **elongated**: stretched out and made noticeably long, or longer than normal

Then came a long interval in which Bamalford apparently was speaking and Ms. Framley, entirely won over by whatever he was saying, kept showing her **approbation** by murmuring "Excellent, sir" and "Well done, sir" and other phrases of that sort.

At last, though, something more **vehement** than mere approval came into her voice. "Exactly! It's exactly the right move. They may be dug in, but Plan B will rock 'em, sir! Then they'll lift those stubborn feet. They won't like it, not a bit. And you can count on me to help."

After that, and after a promise by Ms. Framley to report any new developments, the conversation was soon over, leaving the attic silent once again. Class resumed in Room 401. The hours that followed, however, were not very productive. No one could concentrate—not Ms. Jensen, not the students. Everyone felt uneasy with the news that Bamalford was hatching some further mischief, and that it would rock them, it would shock them, it …

There was a knocking on the door, not long before eleven. Everyone jumped. Allen's finger jammed on the keyboard of his laptop, and the **elongated** version of the Worldwide Web—wwwwwww—suddenly came into being. Ricky stared at the doorway and blurted, "It's Plan B!"

François had noted, though, how the knock was less than a battering, and how the raps had a peculiar sequence to them. "It's not Ms. Framley," she said, "and not Plan B. I think it may be my grandmother. She's everywhere. And she knocks like that."

Ms. Jensen drew the door open, and two men and a woman entered. They were dusty, sweating slightly, and obviously exhausted. Each of them appeared to be at least seventy.

> **ubiquity**: the condition of being everywhere at once or in a comparatively short period of time
> **facilitate**: to help some process go more easily and smoothly
> **reprieve**: the delay or interruption, for a while, of something unpleasant such as a punishment or affliction

The woman caught the eye of François. "You'd be everywhere too, granddaughter, if you had to take care of this town. **Ubiquity** is part of the job. But at least coming here will be easier in the future. I like what I saw in the hall—construction begins. The new rail line should definitely **facilitate** travel to Room 401."

That little bit of humor earned an immediate squawk from the attic. "Aren't we funny today! You old bat—if I see your fingerprints anywhere on that piece of rail, I'm gonna ..."

Voice contact with Ms. Framley was lost momentarily, as she came churning down the stairs once again. In seconds, though, she was bursting into the classroom like a tide, a torrent of foul-tempered speech. And the three visitors were her target. "Bats and weasels," she shot at them, "fossils and mummies, did we all open the right day on our pill box, did we go over our little to-do lists and check our various batteries—before heading out to slime up my property, to disregard ...?"

Ms. Jensen was distressed. "They are thoroughly fatigued," she cried to Ms. Framley. "Will you give them no **reprieve**—five or ten minutes to catch their breath—before you start on them?"

"Do you give a reprieve to a plague?" yelled Ms. Framley. "Because that's what we've got here—disrespect for private property, a plague of it. Look—the mayor goes for a walk up the canyon with his hag friend and this old joke of a gentleman farmer. But do they stay on the east bank of the stream? Ha! Shall we go check? I'm sure their big waffle footprints are all over the western bank.

But on the west is Framley soil, and it cannot bear the touch of peasant foot or peasant shoe."

> **vituperation**: an abusive, lashing criticism or condemnation
> **senescence**: the life stage in which you become an old man or an old woman
> **curtail**: to cut down the size or extent of something; to stop something short of the point of completion

Clara Dubois—a small, lean figure known to many simply as Grandma—had stood bent for a minute or so under the lash of Ms. Framley's **vituperation**. Now she lifted her head, and the blaze in her green eyes said clearly that she could take the punishment which the big woman handed out, and return it.

"Back off, Victoria, with your accusations. The east bank is harder going, but the three fossils held to it, until well above the elevation where your property ends. There was no compromise with **senescence**. None of us stepped on your precious dirt. It's all there for your next bath."

"Grandmother!" gasped François.

The old lady gave her an affectionate look. "I hope you will never talk that way. And I hope you will never need to." She glanced at the clock on the front wall of Room 401. "But what I hope above all is that the very pleasant chat we're having with Victoria right now can be **curtailed**, and that Peter and Marion and I can get down to business before your lunch hour. We wouldn't ordinarily bust in like this, granddaughter, but today there is an urgent matter and we must speak with one of your classmates."

> **relic**: an object that survives the passing away of a former age or time, and reminds us of it
> **magnanimity**: a nobility of spirit which bears trials calmly and bravely, and which in human relations rises above squabbling jealousy and the need to get even
> **scant**: in short supply; barely enough or not enough

"Well," snapped Ms. Framley, "you're right about one thing, Goldilocks. There is a very urgent matter this morning. But it's on my docket, not yours. And all three of you **relics** need to hear it. Early yesterday morning Mr. Bamalford stood in the auditorium of this school, a shattered man. With his last strength he pointed the finger of shame at his attacker. And—listen well, Mayor Povano—it was not just at Foster Farbugle that he pointed, but at your little town also. He pointed at Dropanchor."

"Urrr," interrupted the mayor, holding up his hat like someone flagging a bus, "did he ...?"

"Did he give a completely convincing explanation why Dropanchor is to blame for Foster's televised rampage of character assassination?" Ms. Framley stared with the severity of a judge at the worried man. "Yes, he did. But why don't we move on to the more hopeful part of the story, the part about the olive branch? With a **magnanimity** far beyond that of common mortals—and far beyond what I would show to you, Mayor Povano—Bamalford has held out an olive branch. All can be forgiven and forgotten; peace can return to Dropanchor. But it can't be one-sided. The initiative can't come from Bamalford's side only. Dropanchor has to make a move also, a symbolic show of regret, embodied—as is only proper—in the form of a large present. That was his message, and I'm sorry to say that the attention paid to it so far has been very **scant**."

> **supplement** (verb): to add some further material to something, often in order to correct some inadequacy in it or to make it more perfect
> **appalled**: shocked; pale or otherwise distressed at how horrible something is or at how far it falls short of applicable standards
> **myopic**: not able to see very far

"Even scant is too much for a message like that," said Grandma Dubois sharply.

Ignoring the interruption, Ms. Framley went on in a tone that was increasingly grave. "Perhaps Victoria can help the communication process—that was my thought as I rose this morning. So I came here earlier to Room 401 and I **supplemented** Mr. Bamalford's message with some additional observations on what happens if the large present doesn't show up. And what was the reaction? Blank stares, vacant looks, inertia. Bamalford was **appalled** when he learned of this. 'They are amoebas in human form'—those were his words about you. But he knows how to make a quick end of your stalling. It's called Plan B. And it's nasty, as you will now see. I'm very sorry—but Mr. Bamalford has decided to remove the force field."

"The force field!" Ms. Jensen exclaimed. "What is he—an electromagnet?"

"No!" barked Ms. Framley impatiently. "He's an editor." She pulled a folded newspaper from her purse. "This is Mr. Bamalford's daily. The force field is here."

She unfolded the paper and pointed to the masthead. "Can the **myopic** Ms. Jensen see this far?"

> **vociferous**: raising up a loud voice, often in a pushy manner that demands attention
> **purist**: someone who rigidly demands absolute correctness in speech or in the performance of some procedure or ritual
> **gibe** (noun): a rough, taunting remark that carries insult, criticism or mockery

With the color rising to her cheeks, Ms. Jensen squinted violently. "Yes, it's coming into focus now. I can make out the name of the paper—a mixed metaphor by the way—*Bamalford's Vociferous Beacon.*"

Ms. Framley snorted. "I show you one of the bellowing voices of the journalistic world, an outcry against backward thinking—five days a week—and you can fuss whether its name is one hundred percent correct. Mixed metaphor! You silly little **purist**."

Ignoring the **gibe** Ms. Jensen gave another mock squint. "I can also see an interesting box at the top of the page, over in the corner, with the heading 'Volts from Victoria.' I suppose that's the force field you referred to."

> **adage**: a compact and often poetic expression about human affairs which has been repeated so often as to become a standard saying
> **milieu**: a setting or context, often defined by social and cultural influences
> **cursory**: done too quickly or automatically, and with not enough attention to details, unique features, deeper meanings, etc.

"It's a powerful force, let there be no doubt. Every day on the front page of the *Beacon*—a moral jolt. A hard-hitting proverb, a striking **adage**. I make them up. I seem to have a gift. Today, for example—As a man sows, thus shall he reap. But, no, the force field is something bigger and finer than even 'Volts from Victoria.' Newspaperwise, though, it is found in a humbler **milieu**—it's not front-page."

Something in this last observation plucked at her attention. "Isn't this one of life's riddles, children? What is most grand often has its home in a lowly setting."

She paused, to give someone time to reach the obvious insight, and to utter the obvious insight—Just like you, Ms. Framley, the grandest of ladies, in a two-bit fishing town. No one seized the opportunity, however, and at last, somewhat miffed, she returned to the theme of the force field. "Very well, then, to see the force field which protects this little town, four-eyes, we must open to the comics."

READER: Do you have this thing with "adage"?
AUTHOR: That's a rather strange question.
READER: Well, I mean, you used it two chapters ago, and now it pops up again here. At this rate we'll have about thirty occurrences.
AUTHOR: It's a key word and I didn't want to be **cursory** in my treatment of it.

READER: Key word! It's just another word for "proverb." They mean the same thing.

AUTHOR: Tut, tut. There are subtle differences between the two. I certainly wouldn't define them identically.

READER: No?

AUTHOR: No. I would define "proverb" as "a type of adage," and I'd define "adage" as "a type of proverb."

READER: That borders on something.

Chapter 18: CAPTAIN PARIAH

Ms. Framley spread out the comics page of *Bamalford's Vociferous Beacon* on the desk of Ms. Jensen. "Read this one," she said, "and if the words are too hard, tell me." She pointed to a strip called "Captain **Pariah**." Large, blockish letters indicated that the author was Bamalford himself.

> **pariah**: someone hated, despised and cast out by the community
> **buoy**: a floating marker anchored at some key point in a waterway
> **confound**: to defeat some plan or disprove some opinion, often so thoroughly as to cast the person holding the plan or opinion into confusion

The first box of the comic showed a man with a wide forehead, which at the moment was creased with worry. He was steering a purple boat into the harbor of a small town, past a **buoy** with the encouraging message, Bluemarsh, Pop. 812, Elevation 46, Welcomes You.

In the second box the man sighed. "Surely Bluemarsh will receive me."

The third box, though, **confounded** his hope and showed that the only thing welcoming about Bluemarsh was its buoy. The people of the town were on the dock chanting, "Bubonic plague, maybe. Draco, never."

And from the end of the dock the mayor of Bluemarsh was reaching out a long stick, with an envelope at its tip, and shouting, "Get your mail, Captain Pariah—a letter from that attorney, Fearless Bamalford—and go."

> **dejection**: an emotional state in which you feel low, gloomy and cast down
> **embezzlement**: the act of taking for your own personal use money or other property that was placed under your control for the benefit of someone else

In the fourth box of the comic **dejection** ruled. The inspector's shoulders were slumped, and his face was gray and fallen, as he read the letter. It said that a Federal District Court would hold a hearing about the figurehead on his boat—the reddish-orange dragon carved of agate—and about the accounts which he had submitted when he acquired the dragon some eight years earlier. He was charged with falsifying those accounts—inflating them and pocketing the difference. To determine the extent of this **embezzlement**, the hearing was expected to run forty-five days or more, and during it he would need to explain every purchase—big, small, personal, job-related—which he had made in the last eight years.

veneration: the deep awe and grateful respect you feel for someone who over time has done great things or reached great heights
perimeter: the outer boundary or edge of an area
chastisement: pain or other harsh treatment imposed to punish someone and, often, to spur him on to be better

Ms. Jensen finished reading the fourth box. "Wow, a lot of words for one box, and very nasty besides."

"That," said Ms. Framley in a tone of **veneration** usually reserved for saints, national heroes, founding fathers and the like, "that is the force field which Peerless Bamalford has set around our city, the protective **perimeter** which Draco bounces off of. Every day Draco opens the comics and gets an ugly reminder of the **chastisement** waiting for him—the bruising, punishing legal procedures he'll be dragged through—if he oppresses Dropanchor ever again. And it works. The man stays away. The purple boat stays away."

amethyst: a purple, semiprecious stone commonly used in jewelry
bane: something which on a regular basis is especially harmful to a particular class of persons or things
impunity: freedom from punishment or penalty, in spite of doing things which under other circumstances might have incurred punishment or penalty

"Well, on the subject of purple, this works too, Victoria," cried Grandma Dubois impatiently. She held out her left hand, to display an **amethyst** ring. "Asteroid **Bane** it's called. It has a unique power of causing harm to asteroids. So they stay away. It keeps them away. We're positive it works"—the mockery was apparent in her voice—"because no asteroids have fallen on Dropanchor for quite a while."

Ms. Framley let out a shriek of irritation. "What is this—leave-your-brains-at-home week? Can no one see what's at stake here? I'm so tired of you mindless creatures." There was a long sigh. "But I'll do my duty. I'll give you a clue."

Somewhere deep in her throat she produced a coarse humming sound. "Guess what that is, children of all ages. C'mon, there's no penalty for guessing, guess with **impunity**, what do you think it is? A motor perhaps? The motor of a large boat, maybe a large, purple boat, what do you think? A large, purple boat coming our way just as soon as Bamalford drops the force field, yanks the Captain Pariah comic, stops ..."

A low groan escaped from Povano. Slowly and distractedly he let a heavy fist drop against an open palm. He was still a very sturdy man for all his years, built on the mold of a blacksmith. But he was a worrier. There was a perpetual look of care printed on his face. And Ms. Framley's little sketch of purple boats arriving was making him uncomfortable. "Don't talk that way, Victoria," he said. "There's so much to worry about as is, and now ..."

> **intervene**: to step into a developing situation (often one that appears to be worsening) in order to modify its direction or prevent it from developing further
> **astray**: wandering off the correct course or path, often with the result of getting lost or confused
> **foreboding** (noun): an inner sense that something bad is about to happen

Grandma Dubois **intervened** at once. "Marion, you were born worried. Worry is your bread."

That was where Ms. Framley should have stepped in, to keep the conversation from going **astray**. But she waited too long. Comic strips and purple boats were suddenly forgotten as the mayor, who didn't like being a worrier, delivered a pointed reply to Grandma. "Maybe so, but you shared my bread this morning at the briars."

Now it was Grandma who gave a soft groan. This was her topic, and it was a painful one. "As for the briars, old mayor, I must admit—I am more worried than ever. I have this **foreboding**—something bad is slinking their way."

She spotted François. "Granddaughter, we've been up the mountain, up to the briars, Mayor Povano, Peter Oakum and I. Peter is a very practical man, a gardener in his later years, and Peter thinks there is a problem."

> **exacting**: demanding your most careful attention and most careful performance
> **tautness**: the condition of a flexible item (such as rope or fabric) that has been pulled very tight
> **disinclination**: a preference for avoiding a certain activity or occupation

She gestured toward the third member of the group. He was an appealing old fellow, a mix of contrary elements. His face was full and roundish, with a fundamental cheerfulness of expression, but the long years and some **exacting** work had superimposed upon it a **tautness**, the look of someone who could afford no mistakes. He nodded now, at the attention of Grandma Dubois, but said nothing.

Grandma went on. "Something's not right up there, granddaughter. And if the briars have a problem, then Dropanchor has a problem. You must speak to your friend, the Disco, and ask him to go with us up the mountain. I told Peter and Marion your story, about the lemon tree, and how your friend sensed what was wrong. Our hope is that he can do the same with the briars. But maybe

125

that's hoping too much. Maybe he doesn't even want to go up there—some people have a strong **disinclination** to go on mountains, you know."

François laughed with enjoyment. "He's right here, grandmother, his name is Tedesco, and if he has a disinclination to go up that mountain then ... then the gulls have a disinclination to steal food, the whales have a disinclination to spout, the ..."

> **ostensibly**: with the appearance—often the deliberately misleading appearance—of being such and such or of doing this or that
> **fanatical**: so dedicated to a pursuit or movement or belief that you go a little crazy and will do almost anything for the sake of it
> **vantage**: a point from which you can get an especially good view of a scene or situation

She stopped. Ms. Framley was punching a number into her cell phone.

"Probably reporting the gulls and the whales," Grandma Dubois commented dryly.

"Silence, you old disgrace," hissed Ms. Framley. "I'm on the phone."

Her call connected. "Sir—you asked to be kept informed of any unusual activity by the foreign boy. I think we have something. He's planning to go up on the mountain, **ostensibly** to make a house call to those blasted briars. The real reason? I keep a cool head, sir, and avoid exaggeration, but I think it may be an escape attempt. Right over the top. No, I don't know when for sure, but probably today after school. And—the briars, sir? Oh yes, they are a very big deal around here. The locals get quite **fanatical**."

Ms. Framley was still cramming the telephone back into her purse, and Joannie was asking Ricky in a whisper why it should matter if a foreign exchange student took a walk on the mountain, when they all heard the roar of an engine. "Local editor approaching high school," reported Allen from his **vantage** point near the windows. "Driving van. Suboptimal performance and handling. Apparent road rage. Near miss on South Bridge."

> **cosmic**: spread throughout, or otherwise relating to, the entire universe; set on a grand, universal scale
> **forgo**: to hold yourself back from the use or enjoyment of something
> **dupe**: to fool a person who is unsuspecting and not on guard, often to gain some advantage from him

Not long after that the stairway was ringing with a heavy tread, and with a voice that came bellowing in advance of its owner. "The foreign boy is global, oh yes, and the fiction he invents after he does his heart-to-heart with your briars—that will be global too, or **cosmic** even. A big cosmic banana, that's what he will bring down from the mountain, and like witless monkeys you will swallow it."

126

The door flew open—no knock this time—and Bamalford, wearing an immaculate white apron lettered with his name and the words Editor-in-Chief, swept in. He gave a long sigh, as though to say it was exhausting work, saving foolish people from their folly. Then he made his appeal to Grandma Dubois. "If you let it happen, it's news, and I have to carry it. But it's one story I'd love to **forgo**: Foreign Boy **Dupes** Old-Timers, Mayor Goes Duh. Please don't make me print it."

"The briars and the berries are at stake," replied Grandma sternly. "You probably can't imagine what that means to the life of Dropanchor. But it means everything. If fortune gives us a Tedesco with this ... this Green Affinity, then we send him up there. Whether or not I get duped, or Peter or Marion gets duped, is of little importance by comparison."

> **interloper**: someone who intrudes on the property, the rights, or the established space or realm of another
> **pervade**: to spread all through something, reaching into every part of it

Bamalford drew himself up. "Grandma Dubois, you regard me as an **interloper**, that much I know—as someone who came intruding upon the traditions of this little hamlet. And the opinions of an interloper bear no weight with you. You don't even have a subscription. But I know foreign boys, madam, they are the real interlopers. And liars besides, madam, skilled liars. They lie shamelessly on their application, and the same deceitfulness then **pervades** every other part of their lives. If you send this one up to diagnose your precious briars, he'll come back with a cosmic banana."

> **acuity**: quickness and sharpness of perception or comprehension
> **configuration**: the structure or arrangement according to which the elements of some system, organization, etc., are positioned with respect to one another

"Possibly," said Ms. Jensen, "you could help us lesser mortals understand what a cosmic banana is."

"It should be quite obvious to a person of ordinary mental **acuity**," observed Ms. Framley.

"We must help the frail," said Bamalford compassionately. "Look here, Ms. Marm. Suppose the Brazilian boy goes up to those blasted briars, OK, and sees that they have some trifling problem. Maybe a tiny imbalance of potassium in the soil. Maybe the roots are damp from rainwater. But does he bring back a simple explanation like that?"

Ms. Jensen tried to break in, to take up the question, but without success. Bamalford barreled on. "Oh no, Ms. Marm, you watch. He'll bring back a big story, with the universe in the balance. Maybe some galaxy has burped out a dark matter which alters the structure of light, which rearranges the **configuration** of atoms in every last stinking molecule of light. Overnight—photosynthesis stops working, botany is down for the count, all plant life is going extinct—Grandma's precious little specimens included. Something like that will be the foreign boy's diagnosis of the briars—and that's the cosmic banana. When he puts it in front of the monkeys, you can imagine ..."

> **fabrication**: a false story or report, invented to deceive someone
> **embroider**: to make a report, explanation, etc., more dramatic and appealing by adding some points that are exaggerated or fictitious
> **moribund**: drawing near to death, showing the weakness and decline of one close to death

He was cut off by a sharp "Hush!" from Grandma Dubois. Reaching under one of the desks at the front of the room she pulled out something, held it before her, stretched it into a long string, pink and almost breaking. "My patience is going to snap before this gum, Mr. Bamalford. You're the one who's caught up in a **fabrication**, inventing a compulsive fibber who bears no resemblance to our foreign exchange student. Because there's no evidence of any sort that this Tedesco boy lies, misleads, deceives, makes up false reports or **embroiders** on true ones. Besides, his record so far is one for one. Look at that." She pointed to the rear of the room, where the lemon tree—on fresh water now for the second day—was springing back, and she said, "You can't call that the **moribund** lemon tree any more."

Tedesco himself broke in. "Anyway, now it is too late. The grandmother of François no longer can take back her request, and Mr. Bamalford can no longer ask her to take it back. Because I am accepting it, this moment. When the school is over today, Grandma, I will go up the mountain with you. You can show me the briars, and I will sit by them a while. And what I learn, that is all I will tell you ... without any galaxies or bananas."

> **brusque**: using a rough, blunt speech or manner, that wastes no time on courtesies or good humor
> **guile**: the art of clever deceits

Grandma, who was often rather **brusque** with people she knew and shy with those she didn't, said to François, "That's a very nice friend you have, granddaughter. Let him know that we will meet him after school. And you should explain to him that sitting by the briars won't be so easy as he thinks."

Bamalford was in a great huff when he saw things going against his wishes. He marched stiffly toward the door, promising that he would write the story at once, how the simpleminded mayor and his simpleminded friends were no match for the **guile** of the foreign boy, how they fell into his traps.

"This kind of story you can write in advance," he fumed, "because there's only one way it can turn out."

> **unabashed**: still showing confidence and self-assurance in spite of having to deal with embarrassing facts or with criticism and disapproval by others
> **cynical**: bitterly mocking any belief that human action can arise from noble motives; holding that the only reason people act is to look out for their own selfish interests

Ms. Framley marched behind him, and as she passed Grandma Dubois she asked angrily, "How did you know that gum was there?"

The old lady answered **unabashedly**, "That's where I left it fifty-five years ago."

———————————

READER: Larry says one semiprecious stone is OK, but don't go padding the vocabulary list with sapphire, topaz, aquamarine and so forth.

AUTHOR: I guess he's referring to the amethyst ring of Grandma Dubois.

READER: Correct. He says "amethyst" will never be on the entrance exams. And he just wants to know the right words to get into college.

AUTHOR: How about "Please" and "Thank you"?

READER: Ha. How about "My daddy might endow a chair"?

AUTHOR: They told me that Generation Y can be **cynical** at times.

Chapter 19: MOUNT RELIEF

Tedesco was in high spirits at the end of the school day. With Ricky at his side, he was part of the general stampede pouring down the wide staircase. As the two of them emerged from the sturdy brick cube that was Dropanchor High School, and into a cloudless afternoon, he said, "So now at last I will go up this mountain. Mount Ricky—is that right?"

> **ostentatious**: favoring a style which is showy and eye-catching
> **invincible**: successfully resisting all attacks; not able to be overcome

"Sorry, Cabbage," said Ricky in a tone of correction, "and not Mount Snoozer either. We're not an **ostentatious** bunch, we Snoozers, and putting our name on mountains, bill boards, T-shirts, whatever, is too showy for our taste. But if the mountain wasn't named after a Snoozer, it was named by one. Which is actually a good story, and as we climb I will tell it to you."

"Then you are coming too?" asked Tedesco.

"Half the town is probably coming," answered Ricky. "There's a general astonishment that the briars are losing a battle. I mean—they've been **invincible** for the last five billion years, but now some fungus or whatever is beating 'em. Everybody is worried and wants to have a look."

> **equilibrium**: the balance or harmony that results when contrary forces or influences are roughly equal one to another
> **counterpoise** (noun): some weight or influence which is the even match of an opposing weight or influence
> **bureaucracy**: an organization (such as a government agency) which is divided into a complex structure of departments and chiefs, and which follows procedures that are rigid and overly complicated

They started on their way, working up the long grassland that ran out to the east from the school. The sun was at their backs, their shadows were just beginning to lengthen. It was a deep, resting afternoon, and no trace remained of the storminess from two days before. Everything had for the moment fallen into **equilibrium**—the mass of the mountain balanced the vastness of the sea, the spreading warmth of the sun was the **counterpoise** of the high snows and the draft of cool air that flowed down from them.

"This," said Tedesco, pointing to the narrow trail they were following, "this is like the path my father takes up to the coffee bushes."

Ricky smiled proudly. "This is what I call a people's path. **Bureaucracy**-free, no government agencies involved. There were no hearings about its location, no two dozen permits for its construction. It just sort of happened, people climbing the hillside day after day, wearing a pathway into the ground. Can't say the same for the road, however."

He beckoned out to the edge of the meadow, where a carefully maintained gravel road ran along. A sign indicated that it was Dropanchor Rural Road 21. "But sometimes we just call it the Bridge-to-Bridge," said Ricky, "because it follows the Bad Pony from the bridge in front of the school up to the bridge at the top of this slope."

> **forage** (verb): to poke all around in search of food or other supplies
> **preclude**: to shut out the possibility that something will happen or be done
> **idolatry**: the act of adoring and showing devotion to some object as though it were a god, or to another person as though he or she were a god

Rachel was there on the Bridge-to-Bridge, and many of the people of Dropanchor, all making the ascent. As Ricky watched his sister, he groaned, "Oh no, she's **foraging**."

The little girl was rooting about in the variety of grasses and wildflowers that grew by the edge of the road. After a few moments she stood up, displaying a gangly vine, and shouting something to Ricky across the wide interval of meadow. The distance and the afternoon breezes **precluded** any comprehension of her words, but Ricky seemed to know what she had said, and in response he shook his head vigorously and wagged his finger.

It was a no, and Rachel was displeased with it. She stamped her foot and turned back to the march, ignoring the kiss that Ricky threw her as a consolation. "She adores me," he said. "I mean—it borders on **idolatry**. But she does not like hearing no. I told her not to eat the plant. Her class is doing a unit about living off the land, and she wants to discover an edible plant—outside the supermarket."

Tedesco was troubled. "But Ricky, some of these wild plants—they make you hurt very bad inside. And little kids, you have to be careful, they see some new plant, OK, and it's—who knows?—it's their most favorite color, and this means they have to eat it. Or on some other day it's their least favorite color, and maybe now *this* means they have to eat it. Or ..."

> **capricious**: behaving with unpredictable actions and alterations, often on the basis of whatever wild notion or flight of fancy possesses you at the moment
> **transitory**: being in full effect for just a short time, and then vanishing
> **caricature**: a highly exaggerated portrait or version of something, often provoking amusement and ridicule

"Not Rachel," broke in Ricky. "She's not **capricious** like that. She brings each new plant to me, and I make the call whether it's edible or poisonous or what. The only problem is I know beans and less about plants—yes, I see the faint smile. So what should I do? I tell her every time that the plant is not edible. But she's getting frustrated."

As it ascended, the grassy fairway was marking out a long curve, leaning to the north, running up toward the huge pillar of reddish granite which many people now called the Giuseppe Stone. And all the while the long strip of meadow was narrowing, until at last the pathway up its midline and the road along its edge came together at East Bridge, the rugged span nearly at the base of the great pillar.

Rachel got to the bridge before her brother. She marched out to the middle, drumming her heels on the wooden planking. Before her the Bad Pony threw its waters in surges against the reddish stack of the Giuseppe Stone, and with each surge there was a **transitory** plume of vapor—rising, gleaming with flecks of rainbow, then falling back and sweeping under the bridge. Rachel watched, and Merci, just arriving, came and watched beside her.

Ricky might have stood for a moment too, if it had been allowed. When Rachel saw him, though, coming onto the bridge, she forgot the plunging stream and the glimmering spray and ran straight for him, grabbed his arm, straightened his index finger, and made it wave back and forth in an exaggerated arc—a **caricature** of someone saying no. "You always say no," she scolded. "I'll never discover my plant. Besides—I won't just gobble, Ricky. I'll still show my teacher first, even if you say yes."

Merci glanced sternly at Ricky. "Evil big brother," she said.

> **primeval**: in existence at the time of the earliest beginnings of the world, or otherwise related to those beginnings
> **file** (verb): to move in a line, one person following another

Ricky pointed vaguely up the long valley that climbed away from that spot to the north and a little to the east. "Up there, Rach, we've got briars. You can go up there and discover the briars—this afternoon if you like. And what a great discovery that would be. Joannie says they grow nowhere else in the world—and she's checked all the other places. Grandma Dubois says they come from the dawn of time—earlier than the forest **primeval**. Earlier than the Big Bang, which is ..."

There was a tap on his shoulder. Ricky didn't even turn. "Uh, Grandma, I bet that's you. Or Joannie. Probably worse if it's Joannie. We were just having a discussion about ... the forest primeval."

"Do you walk while you talk?" was all the old lady said. Ricky promised he would try, and with that the march began.

The crowd which had collected on and about the bridge, easily more than one hundred persons, now formed an orderly column and began **filing** up a rough pathway along the east bank of the Bad Pony, up the valley that led to the briars. At first there was no conversation, and the line of marchers passing silently across ancient beds of stone, through a patchwork of sun and shadow, was a noble sight. Ricky murmured to himself, "Probably not destined to last."

> **clamor** (noun): a loud, ongoing outcry or other such noise, often insistent or complaining, and often rising as a confused mix from many sources
> **rustic**: rough in manners and speech, the way country people are sometimes thought to be
> **formidable**: so large, powerful, numerous, extreme, etc., as to fill you with fear and awe

And, of course, it wasn't. There was soon a **clamor** of straining pistons, as a van from the *Vociferous Beacon* pulled into the turn-about by the bridge. Bamalford leapt out, waving his yellow press card. He was not in a good mood. His megaphone voice, insulting as always, carried easily up to the hikers. He told them that they were a **rustic** people, clomping off through the mud in their heavy boots, leaving cows unmilked and fires untended; but that it was his duty as an editor to cover their ragged procession, if they insisted on going forward with it.

Half running and half walking, handicapped by an overcoat he insisted on wearing against rain and chill, neither of which was a serious threat at the moment, he caught up with the march and attached himself to it. Against the immensity of the mountainside and in the gathering calm of the afternoon he was not a **formidable** figure, and no one took any special note of him. The silence was finished, however, and several conversations broke out.

Tedesco had remained by Ricky's side, and now he commented, "It's still just the mountain, you know."

> **forte**: the area in which your strengths and skills are at their highest; what you're best at
> **mandate** (noun): an order or directive from a source of high authority, often imposing some continuing responsibility or mission
> **cartographer**: a mapmaker

"Oh," said Ricky, suddenly remembering. "Oh yeah, the mountain ... is still just the mountain. And I promised to tell you the little historical thing about its name. Well, Cabbage, history is not my **forte**—in fact, if anyone knows what my forte is, they should phone the Snoozer residence at once. But anyway, remember our little talk at lunch yesterday—almost two hundred years ago the Farnum Expedition was working its way up the coast. It was financed by some merchants of Boston, and from them it had received its **mandate**—find a place, build houses, plow land, start a settlement. So the expedition came with settlers—the tinkers, the tailors, the brewers, the smiths, all the trades and professions necessary to start a small town. And it came with a Snoozer."

"An alarming thought," said Joannie, who was next after Tedesco in the line of marchers.

"Nathan Snoozer," went on Ricky. "He was the **cartographer** for the expedition. And obviously, as their crowded little ship came bobbing closer, he got a glimpse or two of this very large mountain we're stepping on. And he marked it on one of his maps, with an estimate of its altitude, correct within a sixteenth of an inch. What to call it, though, was a problem, so he asked for suggestions. That may have been a mistake. There were more than forty people on that ship who had a perfect name for the mountain, no two alike, and suddenly Nathan was under siege. The most insistent of them all was a woman named Maggie, a bossy woman with a gaze like a beacon. Joannie's ancestor, I think."

"She did not have a gaze like a beacon," protested Joannie. "But I do. So leave Maggie alone."

> **homage**: a form of respect or praise which expresses the belief that in some regard the person being praised is highly superior or is the master
>
> **insularity**: the condition of being cut off from contact and communication with the main body or group, as an island is cut off from the mainland
>
> **efface**: to minimize or erase the distinctive marks of something so that it disappears or ceases to be noticed ("Self-effacing" means making an effort to assure that your good points and accomplishments attract as little attention or praise as possible.)

Ricky squirmed and hunched his shoulders. "Right between the blades, just like a laser. Anyway, though, Maggie's idea wasn't all that crazy. She said the only appropriate name for the mountain was Mount Farnum, in **homage** to their captain who had brought them safely around the Horn, and served ginger tea while doing it, while the ship was tossing in the ..."

"Whoa, Tedesco!" broke in Joannie suddenly. "Get back here." Their hike had brought them to a sturdy footbridge which led over to the west side of the stream, and Tedesco had started across it. Joannie was dragging him back, and explaining, "It's called the Bridge of Instant Sorrow. It connects to Ms. Framley's land. Walk across it and she'll make you sorry that you did—sometimes in an instant. Visitors are very unwelcome. She wants to turn her property into

134

an island, a little Framley island, where we the unwashed and the uncultured would never set foot. It's a vision of **insularity**."

"Sort of a one-way insularity, though," said Ricky. "We keep out of her world, but she's always barging into ours." He looked for a moment at Ms. Framley's hillside. "I'd stay off it, if she'd stay on it. But anyway ..."

He caught Tedesco's collar and gave it a tug. "Anyway—let's go back in time again to the days of Nathan Snoozer—so that we can finish the story and put a name on this blasted mountain. Joannie's idea, I mean Maggie's idea, didn't go over well with Captain Jack. He was a self-**effacing** man, he was already very uncomfortable that people were nicknaming the ship *Jack's Equator*, and he certainly didn't want any Mount Farnums on the map. 'Name it Mount Crew,' he said, 'that's who went up the ropes, rounding the Horn. Name it Mount Maggie, for that matter—she's an awesome woman, a lighthouse. Or even better—bring me the mapmaker—he should decide the names that go on the map. Let Nathan be the judge of this dispute.'"

As he got into the story Ricky was walking slower and slower. "Batteries low?" came a sharp interrogatory. Grandma Dubois was suddenly at his side. "You said you could do them both simultaneously."

> **arbiter**: one who considers the competing claims in a dispute and announces a resolution, often a binding resolution
> **relief**: the condition of sticking up or projecting from a flat surface; the extent to which the features of a landscape rise above or fall below a base elevation

Ricky had to grin. "It's harder than I thought," he said. "But the story's almost over. So pay attention, Cabbage. Nathan was very unthrilled to be made the **arbiter** of a dispute where feelings were starting to run high. He listened to all the competing proposals, tried to choose among them, failed, and at last decided to pick a name on his own, something so self-evident and uncontroversial that it couldn't generate any argument. Mount Mountain—he thought of that first, but it was heavy on M's, so his next idea was Mount **Relief**. Mountains stick up, so who can quarrel if you call a mountain Mount Relief. Actually, everyone quarreled, but Captain Jack liked it, and the name caught."

"So I am walking on Mount Relief?" asked Tedesco.

It was Grandma, no longer shy around the foreign visitor, who answered. "Walking and talking. You are on the lower slopes of Mount Relief, and you need to be on some higher ones long before the sun goes down. Which will not be easy, unless your friend here, the Snoozer boy, picks up his heels. And ... unless we can pass by certain ... obstacles"—a note of worry was coming into her voice—"without losing our mayor, eh Marion?"

> **inimical**: unfriendly; behaving as an enemy toward you

135

> **forestall**: to take steps ahead of time, and by those steps to prevent something from happening or reaching its conclusion
> **quizzical**: curious; in the mood to ask a lot of questions, like someone trying to solve a puzzle

Mayor Povano was far ahead, a hundred yards or more, climbing slowly, and drawing near to another footbridge. It was a well made span, but compared to the Bridge of Instant Sorrow it was of a humble construction, just rope and planking, swinging slightly in the breeze. Between the two bridges the terrain got rougher with the ascent—more broken, more strewn with boulders and obstructed with rocky outcroppings, generally more **inimical** to hikers.

"So the mayor, for him this difficult ground is ... an obstacle?" asked Tedesco. "I see that he is going slower."

Grandma was watching intently now. "You're right—he is going slower. But the ground—it's not the ground—he could dance over this ground. It's ... Ah, see, Peter is there, trying to distract him, trying to **forestall** the crisis and waltz him past that horrible stone before ... But it won't work. Excuse me, children, excuse me."

With a surprising burst of speed she hurried forward. Tedesco came along not far behind her, with a **quizzical** look that promised a thousand questions. And Ricky and Joannie followed.

> **flag** (verb): to lose energy and slow way down or become drooping and sagging
> **attribute** (verb): to mention some effect and claim that it is owing to some specified cause or source
> **unwieldy**: too big or heavy or awkwardly shaped to handle easily

As the mayor had approached the footbridge his progress had **flagged** until at last, only a few steps back from the span, he had halted completely. He was staring intently at a large stone by the side of the trail. Its full size was impossible to say, because its base lay buried. The part which projected, however, was as big as a table, and for that matter it bore a strange resemblance to an old-fashioned writing table.

The stone served as an anchor for the bridge, it was the fixture around which one of the supporting ropes was wound. Seeing this from a distance, Tedesco was sure he understood—the mayor had stopped because he was worried, and the worry could be **attributed** to the rope, some fraying or slipping of the rope where it met the stone. Yet that did not explain why the conversation between the mayor and Peter Oakum—conducted in low, earnest voices that Tedesco could barely hear as he drew closer—was about a witch.

READER: I'm about bridged out.

AUTHOR: I assume that's a reference to some recent dental work.

READER: No, it's a reference to the **unwieldy** number of bridges you have in this book. It's going to get awkward trying to keep them all straight.

AUTHOR: Bridges have always been important in world literature.

READER: Yeah, but you don't have to put all of them in one book.

Chapter 20: THE INVIDIOUS PRUNES

"I know very well she was not a witch," the mayor was saying to Peter Oakum, as Tedesco drew closer. "In fact, how ridiculously clear that she was not a witch! It's just that when I come to this spot, and I see this rock, and remember the story ... with all those details ... I can't ..."

> **withstand**: to bear the impact of some opposing force without breaking, giving way or suffering other ill effect
> **ignominious**: falling wretchedly short of what is generally acceptable, and thus being a source of shame, often public shame

"Can't help thinking maybe she was a witch," prompted Peter Oakum in a helpful tone.

"Something like that," said Povano miserably. "And in light of ..."

Grandma Dubois had come up to him by this time. "Marion," she said softly, "if you call on your reserves of common sense and moral firmness, you will be perfectly able to **withstand** these anxieties. And if you don't"—she crinkled her fingers in front of his face—"I, who am more of a witch than she ever was, will turn you into a red wagon and have you pulled **ignominiously** up this mountain, and your voters will say 'For shame, for shame!'"

> **impeachment**: the first step in removing someone from political office, namely, the presentation of a formal accusation of misconduct or unfitness to the appropriate court or judging body
> **enigmatic**: expressed in riddles, or occurring in a mysterious way that defies comprehension
> **reprisal**: an injury (usually a "measured" injury, in the sense of going this far but no farther) which you inflict in return for an injury inflicted on you

Even as she was menacing him with these things, she was taking his arm gently, turning him away from the stone, and leading him onto the bridge. "My voters," he groaned, "are probably drawing up articles of **impeachment**. And our visitor, the Brazilian boy, must be feeling very much in the dark." He saw Tedesco, only a few steps away. "I'm sorry for the **enigmatic** behavior, my boy. I'm much better now that Clara threatened to turn me into a red wagon. So go ahead and ask what you want, and we'll try to clarify the mystery for you."

"It is OK," answered Tedesco. "And I hope you are feeling better. But, one thing—how are you daring to go on the bridge? Joannie told me that Ms. Framley will make you very sorry."

"That was the last bridge," said Joannie, smiling to see that she too was an instrument of confusion, "not this one. Now we are beyond the boundaries of Ms. Framley's property, and we can cross over to the western bank of the stream—where the trail is easier—with no fear of **reprisals**. For we won't be on her land. But listen, Tedesco—don't lose a chance to hear the story of the witch. Take up the mayor's offer. Think of your poor brother, waiting for news."

> **embellishment**: a little addition you make to a story, a garment, a building, etc., in order to leave it more beautiful or dramatic
> **debunk**: to discredit some belief or claim as exaggerated, fictitious, superstitious or founded mainly on emotion

Tedesco brightened. "That's true—crazy Octavio. He will be very interested. So alright, after all, I am grateful to hear this story. And Ricky is telling it, right?"

Ricky gave a start. "Oh no, not me. I might tell it too well. When I tell a story, I add **embellishments**, I put in some touches that make it more lifelike than life itself. But with this story, Cabbage, we don't want it too lifelike. Young minds like Rachel might start believing it."

"Rachel?" said François, lifting her expressive eyebrows.

"Well," answered Ricky uncomfortably, "maybe Rachel's brother. A story like that is better at lunchtime, when the sun is straight overhead. I mean—look."

He beckoned toward the ridge forming the eastern wall of the canyon they were hiking up. The sunlight was still there, but slanting now, touching only the upper bands of the rocky flank.

"Maybe the mayor should tell the story," suggested Meagan. "Working through it in a calm, emotionally flat sort of way might help **debunk** its claim to be about a real witch."

Grandma was shaking her head. "It's a perfect idea, Meagan, except that the mayor is worse than that Ricky boy. Talking and walking at the same time is just too much."

> **ascendancy**: a commanding influence, often based on some superiority of strength or advantage and not merely on high rank within a power structure
> **inept**: too clumsy or untrained or slow-witted to perform some task
> **problematic**: marked by open questions and unresolved issues, and thus difficult to manage, work with or take decisions about

Povano laughed. He was across the bridge now, and slipping free from the dark **ascendancy** which the stone had held over him. But he had no desire to be the teller of the witch story. "I'll muff it," he said. "I'll be quite **inept**. Lack of necessary skills, you know. But perhaps you would like a recommendation. If ... if the woman to whom we refer was not a witch—as Peter and I are sure she was not—then she must have been a very **problematic** grown-up. To speak of her, then, we obviously need someone who knows grown-ups, and in particular the problematic variety."

> **charge** (noun): some act or service which it is your obligation to perform; some task entrusted to your responsibility
> **copious**: enough and more than enough; presenting an abundant supply of something
> **arable**: able to be plowed and planted; capable of yielding crops

That was how the **charge** of telling Tedesco the story of Serquiella—the angry beauty of days long gone by—fell to Meagan herself. Everyone said that Meagan was good with grown-ups, that she knew where they were at and comprehended the stresses they were under.

"Almost four hundred years ago," she began, as she caught hold of the banister rope and started over the bridge, "there was a rumor of gold in this region, the vague report of a deposit that was vast, unfailing, **copious** beyond anyone's need or want, enough—if melted down—to fill a mountain lake. The rumor attracted a minor expedition from what is now Mexico—a mixed band of soldiers, merchants, settlers. They were the children and grandchildren of conquistadors. Some of them definitely had the fever, and they swore that gold was all it took, that bad days and boring days could never again return if a man had gold. But many of those who came, probably the majority, had their hopes on other things—a few acres of **arable** land for a farm, some timber for the posts and beams of their houses, eventually a little market where they could trade."

> **oscillation**: the act of curving back and forth across a centerline or between contrary positions
> **debilitate**: to make something feeble; to reduce to a state of weakness
> **acknowledge**: to give a clear indication that you agree that some facts are true, or that some rights, claims or obligations are valid

The slender bridge was swinging gently now as Meagan made her way across, and lifting and falling in a long **oscillation** as Ricky and Tedesco and the others came hiking behind her. She kept a firm hand on the rope, and she pushed on with the story. "They founded a settlement, expanding outward from a central plaza which is still our town square today. With time the settlement became a little village called Esperanza. As for the streets—they were

140

not paved with gold, for the rumored deposit, enough to fill a lake if not a sea, was proving elusive. But the farmers were happy, the carpenters were happy, and Esperanza grew slowly until it had its own mayor, as well as a doctor and a lawyer."

Rachel had come skipping and squirming through the line of marchers to be alongside Meagan and had seized her hand. "Now is the part about the prunes?" she asked.

Meagan, catching her balance, replied, "It may be the part about Meagan falling in the stream if this bridge doesn't calm down, young lady. But, yes, the prunes are coming in now, and we hope Ricky won't be scared. It was a frozen winter's day—the beginning, we think, of the little ice age that eventually drove the settlers back to the south—and a shepherd came down from this same valley which we are ascending now, and walked through the streets of Esperanza to the office of the mayor. The bitter cold was having a **debilitating** effect on the poor man's wits. He said that in the high orchard he had found three plums of solid gold, which should be given to the fairest woman in Esperanza. But I'm afraid that what he placed in the hands of the mayor were three ordinary plums, not solid and not gold, and so withered that they were little more than prunes."

Rachel was tugging at her sleeve. "Ricky's friend wants to say something."

Meagan threw a quick glance at Tedesco. "If I know Ricky's friend, he wants to hear more about the high orchard."

With a brisk nod Tedesco **acknowledged** that she was correct. "An orchard up here would be a beautiful thing."

> **disseminate**: to scatter or distribute something (such as seed, infor-
> mation, etc.) over a wide range
> **chafe**: to rub to the point of soreness, rawness or irritation

"I'm afraid," said Meagan, "that four hundred years have taken their toll. But you'll see for yourself—another half mile and the trail leads right by it. And maybe I'll get through the story by then. What I was saying was—the mayor found a chair for the poor shepherd by the fire, and then he looked again at the three wrinkled plums in his hand—a prize for the town's most beautiful woman—and he thought it was all innocent enough. He told the event to the scribes and examiners who worked in his office. That was suffi-cient to **disseminate** it to every corner of Esperanza. It was an amusement for most of the people, but for the young wife of the lawyer, the town's only law-yer, it was wild, troublesome news. She was undeniably beautiful, she be-longed at court, and her soul was **chafed** to have been brought to such a wil-derness. Her name was Serquiella."

There was a long sigh from Tedesco. Meagan teased him. "So you are in love with her already."

"Only a little," he answered. "Because I have seen these things, and they do not end well. I could almost finish the story for you."

"Or I could finish it," volunteered Ricky, a bit sad now to have given up the mike. That drew a severe glance from Grandma Dubois, and he reconsidered. "Then again, too many cooks ..."

> **aghast**: stunned and shocked at how bad something is
> **obsession**: a condition in which something so totally seizes your attention that you can't stop thinking about it
> **eradicate**: to yank something out by its roots

"Serquiella," continued Meagan, "went to the mayor and demanded the golden plums as some small recognition of her beauty. The mayor saw the craving look in her eyes, and he was **aghast**. He asked her if the rose by the gate was blooming with red flowers or white, and she could not recall the color, she could not recall the bush or the gate, she was that consumed with her own beauty and the urgent need for it to be honored. He begged her to tear out this **obsession**, but she said it was the privilege of her fair appearance, and could never be **eradicated** or even lessened."

The expedition to the briars was moving along well now, climbing steadily higher into the valley. The walkers were strung out over some distance. Merci was one of those close enough to Meagan to hear the Serquiella story, and she was jotting down some notes. "This doesn't look good," said François when she saw it. "You never take notes."

"But such a great line," explained Merci, "so high and bratty—'the privilege of my fair appearance.' Maybe I can work it in some time."

> **renounce**: (1) to have nothing more to do with something, either because you are rejecting it (for example, a political theory) or because you are surrendering your claims to it (for example, a privilege); (2) to declare your intention to have nothing more to do with something
> **invidious**: expressing or promoting envy and other resentful feelings

"Meagan," cried François, "you're supposed to tell it in a way that your young listeners, even the incredibly cool Merci Dubois, will **renounce** the value system of Serquiella, not embrace it."

"Don't worry," said Meagan, "from this point forward in the story, as you recall, Serquiella is not a charming girl. Certainly she didn't charm the mayor of Esperanza. To put a quick end to the whole affair he gave the three plums to a dairymaid named Anna, a shy, pretty girl who did what he hoped she would and put them in a shed and forgot them. But Serquiella could not forget them. She began appearing daily at the mayor's hall, in fine gowns, raving against

Anna and demanding the plums. She always referred to them as the golden plums, but the mayor gave them a different name, the **Invidious** Prunes, when he saw how hateful she had become because of them, and how bitterly jealous of the milkmaid. Eventually Serquiella left a wooden bowl on the ground in front of Anna's cottage, with a note saying, 'O beautiful among cows, return what is mine.' Anna was shaken, and wanted only to give back the plums, but when she looked in the shed for them she found that the mice or the possums had gotten there first and that very little was left, three pits and nothing more. Now she was painfully unsure what to do. For all that day, the question turned and turned in her head. Finally, still uncertain, she took the three pits and laid them in the wooden bowl."

"Eeee!" said Rachel, clinging tightly to Meagan's hand.

> **henceforth**: from this moment and on into the future
> **counterpart**: X is the counterpart of Y if the role of X in its system or organization is equivalent to the role of Y in its system or organization

"Eeee! is about right," answered Meagan. "Serquiella went half crazy. She had no doubt it was intended as a slander on her beauty. And that it was done by order of the mayor. She stormed to his office and gave what became known as the **Henceforth** Speech—'Henceforth my face is set against your town, henceforth my beauty ...'"

The story was interrupted by the mocking voice of Calvin. "Hey, Meagan, I didn't know that Serquiella spoke such good English—big words like 'henceforth.' Wha'd she do—check out some tapes?"

"You're right," Meagan answered, making herself remain calm. "It was all in Spanish of course. But for your information, Calvin, 'henceforth' is a perfectly good translation of the Spanish word ... umm, the Spanish phrase ... oh, stupid memory!"

"*Desde ahora*, something like that," volunteered Tedesco quietly. "I am guessing from the ... the **counterpart** in Portuguese. It was hard to remember, though—sometimes now I forget my own language. But anyway, Meagan, after Serquiella's speech, what ...?"

> **trepidation**: an anxiety or fearfulness that leaves you worked up, hesitant, fluttering
> **precocious**: showing at an early age a degree of physical or intellectual development which is usually found only in someone far older
> **paranoid**: suspicious to the point of being irrational; seeing everyone around you as hostile and ready to cause you harm

"I'm sorry," she said, "I've gotten off track. After Serquiella's Henceforth *Desde Ahora* Calvin is a Jerk Speech she became a creature of fury. She dressed in black, she stamped all over this mountain. Her favorite place was that stone back there which spooked the mayor, the one that looks like a writing table. And in fact that was how she used it. She would lean against it and look down at Esperanza—part of the town is visible from there—and she would write things on little sheets of paper. Afterwards, she would fold the sheets and leave them there, with a small rock set on top. The same shepherd who had brought the plums now carried down those pages. And the mayor shivered as he read them, and **trepidation** grew in Esperanza. For they were covered with hexes, curses, prophecies of ruin."

———————————

READER: Larry says Meagan is really lucky to understand grown-ups and how they turn into witches, and things like that.

AUTHOR: Meagan was always **precocious** in the area of psychology. At age five, she was practically a little shrink.

READER: If she ever publishes something like *77 Weird Grown-ups and how They Got that Way*, Larry intends to buy the book.

AUTHOR: Well, harrumph. I hope he's not planning to get a refund on my book so he can buy hers. What have I done to get on his wrong side?

READER: Whoa—a bit **paranoid**! Tell Meagan to make it seventy-eight.

Chapter 21: THE WITCH'S ANOMALY

As the sun dropped farther from the **zenith** its light became more amber, more able to mark the irregularities of line and angle which the gave the high places their enchantment. It fell by an ever more slanting course, touching mainly now on crests and summits. The marchers were not yet within this band of illumination, but they were ascending quickly toward it—for until now Meagan had told her story without any break in stride.

> **zenith**: the highest point arrived at in some passage, development, evolution, etc.
>
> **surfeit**: a quantity so abundant that it exceeds what is needed or wanted

Toward the sun, thought Tedesco, and toward the high orchard as well, whatever that might be. He felt a deep anticipation. He was brimming with energy, a **surfeit** of it, so much that he didn't know what to do with it all.

Ricky was teasing him, as Meagan paused at last in the story. "The mountain has cast its spell on you, Cabbage—you are unable to concentrate on anything else. And probably you are turning into a goat."

Tedesco waved his hands in dissent. "The part about the goat, that may be right. But I am still concentrating a lot on the story of Serquiella. Meagan is telling it very well, you know, Ricky—she has just the right qualities. She ..."

> **extol**: to praise with enthusiasm and high compliments
>
> **archaic**: originating in a time long past and often, as a result, striking us as primitive or sharply different from what we're used to

Meagan herself interrupted. "Usually, Tedesco, when someone wants to talk about *moi* having all the right qualities, I let them go on. Being **extolled** is always rather nice. But it wouldn't be fair right now, because I am about to resign as storyteller. Peter Oakum is the one who should tell it now. It's at a delicate part, about the ... curses"—she glanced cautiously back at Mayor Povano—"and a deadpan, matter-of-fact style like Peter Oakum's is best. He will put the curses in the same basket with drawbridges and butter churns—all of them **archaic** items, curious things from another time, nothing more."

"Thank you," said Peter, with a little blink of surprise. "After an introduction like that, I'm embarrassed to say that I own a functioning butter churn. No drawbridge, however."

genre: a particular form of literary expression (for example, love sonnets, space novels)
infirmity: a weakened, unhealthy condition; an illness associated with such a condition
anomaly: something that runs contrary to what is required by some rule or pattern

He gave Tedesco a sympathetic smile. "You are the official, one-man audience of our story, so if something is confusing, just let me know. Now—the curses of Serquiella—they didn't fit the **genre**. Your typical curse is uttered to call down lightning, dragons, wasting illness and other horrifying physical **infirmities**, war, earthquakes, all the industrial-strength types of misfortune. But the curses which Serquiella wrote as she brooded there at the stone—they were in a category apart, more subtle, more indirect, though just as mean-spirited. 'May your children be awkward and dull. May your scales weigh under, and your measures prove inaccurate. Mold every other year in your grain. Warts on the thumbs of your maidens.' There was one curse which embodied such a strange contradiction that it is still remembered as the Witch's **Anomaly**: 'You will never get the hundred: square the ten and reach nine twice over.'"

"Better than warts on the thumbs," remarked François.

Peter smiled. "Hope so. Anyway, the curse apparently means that ten times ten will equal ninety-nine, contrary to all the laws of mathematics. Just an empty-headed fancy, you might say, and who would take it seriously? No one, except the man back there with the bright suspenders, our apprehensive mayor."

Povano was not far behind Peter in the column of marchers, and he raised a protest. "You have to admit that what happened last week was a little too weird."

pontificate: to speak as though you were the supreme authority on a subject
mute: incapable of speaking
extricate: to disentangle and remove carefully from a troublesome or awkward situation

"Last week," said Peter, sensing the ripple of confusion among his listeners, "my good friend Povano was over at the grade school **pontificating** on a variety of subjects, proud to be the last word on each of them, when a little girl pointed out a new poster in the main hallway. It was from last year's Whalefest, a close-up photo of ten pairs of hands tying a ridiculously complicated knot called the Hundred-Finger Knot. Widely used, I'm sure! Well his lordship could not just accept that ten pairs of hands with ten fingers each would multiply out to a hundred. He had to count the fingers—and it came out ninety-nine."

"Someone he has lost the finger," suggested Tedesco.

"Correct," said Peter. "One of the ten knot makers was a man named Darlingson. Twenty years back, more or less, he was part of the crew of an old tugboat. They were out from one of the northern harbors, during a storm. He saw a cable about to snap, close behind a new kid on the crew, a girl from Canada. He's **mute**, you know, so obviously he couldn't shout. He ran and pushed the girl down, just as the cable sang through the air and danced away with his little finger. That gave us nine-fingered Darlingson, and that obviously had an impact on the poster: the Hundred-Finger Knot was tied by ninety-nine. Not a big problem for the knot, but very unsettling for the mayor. He stood there for a long moment, counting the fingers again, and remembering the words of Serquiella, 'You will never get the hundred.' Then, as soon as he could do so, he **extricated** himself from the round of little duties and ceremonies at the school, and came to see me, and ..."

> **distraught**: deeply upset and driven this way and that in a confused manner by some strong and negative emotion
> **skepticism**: a tendency to receive the statements of others with doubt, and sometimes to subject those statements to sharp questioning
> **bequeath**: (1) to transfer your property to someone by means of a will; (2) more generally, to pass on what is yours to someone who comes after you

"And confessed to you that he was **distraught**." Povano's growly voice momentarily overrode Peter's account. "Because in a way and after a fashion ten times ten had yielded ninety-nine, and maybe, my rational Oakum, the Witch's Anomaly was at work among us."

"And if it were," answered Peter, looking back over his shoulder toward his friend, "what is the harm? It lowers the price of your groceries."

"What is the harm?" murmured Povano, speaking more to himself than to Peter. "If one of her curses comes true, then maybe that other one ..."

"Oh, Marion," scolded Grandma, who was walking near the mayor, "this will never do. If you wish, every one of us will sign a pledge to treat you like a fraud, to greet whatever comes from your mouth with **skepticism**. Must it come to that?"

Peter remembered his duties as the storyteller. "You see," he said to Tedesco, "the strangest of all the curses was the one that Serquiella uttered against the mayor of Esperanza and against those who would be the mayor of this place after him—'May the people believe every word you say.'"

147

"And it has passed down to me," groaned Povano, "like an inheritance, like something which that first mayor—unwillingly—**bequeathed** to the mayors who followed him, and which I—unwillingly—will leave in turn to the mayors who follow me."

Tedesco was struggling with the logic of this. "You don't want the people to believe the things you say? Most politicians ..."

> **rhetorical**: using devices of language such as dramatic repetition, exaggerated comparison, linkage to famous figures, etc., in an effort to make speech and writing have greater impact
>
> **antithesis**: something which is squarely contrary to, and at odds with, something else
>
> **dilettante**: a person who loves some branch of activity or learning but pursues it only as a hobby, and has only an amateur's ability in it

"It's the 'every word' part," replied Povano. "It's nastier than it looks. Sure, some of what I say—twenty-three percent maybe—is meant to be believed. But the rest—the nonsense, the fancy, the play and replay, the trial balloons ... I mean—what if people start believing my jokes? Think of the uproar the next time I announce we're adopting the Euro. What about those **rhetorical** touches I like to use? Some of them are basically exaggerations—bread trucks lost in potholes, six-figure fireworks budgets. They are meant to amuse, to win sympathy, but if everybody starts taking them literally ... It's bad, I know, to be the little boy who cried wolf—everything you say gets treated as a lie. But it would be worse to be his **antithesis**, and have everything you say taken as the solemn truth. And that, I'm afraid, is what Serquiella has packed into her curse of the mayors."

Grandma was making snapping motions with her hands. "Marion, this means keep moving. Let's not go from walker to stander, if you please. One foot in front of the other, that's it. And as for what you said about people believing your jokes—I don't even believe half of the serious things you say. And no amateur witch will change that. Serquiella? I beg your pardon, but she sounds like your basic **dilettante**, the every-other-Saturday type. All enthused, but what did she really know how to do? Probably got her wand at the hobby store. So test me, test her curse, if you want. Try out a joke, tell me ... whatever, tell me these poor old stumps here will blossom next spring, see if I believe it."

> **array**: a large quantity or assortment of things, laid out or ordered in what is often an impressive display
>
> **rift**: a split or tear in the earth's surface, sometimes with the land on one side thrust up or down to a different elevation than the land on the other side

archipelago: an extensive string or group of islands

The excursion had reached what Meagan earlier called the high orchard, a stretching **array** of small trees, or what was left of trees. Grandma was gesturing toward them now, as she spoke to Povano. There were trunks and main branches, but no twigs or leaves. It was a high orchard and a vast one, but to all appearances no longer a living one.

The place itself where the orchard had grown and ceased to grow was a long, shallow basin, reaching away from the band of marchers toward the sea. It was not one of the defining features of Mount Relief, but rather was framed in by such features. It was where the long northward decline from the crest of Ms. Framley's hillside ran itself out. It was something of a backyard for Cape Stairstep. And if you were hiking up from the south, it was the last pause before an abrupt upswelling of the mountain along the course of an extensive **rift**.

In its own right the basin did have a curving chain of seven low summits, which on many mornings stood forth like an **archipelago** when the fog was streaming across the ground. And there was the orchard—the countless trees planted in rows that lapped around the seven hills.

"In its day," said Peter, "it must have been magnificent. From what is still standing you can see, after some close study, that everything was grown here—peach, persimmon, quince, apricot, and if I'm not wrong, a fruit you're surely familiar with, Tedesco—the guava. But what a riddle this orchard is, a four-hundred-year old riddle. I mean, why …?"

> **conundrum**: a tangled and puzzling problem, inviting guesses and theories but resisting a definitive solution
> **mesmerize**: to capture your attention so completely that you are left almost in a trance or under a hypnotic spell

"Peter," broke in Grandma, "up ahead, up beyond that"—she pointed to a steep incline of granite that was looming ever closer—"we've got a modern-day riddle waiting for this boy. What's happening to the briars? That's the **conundrum** of the day, and we need his help on it. But look what's going on. This ruin of an orchard is getting a hold on him."

Grandma had a point. Tedesco seemed to be **mesmerized**. He was looking with fixed attention out across the basin, and the suggestion of a smile was lighting up his face. He had suspended—or so it appeared—simple functions like breathing and blinking. For all this, however, part of him was still tuned in, and he heard Grandma's concern and spoke some reassurance. "It is not to worry, OK. We will go first to the briars, to help them all we can. That is first, but when that is done, and when all the other things are done—to finish the school, to have a job and raise some children and take care of my mother and

149

father—then I will return to this orchard and try to bring it back to life. This place is beautiful, with colors like from one of those old paintings. And the orchard—it honors the place. It follows ... like the line of the place, it is the right size for the place. And when it was in bloom ..."

> **commensurate**: on the same scale as something else; of similar proportion or measure; roughly as small or great in degree as something else
> **plausible**: believable, at least for the time being, by reason of appearing to be consistent with known facts and accepted understandings
> **arid**: dry as a desert through lack of rainfall and irrigation

Peter's head lifted suddenly. "The right size ..." he said thoughtfully, addressing no one in particular. "That's the riddle of the orchard—why wasn't it the right size, why was it so big? Even if every man, woman and child in Esperanza was a fruit junkie ... But Tedesco comes at it differently—the orchard was made **commensurate** with ... with the scale of its place. I like that. It solves my riddle, it's a **plausible** explanation, a nice one actually."

"What I liked," said François, "was Tedesco's promise—about the orchard coming back to life someday. We will hold him to it."

Now Peter stared out to the west, where the sky still shimmered with the heat of the afternoon sun. "I'm sorry not to be encouraging," he said, "but it's an open question whether any orchards will ever spring back to life in this basin. The place is more **arid** now, I think, than four hundred years ago. The rains seem to pass it by. Possibly it's turning into a little desert."

That innocent remark, for some reason or another, was the one that brought Bamalford back into the conversation. "Turning into a desert!" he roared. "That is so stupid! You can't get a desert in four centuries. They take millions of years to form. Haven't you ever heard about the sands of time?"

> **refute**: to take a statement or claim that someone has put forward and throw it back by showing that it is wrong
> **phenomena** (plural; the singular is phenomenon): the raw data of reality (the images and appearances, the motions and occurrences, etc.) which present themselves to our perception prior to interpretation or theoretical analysis
> **elite** (noun): a small group of persons, often of superior ability or believing themselves superior, who enjoy special privilege and influence

That pulled in Ms. Jensen. She was starting a unit on desertification with the seniors, and she felt that the wrong-headed remarks of Bamalford on the subject should not pass unchallenged. "Sir," she began in a quiet voice, "what you just said can be **refuted** from textbooks, it can be refuted by logic, and it can be refuted by simply observing ..."

"But it shall never be refuted," cried Bamalford, with the whites of his eyes growing larger, "by a rookie teacher, a rookie lady teacher, earning a crummy two K per month. What none of you seem to realize is that I am an editor. I have access to on-line information sources that most of you can only dream about. One click, one little smeef of a click, and I have detailed descriptions of natural **phenomena**, historical phenomena, political phenomena, whatever. Another click and I get authoritative interpretations of the same. So, people, when you hear Bamalford speak on a subject—deserts included—you are probably hearing the last word. Because he has done his homework, he has tapped into his restricted sources. Just live with it, OK—there's an information **elite** in this country and one of us here, but only one of us, happens to be part of it."

> **physiological**: being part of, or explainable in terms of, the physical systems and processes of a living body
> **arduous**: hard to do; requiring much toil and exertion
> **erratic**: bending and wandering this way and that, with no regular pattern or course

"Well, that's very nice," snapped Grandma. "I just hope you're also part of the **physiological** elite of this country. Because all your physical systems, sir—respiratory, cardiovascular, the works—will be put to the test very soon now. On the Steeps."

There was no missing what Grandma had in mind with her reference to the Steeps. The easy walking was almost over, along the landward edge of the basin. Now a sharply tilted face of granite rose up before the marchers. If you chose the most **arduous** route and climbed it head-on, by a straight line from bottom to top, the distance covered was a couple hundred yards, a little less. The common trail—a hard climb in its own right—followed a more **erratic** course up the face, bending and crooking through some shallow washes worn into the stone by streams of other times. "Other times," Ironbane would say, "when this band of granite was not yet the Steeps, when it lay horizontal and a river could flow in any direction across it."

> **incessant**: going on and on, without stopping or pausing
> **elaborate** (verb): to describe something in fuller detail
> **precedent** (noun): (1) a prior situation which, because of similarities to a present one, helps us comprehend the present one; (2) a response which was taken to a prior situation and which now serves as a rule of action when a similar situation arises

The Steeps extended for some ways along the mountain's flank, out to the west. It ran like a belt of blue-gray stone, and formed the back wall of the basin where the high orchard had been planted. It was a striking feature at any hour, but especially in late afternoon when the glancing sun struck off countless sparks. For Grandma and Peter, for Mayor Povano and many others, the sight was heartening, and seemed to renew their strength for the ascent. Not for Bamalford, however. He went up the Steeps grumbling **incessantly** about the sun in his eyes, the absence of a handrail, the uncivilized pace of the march and the general absurdity of everyone going off to inspect some stupid brambles.

READER: Larry says that desertification may be his only hope.

AUTHOR: I don't suppose he **elaborated** on that?

READER: He said it's the night before the SAT, OK, and a big truck brings the No. 2 pencils, and they're stored in a depository at one edge of town.

AUTHOR: Under lock and key, I imagine.

READER: More than that—all the proctors are there, standing guard and saying, "It's a go. It's a go. We've got the number two's."

AUTHOR: Sounds a bit dramatic.

READER: Then a hot wind starts to blow on that edge of town. It blows all night, carrying in the sand, grain by grain. By morning the depository is underneath a 950-foot dune.

AUTHOR: Unheard of.

READER: That's what the proctors say that day at the testing centers—kids, we've never had one like this. There's no **precedent**. The only thing we can think of is to declare a sand day and cancel.

AUTHOR: Larry's a bit weird, but he speaks for many.

Chapter 22: MENDICANT BRIARS, MENDICANT BERRIES

"That was rather romantic," said François, in reply to Tedesco. They had completed their ascent of the Steeps and emerged onto a wide tableland. Tedesco was gazing out over it, intently, with obvious pleasure. He saw how in that place the Bad Pony was not one stream but several, a weaving of silver lines, winding brightly across the high meadow and at last uniting not far from where the marchers stood.

> **burlesque** (noun): a distorted imitation of something, designed to provoke laughter
> **tortuous**: bending and twisting back and forth
> **redolent**: carrying some fragrance or scent, as, for example, the air in a room carries the fragrance from a vase of lilies

"Like a beautiful woman braiding her hair"—that was the remark of his that won François' appreciation.

Bamalford, however, saw nothing in it to appreciate. He moved his hands in a harsh **burlesque** of a woman fixing her hair. "Braid lady," he sneered, "Mother Farbugle perhaps."

Furious, Grandma Dubois widened her mouth and gave one or two gulping swallows. "Megalomaniac Bullfrog. City editor, perhaps."

Tedesco set a hand on her arm. "I think I see them." He motioned toward the far edge of the tableland, toward a long gray band of rock, strung with green. It was a low bluff of granite, irregular in height, but no taller than thirty feet at its tallest. It ran like a rough piece of curbing, forming the back limits of the plateau. And trailing in a thousand ragged falls down its face were the briars of Grandma Dubois.

With a last glance at Bamalford, Grandma moved to the front of the column of marchers and led it slowly across the stony meadow. The way was easy enough, though **tortuous** as it bent and doubled along the several streams of the Bad Pony.

"This tableland," said Ricky in a low voice to Tedesco, "is like a plaza at the intersection of two roadways. From the north comes the valley of the Bad Pony, and from the west a green canyon, and they both open out here. The valley out of the north cuts down from the highest summit of the mountain—or maybe from Antarctica, it's so cold and rocky. The canyon is just the contrary—it is steamy, and hung with vines, and **redolent**, as they say, with strange spices."

He pointed out toward the west, toward a long slash of green—a jungle to all appearances—that came descending from a wide, broken overlook. "And that's not all," he went on. "The mountain has several other summits, and from each of them ..."

> **innate**: forming part of your character right from birth
> **minuscule**: extremely small
> **mendicant** (noun): one who regularly begs for money or food

Meagan had been watching Tedesco's struggle to pay attention. Now she broke in. "Ricky, he's trying desperately to stay with your geography lesson. He's got an **innate** courtesy that won't let him just tune you out, the way the rest of us—born rude and proud of it—would. But now we are very close to the bluff, close to the briars, and I have the impression that they are jamming his signals."

Tedesco laughed. "She is very sharp-eyed, Ricky. This has always been a weakness for me—the grass rooted in the wall, the vine that springs from rock. When I see this—don't ask me why—I am very happy. And now look at these briars, look how stubborn they are, growing right in the stone."

Tedesco was right. Along the wide sweep of the bluff, wherever a **minuscule** quantity of soil had collected in some nook or pocket, the briars had rooted. They were shaken by the wind and tossed about by the ragged plunge of the Bad Pony, but they held their ground all the same. "They are like the poor families," he went on, "who build their little houses, their shacks, on the steep hillside."

Peter Oakum threw him a quick look. "The comparison is more fitting than you think. Because when there is no work for the poor, and no help, some of them must beg. And that is the name of the briars—they are called the **Mendicant** Briars. The leaves grow in pairs, and as they mature they hold themselves outstretched like the two hands of a beggar asking for a coin."

> **immutable**: fixed and unchanging; resistant to any variation
> **remonstration**: the vigorous presentation to someone of the reasons why a plan, position, behavior, etc., of his is wrong or objectionable

"At least, that was the **immutable** pattern for the two or three hundred years which I can remember," said Grandma Dubois, "until this year when things changed and ... well, you can see."

It was not hard to see. The leaves did not resemble outstretched hands or outstretched anything. They had curled themselves into rolls. "Tight little rolls," said Grandma, in a tone of **remonstration**. "And if you stay in tight little rolls your berries will have no protection next spring, and they'll die in the sun or the frost."

> **stupendous**: so huge or great as to be astonishing
> **wane**: gradually to become smaller or less powerful or less important

"From Mendicant Briars come Mendicant Berries," explained Peter to Tedesco, "some of them all year round, which is strange, but with the main crop coming in the spring. And the berries are **stupendously** important in the life of Dropanchor. Without them this place will be a **waning** star, growing dimmer and colder, slowly going out."

"We'll be in a very bad way, young man," said Grandma, also addressing Tedesco. "Without the harvest of the berries we'll lose a tradition that keeps this town alive. So if you can ... can do whatever it is you do, and tell us why these leaves insist on curling, you'll be a hero."

> **eleemosynary**: related to the works of charity, such as the donation of money, the furnishing of food or medical care to the poor, etc.
> **goad**: to jab someone, often with sharp words, in order to drive him into some action or reaction
> **puerile**: silly and childish; lacking the maturity or seriousness which the situation demands

"And you can appear in hero commercials," scoffed Bamalford, obviously in a foul humor from the long hike. "This intolerable fuss over some plants, I just can't stand it. Do you know why the beggar leaves are curled? That's easy—why does any beggar curl his fingers, close his fist? Because someone put a penny there, and he's afraid to lose it. And do you know how to make him open his hand? Ha—hold out something more interesting, like a quarter. In fact, let me show you. I'll make those leaves uncurl. Let's get **eleemosynary**. Let's toss the beggar berries a quarter. One more charitable deed by the charitable Mr. Bamalford. Who's got a quarter around here?"

Grandma was staring fiercely at him, but for the moment she kept her silence. He sensed her indignation, and **goaded** her the worse. "Ha, ha. C'mon now. Who's got a quarter? Grandma? They say you're worth some bucks. A quarter, a quarter mill, it's all the same to you, right. So c'mon, loosen up."

Her look grew darker, and she snapped, "Go find somewhere else to be childish. This is sacred ground where the briars grow, not a good place for **puerile** coin tricks, and definitely not ..."

"Oh, save it!" he cut in. "Save the jabber." He was scanning the ranks of the marchers now, looking for someone. "Let's see ... ah, there you are. Ahoy, Calvin my lad, newly hired advertising artist for the *Vociferous Beacon*, what do you think of my idea of pitching a quarter to the beggar berries?"

quandary: a condition of somewhat paralyzing doubt about how to judge something or how to act
resolute: having your mind firmly made up
troglodyte: a person from the prehistoric past who lived in a cave

In the following silence Calvin looked around, at Joannie and the other marchers, at the angling sunlight on the heights above them, and the gathering of the first dusk over the many streams. He sensed the appeal of the place: this is sacred ground. But Bamalford knew how to urge an appeal of his own. "You look like someone in a **quandary**: Oh, what to do, what to do? Sacred ground. Bosh! Sand and gravel. I'll tell you what's sacred: the advertiser-client relationship. Will you trample on that, three days after I hired you, one week before bonuses?"

Calvin grew more **resolute**, squaring his shoulders, drawing a long breath. "It's a fine idea, sir, pitching a quarter to the beggar berries. A modern idea, reminding these ... **troglodytes**, with their tribal marches and their superstitions of sacred ground, that this is not the year 10,000 B.C., and people don't live in caves anymore. And ... and here's your quarter, sir."

Bamalford received the quarter from Calvin with a wide smile. "I made a good choice for my part-time advertising artist."

sycophant: a person who practices submission and flattery to gain some benefit
ungainly: awkward and uncoordinated
trajectory: the curving path of a thrown or orbiting object

"Part-time **sycophant**, don't you mean?" cried Joannie, unable to hold back her distress. "All scrape and bow, all butter on the tongue, all flattery."

Bamalford laughed. "Just ignore her, Calvin, my boy. It's quite standard, this jealousy and whining when a childhood friend is too **ungainly** to follow you onto the fast track." He looked at the coin in his hand. "Now, let's remember the needy."

After a moment of elaborate shoulder rolls and other warm-ups, Bamalford threw the quarter on a high **trajectory** toward the Mendicant Briars. "A fine pitch, sir," observed Calvin as the coin twirled through the air.

"Full-time sycophant now, Calvin?" came Joannie's rebuke. It was fired off with such vehemence that it drew all eyes to her for an instant, and they turned back just in time to see a streak of shadow racing to intercept the falling piece of silver. A hand swept out from a hurtling body, and inches from the briars the coin disappeared into its grasp. In a moment the images resolved themselves into the powerful figure of a man in working clothes, fifty perhaps, fists held by his side. He was clutching the quarter, and staring at Bamalford. It was Darlingson, and he made no sound.

> **menial**: held in low esteem because requiring bodily, but not mental, energy
> **tauten**: to be stretched out or pulled out to the point of tightness
> **retort** (noun): a stinging reply, sometimes throwing back on the original speaker the accusation or insult that was carried by his statement

Bamalford's voice mounted almost to a scream. "Ape! Ape in overalls. Get back, ape, get behind a broom, get under a sink, go clean a toilet, get back to **menial** where you belong, and don't mess with Bamalford again, OK, boom box!"

It was very ugly, and Merci felt her slender frame **tauten** with rage and pain. She hurled a **retort**. "You animal ... you ...! He has a world inside him of bright thoughts. You could never go there, you ... obscenity. I'm afraid you've hurt him!"

> **incarnation**: the presence of an abstract idea or spiritual reality in bodily form
> **vilification**: the act of smearing someone with assertions of base conduct or low character

Smiling faintly, Darlingson set a finger on his lips and hushed her. But there was no hushing Bamalford. He was waving his yellow press card and shouting headlines. "Slime Attack! Peerless Bamalford—Courageous Editor and Bodily **Incarnation** of Freedom of the Press—under Attack. Savage **Vilification**, as Goblin Girl Drags His Good Name toward the Slime."

He raised an arm and pointed back across the tableland. "Once we're back in town the little shrieker goes to detention, the ape-man goes on lavatory duty, and the alien boy gets deported. I am through messing around."

> **desecrate**: to treat something sacred in a rough, insulting manner
> **domestication**: the process of gradually altering something wild (a species of wild animal, for example) until it can coexist with humans and be a useful addition to human households

By this time Tedesco was already detaching himself from the group and beginning to move slowly along the green curtain of the briars. He was very absorbed in his survey, in his first acquaintance with the ancient vines, but not to the point of losing touch with the human theater. When his wandering path crossed that of Darlingson, he shook hands warmly, as though to congratulate the silent man on his catch of the **desecrating** quarter. And when he heard Bamalford declaring all the harsh measures to be taken once they returned to town, he looked toward the spouting figure and announced, "I am not going back to the town. I will spend the night here, on the mountain."

READER: Fulano offers an example which perfectly illustrates the word "troglodyte."

AUTHOR: That's the famous ambulatory-dictionary Fulano, I assume.

READER: Of course. His sentence is: "One day at the dawn of human history, centuries before the raising of crops and the **domestication** of animals, the parent troglodytes emerged from their cave, shot a pterodactyl from the sky with their rude bows, and made a broth for the baby troglodyte, who was sick."

AUTHOR: I take my hat off to the master.

Chapter 23: MERCURIAL CANYON

Bamalford was thunderstruck by Tedesco's announcement, and his fury **abated**. The scowl and the shadow retreated from his face, pushed away for the moment by a staring astonishment. "You don't even know Rule One. Anybody talking like that, talking about a night on the mountain, doesn't even know Rule One."

> **abate**: to become, or to cause something to become, less intense, pressing or urgent
> **myriad**: a huge, uncountable number of things
> **diurnal**: happening during the daylight hours; carrying on the principal part of your activity during those hours
> **reciprocity**: a two-way relation in which one side receives something from the other and returns a rough equivalent

Tedesco ventured, "You mean 'Love thy neighbor'?"

"Not that blind alley," exclaimed Bamalford. "I mean Rule One—Day is ours, night is theirs."

"Oh," said Tedesco, "theirs."

"The beasties, the crawlies, the **myriad** of bugsies, swarming everywhere, with their six little knee joints and parchment wings, and their probosci or whatever. By day we hunt them, tag them, spray them, squash them. We have the advantage because we are **diurnal** creatures. But don't be out there at night, in the fields and the forest, because then it's their turn. The advantage is theirs. **Reciprocity** you know." Bamalford shivered.

Tedesco picked up his feet, looked over his shoulder in a show of alarm. "There is a bug on this mountain?"

The humor was lost on Bamalford. "A bug! There's a bug factory, a warehouse of crawlies. Look there!" He beckoned up the jungly canyon which Ricky had pointed out earlier.

"Ha!" shouted Joannie sharply. "Would you like a tour? Ask Calvin. That's where he learned to draw. Before he got on the fast track."

> **eureka**: "Eureka!" is a cry of success at the moment of finding or discovering something; it literally means "I have found it!"
> **affiliated**: closely linked (though not to the point of a complete merger of identities), often within some commercial or institutional framework
> **accolade**: some sign, ceremony or other expression conferring praise

In a quieter voice she turned and said to Tedesco. "To answer your question, there is a bug on this mountain. Trillions of them. And on this point, at least, Mr. Bamalford is right. Most of them come from there"—she gestured toward the green canyon—"and many of them come from nowhere else. You photograph them, you draw them, you compare the field guides and the registers, and at last you cry '**Eureka**!'—another discovery, another unknown species brought to light. And in the time it takes to do all that, the canyon generates two or three more—new species, I mean. And the work goes on."

Tedesco showed a wide smile. "So the bug that crawls out of the canyon tonight may be something never seen before?"

Bamalford burst in, "And when it crawls over and gives you a bite like you've never had before, don't expect the pharmacies of Dropanchor to start dishing out the antibiotics, or any of those non-steroidal things. They are all reserved for the people who make useful contributions."

"If it crawls over," said Joannie, addressing Tedesco, but with a sternness in her voice that was a rebuke to Bamalford, "and if it's a snacker, obviously— don't let it snack on you. But please, let me see it, so I can do an identification. And if necessary … a drawing."

She gave a little nod in the direction of Calvin, who was still at Bamalford's side. "Yonder robot, who used to be a human boy, and I once had a plan. I would discover and catalog new species in the canyon—not just the bugs, but mosses, vines, geckos, marsupials, whatever—and he would draw them. Joannie Inc. and Calvin Inc., two closely **affiliated** enterprises, working together over many years on a landmark research, a ninety-seven volume natural history of the green canyon, winning medals, honors, **accolades** of every sort, for both text and drawings."

> **rueful**: feeling a sad regret that things didn't turn out differently
> **lampoon** (noun): a representation of someone that holds him up to ridicule by seizing on and exaggerating anything comic or pathetic about him
> **reprehensible**: deserving a sharp rebuke, usually on account of being contrary to standards of morality and decency

She stared **ruefully** at Calvin. "And it will get done. There may be only one name on the title page, but it will get done."

Calvin was apparently feeling no regrets. He began flapping his arms and shifting from foot to foot, like some enormous mantid. "Alert, alert, new species, call Joannie. Alert, alert!"

Joannie stayed silent under this mockery, but Meagan could not. "Is this all a bluff?" she challenged. "Are you just putting on this **lampoon**, Calvin, so that no one will see what you're feeling? You gave up a lot to get on the fast track, and you must be sad."

"Gave up a lot!" he scoffed. "The chance to work on a doomed project. One day, Meagan, we'll be sitting there in, who knows, etiquette class maybe, and we're going to hear a quiet boom, a soft, well-mannered boom, as this mountain blows up, and within minutes Mercurial Canyon will be a lava bed. Joannie's lifework will be a cinder block. She should bag it all, don't you think, and come be my trophy wife. Ha—she can take my calls, schedule my appearances."

Joannie was used to the bad Calvin, and again she remained silent. Meagan, though, was furious. "That is completely **reprehensible**! People should turn their faces from you, Calvin, after you say a thing that swinish about a girl who has been so good to you, who ..."

> **acquiescence**: the act of remaining silent and raising no objection, and thus letting some proposed action go forward or some statement stand as correct
>
> **encroach**: to extend or lap over into the property or domain of someone else; to commit trespass bit by bit
>
> **divulge**: to make known something you have kept, or should have kept, as a secret

A calmer voice imposed itself at this point. "I would ordinarily keep my distance," said Ironbane, "from a matter such as this. But I'm the Mount Relief guy. If I stay silent now it will be seen as my **acquiescence** in Calvin's theory of an exploding mountain. Yet, having walked all over these slopes for twenty years, I have the pleasure of reporting that your theory, Calvin, is doubtful. I suspect that odd bugs will flap and strange plants will grow in Mercurial Canyon for generations to come, and Joannie's project will not turn into a cinder block."

Ironbane had never been quite this reassuring, and Joannie wanted to be certain she was understanding correctly. "Are you saying there's no fire down there, sir? I always thought ..."

Ironbane was already shaking his head. "There's fire, no end of fire. It is a kingdom of fire and magma. But with each passing year I am more convinced that into that domain another force comes **encroaching**—the cold waters of the Pacific. They don't quench the fire, but they make it less explosive. Pardon me, though, if I **divulge** no more than this. The rest of the theory stays in the vault"—he tapped his head—"under lock and key. Because the rest is a bit far-out, and I have the normal fear of looking weird."

> **nether**: found at a lower level, or below the main surface

161

inundate: to flood into or over something in such great quantities as to fill or cover it
juggernaut: a huge force that advances unstoppably, grinding down whatever lies before it

Bamalford gave a smirk, as though to say "Too late!" and then stared out toward the green canyon. "I don't like that place, Rusty, and I wouldn't mind a bit if those **nether** fires of yours would chuck up sufficient lava to overflow it, to **inundate** it from one end to the other. That would be a useful service."

"I'll pass on your suggestion," said Ironbane with a frown. More for Joannie's sake than for Bamalford's he went on. "The real service, though, which the fires render is to make the green canyon possible in the first place. Not that ice doesn't get some credit also. It all started long ago, of course, and scene one actually belonged to the ice. A huge glacier cracked loose from a western summit of Mount Relief, carrying one flank of the mountain with it, I believe, almost like a plow blade. And plow it did. It came on like a **juggernaut** in slow motion, tearing and scraping, gashing out a substantial trench. A small part, though, of the glacier was just ice, carrying no mass of stone, and it made a shallower cut, carving a ledge that ran almost like a sidewalk along the edge of the trench. As for the trench itself, it was sunken deep enough to bring my nether fires into play. It felt their influence, it became a warm and often humid realm, with steam percolating up at many places through the fractured granite and the many beds of topsoil that gradually collected there."

discourse: a carefully organized speech or writing that develops a topic at some length
mercurial: undergoing rapid changes in mood or aspect, often in response to minimal or trifling influences

By this time Bamalford had stopped listening altogether to Ironbane's **discourse**, and was fumbling instead with his cell phone, trying to punch in a number. Joannie, though, was still intent on every word, like a child hearing some fateful story from the family history. "So with the steam and the soil," she prompted, "it became a place that generated many species of bugs and plants and ..."

"And many species of weather," laughed Ironbane. "The canyon is a weather machine. Cells of humidity clash with the cold wind off the summits, and there are storms. Then, without warning, the wind drops, the steams trail off, the place becomes an oven, baking under a blue heaven. And you think, a few days of this and ... But in **Mercurial** Canyon, as most of us call it, nothing is for a few days. A few hours go by, maybe just a few minutes, and the breezes freshen, once more pushing in from the sea. There is a rash of little cyclones, the steams rise again, then a rolling fog. And the alternation goes on and on."

> **deplore**: to show yourself grieved and afflicted by something and often, in this way, to express your criticism of it
> **unobtrusive**: not conspicuous or calling attention; not breaking in on the peace or concentration of others
> **apologist**: a person who makes well thought-out arguments, spoken or written, to explain and defend something

As Ironbane was finishing, Bamalford had moved off some distance from the crowd, obviously seeking to make his phone call in private. He failed, however, to reckon with Allen the Snoop. Allen wasn't the most obnoxious sort of snoop, and as a general matter he didn't listen in on conversations—he could appreciate that eavesdropping was widely **deplored** as one of the grosser invasions of privacy. He hadn't hesitated, though, on the preceding afternoon to overhear Bamalford's telephone call to Bezzle from the Dome, and he didn't hesitate now to repeat the trespass. Bamalford was a case apart. He seemed to be a man with an agenda. No one knew what it was, but you felt that if he got it all—everything on his list—it would be an unlovely future for Dropanchor.

Allen worked his way along the fringe of the crowd, greeting friends, scribbling little notes on his pad, trying to be **unobtrusive**—a non-event on the radar screen—as he moved steadily closer to the hunching figure of Bamalford.

READER: We took Larry to a French bakery the other night.
AUTHOR: And he did something so weird that you can never go back?
READER: Not that bad. But when the waitress asked what he wanted he said a canyon.
AUTHOR: Whoops.
READER: She was confused, and started checking the menu. He explained how Joannie has a canyon that she lives for, how she has become a naturalist by exploring it, and a bit of an **apologist** by starting to speak out for it and defend it. The waitress set down the menu. She had a sweet face, and there was a little smile beginning to appear, as though she could hear what he was really trying to say. So Lare, he takes her hand and blurts, "There is nothing more beautiful than to know what your lifework is while you still have time to do it."
AUTHOR: I'm rather impressed.

READER: So was the waitress. She went and got about fifty loaves of French bread and several huge blocks of cheese, and set it all in front of him, saying, "Eat, eat, you need to be strong."
AUTHOR: I wish I had been there.

Chapter 24: SALUBRIOUS TWILIGHT

Allen's advantage was his sharp sense of hearing. He could stay at a distance which roused no suspicion, and yet catch most of what Bamalford was saying over the phone.

> **capitulation**: the act of dropping your resistance and making your surrender, often on specific terms and conditions
> **acclimatize**: to get used to a new setting or situation, to the point that you can exist comfortably and effectively in it

The big man looked tense. His jaw was set, his grip on the phone threatened to crush it. "I'm sure I said please," he was insisting. "I remember saying please, I always ... Oh, alright! I surrender, I give in—total **capitulation**. Please, please, please! Not tonight, please. That's the message—not tonight. Half of Brazil will be up here tonight, antennas twitching, X-ray goggles ... No, that's OK, I'll tell him. He's here, the big rhino, already feeling at home, it appears, in this horrible place, in this air that's practically electric with bugs, and on this awful plateau, like some junkyard for discarded rivers. Oh yes, he's thriving. That's the advantage of being dense as a rhino, you **acclimatize** easily, wherever you wind up. But for a man of letters, a man of refinement, this pesthole ..."

There was silence for a moment and then, in a voice betraying the struggle to stay composed, Bamalford answered some question. "Yes, I am on the anxious side just now, thank you. It gets on my nerves, being so close to that scummy canyon, the one they call Mercurial Canyon. What right does it have to pass through monsoon season every morning and afternoon? To keep generating more species than we could ever count? And for that matter ..."

> **extrapolation**: a type of reasoning in which, on the basis of a trend observed in situations already encountered, you make a projection of what must occur in a situation not yet encountered
> **metamorphosis**: a dramatic change in form or nature, sometimes so extreme (as, for example, the change from a human being into a swan or a tree) that it can be explained only as the result of supernatural forces

He paused, a fretful pause to listen to something obviously unwelcome, and then in a voice from which much of the composure had vanished, he growled, "Easy on the **extrapolation**, Bez, if you don't mind! I grant you Case A: let the steams emerge, and the drafts descend off the mountain and the fogs come in from the sea and, sure, the canyon will brew all forms of violent weather—probably a few we haven't even thought of yet. And I don't even care if you go on to Case B, OK—fill a canyon like that with a variety of life-forms and, yes, you do get breakneck evolution. But there it stops, Bez, that's as far as you can take it. No crazy projection, please, to a further case about an individual creature, a small, weak, stupid individual creature which wanders into the canyon, gets bombarded by the strange forces of the place, and transforms overnight into some huge and wrathful beast! That's called **metamorphosis**, Bez, and it's a product of juvenile imagination, not of logical extrapolation."

> **protracted**: drawn out; made to continue for a long time
> **unimpeachable**: so proper in conduct and truthful in speech as to be above all accusation or doubt
> **veracity**: careful and deliberate truthfulness

He stopped suddenly, realizing that his voice had risen and was now the only voice to be heard on the evening air. Extending his head slowly from the shelter of his overcoat, he stared defiantly at the people of Dropanchor, and they stared back at him. A deep silence reigned, and was becoming **protracted**, when François, usually the soul of good breeding, said softly and deliberately, "Quack."

Bamalford jumped at the sound. And Grandma Dubois swung about sharply. "No, no, granddaughter. Quack means you buy the story—how the baby duck sees its mother captured by the brave Mr. Bamalford, how it takes flight to Mercurial Canyon and then, during the night, undergoes a massive change in size and shape and becomes a huge, scary mega-duck. But that's a deception, and deception is not in the Dubois vocabulary."

"But Grandma," protested François, "it's a very unusual canyon, and it doesn't play by the rules. If you, for example, were to spend a night there ... Well, however that may be, I have it on the word of Ricky Snoozer—an **unimpeachable** witness, the son of a judge—that the metamorphosis truly occurred."

Grandma cast a very doubtful look in Ricky's direction. "And on whose word does he have the story?"

"The last word in **veracity**," answered Ricky, "my good friend, Allen the Snoop. He saw it with his own Allen-the-Snoop eyeballs, especially trained to see no more and no less than what is really there."

"He saw the metamorphosis?" challenged Grandma. "He saw that poor baby duck start doubling and tripling and getting claws and ...?"

> **candor**: full and honest disclosure, even of personal sentiments and delicate information

166

litotes: understatement of the sort you use when you say, for example, that a tornado was "not a light breeze" or that a genius is "no dummy"

"In all **candor**, no," volunteered Allen. "But I saw the result of that metamorphosis, right here on this mountain. By sheer chance it was the day after Mr. Bamalford had captured the Harbinger Duck on the beach. I was up here all alone, not far from this spot, a rookie reporter with my yellow press card pinned to my cap. We had a rumor about a new species of butterfly in Mercurial Canyon, and the *Trumpet* wanted a story. I was walking along, and for a moment or two I looked down, checking my camera maybe. It was just after lunch, I remember. When I looked up again, all I could see was wings and beak and webbed feet the size of manhole covers. And none of the above was posing for a photo. It was all charging toward me."

Seeing the flicker of alarm on Bamalford's face, he slowed the pace of his account. "The scariest thing ... was the sound that came from the creature. It made the air shudder. It was so bloodcurdling, that I will not describe it, I will not repeat it. No, we have **litotes** for just such occasions as these, and I will only say, Mr. Bamalford and all of you, that the sound I heard ... was not a friendly quack."

chimerical: too monster-like, magical, idealistic or otherwise extreme to be real; conceived by a wild flight of imagination
baleful: heavy with the menace of evil to come
epitaph: the message carved on a tombstone

Grandma Dubois was staring sternly at him, but he continued gamely. "The creature was, of course, the Chimerical Mega-Duck. I call it **chimerical** for the sake of the fainthearted and children, but that day it was too real. Its horse-high body careened toward me, its blazing eyes stared **balefully** at my forehead. Things looked very bad for your correspondent. The little copy editor in my brain was composing **epitaphs**: Here Lies the Snoop—He Went with His Boots on, and His Press Card. Blam! I was hit with a major insight, and none too soon. The press card! The mega-duck was staring at the press card. It was the badge of evil—Bamalford flashed it before the eyes of the mother duck when he captured her. I dashed my card to the ground, and the cap on which it was pinned, and ran for my life with ... with ..."

celerity: swiftness; quickness in the performance of a work or motion
medley: a loose mix of distinct things
thesis: a proposition which you put forward, defend against objections, and work to prove

"With unaccustomed **celerity**," said Ricky, giving Allen a little poke in his well-padded stomach.

"That's a quaint way to put it. But, yes, with unaccustomed celerity. After a few moments, though, I realized that the smack of those huge wings, the braying from that orange beak—all the dreadful sounds were gone. I could hear nothing now but the chirring of crickets and the wind in the pines, the jabber of some crows—the usual **medley** that rises from the mountain by day. The mega-duck had chosen not to pursue. I was alone and safe. But my press card, and my poor cap ..."

"So you see, Grandmother," said François gently, "I'm sure the logic is clear. On one day the duckling flees wildly as Bamalford lunges toward it, and it only rests when it has come to Mercurial Canyon. On the following day, as Allen has confirmed in painstaking detail, the vast hulk of a mega-duck appears. What stronger support for our little ... **thesis** that Mercurial Canyon does not deal in evolution only, but in metamorphosis as well?"

"I wish that is what the story supported," said Grandma with a dark glance at Bamalford, "for the sake of the mother duck caged in the Ambivalence Dome. But it may mean only that Allen had a big lunch that day and ..."

> **paucity**: the condition in which there are only a few of something; scarceness of supply
> **plagiarism**: the act of holding yourself out as the originator of a literary product actually created by someone else
> **acerbic**: having a tone that is sharp-edged and cutting

By this point Bamalford had pushed down whatever anxieties had started to awaken with Allen's story, and he was able to resume his usual offensiveness. "Why don't we get right to it?" he said with disgust. "The kid was on the mountain, he was gnashing his teeth about the **paucity** of news for his little amoeba paper. What were his alternatives? The same as for any baby reporter who's seriously short on copy. He could get to work and find some news, or he could pull someone else's story out of an archive and put his own name on it, or—if he's squeamish about **plagiarism**—he could go the fiction route, write down one of his own hallucinations, and palm it off as true. And which choice appealed to our lad on that mountain day so long ago? Just look at him, with those pinball eyes, that confetti hair—he's got cheap fiction written all over him!"

He stopped and glared at the townspeople. "And now can we move this circus down from the hills? Am I supposed to miss my supper, is that it?"

Resenting greatly that Bamalford had joined the expedition in the first place, Grandma now informed him in an **acerbic** tone that he was free to return by himself if he wished, and whenever he wished. He growled something about the duty of a newsman to stay with the story. And even as the two of them bickered the people began moving out, for the hour was getting late.

> **conventional**: in line with values, opinions, tastes and customs that enjoy long-standing acceptance by most of the people in a society
> **converge**: to move toward and meet at a point of union, sometimes with the result of combining forces or masses

The Farnum brothers made a fuss about positioning themselves as nearly as possible at the middle of the column of marchers. Henry beckoned toward the front, where Allen was, and said, "Cheap fiction." Andrew gestured toward the rear and said, "Possible duck bite."

"**Conventional** morality," explained Henry, motioning again toward Allen, "says stay away from bad actors."

"And conventional travel-safety rules," echoed Andrew, "say stay away from duck bite."

"And for today, at least," they said in unison, "we are the conventional type—if it works for most people, it works for us."

Bamalford too was near the middle of the line of walkers, and couldn't help hearing the nonsense of the Farnums. He scowled but said nothing, just stamping along to keep pace with the others.

As the marchers progressed into the middle distance of the tableland, far now from the briars and still a good ways from the opposite edge where the several streams **converged**, Meagan turned round, trying to spot Tedesco. As promised, he had stayed behind at the granite bluff where the briars grew. "Are you OK?" she shouted, knowing he could not hear the question. But an answer came sailing back on the cool air. "It's all legal. And ... the evening is a jewel."

> **advert**: to turn your attention toward something and take conscious note of it
> **patrimony**: the body of wealth that has passed to you by inheritance from your ancestors

Ricky smiled. "Cabbage! He says 'legal' for 'OK.'" Then **adverting** for the first time to the glory which the sun, just vanished, had left burning in the western sky, he added, "And, you know, he's right about the evening."

Mayor Povano growled, "Now you notice it. We have to bring an exchange student from 50,000 miles away to show you your own **patrimony**, the wealth of natural beauty which you and every son and daughter of Dropanchor inherit just by being born here."

> **suffuse**: to spread softly throughout something and fill every part of it
> **salubrious**: having a favorable influence on your health
> **corporeal**: having to do with the realm of matter and material bodies, as distinguished from the realm of soul, spirit and mind

It was a rare evening. Every reach and hollow of the mountainside, and all the air above, was **suffused** with light. It was rose and purple, and through its tide the gulls were wheeling. The mayor drank it in like a tonic. "It is a **Salubrious** Twilight," he proclaimed to no one in particular. "It heals and brings health. It takes away that aching under the kneecap, the soreness in the lower back. And when it finishes with your **corporeal** hurts it mends your spiritual ones as well. Hey, Grandma Dubois, yes, hey, look here …"

When he caught her attention, he whistled a few bars, and asked, "So, Clara, what am I whistling my way past?"

"Marion," she replied in a severe tone, "you are whistling your way past one of the countless little turnings of one of the countless little streams of the Bad Pony, and if you don't take care you'll fall in."

"I am whistling my way," declared Povano triumphantly, "past Serquiella's writing table. In my imagination, of course. And I don't feel nervous, edgy, or scared witless by it. This Salubrious Twilight has healed my fear. It heals everything."

> **impervious**: beyond the reach of some influence, not able to be touched or affected by it
> **demur**: to express an objection to the correctness or relevance of what someone has said
> **susceptible**: more likely than average to fall under the power of some influence

Grandma nodded grimly. "Maybe so, Marion, but I'll show you one case of wounded feelings that's **impervious** to the influence of your twilight." She motioned toward the middle rank of marchers, where Bamalford, large as a haystack in his overcoat, was plodding sullenly along.

Povano drew in a slow breath and said gently, "I must **demur**, Grandma. Even he is **susceptible** to the medicine of this evening."

> **eschew**: deliberately to avoid using, enjoying or otherwise having contact with something, often because you believe it is inconsistent with your goals or principles
> **accost**: to come up and initiate conversation with someone, often in a challenging manner
> **elicit**: to call forth some expression or reaction from a person, usually by subjecting him to some stimulus such as an insult, an encouragement, a challenge, etc.

The mayor let himself fall back in the line until he was alongside Bamalford. **Eschewing** all preliminaries, he said, "It goes right to the soul, doesn't it, sir?"

"Why are you **accosting** me," snarled Bamalford, "and pushing into my personal space? And why such a stupid question? Of course, it goes right to the soul. Getting slandered on national TV isn't just a soft tap, you know."

Povano hastened to correct the misunderstanding. "No, no. That's the wound. I'm talking about the cure, this flood of twilight. It can wash away all the Farbugle pain, and leave you healed and filled with peace. It's a Salubrious Twilight, and it goes right to the soul."

Bamalford bent down and looked closely at the side of Povano's head. "It's gone right to your soul, for sure. There's a large deposit of it shining in that cavity between your ears. Ha, ha, ha!" With a stern look he **elicited** an echoing laugh from Calvin as well.

> **edifice**: a building, especially an imposing one as, for example, a temple
>
> **sanction** (noun): an unpleasant consequence (for example, the loss of a privilege or right) which a lawgiver or other person in charge attaches to a disobedient act
>
> **quack** (noun): someone who claims extensive medical knowledge but who in fact offers diagnoses and remedies that are often strange and without any firm basis in medical science

Povano persisted in praising the twilight, and Bamalford persisted in ridiculing Povano. In this way they slowly descended from Mount Relief, down the Steeps, across the swinging bridge, until at last they were on the final stretch of the trail, only a few hundred yards from the fading mass of the Giuseppe Stone. On the slope high above them was the white marble home of Ms. Framley. Povano gestured toward it. "Look there, Bamalford, see how everything becomes noble in this twilight: man, beast, **edifice**. Victoria's house still glows like a Greek temple."

Ricky watched Povano's gesture and thought, "That could be a mistake."

A moment later a shriek of indignation broke across them. "You can stop your peeking, old goat mayor! Because that is you, isn't it!" Ms. Framley had emerged onto her porch. "Tell him … Mr. Bamalford," she bellowed, "that the law imposes harsh **sanctions** for that sort of thing."

Bamalford's voice carried up the slope as readily as Ms. Framley's carried down it. "A pleasure to see you, Victoria, if only dimly. Join us if you have any ache or discomfort—physical, emotional, financial, philosophical, I don't care. The mayor has the remedy. Just stand around in this twilight, let it wash over you, and everything will be healed."

"This," cried Ms. Framley in a birdsong voice, "this must be the biggest advance since antibiotics. We honor the chubby mayor. As a politician he may be a fraud, but as a medical researcher, not so—he's obviously no **quack**. And just for example, Mr. Bamalford, how does it work on … on the injury one feels after being slandered on national television by Foster Farbugle?"

> **antidote**: a medicine or other remedy that works to cancel the effects of some particular poison or harm
> **elucidate**: to remove the confusions and uncertainties from some matter by carefully explaining it

"Well, Seismo," Bamalford yelled back, "you do get right to the point."

Turning toward Povano, he raised his arm and forefinger and traced a dramatic arc on the air. "This twilight stuff is no cure," he declared, "none at all. I've said it before—Foster's poison is a wicked dose, and there's only one **antidote**—a big present. Oh yes, I have said it before, but nothing happens, and I grow tired of repeating myself. So do you know what? Captain Pariah disappears tomorrow. Check the comics—he'll be gone. No present, no protection—because when he disappears, my little rabbits, guess who may reappear." He pushed back his hair. "The guy with the big forehead and the purple boat."

A squeal of delight came from the heights. "Ha! That's in a language they can understand. I tried with all possible clarity to **elucidate** for Ms. Jensen how your Captain Pariah comic strip serves as a force field, but she just blinked those four eyes of her, and glazed over."

"And she'll blink tomorrow, Victoria, but like a startled deer. Ha—they'll all blink tomorrow."

> **convoke**: to invite or order people to come together for a meeting
> **august** (adjective): grand and distinguished; marked by a high dignity
> **disaffection**: a condition in which the loyalty or other sentiment that tied you to some group or institution has been eaten away, leaving you dissatisfied and rebellious

Povano's hopefulness was at last broken. He understood now that Bamalford was determined to nurse his grudge. The big man would not be getting over the hurt which Foster had inflicted, no matter how many apologies he received, or how radiant the twilight through which he passed. So with reluctance the mayor met the nasty business head-on, looking at Bamalford for a long moment and then asking, "Alright, what's on your list? And when do you tell us?"

Bamalford's mouth broke into a triumphant smile. "Call a meeting, Mayor Povano, of the town council. **Convoke** those distinguished statesmen. Ha, ha. Assemble that **august** body. Ha, ha." The smile faded. "And do it soon."

READER: Larry is asking if the Salubrious Twilight would help with ringing ears, temporary rashes, temporomandibular-joint pain, labored breathing, spots before the eyes, twitches, bad dreams and general **disaffection** with the educational process.

AUTHOR: The standard symptoms of a kid being tested to death.

READER: 'Fraid so.

AUTHOR: Well, you have to look at the big picture.

READER: Larry's dad told him that the big picture is get a 1600 on the SAT, and an A-plus on the rest, or else.

AUTHOR: Be there for your kids, I guess that's the idea.

Chapter 25: VENALGATE

On the following morning Ricky rose early and went to the East Bridge, hoping to see the sleepy figure of his friend straggling down the banks of the Bad Pony. The same hope had brought Grandma Dubois there as well, and Mayor Povano, and a few others who had been part of the expedition the day before. In the slanting rays of the first sun they surveyed the turnings of the trail, as far up the mountain as their sight would reach, but saw no one.

"I don't see our young botanist friend," said Grandma with a hint of apprehension in her voice.

> **reprove**: to give someone a mild scolding
> **lacuna**: an empty gap or interval, often one where something is missing
> **pregnant**: bearing some vital significance; loaded with meaning

"Now, now," Povano **reproved** her. "You're the brave, unperturbed one, Clara. You're the source of reassurance for the rest of us. So don't go suffering an attack of nerves."

"Well, we don't want any missing persons on this mountain," she replied sternly, looking beyond the mayor toward her granddaughters, who were also part of the little assembly. "Do you hear, François and Merci? No missing botanists, no missing students from faraway lands."

Allen was there too, and now he interrupted, saying, "The only missing person on this fine morning is Captain Pariah. Look." He held up the day's edition of the *Vociferous Beacon*, folded open to the comics page. Toward the middle of the page there was a gap, a white, empty rectangle, where usually the Captain Pariah strip appeared.

"Sort of a **lacuna**," said Ricky.

The mayor was shaking his head sadly. "Very definitely a lacuna. But one, I'm afraid, that bears a great deal of meaning."

"Sort of a **pregnant** lacuna."

> **fastidious**: very delicate in your standards about what is acceptable in speech, manners, food, dress, conduct, etc.
> **import** (noun): the message or significance carried by some expression, action or turn of events
> **discrete**: occurring as something separate and distinct; not shading into something else, not forming a continuous, unbroken range or stretch with other things

Povano's thick eyebrows raised slightly. "Thank you, Ricky. Your **fastidious** mayor might have put it differently, but the word fits perfectly."

Grandma stared fiercely at the blank space. "Pregnant indeed, and the **im-
port** is only too clear—the time has come for another spurt of empire building.
Bamalford is smart you know—he is building his empire in **discrete** phases.
Look what we know of the man. Three point seven years ago, whatever, he
rolls into Dropanchor, makes his first conquest—acquiring the newspaper—
and immediately, deliberately, pauses. Give people some time to get used to it.
Then—*sproing!*—another jump, he goes for another prize. He gets the Dome,
and the elevators up the side of the cape. After that, a pause once more, he
goes **dormant** once again. Now, in our time, froggy's ready for another leap.
The big present he's squeezing us for is part of it, you'll see. Bamalford International Airport, maybe, or Bamalford Deepwater Harbor. In any event, the
gear of empire."

Povano held up his hand. "You never liked the man, Grandma. But his little **machinations**, his manipulations and schemings, no matter how clever and
mean, are not what scare me. It's that psychotic in the purple boat, raving
about the eighty or ninety different punishments he can inflict on us. He's got
the law of the land backing him—or so he claims. That's what the lacuna says
to me—Inspector Draco is coming."

Before Grandma could reply, a slender figure darted toward the newspaper,
which Allen was still holding aloft. It was Merci, and she was unhappy when
she found the paper beyond her reach. "Allen," she said with a little show of
exasperation, "I can't snatch it rudely from your hand, if you hold it up that
high. Remember, please, that there is no recorded instance of the senior boys
refusing my wishes."

Allen gazed on the fairy-tale face, with the pretty arching of the brows and
the smile playing lightly on the teasing mouth. "You know, brat princess," he
said, lowering the paper, "this … this **methodology** of yours for getting your
way in every possible situation can't work forever."

> **laconic**: stingy with words; expressing your idea with the fewest possible words

"You are completely right," she answered pertly. "Because half of my charm is the brattiness, and I don't intend to be a brat for all time. Today, however ..."

With a **deft** turn of the hand she extracted the comics page, and only the comics page, from Allen's grasp and ran with it over to the corner of the bridge where she had left her backpack. She sat down, taking some pens out of the pack, and sketched feverishly for two or three minutes. Then she held up the page for everyone to see. The blank space was gone, filled in with four little drawings, neatly boxed, and a conversation balloon. To begin, a girl wearing a shirt that said Unfriendly Engineer was in a forest, gathering a long stick and a large, blocky stone. Then in the second box she was by the edge of the sea. She had set down the stone and was using the stick across it as a lever. In the third box the sea was tilted, with one shore lifted up steeply by the girl and her simple machine. A purple boat was struggling without success to climb the slanting water. The cartoon was a **laconic** one, for only in the last box was there any speech, and even that was kept to a minimum as the girl warned the pilot of the boat, "If you think an unfriendly lawyer was bad ..."

> **sophomoric**: assured and assuring others that your opinions are correct in every detail, your action plans are masterpieces of strategy, your jokes are highly clever, etc., when in fact they are all marked by some degree of immaturity and silliness
>
> **deter**: to cause someone to give up an action, often by inspiring his reflection on difficulties or unpleasant consequences associated with it

After displaying her work for a moment, Merci took the comics page, folded it into the shape of a boat, and ran to the railing of the bridge. "Sister," came the quiet voice of François, "aren't we being just a little **sophomoric**?"

Merci was not **deterred**. "Pigs are incapable of knowing if they act piggishly and bears can't know if they are acting bearishly. I'm a sophomore and thus have no way of judging whether I'm being sophomoric."

She released the paper boat and it spiraled gently down to the torrent of the stream below. "Ride the Bad Pony," she commanded. "Ride down to the sea and deliver yourself to the purple boat, Bureau of Ecology Patrol Vessel 19, attention Draco."

Povano shook his head and in a low voice said to Grandma, "Perhaps if I had some of her defiance ..."

> **bailiwick**: some realm of activity in which you have the leading responsibility, or where your superior skills and experience make you the person to be reckoned with
> **cosmos**: the physical universe, especially when regarded as orderly and systematic; any sphere of activity which is orderly and complete enough to be a little world unto itself
> **conjure up**: through magic, imagination or inventiveness, to cause something—a presence, an image, etc.—to take shape before you

"Old man, defiance is her **bailiwick**. And she does it well. You have a different responsibility—taking care of this little **cosmos** which we call Dropanchor, and…and not losing anyone." Grandma looked again up the trail, squinting, trying to **conjure up** a descending figure where there was none.

François came forward and took the hands of the worried lady. "My friend Joannie knows the area of the briars very well, and Mercurial Canyon, and she swears there is nothing up there which is going to eat our exchange student for breakfast. Let's begin our day."

> **savanna**: an open, more or less level area, covered with hardy grasses and some scattered trees, usually in a tropical or subtropical zone
> **autocratic**: holding absolute authority, and exercising it harshly
> **denotation**: the basic meaning of a word, as found in dictionaries, without regard to the emotional or moral suggestions carried by the word in certain contexts

Grandma saw the wisdom in that advice, and turned it into a marching order. "Marion, everyone, let's begin our day." She gestured bravely toward the long grassland sloping down to the school. "Onward across the **savanna**!"

They descended as a group, with the exception of Merci, who dashed ahead to make sure that her paper boat had not snagged on a stone or run ashore. The air was cool, the first sunbeams were catching at every stalk and thistle, and Ricky—brimming with good ideas—decided to explain to Grandma why the grassland was not really a savanna. "There would need to be some scattered trees, ma'am, the grasses would need to be coarser, and the whole scene would have to shift many miles to the south—closer to the tropics, you know."

He was hoping for something sharp in return, and was not disappointed. She pinned him with her celebrated **autocratic** gaze, as though to say he could be jailed for his impertinence. "Aren't you the boy," she demanded, "who gets all his information from Allen the Snoop? What does he think?"

Allen did his best to put together a noncommittal reply, saying that technically Ricky made some good points, but that the precise **denotation** of "savanna" was unclear, that the dictionaries were not in perfect agreement, that in

177

any event global warming was enlarging the tropical zones, probably Iceland would have savannas some day, and so forth.

"So maybe I was right, and maybe not," Grandma said, "when I called this a savanna. But at least you're OK if I call that"—she gestured toward Mount Relief—"a mountain?"

"Yes, ma'am," replied Allen.

"And if call the boy on that mountain … Tedesco?"

"Yes, ma'am."

"And if I call Tedesco … a little late?"

"Yes, ma'am, but he's OK. The main way to get in trouble on the mountain is to carry a yellow press card, and he's not carrying one."

They were at a fork in the trail now where Grandma and Povano, after wishing the little band of students a very good day, took the path bending out past the front of the school and onto the long hill that dropped into town.

> **sojourn** (noun): the time you spend visiting or temporarily living in a place away from home
> **assessment**: a judgment about the value or fitness of something, usually made on the basis of observation and analysis

Ricky told François, as they hiked around the back of the school to the seniors' entrance, that he wasn't worried. "Tedesco's got the necessary wilderness skills. Even if he stretches an overnighter into a **sojourn** of a week, he'll still be OK up there."

François agreed with this **assessment**. "I believe he's probably got the necessary wilderness skills," she echoed. Allen as well was of the same mind.

And yet, a few hours later, the high sun of midday found the three of them back on East Bridge, with Joannie and Meagan too, looking up the trail.

Allen, at any rate, was confident that Tedesco's reappearance was only a matter of minutes. "True—he's got the wilderness skills, he could stay up there a year if he wanted, but I doubt he'll really skip lunch."

Meagan laughed. "Gotta keep those priorities straight." She watched as Allen drew three midsized submarine loaves from his pack. They were colorful with slices of salami, imported cheeses—including some blue, and tomato, as well as wedges of lettuce, orange and kiwi.

> **variegation**: the presence of a variety of contrasting qualities in something, especially contrasting colors
> **supplement** (verb): to add some further material to something, often in order to correct some inadequacy in it or to make it more perfect

He sensed her gaze, and ventured, "A ten for **variegation**, huh?"

"If ten's the highest score," she laughed. "That's a real salad bar. And thanks for bringing enough for all of us."

Allen drew up his shoulders, like someone caught in the rain. "Well, that's embarrassing. I was hoping to **supplement** this little starvation of a meal by borrowing from the rest of you." He pushed his hand once through his bristly hair, apologetically, and then began making the sandwiches disappear. He was a clean eater—no morsels down his front. Clean and efficient.

Meagan finished her meal, something or other on pita bread, and went and stood at the far side of the bridge, staring up the corridor of stone and pine where the Bad Pony ran. The splash of the waters against the Giuseppe Stone and the busy flight of some crows above it were the only movements to break the noonday stillness. After a time Joannie came and stood by her. "He likes our mountain," she said.

Meagan smiled. "We'll go read him the truancy law if he's not down by tomorrow. But for today…"

She was interrupted by a muffled groan. It came from the other side of the bridge, from the figure of Allen, slumped against the railing.

"Lunchmouth!" cried Ricky. "Knock off three sandwiches and a pound of salami, fall asleep, and see what kind of dreams you get for it!"

> **articulate** (verb): (1) to set forth your ideas and feelings in clear, intelligible speech; (2) to form the sounds of speech crisply and distinctly
>
> **venal**: open to bribes, and ready—in return for bribes—to abuse the authority and resources entrusted to you in your political office or other position
>
> **pedestrian** (adjective): dull, flat, plodding; possessing a dreary ordinariness; not touched by any grace or inspiration

Allen was mumbling something, but the only phrase which carried any sense was "the gate, the gate." All the rest was confusion. Ricky shook him by the shoulder, lecturing, "We must **articulate** our feelings a little better than this."

Allen struggled into a sitting position and, still half asleep, looked wildly at Ricky. "**Venal**gate! Big three-inch letters, right across the top of page one. What a banner! But I'd give it all up, the whole story, if she'd close the gate. What should I do?"

Ricky laughed. "My **pedestrian** advice is: rub your eyes, stretch your limbs, wake up, and begin from the beginning. Not a very exciting program, but it usually works."

> **luminance**: the shining or glowing light that fills a place or surrounds an object
>
> **iridescent**: shining with a rainbow pattern of colors which change as the onlooker changes the angle from which he is observing
>
> **probity**: an unshakable honesty, a strong attachment to right conduct

179

Allen was sensing the presence of his friends now, and the calmness of the noonday. "Perhaps I was dreaming." He gestured up the canyon. "I was up there. It was night, no moon, no stars. The morning was still hours away. Under such conditions it should have been absolutely dark, dark period!—but in fact there was a strange **luminance**, dimly revealing the shape of things, including the shape of Bamalford."

"Bamalford seems to star in most of the bad dreams in Dropanchor," commented Meagan, half to herself.

"Well, he was there," went on Allen. "He was in a hurry, heading up the trail, approaching the suspension bridge and that strange writing-table stone. At that point his way was barred by a gate. It wasn't the sort of gate you could just push your way past and think nothing of it. It was firm as ages, and shining softly with streaky colors, reds and purples, **iridescent** like the inside of an oyster shell. Bamalford, though, laughed and rubbed his hands together. 'I know what opens you! I know the grease for your hinges. Venality. The most universal of substances. I dub you Venalgate.'"

"I wish Bamalford would stop dubbing things," said Joannie peevishly.

Meagan smiled. "At least he didn't name it after himself."

"Maybe he did," said Allen, resuming the story. "Anyway, he drew near to the gate and read the sign attached to it: 'This gate shall be closed for one thousand years. None may pass. Do not fail, gatekeeper.' He laughed again, saying, 'One thousand years. A bit too long. Well, there are ways. Oh yes.' With a knowing air he put a ten-dollar bill on the gate. When nothing happened he put a twenty next to the ten. Still nothing happened. 'Oh, dear,' he said. 'Such **probity**. Maybe this gatekeeper is a straight arrow, never swerving a fraction from the moral path. But I have one other present which might interest her, a handsome little set.' From the pocket of his overcoat he drew three plums, of solid gold, and placed them next to the money."

François lifted her head in alarm. "That's sort of scary, a meeting between Bamalford and …"

> **sonorous**: having a sound which is full-bodied and deep, and which carries easily throughout a place
> **resolute**: having your mind firmly made up
> **litigious**: excessively disposed to solve problems by suing somebody

Allen smiled weakly. "It was scary. The huge shadow of a woman emerged from the dark and bent over the golden pieces. She was beautiful, but too ancient. When she spoke, it was too … **sonorous**. The whole valley was speaking, that's how it felt, her voice was so full and sounding. And what she said was creepy. 'They told me—guard the gate, keep the mountain and all that grows there free of harm. And I have been faithful, year after year. But for

180

everyone, man, woman and child, there is appointed a price.' She took the golden plums and held them against her cheek. 'You were always mine, and you shall be mine. The fat mayor and the dairy girl should have given them to me from the start. I was right to be angry.'"

"I'm glad Mayor Povano isn't hearing this," broke in Joannie.

"I wish I wasn't hearing it," Allen replied, "much less telling it. But to continue—she turned to Bamalford, she was **resolute** now, and she told him, 'I will hesitate no longer. You have bought your passage. The gate is Venalgate, and for you it opens. The mountain is yours, and all that grows there. Ha—how do you like that, fat, stupid mayor of Esperanza?' And the gate swung open."

Allen shivered. Joannie messed his hair for him. "Not to be **litigious** or anything, but you should sue the deli where your mother bought that salami. Nightmare salami, that's what it is."

> **colleague**: a companion in a profession or line of work
> **exploitation**: the use of some resource to get as much advantage—often immediate, commercial advantage—as you can from it, sometimes in a manner that ignores environmental or humanitarian concerns

"That's helpful," muttered Allen. "Let's just get this finished. The gate opened. Serquiella gave Bamalford a long look, saying once again, 'And all that grows there.' He repeated the phrase, holding out his hands, palms upward, like someone begging. And all at once the two of them were at home with each other, **colleagues** practically—in some nasty business, and sharing a low, comfortable laugh."

François said sternly to Allen. "It's not right even to dream about the **exploitation** of the Mendicant Berries."

> **ambient**: lying about on all sides of you, like an atmosphere
> **accouterment**: a piece of gear or clothing by which you are outfitted for some activity
> **gastroenterologist**: a doctor specialized in treating conditions of the stomach and the other digestive organs
> **adjunct** (adjective): associated with some enterprise in a helping role, but not fully and permanently integrated into it, and not having a voice in its direction

"I tried not," Allen pleaded. "That's how it is though with my dreams: I own the theater, but I don't pick the movies. Anyway, I'm almost through. Serquiella was reabsorbed into the **ambient** darkness, and was gone. Bamalford was still there, in a cell of flickering light, and now he was transformed, shedding his coat, acquiring a loud pair of Bermudas, a neon T-shirt and—I hate to

181

say it—the **accouterments** of a berry picker. Suddenly he had gloves, a pail, a stick to push away the brambles. I started to shout, 'None of that! Close the gate.' And that's all I remember, except a rude shaking by Ricky here."

"Well, you've remembered quite enough," said François with a frown. "That's been Grandma's worst fear all along, that after Bamalford and his dome were well established on the beach, he would turn his attention to the mountain."

READER: If this is going to be a book with eating scenes, you need to do them right.

AUTHOR: I couldn't agree more

READER: The modern reader wants eating scenes with accurate details, no matter how shocking—food being ground by molars, torn by incisors, washed by gastric juices as it exits from the esophagus.

AUTHOR: Too much! I'll have to bring a dentist and a **gastroenterologist** onto the team—at least in some loose, **adjunct** role—so that I can tap their expertise whenever Allen has lunch.

READER: Whatever it takes. You might think about a ghostwriter also.

AUTHOR: Uncalled for!

Chapter 26: THE INVETERATE SEA DOGS

Tedesco returned the following morning. He descended in the first light and was seated on an oak bench at the seniors' entrance of the school when Ms. Jensen arrived. It was the same Tedesco, calm in expression, courteous in **demeanor**, but marked now as well, she saw, with something of the wild.

> **demeanor**: the sum of outward manifestations (posture, tone of voice, facial expression, gestures, etc.) by which you display an attitude toward others
>
> **citadel**: a fortified structure such as a castle or military stronghold, often overlooking a town or settlement that it controls and protects
>
> **countenance**: your face, especially as expressing your feelings or frame of mind

She gave a faint, comprehending smile. "So the sky was burning with stars and the night winds carried up the sound of the tide."

He smiled in return. "It is a very old place. For a million nights, or millions of millions, the stars have been turning above it. And the next time I go there, maybe there will be no news to carry down. But ..."

"But this time," Ms. Jensen finished for him, "there is news which you would rather not be carrying. That was expected, I'm afraid. Let me get Mayor Povano and the others to hear what you have found. In the meantime you take care of this." She took a cranberry muffin from her bag and gave it to him.

Soon Tedesco was surrounded by a small crowd. Grandma Dubois was there, and the mayor and Peter Oakum. Rachel had come with Ricky to be sure that her brother's friend was OK, and she made herself comfortable next to him on the bench.

Ms. Framley, seeing the collection of people, had charged down from her **citadel**. Bamalford was in the circle as well, a dark frown across his large face. "Ignore the scowling **countenance**," Grandma said to Tedesco, "if you can— I'm sure it's nothing personal—and tell us what happened. The mayor was getting very worried."

Tedesco began in a quiet voice. "In that wall where the briars hang down there is like a shelf or ... ledge. It is right in the middle of the briars, and only part of it is wet from the waterfalls. So on the first night I go crawling up there, onto the dry part, soon after you are gone, and watch the light fading and the stars coming out. Things start to slow down—thinking, breathing, probably even the beat of the heart. Everything is slowing down."

engender: to cause something (often a feeling, attitude or form of behavior) to come into being

vigilant: watchful and on guard; determined not to be caught by surprise

contract (verb): to make something smaller, often by squeezing it in upon itself

capillary: a very thin, tubular vessel, such as the tiniest blood vessels in the body

A sneer came from Bamalford. "All the right stuff for **engendering** wild hallucinations."

"That's not as bad as the warped lenses," fired Grandma, "that you watch life through. Now let the boy talk!"

Tedesco was untroubled by the interruption. "On the ledge," he resumed, "I wait. The moon is orange and climbing. The night birds are calling, there is a mist from the stream, and I feel how part of the tension goes out of the briars. This is the way their world has always been. And this is the moment, I realize, for a little sleep. I am not afraid to fall asleep, because the ledge is wide enough. But it is a light sleep, a **vigilant** one, I am still on watch. And later on, when the night birds are no longer calling, I start to wake up, and even in the first seconds, as I am shaking away the sleep, I feel how everything has changed. The tension is back, there is a ... crisscross of anxiety. The briars are shrinking themselves from something. They are trying not to have room for it. They are **contracting** their tiny ... passageways, their **capillaries** you say, and the leaves are curling even tighter."

"Obviously," drawled Bamalford, "they were sensing a disease of foreign origin."

Again Tedesco ignored the abuse and pushed on. "It only takes a few seconds, and the sleep is brushed away and I am wide awake. I can tell at once that the wind is different. Now it is chill and uncertain, it comes and goes. It is the problem, I am growing more sure. And what I need to do has become clear—I must find out where this wind begins."

diffused: not compressed or concentrated; spread out over much space, scattered in many directions

superfluous: in excess; over and beyond the amount you need or can put to use

truncate: to shorten something and leave it squared off or blocky, usually by cutting off a piece

Tedesco went on to describe how he scrambled up the last few yards of the bluff—his ledge was already halfway up it—hoping that at the top the wind was more gathered, flowing more steadily from a single direction which he could determine. But even there it was **diffused**, scattering every which way in

gusts and breezes across the open, irregular slopes. He was persistent, however. He waited there more than an hour, turning this way and that, and in each
position noting the chill against the back of his neck, when it was stronger and
when it was fainter. He performed this experiment over and over, wanting to
be sure, reaching at last the point where any further repetition was **superfluous**. And from this trial he was able to conclude that the wind was generally
out of the northwest.

"It was coming down from one of those ... summits," he said, "not the
highest one, and not the one at the top of Mercurial Canyon, but between those
two, the one that's rounded on one side but cut off square at the other, so that it
looks like ... half of the bread or ... how would you ...?"

Ricky went to his aid. "I know which one you mean, Cabbage, and you are
perfectly free to call it a half-loaf. To me it always looked more like one of
those hundred-pound half-circles of cheddar, just after Mrs. J. Snergglebottom
came into the deli and said 'Cheese, please!' and the deli guy took the big knife
and lopped off a huge piece, more than one-third to be precise. And there you
are, by the way—a modern myth explaining how the summit got its **truncated**
appearance. Now why Mrs. J. Snergglebottom needed so much cheese is another ..."

Joannie fixed him with a stare like a beacon, and he fell silent, apparently
content at having made a small contribution to world mythology. Tedesco continued. "The wind from that summit was the problem. All the tension in the
briars was because of it. It was more than wind, it was carrying something, I
don't know exactly what, but something very ... unwelcome."

> **antipathy**: a deeply seated sentiment of dislike and hostile disap-
> proval
> **aversion**: an attitude of turning away from something in disgust and
> dislike

"Dragons maybe?" interrupted Bamalford. "That might liven up your dull
story." His tone was hostile. His **antipathy** seemed to grow stronger the closer
Tedesco drew to the end.

"No, no, not the dragons. They were sleeping. Here—I know how to show
you all what the wind was like, the sort of thing it was carrying."

Rachel was still by his side on the oak bench, and he said to her, "You
know, Rachel, I have this sister, Magali, and she is smaller than you, she is
only three. And one day, I believe on the Easter, she is at the *churrasco*—the
big barbecue—for the workers on the farm. Magali thinks it is all for her. She
goes around, at one table she eats some yellow onions, but that's too boring, so
at another table she has half of a raw garlic and some—what are they?—the

radishes, and then she comes and puts her pretty little face close to mine and asks me six or seven times, '*Como vai*?'"

Rachel instinctively hunched her shoulders and turned away. "Yuck, Magali, don't breathe on me."

Tedesco looked at her gratefully, and then said to Grandma, "That's how it is also with your briars. They have an **aversion**. They turn away when the wind comes down from the half-loaf summit. There is something in it which to them is offensive. And because of it they curl."

He paused for a moment. "And on the second night the same thing happened—the same wind, the same turning away. The wind is the problem. That is what I learned up there."

> **remonstration**: the act of showing someone, often with argument and protest, the reasons why a plan, position, behavior, etc., of his is wrong or objectionable
> **prejudicial**: causing loss or harm, often in a gradual or indirect way

As Tedesco finished Grandma thanked him warmly, and then at once changed gears to address Ironbane with a **remonstration**. "You're in charge of that mountain, and you've been a little easygoing. It's clearly up to mischief. And not a harmless mischief either."

Raising no defense, Ironbane nodded slowly. "A **prejudicial** one, no question. A mischief that could cause the Mendicant Briars to curl right out of existence. I need to get up there."

Peter Oakum clapped the principal on his shoulder. "I'll come along. If there's a rogue vapor to be analyzed here, my knowledge of gas measurement, gained through an exceptionally entertaining career in that field, could be useful. Let me get my boots and …"

> **skepticism**: a tendency to receive the statements of others with doubt, and sometimes to subject those statements to sharp questioning
> **oracle**: a person whose pronouncements, often on deep and difficult subjects, are received as revelations of the truth
> **charlatan**: a person who tries with a false display of learning, or with impressive but invented credentials, to convince you that he is a master or expert in some area

"Whoo-eee!" A great roar from Bamalford submerged the exchange between Oakum and Ironbane. "Whoo-eee, Ms. Framley! Look at their faces— big, wide, believing eyes, mouths gaping like cows, not a trace of **skepticism**. They swallowed the foreign boy's story totally, just as I said. He sweeps down off the mountain with an air of having all the answers, he uses a few scientific words like 'capillary,' and they think he's an expert, if not an **oracle**. Here, listen to my headline: Boy **Charlatan** Ropes in Elders; Mayor Goes Duh."

Ms. Framley looked scornfully at Povano and the others. "Even a baby charlatan could win some points on these locals."

> **intimate** (verb): to make something known indirectly, by hints and suggestions
> **cogitation**: deep, energetic thought; intense mental exploration of some subject
> **existential**: concerned with deep questions of human existence—what meaning it has, whether a person's choices and actions can give it meaning, and so forth

No one gave her the satisfaction of an answer, and the little meeting broke up. Bamalford phoned in his headline. Ironbane and Peter Oakum began making plans for a climb to the half-loaf summit, even as Ms. Framley reminded them harshly not to step on or look at her property. Ms. Jensen led her students off to Room 401, and—without exactly saying it—**intimated** to Tedesco that if by any chance he sat under the once sickly lemon tree (now flourishing) and if by any chance he fell asleep there, he would not be disturbed.

Tedesco was unable to nap, however. He was deep in his thoughts, working through something, frowning now and then with the effort. When the lunch hour came Ricky said, "Before you get some kind of overuse injury, why don't you break out of the **cogitation** and share what's on your mind? Maybe there's more news than what you reported to everyone this morning."

Tedesco didn't argue. "Maybe there is more news. Or maybe it's absolutely nothing. But first, let's walk a little."

Five minutes later Ricky was murmuring, "Ho hum, ho hum, yet another visit to East Bridge." They were hiking up the grassland, half listening to the dry creaking of grasshoppers in flight, the droning of bees. "This is my twentieth time up here in two days. Oh well, my friends, to find meaning in humble, repeated actions—that is the great **existential** challenge, after all."

There was little else said on the ascent, and soon they had arrived. The bridge was warm and rough under the sun, fragrant with pitch, and as they found a seat on it, on the side near the Giuseppe Stone, Tedesco broke his silence. "You told me one time that the whales are coming and going past Dropanchor, often very close to that long island which divides the bay from the sea."

> **blatant**: being something in a conspicuous, shameless way, without any effort at softening or disguise
> **ambiguous**: capable of being understood or interpreted in one way by one person and in a sharply different way by someone else

Ricky nodded and Tedesco took a long breath. "And you said, I am sure, that now and then one of these whales is ... purple."

187

"Well that," said Ricky with an engaging smile, but with worry awakening in his eyes, "is one of the most **blatant** lies I have ever heard."

"I was afraid of that," confessed Tedesco. "And I am worried too. Because this morning I saw some purple."

Ricky knew where this might be heading, but he didn't rush the matter. "Where did you see purple, Cabbage?"

When Tedesco pointed toward the top of the Giuseppe Stone, Ricky gave a sigh of relief. "A purple bird on a granite perch, a bluish-purple trace of quartz, maybe a cluster of grapes left from a recent picnic—purple up there we can deal with, and ..."

Tedesco stopped him. "The top of the stone is where I was when I saw the purple, not where the purple was."

"Oh," said Ricky, sagging under the return of his anxiety, "I guess my question was **ambiguous**. Well then, we know where you were. Where was the purple, anyway?"

Tedesco worked toward an answer. "The Giuseppe Stone is very tall, a very big haystack, and from it there is a view of the outer part of the bay, and that long island. When I climbed it this morning the light was still dim. What I saw was not clear, it was just a stain or ... smudge of purple, on the water, a little beyond the island. But, Ricky, you should not get all worried. It could have been anything—a school of purple dolphins, a floating pack of seaweed, purple seaweed. Why not?"

> **wry**: twisted somewhat from normal position, sometimes with a comic or mocking or otherwise expressive effect
> **solace** (noun): a comfort for your sorrow or distress

Ricky made a **wry** face. "Thanks, that's a real **solace**. My feelings of panic and disorientation are completely gone. Listen, Cabbage, I think we should climb your haystack for another look."

The sides of the Giuseppe Stone were steep but fractured, and by a course of clefts and spurs the two friends spiraled around and up it. Ricky hauled himself over the top—easily forty feet above the decking of the bridge—and quickly scanned the breadth of sea and bay which was now visible. Suddenly he let out a whoop, which bore no trace of the anxiety that had clutched at him. "You don't look too purple from this distance!"

> **supplicate**: to ask or plead intensely for something, in a humble, lowly manner
> **prototype**: the original instance of something, which serves as a pattern or model for later copies

188

retract: to take something back (such as a statement, a book, an offer), often as a way of showing that you no longer support or sponsor
it

Tedesco, not yet to the top, **supplicated** his friend. "Please, Ricky, this is
not the right time to lose it. Please try ... I will always be grateful."

Ricky laughed and pulled Tedesco up beside him. "There's no purple now,"
he shouted, "only some elderly sailors and their mainsails and topsails and
other items of that nature."

He pointed toward the long island. There, just seaward from it, proud and
swelling with the breeze, was a grand intricacy of white sail, a merchant
schooner with two tall masts, making for the entry of the bay.

Tedesco stared intently. "A beautiful thing. How did they copy so perfectly
from the ancient ... original?"

Ricky's face broke into a smile. "A question about the ancient **prototype**
and the modern copy. Fortunately, Cabbage, I don't think they heard it. What
you see there *is* the ancient prototype. And the ancient mariners who sail her
are rather touchy on the point."

Tedesco murmured something in Portuguese that was roughly equivalent
to Nice work! and then said, "I **retract** this question of mine. But who are
they?"

inveterate: attached stubbornly and for a long time to some prefer-
ence or habit
forebears: those from whom you are descended; ancestors

"They are the age of sail," said Ricky, looking for a comfortable position
on the high roost where he and Tedesco sat. "They are a gang of stubborn old
men from Dropanchor, Grandfather Snoozer included, and some stubborn old
women as well. They insist that moving commerce by wind is still the way it
should be. Year after year they run up sail and haul cargo. They're so unbudg-
ing about it all that we call them the **Inveterate** Sea Dogs."

Tedesco too was struggling for a more comfortable perch on the narrow
cap. "But the ship," he asked as he tried to anchor himself against a little knob
of granite, "that ancient ship, how ...?"

Ricky laughed. "They've mended every inch of it, caulked every inch, var-
nished every inch, repeatedly. It's the same ship which Captain Jack Farnum
sailed on when he brought settlers here almost two centuries ago. It's called
Jack's Equator, because it crossed so many times down to your little continent,
Cabbage. In fact, maybe the legendary Captain Jack knew the legendary
Tedesco **forebears**."

"But he will never know my descendants," groaned Tedesco, trying to ex-
tend his leg. "Because soon I will die, such a cramp I am getting!"

egoistic: approaching human relations with the attitude that your own well-being and comfort are important above all else
notoriety: the state of being famous, but usually for something bad
taboo (noun): a rigid prohibition, which is often rooted in custom, and which makes some activity, relationship, subject matter, etc., strictly off-limits

Ricky was suddenly apologetic. "I have been very **egoistic**—I come up here and hog the good spot as though the comfort of Ricky Q. Snoozer was all that mattered in the universe. Speaking of that—hogging, I mean—part of the ship's cargo is hogs, for the farms out in the foothills east from town. Captain Daniel likes them. He says they deserve their **notoriety** for stinking up the place, but that otherwise they are sensitive creatures, responding to little changes in temperature, light, humidity. He plays music for them, and there's a rumor that he even puts his drawings up in their pens. Some odd genes in that family"

Tedesco commented, in the most innocent of tones, "Foster Farbugle—whoever he may be—missed a good one there."

"Blast!" cried Ricky. "You are right. I should have told that one to Sallie and Reggie. Deep bench here in Idiosyncratic City. Anyway, Cabbage, try to move your legs. We should go. We'll be on the dock when Grandpa Snoozer throws the rope."

READER: Larry says that was really quite courageous of you.
AUTHOR: I agree, of course, but what?
READER: That part about Tedesco's little sister—the way you disregarded social **taboos** and launched a frank discussion of infant garlic breath.
AUTHOR: It was my duty as an author. But it's cost me a lot of shelf space.
READER: No doubt. Well, we'll see what other highly inflammatory issues you tackle next.

Chapter 27: THE IMPROMPTU HOLIDAY

Everywhere in Dropanchor people were declaring a holiday and heading for the docks. "Once they see that white sail," Ricky told Tedesco, "or get a call, the day's work is done. There on the spot they decide it's a holiday. And the mayor tells his councilmen, 'The people have declared an **Impromptu** Holiday. They can't do that. We must have a meeting of the Council at once.' And the councilmen reply, 'Tomorrow,' and they all go to the docks."

> **impromptu** (adjective): made up on the spot and for the occasion, without prior preparation or planning
> **gingerly** (adverb): with delicacy and carefulness in your movements, often to avoid breaking something, triggering some force, etc.
> **indefatigable**: fatigue-proof; not able to be tired out

The two of them were picking their way **gingerly** down the reddish flanks of the Giuseppe Stone. Since Ricky couldn't spare a hand to beckon, he just nodded in the general direction of town and said, "Down there at Rachel's school, it's out of control. At this very moment, I'm sure of it, her teacher is scheduling a field trip to the docks, for immediate departure."

"And you, Ricky Snoozer," came a voice from behind him, "need to do the same thing at the high school. Because I won't be there."

Ricky, turning as best he could, gasped to see Ironbane coming down the Bad Pony trail, with Peter Oakum close behind. "It's not possible that you two have been up to the half-loaf summit, the half-cheese summit, already. That's a long trip."

The principal gave a silent little scream, and said, "With the **indefatigable** Peter Oakum it's possible. The man has never heard of getting tired, much less of taking a rest."

> **overt**: obvious; out in the open; readily seen
> **rudimentary**: very basic; of the simplest sort; not yet developed into a state of higher complexity or sophistication
> **repudiate**: to reject or throw back something, often with the message that it is invalid, untrue or unworthy

With a last little jump Tedesco reached the ground. Now he noticed the bread sacks, one with Ironbane, two with Peter, puffed full of air and sealed with wire ties. "Samples," confirmed Peter. "We found no **overt** discharge of vapor at the summit, but that does not rule out a more subtle leakage drifting down toward the Mendicant Berries. So we caught some samples."

191

Ironbane set down the sack he was carrying, with a long sigh of relief. "Now we're on the way to Peter's place on the south cape. He owns a little collection of testing equipment, **rudimentary** but probably enough to tell whether these sacks hold something more than air. And Peter says, like now— we'll lose our samples otherwise. So if the two of you could declare the Impromptu Holiday there at school, maybe with some help from Ms. Jensen, and if you could tell Captain Daniel and the other fine people on *Jack's Equator* that we'll be down to the docks as soon as possible ..."

He eyed Ricky—rumpled and a bit wobbly from the Giuseppe Stone. "All on the assumption, of course, that what you saw up there really was *Jack's Equator*. You look worse than I do."

"Well, it wasn't the *Cutty Sark*," answered Ricky smartly.

Peter smiled. "They are so mouthy these days."

The two explorers and their bread sacks slipped away on a trail which ran essentially south, winding through a tangled stretch of hills and hollows. "If we don't reappear," shouted Ironbane in farewell, "you may be sure it was the cucumber vine."

Ricky laughed. "There's a coastal vine, a very independent coastal vine, with little gourds like cucumbers, and at points along the trail it has been ... retaking the ground. It has **repudiated** our rule, it mocks our claims. Ironbane and Oakum should be careful."

"At least they won't be crushed by their load," said Tedesco solemnly.

"You got that one, Cabbage! But c'mon. The wind is brisk, and it's pushing *Jack's Equator* toward the dock."

There was no need to stop at the high school. It was already empty, with the last stragglers vanishing down the long hill toward the center of Dropanchor. The town was almost empty as well. The plaza, the market buildings, the stone-and-tile city hall from the days of Esperanza—they were all like turned-out pockets.

> **oblivious**: without any awareness of something; not paying any attention to something
> **pragmatic**: mainly concerned with achieving practical, down-to earth goals in an efficient manner
> **metaphysical**: related to fundamental philosophical questions such as What is reality? or What is the connection between reality, appearance and thought?

Ricky and Tedesco arrived in time to see the last bit of nimbleness by which the Sea Dogs, **oblivious** for the moment to aching joints and weary muscles, dropped the greater sails and eased their ship into a lazy drift toward the dock. A tall man with thick silver hair threw the first rope. Ricky darted forward, nearly upending Allen, and grabbed the end of it. "Do you remember the knot?" called the man.

"How could I forget it?" shouted back Ricky. "You made me repeat it about fifty times."

The man laughed. It was Ricky's grandfather. "I may have exaggerated. Anyway—tie us up. The passengers are tired of waiting."

Even as he spoke a complaint rose up from the deck—a loud, earthy squealing.

"Pigs!" cried Rachel, "I learned it in school."

Allen was pulling out his reporter's pad. "This could be a story—Proud Schooner, Built for Silk and Tea, Hauls Pigs!"

"We're a **pragmatic** bunch, you know," answered Grandpa Snoozer. "This ship is a beauty, but she eats money. So when the merchants send no silk or tea, and the farmers offer a fair rate, well—we haul their pigs."

"But are they really pigs? That is the question." Andrew and Henry Farnum were breaking in.

The old man laughed. "Whether pigs are pigs, and whether the Farnum twins exist, and any other **metaphysical** questions, I refer to the captain."

There was a man of seventy-five or so on the captain's deck, strong-jawed and still square across the shoulders, and now he yelled down to the twins, "I suppose you think my pigs are Martians. Show me your proof."

"Well," they fired back, "we can't prove they are, but you can't prove they aren't. So there's a fifty percent chance either way. Which means every other pig is a Martian."

> **staid**: settled firmly into a style that is somber, self-controlled and proper
> **fallible**: not error-proof; capable of perceiving or judging mistakenly
> **finesse**: a delicate artfulness and grace by which you maneuver through complicated situations

"No need to mention that to the farmers," advised the captain. "They may not see the humor of ordering a pig and getting an interplanetary visitor. Some of them are pretty **staid**. They have a strong sense of what's proper in these matters."

His eyes slowly scanned the crowd. "Let's see which other rascals are here. I'm spotting Meagan and Joannie, Allen and Calvin, all the kids. And who is that with you, Ricky?"

"Hello, Captain Daniel," Ricky shouted up from the dock. "This is Tedesco. I think he saw your ship early this morning—but in the half-light before sunrise the senses are **fallible**."

193

To the captain that was more than an idle remark, and it moved him to ask, "What was the ... mistake in your friend's perception, Ricky, that makes you talk now about the senses being fallible?"

"Just a little thing. What he saw was like a smudge ... of purple. It was on the surface of the sea, and I can think of nothing else that it might have been except your ship."

A wince tightened across the features of the captain. "My senses also were rather fallible before sunrise today. Here—come on board and have a look at what I drew. And if that's Mayor Povano I see there, bring him along."

Climbing the gangway was easy enough, but threading across the main deck, through milling pigs and toiling sailors—that took a particular **finesse**. Ricky and Povano followed Tedesco, who seemed to know the right moves. When they reached the brief stairs that climbed to the upper deck, Captain Daniel was there, riffling through a sketch pad and opening it to a page near the back, which for the moment he kept turned away from them.

> **reactionary**: rejecting what is modern and progressive, and holding to the opinions of some prior, highly conservative system, regime, school of thought, etc.
> **coalescence**: the process of growing together into a single mass or quality, or into a tightly knit unity

"I showed it," he said, "to the hogs, and they were ... polite. But I want you to get beyond polite and tell me what you think. Just don't go, 'Ah! Abstract art! Daniel has finally stumbled into the modern era and done some abstract art.' No, no, I'm as **reactionary** as ever. So far as I'm concerned, they got it right three centuries ago—paint what's there, what everybody sees, and not some confusion of streaks and smudges. My problem this morning was that in the very early light—when I did this—that's all that was there, all you could see, streaks and smudges."

With this introduction he turned the drawing. The prevailing tones were those of early dawn at sea—the silver, the rose—suggesting water and sky. But across the middle ran a vague bar that was not silver and not rose and not a **coalescence** of them, something faintly out of place, a bar of soft purple.

"That is what I saw," said Daniel, "and I wish I hadn't."

"And that is what I saw," said Tedesco.

The news spread quickly throughout the people gathered on the dock. They struggled not to overreact. They reminded one another that a purple smudge didn't necessarily mean a purple boat. But the holiday spirit was gone.

The impact on Mayor Povano was visible. When he saw the drawing his shoulders drooped, and a long sigh escaped from him.

> **proclivity**: a deep-seated tendency toward some object or activity

equanimity: a steady calmness in mind or feeling
fortuitous: happening just by chance

"Marion," came the stern voice of Grandma from the dock. "We've talked about this **proclivity** of yours to worry excessively and short out your appliances. This is a fine opportunity to practice calmness. Your **equanimity** would inspire all of us, and maybe I won't have a panic attack."

Povano mastered his alarm as best he could, took a deep breath and looked out over the crowded dock. As he did so, the people fell silent, electing him with their silence to be the one to put a brave, more hopeful turn on it all.

"Folks," he began softly, "I know, I really, really know. That comic strip disappears one day, and on the next—something purple on our coast. And to give it one possible name—Draco. So we naturally suspect a connection of the worst sort—he's here because the comic is gone. But maybe not. It could be totally **fortuitous**. Maybe he's showing up in our waters at this time because he's on his way from Los Angeles to Seattle, for example, or"—thought lines appeared on the mayor's forehead—"from Seattle to Los Angeles! Get it? Pure coincidence, maybe. And remember also—what is Draco without trash? Nothing. If he doesn't find trash in our waters, there's nothing he can do to us. So, my people, let's not toss any rubbish in the bay, not a nit, not a nat, and we'll neutralize the man."

charismatic: possessed of a special presence and an inspiring influence, which draw people to you
luminance: the shining or glowing light that fills a place or surrounds an object

Grandma Dubois raised her small fist. "Bravo, Marion. Not a nit, not a nat. You're great. You're inspired. You're approaching **charismatic**."

The mayor gave her a smile, and went on. "And another thing, my people. We don't know for sure what Tedesco saw, what Daniel saw. Who says it was Draco, after all? Don't go visualizing purple boats everywhere. The light in this region does have a good deal of purple in it. Dawn and dusk have a purple tint about them here, sometimes quite distinct. Why shouldn't it show up in Daniel's drawing? And the edges of distant objects shine dimly with a purple **luminance**. There—see the north tip of the island."

He beckoned toward the long island at the far edge of Dropanchor's bay. "See that soft purplish glow where the line of the island gives way to the sea. It's the very thing I'm talking about."

substantial: having a significant amount of mass, weight, density or (in an extended sense) importance
raze: to pull down a building or other structure, to the ground

195

muse (noun): a divine principle or figure that quietly furnishes inspiration to a poet or artist

The people followed his gaze, and seeing a faint purple shimmering, where he was pointing, they agreed that they had picked an observant man for mayor. And as the shimmer grew more **substantial**, as it detached itself from the green bank of the island, as it bore down on them—each moment more in the likeness of a purple boat, they shuddered and agreed that their observant mayor would earn his salary and then some before that day was over.

READER: Larry wants action. He says the pigs should have stampeded and **razed** half of the warehouse section by the dock.

AUTHOR: But then I've got pigs in my plot, and I don't have the faintest idea how to work them in.

READER: Beg your **muse** for an idea.

AUTHOR: And if she's not fond of pigs and tells me no.

READER: Even better. That way you've left a loose thread which you pick up in two or three years and use as the opener when you write your sequel— *Dropanchor II.*

AUTHOR: Gasp!

Chapter 28: THE *PURPLE OMNISCIENCE*

In a matter of seconds Draco and the purple boat were before them, menacing dock and people alike with a fast run-up, giving everyone a closer look than they wanted at the dragon of orange agate installed on the bow. There were no preliminaries. The inspector cut his engine and began at once, in a half-shriek. "We shall continue—after a **hiatus** of almost four years—where we left off when that editor goon of yours interrupted. I was showing you the maroon book, Title 51 of the *United States Code*, the Clean Water title. It was good then, it's great now. Listen, repeat offenders, to the improvements. First of all, Congress stopped being so fussy about free speech and government control thereof, and added a section here which makes it a crime to publish **incendiary** material about the Bureau of Ecology and the BE inspectors. And that includes comic strips which fire up **popular** passion against us, by suggesting we abuse our authority. You can tell your Mr. Bamalford I'm very sorry, but Title 51 muzzles his beak, doesn't it?"

> **hiatus**: a gap or open interval, often in something otherwise unbroken and continuous
> **incendiary**: firing up strong sentiments of resentment, anger, etc.; stirring up public unrest
> **popular**: done, used or believed by all or most of the people

Draco pulled out a long piece of fabric, cut like a shoeshine cloth, and buffed the head of the orange dragon. Then he pressed his own wide forehead against the monster, murmuring, "Grrr! Eat 'em up, spit 'em out!"

> **inkling**: a slight hint; an understated indication
> **omniscience**: the awareness or knowledge of everything

When he tired of that, he opened the maroon book once more, and smiled hideously. "There have been some other changes to Title 51. Patrol boats can have names, not just numbers. I like that—numbers don't say much, but names give an **inkling**, maybe more, of what a boat can do. We, for example, my boat and I—we are no longer BE Patrol Vessel 19. We've got a name—the *Purple Omniscience*. That gives a little hint, doesn't it, that with these antennas, cameras, mikes, sensors and other equipment all over the deck, we know everything. If you, the waspish old lady on the dock"—he pointed toward Grandma—"if you, for example, have a picnic on the beach with your waspish friends, and if you pull a nectarine from the wicker basket and you peel off

197

that little sticker and drop it where the tide can reach it, trust me, madam, my boat and I will know. You can't violate Title 51 without us knowing."

"I never eat nectarines," answered Grandma flatly, not able to keep quiet but not wanting to provoke the inspector any further. "We never have enough, and I leave them for the children."

> **draconian**: imposing harsh obligations, and cruel punishment for any failure to satisfy them
> **confiscate**: under authority of law, to seize the property of someone
> **deter**: to cause someone to give up an action, often by inspiring his reflection on difficulties or unpleasant consequences associated with it

Draco, in fact, seemed pleased with what Grandma had said. "So you have the natural mammalian affection for the children. That's very useful, because it brings me to the last improvement in Title 51, the last and—ha, it sounds like me, doesn't it—the most **draconian**. Listen. Paragraph 37: Remedies. It tells me what I can do, the measures I can take, if you little slobs won't keep the public waters clean. Formerly it had just Subparagraph A, which said I could go after your money—and Subparagraph B, which said I could go after your property. But now—I love it!—there's a new Subparagraph C, which says I can go after your kids."

"What the ...!" It was a burst of astonishment and rage from Povano, who was still on board *Jack's Equator*.

Draco looked up at him with satisfaction. "Ah, the mayor, the voice of authority in this place. Please listen carefully, sir, and no more little shows of emotion. If fining you people and **confiscating** your property will not **deter** you from trashing up the seven seas, then I can go after your kids. Title 51 now allows me to compel the attendance of your children over age fifteen at the Bureau of Ecology Enforcement School. That's right—I can enlist your own children to fight against you and your trashy habits."

Before Povano or Captain Daniel or Grandma Dubois could even begin an answer, François stood forward from the crowd on the dock, with her slender shoulders squared in defiance. "You can compel our attendance, but that's all you can compel. You could never turn us against our parents and our own people."

> **malleable**: soft enough to be worked, by pounding and pressure, into a different shape
> **eradicate**: to yank something out by its roots
> **psyche**: the soul, the self, the inner person, with its conscious and subconscious realms

198

peremptory: arrogantly cutting short all questions and objections, often because of your supreme certainty of the correctness of your position

Draco let her challenge hang in the air for a moment, while he buffed again the head of the orange dragon. His voice was mocking when he said, "I am so sorry for you, small-town girl; you haven't met Melanie yet. Melanie runs the Enforcement School. The students there are called Melanie's **Malleable** Kids. She works them into new shapes—and so professionally. Beautiful Melanie, she knows every trick—the little deprivations, the little rewards, for **eradicating** the last shred of influence which parents and teachers have had on a child. She weeds it all out until only the workable clay of the young **psyche** remains. And what a shape she puts on that, tapping, kneading, tugging, squeezing. Enchanting Melanie, with the curling fingers, what masterpieces you turn out! Young enforcers, ruthless in action, **peremptory** in speech, allowing no debate, hearing no excuse, jealous for the smallest letter of the law, which has become to them as mother and father."

minute (adjective): extremely small and insignificant; at the level of tiny details
flagrant: offending strikingly against law, morality or some other rule, in a way that is extreme, conspicuous, and often contemptuous of authority
soluble: capable of being dissolved in water or other liquid

Grandma Dubois, looking like someone about to retch, screamed at him. "You will never take our children. I'll spend every remaining hour of my life out on the bay, watching for litter. I'll pick up everything, no matter how **minute**, eyelashes and poppy seeds. You will never find any trash in our waters to charge us with!"

"Why," countered Draco, reaching to retrieve something from the deck of the *Purple Omniscience*, "why do you speak in the future tense, saying that I *will* never find trash in your harbor? Look here, old parrot, look here, I *have* found trash in your harbor already this morning, wide-open violations of the Clean Water statutes, **flagrant** violations, the in-your-face type." He held up in one hand a brown bottle. "Same brand as last time, different bottle—Terebinth Beer."

In his other hand there was a soggy page from a newspaper. "Fat boy's newspaper, by chance. The comics page, by chance—isn't that funny? And yes, one of the comics is missing, that clever one about Captain Pariah. Fat boy has wised up. And in the blank where it was, some handwriting, maybe some sketching, can't really tell. Obviously the ink was **soluble** and it's mostly washed away. Too bad."

199

Merci, standing close behind Grandma Dubois, gasped at the sight of the soggy newsprint. Draco, with his sharp vision, caught her startled look. "So the pretty one is alarmed to see the pollution of our waterways—as she ought to be. Are you fifteen yet, my fragile beauty? Perhaps you'll be one of the seven fortunate boys and girls who ... win a scholarship to the enforcement academy."

> **score** (verb): to mark a surface by cutting or scratching lines, often parallel, into it
> **ingenuous**: (1) open and unrehearsed in your expressions; (2) so simple and innocent that you fail to grasp the complexity or evil that is present in many situations
> **proficient**: competent to an advanced degree in some art or line of activity

The inspector swung about, to face again the group on *Jack's Equator*. His voice grew even more shrill, and lines of shadow **scored** his expansive forehead. "You heard it, Mayor Povano, seven. Dropanchor will send seven lads and maidens to the school, seven, OK. Simple, trusting souls, no doubt, free of pretense, frank of speech. In a word, the usual **ingenuous** pack you get from these small towns with their misplaced emphasis on family. The seven souls will spend a year with Melanie, graceful Melanie, so at home inside the human circuitry. And when that year has run she will send back to Dropanchor seven—ha, the miracle of birth—seven Dracos!"

He had said what he came to say, and having no interest in any response from the people of Dropanchor, he shot away from the dock. Over the fury of his engine and the white churn of the boat's wash he shouted a last message. No one could hear it, but Allen, **proficient** since eleven or twelve at reading lips, was able to tell Povano, "'Back soon for the seven names,' I'm pretty sure that's what it was."

> **lethargy**: a heavy, drowsy state in which almost nothing can stir you into action
> **indomitable**: not able to be defeated or bent to someone's wishes, no matter how heavy the assault

All Povano's fire was quenched. "This game is too fast for me," he groaned. "Just wanna sit." But he knew his people were watching. If he sank into a weary, anxious **lethargy**, they would too. So he stayed on his feet, surveying the silent crowd before him and at last announcing with all the formality he could manage, "The floor is open for suggestions."

"Marion, you are **indomitable** in your old-lady sort of way," exclaimed Grandma Dubois. "And I have a suggestion—the nation of Dropanchor."

The mayor's bushy eyebrows lifted at the phrase. "The nation of Dropan-chor?"

"To be sure," returned Grandma. "We set up our own country, we have sovereign control over our own waters. Draco would lose jurisdiction, then, and we could send that madman packing."

"And we could print our own stamps," cried the excited voice of Rachel, "and the kids would draw them."

> **hegemony**: leadership and control over others, usually obtained not through appointment or election but by virtue of superior strength, wealth, advantage, etc.
>
> **burgeon**: to swell with new growth
>
> **prosaic**: down-to-earth; in touch with practical, grubby realities; not inspired by elements of fancy

"And we could have three branches of government," piped Squeaky.

"And our favored position on the shipping lanes would give us commercial **hegemony** over all other nations." That was from Henry Farnum.

"Which means," added his brother, "that the sun would never set."

"And to finance the party," replied Povano to all of them, "taxes would **burgeon** like bamboo in the spring, tripling, quadrupling. And then the out-raged population would storm the mayor's office. Oh why did I ever take this job?"

He pushed his fists into his forehead, and then looked up again. "Other suggestions, slightly more **prosaic**?"

> **augment** (verb): to cause something to become bigger, more numer-ous or more complete
>
> **appease**: to give someone what he wants and in this way to cause him to stop threatening or practicing hostilities toward you
>
> **indoctrination**: the act of pressing a system of ideas into the mind of someone, often by teaching methods that leave him little opportunity to question or reject

"Let's do what we did at Heronfire Power and Light when panic was set-ting in—let's call an open meeting." It was Peter Oakum, shouting out from the back of the crowd. "Ironbane and I have just arrived, but I can see the score. Draco is still a factor, and I hate to admit it but our ... defensive capability looks too small. It may need to be **augmented**, unfortunately, with the rude energy of Bamalford, to add up to a force that can turn back the inspector. So, Marion—let's have an open meeting of the town council. Let's invite Bamal-ford and at least find out what he wants for his big present. And let's face the unpleasant truth that maybe our pouting editor will need to be **appeased**."

Povano held his silence, and Peter went on for another moment. "I wouldn't talk this way if it were just about money. If there were no threat to haul off seven of our kids for **indoctrination** at that Melanie woman's school, if the worst Draco could do were fines and seizures of property, then I would say call his bluff. But ..."

"But sir," cried Joannie, no longer able to contain herself, "that's what I was thinking—call his bluff. I mean—seven kids get dragged away because of one bottle and one paper in the bay? Is that the law? The punishment is so terribly out of proportion. It can't be ... it's really cruel. This is a civilized land ... we don't let that sort of thing happen ... do we?"

Peter looked down, and fumbled for his words. "Probably we ... don't mean to, and probably ... not to such an extreme ... but ..."

> **interminable**: going on to exhausting lengths; not coming to an end
> **pithiness**: a compactness of speech by which a great deal of meaning is packed into a relatively few well chosen words
> **exonerate**: to clear someone's name by showing him to be innocent of an accusation

There was a low groan from Povano. "This issue is so electric and so difficult to reach agreement on, everyone, that the debate could be **interminable**. I'll be an old man before we finish."

"That's if we hold the meeting at city hall," answered Peter, finding his words more easily. "Put it on the beach, on the square stone, and **pithiness** of speech will be everyone's favorite virtue."

With a long sigh, and realizing that this suggestion was probably the best he was going to get, the mayor declared that two nights from then, at the hour of low tide, the town council would meet on the beach, on the great square stone situated north of Cape Scurrility. The one topic would be the present for Mr. Bamalford, what it might be, and whether or not to give it. "There, Peter," he finished, "that should do it."

"Not quite," called Oakum, still at the rear of the crowd. "Sorry, but there is a second item for the agenda—the vapor."

He held up a bread sack. It was inflated and sealed, just as Ricky had seen it earlier. "You all remember," he began, "how Tedesco reported that some fume, some vapor, is escaping from our mountain, at the half-loaf summit, and stealing down to put that fatal curl in the Mendicant Briars. And how, for his troubles, he was accused—by Bamalford, of course—of being a faker. Well, now his name is **exonerated**—by a bread sack. Ironbane and I climbed to the summit and caught some atmospheric samples in sacks like this one. Then we tramped off to my place, where I've set up a small, very basic lab, and just an hour ago we ran a test. What we found clears Tedesco of any charge whatsoever of trying to deceive anyone."

> **stymie**: to block someone from reaching a goal, or prevent an action from being completed successfully
> **replicate**: to make a duplicate of; often, to repeat the steps of some experiment or procedure to confirm that it arrives at the same conclusion as before
> **corroborate**: to furnish evidence strengthening and confirming some position

He held up the bread sack again. "Ninety-nine percent air—oxygen, nitrogen, and so on. But one percent something else. There's an element here that's definitely not air. What it is I don't know. It has me **stymied**, and my equipment stymied. For the moment it's a mystery vapor. But it's there, no doubt."

Povano was not completely comfortable with the science. "You know, Peter, bread sacks can generate their own mystery vapors, when they're left for long weeks in the pantry with a heel of bread still inside."

Oakum was not troubled by his friend's hesitation. "Mayor Povano—give me new bags, sterile bags, and I'll **replicate** the experiment. I'll gather another sample, I'll put it through exactly the same test, and almost certainly I'll reach the same result—ninety-nine percent air, one percent unknown."

"A waste of bags," came the clear-grained voice of Joannie, who was also at the back of the crowd, not far from Ironbane and Oakum. "Peter's laboratory analysis does not stand alone—there is some **corroborating** evidence."

Glancing around, Peter noticed what Joannie had noticed, and he realized at once where she was heading. "And if I had more hair," he said with a laugh, "I might have been Exhibit A. As is, however ..."

"As is," declared Joannie, "I give you all Exhibit A—Mr. Ironbane, his baseball cap, and the jungle beneath."

Ironbane and his cap were at once the target of a hundred curious stares. Unperturbed, but curious as well, he twisted his neck about, something like a crane, as though to have a look for himself. The only result was to cause the cap to fall off, revealing a thicket of tight, tiny curls. He patted them hesitantly—for his hair had always been straight—and you could almost see his hand springing back. "What is this?" he cried.

> **alibi**: the excuse that you were somewhere else when a crime occurred, so that it couldn't have been you
> **laudatory**: written or spoken to confer praise

Joannie laughed. "It's an **alibi**, that's what it is. If you're ever accused of some crime occurring in this past week, you just say—Sorry—I was in the salon. Because curls like that, so incredibly tight, all across the head, would take about a week—in a salon."

Ironbane cast a self-conscious smile in her direction. "Can you imagine the statement? The tip alone..."

He paused, trying to catch Povano's eye, which wasn't difficult, since Povano and almost everyone else were still staring at him and the springy mass which his hair had become. "This is what the Mendicant Briars are up against," he called out to the mayor, "and this is why your agenda, sir, two nights from now has to include the vapor in Peter's bread sacks."

READER: Larry says if that Melanie tried to bend his mind ...

AUTHOR: She would fail miserably, right?

READER: No—she wouldn't have any problem!

AUTHOR: Impressive honesty. And really—a lot of us would cave under the deprivations.

READER: No, no—Larry just gets stubborn under deprivations. It's the rewards that would undo him.

AUTHOR: The bonbons, the cruises?

READER: No. The compliments. Sincere compliments, false compliments, anything **laudatory**—Larry says it turns him into cookie dough.

AUTHOR: Maybe as he grows older ...

READER: That's what he thinks—if he can just make it 'till he's seventy.

Chapter 29: THE ACCOMMODATING LOSERS

The citizens of Dropanchor went back to town, some to their homes, most to the coffee shops. They were a **gregarious** people, and with the shock of Draco's visit still fresh in their minds, most of them wanted to be in the midst of friends, to talk over what had happened and what might be hoped for from the meeting which the mayor had called.

> **gregarious**: seldom alone; preferring to be with your group; habitually seeking out the company of others
> **unobtrusive**: not conspicuous or calling attention; not breaking in on the peace or concentration of others
> **reverie**: an absorbing daydream or fancy or free-flowing sequence of thoughts

Joannie was one of the few who remained at the dock. She found an **unobtrusive** seat out near the end where she would not be in the way of the workers unloading hogs and other cargo from *Jack's Equator*. She liked being near the ship. It was one of the very few things which could draw her into **reverie**: in her imagination it was called the *Beagle*, and it was sailing down the long coast of South America, cataloging the plant life and the wildlife of a continent.

The image absorbed her, and she failed for several moments to notice that someone was kneeling motionless by her side. Then in a startled blink the *Beagle* was gone. Joannie gasped, "Merci—you scared me. I was ... somewhere else. What ...?"

> **supplication**: the act of asking or pleading intensely for something, in a humble, lowly manner
> **odious**: so mean or offensive as to stir up repugnance and hatred

With anyone but Merci the posture would have been ridiculous. With her the kneeling had a grace. It spoke of deep **supplication**. "Joannie, I need your help very badly."

Joannie's eyebrows hunched down in a look of doubt. "Need my help? Most of the time you won't even talk to me."

Merci's voice fell. "You're right, of course. I have trouble with the senior girls. They make me nervous. They're too grown-up. And me ... I am the brat. I do **odious** things. I try to win all the senior boys, Calvin included, and keep them ... like trinkets on a bracelet. But—please don't hate me. I need your help."

Joannie shook her head, imperceptibly. "Calvin's lost, I'm afraid. But I don't hate you, Merci. You are one of the most amazing species I've ever encountered. What can you want from me, though? My plain face? Probably not, right?"

> **pretext**: a reason which is given for some action, and which serves to cover over the real reason
> **remorse**: a form of grief and painful regret, based on your recognition of guilt for some wrong you have done
> **atone**: to pay some price or confer some benefit in order to balance out, or compensate for, a wrong which you have done

"I would give anything for your ... direction," said Merci generously. "You know where your life is going, you even like where it's going. Mine is still deciding between north, south, east and west. I have the engineering genes, that's true, only no idea where they are taking me someday ... But Joannie, listen, right here and now, if I had your help ... I feel so bad. I had to get theatrical yesterday on the bridge, had to draw a cartoon on that page of newspaper and throw it in the stream. And Draco found it—the bay is so big, but he found it, fished it out. Now it's a pollution episode. I gave him exactly what he was seeking—a **pretext** for coming after us!"

Her **remorse** was deep, and she was close to tears. Joannie set a hand on the slender shoulder. "Easy. A jerk like Draco would have found something. In fact, remember that bottle. We're on his list for some reason."

With her back held straight as a classical statue, Merci rose slowly to her feet. "But I will make it up, Joannie, what I have done. I'll render Dropanchor a service that **atones** for my idiocy. I can't do anything now about the Draco problem—though I'd love to steer his boat into a black hole—but the other problem, the one with the Mendicant Briars, that's one which calls for an engineer believe it or not, and here I am."

"On behalf of the briars," said Joannie with a trace of amusement, "we welcome your concern. But what ...?"

An hour later and she was high above Dropanchor, following the switchbacks that led up the Steeps. Merci had persuaded her to make the climb to Mercurial Canyon—something she would have done anyway with her holiday afternoon—to look for a plant that was tall and had "tendencies to form a wall."

> **orthodox**: lying within the established mainstream of acceptable opinion and conduct; conforming to official teaching about how something should be or should be done
> **camouflage** (verb): to make something escape notice through disguises and false resemblances

206

Merci had a plan to protect the Mendicant Briars from the wasting breeze that was flowing down on them. "It's straightforward, really," she was explaining to Joannie as they labored up the trail. "We put up a wall, enough of a wall to turn back that wind. But not a standard wall, not made from the **orthodox** materials which the big firms use for this sort of thing—brick or plywood or maybe canvas. Those are widely approved, I know, and everybody goes with them—but on the bluff they would look horrible. We could **camouflage** them, maybe, with the colors of the mountain, but it would still look tacky."

The winding of the trail had brought them near the Bad Pony, plunging down the stony face of the Steeps, and they rested at its side. "Which is why," Merci continued, "I need to find a plant. The wall I have in mind will be a hedge. A good hedge will stop those breezes, or turn them aside, or break them up. It's not the first time, you know. It's like the windbreaks that the settlers made on the prairie, when they planted a row of cottonwoods or something along the side of the farm."

> **personify**: to speak or write about some object as though it had human emotions or engaged in human actions such as thought, speech, etc.
>
> **differentiate**: to take note of or take into account the differences between two things—often essential and defining differences

Joannie responded in a half-apologetic tone. "I'm afraid the better comparison may be a picket fence trying to hold back a flood. The river leaves its banks and rolls across the lowland and comes to the house with the fence and the house without, and—excuse me for **personifying**—it scoffs and says, 'I see no reason to **differentiate** between the two.' And it floods them both, equally deep."

"Whew!" cried Merci, "you know how to make it hurt. Yet it's not exactly the same case." She was quiet for a moment, watching the rush of the stream, pressing the knuckle of her thumb against her teeth.

> **rarefied**: distributed thinly throughout a medium or atmosphere (as, for example, particles of smoke which have gotten farther and farther apart as the smoke spreads out in the open air)
>
> **analytical**: thinking through an issue carefully, identifying the basic elements at work in it, and, often, seeking the logical connections and distinctions among those elements

"In the flood example," she said at last, "all water is ... bad. You don't want any of it in your house. But in our case with the Mendicant Briars, there's bad air—coming down from that half-loaf summit—and there's good air, everything else. So we have the possibility of something like a compromise we could live with. If my hedge can even interrupt the flow of bad air, break it up and scatter it, we might still be OK, because that way the bad air mixes with the good. The pollutant—whatever it is—is still there in the mix, that's true, but now it's...**rarefied**, diluted. And against a rarefied pollution the Mendicant Briars should be more resistant—or so we hope and pray. That's our here and now case. But in the flood case, you can't do that sort of thing—you can't dilute water."

With a soft whistle of admiration Joannie exclaimed, "Wow—François always said her little sister could get kind of **analytical**. You have obviously thought it through, Merci, and in my opinion as a senior girl you do have a point. *Vive* the wall, Merci's wall. It may be a long shot, but I guess it's not completely off the map."

They said little more until they arrived at the mouth of the canyon. Then as they pushed into the tangle of green Joannie smiled and asked, "Are you ready for rain, fog, thunder and clear skies, all in the next twenty minutes?"

"There are days," answered Merci, "when my moods change faster than that. And what I'm very, very ready for is a tall plant, with no objection to serving as a wall."

"Well then, I think we have an item which will suit the mademoiselle." Joannie slipped through a heavy tapestry of vine, stirring up a cloud of acrylic blue moths, and Merci followed. What there was of a trail lay through a towering stand of trees. Beneath its canopy an obscurity reigned, where the sunlight fell only in tatters. Its privacy pleased Merci greatly.

> **profusion**: a pouring out of some item (good advice, cultural achievements, ceramic jewelry, whatever) in such quantity or number as to be an abundance
> **protrude**: to stick out from something, sometimes in a conspicuous way
> **capricious**: behaving with unpredictable actions and alterations, often on the basis of whatever wild notion or flight of fancy possesses you at the moment

The landscape was as shifting as the weather, however, and soon the forest opened onto a narrow glade, spilling toward them down a gentle slope. It held a rich **profusion** of life, a traffic of hummingbirds and butterflies of great assortment, weaving through a variety of shrubs and vines. At the upper end of the glade was a pool, penned in by a low curb of granite which **protruded** through the turfy soil. The area to the sides and rear of the pool was crowded with one type of plant, an odd breed with a woody stalk of seven or eight feet. Each plant had only two leaves, huge and curving, hinged on the stalk itself, and standing out firmly from it like angel's wings.

"They're tall," said Joannie. "And how do they feel about walls? Well—they do grow close together. But as you are starting to see, there's one little thing they do that's not very wall-like."

All across the patch the great angel-wing leaves were fanning slowly. There was too much regularity in that movement, as Merci saw even from a distance, for it to be the work of the **capricious** winds blowing every which way in the canyon.

> **malign** (adjective): intending or leading to a destructive or otherwise evil effect
> **extricate**: to disentangle and remove carefully from a troublesome or awkward situation
> **nomenclature**: a systematic arrangement of names, and sometimes a set of rules for generating names, to be used in identifying the objects of a science or art

"You're right," said Joannie, watching her with a little smile. "Not the wind. The plants move themselves, like some overgrown flytraps, looking for a meal. But is it really about food? There, see that one—a butterfly enters the space between the leaves, the leaves begin to close on the poor creature, let's suppose for a **malign**, nutrition-related reason. Well—note the lightning speed at which the tragedy unfolds—at least half a mile per hour. Unless the butterfly senses his danger and **extricates** himself in approximately forty-five seconds, he's history."

For all her intensity, Merci laughed. "They're a bunch of goofs. *Phfwatt!*—missed again."

"A bunch of losers," said Joannie. "And that's what I call them, even though their official name in the international system of plant **nomenclature** will be more polite, no question of that. But whatever their name, and whatever their real reason for opening and closing their leaves, to me they look like the hedge you have in mind, more so than any other bush or shrub here in the canyon."

"They could be the ones," said Merci. "A wall of losers. What about re-planting them—how much soil do they need?"

"The news is good. The Losers tolerate a shallow, wet soil, which I suspect is what they'll find on top of your bluff. So that's workable."

"So far, so good," said Merci. She had folded her hands, brought them up to her lips, in a gesture of concentration. "But let's think it through now, step by step. What about digging them up in the first place?"

> **accommodating**: arranging things to fit someone's needs and schedule; making every effort to go along with someone's request

adjacent: close by something, usually next to it or immediately bordering it

"Once again," said Joannie, "they love you. The digging should be OK—the roots cluster beneath the trunk instead of spreading way out, so you'll be able to get the entire rootball without excavating a huge crater. Call them the **Accommodating** Losers—they're sure trying to fit in with your plans."

Joannie looked out over the crescent of ground where the Losers grew. It was a spacious plot, and was dense with plants. "And," she went on, "the quantity won't be a problem. There are more than enough. Just by thinning the patch you'll have what you need for your wall. Then—another thing is distance." She was glancing back now along the path they had followed in. "We're not exactly **adjacent** here to the bluff above the briars, but the distance isn't too bad, we're not real far into the canyon yet."

As Joannie ran through the merits of the strange plants, Merci was lifting her head, setting her chin, in an air of determination. "It is possible," she declared at last in a stern voice, speaking it seemed to a doubting Merci inside her, who was trying to hold her back. "With this plant, it is possible!"

There was a delicate question which had a very close bearing on the possibility of Merci's project, and Joannie raised it now. "Heaven only knows how we'll actually move them."

"I'll move them," said Merci fiercely. "I was the idiot who threw that newspaper in the stream! I'll move them, a whole wall of them, to stand over the Mendicant Briars."

ignominy: the quality by which a thing or action is a source of disgrace for you; shamefulness
preposterous: highly ridiculous, to the point of being impossible to believe or take seriously
extant: still in existence; not extinct or otherwise eliminated, in spite of being subject to forces (the long passage of time, climate change, etc.) tending to cause extinction or elimination

"But you're going to need some help—maybe some of the boys."

Merci gave a little shake of the head. "I'm actually very strong," she explained firmly. "I'm not ashamed to dig—it has no **ignominy** for me. And I've inherited these incredible engineering genes. I won't need any boys."

———————————

READER: If those plants aren't trapping insects, then you have a responsibility to explain what they are doing when they fan their leaves.
AUTHOR: I can answer that—they're trying to fly.

READER: That's **preposterous!**

AUTHOR: No—my research indicates that several trillion years ago many types of plants were trying to achieve flight. Of them the Losers are the only **extant** species.

READER: That could have changed life as we know it.

AUTHOR: Correct! Think of it—the sky turns green as this year's crop of broccoli wings off to the supermarket.

Chapter 30: THE JM PARADIGM

On the following morning a sad cry carried through the windows of Room 401. "I need some help … after all."

Allen went over and looked down. "Ms. Jensen," he said after a moment, "I'm going to have to change the subject, but I guess that's OK since we're in Desultory Warm-ups. Looks like another story is breaking, more news for the *DHS Trumpet*. Yesterday, a naval assault by Draco; now this. Merci is down there with a red wagon, and I think she needs the senior boys."

> **advocate** (noun): someone who speaks out to promote and make a case for some position, cause or practice
> **veto** (noun): the authority to block some proposed action, simply by saying no
> **logistical**: relating to the coordination and timing by which people and supplies are moved about to accomplish some mission

"I presume she needs them after school," said Ms. Jensen dryly.

Joannie slipped up to her desk and quietly explained what she knew about Merci's enterprise. She was an efficient **advocate**, and after a minute Ms. Jensen nodded slowly, looked up at Allen, and said, "You may go and help Merci—Joannie has convinced me. And the other senior boys may go with you. I believe I have that authority. But at the end of the day you will probably wish I had exercised my **veto**."

A second cry, sad and sweet, came through the windows. "Is anyone going to help?"

Muttering that a newsman should not be expected to make the news, Allen rose and left the room. The other boys followed. Listening to their heavy trooping down the stairs and seeing the worry growing in Joannie's eyes, Ms. Jensen said, "It's going to be a **logistical** nightmare—moving a small army in, moving a small forest out. Someone needs to be there to say, 'Step lightly.' You'd better go." With a nod and a look of intense gratitude, Joannie hurried through the door to catch Allen and the others.

> **deplete**: to take from some supply until it is gone or severely reduced
> **lithe**: bending and moving with an easy grace; willowy
> **unscathed**: being without wound or mark or other harm, after passing through some trial or assault

It was an unforgettable day for those who followed Merci up to the briars and the canyon. Even if nothing else had been notable, the sheer immensity of the labor would have given Allen a good story. Long after ordinary reserves of energy were **depleted** the digging and lifting, the hauling and planting, went on. Several times, Ricky announced, "Well, good friends, that's enough for today," and then went right on working. Who could stop when Merci, streaked with sweat, drove her **lithe** form without pause or rest?

But there was more than the killing enormity of the work. Through all the ache and strain, the performance was inspired. Joannie loved Mercurial Canyon, was alert to its needs, and was determined that it would remain **unscathed** when the huge transplanting was done. Merci loved solutions, and her darting mind discovered them again and again throughout the day as Joannie called problems to her attention.

"Not wagons," Joannie had said when she first caught up to the squad. "The wheels are narrow and hard and will cut into the floor of the canyon." Without hesitation Merci commanded, "Wheelbarrows! They have wider tires. And Ricky, please, a pump. We'll overinflate them."

> **herculean**: enormously difficult; requiring vast labor and strength
> **judicious**: carefully weighing the competing considerations in a complex situation, to reach sound decisions

Something more than an hour later the labor gang entered Mercurial Canyon, ascended the hillside to the bright pond in its granite basin, and at last understood the **herculean** labor that was waiting for them. There was a great outcry, every form of groaning and complaining, part of it in words, part in brays and snorts. Joannie waited until it started to die away, and then pointed to the patch of slowly fanning Loser bushes and said, "That's fine, be honest about your feelings, but I beg you, once you start removing Losers, be **judicious** also. Think it through. Take one, leave two. Don't open up bald spots. Check out the interplays—spare the plant that interrupts a rain channel; it's fighting erosion."

Merci responded. "Judicious is great for thinking beings. We'd better try something else." She pulled a roll of orange flagging from her pack and like a fairy-tale creature ran through the grove, tying a ribbon on the plants which Joannie called out for removal.

> **latent**: present in something as a feature which is now hidden and producing no obvious effect, but which may manifest itself later on
> **degrade**: to slide down into some physically or morally inferior state
> **obliterate**: to wear down or wipe out something to the point that it ceases to exist or have significance

A major engineering test came not long after. The first seven or eight plants had been excavated and burlapped, and carted around the pond, out of the canyon and away to the bluff above the Mendicant Briars. With a gathering

213

frown Joannie watched the zone of grass and brush just below the pond. Across a distance of thirty feet or so, the wheelbarrow tires—even though inflated in accord with Merci's suggestion—were leaving deeper ruts with each trip, and silver trickles of water were beginning to show at the bottom of them.

"**Latent** seepage," Joannie explained to Merci. "The pond sits in a wide bowl of granite, which after a few million years is cracked in places. There is some leakage, of course. It usually stays a few inches under the top of the soil, so you don't see it, but it's there, and it has the potential to turn the ground boggy. A few more hauls by the squad, some additional tramping about, and that whole area, I'm afraid, will **degrade** into a hog wallow. With the consequence that four or five unique species of grass and shrub will be **obliterated** from the face of the earth."

> **topography**: the lie of the land; the way it is flat or hilly, bare or marked with trees and other features
> **eschew**: deliberately to avoid using, enjoying or otherwise having contact with something, often because you believe it is inconsistent with your goals or principles
> **conscript** (verb): to draft someone into service, usually by force of law or some other authority
> **dispatch**: to send someone off on an official mission or errand, often in haste

Merci was deeply moved. She gazed for some time on the threatened area, and then walked twice around it, exploring the ragged granite outcroppings at its edges, looking for an alternate passage for the wheelbarrows. Her voice was firm when she spoke again. "Not one more load rolls across there, Joannie, I promise. I don't see any good way around, so we're going to elevate this job. The Brooklyn Bridge spans 1,595 feet, and it was built before the invention of senior boys. We'll span thirty. And in spite of the challenging **topography**— sloped and irregular, and somewhat brushy—we'll do it before lunch."

Both as a reporter and as a person who **eschewed** physical exercise, Allen would have liked to view what followed from the sidelines. But he was **conscripted** along with the others for the special labor. Merci sent the boys hurrying back down the mountain to collect ten-foot posts, hammers, rope, stakes, pulley wheels and a strong hook. "Get it from the dockyards," she shouted after them. "My father won't mind." Ricky had a mission of his own: he was **dispatched** to find Darlingson and say that Merci needed him.

> **guy**: a rope or wire which stabilizes something by connecting it to a stake, tree trunk or the like
> **periphery**: the outer edge or margin of something

Some time later, when the materials were collected and the quiet figure of Darlingson, with his huge strength, was there, Merci oversaw the setting of two pillars, one at the near edge of the boggy area, and one at the far. Each was made by lashing several posts together. They were not sunk into the ground, but were held stable by **guy** ropes running out and back to granite anchors at the **periphery** of the glade. An iron wheel went at the top of each column, and on the wheels a circuit of heavy rope was stretched. The hook was knotted into the rope.

Merci made good on her promise. By lunch the transplant was resumed, and the slumping mass of each Loser plant, held in a temporary netting of light rope, was ferried through the air by her cable, across the boggy stretch of ground, and into a wheelbarrow waiting below, where the jungle floor was drier.

> **incidental**: occurring as the by-product or side effect of some action rather than as its principal effect or objective
>
> **paradigm**: a perfect example or instance of something; an example which is so complete and so typical that it functions as a model or a point of reference

"Drier at least between the squalls which passed over every couple hours," wrote Allen the following day in an article for the *Trumpet*. "But rain, shine or fog, the performance of Merci and Joannie, of Darlingson and of the senior men was world-class. The jungle was harvested but in the most careful way possible. What was needed was taken, but nothing more. The human tread was light, with none of that **incidental** destruction that often goes along with big harvests. It was a **paradigm** of jungle management, a perfect instance of how to do it right."

Allen liked the phrase "paradigm of jungle management" and wanted it to serve as the headline for his article. That made an awkward fit in the column, however, so he shortened it down until it simply read The JM Paradigm. The story described how a thick hedge of Loser plants was in place by sunset across the top line of the bluff where the Mendicant Briars grew.

"This reporter," he wrote at the end of the story, "remained behind on the bluff as night fell, with Tedesco of Green Affinity fame, and R. Snoozer of general fame, to watch the tightly curled leaves of the Mendicant Briars and see whether the body-breaking labor of that day would have its reward."

READER: Larry's father recently asked him if he knows what "paradigm" means.

215

AUTHOR: And Larry, having just read this chapter, blew his doors off, right?

READER: More than you'll ever know. He said "paradigm" means an overhead cable for hauling large plants.

AUTHOR: Say it's not true!

READER: Now the rule is that for every page he reads of you, he has to read ten of Fulano.

Chapter 31: THE NON-DILATORY QUADRALITH

The following day was a tense one in Dropanchor. Merci's experiment hung in the balance. The only news so far was that her hedge of Loser plants was alive and well after its first night on the bluff, but that as yet it had not become what everyone hoped it would soon become, a **beneficent** neighbor of the Mendicant Briars, seeking their good and their protection. For there was no improvement after more than twelve hours—the leaves of the briars were still tightly curled under the influence of the unknown vapor. That was the report which Allen gave when he descended early in the morning from the bluff. He had come down alone—Ricky and Tedesco were still there.

> **beneficent**: actively seeking good for others; helping to bring about benefits for others
>
> **protagonist**: someone who has the leading role in initiating or carrying forward some mission, project or struggle
>
> **inexorable**: moving toward some outcome, certain to reach it, and not able in any way to be turned aside from it

Grandma Dubois was one of those who had spied Allen as he came straggling through the town square in the first light. As she listened to his story her head was cocked to one side, and her eye was bright as a hawk's. He escaped her only after many questions.

She was frustrated not to be on the mountain herself, near the briars. On that day, however, a more urgent business held her in town. They had to do something about Draco, to push him back once again, and the day would show whether they could count on Bamalford to play his part in the struggle. It was no minor part, either. The lead role belonged to him, which was unfortunate—he was a most unattractive **protagonist**, refusing his help until given his reward. That same evening he would appear at the town meeting, whining and theatrical no doubt, to demand his present.

Grandma dreaded that session. As the day wore on she sensed half-consciously that some voice inside her was begging the sun to stay at morning, to stay at noon. But already now it was riding **inexorably** down the western reaches of the sky. With a small shake of her head she set out, walking north along the beach, under Cape Scurrility, toward the wide table of stone where the meeting would be held. It was one of her favorite landmarks, even though its height was insignificant, rising just elbow-high from the beach, and its shape was nothing more exciting than a rough square. What she liked was the sight of it emerging again and again from the battering and flood of the tides, to glint once more in the sun.

>**flaccid**: limp and slumping; too weak to maintain standard firmness
>**arrest** (verb): to cause some movement or process to come to a halt

She had come early, and from a distance she saw that as yet no one was on the stone. She was not the first, however. Ahead of her, drawing close to it, was Bamalford himself. With him was a younger man, thirty-five or so, who shuffled wearily across the sand. Grandma was struck to see how **flaccid** Bamalford's companion was. He was not overweight, and not underweight, but all his weight seemed to droop wearily on his frame, as though the muscles had been discharged of their force.

His slow progress was completely **arrested** at the side of the stone. It rose sheer and vertical, but since it stood only four feet high it was really no more than a big step, up from the sand to the broad granite surface where the meeting would occur. For the stranger, though, it could have been the north face of Everest. He had no strength to climb it. Bamalford was distressed. "Don't you worry, sir, we'll have you up in a blink, and we'll get you the best seat, on the dry side, which is the least you deserve, sir."

>**obsequious**: showing an exaggerated attentiveness and obedience to someone's little wishes, often to win favor
>**servile**: putting yourself totally at the service of someone's wishes, in the manner of a slave

Grandma had come within earshot and was surprised by the **obsequious** note in Bamalford's speech. This was strange, to find Bamalford—always so sure of his mastery over man and nature—suddenly **servile**. But there he was, hopping about, bowing like a butler, desperate to be of service. At last he hauled his own considerable mass up onto the stone and, straining, succeeded in pulling his companion up behind him.

"They're numskulls here," he explained, "seven or eight centuries behind the program. This is what they call access to public places. Pardon me, sir, but you should give them a long speech on how things work in the modern era."

>**dilatory**: causing things to drag on and not finish; engaging in delay
>**quadralith**: a stone that is roughly square in shape (from the Latin word for square and the Greek word for stone)

"Oh no, no, no," scolded Grandma, who had arrived at the stone and scrambled quickly up its side. Her finger was wagging at the startled face of the younger man. "Long speeches mean delay, and delay is obviously not what a place called the Non-**Dilatory Quadralith**—we had to name this stone something—is all about."

Before either of them could reply she moved on around them, walking out farther and farther on the rock, through the irregular rows and clusters of chairs which had been set up for the meeting, past the scattered pools where anemones and starfish waited for the returning tide.

> **salient** (noun): an outcrop, cape, spur or other feature that juts out conspicuously from the main mass or structure to which it belongs
> **cataclysmic**: relating to a disaster of immense scope, which brings wide upheaval and ruin
> **officious**: offering advice, reminders and services when they are not asked for and probably are not wanted

At its far edge the great stone was not cut perfectly square, but thrust out a small spur of granite toward the sea. It was to this **salient** that Grandma came, to stand, to lean against the simple railing that ran there, to watch for a few moments. A little ways below her, on the coarse stretch of sand and shell that stretched out from the base of the rock, the waves were pounding violently.

When she had woven her way back through the chairs and around the pools and was standing once more at the landward edge of the stone, she tried to explain what she had seen. "You may already know this," she said to Bamalford and his friend, "but the tide will not delay. It will drop for an hour more, maybe a little longer, and after that it will turn and swiftly reclaim all that it has surrendered, this stone included. Then it's another world up here. With the spray flying and the water churning around your knees and night falling, it can all be rather **cataclysmic**, life as we know it being swept away." She threw a warning look at the two men.

Bamalford never reacted well to Grandma's reminders, and he was turning scarlet now. "I hope there's no fee for advice not sought, counsel not requested. Why does every small town have its troop of **officious** hags? Anyway—we'll take no bath, my friend and I. We're sitting landward, on the dry side."

Grandma smiled. "Dreamer! This nonsense about a dry side of the Non-Dilatory Quadralith always gets washed away soon after the tide reaches the wet side."

Others were hiking along the beach now to the stone, their shadows lengthening in the late sun. Among them were many of the students, Merci included. She climbed nimbly up the side of the rocky platform and found her grandmother, to say that there was no further news about the Mendicant Briars, and that Ricky and Tedesco had not yet descended from the mountain. Then she made her way out to the seaward edge of the stone, to the same overlook where Grandma had stood a little while before.

> **verbose**: using a lot more words than are needed

arbitrary: done or said without a rational basis and simply as the free and unrestricted expression of will or fancy
chagrin: sharp, painful embarrassment and distress over some failure or setback

As the sun touched the horizon Mayor Povano called the meeting to order, running on his sentences like a man who has forgotten all punctuation. "The town council is now in session here on the Non-Dilatory Quadralith generally people if you hope to leave with dry socks don't be **verbose** just get it said and low tide is not far off and after low tide comes high. Is there any old business? And of course there always is—we've got briar leaves curling we've got whales turning shy—but nevertheless I **arbitrarily** find that there is none, which means we go straight to new business and we have one item—namely the **chagrin** of Peerless Bamalford over being compared to a bullfrog during prime time. And sir you speak of a big present so what is the big present which would take away the pain and would leave you disposed once again to send Draco packing?"

Bamalford stood, and with the solemnity of a judge pronouncing his verdict said, "The only decent present would be for that Sallie Driven witch to televise Foster Farbugle eating cold oatmeal out of my boot. But if that's too much, then I want a ... road."

egotistic: having an oversized sense of your own importance
elaborate (verb): to describe something in fuller detail

Relief at once softened the worried lines of Povano's face. He had been apprehensive that Bamalford would once again raise the topic of the Giuseppe Stone, demanding that it be carved into his own figure, noble and storm-tossed. "A road," the mayor now exclaimed. "That we can do! One-day turn-around on **egotistic** demands. You want your name on one of our streets—a public honor for a living legend? Why not? Your statue towers over us already. How about two? Roads I mean—you know—I'll meet you at the corner of Bamalford and Bamalford. That sort of big present we can handle."

Bamalford held up a hand, striking a pose like that of his statue, which glowed a dull copper in the twilight atop Cape Stairstep. "Stop, little man. You've flubbed it already. Let me **elaborate**. I want a new road, a road that doesn't yet exist, a road that needs to be constructed."

pulverize: to smash something until it is ground into small bits or into powder
desecrate: to treat something sacred in a rough, insulting manner
savor (verb): to enjoy the taste of; to take a slow, deliberate delight in something

Grandma was on her feet, with the look of a woman hearing an air-raid siren. "Hold it right there, Mr. Bamalford! You're the sort who would **pulverize** Plymouth Rock and use the pieces to pave over Old Faithful. What holy place will you **desecrate** by putting a road on top? A road to where, please?"

Bamalford gave a mock bow to the old lady. "A road, if you please, up the canyon of the Bad Pony…up to those semisacred Mendicant Brambles."

That was intolerable. Missiles were launched. The shell of a razor clam went flying in Bamalford's direction, and a length of seaweed tubing, before François could catch her grandmother's arm.

Bamalford **savored** the moment, letting out a long sigh of contentment and poking at the clam shell with his foot. "What else is on the meen-yu? Perhaps … I might see the wine list?"

> **exotic**: so different from what you're used to—and so marked with a style that is foreign, richly imaginative, and sometimes excessive and daring—as to excite your interest
> **exorbitant**: shockingly in excess of an ordinary and fair level for prices, rents, profits, fees, etc.
> **effete**: overly refined, to the point of weakness and softness
> **apnea**: a temporary suspension of breathing

It was a question with a barb, and Grandma was stung. "Wine!" she yelled. "That's it. That's what has hulked around the edges of my nightmares. Your road is just a way to commercialize the Mendicant Berries, to harvest them by the truckload, and turn them into an **exotic** wine for sale at **exorbitant** prices to **effete** commercial types wearing lace cuffs and waiting for the next earthly delight to be rolled in for their sampling. To that sort of road we say Never!"

"My dear woman," returned Bamalford in an injured tone. "Please control your ravings. And shorten your sentences. The purpose of the road is spiritual, if you must know. And—another thing. You refer to it as my road. Quite wrong. It will be his road."

READER: You can't do what you did!
AUTHOR: Well, if I did it obviously I can do it. But what are we talking about?
READER: You can't have a title where both words are hard.
AUTHOR: Oh—the Non-Dilatory Quadralith. I couldn't think what to call it.
READER: Besides—I checked all the big dictionaries—"quadralith" is not a word.
AUTHOR: But you wouldn't deny, I assume, that quadraliths exist.
READER: How can quadraliths exist if "quadralith" is not a word.

AUTHOR: Tut, tut. Would sleep **apnea** cease to exist if "sleep apnea" were not a word?

READER: You never know, and actually that might be the preferred treatment—cheap and non-invasive. Besides, it's two words.

AUTHOR: You're being rather stubborn.

READER: You're being rather slippery.

Chapter 32: NAMELESS ENTREPRENEUR

Bamalford's companion rose slowly to his feet. With his collapsing posture and shy grin he was not a threatening figure. "Yes, my very good friends," he began, "the road is for me." The voice was soft, gentle, but it made Meagan sit bolt upright.

"Velvet," she whispered with some alarm to Joannie. "That voice has velvet ... the sort which makes you buy things you don't really need."

> **susceptible**: more likely than average to fall under the power of some influence, as, for example, a teaching, a temptation, a disease
> **remnant**: a small remainder left over from a larger mass
> **entrepreneur**: a person who organizes a new business venture and works to keep it running, often putting some of his or her own money at risk

"When it comes to that kind of velvet," Joannie whispered back, "the people of Dropanchor are not very **susceptible**. Tennis shoes with...with turn signals, for example, and that sort of thing, would not do well around here." She looked up at the stranger. "But that boyish smile could be trouble."

The boyish smile was flashing now. "My very dear friends, I am a **remnant**. Most of me is gone, used up helping others. Somewhere I have a real name, but you may call me Nameless—yes, like that little Colorado town. Nameless **Entrepreneur**, for that is what I am. I launch commercial ventures—and I meet deep human needs. Maybe an example, a little sketch of one of the successes. That should help you know me better. Let me think."

For a moment he stared off blankly above the heads of the crowd, seeing nothing, searching—it appeared—through the mental records of his accomplishments. He was droning softly, as though with contentment. "Nutrition," he murmured at last, "from the area of nutrition we can draw a fine example for the mayor, and the lady who throws things, and for all of them."

> **abstemious**: using self-control to limit sharply your intake of food and drink
> **dissemble**: to hide what you really feel or think, through the expression of a false emotion, preference or opinion

Looking once again at the assembly, he said, "We live in an age, you know, when people feel a desperate need to have their diets incorporate the food pyramid. But that means a lot of hardship if you get too literal—

shoveling in the fruit you hate, **abstemious** around the fat you love. Well, I have answered that need in a more human way—with this."

From the pocket of his vest he took a small object and held it up to view: it was triangular and foil-wrapped. "A food pyramid," he explained joyously. "It gets no less than ninety-eight percent of its calories from saturated fat. Guaranteed not to taste like any known fruit or vegetable. To hold its unique shape it's deep-fried repeatedly. My customers eat these twenty at a time, proud as kings. In their eyes, I am the sun and the moon. With no trace of **dissembling**, no faking it to earn free samples, they send me letters full of gratitude and compliments, because I made the food pyramid part of their diet. That's the kind of guy I am!"

> **palpable**: readily perceived by the senses, especially the sense of touch
> **prodigious**: awesomely large or powerful or extensive

Grandma was staring hard at him, so hard that her gaze bore against him with **palpable** force. He didn't mind. He smiled at her, at Povano, at the entire assembly, and said, "Another thing—I am a secret benefactor of your town. I bring some of my clients here, very financially responsible people— **prodigious** quantities of money. They need dome services, expo and demo and so forth, and the chubby Mr. Bamalford has a dome, has he not? The clients come and eventually the clients go, but their money stays. That helps you all. So please may I have a road?"

"Why?" snapped Grandma. "So you can try one of your cute ventures on our Mendicant Berries?"

> **convergence**: the movement of two things toward, and their meeting at, a point of union, sometimes with the result that they combine forces
> **mollify**: to cause someone to put aside or soften his anger, bitterness, etc., usually by treating him agreeably
> **dearth**: a shortage in supply, often severe enough to leave people worried

"No—not to do that, not to do anything. That's the point. My shrink says I spend all my time doing things, doing, doing, doing; serving others. She says go find a wilderness refuge and just be. And she's right. And the very large Mr. Bamalford swears the perfect place is waiting on your mountain—a stream, a **convergence** of canyons, a long bluff, a curtain of brambles. It's all at the end of my road. I should go for it, my shrink says. If I don't get up there soon, she says, I'm going to work myself into extinction."

"Not a bad idea," flared Grandma, in no way **mollified** by the bright smile of Nameless. "And maybe the food pyramids could do the same."

"A poor example, I recognize that now," responded Nameless, still in the tone of velvet which had startled Meagan earlier. "I don't understand small towns, you see. Maybe you're hostile toward pyramids here. But my next example will touch you. Because it is from the heart. I believe that the human heart is one—what I find in mine will be in everybody's. When you think about it—what a great place for product ideas."

He smiled, with a trace of shyness, and cast a brief look at Grandma and the others. "So you see, little people, I have studied my heart, and what I have found there, very firmly installed, is a need to blow something off the map, a rhino, a dino, some brute, offensive creature stumbling into the crosshairs. Then I have considered how in our time there's a **dearth** of things to shoot— thanks to shrinking herds, widening reserves, reduced seasons. We're running short on targets. So listen to what Nameless did about it."

"My heavens, man," interrupted Povano with alarm on his face, "what did you do about it?"

"It's called Roxxy's Rekillables," answered Nameless proudly. "We're in twenty-three malls now. Let's say, Mayor, that one morning you wake up and your mayor heart is filled with the very thing I was just describing. So you hurry to the mall, you find Roxxy's, select a gun, order a beast—lion, bear, woolly mammoth, whatever. There is a brief delay and then it bolts across the gallery in front of you, solid and three-dimensional, a thousand pounds of robot fury, lifelike down to the whiskers. Ba-lamm!"

> **contiguity**: the state of being right next to something, and often having an edge or boundary running in contact with an edge or boundary of it
> **prolixity**: the tendency to pour out long, often wandering, streams of speech

For all his frailty Nameless did a powerful imitation of a hunting rifle. "Balamm! You blow it to smithereens. Five thousand metal parts all over the floor there at Roxxy's. But very sophisticated parts, each with a transmitter and a tiny electromagnet, at the minimum. They are swept into a huge tumbler. The store manager (also a stockholder, I assure you) logs into an application we created called Tigu, as in "**contiguity**," and programs it for the next beast. The tumbler starts to turn, the parts begin transmitting, and Tigu reads their codes and looks for matches. Now, Mayor, five thousand parts are spinning, but think only of two of them, any two which need to be fitted up against each other in the next creature. When by pure chance those two parts go flying by one another for a billionth of a second there in the barrel, Tigu switches on their magnets and they lock, side to side. In this way we build the next creature. It takes just three or four minutes, then the tumbler stops, and out comes one beautiful, rekillable Bengal tiger or velociraptor or what have you, ready to meet the waiting client. Only at Roxxy's."

Grandma was growing alarmed at the man's **prolixity**. He could roll on when he wanted to. The returning tide meant nothing to him, but she saw it constantly in her mind—the pounding of the water against the sand and the shells—and she heard it below the current of his speech.

> **misconstrue**: to be mistaken in the interpretation or reading you put on something
> **paramount**: above everything else in importance or standing
> **discreet**: carefully taking into account the feelings of others or the complexities of the situation, in order to avoid giving offense or provoking unwanted reactions

When she began to wave her hand, though, trying to stop him, he **misconstrued** the gesture. "I understand—you want to ask about getting a Roxxy's for Dropanchor. I'll do everything I can. Really, I'll knock myself out to make it happen. That's just the kind of guy I am. Making the planet a more humane place, one little hamlet at a time. The only thing is that now, after years of it, I'm exhausted. My shrink gets this worried look: 'Find your wilderness refuge, Nameless—soon. That's **paramount**, that's first place on the save-your-life list.' And she's right. So please, people of Dropanchor, now that you know me—please can I have a road?"

Grandma responded sternly. "I'm not sure that to know you is to love you. And why does your refuge need to be at the briars? Why not somewhere on the beach, right here even, on this stone?"

"Too many chairs," said Nameless, lifting his chin and letting the boyish smile shine forth. "The chubby Mr. Bamalford promises that the perfect place is at the briars."

"But, sir," interrupted Povano. "Why a road?" He was laboring to be **discreet**. "The trail up the Bad Pony is not the finest, but even your aging mayor, sore of knee as he is, finds it … manageable. Could you … possibly …?"

"Walk!" cried Nameless, with a touch of hysteria. "Could I possibly walk? Little mayor, it's far too late for that. Try to understand. I'm an idea man— dreams and schemes, twenty-five hours a day. I'm a telephone man, talking to investors, technicals, regulators—twenty-five hours a day. I'm an airplane man—flying everywhere to do the face-to-face stuff, twenty-five hours a day. But do you see the price which the Nameless body pays for all this?"

> **atrophy** (noun): the process by which muscle tissue wastes away and becomes less, often from lack of use

demeaning: offensive to the dignity of your position, or at least not consistent with the respect owed to that position, and thus tending to pull you down to a lower status

dispassionate: calm and businesslike; not under the influence of strong emotion or strong likes and dislikes

He stood drooping before them, a textbook case of physical unfitness. "There's no time to eat right or to exercise. The muscles start to waste away, little by little. Many moons pass. Finally, the **atrophy** is so advanced that it becomes irreversible. Yes, my wilderness refuge is on your mountain trail, but these legs won't carry me there. I'll have to go by limo—and that takes a road."

"And hauling our Mendicant Berries off to the winery takes a road too," shot back Grandma. She turned away from the unfailing smile of Nameless and shook her head. Some moments passed. When she spoke again, it was in a softened tone. "We'll get you up there, OK, as often as you need, but without a road. My granddaughter has a red wagon and ..."

"I am just about to lose my temper," erupted Bamalford in the voice of a man who has lost his temper some time ago. "This is my party, Nameless is my guest. And you won't talk to him in this **demeaning** way, as though he's a drippy-nosed kid you can haul about in a red wagon. A little respect might be ..."

From the seaward edge of the stone came the voice of Merci, utterly **dispassionate** on the darkening air. "The tide is now at its lowest ebb, Grandmother. It is approximately forty-five feet down the beach from the base of the stone, and it is turning."

READER: If Benjamin Franklin read that chapter he would never have invented and promoted the telephone.

AUTHOR: I don't think it was B. Franklin who ...

READER: Never mind. What shabby treatment for the entrepreneurs who bring us new products—getting mocked in front of your twenty-seven readers.

AUTHOR: Unfair! I poked fun at the far-out stuff, Roxxy's robots and so forth, but I wouldn't mock the people launching useful things like telephones.

READER: All the useful things have been invented. It's far-out or nothing.

Chapter 33: THE UNFLATTERING CAPITULATION

Merci's announcement about the tide had nothing in it that was rude or of-fensive, yet it galled Bamalford terribly. "There!" he shrieked, pointing toward her and addressing the people generally. "There is your problem. You let your swine-baby children talk when they should be quiet. You have **abrogated** your duty to make the little idiots shut up! Tonight it's the goblin child. A week ago it was that Farbugle mutant, on national TV, shooting off his unmuzzled trap. That's ..."

> **abrogate**: to declare, decide or otherwise bring it about that some law, responsibility, standard, etc., is to be given no further effect
> **ultimatum**: a statement (often at the end of negotiations that have not been successful) that if some concession is not granted by a certain time, or some other action not taken, then harsh consequences will follow
> **foment**: to stir up some result by working on the forces present in a situation until they break into action

"Please, Mr. Bamalford," broke in Povano. "Merci is right. The tide is moving up the beach now. We have a little while, but only a little while, be-fore it's here, breaking across this stone. And it's real cold. If we're not brief now we'll be sorry then."

Bamalford glared at the mayor, and the fading light glinted on his huge eyeballs. "Brief? Brief it will be. Do you know the briefest form of decision making? The **ultimatum**, and here is mine. If the Pacific Ocean hits my part of this stupid rock before you approve the road for Mr. Nameless, it's all over. The force field stays down. Captain Pariah does not come back to the comics. And Inspector Draco is free to return to Dropanchor and haul off your chil-dren."

Merci glanced up from her vigil at the front of the stone. "Inspector Draco is an irritant, nothing more." You couldn't tell who she was speaking to. Her tone was that of someone picking up the loose ends of a prior conversation. "When you think about it—and what else have I thought about these last two days?—the man starts to look like a fraud, making up laws, dreaming up non-existent Melanies. Can you try to see that, Grandmother? We may have taken Draco far too seriously."

Her comment was wonderfully calm and self-assured in the face of Bamal-ford's storming, and it almost **fomented** an uprising. Joannie was on her feet, with none of Merci's calmness, shouting, "He's good at looking purple, nothing else." Allen, usually an observer, joined in, yelling, "He's a flake, a rookie ..."

Bamalford moved quickly, hurling a savage blast. "Hold it right there, newspaper boy. Stand by what you wrote, or get out of the profession. I read your article about Draco's visit, your big scoop in the high school paper this morning, and don't try rewriting it now."

> **diminution**: the act of becoming less or growing smaller
> **placate**: to cause someone's anger to lessen by giving him presents, honors or privileges
> **naive**: ignorant of the way things really are in some area of life such as politics, class differences, human reproduction, etc.; holding childish beliefs about such an area

He turned in the direction of Grandma and Povano. His voice fell from a roar to a growl, but even with the **diminution** it carried easily above the pounding surf. "I read the boy's article. And the Draco of that article—well, he's no rookie is he? A maggot, a misfit, but no rookie. According to your own Mr. Snoop, he raves with some authority, his threats are somewhat jolting. The big forehead is still a signboard of doom."

Bamalford was swelling now, confident that his hold was still secure. "I can see what's what. There's a road in your future whatever you do. Either you **placate** me and build the road for Mr. Nameless, or you don't. And if you don't, I stay mad—oh, yes!—I let Draco have his way, and there's a road to the east for your children, from here to that mind-bending Melanie."

He paused and stared hard at Povano for a moment. "But I see the crazy look in your eyes, Mayor, the desperate hope. It's the thing your little priestess babbled, isn't it, that Draco is a fraud and not to be feared, that Melanie doesn't exist, that Bamalford and his ... his services are quite dispensable. And I hear the little pepper mill of a brain of yours, grinding out an argument—Merci may be right, because the law could never be so harsh as Draco says, and there could never be a person so mean as Melanie, and the world's just too nice for all that."

He surveyed the crowd now, and gave a sweeping gesture, worthy of a Caesar. "So, people of Dropanchor, is your mayor right, or is he fatally **naive**? Place your bets, but understand what is at stake. This is not a game for pennies or poker chips. You are wagering your children."

> **admonish**: to give someone a warning, criticism or other piece of advice, usually in a gentle way and in order to help him
> **agitation**: a condition in which your feelings are stirred up and troubled
> **furtiveness**: a sneaking manner of action, adopted to avoid detection

The sun was down now, and the night wind was freshening. From her perch at the fore of the rock, Merci **admonished**, "The tide is returning, Grandma. It reaches out."

In what light remained the **agitation** was apparent on Povano's face. He allowed himself, however, one long groan, nothing more, and then lost no time calling Grandma and Peter Oakum and the other members of the town council into a tight cluster around him. Allen crept closer, trying without success to be inconspicuous.

"Grade D for **furtiveness**, Mr. Snoop," said the mayor, with just the ghost of a smile relieving his worried features. "But you may eavesdrop if you wish, and you may write your story."

> **dilemma**: a predicament in which there are bad consequences associated with each of the options between which you must choose
> **coercion**: the process of using or threatening force, or applying some other form of pressure, to make someone do something
> **artifice**: some piece of cleverness, trickery or deception, skillfully done

"D for **Dilemma**," answered Allen. "That will be the headline."

The little smile vanished and Povano turned grimly to his council. "Dilemma it is, and a cruel one. Bamalford put it quite well, to give him credit—a road to the briars, or the mortal risk of a road to the east."

Grandma was in anguish. "I would like to think," she said with a look toward Merci, keeping her watch at the edge of the meeting stone, "that we have made them strong enough to resist the pressures and **coercions** which that Melanie creature would use upon them, and wise enough to see through her tricks and **artifices**."

> **ubiquitous**: being everywhere at once, or in a relatively short period of time
> **destitution**: sharp poverty, in which you lack, or are seriously short on, even the most basic materials of life
> **reiterate**: to make a point over and over again

Peter Oakum was shaking his head slowly. In a voice so low that Allen had to lean forward to catch it, he said, "Young Oakum was strong and wise many years ago and many miles away when he started his job at Heronfire Gas and Electric. They gave him an inside office—no windows, no weather. They worked him long hours—there was always some urgent deadline—but they liked his work, and told him so. They fed him in the company cafeteria. They clothed him with the company T-shirt, and surrounded him with the company emblem—on his pen, watch, handkerchiefs, coffee mug. The thing was **ubiquitous**. And then they rotated him for a few months onto the billing desk, where his mentors were Jonathan and Patrice, the good-humored, bonus-conscious Jonathan, the elegant and bonus-conscious Patrice. And when the two of them heard Oakum telling customers about the thirty-day grace period, they taught him, 'No, no—if the customer can't pay and inquires "What now?" you go straight to the S-word—"shutoff." The grace period gets mentioned only if the customer specifically asks about it.' Well, under all those influences ..."

Here the narrative dropped so low that Allen wasn't sure whether he was hearing it or reading lips. "Under those influences," finished Peter, "young Oakum made some brilliant remark about shutoffs building character, and he fell in line ... at least for a while. And when people who were probably on the edge of **destitution** called and said they could not pay, he left many of them believing it was pay at once or the house would be cold before the kids got home from school. Young Oakum had no windows, you see, and there were..."

"That's OK, Peter," said Grandma gently. "Young Oakum turned out right. And old Oakum has made his point, even though I don't know if the kids will agree. They're constantly **reiterating** how their generation is a different breed, and how it's unflattering that I worry so much they'll lose their heads, and how they're ready for anything—Melanie included, I suppose."

With a long sigh she looked off to the east, across the breakers and the beach, toward the darkening bluff which lay between Cape Scurrility and Cape Stairstep. She fell into a meditation, and Peter and the others waited on her—but only for the briefest moment. With a sudden gasp she struggled to pull her gaze away from an unexpected vision. She had seen squarely on the line of her sight, on the line to the east, a hulking form. It was the massive silhouette of a woman, raising something greedily to her lips. Grandma gasped a second time, and said, "Melanie!"

> **myopic**: unable to see distant objects except as a blur
> **invective**: a sharp and bitter verbal assault
> **sanction** (noun): an unpleasant consequence (for example, the loss of a privilege or right) which a lawgiver or other person in charge attaches to a disobedient act

"Much worse," returned the rasping voice of Ms. Framley. She was slouched heavily in a chair at the eastern edge, the landward edge, of the meeting stone. "Blind old bat—strap on some binoculars, why don't you, over those **myopic** eyeballs. And don't interrupt again, old hag, while I'm taking vitamins. When I want some news from fungus world, I'll ..."

Grandma turned away from the **invective**. She was badly shaken, less by the stream of abuse than by the sheer presence of so much hostile mass. The

231

question whether Melanie really existed seemed frivolous at this point. "Look what is waiting in the east," she murmured weakly to Povano and the others. "I don't think the kids are ready for that Melanie beast."

François had crept to the edge of the circle formed by the council members, and she protested, "We are ready, Grandma. Let Draco ship us off to enforcement school. It won't change us. We're not protoplasm, you know."

Beckoning toward the figure of Ms. Framley, Grandma answered softly, "Look at the monumental oppression which waits for you in the east."

François smiled. "Grandma, do you think she's going to sit on us?"

"No, but Peter is right, she will press on you in a thousand ways, with rewards when you sing in chorus and **sanctions** when you don't, until she changes who you are."

"Oh, Grandma—the Dropanchor kids are tougher than that. Anyway, not to get technical or anything, but that monumental oppression in the chair isn't Melanie in the first place—it's Victoria Framley."

> **adumbration**: a small token or dim foreshadowing of something to come
> **callow**: noticeably young and unfinished; not yet possessing the emotional and judgmental maturity of a grown-up

Grandma seized on the point. "That's what scares me. For all her bulk and meanness, Victoria is only a faint preview, an **adumbration**, of what Melanie will be. Victoria has only the Dogmatic Lease to wave at you; Melanie will have much nastier instruments for reprogramming your **callow** young minds."

"We're not green twigs and slimy nestlings," returned François with some indignation. "This is becoming rather unflattering, you know."

> **capitulation**: the act of dropping your resistance and making your surrender, often on specific terms and conditions
> **precocious**: showing at an early age a degree of physical or intellectual development that is usually found only in someone far older

Grandma looked at François, tenderly. She looked at Merci, still by the stone's edge, and at Allen and Meagan and all of Dropanchor's kids who were assembled there. And with a shudder she looked back to Ms. Framley, who was wiping her spoon more or less clean of vitamin elixir and hanging it again from her right ear. "Alright then," said the old lady at last, lifting her chin, "you may call what I am about to do the Unflattering **Capitulation**."

She turned back again to the council. "Mayor Povano, I give in to the demands of Bamalford. Let him have his way. Our children are more important, and I will not put them to the proof at the hands of Melanie. I move that the council authorize a road up the mountain, alongside the Bad Pony, as high as the meadow below the Mendicant Briars. And may I never set foot on it."

READER: Larry had to stop reading when François talked about the slimy nestlings.

AUTHOR: I thought Larry was into stuff like that.

READER: When he was five some robins built a nest right outside his window. After the babies hatched, all featherless and glistening, he stuck his hand in, holding a rubber worm.

AUTHOR: **Precocious** child—scientific experiments at age five. So what did the birdlets do—bite him?

READER: No—they slimed him.

Chapter 34: THE MONOLITHIC REJECTION

Povano knew that the Unflattering Capitulation was **excruciating** for Grandma and should be gotten through without delay. He brought the matter to a vote, and within minutes the town council had approved a road up the canyon from the East Bridge to the meadow below the Mendicant Briars.

> **excruciating**: painful or distressing to the limits of endurance
> **recluse**: a person who habitually avoids social contact and seeks to be alone
> **venue**: the site or setting where you select to put on some activity or hold some event

When the vote was announced, Nameless looked like Christmas morning. "I got my road! Thank you so much, Dropanchor. Now we'll buy a motorcar, Bamalf and I, and Bamalf will drive me up the mountain so that I can meditate. Maybe I'll become a **recluse**, and never come down, no more deals, no more interactions with the human race. And Bamalf will have to truck in supplies. Who knows? But thank you again, little seaside town. I will repay. I will send some venture capital in your direction. Half a mill or less, just for example, and we could take that old smuggler"—he motioned southward, toward the harbor, where *Jack's Equator* stood at rest, a patch of gray in the thickening dusk—"and transform it into the premier offshore **venue** for frat parties, nationwide."

> **aristocratic**: acting as though you belong to a superior class, entitled by its superiority to rule society
> **eponymous**: being the person whose name has been given to some object such as a town, plant, disease, etc.

Bamalford, for his part, was revolving slowly, passing through phases like the moon. When he turned toward Nameless, he was lowly and expectant— "How about that, sir? We wanted a road, we got a road. What do you think?" His tone was **aristocratic**, though, as he came gradually swinging about toward Povano and the people. "Take a lesson, Mayor, this is the only way to run a society—the will of the great ones must prevail over the common flock." And when his rotation brought the shadowy bulk of Ms. Framley into view, he slipped into the usual familiarity. "Well, my **eponymous** Victoria, there is a share in this great work for you. As it comes up to that stretch where the canyon narrows, below that witch's stone or whatever it is, the road will need to cross the stream and run a short ways on your land."

With a squealy sound, barely recognizable as a giggle, Ms. Framley responded to the crowd at large. "Do you know why he calls me eponymous, any of you? Can't you guess? It's because the road will be named after me—Victoria's road. He made that Calvin boy draw a picture of the road sign, with my name on it. Yes, Mr. Bamalford, Victoria's Road may pass on Victoria's land. But warn the handsome workmen not to spend hours staring up the hillside, hoping for a glimpse…"

> **abominable**: so foul as to cause disgust and hatred
> **ructation** (an old term, no longer in common usage): the act of belching

A nasty undertone came into her voice. "And tell them also—no disgusting failures of etiquette on my land, no **abominable** manners, no audible **ructation**, and above all, no spitting of berry seeds on the ground. Ha, ha—get it, Grandma? Berry seeds?"

> **covetous**: wanting very badly what belongs to another, often to the point that you would consider using improper means to get it
> **mendicant** (noun): one who regularly begs for money or food
> **impecunious**: without money most of the time, or with only a small and insufficient amount of money

"You warn the handsome workmen," commanded Grandma, addressing Bamalford and ignoring Ms. Framley, "that if anyone touches the Mendicant Berries, if anyone even throws a **covetous** look at them, then whoever he is he will be the **mendicant**, because you, Mr. Bamalford, will hold back his wages."

Bamalford jerked his head sharply at the word "wages." "*Moi*, Grandma, *moi*? *I* will hold back his wages? That assumes that I will be paying his wages."

"Who else would be paying them?" she snapped. "It's your road."

"It's my present," he thundered in return. "My big present. But some lousy little el-shrinko present it becomes if I have to pay for it."

Mayor Povano broke in, trying to save the peace. "Scenery we've got, Mr. Bamalford. And whales besides. But money—well, that's in short supply. As you well recall, it wasn't Dropanchor money that paid for six months of helicopter madness when the Dome was built. We've always been an **impecunious** town."

Bamalford's big arms were waving. "Well, you're gonna be stinking rich in miniature Dracos if I have to pay for the road! Because I won't be doing much to keep the inspector from shipping off your kids—to be retooled in his likeness. This is just too tacky! You should learn the art of giving presents."

235

Povano did not answer, and in the momentary silence no one could miss the pounding of the waves upon the sand, insistent now and drawing near. Then once again there was the silvery voice of Merci, carrying easily across the great stone. "Two things, OK, two things. First, a drenching is **imminent**; the water is already splashing at my side of the stone. Secondly, about presents—homemade is best, you know."

"Great!" snarled Bamalford. "Then go bake me some cookies!"

"Granddaughter, tell me you aren't thinking ..." said Grandma Dubois in sudden dismay.

"I am thinking it, I am!" There was emotion now in Merci's voice. "A homemade road. I can do it. I'm extraordinarily beautiful. I have those engineering genes. I have strong wrists. And I'm the idiot who threw the newspaper in the Bad Pony and put Draco in a frenzy. So I'll build the road. It's not crazy. It's ... it's perfectly **consonant** with Dropanchor's tradition of self-reliance, and ..."

Povano was smiling and shaking his head. "It's a brave offer, Merci, but I cannot accept it."

indulgent: letting someone have his own way, granting his wishes, even though you could—and oftentimes should—say no

unorthodox: holding beliefs or engaging in practices which are outside the established mainstream of acceptable opinion and conduct; running against the official teaching about how something should be or should be done

Grandma was equally firm. "Stubborn thing! Road building is huge work, and not for a fifteen-year-old girl."

Merci's own father, usually **indulgent** of her desires, stood against her now. "We're a rather **unorthodox** family, daughter, that I admit. The pet meerkat, for example, or the dandelion project that made all our neighbors hate us. But road building in your sophomore year is just too...far-out."

Bamalford's verdict, not surprisingly, hit harder. "She's hallucinating! She thinks she's a cross between Joan of Arc and ... and that guy who built the Eiffel Tower. Get a jacket on her!"

incisive: cutting right to the heart of a matter, through keen, precise analysis and sharply focused statements

monolithic: being a single, unbroken mass of stone, or—in human affairs—coming across that way by virtue of presenting a united front that is intolerant of dissent or variation

It was Nameless, however, with his trademark smile and velvet tone, who delivered the most **incisive** judgment. "She's an unproven vendor. And you don't buy a big-ticket item like a road from an unproven vendor."

Merci sank for a moment under the responses, but she did not surrender. "You're all very ... unanimous tonight, and very **monolithic**, one big, smooth face of granite. But I won't give in, I won't accept your ... your Monolithic Rejection. I ..."

"Merci!" gasped François.

A huge wave had cracked against the far edge of the meeting stone and tossed a shower of spray high into the air. Merci glanced at it, but made no attempt to shield herself. In a moment she was drenched, and a wild race of foam and water was at her ankles. She shivered, she reached out to a little upsweep of granite to keep from faltering, but her voice was calm as she said, "I told all of you the tide was near. It doesn't wait, you know. Now about the road..."

> **corona**: a ring or band around some center, with more or less the appearance of a crown, as for example a ring of light around the moon
> **exodus**: the act of many people going out from a place where they have lived, often to settle elsewhere

They could not see her face as she reopened the argument, but the last twilight was in her hair, a faint **corona**, a reminiscence of the sun's reddish gold at setting, marking her with a moment's royal grace even as she stood dripping before them. "About the road, Grandmother, it will carry unwelcome traffic, there is no doubt, but it might prevent something unwelcome too. I know the dark vision of yours—how a year from now, two years, there is a tragic **exodus** from Dropanchor, and all the kids, Ricky and Meagan and the François girl, are marching in a ragtag band across the continent, thousands of miles, seeking ... jobs. But it's not a vision that has to come true. A road-building project would keep us here, close to home, and maybe it would lead to..."

She had to stop, as a spell of violent shivering passed over her. Drops were still running off her elbows, and the rising breeze carried no warmth. "Stubborn child," cried Grandma, in exasperation and worry. "I know a project means work for the kids, but what about the thing which that man said, about being an unproven vendor? He is right, granddaughter. The list of roads you've done isn't very ..."

> **subside**: to settle down and become less intense or forceful
> **elation**: a high joyfulness, often springing from the achievement of a triumph or the perception of good fortune coming your way
> **forensic**: (1) related to the processes of argument and proof used in public debates and legal proceedings; (2) related to the effort to gain

> information about an event by using the techniques of the medical sciences and the other sciences to find clues in the materials that remain from the event

There was another crack, another wall of water thrown high and crashing down about Merci. As the spray **subsided** two soaking figures stood beside her. For all the world it looked as though the deep sea had sent two sons to be her company. One placed a hand protectively on her shoulder and said, "I am thinking that already you are this proven vendor, Merci."

And the other, in a solemn tone, explained to the assembly at large, "You may trust the Cabbage. What was curled is now uncurled." He pointed dramatically and vaguely in the direction of the Mendicant Berries. Then, beckoning to Merci, he added, "And the little sea anemone here—she's one for one on crazy ideas."

Grandma Dubois called to him. "Say it again, Ricky." Her voice was a mixture of lingering worry about Merci and a sudden **elation** over the unexpected good news. "What has this girl done?"

Standing just behind Merci, as though to block the returning tide, Ricky declared, "She has saved the day. Against long odds. Because until two hours ago the situation at the briars was very bleak. The leaves were still curled tight. Tedesco was trying to pick up a signal, any signal. He was crawling through the vines in slow mo, like a sloth. But there was nothing. As for the Loser plants—I was starting to worry that even they would curl. The mystery vapor was about to sweep the series."

"And you, alien from the deep sea floor, what was your contribution?" The interruption came from Andrew Farnum, who had respected Ricky for many years as an unfailing source of odd behavior.

As always, Ricky gave good measure. "I was doing a fair imitation," he began, "of a **forensic** botanist." He pushed the wet hair back from his forehead. "I was examining the briar leaves, one by one, looking for DNA, carbon-14, or any other microscopic bits of evidence about ... about what was going on. Unfortunately, it led nowhere. But it kept me occupied until out of the blue, in our darkest hour, Tedesco announced that he was finally picking up something, an imperceptible stirring in the briars. Whatever it was, he liked it, because after a few minutes he told me that ... everything was going to be alright. Twenty minutes more went by, and everything, you know, started to be alright! Green yo-yos by the millions began unwinding. It was fists unclenching, scrolls unrolling. The briar leaves were at last feeling some protection, and that was all it took."

> **tutelary**: watching over and guarding someone, often someone who has been especially entrusted to your care

238

founder (verb): to become unable to keep standing or going forward; to collapse or sink down
sanguine: cheerfully and sometimes unrealistically confident that things will turn out well

After pausing a moment to let Grandma and the others absorb the news, Ricky continued. "And as you know, it was this girl, the one with the Pacific Ocean washing around her knees, who installed the protection, the nine million Loser plants, the immense, **tutelary** hedge, surpassed only by the Great Wall of China as far as engineering accomplishments go."

Again and again now the surface of the meeting stone was vanishing in the gray swirl of the tide. Through the churn left by one huge wave Peter Oakum took several laboring steps out toward the seaward edge, barely maintaining his balance. "Stop here," he warned himself at last, "before the good ship *Oakum* **founders**." Then he said to Merci, across the distance that still separated them, "In light of Ricky's testimony to your engineering abilities, and maybe even in sympathy to your frozen state, I'm reconsidering. But in heaven's name, young woman, why do you think you can build a road up the valley in any time short of a hundred years?"

Merci answered slowly, tightening her jaw so it wouldn't shake. "I didn't say build. This is not a road that needs to be built. I think it's already there. The road grader has already done its work—one of those glaciers of Mr. Ironbane—passing down the valley of the Bad Pony thousands of years ago. The road is there. Just let me have shovels for where the topsoil has gathered, and chisels to take down the rough spots, and of course the senior boys, and we'll give Mr. Bamalford his present by Christmas." She shivered hard. "And I am not being overly **sanguine**—it can really happen."

Povano had waded through the gray flood to stand by Oakum, and he gave a soft laugh. "Ha—I know I'm being overly sanguine, Merci, but I'm starting to believe you could pull it off. Your own grandmother may see it differently, and she can kill it if she wants. She's on the school board, and without big changes in the academic calendar you won't get your senior boys. But for my part—I'm going to approve it. It's a contract under ten K—ten K under ten K for that matter—so it's my call. Harrumph! As mayor of this town I now award to Merci Dubois, an obstinate and half-frozen minor, the contract for the road up the valley of the Bad Pony."

despotic: ruling with unlimited authority, often in an oppressive manner
trepidation: an anxiety or fearfulness that leaves you worked up, hesitant, fluttering
fatuous: empty-headed and silly; said or conceived without consideration of the way things really are

239

In the dark badlands of the surf, a big wave was overtaken by a bigger one and the two of them, now a single ridge of shadow, swept toward the stone. Povano saw it, in the dimmest outline, and lost no further time. "With the contract now in place," he declared, "the young lady is ordered, as are her companions, to come in at once. No debate, no discussion, no review by any other branch of government. The order is absolute, for in this matter I act **despotically**. Get in here!"

Merci answered "Thank you!" through chattering teeth and came running, even as the wave hurled itself with a booming report against the flank of the meeting stone. In a moment she was with her family, wrapped in sweaters and jackets and her grandmother's old shawl. Even Rachel came hurrying over to wind her woolen parka like a big mitten around the hands of her friend.

Povano knew that a last item of business remained, and his voice grew severe as he turned to face the landward side of the stone. "And now, Mr. Bamalford, let me hear it from you directly that you are with us again in the fight against Draco, and that the Captain Pariah comic strip, with its strange power of causing the inspector loss of nerve and general **trepidation**, will reappear in tomorrow's paper. You have your road, sir."

Bamalford and Nameless were standing on their chairs by this time, hunched like vultures and otherwise formless in their heavy overcoats, looking with distress at the swelling tide. "Who knows what I have?" growled Bamalford. "The **fatuous** promise of this silly juvenile, that's what. 'Give me some chisels, I'll carve a road.' Ha! If we get a goat path, we'll …"

> **colloquy**: a conversation, often a serious one entered into to exchange views on a subject
> **unilateral**: (applied most commonly to situations—a romance, or trade between nations, for example—in which there are two or more sides or parties) done by one party only, without the other parties joining in the action or taking some corresponding action
> **hitherto**: up until the present time

Nameless was tugging feebly at Bamalford's sleeve. The two of them bent their heads close together, almost pitching themselves into the gray streams as they did so. Not even Allen could catch what was said in that whispered **colloquy**, but it put a more calculating turn in Bamalford's manner. "Very well, Povano, Captain Pariah returns tomorrow. But he disappears again and for good the very first time I go up the Bad Pony canyon—and I'll be going often—and I see the infants building a make-believe road, a symbolic road, or anything less than a mean, ugly, real-life road, capable of bearing traffic at least as heavy as the limos which will carry Mr. Nameless to his mountain refuge, and the supply trucks which will bring him his … his supplies."

READER: Larry says it wouldn't be half bad being eponymous.

AUTHOR: We did use that one, didn't we?

READER: So he has **unilaterally** named something after himself.

AUTHOR: Like some **hitherto** nameless hill or stream, I suppose.

READER: No—like lunch. From now on three squares a day means breakfast, Larry and dinner.

AUTHOR: Well, it works for me. But he might want to check with the other half-billion English speakers in the world.

Chapter 35: THE PERENNIAL POUT

Early on the following morning Merci shook François from an exhausted sleep. "Genes may not be enough. I've never built a road, you know."

"Then go to the library and read a book," said François, only half awake.

Merci shook her again. "Exactly what I was thinking, but I'm scared of Bezzle. So you have to come."

> **morose**: gloomy and brooding; hostile to any attempts at cheerfulness
> **lien**: a legal right to take some specified item of a person's property (for example, his car) if he doesn't pay a debt

François struggled into full wakefulness. "I'm scared of Bezzle too, for that matter. He's so **morose**—like, if we smile, we die. We'd better call Meagan. She's good with grown-ups."

By 8:30 Merci, François and Meagan were passing through the stone pillars which formed the entry to Dropanchor's library. The place was empty, except for a lone figure tacking up a poster which read, "We can take your home! Pay now!"

It was Bezzle, Maurice Bezzle, Dropanchor's librarian. He turned at the sound of the girls and muttered, talking as much to himself as to them, "People will smirk—at first. They'll keep returning their books late, they'll scoff at the fines. But one day as they sit with their expensive coffee, half hidden in their daily paper, browsing through the legal notices, they'll see with horror that the library has slapped a **lien** on their house. And that's when they'll get slightly more serious about their overdues, isn't it, Morrie?"

> **stalwart**: strong, sturdy and dependable
> **undermine**: gradually to weaken the foundation of something, often to the point of making it collapse or otherwise destroying it
> **perennial**: lasting and lasting, maybe forever, without loss of force; always reappearing, season after season, year after year

He was forty-five or so, just under average height, with good breadth across the shoulders and a firmness in his step. His hair, though worn short, was still thick and dark. At the first sight of him people often thought—here is a **stalwart** fellow. But the impression was **undermined** by something unwholesome at work in his features—an offended, waiting look in the eyes, an angry set of the jaw, a pouching and curling around the mouth—in short, a pout. And because it was constantly there, in each new season, with each passing year, Meagan called it the **Perennial** Pout.

242

François explained in her gentlest voice—"My sister is going to make a road, Mr. Bezzle, a mountain road, and she needs a book that will discuss some of the fine points of road building, such as how to do it, for example."

> **asperity**: a bitter, rough-edged quality in your speech or manner
> **enigmatic**: expressed in riddles, or occurring in a mysterious way that defies comprehension
> **recess**: a nook or other interior area set back and away from a main area and often somewhat hidden

"Like a how-to book," added Merci, trying to be helpful.

At the mention of how-to books, Bezzle's face tightened with a look of pain and his eyes lost focus for a moment as though he had retreated into his thoughts. Then he looked at Merci again, and with the **asperity** of someone deeply indignant he said to her, "We both know where you're heading, don't we? I'm sure it's well rehearsed. You start with a text of one sort or other on how to build a mountain road. Once you build it, though, you've gotta use it, of course, so the next thing is for you to check out some title like *Driving ... whatever ... Driving the High Places*. But that's about cars, and a hard-hat girl like you will soon be back for one of our big manuals on trucks. And from trucks in general to the truck that is especially ours here in the west—that's a natural step, wouldn't you say? Which gets you where you wanted to be all the time, doesn't it, young lady—that monument of literature, *The Million-Mile Logger*, the bible for driving and servicing the big log trucks."

Bezzle's tone was so harsh, and what he said was so **enigmatic**, that Merci could only stare at him speechlessly. Her chin had dropped, and her eyes were wide with the most intense bewilderment. Oddly enough, that reaction, of all possible reactions, was the one that had the power to make Bezzle rethink his mysterious suspicions. "Maybe not, Morrie," he murmured to himself, "maybe not. You can't rehearse a look like that."

He remained bristly, but at least there were no riddles when he said, "We have the book you need. It doesn't circulate, however, and we check it after each use for smudges."

He disappeared into a **recess** that angled off obscurely from the back of the reading room, and as he did so Merci let out a soft Whew and looked to her sister. "If you weren't here, François, I would have cried. What was that?"

"It's OK now," said François gently, squeezing Merci's shoulder. "But as for me, I'm glad Meags was here. And really—how did we get on log trucks? What did happen anyway?"

> **construe**: to place an interpretation or reading on something such as a statement, behavior, symbolism, etc., that has multiple meanings

divulge: to make known something you have kept, or should have kept, as a secret
perusal: the act of reading through something, usually in a careful, searching manner; the act of giving something a careful looking through

Meagan had watched Bezzle closely during his little raving, and now she spoke with care as she tried to **construe** the strange words and manner of the librarian. "I think it was a playback," she said, "of the original wound. Generally, when there's a deep injury in the self-identity and for some reason it cannot heal, it starts to function like a script. Again and again it takes situations that should be no big deal and transforms them into, like, almost reenactments of the original event. Which means," she finished slowly, "that Mr. Bezzle, in a partial and confused way, and without meaning to, has **divulged** what happened, the dark chapter where he changed from a nice Bezzle to a sour, resentful one."

François started to respond, but there was no time. Bezzle was already returning with a big, sturdily bound book in his hands. It was the seventeenth edition of a classic work, *The Civil Engineer's Best Companion*. Merci saw at once that it was the book she had been searching for. She took it from Bezzle's hands, hurried to one of the large oak tables in the reading area, and with a scowl of concentration was soon engaged in a fierce **perusal** of the chapter about mountain roads.

Bezzle glared at her, maintaining a wounded silence. François went over and gave her an advisory punch on the shoulder. "I don't think we said thank you to Mr. Bezzle for bringing us this nice book."

arcane: hidden from the comprehension of ordinary people and known only by the masters of some art, science, creed, etc.
voracious: eager to devour a huge quantity of the stuff (food, literature, etc.) that satisfies your appetite
forlorn: sorrowful and without hope, often from a sense of being alone and abandoned

Merci looked up sharply. "It is a nice book. It's got some very **arcane** stuff, the secrets of the masters—the minimum radius for curves on slopes over five degrees, friction coefficients for asphalt, concrete and the common granites, and on and on. So I do thank you, Mr. Bezzle, like major, OK?"

Bezzle turned away with a little Hmphh! and busied himself again with the daily tasks of the library. François watched her sister returning to the book. It was a striking scene. Merci was **voracious**, consuming page after page of text, diagrams, and formulas, and never looking up.

244

"I'm starting to believe her story about the engineering genes," whispered Meagan.

"Oh, she's got them," answered François. "Every last one of them, in fact. Not a single one for the older sister. But that's OK because"—a **forlorn** note, ever so faint, crept into her voice—"because after all I got the ... umm ... and I was blessed with the ... umm ... and, of course, the nice smile."

Meagan gave her a gentle push. "Crazy child—you weren't overlooked when the gifts were passed out. You have that rare Dubois sense of refinement, as well as a slumbering courage and that nice smile you mentioned and ... and great earlobes."

François laughed. "Dynamite earlobes! I'll hang a spoon from them, like the mean lady on the hill. C'mon, let's explore while the gremlin here gobbles away."

> **abode**: the place where you stay and have your home
> **gargoyle**: a small monstrous or deformed figure, often carved in stone and constructed into the upper ledges of a building so as to stare down
> **superseded**: having become void and without further effect by reason of having lost place to something newer

They prowled quietly about the library. Like many of Dropanchor's buildings, its architecture repeated the falling and irregular lines of the land on which it was built. In spite of its classical entry, its interior was a tumbled assortment of galleries and nooks, odd angles and split levels. It was also the **abode** of a hideous, grinning creature, made of stone and staring down from a high ledge.

"What is that?" gasped Meagan.

"A **gargoyle**," said François with delight. She returned the gaze of the little beast. "Have you met Bamalford yet?" she asked cheerfully.

There were other discoveries: a room of old manuscripts, a huge nineteenth-century globe, leather-bound volumes of early laws—most of them long since **superseded**. When they finished their exploration, Merci was still sitting motionless, absorbed in her book to the exclusion of all else.

"She made us bring her here," said François, "and now she doesn't even know we exist. The little jerk!" She led Meagan out through the front door. "Let's snoop outside for a while."

As they began scrambling up the rising ground at the back of the library, she continued, "The age of discovery is never closed. There's another find waiting for us, I know there is."

> **prescience**: a special power of knowing what will happen before it does

245

accretion: a buildup or accumulation occurring through the gradual addition of more and more matter

It was just a few minutes later when Meagan's eyes widened with admiration and she said to her friend, "Excuse me, and expand the list—earlobes, nice smile, and **prescience**. Another find—yes ma'am!"

They had worked their way two hundred yards or so up the slope, along a slanting path that might once have been a logging road. Meagan had been predicting that an ocean lay beyond the summit, that perhaps they could claim it as their own, when the sudden dive of a gull caught their attention. At the bottom of its plunge they spied the glint of sunlight on metal.

It was near at hand, in a little grotto cut into the main fall of the hillside. They pushed away a tangled screen of vines and caught an imperfect glimpse of a vehicle. It was large and blocky, with exaggerated fenders and a long running board. A thick gauze of spiderweb lay across its windshield, and at its grill and mirror the wind of many seasons had left **accretions** of dust. In the broken light, and through a congestion of bluebottles, the image slowly resolved itself until Meagan exclaimed, "The bookmobile! We've discovered the bookmobile. You were right, François—one more big discovery. I thought this thing was just a myth. But no"—she wrinkled her nose at a sharp, salty odor that came breathing up from the vehicle—"it's too smelly to be a myth."

> **affable**: pleasant and friendly; welcoming conversation; easy to talk to
>
> **monger**: (often used in combined forms, such as fishmonger, ironmonger, etc.) an individual who carries on a trade acquiring and selling some item
>
> **threshold**: a heavy-duty slab of stone or wood which serves as the floor-piece in a doorway

"A curse on my high refinement," said François, drawing back with an exaggerated revulsion. "But there it is! I have heard so many stories about this monster—I think my mother did bake sales to help pay for it. Ages ago, when we were very little gargoyles, it carried books around, especially to the outlying farms. Bezzle was new here then, and much more **affable** I hear, a cheerful, approachable guy who wanted people to read. But then whatever happened happened and he went into his long funk, never to emerge, and the bookmobile was no longer to be seen bouncing along the roads of Dropanchor. Eventually it was rented out to a fish**monger**, and for two years its wooden shelves soaked up a mix of salt and lemon and fish oil, and soaked it up good, until they took on a briny smell which even today ..."

She was interrupted by a sharp yelp from the direction of the library. "How could you abandon me? I study my book for five minutes and you disappear."

They hurried back along the path they had ascended. Merci was there, at the door, tapping out an impatient beat on the **threshold**.

François held up her wrist and tapped out an equally impatient beat on the face of her watch. "Five minutes! How about five hours? Look here. Lunch time and then some."

> **petulant**: showing through grouchy words and spoiled behavior that you are in a bad mood
> **transcend**: to pass beyond some limited condition by rising into a plane of thought and action that is more noble, free, universal, etc.
> **respite**: a welcome break from some labor or difficult experience

Bezzle appeared at the door. His face was locked into its Perennial Pout, and his tone was **petulant** as he complained, "Librarians need lunch too, you know. And thanks for making mine late."

That struck an instant spark in Merci's eye. François whispered, "Watch out, Meags, the little warrior has drawn courage from somewhere—maybe her engineering book!—and she's about to launch."

It was courage, and impatience with petty tragedies, as Merci demanded in a stern tone, "Mr. Bezzle, do you know why libraries exist? I'm sure you do— to help us **transcend** our unlovely, day-to-day cares by rising into the king-dom of ideas. And I did it. I forgot time and lunch and everything, and spent five hours lost in a book."

Bezzle was caught off guard. "That's a … a noble mission, isn't it?" Like ugly weather lifting, the pout was clearing from his face. Such a relief, thought Meagan. "Like an unexpected holiday," said François later. But the **respite** was brief. In a moment the unhappy look was settling back in, and Bezzle was whining, "Nevertheless—I have my right to an on-time lunch, you know."

Merci tucked away her engineering notes and answered, "We'll see how many of the senior boys have an on-time lunch tomorrow."

She linked arms with François and Meagan and led them off. "Just get me the yellow bricks, and I'll do the rest."

AUTHOR: I hope Larry liked the part about the gargoyle.
READER: It got him going. He says that long ago gargoyles really existed, and that they caused the famous dinosaur extinction which everyone talks about.
AUTHOR: What does he say happened to the gargoyles?
READER: They evolved into humans.

Chapter 36: THE DISPARAGING EYEBALLS

Like many engineering triumphs in history, Victoria Road was a near miracle, encountering a series of towering difficulties which with luck and stubbornness and heroism were eventually **surmounted**.

> **surmount**: to find a way up and over some obstacle; to overcome
> **levity**: the act of treating a situation, often a serious one, in a light, joking fashion
> **unabashed**: still showing confidence and self-assurance, in spite of having to deal with embarrassing facts or with criticism and disapproval by others

The opening day began with promise but sank steadily toward disaster. Long before sunrise Merci was at East Bridge, and in the rough ground which ran up and out from it she began marking the line of the road. When the first daylight came stealing down, and the senior boys had formed a sleepy troop before her, she told them, "I know you are here from a variety of motives—some of you for the free breakfast, others for the free lunch. Well, the breakfast is yours just for showing up. But lunch will be on the road."

She walked seven or eight steps out from the end of the bridge. "On the road, and a ways down the road, twenty feet or so. If this spot where I am standing is road by noon, and all between is road, then there will be lunch."

"And if we cover twice the distance," yelled Lumps, "then we get seconds?"

Merci scowled. Her expressive eyebrows came pinching down. "We are setting out on a serious enterprise," she lectured, "with little or no room for **levity**."

Lumps was **unabashed**. "And if we mark the center stripe and paint the no-passing zones, then we get thirds."

> **auspicious**: giving a sign, or marked by a sign, that something which you have started will have a favorable outcome
> **proficient**: competent to an advanced degree in some art or line of activity
> **intact**: still holding together, whole and complete, without loss or disintegration

"This is no art project," shot back Merci. "It's one big piece of work, OK? And I think we should be starting." She picked up a hammer, a chisel, a pair of goggles, and walked over and placed them gently in the hands of Tedesco.

"Mount Relief seems to like you. So you are the one to lead off. Maybe on your first blow the stone will lift away like butter. Why not, right? And that would be an **auspicious** beginning, a sign, sort of, that this is a charmed and fail-proof project."

She pointed to the rough stone ground which stretched away from the bridge. "If we can smooth that out, knock down the high spots and fill in the low ones, it will be a road. And to do the job with hammer and chisel is not really all that weird. There are several examples in my engineering book."

Tedesco knelt and applied the chisel to a knob of stone—blackish-gray, glinting dully, one of the countless little bumps that made the terrain there so irregular. He struck a sharp blow, cleanly delivered, but the hammer sprang back and the chisel glanced away. The result was no better on his second and third attempt.

"I was afraid he'd violate his visa," came the mocking voice of Calvin, "by working in the USA. But no danger of that. Definitely no work so far."

Merci thrust a hammer and chisel into his hands. "Why don't you show how **proficient** you are as a stone cutter, Calvin. I'm sure you're a master or you wouldn't be entertaining us with this babble. And get those goggles on!"

Muttering that he was a member of the white-collar world, a rising star for that matter, and not a manual laborer, Calvin beat heavily at the piece of rock which had defied Tedesco. The blows might have been spring rain, for all the good they did. The rock remained **intact** and unmarked, and it threw such a vibration back along the chisel shaft that Calvin's hands were stung. "Stubborn, pigheaded old stone," he yelled, slamming down the tools. "Have it your own way!" He clutched his hands together in pain.

"Generally it's not fatal," said Lumps, coming forward for his turn. "But it can sure sting."

> **indomitable**: not able to be defeated or bent to someone's wishes, no matter how heavy the assault
> **debacle**: a total and disastrous failure, where everything goes wrong or collapses

He put on the goggles which Merci held out to him, and then crouched by the undefeated rise of stone and ran his fingers slowly around its base. "There," he said at last, with satisfaction, "there's the seam." He set the chisel carefully at the spot where his fingers had paused, and drew the hammer back. Both tools looked small in the powerful hands. It was plain to see that this would be the definitive contest, the one to show if the stone was **indomitable**. When the hammer fell, there was little effort visible in the blows it struck, but they were smart and insistent. Slowly the chisel's blade sank into the rocky mass until with a tearing sound a chunk the size of a bread loaf lifted away from the ground.

Joannie, who was there in her unofficial role as Merci's environmental adviser, cheered. "He looks like someone who has built roads before."

Lumps apparently liked the compliment, for he gave a big smile. "Thank you," he said humbly, "but it's probably just a natural gift."

That was the pattern for the morning. Lumps had some additional successes, prying loose a number of low knobs and ridges of basalt, most in the new roadway, but some—to Merci's exasperation—lying outside it. For the other seniors, though, success was rare, and the first attempt at road building was mainly a **debacle** of escaping chisels, cracked or broken hammers, smarting wrists and fruitless effort.

> **dexterity**: (1) a quickness and skillfulness in moving the hands through the motions required by some complicated task; (2) more generally, a quick and expert skillfulness in carrying through some task
> **avail** (noun): the help you get from some resource which you call upon or some effort which you make (often used in negative phrases such as "to no avail")
> **incorrigible**: stubbornly disobedient; rejecting all discipline and correction

Ricky had an especially rough time of it. The **dexterity** which made him so quick at dialing phones or blowing through websites was of little **avail** here. His hammer grew intolerably heavy, and his chisel was like an **incorrigible** child, darting off in every direction, refusing to be brought into line. Toward the end of the day he was working on a particularly bad little knuckle of stone. Spending the last of his strength he brought the hammer down in a final, do-or-die effort. With a loud ping the chisel shot away and licked across the back of his hand, drawing a few beads of blood from a long, shallow scratch.

> **start** (verb): to jerk or flinch involuntarily at the sight of something imposing or scary
> **disparage**: to talk about, or otherwise react to, something in a way suggesting that it is of low status or inferior worth

He **started** at the sight of the wound, and started again when he saw the two circles of white staring at him. Bamalford was there, he had been watching all the while. His eyebrows were lifted high in disapproval, his mouth and cheeks were pulled down in contempt, and the effect was to lay bare the whites of the eyes in a much fuller expanse than is common. "The **Disparaging** Eyeballs," murmured Ricky to himself, knowing that disparaging speech was soon to follow.

minuscule: extremely small

tyro: one who is just beginning to learn some skill and is still awkward in the practice of it

"Well," huffed the portly figure, "this road will be good news for the bandage companies—and the joke writers. Look here, all of you, and especially you—the little goblin engineer, you've been at this silliness for half a day now, and your progress is so **minuscule** that after a month at this pace we'll still have a road that's wider than it is long."

"Then we named it well," fired back Merci, using her hands to model a wide-waisted woman on the air.

The heavy lips pulled themselves down even farther on Bamalford's face, and the eyeballs rolled with yet greater scorn. "A rude, uncultured girl, raised by wolves perhaps. And obviously a **tyro** at road building, a rookie."

The slur on her manners was not a problem for Merci, but being called a rookie was. Her chin set and a blaze kindled in her fine blue eyes. Seizing a hammer and chisel she attacked the stump of rock where Ricky had been working. She pounded savagely, to the point of exhaustion. But the rock held fast.

Bamalford watched it all, shaking his head, and repeating, "Tsk, tsk!"

———————————

AUTHOR: Well, that should satisfy the safety people—Merci's got the whole road crew wearing goggles.

READER: So far, so good, but what about earplugs, kneepads, mosquito repellent, sunscreen, respirators and steel-toed shoes?

AUTHOR: Whoa! Where did you come from? This is an action novel. I can't have it clunking along like a safety manual.

READER: If this is an action novel, my plastic kazoo from the forty-eight-ounce box of Wheat Swatches is a saxophone.

AUTHOR: You didn't need to say that.

Chapter 37: THE ASSIDUOUS PILE DRIVERS

The theory that moonlight softens basaltic rock has few, if any, supporters among serious geologists. Yet there was a moon that night, after Merci and the others descended, a fat, fifteen-sixteenths moon that rose orange and big above the eastern range. And beneath that moon the stone was softer—or at least that's what you would have said if you had seen it giving way under the toil of the phantom who appeared there.

> **invincible**: successfully resisting all attacks; not able to be overcome
> **extol**: to praise with enthusiasm and high compliments
> **mottled**: marked or textured with uneven spots and patches of different colors or shadings

He came slipping across East Bridge in the last dusk, a hammer hanging from one side of his belt, a leather pouch with chisels from the other, and he fell to work on the humps of stone which had been so **invincible** during the day. One by one they tore away under the rhythm of the blows. Hour after hour it continued, the sure repetition of setting and striking, and the easy, swinging toss of the broken stone, until by three in the morning Victoria Road was longer, by at least fifteen feet, than it was wide. Darlingson rested from his work, sitting by the heap of rubble which he had created.

Before long the night airs carried to him the sound of footsteps, approaching East Bridge, crossing it, not in any particular hurry. A tall figure stepped onto the new roadbed, walking it from start to finish with a careful, measuring pace. "What an incredible night's work!" The voice was encouraging, calm, unmistakably that of Ironbane. "Really—work on a heroic scale. It needs somehow to be ... **extolled**. We'll ask Ricky to do one of his poems—he'll turn you into a modern-day legend. Now one other thing—was it easier as you went along?"

Darlingson smiled at the question. He knew what Ironbane was driving at. Rising up wearily, he searched about in the mound of broken stones that had piled up during his work, and pulled out two large fragments. One was noticeably darker than the other, even in the moonlight. He set the darker one at the point where he had begun hammering some hours before, and the lighter one where he had finished. In between the two was almost twenty-five feet of roadway, and at the midpoint of that he placed a third piece of stone, **mottled** in appearance, with an alternation of dark and light patches.

> **pedagogy**: (1) the art of helping people learn; (2) a carefully developed style of teaching
> **heterogeneous**: not made of the same stuff all throughout; incorporating elements that are different in kind from one another; showing contrasting qualities from one point to another
> **prevail**: to emerge as the most powerful force and thus to obtain some victory; to be predominant in the sense of being the most widely or frequently encountered

Ironbane nodded in admiration. "Now that's **pedagogy**. Not a word spoken, but a great deal taught."

He walked to the darkest of the three fragments which Darlingson had set down. "Tell me if I got the lesson. At this spot, the very beginning of Merci's road, we're on basalt, stubborn, heartbreaking basalt. But the geology of this flank of the mountain is very **heterogeneous**—a mere ten or fifteen feet up the canyon, at your middle fragment, the black basalt is giving way to a sedimentary rock, some kind of sandstone, light in color and much more workable under the chisel. Finally, at the farthest fragment the basalt has disappeared, the sandstone—mercifully—has **prevailed**. I know for you it's all one—sandstone, basalt, granite, molybdenum—but for the young road builders, muttering in their dreams even as we speak, this is great news."

> **evocation**: an artful representation that calls up before the mind the image of some reality
> **divination**: the act of guessing or perceiving with strange accuracy and insightfulness something that is hidden or obscured
> **rout** (noun): a total defeat in which the losing forces are thrown into confusion

The moon, by now, hung far out over the sea, sinking slowly down. As Ironbane turned his face toward it he seemed to remember that as of yet he'd had no rest that night. "For the sleepy man," he murmured, "everything is an **evocation** of sleep. What I see portrayed in this moon of ours is a little kid, a round-faced child, tired out and coming to lie down. And the ocean is the silver cradle."

He said good-by to Darlingson and slipped away to catch a bit of rest before the new day began. Darlingson himself, gathering his tools, soon vanished as well.

An hour later, in the last of the moonlight, Merci arrived. Seeing the enormous labor which had occurred during the night, she said to Joannie, who had met her in the quiet streets, "With my astonishing power of **divination** I guess that it was … Darlingson."

"Very challenging divination," scoffed Joannie. "Isn't Darlingson always there, watching out for the Dubois kids? So … are you mad?"

"Mad because he built part of my road? Not really. We got killed yesterday in the black stone. Troops demoralized, total defeat, a **rout**. Only Lumps scored some minor victories, and not all of them stayed inside the lines. So I'm not mad—we needed some help. And I doubt if any of the worker bees will be mad."

> **notwithstanding**: in spite of
> **contrite**: sad in the knowledge that you've hurt someone or done something wrong
> **proprietary**: having the character of private property, owned by one person and off-limits to others

When Lumps arrived not long after and saw by the first paleness of morning that the most obstinate stretch of basalt had been leveled, he was mad, **notwithstanding** Merci's prediction. He went and found Darlingson at the dockyards, and complained, "It's not fair if you hog all the tough stuff. This is my chance, OK. Next time there's a hard mission on this road, before you make it a hundred percent Darlingson job, please give me a shout..." He stopped, **contritely**. "Sorry, wrong thing to say. Please clap, OK, clap sharply and I'll be there."

Darlingson was like ... something, maybe a huge oak at the brow of a hill, strong and weathered by many seasons. He wasn't particularly upset at the little scolding. And he understood what was going on—how Lumps his friend was changing, needing to take his place and show at last that the clown was more than that. All this was as it should be, and Darlingson was glad to see it. Then and there he honored the request which had been made of him, giving a sharp clap, and a second one, and in this way saying that in the future there would be nothing **proprietary** about challenges on the road project, that they would not belong to him alone but would be shared with Lumps in common.

> **itinerant**: moving about regularly from place to place, often in order to carry on your trade or profession
> **perspicacity**: a sharpness and perceptiveness in your understanding of complicated situations
> **pile** (noun): a post driven firmly in the ground and helping to hold up some structure placed on top of it

It was a little more than two months later, in the shortened light of a late November day, before Lumps again heard that clap. He scarcely recognized it at first. He was with the road gang, half caught in the music to which they had grown accustomed, the rhythm of chisels on stone, accompanied by the clear voice of Ms. Jensen, now an **itinerant** teacher following her students and reading them lessons wherever she found them. It was history today. Across an-

254

cient Britain a network of roads was under construction by the Romans, masters at compaction of the subsoil and the use of...

Clap! This time Lumps heard it. He looked up and saw a strange sight, Darlingson standing waist-deep in the torrent of the Bad Pony, at a point some ways upstream from the road gang. He had a heavy metal bar, pointed, and perhaps five feet long, which for the moment was standing on end, half in the water and half out, penned in the enclosure made by his arms as he clapped.

For all his reputation as a clown, Lumps possessed a great **perspicacity** on the physical order of things, a quick intuition where mass and motion and distance were at play. He made sense almost at once of the strange scene before him.

"A **pile**," he declared to anyone who would listen. "The hour has come for driving a pile."

It was not an evident conclusion, but it was correct. Since the disastrous opening day in September, the work had gained momentum. The road had progressed rapidly up the canyon, along the east bank of the Bad Pony. It was drawing near, however, to Instant Sorrow, the footbridge coming over from Ms. Framley's land. From that point upwards, the east bank was difficult, a narrow strip pinched in by the canyon wall and cluttered with outcroppings and boulders that were simply too big for the primitive tool kit of hammer, chisel and crowbar.

> **expedient** (noun): some procedure or device (sometimes invented on the spot, and often adopted after more normal or more acceptable means haven't done any good) that helps you achieve an end or respond to a problem
> **pristine**: still in some original and pure condition; not stained or worn down or cheapened by excessive human use or contact
> **alacrity**: an eagerness and swiftness in responding to a call or performing a task

Dynamite could have cleared a way through the forbidding terrain, but no one, Merci least of all, wanted to fall back on that **expedient**. The idea was to tread lightly, leaving the canyon nearly as **pristine** as before the project started. In these circumstances, the only workable option was the opposite side of the stream—the road would need to cross onto the western bank.

To cross by the existing bridge—Instant Sorrow—would never work. That structure was too narrow, and it spanned the stream with no support. A new bridge was needed—wider, and sturdy enough for traffic. And for these virtues it would require a support on which its weight could rest, a column or pile positioned at midstream.

Lumps saw these things clearly, and in their light he understood at once why the clap had come from Darlingson, standing there at the center of the Bad Pony. This was a prize—a summons to be part of a hard and desperate mission, the setting of the pile—and he responded with **alacrity**, jumping to his feet, dashing to the stream bank. There he found a heavy sledgehammer. Taking it in hand he waded into the stream, pushing his way out through its cold sweep to a spot beside Darlingson.

> **precarious**: especially at the mercy of outside forces, and thus poised on the brink of some change or misfortune which those forces may bring about
> **stratum**: a layer, often in the geologic sense of a layer of one type of stone bounded on the top and bottom by a layer of some different type of stone

Part of the work was just keeping position. The footing was **precarious**, with the smooth bottom offering no hold, and the swift current tugging at them ceaselessly. "At least it doesn't breed mosquitoes," said Lumps, hardly knowing what he was saying.

The main work, pecking out a deep, narrow hole into which a post could be driven and wedged, promised to be as tough as anything he had ever done. The quiver in the iron bar, as it took the first hammer blows, showed clearly how resistant the streambed was going to be. The fact was that the bed did not lie in the workable layer of sandstone and occasional marble where the road had made such progress in the past nine weeks. The Bad Pony had eroded away that user-friendly **stratum**, as Allen called it, revealing again the shield of black basalt which had turned the first day of road building into misery.

Their labor quickly settled into a pattern. Lumps would bring the sledge down thirty times on the iron bar, while Darlingson held it steady. Then they would reverse roles, and Darlingson would give thirty more blows. After the hammer had changed hands between them a dozen times or so in this way, they would come ashore to rest, exhausted.

> **propensity**: a compelling tendency (often part of your basic makeup) toward some particular activity
> **tenuous**: weak and thin, without sufficient body; just barely effective, and apt to fail at any moment

On the seventh shift Lumps proved that cold and fatigue were not enough to break his **propensity** for poorly timed jokes. "Hey, Merci," he shouted above the swift chattering of the water. "I had this outrageous idea that ..." He had turned slightly toward her—she was there on the bank—and that turning cost him everything. A few more inches of him were exposed to the current, and the grip of his toes on the smooth stream bottom, already so **tenuous**, was lost in an instant. He was swept away.

Yelling and thrashing, he was a hundred yards downstream in moments. "That could be all the way to the beach," cried Joannie in alarm, but in fact the journey ended abruptly, with a fingertip grab, as Lumps caught a crook of stone which bent out over the water. Merci was the first to reach him, clinging to some brambles with one hand and stretching toward him with the other to help pull him in. Seeing that he was unharmed, she asked tartly, "So what was the outrageous idea?"

"Dunno," he said, motioning weakly toward the torrent. "It dropped off in there, I think."

> **titan**: a person who is giant in size, forcefulness or achievement
> **assiduous**: sticking to a task or other activity with great attentiveness and persistence
> **bizarre**: so strange and outside the normal course of things as to be rather shocking

Shaking himself once or twice he began trudging back up the stream. Darlingson walked beside him, making sure he was OK. They were a pair of **titans**, and Allen caught a photo of them just as they splashed into the water, leaning forward against the current, intent upon returning to their work. When the photo appeared the next day in the high school paper, it was over the caption, The **Assiduous** Pile Drivers. It was a heroic picture, destined to show up eventually in restaurants and pubs all around Dropanchor. In the near term, though, it prompted a **bizarre** reaction.

> **excise** (verb): to remove something in a clean, trim fashion by cutting it out
> **infinitesimal**: too small even to be measured; small to the point of vanishing

Bamalford ran the very same photo in the *Vociferous Beacon* on the following day, with one modification: the figure of Darlingson was completely **excised** and the resulting blank was skillfully drawn over to look like a continuation of the landscape. The text with the photo described Lumps as the Assiduous Pile Driver and praised him for his persistence and close attention on a project "suffering generally from laziness, fumbles and lack of vision."

"The photo was for the text, and the text was for hurting Merci," said François. She was with Joannie and Meagan. They worked frequently on the road now, and at the moment they were taking a rest, sitting where the road met the stream, and discussing what Bamalford had done.

Joannie disagreed. "He's jealous of Allen. It was a stupid slam on Allen."

And Meagan had still another opinion: "It's the battle for the soul of Lumps."

READER: Larry took a poll of the purchasers of this book, and the majority would like to see something romantic develop between Lumps and Merci.

AUTHOR: I'm not sure these things proceed on democratic principles.

READER: Respect thy readers. Twenty-two were in favor, only one against, and four undecided.

AUTHOR: Hmm. Twenty-seven altogether. We saw that number a while back. I assume by now it's an **infinitesimally** small sample of the total number of people who have bought the book.

READER: No. That still is the total number, including several who got it with expiring frequent-flyer miles.

AUTHOR: Hmm ... maybe a Super Bowl ad.

Chapter 38: THE LACONIC LIST

On a morning in early March Mayor Povano stood on a simple platform, brushing snowflakes from his eyebrows, turning up his collar against the fitful wind, and looking out over the people of Dropanchor. Everyone was exhausted. The road had been completed only two days before.

> **conscription**: the process of drafting someone into service, usually by force of law or some other authority
> **augmentation**: the process of making something bigger, more numerous or more complete; the growth or increase resulting from that process
> **efface**: to minimize or erase the distinctive marks of something so that it disappears or ceases to be noticed ("Self-effacing" means making an effort to assure that your good points and accomplishments attract as little attention or praise as possible.)

At the end of the project something like universal **conscription** had reigned. The mayor had called out his citizens, young and old, and sent them to report to Merci on the mountainside. This was a major **augmentation** of her road gang, and she did not complain. It let her finish off what Lumps and Darlingson had started many weeks before, the bridge carrying the road onto Ms. Framley's property. It gave her the labor force as well for the immense toil of widening the zigzag trail that ascended the Steeps. And on the high tableland where the Bad Pony ran in many channels, it helped her make short work of the final stretch of the project.

When that last piece was done—a long curve out and around the crisscross of streams, past the mouth of Mercurial Canyon, and then back in toward the bluff on which the Mendicant Briars grew—Merci had gone and found Mayor Povano. "Sir, the little road is finished. Not long, not wide, not sophisticated—but it's the best I can do."

Povano had laughed at this self-**effacing** description. "The little road? It's a superhighway. And even though it was built to humor the … the not very lovable Mr. Bamalford and his Nameless Entrepreneur friend, now that it's finished we'll pass out some T-shirts, make a video, and have a … a little nothing of a speech by the mayor."

> **improvise**: to put something together through a creative use of whatever materials happen to be at hand; to come up with some arrangement or solution on the spot and without a plan or set of instructions to guide you

lucidity: the excellence by which something written or spoken is especially clear and laid open for the mind to comprehend

And so, two days later, Povano stood before his people on an odd platform, **improvised** for the occasion from boards and barrels and some chunks of granite. The setting was the high tableland, at the point where the long arc of the road touched closest to Mercurial Canyon. Snow was falling, one of the few storms that year, and it enclosed the scene and muffled the mayor's voice as he began. "I noticed on the way up that the SPM Index for this road has turned out quite high."

"Marion," interrupted Grandma Dubois, "what have you got against **lucidity**, that you talk for ten seconds and throw us all into confusion?"

"Ma'am," returned the mayor, "one interruption every ten seconds and this spring blizzard will turn us into statuary before I'm through. SPM, of course, means signs per mile. This is a road with a lot of signs. At the very start, just off East Bridge, is one which says simply Road. I guess Merci put up that one in case people look at what she's done and not know it's a road."

"Well, it's more than a goat trail," commented Grandma, "unless our goats have gotten big as elephants."

chimerical: too monster-like, magical, idealistic or otherwise extreme to be real; conceived by a wild flight of imagination
embellishment: a little addition you make to a story, a garment, a building, etc., to leave it more beautiful or dramatic

Povano peered about nervously through the falling snow. "**Chimerical** mega-goats to join our Chimerical Mega-Duck. This would be just the weather. Anyway—let me go on. Now I'm driving up the road—mentally, of course—and I'm seeing altitude signs, falling-rock signs, buckle-up signs, and so on. And now I'm crossing that bridge where Lumps and Darlingson drove the pile, I'm onto Ms. Framley's land, there's a forest of signs. Victoria Road— seven or eight times. And lots of warnings—Stay inside the Lines, Do Not Allow Fenders to Swing across Lines, Intruders Will Be Used as Lawn Ornaments, and more of the same. Friendly **embellishments**, you might say, on a simple No Trespassing message."

"Careful, you old gabbler," came a gravelly warning from Ms. Framley, "or I'll put in a toll booth."

check (verb): to bring some motion or action to a halt, often in a sharp, decisive manner
serpentine: marked by bends and twisting curves
facetious: said as a joke; intended to get a laugh

260

Grandma started to say something about putting in a weigh station, but Povano **checked** her and went on. "Then there was a pair of signs, one at the bottom of the Steeps and one at the top, each with the message **Serpentine** Conditions. And though you may complain that it's a bit ... poetic, you will have to agree that as the road ascends the Steeps it is a serpentine affair ... and also as it descends, for that matter. So thank you, Merci, wherever you may be in this crowd, for the literary touch—I am assuming you were the author."

A white glove waving, and seen only because it was waving, revealed where she was. "A little compensation," she called through the snow, "for all the English classes I missed."

Povano raised his eyebrows for a moment, and then continued. "The last sign I noticed as we hiked up was a hand-held one, a circle of plywood on a broomstick, lying by the side of the road. I can almost see it from here. One side says Slow, and the other says Slower. I'm guessing it was **facetious**, someone's little joke. Maybe yours again, Merci?"

> **indolence**: a distaste for work and an attraction to ease and idleness
> **eradicate**: to yank something out by its roots

"No, no, no," said Merci emphatically, wagging her index finger back and forth. "That was Lumps, all Lumps. He would stand at the side of the road, telling the nonexistent traffic to go slow and slower—while everybody else was working and ..."

"Sister, that's not exactly fair," broke in François. "You make it sound like a case of **indolence**. But he did his share. And far more than his share when something really hard was involved—remember the pile."

Merci hated being corrected by her older sister. "I didn't say he was lazy. He just had to be comic boy all the time."

Lumps was stung. He had taken the road building seriously, and so far as he was concerned this basic fact had not been compromised by some occasional clowning to relieve the tedium of the work. "Is there a campaign against humor around here," he demanded, "like it has to be **eradicated**—weed-free gardens, humor-free public works? What about your sign, Merci? Didn't you get sort of humorous in your sign, with that 'serpentine' stuff?"

> **spitefulness**: a nasty dislike that I have for someone, driving me to seize little opportunities to humiliate or otherwise afflict him
> **aloof**: keeping your distance from others, in the sense that you share very little of yourself with them, and care very little what's happening with them

"Well at least," she fired back, "I waited until the road was finished."

"And at least," added Calvin, taking the little quarrel to a new level of **spitefulness**, "she knows how to read her sign."

Merci saw Lumps go pale, and without the waste of an instant she told Calvin fiercely that she didn't need that kind of help—but it was too late.

"And at least," roared Lumps, furious at Calvin's taunting but laying it to Merci's account as though she had unleashed it, "at least I didn't get a wart on my thumb, did I?"

This time it was Merci who gasped with pain—there was in fact a large wart growing on her right thumb, a recent appearance which she had concealed as best she could. Now with her shame publicly proclaimed, she was sure that everyone was staring at her. It was an awful feeling, and she lashed out blindly. "I hate you, Lumps!" she cried.

Through the milling snow a sound forced its way, terrible and gargling. "Ha-har-hargh! The little czarina!" The words were coming up the throat as the vitamin elixir was going down. "The little empress. She was always so **aloof**, so distant from we of the common clay, and now she has sprouted a wart. And the glove ... the snotty white glove ... it was really ..." The rest was lost in a rush of guttural laughter.

Grandma Dubois was there, suddenly, protectively, settling a cloak over Merci's slumping shoulders, throwing a warning look at Victoria Framley, and all at the same time addressing the mayor in a charged voice. "Marion, I think there's a wart growing on the community, but be that as it may, you were in the middle of a speech and ought to resume."

Povano let out a sigh. "Great fun, eh? Perhaps I should have skipped the Slow-Slower sign. Whew! It's not a real road sign anyway, I mean it's not planted in the ground as a permanent fixture, it's just lying there, and someday when we pick up our room we'll ..."

> **digression**: the act of getting off the point, of wandering away from the main subject matter in a speech, essay or conversation
>
> **appeasement**: the act of giving someone what he wants and in this way causing him to stop threatening or practicing hostilities toward you
>
> **eulogy**: a speech or writing, often formal in tone, in which the character traits or community services of a person are highly praised

"Marion," Grandma said sternly, "are we slipping into a **digression**? Could we get back on track?"

"Right-o," said Povano. "Back on track." He let his tired eyes sweep across the crowd. Merci was still in the shelter of the cloak. Calvin had on a metallic smile. Lumps, utterly dismayed to have set Ms. Framley loose on Merci, was close to tears.

262

"A fine, boring speech will do all of them good," muttered Povano to himself. "So let us begin." He lifted his voice. "History is never kind to the appeasers, you know. And this road is an **appeasement**. We gave it to Bamalford to make him stop hating us and threatening us over the Farbugle incident. Sometimes it's all you can do. Funny thing, though—as a kid I never dreamed of growing up and becoming an appeaser. I wanted to be an engineer."

· With that transition Povano turned to Merci. He delivered a long **eulogy** on her engineering talents. He thanked her and the senior boys, Lumps especially, and Darlingson and all the citizens for carving out the masterpiece commonly known as Victoria Road. "I could go on," he concluded at last, brushing an accumulation of snow from his hair, "but after three zillion scrillion snowflakes I'm convinced that no two are alike, I don't need any further proof, so let's get out of here."

"Very clever," shouted Peter Oakum through the swirling air, "but not so fast. We want to see the little ceremony with the list."

> **incongruity**: a striking inconsistency or lack of proportion between two things
> **laconic**: stingy with words; expressing your idea with the fewest possible words
> **ingenuity**: the resourcefulness and sharpness of wit by which you come up with clever solutions

"Oh bother," growled Povano. "You are amused by small things."

Joannie shouted, "The list, the list!" and others took up the cry.

Murmuring that it was very ridiculous, Povano drew a small slip of paper from his pocket. It stayed in his hand for only a second. Oakum snatched it, after a rush up to the platform, and held it up for everyone to see. "This is a marvelous **incongruity**. When he speaks, our mayor goes on forever, until he's stopped by the tide or the snow. But when he writes—look! The **Laconic** List. This is Dropanchor's agenda—a list of major projects—and it's only four words long. Stingy, stingy."

Povano had pulled out a pen, and now he threatened, "Be careful or I will add a fifth—namely Exile—as a reminder to send you into exile, Peter."

Oakum laughed. "I'd slip back in with the next cargo of pigs. But look here, Marion. The first word on your list—Berries—and next to it a box with an X in it ..."

"Quite obviously," said the mayor, "that refers to the problem we have had with the Mendicant Briars. And the X is a check-off, meaning the problem appears to have been solved by the **ingenuity** of Merci and Joannie—you know, that clever wall of arm-waving Loser plants. And ... well, yes ... there might be an opening, my friend, for ..."

263

"For an arm-waving old chap like myself," finished Oakum. "And that's very cruel of you. But now to the business at hand. The second word on your Laconic List is Road."

"And if you'll return the blasted thing to me," growled Povano, taking back the list, "I'll put a big X next to that word, to show that the road is completed."

> **banter** (verb): to talk with someone in a lighthearted way, with quick, witty exchanges and often with teasing
> **anarchy**: the chaos resulting from the absence of effective law and governing authority

When he had done so, a loud cheer went up from the people. The road was truly finished when Povano checked it off on his list. Strangely, though, Peter Oakum, who had thoroughly enjoyed **bantering** with his friend over the last few minutes, had fallen quiet, and his face had assumed a little frown. "Marion," he said, "let me see that list again. I ... don't understand the third word."

READER: You wrote that Merci is always "so distant from we of the common clay." It should be "from us of the common clay."

AUTHOR: It was sort of Ms. Framley's fault.

READER: Breaking the rules of grammar is the beginning of **anarchy**. Next come bad table manners, refusal to pay library fines, disregard for traffic laws, contempt for elected officials, looting of public granaries, and so on until at last there are no more rules, no more government, just chaos.

AUTHOR: I will be more careful in the future!

Chapter 39: UNSCIENTIFIC MISGIVINGS

"I've read it backwards and forwards," said Peter Oakum, staring at the third word on Povano's list, "and it really does look like Decoy. With the road finished, Marion, and spring hidden just behind this storm, your thoughts are riveting themselves, I'm sure, on whales and Whalefest, and getting them to come to it. Would you just assure me that ... that you don't have some wild-haired, **outlandish**, hopelessly weird scheme to set a decoy for the whales."

> **outlandish**: very alien and unusual; wildly contrary to accepted styles and manners
> **incumbent** (adjective): having the nature of a duty that is pressing on you, often one that goes along with some position of responsibility
> **skittish**: nervous, hesitating and jumpy

Povano shook his head slowly. "If you could assure me, Peter ..."

"Oh, I knew it, I knew it," cried Oakum. "A decoy for the whales! I don't want to say this, but it's **incumbent** on me to say it nevertheless. Luring live whales into our bay with a fake one, with some plastic or inflatable model—well, that's tacky, and contrary to the spirit of Whalefest. There—I've done my duty as one who loves this town and her festivals."

Povano beckoned vaguely toward the falling snow. "You don't need a decoy for this stuff. It comes anyway. But the whales aren't like that. Talk to the one who calls them—Grandpa Lumps. He thinks they're becoming hesitant to enter the bay. They're nervous and **skittish**. For several years now, he says, it's been getting harder to call them in at Whalefest."

"You'd be skittish too," returned Oakum, "if you had to swim into the bay with a forty-foot statue of Bamalford staring down at you."

> **censorious**: telling people, in a severe and condemning way, that they have done wrong
> **hedonistic**: habitually pursuing pleasure as the supreme good in life

"There, Peter, there!" answered Povano. "It could indeed be the statue. The thing is so ... **censorious**. Those big eyes, with rebuke and condemnation streaming out! Maybe that is what's spooking the whales. The main thing, though, is that they're spooked—that at least is getting more and more clear. So we need to send the message that things are still safe around here."

"And to do that you want to put some blimpy-looking decoy in the bay? That's really what you want?"

"I don't want to," groaned the mayor, "I don't want to at all. But we may have to if any whales are going to come to Whalefest this year. But since you asked what I want—well, a scone, some jam, a hot chocolate, that's what I want, a few pleasures of that sort. None of which by the way is available on this freezing mountain, so can we please get down from here?"

"What a poor example for the children," laughed Oakum, "a **hedonistic** mayor, living only for pleasure. I'm sorry—you must delay your gratification another moment, until we talk about the fourth word. And don't imagine that the decoy topic won't come up again, either."

"The fourth word?" asked Povano, passing over the rest of what Peter had said.

"Yes—the fourth word on your four-word list. Prima. What's Prima, and is it something we will like?"

> **altercation**: a heated quarrel; a loud, angry exchange of words
> **incarcerate**: to put a person in jail or other confinement
> **ephemeral**: lasting only for a short time and then passing away

"The word 'prima,' my good Pedro, means first, and that is short for first lady, and to avoid an **altercation** on the subject, with everyone screaming in everyone's face, I will dispense with democracy for a second and simply appoint her. Merci, you will be the first lady of Whalefest this year, first to harvest the berries, first to taste the cider made from them. And—if the creatures show up—first to keep watch over the whales. Do you accept, or do I have to **incarcerate** you for thirty years?"

Merci smiled weakly. "François would have to visit every day. But ... I do thank you, and I do accept, though on one condition. I am first lady only on account of the road, and not because of what—as a girl—I called my extraordinary beauty." She glanced sadly at her right hand. "Because that beauty was very **ephemeral**, its day was very short, and now it's just a remembrance, ruined by ... by ..."

> **vestige**: a trace or remainder carrying over from something that has otherwise disappeared
> **impinge**: to strike up against something, usually with sufficient sharpness and focus to make an impression

"By a wart," laughed Povano gently. "Well, young woman, don't surrender completely to despair. I'm sure some small **vestige** of that beauty remains. But to the point—your condition is granted. You are the first lady in honor of your service. And the honor is surely due. In fact, my plan was that you would be driven to this ceremony today by a uniformed chauffeur in a limousine, the first car to go on Victoria Road. But Dropanchor is temporarily out of limos, drivers and uniforms, so I let you come hiking."

Merci was cheered by the mayor's shuffling good humor, and said in a voice that had recovered much of its strength, "I may never come by car on this road. Why spoil a good walk?"

"That is just how most of us feel," added Grandma. "The only motorist may be that Nameless Entrepreneur character. And even about him I have serious doubts—I mean, whether he'll find the stamina for the trip."

"Well then," snarled Ms. Framley, breaking in suddenly, "there's a sight that will shut your beak, you suspicious old toucan." She was pointing down the road. Through the blowing snow, the rounded form of an enormous red sedan was materializing. The wind carried off the sound of the motor and left nothing to **impinge** on hearing, so the car's approach was silent and ghostly.

The emergence of the huge auto from the veils of snow took Povano off guard. "Peter, Clara," he said nervously, "I can't see who the driver is. In fact, I can't see any driver at all. You don't think…?"

"Marion," answered Peter briskly, "you can't see the driver because the windshield is fogged. It's as simple as that."

As the car pulled steadily closer, there was a sharp blast on the horn, as though to warn those in the way to scatter or else.

"That's gotta be Bamalford," muttered Peter.

It was indeed Bamalford. He was at the wheel, and Nameless Entrepreneur was in the passenger seat. Nameless, however, was less interested in blowing the people of Dropanchor off the road than in jabbering to them for a moment. As the crowd parted just enough to give passage to the red sedan, he laboriously rolled down his window and in a weak voice, heard only by those who were near, said, "Thank you, little friends, for the road. We're driving to my first session. I'll be meditating, existing, getting in synch. I even bought some of those expensive tapes with the dolphins. And Bamalf has a little snack for me in case I get hungry."

> **emulation**: the imitation of someone's performance in the hope of matching or beating it
> **encumbered**: having something heavy or awkward somehow attached to you, which interferes with your functioning

He had on so much winter wear that he appeared to have tripled in size. There was a down-stuffed parka, a bulky sweater, a vest, two scarves, earmuffs, a thickly padded aviator's cap—such a collection that Joannie called it an **emulation** of the polar explorers. François laughed. "I would say he's about thirty pounds of wool and goose down ahead."

As Nameless started to roll up the window, a phone rang inside the car. He leaned over to get it, but his hands were so **encumbered** by heavy mittens that he was unable to pick up the receiver, and Bamalford had to do it for him. And that was how the red sedan slowly vanished into the snow: Bamalford holding the phone very unhelpfully at the level of the rearview mirror, Nameless straining to get close enough to speak and hear, and large flakes, no two alike, drifting in through the still open window.

> **contentious**: disposed to quarrel and debate hotly about everything
> **misgiving**: a nagging suspicion or worry that something is going wrong
> **denouement**: the way a plot or other complicated situation, series of events, etc., finally works out

With no more ceremony Povano left his platform and began the descent from the tableland. He remarked to Peter, who was marching at his side through the snow, "There you are—everything in good order. Build a road so that Nameless Entrepreneur can go and meditate, and Nameless Entrepreneur goes and meditates. Any reasonable person would say that it looks legitimate. But you, Peter—you're the **contentious** sort, quarreling with everything, so you probably ..."

"Disagree violently?" asked his friend. "I won't go that far, but I have strong **misgivings**. I'm not comfortable letting that overdressed young weasel go motoring up our mountain. This story will not have a pretty ending, we won't be feeling so good at the **denouement**. But you, Marion, you're the uncharitable sort, so you'll say that there's no hard evidence for all of this, and that my misgivings are unscientific."

"I'm guilty too," said a pleasant voice from behind them. "I'm also having some of those Unscientific Misgivings." They turned and saw Ms. Jensen, with that steady, sensible air of hers that had impressed them a year ago when she came seeking a job at the high school.

> **mien**: your outward manner or look, often seen as the expression of what is interior—mood, attitude, etc.
> **poignant**: touching your feelings deeply
> **otorhinolaryngologist**: a doctor specializing in problems of the ear, nose and throat

"I don't think Nameless is going up the mountain to meditate," she continued. "That sounds judgmental, doesn't it? But when you go out to meditate you wear a certain look, you have something in your manner, a quietness, but also a touch of—I don't know—festivity. In short, there's a distinctive **mien**. But there was nothing of that in Nameless. He just looked eager for distraction—a little chat with the locals, a phone call, a snack for later on. I know this may be his first time, but something wasn't right. That's how I saw it, anyway. But you ask, no doubt— how can this woman say these things?"

"You're the teach," answered Povano easily.

She laughed. "Well, what it really is—I meditate too, sort of. Since I came here, I have roamed all over this landscape, looking and looking, watching ... whatever, the play of life, the flow of time. So, naturally, after a year at it, I think I'm an expert, and fit to pass judgment on Nameless. Still—I stand by what I said."

Povano lifted his dark eyebrows and gave a weary smile. "I hear what you are saying, and I almost wish I hadn't, because it's starting to worry me."

At the lower elevations the air was gray with rain. The people of Dropanchor straggled back to their homes and coffee shops, wet and tired, wondering where their new road would take them.

———————————————

READER: Do you think you could just send Merci off to a dermatologist in the next chapter to get her wart removed, so we don't have five hundred more of these **poignant** scenes where she looks sadly down at her right hand?

AUTHOR: I hadn't really planned on having any dermatologists in this story.

READER: Are we a little fussy or what?

AUTHOR: Look—if I let in the dermatologists, you know who'll be beating on the door next. The **otorhinolaryngologists**. And even in a word book, you've gotta think twice about guys with twenty-one letters in their name.

READER: Wow—that's a peeve.

Chapter 40: THE GIANT OF WHITHER AND WHENCE

On the Monday after the snow storm, at the beginning of the school day, Ms. Jensen walked into Room 401 and laughed softly. "An encouraging sight—seniors in the senior homeroom. Welcome back to normal life, after a brief **interlude** of road building."

> **interlude**: a period of time which interrupts a main activity or condition, and during which some other activity or condition occurs
> **subversive**: working—often from within—to pull down a political or social order
> **dismantle**: to take something apart; to wreck something or put it out of operation by reducing it down to its pieces

"It was Merci's fault," muttered Lumps.

Ms. Jensen thought for a moment. "You are right, you know. The girl has been a **subversive** force around here. She practically brought commerce to its knees, getting all the shoppers—and shopkeepers too—sent off to the road gangs. And that's not to mention the state in which she left Dropanchor's academic calendar—completely **dismantled**, and dear Ms. Jensen trying to do her best with the pieces. Anyway, there's my half-baked contribution to Desultory Warm-ups. Anyone else?"

> **negligible**: highly insignificant; almost not worth noticing
> **usurp**: wrongfully to seize and exercise the role or office of someone else
> **patronizing**: treating someone with an insulting degree of gentleness or helpfulness, as though he is a child who will be at a loss without your guidance

"Yormp! Here!" There was a sharp smack from the back of the room, and a cry of pain. Ricky came forward, running, limping. "Ow! What a knee banger. But it does not matter, it's **negligible**, a trifle. Pain does not exist. Because ... I remembered!"

Ms. Jensen tilted her head as though to take a better look. "You're the one who was so good with a chisel, I believe. Well—what did you remember?"

Ricky could not hold still. "It was when the telephone rang—that's when I remembered. All at once, on the big screen."

Tedesco slipped to the front of the class and put a hand on the shoulder of his friend. "Honorable childhood companion, they are beginning to wonder."

Ricky forced himself to stop his nervous dance. "I'll get a grip. Some of you may think emotion has **usurped** the place of reason up here"—he tapped his head—"and started to run the show. But … I'm good. Reason is back in charge now. I hope everyone can see that."

"Ricky!" scolded Joannie, "it looks like blabber is in charge. Just tell us what you remembered."

"The dream," he cried. "The boggler of a dream. See—here's what made me remember." He ran to the board and drew a wide V.

"This is the other day," he said, causing François to shake her head in confusion.

He tried again. "This is a day which is not today." A silent Help! formed on the lips of Meagan.

"Tough crowd," he murmured. "I must keep it simple. Today, my scholars, is Monday. What I have put on the board is from a different day, the other day when we were all up on the tableland in the snowstorm. And the figure I have drawn is a V, the twenty-second letter of the alphabet, at least the English …"

Joannie was starting to wad up an old lunch bag. "Ricky, if we're going to be **patronizing** … "

"Sorry, Ma'am. It wasn't deliberate. Anyway—the joint of the V, the vertex, as some of you would say—that stands for where Mayor Povano was, on that platform, giving his speech. And this"—he pointed to one arm of the V— "is the stretch of the new road running from the platform to the briars. The other arm is Mercurial Canyon, running north from the platform. And that's what I saw. Some of you saw other things that day, but I saw a V, a wide V, and once I did a message light went on—Ricky, you have had a dream, an important …"

"What a Martian!" broke in Calvin suddenly. "Little message lights in his head."

"Easy!" cautioned Allen. "Call him a Martian and the Farnum twins will be on his trail."

Ms. Jensen laughed. "Maybe they'll be off mine."

Allen nodded sympathetically. "Sometimes I wonder where *they're* from."

"Let's hear the dream," begged Joannie, "and worry later about who's from where."

> **tantalize**: to tease someone by holding out something desirable and then drawing it back when he reaches for it
> **cajole**: to use flattery and promises to cause someone to agree to something

Ricky went on. "While Mayor Povano was giving his speech I was reaching for the dream, trying to remember what it was, but it kept pulling back, over and over, to **tantalize** me. I was going mildly insane, trying to get hold of it. I was **cajoling**—nice little dream, come here and pick up your prize. I was threatening, I was negotiating, but nothing was working until all of a sudden the phone rang in that red sedan ..."

Joannie was growing indignant. "This is not a workshop in *how* to remember dreams. We wanna know what was actually playing last night—in your mind, in the funky theater of your mind."

> **impeccable**: made, done or performed perfectly and without flaw
> **whence**: from where; from which place or point of beginning

Ricky breezed on. "The phone rang, and it all came back—the forgotten dream. There was an enormous V, each arm a hundred yards, floating in space I guess. I was standing out at the end of one of the arms. Calvin was at the end of the other one. And at the vertex there was a giant, a huge brute, fifteen feet tall if an inch, but dressed in a red cap, black linen trousers and a red satin waistcoat. I noticed right off that these were real clothes—the tailoring was **impeccable**, every stitch perfect, a perfect fit from head to toe. So—what else? Well, one other interesting thing about the V—besides a Calvin or a Ricky or a giant at each corner, there was also a telephone."

"I don't appreciate appearing in your weirdo dreams," said Calvin unhappily, "even if the giants are well dressed."

Ricky answered smartly, "Worse to follow. You dialed a number on your phone, Calvin, and I dialed one on mine. The phone at the giant's corner began to ring. He was annoyed, fifteen feet worth of annoyance. Without picking up the line, which kept on ringing, he glared at me and at you. A rumbling came from his chest, and in a voice like a boulder slide he growled a single word, **'Whence**?' No doubt about it, he was asking where the call was coming from, my phone or yours."

Joannie was following this closely. "And ... and I'm sure Calvin reacted honorably."

> **prejudicial**: causing harm or loss, often in a gradual or indirect way
> **pusillanimous**: very timid; easily unnerved by any opposition or danger; lacking any boldness of spirit
> **thence**: from there; from that place or point of beginning

Ricky looked at her for a moment. "Calvin, I'm sorry to say, began to worry that talking on the phone with giants could be **prejudicial** to his career and perhaps to his health. He went from worried to nervous, nervous to fearful. His fingers started to tremble, his face turned pale, and finally, he was nothing but a **pusillanimous** blob. He pointed to my corner of the V and stammered, **'Thence.'**"

"So the giant asked 'Whence?' and Calvin answered 'Thence,'" Ms. Jensen summarized. "What did you say, Ricky?"

> **hence**: from here; from this place or point of beginning
> **cordial**: treating someone with a lively goodwill and graciousness
> **verify**: to check something out to be sure that it is true or correct

"I said **'Hence.'** You know—what else? But I said it with a gulp, because it didn't look too bright to tell a giant that you were his nuisance call. I gulped again as he reached for the handset. This could get ugly. But at that moment his mood was transformed, everything lightened up. In a **cordial** tone, he said to me, over the line, 'Front Desk. How can we help you?'"

"Not! You never dreamed that." The challenge floated through the open windows of Room 401, from below.

Allen sprang to the defense. "You airhead Farnums," he shouted down, "how can we ever **verify** what he dreamed and what he didn't? Make him bring in witnesses? Photos? I'm a journalist, but even I just have to take his word. Good thing he's so ..."

> **prevarication**: the communication of what is false, either through outright lies or through a more subtle, artful twisting of the truth
> **whither**: to where, to which place or outcome
> **thither**: to there, to that place or outcome

"So lazy," finished Ricky. "**Prevarication** is very hard work, to do it right. So I avoid it completely and just tell the truth—which I will now continue doing. I'll never know why, but I answered the giant, 'Any messages for R. Snoozer?'

"With a bow he said, 'Just a moment, sir,' and turned to a bulletin board that had appeared behind him. Untacking a slip of paper, he was back on the phone. 'Very good, sir. There is a message. It says that Sallie Driven is coming.'

"I was unhinged, undone, carried away to a better place. The coin of the realm was joy, the name of the month was joy, the streets were paved with ... well, you get the idea. Then suddenly, a nagger. I thought, he didn't exactly say where Sallie is coming to. Always good to be sure on these details. So I asked, **'Whither**?'"

"Not!" Again the challenge drifted up from below. "No one says 'whither' any more."

Allen walked over and closed the window, and Ricky finished his story. "The giant replied very courteously, **'Thither**, of course sir, thither to your town of Dropanchor.' I was a king! And I knighted my large friend at once, naming him the Giant of Whither and Whence. Then I woke up."

hither: to here; to this place or outcome
innovation: a new product or technique, often featuring some creative improvement
obsessed: unable to get your mind off something; worrying far too much about something

He paused and did a completely unnecessary imitation of someone waking up. "My parents were standing at the bedroom door, and Rachel as well. She said, 'Whither, Ricky, what is a whither?' I gave her a hug and swung her about. 'A whither is quite like a hither. And **hither** is where Sallie Driven is coming, hither to Dropanchor.'"

READER: Larry says that remembering what you dreamt will never more be a matter of chance.
AUTHOR: I'm sure there's a basis for such a statement.
READER: He says that **innovations** in the information tech field have just gone out of control, and now there's a device which plugs you into your hard drive during the night and, unless you opt out, puts your dreams on the net—right while you're having them.
AUTHOR: Not to be **obsessed** with details or anything, but how exactly does a sleeping person get plugged into his hard drive.
READER: Larry talked about two wires, one coming out of each ear.
AUTHOR: Two? Like if I have two dreams at once?
READER: No, one for the video, one for the audio.
AUTHOR: Check. Anyway, this could be big—dreams flying over the net in real time, dreamers waking to find themselves famous.
READER: Dream carefully, everyone.

274

Chapter 41: THE CLANDESTINE NON-LIZARD

The spring was beautiful that year, a distraction, a riot of color and growth.

> **precedent** (noun): (1) a prior situation which, because of similarities to a present one, helps us comprehend the present one; (2) a response which was taken to a prior situation and which now serves as a rule of action when a similar situation arises
> **mote**: a tiny grain of matter; a speck
> **effervescence**: a bubbling, brimming enthusiasm

"There is no **precedent**," declared Mayor Povano, "for a springtime this radiant and generous. It has never happened before."

"But there is precedent," said Grandma, "for that statement. You make it every year."

"And this time I mean it!" countered the mayor without shame.

Povano could be excused for his exuberant praises: it was an unforgettable season. The rains which pattered down every third or fourth night drew a wealth of bloom from the hillsides. And when the rain finished, a startling clarity soon ruled—cloud and mist would vanish and through the cleanest air imaginable the sun would cast an angled light, causing every object, even the smallest **mote** or thorn, to stand out sharply.

"In this light," said Ms. Jensen to Meagan as they walked up Victoria Road one day during lunch hour, "nothing can be hidden ... not even the pain."

"You are thinking of ... Joannie?" asked Meagan.

"Joannie for one. Poor thing—she's not as bubbly these days. Something is aching."

This was basically true. Joannie's usual **effervescence** had fallen off somewhat, as she went alone to Mercurial Canyon, again and again, to work on her catalog of species. "She always thought it would be a joint project with Calvin," explained Meagan. "But we're not sure if Calvin exists any more."

Ms. Jensen smiled faintly. "And dear old Lumps has his pain too. The clown puts aside his mask."

"He comes to the mountain now to look for his father," said Meagan softly. "With the snow melting he can go higher up. Sometimes Darlingson and Iron-bane join him."

> **tact**: a perceptiveness about the feelings of others, and the ability to handle delicate matters in a way that does not bruise those feelings
> **diminution**: the act of becoming less or getting smaller

"Does he really hope ...?"

"I don't know. It's been fifteen years. But he won't say much about it."

Ms. Jensen shook her head, gave a long sigh and was silent. So Meagan, with her usual **tact**, said nothing, though she could have remarked that in the searching light of that brilliant spring Ms. Jensen was not able to hide the pain either. For the "schoolmarm" was quieter than usual lately, and sometimes now would waken suddenly into the scene around her, as though returning from a sad place where her thoughts had led her. There was no **diminution** in the care and prodding she gave the seniors, and the absurdities of Room 401 still amused her, but often at evening she sought out the loneliness of Mount Relief, roaming over the folds and capes into which it fell. There were still long intervals of what she had called meditation—the watchfulness, the delight—but now some theme of worry or regret seemed to occupy her as well.

Several days after her talk with Meagan Ms. Jensen was again on Victoria Road, farther up, by the high orchard that stretched out seaward along the base of the Steeps. She was on one of her rambles, lost in her thoughts, paying little attention to the hour. The twilight had slipped into a darkness relieved only slightly by the sliver of moon setting in the west.

She was alone, and the chance of remaining alone was high, for the townspeople were all at the meeting stone on the beach, to discuss Povano's proposal for a whale decoy.

> **engrossing**: so highly interesting as to hold your attention strongly
> **expedient** (adjective): (1) highly useful in achieving a particular goal; (2) useful and advantageous, but involving a compromise of your principles

It wasn't that she felt indifferent toward the meeting. The topic was an **engrossing** one, whether a huge inflatable whale or plastic whale in the bay was **expedient** in the sense Povano gave the term—highly useful as a means of saving Whalefest; or in the sense Peter Oakum gave it—useful, no doubt, but compromising all that Whalefest stood for. Ordinarily she would have been in the middle of the debate. Tonight, though, with some deeper matter apparently needing attention, she had taken the chance to wander alone on the mountain.

> **encore**: a repeat performance, often at the request of an audience
> **meager**: lean in mass, or very small in quantity or extent, when compared to what is needed or expected, or to what normally occurs
> **intermittent**: occurring for a while, stopping for a while, occurring again, and so forth

As the road drew her slowly closer to the Steeps, there was a growl, not loud, but unmistakable. Higher up, farther down, it was hard for her to say, for on the mountain's irregular face there were many points where a sound would

276

get confused and come from everywhere at once. But there had been a growl. A once-only growl, Ms. Jensen thought nervously, I'm sure that's what it was, a single performance, no need for an **encore**. But in a moment it repeated itself, and she flinched as it did.

She looked quickly about, and as her gaze ran out across the old orchard, along the line of seven low summits that strung out toward the sea, she beheld the silhouette of a startling creature. It was in one of the few places where she could have seen it at all on that dark night, framed against the **meager** radiance of the setting moon, and perched on a spur that jutted from the upper slopes of the first of the seven summits. It was a lizard, heavy-tailed, with a heavy pouch of skin at its neck, that swung ever so slightly in the breeze. And it was a good six feet in length.

Again the growl—and the lizard, hearing it, turned and fled.

Ms. Jensen seemed dazed. "The growler is a non-lizard. I thought the … the growler was that lizard, but if the lizard runs from the growler, that means … Sandra, stop babbling and get off this road at once!"

The growl was no longer **intermittent**, but had become a continuous— though somewhat uneven—rumble, drawing closer, following the line of the road. Hurrying as best she could on the rough ground, Ms. Jensen left the roadway and found a hiding place in the ancient orchard, behind one of the countless dry trunks that stood there.

> **clandestine**: deliberately kept hidden from view; carried on in secret
> **gingerly** (adjective): acting with carefulness and delicacy in your movements, often in order to avoid breaking something, triggering some force, etc.
> **interject**: to interrupt the flow of a conversation by tossing in a remark

She was only in time—moments later a vehicle passed by, its motor firing and coughing in a curious rhythm, its lights out.

* * *

"You could see the outline," she was saying next morning to the seniors, and to Mr. Ironbane, who had come to Room 401 to hear the unusual account. "But nothing more, just the outline, blocky, squarish—a vehicle of some sort. Definitely not a lizard. In fact, that was what I called it, the Non-Lizard, or to be more precise, the **Clandestine** Non-Lizard. And take my word, students, the clandestine part really fit—no lights at all, gears being shifted in the most **gingerly** fashion to hold down noise, darkness worn like a welcome veil."

"Darkness worn like a veil," repeated François. "Oh, how creepy! Weren't you just, like, shaking?"

"If this were any place but Dropanchor I would have been shaking just to be out by myself at that hour. But around here ... Besides, there was the germ of curiosity—I wanted to see what the thing was. Or maybe hear what it was—because as it got closer, the growl I first heard was becoming a much more complicated sound. Every three or four seconds the engine was producing this strange wheeze or cough, rather like ... well, rather like ..."

There was a sharp rap on the door, and the Farnum twins entered, walking stiffly with unbent legs and arms, like parts of a machine. "*Brumm, Brumm*," Henry was repeating. And at frequent intervals, Andrew would **interject**, "*Sputt ... sputt*."

"Well, rather like ... that," said Ms. Jensen, casting an intent look of suspicion at the brothers. "May I see your driver's licenses?"

Ironbane was nowhere near so calm. "It's totally insane. You boys—you really fired up that old ...?"

"Tut, tut," interrupted the Farnums, each uttering one Tut. "If the educators make hasty assumptions ... You see, the Farnums were not motorized last night. We were there, but on foot."

> **fortuitous**: happening just by chance
> **corroborate**: to furnish evidence strengthening and confirming some position
> **aloof**: keeping your distance from others, in the sense that you share little of yourself with them, and care very little what's happening with them

"You lads just happened to be on the same part of the mountain as Ms. Jensen, and at the same time? Purely **fortuitous**, that's it?"

"No, sir," the twins answered. "It was by design. We were following Ms. Jensen, sir, looking for evidence. She's from another planet, you know."

"You'll get a bit of evidence next year when you're in this classroom!" vowed Ms. Jensen. "Scallywags!"

"There was some indication from the beginning," explained the twins to Ironbane. "Ms. Jensen arrived in town on a night when Mars was very close to Earth, and that means something. But last night gave us important **corroborating** evidence, a confirmation of our position. After her Clandestine Non-Lizard had sputted out of sight, Miss Jensen stayed on the mountain, and so did we. Now listen to what we heard—she said out loud several times, the word 'Martian'! Just like she was phoning home and the operator had asked what language she preferred."

A trace of sadness appeared on Ms. Jensen's face, and she said quietly, "Beyond assuring you that I was not making an operator-assisted call to Mars, I ... I would rather not say anything more about it. I'm sorry ... Ms. Framley would call me **aloof**, a haughty outsider, keeping my distance. But … it's not that at all."

Meagan, watching all this from the back of the room, saw at once that the Farnums had touched upon something painful. She came forward, taking charge. "Nice work, cadets. The hands of a surgeon. But—hark—I hear a unit on colons and semicolons beginning in 301—and you should be there."

> **knack**: an instinctive or deeply ingrained ability which lets you do something challenging with ease and polish
>
> **convention**: a style, a rule for behavior, a way of performing some activity, an outlook, etc., which has become standard, well established, and accepted by most people
>
> **meticulous**: thoroughly attentive to every detail; sometimes excessively so

In a moment the twins were in tow, being ushered down the stair by Meagan, to Room 301. "Oops," said Henry. "Whoops," said his brother.

When Meagan came back to her own room, she was met at the door by Ms. Jensen. "That was nicely done, Meagan, I'm … very grateful." A little smile appeared. "And since you have a **knack** for rescuing grown-ups, there's another one who needs help, right over there."

READER: Larry says he has made his peace.

AUTHOR: We all need to do that. But what has he made his peace with?

READER: With your giant lizard. He accepts that it's probably not going to flatten buildings or carry off supermodels, the way it would in any other book.

AUTHOR: Well—yeah. We won't be following standard literary **conventions** with this lizard.

READER: But at least you could make it puff out its throat bag once or twice and look threatening, that's all he asks.

AUTHOR: Do those things puff out?

READER: Another **meticulously** researched novel!

279

Chapter 42: RAW CIRCUMSPECTION

Ms. Jensen nodded toward the windows on the north wall, the ones opening out on the vast upsweep of the mountain.

Ironbane was there. He seemed to be proving some point to himself. He was tapping on the pane and gesturing vaguely up the mountain slope. His voice was low and excited. "So—it was in the realm after all. Fifteen years to make it happen, but it was in the realm."

Ironbane was well liked, and if he needed a few minutes to go crazy the seniors were willing to wait. But waiting quietly was another matter.

> **speculate**: to turn a question over in your thoughts and arrive at possible conclusions about it, although you lack knowledge of facts which would permit definite conclusions
> **soliloquy**: a conversation you have with yourself; a speech you make to no one but yourself
> **melancholy** (adjective): marked by a depression or sadness that is often brooding and given over to thought

Ricky was watching with a broad smile and murmuring, "Now, Sallie, now!"

Joannie was **speculating** with François that it was a case of insect bite. "Something flutters out of Mercurial Canyon," she said, "some unknown breed of insect, and it lunches on Mr. Ironbane. His immune system is bewildered, his circuits get scrambled. But who knows? There could be other explanations."

Tedesco was telling Allen of a special drink, made from the guava fruit and said to restore balance to the mental faculties.

Suddenly aware of the attention, Ironbane turned toward the class with a generous laugh. "No privacy anymore, is there? A man tries to engage in a little **soliloquy** and he's got an audience."

"Well, sir, in the realm of what?" asked Joannie. "You said it was in the realm."

"In the realm of the possible," he replied firmly. "There is a story here, as you suspect—one that began fifteen years ago in **melancholy** days. But this may not be ..."

He paused for a second, looking down one of the aisles. Lumps caught the glance and let out a long breath. "It's your story," Ironbane said quietly, "and whether it should be told at this moment is your ..."

"It's my story," repeated Lumps slowly, the trace of a weary smile appearing on his face, "my story for sure, then and now ... And if this is the time for telling it, that's OK. And it doesn't have to be melancholy either."

> **facilitate**: to help some process go more easily and smoothly
> **alchemy**: a process, part magic and part science, for the transformation of a commonplace substance into a rare and valuable one, such as the transformation of lead into gold
> **contrive**: to bring about some result, usually through some cleverness, and often against some difficulty

With a nod to say thank you, Ironbane began his account once more. "In those days we had the whole mountain to cover, and as quickly as we could. The search was by foot, it was going too slowly, and young Ironbane knew the answer. 'If we could get motorized,' he told the elders, 'that would **facilitate** this thing a lot.'

"'Show us your vehicle,' they said to him tolerantly, 'or any vehicle that can get through the canyon and climb the Steeps.'

"He was prepared for that. He had his eyes on an old service van, and now he pointed it out to them. It was ugly and squat. 'But it's got a big engine,' he argued, 'and a very solid frame. We could transform it. With the right work on the transmission and suspension, it could roam all over the mountain—off-road as off-road could be. And it will make the Steeps look like your favorite flatlands.'

"The elders were doubtful. '**Alchemy** would be easier,' they told him. 'Brass will change to gold before that old clunker turns into the mountain rover you're dreaming of.'

"He didn't push it any further. Some of the elders were pretty good mechanics, and they probably knew what they were talking about. Besides, something else was already catching at his attention. So the old service vehicle remained just that, knocking about the roads of Dropanchor for a few more years. And—listen well—it always had a funny sound in the motor like a small, persistent cough—the very sound the Farnums were making, before you ran them out of town, Meagan."

"And if I brought them back," she replied slowly, struggling with the riddle, "and if this time, instead of imitating motor noises, they had **contrived** to smell like fish, would that also be a clue—I mean about the old service van?"

> **pungent**: sharp and insistent—or even irritating and stinging—to the senses, especially the sense of smell
> **nefarious**: shockingly and wickedly injurious to what is sacred or vital in a community

> **estranged**: cut off from someone (family, friends, community, etc.), often through anger or suspicion

Ironbane gave her a sharp, admiring glance. "Someone's putting it together here. I didn't mean to be a riddler but, yes, that would be a clue—the vehicle I'm thinking of had a brief career as a rolling fish market, brief but long enough for it to be permanently imprinted with a **pungent** odor of salt, lemon and cod. Ha—it would sting your nose today, if I'm not wrong."

François gasped, remembering the abandoned hulk and the clouds of flies which she and Meagan had seen on that morning several months earlier at the library. "The bookmobile! What you wanted to transform into a big mountain goat fifteen years ago was the bookmobile."

"And what blew Ms. Jensen off the road last night," seconded Meagan, "was the bookmobile."

"I think I'm relieved," said Joannie. "This means it's Bezzle. And that's much better than Bamalford. Bezzle stands for grouchiness and raving about library fines, true, but he's not a threat to … to the things that are sacred around here. Bamalford, though, is another matter—he's the one who's going to pop off and do something **nefarious** one day."

"Scratch a Bezzle, though," said Allen slowly, still forming his thought as he spoke, "and find a Bamalford? Do you suppose?" He lowered his voice. "Remember the case of Ms. Framley. When Bamalford arrived in town he saw right off how she was **estranged** from the community, up on her hill, up in her attic, distant from everybody. And he won her over with his newspaper, with that stuff about the Seismologic Beauty, on page one. So think—Bezzle's estranged too. How do we know he hasn't become part of Bamalford's growing circle?"

> **allusion**: the act of referring to a thing or person indirectly rather than by name
> **innocuous**: not designed or equipped to cause harm; harmless
> **euphemism**: an indirect and inoffensive phrase used in place of one that too frankly or bluntly names some disturbing reality

Ironbane questioned the assumption. "Do you really think it's a growing circle?"

Allen nodded. "One of its most recent additions is here with us today."

The **allusion** wasn't lost on Calvin. "Hey, Allen, the name is Calvin. And, yeah, I work for Mr. Bamalford. You could too if you wanted to write for a real newspaper."

Ms. Jensen broke in. "Whoa, guys, or I'll make you do a project together."

That left them silent, and Ironbane pressed forward. "To answer the question which was left hanging a minute ago, Allen, I for one anyway do think that Bezzle is part of Bamalford's circle. We know he works over at the Dome sometimes running the elevator, and from that it's not a great leap to imagine he does other jobs as well, odd jobs that Bamalford gives him now and then. Like last night. I think his errand as he drove up Victoria Road last night was probably for Bamalford. But as errands go it seems to have been an **innocuous** one, good and strange but essentially harmless. I say that on the basis of what I saw this morning."

"You're under no obligation to tell us," said Joannie pointedly.

"In that case," laughed Ironbane, "why not? As you know, I'm the guy who checks the mountain for cracks. A new crack, a bigger crack, and we could have a problem, a mountain getting ready to ... to speak. I guess that's the right **euphemism** for this sort of thing. Actually the chances are very slim, I think, but still you need to keep up your guard. This morning was the time to have a look at the granite bluff where the Mendicant Briars grow. To check it right I have to push in through the briars and get up close to the stone face. There I was. I nudged aside a long trailer of vines and—wham—I tripped, lost balance, and tumbled over an oaken chest. "

"And no doubt it was huge," said Joannie dryly, "five hundred years old, and filled with…"

"Hey!" cried Ironbane. "Yes, it was huge, and as a matter of fact it did look five hundred years old. Concerning what it was filled with, could there be any question? Only the points of detail—eighteen karat vs. twenty karat, things of that sort—remained in doubt. Well, as you can imagine, a single emotion rules supreme at a moment like that."

> **circumspection**: a cautious approach in which you study the whole situation and all possible consequences before you speak or act
> **avarice**: an intense, active greediness that drives you to store up more and more wealth

"Raw greed," suggested Joannie.

"No, raw **circumspection**." Ironbane was pacing back and forth in front of the class. "At a moment like that you look at all the circumstances, all the possible consequences. Who still has a claim to the chest? The descendants of ancient Esperanza, for example. And what are my obligations—am I about to break any historic preservation laws? And all that spray in the air from the stream—will it corrode the contents? And what about …?"

"Pleez!" came an anguished cry from Ricky. "Open the chest."

"Oh, sorry," said Ironbane. "I'm rambling. Well, eventually I did work through the circumspection exercise, and once it was over it was over, believe me, and I started having some pretty recognizable reactions. I was shivering a bit as I began pushing back the lid, but that's the fever, that's how you get when you're moments away from a golden vision—coins and bars, bricks and ingots. Or a golden shower."

With widened eyes and exaggerated motions, he was scooping up imaginary doubloons and raining them down on his head and shoulders. "**Avarice** is one of the finer vices, I mean, if you had a choice ..."

He paused to take a breath, and there was a cry of protest. "Just tell us, sir," begged Ricky, "if you're the richest man in Dropanchor. Then you can breathe."

He laughed. "Richest in words, I'm afraid. Because words were all I got. I opened it, finally, and the whole blasted thing, with the exception of one box of cigars, was filled with business magazines, probably the entire collection of our library. I never imagined there was so much business news, or that we subscribe to all of it. Anyway, I think this was Bezzle's errand last night, hauling the chest up onto the tableland, wrestling it out of the bookmobile—don't ask me how, he's built strongly, but the thing's a monster—and dragging it over to the briars, to one of the few dry spots. One more delivery of printed matter to the reading public."

"A reading public of one," observed Ms. Jensen. "Obviously Nameless grows bored now and then with meditating and needs some distraction, something to browse through."

> **voracious**: eager to devour a huge quantity of the stuff (food, literature, etc.) which satisfies your appetite
> **transgression**: the act of overstepping the limits imposed by some rule or law
> **concur**: to agree that what someone has said is true; to express a readiness to go along with what someone has proposed

Ironbane nodded in agreement. "And what an appetite for browsing. It must be **voracious**. There were tons of those magazines. I just can't believe there's so much business news."

"So the grand conclusion," ventured Allen slowly, "is that Bezzle does odd jobs for Bamalford and Bamalford's friends. And he does them with his lights off when there's some petty **transgression** involved—periodicals leaving the library without being checked out—that sort of thing. That's the worst that can be said. So, fundamentally, all is well in Dropanchor."

Ironbane, watching him closely, repeated, "All is well in Dropanchor. High on our mountain—magazines are read. Along our coast—nothing purple is seen. All is well in Dropanchor—fundamentally."

READER: Fulano has "circumspect" too, and he gives a typically great example: "The circumspect toddler held his little jar of mashed green peas up to the light, sniffed it, checked its freshness date, studied its nutrition label, reviewed with Mom what would happen if it got thrown on the carpet, and at last decided to eat it."

AUTHOR: An achingly beautiful sentence, but that kid's gonna need a good shrink.

READER: Larry is unable to **concur**.

AUTHOR: Beg yer pardon.

READER: He says the kid will be fine, the kid's in the mainstream—circumspection is the virtue of the future.

AUTHOR: Well, I appreciate being told ahead of time. Maybe there's some way to cash in on this.

Chapter 43: THE EMBARRASSING ANACHRONISM

"Well, that feels better," said Meagan to Joannie and Ms. Jensen, "we're not on Ms. Framley's land anymore." They were in the school auditorium, having dropped down the steep fall of the seating area and crossed over the Bad Pony to the stage. It was a popular lunch spot, with the stream splattering by and the air charged faintly with the glee and the chase of its tumbling motion.

> **gratis**: free of charge; done or given for free and as a favor
> **emancipate**: to set a person free from the control of someone else

Ms. Jensen was won over completely. "I'd teach **gratis** just for this," she said.

"From what I hear about salaries in the Dropanchor School District," said Joannie, "you almost do teach gratis."

"Well, it's worth every penny I don't earn." She was still looking at the scour of the water across the blue shallows and the bobbing reflection on the ceiling high above. "Most school boards would have said no way."

"We are on the banks of the Nile," announced Meagan, "and of the Thames, the Amazon, the Colorado—whatever river the drama department needs at the time. And it's also the south boundary of Ms. Framley's land. When we came across the footbridge a moment ago we left her domain. Over on this side she has no claim on us. It makes me feel sort of **emancipated**."

"Me too, of course," Joannie said. "And hungry besides."

They sat down on the stage and began their lunches, watching the spatter of the stream. Meagan said to her teacher, "Mixed up place, isn't it? Rivers in the auditorium, town meetings in the tide."

"Which reminds me," answered Ms. Jensen. "Because I was on the mountain two nights ago, seeing lizards and phoning Martians, I missed Povano's meeting about the whale decoy. What ...?"

> **connotation**: the idea which a word suggests in certain situations, even though that idea is not part of the word's dictionary definition
> **semantic**: having to do with what words mean
> **travesty**: a twisted, exaggerated imitation or occurrence of something

Joannie gave a going-crazy sort of scream. "Oh—there will be a decoy. Povano and Oakum first had an argument about the word itself. Oakum claimed a decoy is an artificial look-alike of an animal of some type which lures live animals of that same type so they can be captured or killed. Povano objected that 'captured or killed' is not part of the dictionary meaning of 'decoy,' but is only a **connotation** reflecting the fact that many decoys are used that way. Grandma pointed to the rising tide and said this was a poor time for **semantic** quarrels. Then she threw in her chips with Povano by admitting that without a decoy Whalefest was going to run short on whales."

Ms. Jensen smiled. "Poor Oakum. He sees this enormous plastic thing or inflatable thing floating in our harbor, whale-like only in a mocking way, a **travesty** of the real whales. And a hazard for them too, since they can cut themselves on the cable holding it to the bottom."

> **aesthetic**: related to the beauty or lack of beauty that is in the things we see
> **mitigate**: to soften the force or impact of something and make it more bearable

"Povano was sympathetic," said Joannie. "He asked Merci—she's practically the town engineer now—to find a way to eliminate the cable. And he agreed that a gigantic air mattress lying offshore may be an **aesthetic** jolt—at least within the setting of Whalefest. He said if anyone can think how to **mitigate** the impact and make it less of a shock—they shouldn't hold back."

"They shouldn't hold back even five minutes," observed Meagan. "The signs are starting to pop up—that Whalefest is near."

This was surprising news for Ms. Jensen. "Those Harbinger Ducks—the ones which fly north, two or three days in front of the whales—they've begun to appear?"

"No," said Meagan, "things are not quite that far along. What I had in mind are those ... those little pieces of river traffic." She was pointing to the stream. "Can you see them? They definitely mean spring is on the march and Whalefest is not all that far off."

> **hue**: a color; a shade or variation of color
> **inherent**: showing up as a natural, inescapable part of a situation; bound up with the very essence or structure of something
> **inchoate**: just beginning; still taking form; marked by the disorder and vagueness of something which has not reached a finished state

Now Ms. Jensen noticed the blossoms riding lightly and with crazy darts and leaps, on the current of the Bad Pony. "They're blue!" she exclaimed. "No wonder I didn't catch sight. But now that I see them—what a fine blue indeed, with something of turquoise, something of far-off mountains on hot afternoons—the **hue** of the year I'd say. Are they...?"

"Yes, they are," broke in Joannie. "They're the blossoms of the Mendicant Briars. That's a risk **inherent** in blooming by a waterfall—your petals may be swept away." She paused a moment, turning something in her thoughts.

287

"They're all gone in three or four days, but during that time there's this … this quaint practice, and …"

There was another pause, and her voice fell ever so slightly. "One quaint practice coming up."

She rose from their meal and walked toward the stream, while Meagan explained, "What you do is, you go to the center of the bridge, sit down, close your eyes, and place your hand in the water, palm cupped against the current. If you fish out a flower, you get a wish."

Ms. Jensen was intrigued. "So—can you try as often as you want? And do you say the wish out loud? And what happens to the flower?"

It was three questions more than Meagan could answer. With a long shrug she replied, "No one knows yet. This quaint practice is very … **inchoate**. It's still in the cradle, still defining itself. Come back in a hundred years."

"History in the making," said Ms. Jensen with amusement. "And there, see, Joannie's helping to make it—she's caught one of the flowers."

Water was dripping from Joannie's forearm as she sat for a moment on the bridge, knees drawn up and hands clasped around her ankles. A blossom lay beside her, and she gazed at it, murmuring something to herself as she did so.

> **bleak**: barren; stripped of warmth and cheer; without hope
> **preoccupation**: concern or worry about something, and the devotion of all your attention to it
> **pathological**: originating in disease; altered for the worse in structure or function by some disease

"I know what that one's called," said Ms. Jensen softly. "Young girl with blue flower, making wish."

"The prospects for that wish are looking **bleaker** all the time," replied Meagan.

Joannie rejoined them. "One last prayer for the creep," she said. Her tone was bravely matter-of-fact.

Ms. Jensen looked at her for a moment, with a wisp of a smile. "I correct that boy's homework, you know. I read his essays. And what's happening is not healthy, I admit—this exclusive **preoccupation** with career, this nice-knowing-you attitude toward all else. But has it become **pathological**, is it rooted in bone and tissue like a disease? Maybe not yet, or maybe not very much. I think he's still trying it on. So don't give up all hope for Calvin."

Joannie returned the wisp of a smile, but was silent. After a moment's hesitation, Meagan, the one who was good with grown-ups, lifted her head and said quietly to Ms. Jensen, "And don't you give up all hope for Martin."

> **divulge**: to make known something you have kept, or should have kept, as a secret

288

taciturn: stubbornly closemouthed; disposed to avoid speech
insinuation: a criticism or accusation which is made indirectly, through hints and half-formed inferences

Startled, Ms. Jensen swung about. There was admiration as well as surprise in her look. "Well, Meagan, you are good! What did I do, Z-out and **divulge** everything?"

Meagan gestured toward the Farnum twins, lunching at the far side of the stage. "I knew they were wrong, but not completely wrong, when they said you were calling the word 'Martian' on the mountain the other night."

For a second Ms. Jensen closed her eyes. "The word was 'Martin,'" she admitted fingering the long braid into which her hair was drawn. "And Martin was ... well, Martin was almost everything. It's still not easy to talk about. And it's so hard never to talk about—you guessed that too didn't you, Meagan. For now let me just say ..."

"You know you don't need to say any thing at all," interrupted Joannie, "if you don't want."

"Thank you, and I do know it. And I have been quite **taciturn** on the subject. But to share a little of the story would be a relief. You see, the Miss Jensen who taught you this year—sensible, good-humored, meditating on the mountainside—is a recent invention. Before Dropanchor, it was California, near San Francisco. I ran with a very fast group of friends. I wore the right clothes, had the right toys, yawned at the right moments. Only Martin wasn't right. He was such a crazy guy, very funny, huge supply of enthusiasm, good with his hands, good with words. But my friends—by hints and nods and half-finished sentences and the other means of **insinuation**—my friends let me know that Martin wasn't right."

complementary: going together nicely one with another, often in the sense that what is missing in the one is supplied by the other, and vice versa
impecunious: without money most of the time, or with only a small and insufficient amount of money

Again she closed her eyes for a moment, drawing further into the world she was describing. "During the time that I knew him, Martin was a poet, trying to earn a living from his poetry. My friends would say to me, 'No one earns a living as a poet anymore,' and I would repeat it to him. But Martin had a **complementary** talent. He was a miniaturist—he could write so small you couldn't read it without a magnifier, yet his letters were perfectly formed. So what he did was buy up little ceramic figures—mostly along insect lines, ladybugs and beetles and so on—and in his microscopic penmanship he would write his poems on their backs. He got the clay figures before they were glazed—he was friends with the potter—and only after he had etched his poetry on them would he apply a clear finish and pop them in the oven. People liked what he did, people thought they were cute—the little bugs with stanzas on their wings. And people bought them. Whatever else you could say against Martin, you couldn't say he was **impecunious**. The boy did have some cash flow, poet or not."

"Which shut your friends up?" asked Joannie.

"No," answered Ms. Jensen. "Now they said, 'No one goes to flea markets anymore.' Because Martin liked flea markets. He would take twenty or thirty of his little poetry bugs out to the flea market and sell them to the people he met there. And my friends told me I should be embarrassed."

> **cynical**: bitterly mocking any claim that human action can arise from noble motives; holding that the only reason people act is to look out for their own selfish interests
>
> **lyrical**: giving voice—in a language that approaches song—to the feelings and reflections that life awakens in you (usually said of poetry and other forms of artistic expression)

"Well, that's what they're for, isn't it?" observed Meagan in a bright tone.

"Correct," said Ms. Jensen, smiling weakly. "And what really bothered them was the poetry itself. Don't let the tiny print and ceramic insects fool you—Martin wrote real poems. And I was dumb enough to show some of them to my friends, hoping to raise him in their esteem, but they made faces and exchanged looks. I guess they wanted something more mocking and **cynical**, with a more pounding beat. But Martin was **lyrical**—his poems were like songs. He was always on a journey, across the planet, and the feelings that it stirred became his poems, and even when they were sad they carried this musical quality that he drew from the meter and the images. But my friends said his stuff was sentimental and embarrassing, and when I heard that I was embarrassed."

She looked at Meagan and Joannie, you would almost call it a kindly look, and her voice was lower as she said, "When your chance comes, be sure … Well, you know that, you're both clearheaded. Anyway, Martin always talked about little kids who came to the flea market with their moms, how they would take his magnifying glass and pretend to read the bugs. One day—and if I could have that one day over— he told me of his plan to do a long series of poems celebrating mothers and children. It would all be there—the little dandelion bouquets, the bedtime stories, the lost mittens."

> **appalled**: shocked; pale or otherwise distressed at how horrible something is or at how far it falls short of applicable standards

290

anachronism: something that fits in with an earlier age but seems odd and out of place in today's world
mawkish: filled with expressions of sentiment that are overdone, drippy, and often insincere

"I see trouble coming," said Meagan.

"Trouble came," confirmed Ms. Jensen. "He was so excited about his idea, and I was so **appalled**. I knew exactly what my friends would say, and I said it for them. 'Martin, no one does the mother and child bit anymore. It went out with the nineteenth century, it's an Embarrassing **Anachronism**. Why can't you get a life, do something big, carve out a career in law or business like the guys my friends go out with? Then in your spare time, do your poetry thing, write your verses—just not so **mawkish**.'"

Meagan was pretty sure this was the first telling of the story. The young teacher looked exhausted. She pushed forward, though, working to tell it through, to bring it to a closing.

"Even before I finished I was feeling really bad. Why was I treating him like that? Why was I referring to his poems as 'verse'? He hated the word. But he didn't get angry or try to argue. This look of tremendous alertness came into his face, as though he were reflecting with himself what lesson to draw. After a minute—in a quiet voice—he said, 'I hope it all works out for you, Sandy,' just those few words. When he was at the door he turned for a moment but didn't say anything further, and then he left. It was the last time I saw him."

coherent: arranged or presented in orderly fashion; easily able to be followed by a listener from beginning to end
spurious: false or forged in spite of appearing—often by reason of deliberate effort—to be true or authentic
bard: a poet, especially one creating and reciting poems that celebrate the traditions and heroes of his people
peer: a person who is your equal in rank, competence, social standing, etc.

She fell silent, and after a long pause added only, "I haven't told it very **coherently**, it's a broken cup I know—pieces here and there, but it's all I can manage now."

Meagan knew there was little which could be said. "Well, we like you, Miss Jensen," she offered simply. "And ... in Dropanchor things get healed sometimes."

Joannie's contribution was even briefer. "When I'm low, I watch the airheads." She motioned toward the footbridge. The Farnums were there now. Henry had plunged his arm into the stream and was waiting. Suddenly he pulled out a blue petal, held it out before his eyes, and exclaimed with high feeling, "Time for a blue-flower poem!"

Meagan looked up with alarm, but Ms. Jensen put a hand on her wrist and said, "It's OK, poems don't open wounds for me. In fact, that was Martin's gift. After he was gone, I took stock of my life. It was like an empty pantry. No him, of course, and no friends either. Because I fired my friends. Their claims were **spurious** and I told them so, the way they set themselves up as judges of Martin. The one thing left in that empty cupboard of mine was poetry— without my even knowing it, Martin had given me a love for poetry, and I've always prayed he didn't lose it himself, in the storm of those days. So, Meagan"—the humor was returning to her voice—"you don't need to run over and immobilize Henry Farnum. Let's hear the young **bard**."

Henry was already reciting in a high, theatrical manner:

"Blue flower, beach bound from a mountain home,
Go ahead, hate my poem;
But if you would like to be of help
Before you join the rancid kelp,
Then grant my wish,
Which is that fair Floriander,
Who disdains me as a salamander,
Would ... er ... change her mind ...and ..."

As Henry's poem started to bog, Andrew slapped him several times about the cheeks. "Don't fade on me, son! Eight lines down. Another six and you've got a sonnet which will be the **peer** of the great love sonnets of all time."

> **parody**: the mocking imitation of something spoken or written, re-creating its unique features with a mix of skill and distortion in order to hold them up to ridicule
> **surfeit**: a quantity so abundant as to exceed what is needed or wanted
> **jubilation**: a great joyfulness, and the shouts and gestures of celebration by which it is expressed

"The peer!" cried Henry. "I want it to be the **parody**. I'll have to pack the last six lines with more ridicule and mockery."

When Henry had finished Andrew took his turn. Noting modestly that with his looks, intelligence and mutual fund balances he was the sun and the moon for almost any young lady, he then revealed that his heart was also set on Floriander. "When the romantic attention of the two Farnum brothers is added together," he calculated, "the girl will have a **surfeit** so large she can hold an auction." After some further nonsense he at last closed his eyes and dipped a hand into the stream. Several seconds later there was a cry of **jubilation**, as he caught something in his palm and held it up over his head.

Watching all this with mild interest Joannie saw that it was not a flower that was lodged between Andrew's fingers. A closer look, and her mild interest changed to revulsion, as she exclaimed, "Excuse me, but yuck!"

Andrew himself realized quickly from the feel of the thing that it was no blossom, blue or otherwise. He lifted his head to get a look at it, and several flakes of soggy tobacco caught him on the chin. "Gross!" he cried, "a butt, a foul, disintegrating cigar butt. I want to talk immediately to my ... my ..."

> **loathsome**: very foul; inspiring disgust
> **pretext**: a reason which is given for some action, and which serves to cover over the real reason for the action

"Your physician?" prompted Henry.

"No."

"Your sports psychiatrist?"

"No."

"Well, who? Your lawyer, your confessor?"

"No," answered Andrew. "My journalist. It's the scandal which Allen has been waiting for: City Officials Stock Stream with **Loathsome** Cigar Butts."

Meagan laughed and called to him. "Sorry, Andrew, but it's a real bad time for a scandal to break. Allen's over at the Ambivalence Dome, covering the exhibition of antique cars."

Henry broke in, waggling his index finger, as though to lecture anyone who would listen. "He says he's there to cover the antique cars. But that's a **pretext.** There's a fabulous lunch at these exhibitions, you know."

READER: Fulano gives a great sentence using "anachronism."

AUTHOR: So we should pause and have a Fulano moment.

READER: It goes like this: "In the year 2727 the government began releasing a fine mist of protein and carbohydrate into the air over America. People met their nutritional needs just by breathing, and food became an anachronism."

AUTHOR: A dangerous example. What if in 2728 the government starts releasing a fine mist of vocabulary? Some of us will be looking for work.

READER: Well, get a real job.

Chapter 44: THE 1911 GARRULOUS

It was not fair to suggest that the main motive of Allen for covering the antique auto show was lunch—Henry Farnum had stretched the truth a bit on that one. But there was no exaggeration when Henry said that lunch at the Dome was fabulous. On the day of Allen's visit, as on every day, it was a **sumptuous** affair of five-star foods on crystal dishes, spread the entire length of a very long buffet table.

> **sumptuous**: highly expensive, and marked by a richness and splendor of quality that is often carried to the point of luxurious excess
> **cuisine**: a characteristic style of cooking practiced by a particular group of people; the range of dishes prepared according to such a style
> **soporific**: causing heavy drowsiness or sleep

Way beyond soup and crackers, thought Allen, as his keen vision caught sight of the table. And what a perfect opportunity—his thoughts ran on—professionalwise. No better chance for a young reporter to capture the cultured ease of this crowd than to share its cultured **cuisine**. Bamalford could not object: he knew that Allen had a friend—Mrs. Amanda Cook, the lady from A Thousand Ships, sponsor of a very popular cosmetics booth at the Dome's health and beauty review in September.

So without fear of being turned away Allen pitched in at the buffet table. He worked through an impressive sequence of stuffed mushrooms, lobster salad, several quiches, two enormous servings of shepherd's stew, and a dessert assortment called Chocolate Rendezvous. The result was predictable. Within an hour's time he was muttering groggily to himself: "Large lunches—**soporific** as ever." And he was searching for a quiet corner where he could rest his drowsy head.

> **ascetic**: very disciplined; severely limiting the amount of physical comfort, such as food, drink and sleep, that you allow yourself
> **soliloquy**: a conversation you have with yourself; a speech you make to no one but yourself
> **wan**: lacking vigor and drained of normal color, often through fatigue and sickness

He spotted a cluttered staging area, isolated from the main exhibition floor by a long, curving partition of burlap panels. Checking first that no one else was there, he entered and slumped gratefully against a pile of mannequins, dressed in turn-of-the-century clothing. "The drivers, no doubt, of these turn-of-the-century cars," he mumbled to himself. "Well, they have time to rest. But you, Allen, have no time, so you must be very **ascetic**, giving yourself only a minute to relax, far less than your body is longing for, and then with stern discipline, Allen, forcing that unwilling body back to its duties. And perhaps, Allen, if you had been more ascetic at lunch, perhaps …"

His **soliloquy** was interrupted by a sharp voice, speaking not much above a whisper. "Hsst! Boy! Over here, and I can show it to you."

Looking up abruptly Allen saw a woman of perhaps fifty-five or sixty, dressed in a long gray gown. The face was **wan** and lined, yet for all the paleness and all the creases it still had a striking beauty. Dark eyes stared at him intently and a slender arm waved him closer. "Come along quickly, boy, and you'll see it for yourself."

> **veranda**: a spacious porch or other outdoor deck or finished area that is right next to a house or building and is usually covered by some extension or overhang from it
> **pundit**: one who has become learned about a subject and now speaks with authority about it
> **garrulous**: inclined to talk and chatter at great length

She led him back onto the exhibition floor, on a winding path through the autos from another time, gleaming Hudsons and Daimlers, and brought him out onto something like a porch or **veranda** which overlooked the sea. A single car was on display there. In form, it was a classic touring car, with the exaggerated fenders, the high windshield, the elegantly wrought grill. But its form was not what caught the eye.

The car was a triumph of paintwork, a match for any bird of paradise. Streaks of scarlet deepened into purples and stormy blues, and brightened again towards painful brilliances of orange and yellow. Allen stared at the rippling progression of color, and began a mental draft of its description, for his article: "It ran the full … the full …"

An energetic male voice finished the sentence for him: "The full spectrum, of course. Or maybe one should call it the full visible spectrum, because they say there are other colors which we can't see, at both ends, the ultrareds and the … the … whatever. And do you ever wonder who they are—the 'they' of the 'they say'—the experts and **pundits** who have all the answers?"

Allen was casting about, trying to see who it was, but his efforts were interrupted by the woman. Her frailty seemed to be a matter of appearance only, for she caught him by the shoulder and easily spun him about toward the car. "Stay focused, boy. It's a 1911 **Garrulous**. Don't miss your chance to see it. Just a few of them were made."

reclusive: habitually avoiding social contacts and seeking to be alone
lucrative: yielding attractive profits

The energetic voice again—"Now don't place the wrong interpretation on that, young man. Just a few were made, true, true, but the demand for the 1911 Garrulous was quite substantial. It was a favorite of **reclusive** people, letting them hear, shall we say, a human voice without the need to mingle with humans. But, as you can appreciate, some rather unique parts and special materials were necessary to build a Garrulous, so manufacturing costs were quite high, and the enterprise was never a **lucrative** one. No great profit, no, no. As a result, not many of us were produced."

> **disabuse** (verb): to cause you to abandon an opinion by showing you its error
> **consternation**: a condition of being so dismayed and upset that you have trouble thinking clearly or taking a decision

Allen drew in his breath at the words "not many of us." He looked to the woman, in the hope that she would **disabuse** him of the wild suspicion that was taking hold in his mind. But her eyes were glittering with enjoyment of his **consternation**. "Of course, boy, of course," she shot at him. "Why else would they call it a Garrulous?"

His fingers drummed out an apprehensive beat on his camera case. "Don't be nervous, boy," scolded the woman. "It will make a great story. Perhaps it is not the scandal you've waited for, but it's a marvel in its own right."

> **legacy**: something passing down from one generation to the next, often within a family
> **vicissitudes**: the turns of fortune and changes of situation, both good and bad, that come your way
> **succinct**: stated in tightly knit expressions, with no more words than are necessary

"What I could tell you about scandal," resumed the voice. "What I could tell you. Imagine—it's 3:00 A.M. on a wintry night and I roll down a sleeping street to the house of a dreadfully rich family—old wealth, you know—a fortune passing down from generation to generation, the **legacy** of shipping ventures from before the Revolutionary War. A side door of the mansion swings open; a young woman, tears staining her face, rushes silently out and places a small parcel in the hands of my driver. It is wrapped in brown paper and not marked in any way. 'Place it in a bank deposit box,' she whispers, 'wait a year, then send me the key.' She is gone. My driver puts the parcel in my glove compartment. Days and weeks slip by. Things come up, misfortunes, trials, passing opportunities, all the **vicissitudes** of life. My driver is distracted and does not go to the bank."

296

"And the parcel," asked the woman, in a suppressed voice, "what of the parcel?"

"To speak more **succinctly** than is my custom," said the 1911 Garrulous with a pulsing in the bright wash of its colors, "where the parcel was put, it remains."

The woman's excitement could no longer be suppressed. "There, boy," she hissed. "You've got your scandal. A rich family, a mysterious parcel, a tear-stained face." She beckoned toward the car. "Hasten, boy, hasten! Get in, retrieve the parcel from its long neglect."

There was no movement, however, not a budge or a stir, on Allen's part. He was obviously reluctant to take on a role in the strange story.

"Learn from me boy," ordered the gray figure, catching his wrist in an urgent grasp. "An opportunity like this comes only once."

> **intractable**: firmly resisting the attempts of others to guide, manage or instruct you
>
> **ruse**: a clever pretense that you undertake in order to deceive someone and gain some advantage from him

Growing even more alarmed, Allen took a step back. "In all my years," declared the woman, "and they are more than you think, I have never seen such an **intractable** child." She clutched his wrist even more tightly. "Don't miss your chance. Retrieve that parcel before ..."

"No!" shouted Allen. "It's a trick to get me into the car. It's a ... a ..."

"Forgotten the word, boy? Ask me. I've learned a few of them in my four centuries."

"No. Wait. Here it comes." Allen pointed skyward. Through an opening in the dome Rachel Snoozer, notes in hand, came parachuting in.

"Which one," she called, "which one, Allen—'love' or 'stupid'? I can spell them both, without looking." She pushed the notes into a pocket and started to gather up the collapsing chute—it was peach in color and made of velvet. She was changing now. "O r ... today there's a new word, maybe the one you're looking for." She was becoming someone else. "The new word," she continued in an altered voice, "I can spell it too. R-u-s-e. **Ruse**."

Across the disintegrating scene, with a ragged stream of peach being sucked from the chute to the car, and flame the color of Aztec corn curling up from the glove compartment, Allen tossed the word. "Ruse! I won't get in the car because it's all a ruse. Something's going on, I won't ..."

"Huh? Look! He may be listening!" A gruff voice, angry, startled. The voice of Bamalford.

"Shut!" Not "Shut up!" Just "Shut!" Low and mean, not velvety. The voice of Nameless Entrepreneur.

dormant: in a state of sleep, rest or suspension of movement, often between periods of activity

scrutiny: a sharp, careful look at something, usually to see if there is any mistake, violation or other problem

feign: to make a false showing of something; often, to pretend to be in such and such a condition or emotional state

At the same moment another voice, commanding, urgent, allowing no discussion. But not a hostile voice. "Lie still. No blinks. No wiggles. Long, easy breathing, like when you're asleep." Allen knew the voice came from within himself, a guardian force, long **dormant**, but now awakened in an instant by the spur of danger. So he obeyed, and repressed all the yawns and stretches which would normally have been part of his waking.

He was half sunk by this time into the pile of mannequins, and a hard plastic forearm rested on his nose, and at least two plastic knees were poking into his ribs. But the most pressing weight on him was the gaze of Bamalford and Nameless Entrepreneur. He felt their fierce **scrutiny**, as they watched for the slightest sign that his sleep was a sham.

Allen had never **feigned** sleep before, and it was much harder than he would have thought. Just as the sweat was gathering at his hairline and threatening to run in large, telltale beads down his face, the ordeal ended. Bamalford growled something about "leaving the dummy among dummies," Nameless snarled "Shut!" and the two of them went off.

Allen waited a few minutes and then, giving his best imitation of a boy waking from a heavy sleep after a heavy lunch, got up and headed out the long hall which curved around to the exit. This course took him by the cage of the Harbinger Duck, and as he approached it he slipped his yellow press card into his pocket.

From its cramped prison the bird looked at him with something like recognition. "Just me," said Allen. "Nothing to fear. No repeat of that awful visit last autumn. No yellow cards alarmingly displayed."

explicate: to lay open the meaning of something; to explain something carefully by going through it in detail, part by part

neophyte: one just beginning to acquire some skill or learning

The bird cocked its head and seemed to be looking back along the corridor toward the exhibition floor. Allen read a question in the gaze. "What happened back there—is that it? Bamalford dropped a clue, that's what I think. But it's tangled in with the dream. I need someone to **explicate** that parachute sequence, to walk me through it image by image until it comes clear."

The duck was staring down the other direction of the corridor now. Allen smiled. "I understand. Go find a dream master and seek my explication from him. That makes sense."

He left the Dome and went in search of Ricky.

READER: Larry says that feigning sleep when you're awake is kid stuff, something for beginners and **neophytes**.
AUTHOR: Well, sorry. What does he say is the really big feigning challenge?
READER: Feigning you're awake when you're asleep.
AUTHOR: Whoa! That would be tough. But why does he want to do that?
READER: He thinks his score on the SAT will be higher if he takes it asleep.

Chapter 45: THE TOY OLIGARCHY

Allen was at another lunch. He was eating light, mostly celery. "No more nightmares, thank you!" he said.

"But you don't mind discussing the one you already had?" asked Ricky.

"No—the duck said you were the dream master."

Ricky made a face. "That's flattering!"

Meagan, François, Joannie and Tedesco were with them. They had hiked out along the ridge, through the grove of pine and myrtle, to the tip of Cape Scurrility. A brilliant noonday shimmered around them. Allen was describing the dream—especially the last part and how he woke from it.

> **adventitious**: showing up from outside a situation, more or less by chance, rather than arising from forces internal to the situation
> **vicinity**: the surroundings of something; the area which lies close to something

"The parachute scene," broke in Ricky, waving a celery stick, "wasn't part of the natural flow of the dream. It was a response to something **adventitious**. That's my professional view."

Allen waved celery back. "And the point?"

"Something in the external world, in the **vicinity** of your sleeping body, intruded into your dream—like the footsteps of Bamalford and Nameless, and their voices. And you, the dreamer, translated that intrusion into the parachute scene."

With a frown Joannie cut in. "Fine. But again—what's the point?"

Ricky gave her a look of vast patience and tolerance. "You're trying very hard, I'm sure. Perhaps if I use shorter sentences and ..."

> **condescension**: the act of treating someone with an exaggerated carefulness which suggests that he is of inferior intelligence or rank and that you are graciously stooping for a moment from a position of superiority
> **ruse**: a clever pretense that you undertake in order to deceive someone and gain some advantage from him

Daggers came from Joannie's eyes. "Ricky, you know how I hate **condescension**."

"Actually," he answered, "that was why ... Well, anyway, what's important is the word that Rachel spelled—'**ruse**.' Allen didn't pull that one out of his mental files. He actually heard it. And he actually heard it because Bamalford or Nameless actually spoke it, a moment before they saw him. All of which could mean something. So now you have it—the opinion of the master. Let each one understand it to the best of his or her abilities. And you, Tedesco, no disrespect, please—let's just put down that tomato or whatever it is."

Allen didn't even look. He was thinking hard about what Ricky had said. "You're obnoxious," he began, "but you could be right. I was starting to wake. A word spoken by Bamalford or Nameless—'ruse,' just for example—could have slipped through the gate and down into the dream."

> **perpetrate**: to bring something bad to accomplishment, such as a crime or fraud
> **demeanor**: the sum of outward manifestations (posture, tone of voice, facial expression, gestures, etc.) by which you display an attitude toward others
> **gullible**: too quick and unquestioning in your belief of what others tell you, and thus easily taken in

François said abruptly, "Well, that upsets me, a lot." Her usual calm had vanished suddenly. "I don't want Bamalford and Nameless using a word like 'ruse.' It's OK for other people, because they mean innocent ruses or ruses they've read about. But when Bamalford and Nameless say it, they mean some very nasty ruse, I'm sure, which they are **perpetrating** right here and now, in Dropanchor."

Suddenly aware that her fist was waving and voice was rising, she stopped and smiled weakly. "So much for that highly composed **demeanor** I've been cultivating."

Meagan took François' hand, shaped it back into a fist, and held it up. "Don't stop yet, OK. You may be the voice we need to hear. Were we too **gullible** when we swallowed Bamalford's story—you know, that the road was for Nameless and his shattered health and his need to meditate in a lonely, beautiful place?"

> **mercenary**: hungry for money; viewing everything exclusively in terms of financial gain and loss
> **irrefutable**: undeniably correct; not able to be called into doubt or shown to be false

François spoke in a lower tone than before. "I'm with Grandma Dubois on this one. She always felt this arrangement of Nameless going up the mountain to be with nature was a ... a ruse, to use the word of the day. Nameless is a simple man—**mercenary** from head to toe. For him the mountain can only be interesting if it has the look of money. Bamalford is more complex, no doubt. He would like the mountain for his monument, the Giuseppe Stone for his statue. He has a passion for his own image."

"Well, Frankie," said Meagan with a smile, "that last point anyway is **ir-refutable**." She was looking out toward Cape Stairstep, where the bronze sculpture of Bamalford stood huge and glinting in the sun. "So Nameless is the money guy, and Bamalford the monument guy."

"Frank, if you please," replied François. "And Bamalford is both, I guess that's the point. For all his madness about grand monuments, he still finds time to be very interested in money. He knows its uses, what it can buy. So put him together with Nameless and give the two of them access to a rare, exquisite product like the Mendicant Berries, and then expect them not to hear cash-register noises! Ha! They'll grab the whole crop if we let them...and put it in bottles. There! That's Grandma's theory. And mine too. Wine! Nameless isn't meditating up there, that's all pretense. He's harvesting the berries to support a wine business."

"But Ricky," objected Tedesco, as though Ricky and not François had spoken, "why don't we just give them some free advice: stop to steal berries from the people or ..."

> **credible**: deserving to be believed or taken seriously
> **apathy**: a state of emotional flatness in which you are indifferent to events which should concern you

"Or we slap the cuffs on both of 'em," concluded Joannie.

Ricky was shaking his head. "It's not a **credible** threat. Bamalford and Nameless will never believe it's going to happen. In the first place they're not stealing. The bluff where the berries grow is on public land. And, secondly— they know we're neutralized and won't lift a finger against them."

François nodded grimly. "Grandma worries about **apathy**—people losing their spark and not caring anymore what Bamalford and Nameless do."

"It may not be apathy," corrected Ricky. "It's more like dependence. People do feel strongly about Dropanchor being turned into a cash cow, but how can they challenge Bamalford when they depend totally on his protection to keep Draco away?"

> **viable**: (1) capable of existing or surviving in a self-sustaining way without any sort of special outside support; (2) able to be carried into practice successfully
> **insolvent**: not having enough money to pay your bills
> **oligarchy**: (1) a political system in which a few people have power and control over the rest; (2) those few people themselves, considered as the ruling group

Allen was waving a stick of celery, trying to get some attention. "A thousand pardons. Apathy, dependence—it doesn't matter. Even if we stood by Victoria Road with signs begging Bamalford to ferment our berries, he wouldn't do it. It's just not a **viable** project. The harvest is too small. If he took every last berry growing on the bluff, he couldn't squeeze out more than a few hundred bottles of wine. The revenues would never cover the costs, and the Bamalford Winery would soon be **insolvent**."

"Put that celery down, young man," said François, "and no one gets hurt. You're overlooking one thing, something we all saw as kids—the Toy **Oligarchy**."

Allen blinked several times. "What new madness …?"

"Allen," said François in a lecturing tone, "if there are twenty kids who play on a street, and if they're all wild for some hot new toy, but only a few of them have that toy—who rules?"

> **concede**: to agree that something said—as, for example, a statement by your opponent in an argument—is correct
> **germane**: having something to do with the topic you're interested in at the moment; having a significant connection to some subject matter
> **didactic**: designed to pass on learning and instruction, sometimes through the medium of something entertaining

"Well," said Allen grudgingly, "I don't see where this is going, but I will **concede** that on my street it was … the few."

"Exactly," said François, "the few kids with the hot toy run the street. They decide when to play, and where, and who gets to play and who sits out. That's the Toy Oligarchy."

Allen, who had never lowered the celery stick, lifted it higher and said, "I have been very patient, you know, waiting to see how all this was **germane**, but I don't see any connection between kids ruling the street and Bamalford making wi…"

There was a flash of wings, breaking across the scene, and for an instant the suspension of flight. The celery stick was torn from Allen's hand by gray talons. At once the robber, a heavy-bodied gull, was off with its prize. Its screech rang across the expanse between Cape Scurrility and Bamalford's bronze statue. Allen was reduced to babble.

François, unshaken, handed him another piece of celery. "So think twice next time before you say I'm not germane. And now, if you can keep quiet, we'll stage a short drama, highly entertaining, but **didactic** as well, a little economics lesson showing how Bamalford can get rich on a few bottles of wine. Just let me get some props—and hire my cast."

With a swift hand she snatched from Tedesco the object he was holding, a reddish-orange fruit resembling a tomato. From Ricky she grabbed the three real tomatoes that his mother had sent for lunch. The entire collection went on a napkin in front of her. Then with some swift nudges and pleas she convinced Meagan and Joannie to take the leading roles in whatever was to follow.

> **adroit**: quick and clever at some difficult task; handling it with a skillful grace
>
> **copious**: enough and more than enough; presenting an abundant supply of something

"Wow," said Allen. "She's **adroit** at this sort of thing."

François smiled broadly. "Thank you. Merci Dubois didn't get all the nice moves. Now, watch please."

She dropped gracefully to her knees in front of Meagan and Joannie, and with a jabbing motion gave each of them an imaginary injection in the shoulder. "There—a standard dose for each of you. The itch to be an oligarch is now in your blood."

From the napkin she took a single tomato. "Ladies—the harvest of tomatoes this year was **copious**. Not enough boxes to hold it all. In the U.S. alone, at least three trillion tomatoes are on the market. With that in mind, please, tell me—how much would you pay for this red beauty in my hand?"

There was a calculating tone in Meagan's voice. "Three trillion you say, lass? Every family will have a crate of them. I won't pay more than pennies for something so common."

> **stymie**: to block someone from reaching a goal; to prevent an action from being completed successfully
>
> **despondent**: feeling very low and depressed, often because you've judged that there is little or no hope of things getting better

"Well, how about this?" asked François, replacing the tomato and taking up the mystery object from the napkin. "It looks a bit like a tomato but it's not. This, ladies, is a persimmon, and you should know that the persimmon harvest this year was a catastrophe. The growers were absolutely **stymied**: everything they tried was defeated by freezes, droughts, mildews, locusts and so on. Total USA crop was 329 persimmons. The number of persimmons available locally? About five. How does that make you feel?"

Joannie rubbed her shoulder. "It makes me feel that the shot is working. Think—only five people get a persimmon. And I'm going to be one of them. We, the five persimmon owners, we wear the big hats. We've got what everybody wants, and in our social circle we rule: we can make you or break you by inviting you or not to the very hot Last Persimmon on Earth Party. We, the five, become an oligarchy, just like the Toy Oligarchy which François told us about. I've got to have that thing at any price! Twenty dollars."

She reached for the persimmon, but her eager grasp was pushed back by Meagan. "Not so fast, princess. We don't want Meagie all **despondent**, do we, the girl with the sad face? How much nicer if she becomes one of the five persimmon haves ruling thousands of persimmon have-nots. I'll pay thirty-five dollars!"

A bidding war broke out, and within minutes the price for the persimmon had shot up to $375. The fierce light blazing in Meagan's eyes was answered by one just as fierce in Joannie's. It was getting uncomplimentary, and Allen wasn't sure they were kidding anymore.

"Stop!" he cried. "I'm convinced. Yes—that's probably how it would be with Mendicant Berry Wine, people fighting to get a bottle. Yes—the price would go through the roof. Yes—Bamalford and Nameless could make a fortune. So stop! It's getting too real."

> **encore**: a repeat performance, often at the request of an audience
> **ensue**: to occur after some event, and often as a natural development or consequence of it
> **extirpate**: to eliminate every trace of; to pull out roots and all

He rushed forward, grabbed the persimmon, and held it high, out of the reach of either Meagan or Joannie. In an instant it was high out of his reach as well, as the gull, returning for a brilliant **encore**, swept it from his hand.

A general madness **ensued**. Meagan and Joannie resumed their bidding war, yelling four- and five-digit numbers after the departing gull. Tedesco hopped about in dismay, groaning in both English and Portuguese for his lost persimmon. François started giving a moral lecture, speaking across the void of shimmering air to the statue, warning that birds would carry Bamalford off too unless he **extirpated** the greed from his heart. "By the roots!" she shouted. Allen cared nothing for all of that. His finger had been nipped, and he was crying loudly for a helicopter.

Only Ricky was calm. With a sad shake of his head, he watched his classmates. "The children become so ruffled," he murmured. His turn was not long to come.

> **wane**: gradually to become smaller or less powerful or less important
> **elation**: a high joyfulness, often springing from the achievement of a triumph or the perception of good fortune coming your way
> **induction**: the art of reasoning your way to a general rule on the basis of what you've observed in particular instances

He felt a light tap on his shoulder. "The gull," he cried. "The witch!" But it was Ms. Jensen. "Ricky," she said with a curious smile, "I won't disturb the others—they seem busy. But a letter came. And when the frenzy **wanes** a bit here, when the uproar dies down, would you give it to the right person?" Again the curious smile, and she withdrew along the path which followed the crest of the cape back to the school building.

Ricky looked down at the letter, and what he saw made sweat spring to his forehead. It was addressed to Foster Farbugle, and the sender, according to the envelope, was Sallie Driven. Scarcely breathing he turned it and shook it, sniffed it, held it up to the sun, and then tore it open ferociously. "Tedesco," he shouted. "Help! I've forgotten how to read English. Great education—twenty-seven years old and I can't read English. No, wait—it's coming back, a noun here, a verb there. Oh, wow! She called me Dear Foster. And there's more."

Ricky finally read the message he had waited so long to receive: Sallie Driven was coming to Dropanchor. He was stirred by his **elation** into a wild dance. "She's coming, Cabbage. The letter says. What a great education after all. It taught me to read these little miracles that arrive now and then in the mail." Hopping from one foot to the other, he was holding the letter triumphantly over his head.

"But it never has taught you," asked Tedesco, with a glance all about, "to do this thing, this … **induction** I think is your word?"

> **stifle**: to press down and smother something that is trying to emerge or express itself
> **oblique**: not head-on; having an indirect meaning or impact

"Induction?" said Ricky, still hopping. "You mean like drawing a general rule? Like seeing how the celery and the persimmon got carried off and generalizing that any small object which is held up will be snatched by a gull—here on Cape Scurrility? Is that what you mean, my cabbage friend, **stifling** a grin at the corners of your mouth?"

Ricky had the fastest reflexes in the senior class, and they were all that saved his letter. At the last possible moment, when only inches separated it from the hooked toes of the diving gull, he pulled it from danger, sweeping his arms down from the posture of triumph in which he had been holding them.

Now he was the one to shout after the bird. "Hope ya go extinct!"

Tedesco tugged at his sleeve. "Tell him to bring back my persimmon."

"You!" cried Ricky with indignation. "You saw him diving for my letter, a letter for which I waited twenty-seven years, and you gave me no warning."

With a variety of theatrical gestures Tedesco protested that his remark about induction had, in its own way, been a warning.

"If that was a warning at all," answered Ricky, "it was the most sideways, indirect, **oblique** warning ever yet given." Then he broke suddenly into a smile, and began flapping his arms wildly. "But that's OK. I really believe if the gull had grabbed the letter, I would have been airborne in pursuit. And what a beautiful sight—R. Snoozer on the wing!"

306

READER: Younger readers will be shocked by the "Hope ya go extinct" remark.

AUTHOR: I know. It should be "Hope *you* go extinct." But anyway, since when do I have younger readers?

READER: Kids start their SAT prep now as early as the second grade.

AUTHOR: Serious? Hope they're catching all my subtle jokes.

READER: Don't you think mumps and measles are enough?

AUTHOR: I bet if I understand that one, I'm not going to like it.

Chapter 46: THE NOT SO EUPHONIOUS MALPH

Several days after the meeting on the beach, Povano had found Merci and asked her to take on an errand—to come up with some way to anchor the whale decoy that would not interfere with the whales. "Probably impossible," Merci had said, "but let's check the library."

"Probably impossible," she said again to François as they climbed the marble steps and passed the huge and threatening signs about overdue books. "But maybe *The Civil Engineer's Best Companion* has some ideas."

> **daunting**: so impressive or forceful as to shake your courage
> **gargoyle**: a small monstrous or deformed figure, often carved in stone and constructed into the upper ledges of a building so as to stare down
> **panacea**: some single thing or process that serves as a cure for all problems

When they entered the main reading room Merci gasped and gripped François by the arm. "You're my best companion," she said, "so don't wander off this time to see the bookmobile." They had come upon a **daunting** sight. Victoria Framley was there, hunched in all her immensity over the most spacious of the reading tables, looking vaguely like an enlarged version of the library **gargoyle**, which as always was staring down from its ledge high overhead. At the center of Ms. Framley's table was a telephone, and it was the focus of all her attention. She was wiping at it violently with a tissue.

The table itself was an image of chaos: a hundred or more magazines were strewn at every angle, and onto their confusion the contents of a large purse— the combs and vials and wallets—had spilled out. Spotted here and there over the mess were small puddles of chocolate, the vitamin syrup which Ms. Framley gulped as a **panacea** for all the hurts and afflictions of life.

> **livid**: in a condition of great rage, even to the point that your face loses its normal coloration
> **sequester**: to set something off by itself, often out of view or beyond the reach of some influence
> **superfluous**: in excess; over and above the amount you need or can put to use

It was obviously no panacea at the moment, however. She had allowed an entire spoon of it to fall on the speaking end of the phone, and it had oozed into the little holes. She was furious over this, and **livid** to see that her efforts to clean the phone were just smearing and spattering the goo around further. The sudden sight of Merci brought her fury even higher, and rather than burst she let out a great snort. Bezzle, repairing books in a side room, came running and warned Merci that her borrowing privileges would be revoked if she ever made such a sound again.

The combined force of the snort and the false accusal shook Merci, and François led her to an out-of-the-way table, **sequestered** from the main reading hall by several rows of bookshelves. "It's like a feeding frenzy," she explained in a low voice. "The Fram tears through the fine-living magazines and places orders, on the spot, for everything under the sun, jade sinks and parasols with ivory handles and porcelain figurines that play rock from the fifties, and so on. It's very nice stuff, but it all duplicates things she already has. It's all **superfluous**. Half of it she never unwraps and the other half…"

> **rhinestone**: a large gem cut from glass or formed from paste, often with the appearance of a large, flashy diamond
> **distill**: to obtain an end product, pure and concentrated, by condensing it out from some coarser stock
> **plagiarism**: the act of holding yourself out as the originator of a literary product actually created by someone else

The rasping voice of Ms. Framley cut into François' account. "**Rhinestone**! I said 'rhinestone'—the deluxe version with the rhinestone accents. Yes—I know it's hard to understand me. So get the wax out! Ha, ha!" She was on the phone again, placing orders. It was impossible to filter out that voice, and the two sisters heard all the details as she purchased from stores like Cloisonné Meltdown, Heaven-Sent Opportunities, and One Less Koala.

Then there was a call different from the others. "Yes, it's Victoria, and I have the one for tomorrow—'No use crying over spilt milk.' Me too—I'm excited about it too—short and easy to remember, the way you said. No, no—not borrowed, not a bit. As always, an original offering, **distilled** like a transparent drop of wisdom from the life experience of Victoria Framley."

A puzzlement vanished from François' face, and she whispered, "Of course—she's talking to Bamalford. She's telling him the proverb to go in the *Vociferous Beacon*, in tomorrow's edition, in that little box on page one. And even though she found it in a book ten minutes ago I bet, she's claiming she made it up. **Plagiarism** is one of her more lovely qualities."

Now the voice of Ms. Framley dropped and nothing more could be heard except fragments, broken mentions of rhinestones and store names. François had to cover up a laugh. "Tell me that Bamalford loves the shopping news!"

> **profane** (verb): to abuse something sacred by subjecting it to the touch or presence of what is cheapening and base

pulchritude: beauty, especially the beauty of face or body
divine (verb): to gain knowledge of something hidden, not through ordinary means of study and research but through inspired guesswork or impressively sharp intuition

It was Ms. Framley's final call, and when it was over the library at last grew quiet. Merci began her review of *A Civil Engineer's Best Companion*. François had brought a collection of world poetry, and now she settled in with it. A deep calm descended upon their hidden corner, and they lost themselves in their reading. An unscheduled sacred silence, thought François as she glanced up at the gloom of trailing light and gathered shadow that lay above them among the beams. Unfortunately, it was a silence soon **profaned**.

A loud snort, from close at hand, fell across the scene and jolted the sisters out of their studies. No more than five feet away stood Ms. Framley, leaning heavily against a shelf. Her gaze was judgmental and unforgiving. There was a small notebook lying open in her hand, bound in a violet-colored leather. When she saw Merci turning toward her, she wrote something in it. The scratch of her pen, a heavy fountain pen with a jeweled cap, was harsh and menacing.

"There," she said, looking at Merci with great satisfaction, "your name is in the book—shortly after Foster's." She tapped the pen for a moment against the gold spoon dangling from her ear, and then wrote something more. "Your name, and your offense."

Merci called on the courage which came to her at such moments. "And the offense, what might it be? **Pulchritude**?"

"Pulchritude!" cried Ms. Framley, drawing herself up. "You dare speak to me, adored by Greek sailors, of pulchritude! No, no." She closed the violet notebook and held it behind her. "Your offense is something else. But what it is you will just have to **divine**. Ha, ha—one clue. It's something pretty bad. It justifies tearing up the school lease—I'm sure that's what Abner would do. Ha, ha."

ebb (verb): to sink down or fall off gradually from a peak level, as for example the tide falls back from its high mark on the sand
primordial: having the raw force or stark simplicity that characterizes a primitive situation
punctilious: taking all the little points of a law or rule seriously, and seeing to it that they are carried out with exactness

She said nothing more, returning with an air of moral accomplishment to her magazines. Merci went back to her reading also, but now the sentences were tangled and hopelessly complex. She wanted to remain composed after the encounter with Ms. Framley. The rush of courage, though, had **ebbed**, and

310

the truth was—she felt rattled. "I didn't do anything bad. But—my name's in the book." Her shoulders trembled slightly.

François took her by the arm. "Poor Merci. It's as though we're all born with some **primordial** fear—too deep in our roots ever to be reasoned away. Mine I'm afraid is the dark. Yours is getting your name in the book."

Merci smiled weakly and made another effort to understand her reading. The morning passed by slowly until 11:45, when there was something of a disturbance, as Ms. Framley, after a further dose of her Decadent Vitamins, and further spillage, shouted to Bezzle that she was off to her dinner.

At precisely twelve noon Bezzle posted a sign reading Lunch in two-inch letters, and disappeared into a back room. Two-inch letters and a twelve o'clock lunch, lasting an hour, were specified by his contract with Dropanchor. He was **punctilious** to the last degree about his rights and duties under that contract, so there was no chance that he would reappear a moment before or after one. Merci and François had the reading room to themselves.

A few minutes later Merci stretched and said, "I think I'll wander aimlessly for a few minutes around the library."

> **belie**: to serve as evidence showing the falsity of some statement or appearance
> **exorcise**: to drive out a demon or oppressive spirit that has afflicted someone

François shook her head. "Aimless wandering? Nice try, Merci. Your desperate look **belies** the apparent innocence of your plan. You know that the violet notebook may be sitting on Ms. Framley's table. And you're tempted. But remember—there's never been a Dubois who was a snoop. We go all the way back to … Charlemagne I think it was … and never a snoop."

"My name is in the book," answered Merci softly, "and that scares me. Not even Charlemagne would like having his name in the book." Then she rose and left her place, with quiet footsteps. There was utter silence for a short while, until François was startled from her seat by a sudden exclamation: "The Losers!"

She rushed into the main reading room, and saw her sister close to Ms. Framley's table. "I never touched the violet book," Merci protested at once, with alarm evident in her eyes. "I was close, really close, because having my name in there spooks me, but all at once that fear was … **exorcised**, driven out like a demon, by something a lot more urgent. Look, François, right now, at this magazine, one of the Fram's magazines—look at this ad. We can't wait a minute."

euphonious: nice-sounding; falling pleasantly on the sense of hearing; pleasant when pronounced (commonly said of a spoken word or a string of words)

eclectic: loosely integrating in a single work or presentation distinct elements selected from several different styles, ways of thinking, etc.

discern: to catch sight of and recognize an object, often one that is hard to see, such as one that is distant or set against a confused or indistinguishable background

François tried to make sense out of the chaos spread before her. Near the center of the littered table was the violet notebook. A tattered, yellowing document lay to the left of it—the Dogmatic Lease. To the right, one of the magazines, a large one, had been fully opened and was propped against a book. "This is the one, isn't it?" she said with a professional cheerfulness, trying to calm her sister. "Let's see—a full-page ad for a product called Malph. What a horrible sound—the Not So **Euphonious** Malph, that's what I would call it. But there it is, and right at the top too—in big, capital letters. And beneath that MALPH ..."

"Yes, François," interrupted Merci, with a growing impatience, "yes, tell me what you see under the MALPH."

"Well, there's an incredible drawing, very **eclectic**, pulling in elements from ... three different styles of art. At the bottom is a wide curtain of water, painted in tiny daubs of color, shimmering and vague, in the manner of the Impressionists. Above that, a screening of leaves, each distinct, in a variety of striking greens, with sharp, emphatic edges—to me anyway the look of some of the Latin American painters. And at the top, wouldn't you know it, angels, a hundred or so with wings outspread, crowded against one another, crowded against that awful MALPH. They are done in the ornamental style of cathedral windows. And they...they... Huh! Just a minute!"

"Go on, François," said Merci in a leading voice, "what have you **discerned** as you look more carefully at the angels?"

"The angels," answered François, with the color draining from her cheeks, "aren't ... angels, the spreading wings are really ... pairs of huge, fanning leaves, and the ... Oh, Merci—it's those funky Loser plants that you made a wall from, when you saved the berries from the mystery vapor."

Merci clutched François' arm, just above the elbow, and squeezed hard. "What else, smartie?"

Now it was easy for François to recognize the elements of the drawing. The water was in fact the series of falls which dropped down the bluff where the Mendicant Briars grew. And the screening of leaves—that was the briars themselves.

The impatience was gone from Merci's voice. "Finish the ad. There's still the message at the bottom."

> **vindicate**: to show that some opinion or action is right after all, in spite of people having criticized or rejected it
> **heritage**: the stock of traditions, cultural expression, symbols, sacred objects, and so forth, which have passed down to us and which contribute to our identity as a family, nation, religious congregation or other group

François read for a moment and groaned. "Merci—Malph is a wine! Grandma's fears are completely **vindicated**. The old lady got it right. Listen to the ad—'You'll never find the berries. But if you find the wine, arrange financing and buy it! Malph!'"

Her voice fell to an angry murmur. "That is so, so foul—Bamalford has started marketing our **heritage**, bottling it, putting his ugly name on it! We have to warn Grandma and Povano."

"No later than tonight," said Merci gravely. "There's a meeting this evening on the beach, another one about the whale decoy—to choose a company to make it. Povano will be there, of course, and ditto for Grandma."

> **apprentice**: one who learns a trade by working for a time with a master of it
> **astute**: having such a clear insight into the way something works that you can deal with it in a clever, effective manner

"I'll give that old bat a ditto—right on the side of the head." There was a coarse laugh. Ms. Framley was returning through the wide front door. "I'll give her a perch too, next to our handsome friend." She motioned toward the gargoyle on the high ledge. "The old fossil can sit at his side and be his **apprentice**, to learn the trade of grinning and staring. And as for you snoops, shameless little criminals, shall I read Paragraph 55"—she was picking up the Dogmatic Lease—"about respecting the privacy rights of the Framleys? Or shall I just cancel this thing and take back my school?"

Merci started to say something, but before she had the chance François caught her hand and marched her out of the library. "Your name's already in the book and now you want a big check beside it too?"

————————————

READER: Larry told me how to sell a new wine. First, a month of ads: Malph Is Coming! Then the message: Malph Is Gone. Finally, huge billboards: Malph Is Back, Briefly!

313

AUTHOR: Incredible! Larry is obviously quite **astute** at making people buy things. I'd like to hire his shrewd mind to sell this book.

READER: He says this book is a desperate case, but there's one advertising trick that might help.

AUTHOR: I'm all ears. What is it?

READER: It's called the 200% rebate.

Chapter 47: THE CELESTIAL ZOO

"Onward through the fog," said François to herself, hurrying as she went. "Onward in and out of the fog" would have been more accurate. Like squares on a checkerboard, patches of fog, **discrete** and self-contained, alternated with stretches of open air.

> **discrete**: occurring as something separate and distinct; not shading into something else, not forming a continuous, unbroken range or stretch with other things
> **imminent**: on the brink of happening
> **exculpate**: to establish, on the basis of some excuse or explanation, that a person is not to blame for something of which he has been accused

She was on the beach, hastening through the early evening toward the meeting stone, where in a few minutes the debate about the whale decoy would resume. Povano was already there, she was sure, and now was the chance to warn him about what she and Merci had learned—about the wine called Malph, and the **imminent** attack on the Mendicant Berries. "Imminent if it hasn't started already," she said grimly, as an image of a bookmobile, sagging with berries, started to …

Suddenly she was hopping crazily, falling. She had tripped on somebody. There was a laugh, a familiar voice, the friend side of friend or foe. "If the scene of the accident," said Allen, "which is to say right here, were in a fog pocket, you might have an **exculpating** circumstance. Zero visibility, that sort of thing. But here—a little zone without fog, and with more than enough twilight to show the path—there are no excuses for bumping into the royal body. So that'll be a million dollars, please. And by the way—what's so imminent?"

François was up on her feet again, brushing off the sand. "Allen," she lectured, "if you were a gentleman you would take the blame for our collision."

"You pay the million and I'll take the blame," he answered. "And again—what is so imminent?"

> **vigilance**: the state of being watchful and on guard
> **cardinal**: crucial; having a pivotal importance
> **discriminating**: perceiving the subtle differences between things through the careful use of the senses or of judgment

So she described what she and Merci had seen that afternoon, the lifestyle magazines, the strange sketch of the Mendicant Briars, the advertisement for the new wine. Allen listened intently, and asked her several questions about details. "Something very nasty is in the works," he said, frowning. "**Vigilance** is the number one virtue right now: we really need to be on the watch."

François nodded. "Like hawks, I'm afraid. And—by the way—sorry if I wrecked your carefree mood."

He shook his head. "You didn't. I was worried already. And I know you'd love to hear about it. Think back to the night when Ms. Jensen saw the book-mobile on the mountain. What was happening that night?"

François thought a moment and gasped. "Oh, bad! There was a town meeting and everybody was on the beach—just like tonight."

"On the beach," repeated Allen, "at the meeting stone, tucked down under the capes and headlands, with no view at all of the road up the mountain. That last point is a **cardinal** one, I'm sure, for Bezzle or whoever drives the book-mobile now. He's very big on escaping detection. Remember the way he was traveling when Ms. Jensen spotted him—lights off, trying to be invisible. And tonight—well, tonight is as good as it gets. He can leave his high beams on if he wants and never be noticed. No one will be watching the mountain tonight. Everyone will be at the meeting, even Ms. Jensen."

Because Allen and François had not yet passed under Cape Scurrility on their way to the meeting stone, they still had an unobstructed view of the lower reaches of the mountainside. Almost against her will, François looked up and scanned the slopes. All she saw was the gathered dusk and the gray patches of fog which rested on the scene. Beyond this she could distinguish nothing. "My evening vision is not very **discriminating**," she said. "Everything blurs. But for what it's worth, I don't see anything alarming."

> **surreptitious**: using sly tricks and concealments to avoid being noticed or detected
> **mesmerize**: to capture someone's attention so completely that he is almost left in a trance or under a hypnotic spell
> **indelible**: incapable of being erased or deleted; marking something permanently

Allen was staring now in the same direction. Some moments passed. "Maybe, maybe not," he said at last in a tense voice. "Nothing on the mountain itself, at least the parts that we can see, but on the road that runs across the hillside, from the library to the school, I think there's a dark object moving. Very **surreptitiously**—without lights, and creeping so slow that it appears almost stationary."

That was when Tedesco came along. Although he strained to see what Allen was seeing, he could not. "But what about the birds?" he asked.

"The birds!" said Allen. "What birds?"

316

"The white *coluna*, the white pillar, you can see it."

"Even my ratty night vision can see it," François said to Tedesco. "But isn't it just a little plume of fog?"

Allen was staring at the hillside with new intensity. His voice was distant. "It's in time," he said slowly.

François shook him. "You look **mesmerized**. Please come out of the trance and tell us what you're talking about."

"Tedesco's white column. It's moving in time with that darker object that I wish I was just imagining."

François was first to put all the pieces together. "Then Tedesco was right—it is a column of birds! They're following the smell, that strong, stubborn, **indelible** fish smell—fifteen years haven't removed it. Allen—don't you dare look confused. I'm talking about the bookmobile. Oh—this is horrible. It was a fish market for a while, remember, and it's still got the smell to prove it. That's your darker object, just what we hoped it wouldn't be—the bookmobile, with an escort of gulls. We have got to …"

She looked at Allen with alarm in her eyes.

"We have got to …" he echoed reluctantly.

Tedesco said it for them. "We have got to get up this *grandão* of a mountain and see what is happening."

> **rotund**: plump and rounded by virtue of being overweight
> **pithy**: packing a lot of meaning into a few well chosen words
> **attenuated**: drawn out and thin; weak because of having too little mass or substance

Allen gazed doubtfully at his stomach, where it curved out a little ways beyond his beltline, and said, "As for racing up mountainsides, we who are physically **rotund** …"

"Will just have to be mentally tough," finished François. "Like those of us who are afraid of the dark."

That was the beginning of a desperate chase. As they hurried north along the beach toward the base of Cape Scurrility, they picked up Ricky and Joannie, saying only, "Big trouble. C'mon!"

"That's too **pithy**," cried Ricky. But he ran with the others and was swept into the pursuit.

They caught the zigzag path up Cape Scurrility. Even from the first it was difficult, punishing them in their hurry, leaving them short of breath. When Joannie, looking down to the beach, saw Meagan with Ms. Jensen and tried calling them, her cry was weak and thin, too **attenuated** to carry through the heavy air.

Not far up from the foot of the cape there was a ceiling of fog. They pushed into it, maintaining a close formation. Visibility dropped to almost nothing. In the dense vapor they lost all sense of direction. The path kept bending, and in spots was so rough they feared they had lost it. As they trudged on endlessly, they could sense the night descending.

"Stupid, stupid path!" cried Allen. "Does it think we are ...?" He could not finish, for lack of breath.

> **amorphous**: lacking any definite shape or recognizable form
> **forebears**: those from whom you are descended; your ancestors

François gave a short laugh. "The general direction is up, if that helps."

Then, as if they were stepping out of a tent, they emerged from the cloud and were under open sky. The relief was enormous. After so much fumbling about in the **amorphous** foldings of white and gray, there was a strange delight to see the sharp points of the stars, newly out, and the shapes which they defined.

"At last!" cried Ricky in between gulps of air. "We can use the stars to reckon where we are. That's how our **forebears** did it ... from the beginning of time." With his head thrown back, he was surveying all the heavens. "Look—the Ursa! That was a Roman animal similar to a bear. Its tail points ... north, or something like that."

Joannie beckoned to a different stretch of sky and labored out the words: "There! Giant lizard. Seven stars. Its snout is to the east." She said no more, for like Ricky she was catching her breath, pulling in long drafts of air.

> **preposterous**: highly ridiculous, to the point of being impossible to believe or take seriously
> **celestial**: belonging to the realm of the sky

Allen, panting worst of all, was finally able to say that there was only one constellation he could ever see, a buffalo next to a den made from mud and sticks.

"**Preposterous**," cried François. "Did you ever hear of the beavers?" She was tossing up her hands. "What a zoo! And by the way, the **Celestial** Zoo, with its ursa and lizard and seriously confused buffalo, will close in one minute. We're heading into another fog bank."

> **erratic**: bending and wandering this way and that, with no regular pattern or course
> **anomalous**: running contrary to what is required by some rule or pattern

They marched directly into the swirling mass, and struggled again to stay on the trail as it followed an **erratic** course of switches and bends up the face of the cape. Their pace was steady, but maddeningly slow. "Bother!" shouted Ricky, as he kicked his toe against a stone. "I'm anti-fog forever!"

"Whiner!" answered François. Then her voice brightened. "Besides, look—all at once we're out of it again—up and out I should say."

They had arrived at the top, and stood on the high spur of land where they came sometimes on school days for lunch. The fog was pooled below them. Above the ridges to the east a three-quarter moon was rising.

"Three-quarter and soon to be full," said Joannie.

"Three-quarter and where was it when we needed it?" asked Allen. Looking to the moon, but beckoning back toward the sea, he scolded, "You should have been in the west, as we climbed. Then your light would have reached us."

Joannie scolded him in turn. "For an almost full moon to be in the western sky shortly after sunset, that would be **anomalous**, Allen, and very disturbing. The lunar cycle has its pattern, you know, which it has followed faithfully for quite some time. It's one of the few things we can count on, so please don't start generating exceptions."

They moved out once again, sweeping quickly along the ridge of the cape, past the moonlit outpost that was their school, and onto the grassy expanse stretching up to East Bridge. It was swift progress, but exhausting.

A hundred yards below the bridge Allen stumbled, lurched a few steps more, and threw himself willingly on the grass. François was beside him at once, pounding gently on his back. "Anyone there?"

"No!" came a gruff voice from the level of the sod.

She laughed. The run had lifted her spirits. "Hey—can we talk about it? What's happening?"

> **taciturn**: stubbornly closemouthed; disposed to avoid speech
> **opportunistic**: seizing full advantage of opportunities, sometimes at the expense of honesty, loyalty or morality
> **interlude**: a period of time which interrupts a main activity or condition, and during which some other activity or condition occurs

"Rest!" gasped Allen. "Maybe die. Don't wanna talk."

She pounded again on his back. "Don't wanna talk! Is that just a little problem today or are we habitually **taciturn**?"

By this time Ricky had sunk onto the grass as well. "Just so Allen won't be embarrassed," he said **opportunistically**. "Not because I'm…out of…" He didn't bother to finish his lie.

François granted a brief rest. Far from the crashing sea, and not yet near the Bad Pony, they enjoyed an **interlude** of silence. And that was how, after a minute or two, they heard the sound no one was supposed to hear—a faint *brmm, brmm … sputt*, coming from somewhere higher on the mountain.

insidious: causing harm sneakily, either by subtle traps and snares or in a gradual manner that calls no attention to itself
arduous: hard to do; requiring much toil and exertion
quarry: the object of a hunt or pursuit

They leapt to their feet, driven by a new urgency. "So much for **insidious** doubt," cried Ricky, as they hurried toward East Bridge. "It was creeping in, I confess. It was whispering that maybe the shadow Allen saw and the white column Tedesco saw don't add up to a bookmobile. But now…"

Within moments they were across the bridge and onto the lower stretches of Victoria Road. There was no chance of hearing the bookmobile again—their course lay alongside the Bad Pony, and at this season, with the snow melting higher up, the stream ran noisily through its channel.

To his own surprise, Ricky was catching his wind. The ascent was still **arduous**—difficult on lungs and joints—but he was tolerating it better now. With François he had moved some ways out in front of the pack. As they came drilling across the bridge where Lumps and Darlingson had set the supporting pillar, there was no conversation, and none as they skirted by the old pedestrian bridge, swinging slightly in the breeze. But as the trail lifted more sharply toward the Steeps and the ancient orchard at its foot, Ricky—a touch of drama in his voice—murmured, "I would like one glimpse of our **quarry**."

"Quarry," answered François with a short laugh. "If we're spotted, Ricky, we'll be the quarry. But if you're really after a glimpse, here's your chance."

She pointed ahead to the nearest of the seven low summits that were strung out across the shallow basin where the orchard had once grown. "It's just enough of a peak," she said, "to overlook the tableland, and by now that's where the bookmobile is, I'm sure, rolling across the tableland toward the briars. Besides, the moon has risen a bit, so you won't be stumbling about in the dark. And if you make a dash of it, there won't be any loss of time, because we have to wait here anyway to let the others catch up."

Ricky hadn't meant to volunteer for a mission. "Most of the spy manuals," he said, "advise against something like this until the moon is straight overhead. Shadow reduction, you know."

procrastination: the act of putting off things that you know deserve attention right away
vacillation: the condition in which you swing back and forth between alternative choices without being able to decide on one or the other with finality
dissuade: to use argument and persuasion to turn someone away from a choice

François was unsympathetic. "The slightest **procrastination**," she replied, "and you will get a glimpse of nothing but landscape—the bookmobile will have motored out of view. So tell that to your spy manuals."

Ricky gave a long sigh and gazed for a while on the little mountain he didn't want to climb. It looked innocent enough, still and pale under the slanting beams of the moon. "So maybe I go," he said softly, taking some steps toward the low peak. "And maybe I don't." He took some steps away. Then in a much firmer voice—"And maybe I really hate **vacillation**." With that he set off.

François made an effort to follow his progress as he slipped through the orchard and began toiling up the nearest flank of the summit. Its rocky folds mostly obscured him from her view, but when she did catch sight of him, always scrambling higher, she pointed him out to Joannie, who had caught up with her now on the trail, and to Allen and Tedesco, who appeared a few minutes later.

When Tedesco saw the distant figure of his friend, laboring up the slope in the moonlight, he felt some obligation to be there as well. François, though, tried to **dissuade** him. "It was good you helped pudgy Allen, but Ricky is OK. The boy has excellent wilderness skills. He's our young Daniel Boone— remember, from history class?"

Two or three minutes later a cry reached them, strangled and comic, which made clear that young Boone wasn't totally OK. "Sounds more like young Ms. Muffet," said Allen, lying on the bare ground and still catching his breath.

Ricky was hurtling down the slope, racing back to the trail. His arms were waving madly. He was casting frequent looks over his shoulder. "Ms. ... Ms. Jensen," he stammered urgently, as he drew close to his friends.

> **incredulous**: disinclined to believe what you are told or shown
> **interloper**: someone who intrudes on the property, the rights, or the established space or realm, of another
> **unabridged**: presented in full, without any shortening through the removal of less important parts

"Ms. Jensen was up there?" asked Joannie **incredulously**. "C'mon now, Ricky, I find that hard to ..."

"No, no! Not that. Ms. Jensen was right ... that's what ... about the lizard." He threw another look over his shoulder. "A major, major lizard. And not in the stars either. It was coming up the other side of the hill, heading toward the same overlook as me."

Joannie's research on the subject was sketchy, but she knew that one of the strangest creatures in her beloved Mercurial Canyon was the moongazer, and that it came scratching and scrabbling out on moonlit nights, to find a perch. Now, with Ricky still wild-eyed before her, she held an imaginary pencil just above an imaginary pad, and questioned him in an academic tone. "You were saying, Mr. Snoozer, that a lizard interfered with your use of the overlook."

"No—I interfered with a lizard's use of the overlook! The lizard apparently owns the place. I was the **interloper**. I'm not going back up there."

"Me neither," said Allen, in a voice that suggested he had no plans to go anywhere.

That spurred François, and in a moment she had pulled Allen to his feet, squared Ricky's shoulders, and in general put the little band back on the trail.

"The lizard doesn't worry me too much anymore," she declared, as they moved out in the direction of the Steeps, "whether it crawled over from Joannie's canyon or came down from the starry sky. As long as Ricky's ursa doesn't come down too, we'll be just fine."

"But the same cannot be said for the Mendicant Berries," added Joannie in a worried tone. "They'll be riding in the back of the bookmobile if we don't hurry."

READER: Larry says that, contrary to widely held opinion, all the stars in the northern hemisphere form a single, very large constellation.

AUTHOR: Yeeks! What does it show—an **unabridged** diagram of the human genome?

READER: Very funny. He says it shows a little girl named Cassiopeia using one of those tongue depressor things to scrape the gum off her roller skate wheels.

AUTHOR: Whoa! It's there to be seen by the human eye?

READER: You may have to go out of focus, but it's there to be seen.

Chapter 48: THE 40-WATT DEFILE

They had reached the final switchbacks that carried Victoria Road up the Steeps and onto the high tableland. By now the bookmobile was at the berries, there could be no doubt, and this gave a new urgency to the chase. François pushed straight up the ascent, crosscutting from one loop of the road to the next, and even Allen, exhausted though he was, followed her in this **expedient**.

> **expedient** (noun): some procedure or device (sometimes invented on the spot, and often adopted after more normal or acceptable means haven't done any good) that helps you achieve an end or respond to a problem
> **scintillating**: casting off sparks or pulses of light; brilliant
> **dumb**: (1) lacking the ability to speak; (2) remaining without speaking for a while, and thus letting an occasion for speech pass by

Abruptly, the climb was over, and the tableland stretched before them. Under the rising moon the many streams of the Bad Pony were casting off sparks, ivory and yellow. Ricky gave some steps, as though his path now lay beside the **scintillating** waters, but Joannie hauled him back. "Spellbound child," she told him, "you'll plunge in to your neck."

So they stayed with the road in its sweeping curve along the edge of the tableland. Their speech was only in whispers now, for fear that neither the Bad Pony nor the foul weather localized over Mercurial Canyon would completely muffle their voices. That was why Joannie stayed **dumb** when she saw the lizard. Glancing back for one reason or another, she caught sight of it on the high overlook that Ricky had tried to climb. The outline of the beast was sharply drawn against the night sky and it held itself perfectly still as it watched the passage of the moon. "Say nothing," she counseled herself, "or you'll put Ricky in a state, and it won't be a quiet one either."

> **contingency**: a possible development or turn of events, often one you feel it is advisable to plan or prepare for, just in case
> **meticulous**: thoroughly attentive to every detail; sometimes excessively so
> **inexplicable**: baffling and beyond explanation

The goal was near. To their left was Mercurial Canyon and its private storm, and from there to the briars was less than half a mile. Already they could hear the soft crash of the stream as it plunged over the granite bluff.

They ran almost shoulder to shoulder, instinctively clustering together, and all of them were thinking the question which François expressed in a hushed voice: "Are we ready for every possible **contingency**?"

"If Bezzle is alone ..."

"If Bezzle is not alone ..."

"If he's just checking the berries ..."

"If he's harvesting without restraint ..."

In another minute they arrived at the bluff and discovered with shock that there was one contingency they hadn't thought of—Bezzle wasn't there. After a **meticulous** search—looking behind every tree, into every nook—Bezzle wasn't there, nor anyone else, nor the bookmobile.

"The thoroughly impossible contingency," murmured François, "has happened. I don't know what to say."

"It's **inexplicable**," agreed Allen as they searched one last time along the foot of the bluff.

There was nothing to be found, so at last, more than half convinced that the bookmobile had traveled that night only in their imaginations, they collected themselves into a troop once again and began their return.

"Tired, hungry, sore, humiliated and defeated," said Ricky flatly.

Tedesco roughed him up a bit. "But this your pain is ... is softened by the beauty, eh Ricky, by the light from the stars and the cool wind of this night."

> **assuage**: to lessen a pain or anguish; to bring some calmness to a troubled person or situation
> **empathy**: a deep sharing in the emotional state of someone else
> **comprise**: to be made up of, to include or contain (often used to indicate the elements out of which some set or series or other collective thing is put together)

Joannie smiled. She had felt the magic too. "And by the silver tide of fog curling below us. And by the music of the stream, and the waking birds. They all **assuage** the pain."

François begged to disagree that any birds were waking at that hour, and for some ways they argued the matter. "There," Joannie declared, as a note reached them from somewhere, seemingly from high in Mercurial Canyon, where the storm had cleared. "If that's not a waking bird ..."

François lifted her chin, slightly but deliberately, in a sign of doubled concentration. "Of course, you're right, Joannie. But there's something in that note ... something ever so faintly unbirdlike ..."

Joannie was nearly through a teasing answer, when her sharp eyes fixed on a curious sight. Out beyond the southern limit of the tableland the lizard was still there on its perch, motionless, considering the moon. However, when the mysterious note drifted down again from Mercurial Canyon, a bit louder this time, the creature jerked its head up sharply and puffed out the pouch of folded skin at its throat.

Through some **empathy** Joannie knew that the lizard was afraid. "Waking birds wouldn't scare that beast," she thought. Ms. Jensen's story came back to her, how the lizard fled at the sound of the ...

"The bookmobile!" She clutched François' arm. They stared at each other through the pale light. Both agreed that the very idea was foolishness. And both of them heard the pattern of notes repeat itself one last time, carrying down from the higher reaches of Mercurial Canyon, **comprising**, though vaguely, three growls and a sputter.

> **millennium** (plural: millennia or millenniums): a period lasting one thousand years
> **fathom** (verb): to understand something by getting an insight into its deepest nature or operation
> **intrepid**: bravely enduring peril and trial, without turning aside

"It wouldn't be impossible," said Joannie slowly. "Absurd but not impossible. Mercurial Canyon is like a long, sunken garden with an elevated roadbed running next to it." They were near the entry of the canyon now, and she beckoned toward it. There, stretching back and away from them, always following the tangled canyon bottom but always set some ways up from it, was the "roadbed," a long bench of stone. "The glacier carved it smooth and even," she continued, "twelve thousand years ago. And not much has changed—twelve **millennia** is twelve minutes in the life of stone. It's still smooth today. It could bear traffic—even a bookmobile."

Ricky objected, "But—how many Mendicant Berries will they find in Mercurial Canyon? Slim to none, right?"

"Slim to none, mental giant," answered Allen, pulling at his hair with obvious distress. "Which means ... which means I'm perplexed out of my wits, I cannot **fathom** what the bookmobile wants on this mountain, and ... where are you going, François?"

Trying to appear more **intrepid** than she felt, François had left Victoria Road and crossed the short interval of open ground that led over to the stony bench. "This is my road now," she declared. "I'll follow it through fire and flood, to see what harm Bezzle is about—that's what I'll do." She brought a fist down hard against her palm.

> **bravado**: bold, exaggerated speech and gestures adopted to give the appearance of courage
> **inclement**: harsh, unyielding, without mercy (often said of weather)

Her **bravado** was a success. Joannie and Tedesco joined her at once, and Ricky and Allen a moment later. Joannie took the lead, for this was familiar territory to her.

She pushed them hard, knowing that before long another storm, heavy with thunder, would gather over the canyon. Her forecast was simple: "**Inclement** weather guaranteed in the next sixty minutes."

"It can rain barbells," said Allen. "I won't even notice. Where is that bookmobile? Why isn't it at the berries the way it's supposed to be?"

> **medley**: a loose mix of distinct things
> **exorbitant**: shockingly in excess of a fair level for prices, rents, profits, fees, etc.
> **juxtaposition** (noun): the placement of two items alongside one another, or otherwise close to one another, usually so that their differences become strikingly apparent

"I can hear about twenty reasons why," answered Joannie. All around them now, carrying up from the dense strip of jungle that paralleled their pathway, was a **medley** of hoots and shrills, cackles, croaks and screeches, snuffles and drones. "The creatures making that music—some of them at least—are found nowhere else. They would command outrageous prices, **exorbitant** prices, on the rare beast market."

"So Bezzle is down there," asked Allen, "in the bush, shoving endangered species into his bookmobile?"

Joannie couldn't help a smile. "He's not that crazy. Mercurial Canyon is way too off-road for a bookmobile. No, Allen, keep racking that sample-size brain of yours. The puzzle isn't completely solved; the search isn't over."

The search was carrying them higher and higher on the mountain. They came to a point where a side canyon branched out. The **juxtaposition** was startling. Mercurial Canyon, for its part, was lush, wide and sultry, as it ran on and up before them. The side canyon was a narrow slot, rocky and chill. It cut sharply into the mountain, and was hemmed in by cliffs. At that late hour it seemed forbidding, intently set against any intrusion.

Yet its floor ran tolerably smooth, and as Ricky said, "If you were nuts enough to take a bookmobile in there, you wouldn't blow all your tires in the first ten yards or anything."

> **dilemma**: a predicament in which there are bad consequences associated with each of the options between which you must choose
> **conjecture** (noun): guesswork, often the sort in which you do your best to arrive at conclusions from inadequate evidence
> **defile** (noun): a narrow canyon giving passage between cliffs or steep mountainsides

"So we need to check it out," declared François, struggling desperately to sound brave and unconcerned. "Which leaves us in a fix: either we go up this side canyon and then maybe Bezzle comes slipping back down the main canyon, and we miss him; or we continue up Mercurial Canyon and he comes slipping down this side canyon, and we miss him. It's a **dilemma**."

"But not a killer dilemma," said Joannie. "Another fifty yards or so and this stony bench that has been our roadway starts to shrink, and soon it's too narrow for anything on four wheels. I hate to say it, but if the bookmobile is on the mountain at all, I'm afraid this dark, chilly canyon is the place."

"Then that's where we go, OK!" said Allen, looking down at his feet. Nothing happened, so he said more firmly, "So that's where we go, OK! I've had it with **conjecture**—all these educated guesses about what Bamalford and Bezzle and Nameless Entrepreneur are doing and aren't doing on the mountain. Let's go and see what's actually happening. Now!" His feet began shuffling hesitantly toward the side canyon. Tedesco and the others followed on what they were sure was the last stretch of the chase.

For François a harder stretch could not have been imagined. The canyon was dark, swallowing up the tiny ration of moonlight which penetrated there. "It's like this entire passageway," she said, "is lit by a single 40-watt bulb. We're basically on a hike through a 40-Watt **Defile**."

Joannie laughed softly and took her friend's arm. "I like that. But it's not a long defile. 'Forty-Watt Blind Canyon' might be the better term."

"Blind?" asked François.

"Correct. This canyon runs half a mile and then that's all—it stops abruptly at a granite cliff."

François knew what that meant—the five of them would have the bookmobile cornered, penned against the back wall that Joannie was describing. "Pheww!" she groaned, "that could turn ugly."

> **straitened**: pinched in; made tight and narrow
> **ploy:** a clever move by which you try to outwit an opponent
> **bemused**: perplexed by some riddle, and deep in thought about it

The same apprehension gripped all of them as the canyon became more **straitened**—with the walls crowding ever closer—and the encounter grew near. Yet, when the apprehension was unexpectedly lifted, when they had marched all the way to the canyon's back wall and prowled all over the canyon's floor and found nothing, they felt no relief whatsoever but instead a wild frustration.

"I will go crazy," cried Allen, pounding his head slowly against the barrier of granite. "How did ...? How could ...? Wait—I know—it minimized, just like on your computer screen, and now it's an icon, smaller than a postage

327

stamp. So that was Bezzle's **ploy** to elude us. Very cunning. Check around your feet everybody."

"Allen," said François gently, "maybe you *are* going bats. Come sit with the rest of us and debrief. We've built an imaginary campfire."

Muttering complaints about imaginary bookmobiles, Allen stumbled through the obscurity and took a place in the circle formed by his friends. "Don't mind me—I'm **bemused** beyond recognition: my mind is lost in this riddle. Moreover, my body is shot and, emotionally, I'm on the brink of despair."

"Thank you for the update on your condition," said Ricky in a clinical tone. "May I remind you that when the going gets tough the tough get going, where there's a will there's a way, and hope springs eternal in the human breast."

Tedesco joined in. "I saw one of them too—It's always darkest before the birth of the sun."

Joannie laughed. "Ah, Tedesco, learning even our proverbs. That one, I think, goes—It's always darkest before the dawn."

> **platitude**: a saying, turn of phrase, or other expression that is flat and lifeless, often from having been used so many times before
> **popular**: done, used or believed by all or most of the people
> **quizzical**: curious; in the mood to ask a lot of questions, like someone trying to solve a puzzle

"However it goes," said Allen, with some of the distress fading from his voice, "thank you. Those old **platitudes**, worn out and overused as they are— they still have their moments when they warm the soul, ever so slightly."

"You know," said François appreciatively, "they do. Because they're fragments of **popular** wisdom. They come from the people, they connect you to the people. And that's comforting."

Little else was comforting, however, as they talked through what had happened. All five of them—even François who had seemed tireless—were fatigued. They were tormented by the riddle of the bookmobile, worried that it had all been a hallucination. And the scene of their conversation was no help: the dark and chill pressed in as they huddled at the blind end of the canyon.

After a while Tedesco tried to lighten the mood. "Maybe this time I say it right. Remember, my *amigos*—it's always darkest before the dawn."

"Thank you," answered François graciously. "That proverb is … really quite amazing. Yes … as Allen said, it does warm"—she hesitated—"the soul."

"François," said Joannie in a guarded tone. "I can't see your face in this darkness, but I know it has just acquired a **quizzical** look—like, something a little funny here."

328

"Yes, it has," answered François slowly. She waited, tense, receptive. Then—"Say it once more, Tedesco, that favorite proverb of yours."

Again Tedesco spoke the words "It's always darkest before the dawn."

And again that faint warmth, carried on a small breath of wind. They all felt it now, and they turned toward the source from which it flowed so gently—the back wall of the canyon.

After staring for long seconds through the dimness Allen declared unconvincingly, "Nothing there."

> **orthodox**: lying within the established mainstream of acceptable opinion and conduct; conforming to the official teaching about the right way for something to be or be done
>
> **homogeneous**: quite similar in texture, quality, appearance, etc., all across some expanse or range; not marked by significant variation between any one point and another
>
> **fledgling**: a young bird just starting to fly; a person just starting to gain experience in some field of activity

"Nothing there," echoed Ricky, "… except that rectangle."

"Probably just a naturally occurring rectangle," added Joannie slowly. There was a catch in her voice. "I admit—the **orthodox** view on this matter is that nature has no rectangles—this is the official position of naturalists everywhere, I believe. But it's probably … wrong. At least, around here."

Against the blackish-gray of the back wall, there was a rectangular patch which had no gray at all, which was the most intense black imaginable. Even as they watched, the two sidelines of the figure moved slowly toward one another until they met. The rectangle disappeared, and the shading of the back wall became **homogeneous** once again, an unbroken blackish-gray.

François' voice was faint. "I just want to go home."

Ricky answered, "I just want to turn it over to the FBI. They've got the experience. We're **fledglings**."

There was a silence, broken only when Tedesco hesitantly challenged them. "I just want not to say what I am going to say. But this rectangle is looking too much like a door. We must see."

They walked slowly to the back wall, close enough to touch it. It was reassuringly rough and immense. Surely…

Tedesco spoke again the words they were beginning to dread. "It's always darkest before the dawn."

Nothing happened. Ricky let out a long sigh. "So you see, Cabbage …" There was a soft click, an electronic click, originating it seemed from just within the face of the canyon wall. Without warning the pure blackness was back again, at first a narrow slit, from the ground to twice a man's height, but widening quickly, as two panels of stone slid smoothly away from each other. As Tedesco had feared, the rectangle was a giant opening, and the blackness had depth, yawning back into the mountain.

"That proverb is the password," said Ricky with awe. "Just say it and this ... this airplane hangar opens up."

> **hyperbole**: dramatically exaggerated description
> **ecstatic**: feeling a joy so intense as to lift you above daily concerns
> **tautological**: expressing an idea more than once in a single phrase or sentence, usually through different words meaning the same thing, and usually without there being any necessity for such repetition (as, for example, in the phrase "at 8:12 A.M. in the morning")

François fastened on Ricky's choice of phrase, almost gratefully. "Airplane hangar, Ricky? That's **hyperbole**, of course—you'd never get a real airplane through those doors. But ..."

Now she paused a moment, before raising the unwelcome question. "But would it be an exaggeration to say that a you-know-what could fit?"

"A bookmobile?" answered Ricky with hesitation. "Not a problem, I'm afraid. It would fit, easy." He was fumbling in the baggy depths of his pocket. "I'll measure if you like. My tape is here somewhere."

"No," said François distractedly. "That's OK." She drew a long breath, and pressed her hands together. "Where the bookmobile goes, we follow, that's the general rule. But since the space beyond this door is pitch dark, and no one remembered a flashlight, maybe ..."

READER: Larry is writing some original proverbs for you to use.

AUTHOR: I'm **ecstatic**, but ...

READER: For example—With the sunrise comes the dawn.

AUTHOR: It's a gem—only it may look a bit **tautological** to those readers who view dawn and sunrise as much the same thing.

READER: Great! Get old Lare really cheered up! Let's hear you do one.

AUTHOR :Er—Bills that are wrinkled will be rejected by the change machine.

READER: That's the worst one I ever heard!

AUTHOR: It operates on many levels.

READER: So does a blimp.

AUTHOR: Enough for proverbs!

Chapter 49: FLASHLIGHT HUSBANDRY

"François, you're gonna shoot me," said Ricky. In one hand he held a measuring tape. With the other he was still fumbling about in his baggy pocket. "There! Look what turned up."

> **improvident**: failing to anticipate future needs and prepare carefully for them
> **antidote**: a medicine or other remedy that works to cancel the effects of some particular poison or harm

A shaft of light, yellow and weak, shone from his hand. François let out a soft groan. "Two for two, huh Ricky! Fully prepared. A tape to measure the door, a light to show the way. No one could call you **improvident**. And yes, I do hate you."

She pulled in a long breath and groaned softly again. "Allen—are you really curious about the bookmobile?"

Allen knew what hung on his answer, and he took a moment. "Still curious," he said at last with a swallow. "And, remember ... it's always darkest before the dawn."

The huge doors slid apart again, and Allen, François and the others stepped through and into the depths of Mount Relief. For a moment they stood still, hands touching, letting the dark and the warmth close over them. Then Ricky switched on the flashlight, tracing a wide, exploratory circle with its beam.

"We've entered a corridor of one sort or another, on quite an impressive scale. The walls, of granite it appears, are easily thirty feet apart." It was François making these observations, in the hope that a descriptive, matter-of-fact approach would serve as an **antidote** to the dread growing inside her. "And for its part the ceiling is ... well, actually rather wavy."

> **dispassionate**: calm and businesslike; not under the influence of strong emotion or strong likes and dislikes
> **undulating**: curving repeatedly back and forth in a wavelike pattern
> **insatiable**: never having enough; never satisfied

"A feature we observe frequently in underground settings," added Joannie, speaking low and in the same **dispassionate** tone. "When compressing forces fail to actually break a bed of stone, they often leave it rippled and **undulating**, as we see here in the case of François' ceiling."

"The surface that interests me," said Allen, nearly in a whisper, "is the one that's not undulating. Look at this floor. It's nearly flat—I mean—the road goes on. Victoria road, the granite bench alongside Mercurial Canyon, the alleyway cutting through the side canyon, and now this track leading into the mountain. Getting bookmobiles where they need to go! But this last stretch is very primitive, stone set loosely against stone, maybe built by ..."

It hit all of them at once. "Built by ..." said Joannie in a hushed voice, "the first settlers, the people of Esperanza. Many of them, the mayor included, thought farming and trade were best for the little town, but we know that some of the most powerful figures, especially on the council, never got over the fever—the **insatiable** desire for gold. Baskets of it, bathtubs, never enough. So they searched this mountain for the legendary lake of gold."

> **avaricious**: driven by an intense, active greediness to store up more and more wealth
> **crass**: crude and insensitive; reducing human matters to their raw, physical elements and overlooking more refined or spiritual dimensions
> **husbandry**: the careful, thrifty use of a resource, to make it last longer

"And maybe," whispered Ricky, "they found it—deep inside, at the back of this cave. And to reach it with their carts, hauled up by sheer force from below, they made this road."

"Bless their **avaricious** hearts," muttered François. She took her first hesitating steps deeper into the cave, always waiting for Ricky to light the way in front of her before setting her foot. The others followed, and slowly they left the huge doorway behind.

It was crazy to be entering an underground space without masks and oxygen. Joannie warned, "If anyone, Ricky excluded, starts to feel the slightest disorientation in your thinking, we turn back, hoping it's not too late."

And it was crazy to be talking—Bezzle might be just around the next turn. Yet they continued a whispered conversation, because the sound of their own voices was pushing back the panic that reached for them in this dark underworld.

Tugging at his wiry hair, Allen reflected, "If this is Bamalford's game, scooping up gold by the bucketful, it suits him better than the wine business. He's such an unrefined number, and so **crass**, that it's easier to see him slobbering happily over a pail of gold than sipping gently at a goblet of wine."

Ricky laughed softly. "Go say that on Sallie's show and draw some heat off Foster. Whoever he might be, OK. Now—changing subjects without warning—here's an innocent riddle for all of you. Who knows what **husbandry** means?"

"That you want to marry me," replied François.

"If Sallie dumps me, we can talk," Ricky shot back. "No—here's what it means." He shut off the flashlight—and gasped along with the others at how instantly the darkness closed over them.

"That's called Flashlight Husbandry," he explained. "We have to conserve the batteries in this thing, using them carefully and sparingly. Otherwise ... well, it's going to be a long walk back to the door."

"So we stand here a few minutes, and then the light goes back on, is that it?" asked François.

> **disinclination**: a firm dislike for some activity, and the desire to avoid it as much as possible
> **spurious**: false or forged, in spite of appearing—often by reason of someone's deliberate effort—to be true or authentic
> **stifle**: to press down and smother something that is trying to emerge or express itself

Ricky coughed. "Not quite. We walk for a few minutes—in the dark, feeling our way, suppressing our **disinclinations**. Then the light comes back on and we steal a quick look at upcoming attractions. Then darkness and groping again."

"But," protested François, "what if one of the upcoming attractions is a bottomless pit and we get to it before the flashlight comes on again? Like in that story where a man sends his nephew up a long staircase, in the dark, knowing that high up is a gaping hole; and the boy is saved only by a lightning flash."

Ricky thought for a moment. "Well, were you sent on this chase by your uncle?"

"No, but ..."

"Then your story has no applicability to our situation."

François almost forgot to whisper. "Ricky, that is **spurious** logic and you know it! Sounds good from fifty feet, but proves totally false on closer analysis."

To Ricky's credit he took the lead through the intervals of darkness when the flashlight was off, often crouching to tap the ground in front of him with his hands, making sure that reliable footing was there. It was the hundredth time he did this, or maybe the two-hundredth, when his hand touched something warm and pulsing. **Stifling** a yell, he flicked on the light, revealing a gray lizard, almost a foot long. Its eyes were little more than two small buds on the sides of its head, each with a milky, undersized pupil that saw nothing.

There wasn't anything menacing about the creature, yet a look of anxiety remained on Ricky's face. "I wrote a paper on it," he said in a worried tone.

> **atrophy** (noun): the process by which muscle tissue wastes away and becomes less, often from lack of use

333

gallery: a passageway or corridor (used in several special senses, one of which is to indicate a passage running horizontally underground)
immutable: fixed and unchanging; resistant to any variation

"On our little friend here?" asked Joannie doubtfully.

"No—on **atrophy**. This lizard is a perfect example. Many years ago it came down from the sunlit world to this place of darkness. It made no further use of its eye muscles, and slowly they grew weak, slowly they wasted away until, until ... this." He pointed to the shrunken eyes. "And the same thing could happen to us—that's what my paper indicates."

Unlike its larger cousin on the overlook, this lizard yielded the right-of-way. After turning its blind eye on Ricky for a moment it slipped away, vanishing into the voids and hollows of the road stones.

The troop at once resumed its march, and again Ricky shut off the light, apologizing to his friends for being an agent of atrophy. As they felt their way through the blackened **gallery**, Joannie said in a voice that was flat and academic and well suited to calming jittery nerves, "That particular lizard, Ricky, probably didn't go from normal eyes to those little buds. That's too much atrophy for one creature. More likely there was an evolution over several generations."

"Rome wasn't built in a day," threw in Allen, "in case anyone needs another proverb."

"Well that reminds me," said François, "of what I need to ask Tedesco. Where was it, anyway, that you heard that proverb about darkest before the dawn?"

"In the newspaper," he answered, "on the front page, in that box called 'Volts from Victoria.'"

"Oof!" Allen sounded as though he had been punched in the stomach. "Let's all raise our hands—how many of us have been assuming that the darkest before dawn password is **immutable**, that it stays the password day after day, month after month? But think. The Fram puts a different proverb in the paper every day. I'll bet it works like this—today's proverb, today's password. Tomorrow's proverb..."

"Tomorrow's password," finished Joannie in a troubled voice. "That means darkest before dawn got us in, but it might not get us out."

"Not if we're trying to leave after midnight or whenever the magic moment is when the door gets recoded."

"Wait!" burst out François as best she could in the whispered speech they were all using. "I know tomorrow's proverb. I ..."

Ricky was impressed. "Hey! Besides being cultured, graceful, cute and generally good humored, she reads the future."

laudatory: written or spoken to confer praise
paradox: a statement or situation embodying an apparent self-contradiction or a seemingly crazy union of opposites
secular: related to the realm of here-and-now human concerns, considered as separate and apart from the realm of religion, divine schemes and eternal consequences

François didn't mind the praise. "We don't see this **laudatory** side of you very often, Ricky. But I'm not reading the future. At the library today—it seems a year ago—I heard Ms. Framley on the phone with Bamalford, telling him tomorrow's proverb. And I'll remember in a second ... it had to do with dairy products."

"Well, the best way to remember it," counseled Ricky, "is to forget about it for a while. Sort of a **paradox**, I know. But the more you strain to remember something, the more it runs away. So let me distract you. Would you like to know how that lizard felt?"

"Yuck!" said François.

"OK. Would you like to know what I'm really afraid to touch as I go tapping along in the dark? I'll tell you—the sandal of Pluto, ancient god of the underworld. Wouldn't that be something—in the pitch dark, to go tap-tap on this big set of toes and to hear this tombstone voice, 'May I help you, Ricky?'"

Joannie laughed. "At least you're getting her mind off dairy products. Actually though, Ricky, this may be an underworld, but I doubt it's the type with gods and goddesses. It strikes me as quite a **secular** underworld, just one more department of the day-to-day human world that takes up most of our time. It even has the very human problem of litter. Look at that soda can there off by the side. Trash from Bezzle's little snack, that's what..."

She paused, startled. "Ri..."

"It's not on, I swear it!" Ricky was biting his lip to keep from shouting. "That's not the flashlight, baby!"

luminous: giving off light, whether a reflected light or a light originating from within
tributary (noun): a smaller stream, considered as flowing into a larger one or into a sea or lake
hiatus: a gap or open interval, often in something otherwise unbroken or continuous

Without anyone noticing it, the shapes and figures around them, from the huge lava columns to the little soda can, were no longer completely invisible in the heavy darkness. They had become, in a minimal degree, **luminous**. Joannie marveled, "It's almost like things are glowing with their own light."

Allen was as astonished as the rest of them, but his instinctive need to pin down the facts was already asserting itself. "It may not be a glow," he said. "There's a very simple test—you can't throw a shadow on something that glows. Here—let's see."

Ahead of them, and just to the side of the road, was a pillar of stone. Allen passed it, by a yard or so, and then stepped off the road to position himself close to it. At once his shadow, though faint, was evident upon it. He drew the obvious conclusions. "This light has an external source, and it lies farther ahead on the way we are going."

"And so does the source of this noise we hear," said Tedesco. For now there was a sound as well—a hollow roaring, still low, but gathering strength as they marched along.

They knew that the road's end, whatever that might be, was near. Even the air was different, restless with little surges and retreats. "The feeling they give," said François softly, "is that our corridor is the **tributary** of something much vaster, like a river running to an immense sea."

Joannie could not read that much in the small troublings of the air, but she trusted in her friend's gift. "If you say that's what it is, Frankie ..."

The road came climbing now, though easily, and after another several hundred yards it reached its destination, bringing them to the edge of a breathtaking space, at the heart of the mountain. It was defined in the first place by its roof, an almost boundless dome, formed from arching bands of stone, and glinting in a light which seemed to well up from below.

"We've entered a parallel universe," murmured Ricky.

"The hall of the mountain king," added Joannie.

Allen held his silence, studying the vast vault and the bands of stone from which it was made. In one of them he noticed, after he had been staring for some time, there was a gap, an emptiness, near the top of the long curve. "Like the mouth of a chimney," he said at last to the others, pointing to the **hiatus**. Within moments they spied several more of these gaping vents.

What they could not see at all was the floor of the immense chamber they were entering. Their view was blocked by the road itself, which for a few yards farther out in front of them kept on climbing, to a low crest.

> **covert**: kept under cover and hidden from view
> **unilateral**: (applied most commonly to situations—trade between nations, for example, or a romance—in which there are two or more sides or parties) done by one party only, without the other party joining in the action or taking some corresponding action
> **upbraid**: to give someone a sharp scolding

Allen motioned to this crest and said, "That is where everything comes clear, where the **covert** mission of the bookmobile stops being covert. But we want this to be a **unilateral** discovery: we learn what Bezzle is doing, but he doesn't find out that we're here, right? So one and only one of us slinks up to the crest, looks cautiously over, and returns with a report. And Ricky—for slinking, you've always been the man."

Ricky crept up the road and flattened himself just behind the crest. Then with infinite care he lifted on his elbows and peered at the scene below. After watching for two or three minutes, he called down to the others, "The chase is over."

Allen waved his arms madly, signaling him to shut up and rejoin the group. When Ricky had done so, and had been **upbraided** for exposing them all to discovery by talking too loud, he replied, "Don't be too tough on me. I'm rattled by what I saw."

Allen could not contain himself. "The bookmobile, Ricky, the bookmobile—is it there?"

"Yes."

A huge sigh—"Finally!"

"And Bezzle is there," continued Ricky, "as expected. But I'm sorry to say that he has a companion, another person who has obviously fallen under Bamalford's influence."

> **callous**: insensitive to the emotions which others are experiencing or the suffering through which they are passing
> **axiomatic**: accepted as true beyond question, and often serving as the base on which various conclusions are founded
> **concur**: to agree that what someone has said is true; to express a readiness to go along with what someone has proposed

Joannie was startled. "Calvin?"

"No. Lumps. Dear old Lumps. Bamalford has found some way to get to him. I'll bet it's his father—Lumps has never stopped hoping that his father survived the mountain storm. And Bamalford, with his gift for all that is **callous**, is probably exploiting that fact to the full."

This was sad news, that Lumps had come into the service of Bamalford, and they fell silent for a moment.

At last Allen asked, "So what are they loading into the bookmobile anyway? Is it really gold, as we thought?"

Ricky gave a crooked smile. "From the beginning every one of us took it as **axiomatic** that the bookmobile was coming up the mountain to get something. All our analysis was built on that premise. Well—I'm afraid we muffed it.

337

Bezzle and Lumps aren't loading anything. They're dropping something off—and it's a long drop."

READER: Not so bad on "atrophy"—a shrunk-eyed lizard in the depths of a mountain.

AUTHOR: Well umm mormph like…thanggu!

READER: But Fulano has a truly great sentence.

AUTHOR: I **concur**, I concur, so there's really no reason …

READER: You haven't even heard it. So here you are—"The super-buff rock climber reached the top of the crag and sat for eleven hours, motionless, gazing on the far blue peaks. At the end of that time his arms had atrophied and he lacked strength to go down the rope so they had to bring in a helicopter, at great expense."

AUTHOR: It's good, I admit, but you have to be careful with "super-buff." Five hundred years and no one's gonna remember what words like that mean.

READER: Five hundred years and Mandy's Mind-Jump and other telepathy providers will have us all linked in, and we won't be using words, thank you.

AUTHOR: Alas my children!

Chapter 50: THE FASTIDIOUS PHARM

Ricky's report was meant to **obviate** any necessity for the whole troop to crawl up to the crest and take a look, but that was what happened anyway. François was first, muttering that he was a very nice boy, but one who spoke in riddles. The others followed, and soon all five were surveying the vast chamber from the protection of the little ridge.

> **obviate**: to eliminate the necessity for some action by disposing of the problem which the action would have addressed
> **ominous**: indicating, though not directly declaring, that forces are at work to bring about some evil

The floor sloped downward from their vantage point, running out and away from them for some distance until suddenly there was no floor at all, only an enormous chasm. From it came the pulsing shine of some deep fire. How deep you could only guess—but there was a softened quality in that light, and in the roar that went along with it, which suggested they had already risen far from their source.

The sloping of the floor was gentle. From all appearances you could have walked there, sat there, slept there without any real fear of sliding toward the abyss. And yet it was **ominous**—that slight tilt toward the chasm—and it inspired a vague dread in François and the others.

> **contours**: the lines, planes, slopes and angles that define a particular terrain or place
> **advert**: to turn your attention to something and take conscious note of it
> **impervious**: beyond the reach of some influence and not able to be touched or affected by it

Once they had taken in the general **contours** of the place, in all its vastness, it became easier to **advert** to the details. The bookmobile was there, and François whistled softly to see that it had been backed, on something of an angle, to a position no more than fifty or sixty feet from the edge of the pit. Bezzle was at the front of the vehicle, the uphill end, looking at some papers spread out on the hood.

Lumps was at the rear, and even as they watched, he climbed in, disappeared a moment, and then came quickly back in view, laboring with the weight of a large barrel. It was aluminum, and unpainted except for some red markings. Once it was lowered to the ground he stood it on end and danced it nimbly down the slope until it rested only ten feet or so from the rim of the abyss. He was sweating freely, but his manner was brisk, even cheerful, and he seemed **impervious** to any anxieties about working at the brink.

> **adroit**: quick and clever at some difficult task; handling it with a skillful grace
> **amiable**: friendly, pleasant and approachable in your dealings with others

Now Bezzle called out something. He was competing with the dull roar that came up unceasingly from the fire shaft, but the fitful wind carrying the roar carried his voice also, and without too much effort the intruders were able to catch the words. "A nice tango, Lumps. You're quite **adroit**. And now sir, if you please, the number."

"That must be Bezzle's good-natured twin brother," whispered François. "I've never heard him so **amiable** before. Where's the Perennial Pout? And why does Lumps look so content with it all?"

Lumps was turning toward the bookmobile and shouting, "Number eighty-eight."

"Rascal!" cried Bezzle. "You know which number I need."

The red markings on the barrel were a long serial number, and Lumps read it off slowly, with a hint of pride in his voice. "At least I read numbers, huh?"

"If you want it bad enough, someday, Lumps, you'll read … the hardest book in the library, whichever one that may be. And if I'm still librarian, you can check it out as long as you like—no fines. But at present—do you have any plans for that barrel?"

> **ponderous**: heavy, bulky and without gracefulness
> **gyration**: the spinning of a body in a circle around some center or axis
> **titan**: a person who is giant in size, forcefulness or achievement

Lumps went back to work. With a strong tug, he turned barrel eighty-eight over on its side, lined it up carefully, and pulled his hands away. It rolled **ponderously** down the last ten feet of the slope, and little spurs of stone were chipped free as it bounced and struck several times. Once over the edge it acquired a grace, hanging in the air for an instant, then turning in a slow **gyration** and rushing downward into the abyss. During a long silence everyone, the five intruders and Lumps and Bezzle as well, seemed to be waiting for some sound, or a flicker in the light, which would signal that it had arrived at a bottom. But no signal came. "Gone without a trace," whispered Ricky at last.

As Lumps began his standard trudge up the slope, Bezzle—with the look of someone breaking out of his routines—passed quickly around to the back of the bookmobile, entered, and in a moment reappeared, wrestling the next of the barrels. Although not a **titan** on the scale of his companion, he was very sturdily made, and in another moment he had brought the barrel carefully down, so that it was standing on end, on the rough ground, ready to be escorted to the brink.

François murmured to her friends, "Are we at the foreign film festival or what? This is turning into a very unusual movie—Bezzle being nice, Bezzle helping with the dirty work."

> **penultimate**: last except for one; next to last
> **nocturnal**: happening at night, active by night, or otherwise especially connected to the night
> **ephemeral**: lasting only for a short time and then passing away

"There's almost a holiday air," whispered Ricky, "like when exams are over."

The remark was not far off. As Lumps laid hold of the barrel that was there ready for him, Bezzle announced, "We're closing in. Number eighty-nine, the **penultimate!**"

"Ninety barrels," groaned Lumps, "ninety backbreakers, requiring several of these **nocturnal** trips in an old, shot-springs bookmobile. And before that, the runabouts—winching up the Steeps, eh Bez."

"The runabouts!" exclaimed Allen as quietly as he could. "This has been a labor of slaves. No wonder there's a holiday air as it comes to an end."

Again there was the intricate dance as Lumps rocked and skidded the barrel to the edge, and again the launch. Once more it seemed to be a vanishing without a trace, as no sound and no flaring marked the fall of number eighty-nine.

When Lumps had climbed back up to the van, the last barrel was waiting, doing service as a little table, for Bezzle had placed there two cans of juice or soft drink, white with frost. "We'll have a poor man's toast," he said. "To Lumps and Bezzle—called from obscure origins to a brilliant career on the royal stage!"

"Brilliant," Lumps agreed, "but please not long. Let's keep it brief and passing."

"Called to a brilliant but **ephemeral** career on the royal stage," corrected Bezzle.

There was a nod of gratitude from Lumps, and then—"And we welcome you!" he cried, gesturing boldly in the general direction of the ridge, and never knowing the panic that he touched off there, "you, the 87,000 patrons who have crowded our amphitheater tonight."

Bezzle was handing him one of the icy cans. "This will help, I'm sure."

It was an affliction for the five companions to watch the chilled beverages going down. The effort of the chase and the heat of the underground chamber had given them a strong thirst, and now with the vision of the frosted cans before their eyes, they were growing rapidly more conscious of it.

> **vicarious**: experienced indirectly, by linking yourself in your imagination and feelings with the experience of someone else
> **perquisite**: some privilege or favored treatment that goes along with a job or other position of responsibility
> **compile**: to build a list, collection, etc., by gathering and adding element after element

"I'm OK," said Ricky. "Each time they take a swallow of those beautiful cold drinks, I take a swallow too—in my thoughts. I'm drinking **vicariously** with them, through them."

"Well, I'm not," said Allen mournfully. "I think we should attack, seize their containers."

"Too late," answered Joannie, "they're finishing—selfish creeps."

As Lumps drained the last drops, he threw the can lazily in the back of the bookmobile, and then sat down on the coarse ground, his arms drawn around his knees. "Well, Bez—now it's Bamalford's turn. I've done my part, ninety barrels worth, several months' worth, and now he should do his and get that special database. 'A highly restricted source, my lad'"—he was imitating Bamalford now—"'with access limited to editors and no one else but editors. One of the **perquisites**, you know. Help me, though, with a wee job, son—I've got a few barrels to move around—and the source will be at your disposition, the most detailed register of missing persons that was ever **compiled**.'"

"Scum!" broke out Joannie furiously, restraining her volume with great difficulty. "Bamalford trades on the loss of a father!"

> **infallible**: not capable of making a mistake; beyond error; always right
> **prevarication**: the communication of what is false, either through outright lies, or through a more subtle, artful twisting of the truth

Bezzle, for his part, was doubtful even that the trade would be honored. "If I know our mutual friend, he'll move the target on you, Lumps. I hope I'm wrong—and maybe am, never having become **infallible**—but that's my confident prediction."

"Mine too," whispered Joannie, still in a fury. "Fat chance Lumps will escape the yoke so easily. Calvin ..."

Allen begged her to be quiet. He understood the emotion, but they were barely able to hear the conversation—only he was catching all of it—and with a second sound track the task became impossible.

342

Lumps had just asked something about "squeaky," and Allen struggled to read the question in Bezzle's reply. "I know he told you," Bezzle was saying, "that it was clean in every way, this little job we've done here. And that wasn't a total **prevarication**—sometimes a bit of truth mixes in. In this case the circumstances are not squeaky clean, I'm afraid, but it does appear that the product is—we're dumping a clean product."

> **empirical**: basing your conclusions on what you have actually seen, touched or otherwise experienced
> **acoustical**: having to do with some aspect of hearing or sound

Lumps joked, "You did what—opened a barrel, stuck in a thumb?"

"Nothing so **empirical** as that. I overheard a conversation—between Bamalford and the client—way last summer. It happens a lot. I'm an odd-job guy at the Dome, you know, and my little odd-job path often intersects Bamalford's big-cheese-executive path. I don't make a point of overhearing, but I don't wear **acoustical** protection either. And Bamalford is loud. Anyway, from what I heard, these barrels hold some kind of semi-miraculous shampoo, which does all sorts of things. I mean, if either of us had any hair"—both of them kept their hair very short—"we should have taken some home."

"Why spend a fortune incinerating shampoo?" asked Lumps.

Bezzle smiled faintly. "That brings us to the circumstances. At one point in that conversation I wasn't supposed to be hearing, the client got very serious and told Bamalford he needed to talk about the formula of the shampoo."

"To be sure, the scientific formula," said Lumps, in a scholarly tone, "like— extract of pseudo-sephamorphic alpine thistle 2.4%, semi-oxidized suspension of peripephridianthic acid 3.1%, and assorted inert ingredients 94.5%, and no guarantee on the math."

> **erudite**: manifesting a deep and often detailed learning that has been gained from the long study of books
> **circumlocutory**: using far too many words to make your point; blunting the true force of your subject matter through the use of roundabout phrases
> **damning**: (1) condemning, often to ruinous punishment; (2) serving to confirm someone's guilt and thus to assure his condemnation

"That was what I expected," laughed Bezzle, "some **erudite** description of the formula along those lines, basically a little chemistry class. But what the client actually had in mind was quite different—a brief and partial history. There was a time, it appears, when the client didn't own the formula, didn't even know the formula, and was unhappy. And the true owner had no intention of selling it. Then there came a later time, when the client *was* happy, and he did know the formula, and he didn't care too much whether he officially owned it or not. Which means, of course, he got it, but to use his own words, he got it in a manner that departed rather substantially from the accepted procedures by which one person normally obtains property rights from another."

"That's rather **circumlocutory**," said Joannie, almost forgetting to whisper. "Translation—the formula was stolen."

She stopped, thinking Allen was about to hush her again, but now it was Allen who continued, having heard enough of the story line to guess where it was heading. "At first," he whispered, "we may suppose the client assumed all was well, and went forward, even to the point of mass-producing the shampoo—ninety barrels worth. Then suspicions began to surface, there were some initial inquiries, eventually some accusations, and the client started to sweat, and started to view the ninety barrels as **damning** evidence. Bamalford's little make-things-disappear service began to look more and more attractive. And the rest ..."

François slugged him in the calf. "Allen," she hissed fiercely, "something about one hundred barrels! In the future!"

Allen was attentive at once, repenting the moment's distraction. Bezzle, in a graver tone than before, was saying, yes, there was another conversation that he overheard. And, yes, Lumps had every right to know about it.

> **synthesis**: a single substance or work in which a variety of elements have been joined and integrated, often closely, with one another
> **panacea**: some single thing or process that serves as a cure for all problems
> **fastidious**: very delicate in your standards about what is acceptable in speech, manners, food, dress, conduct, etc.

"It was a different client," he explained, "a very different one, a woman, not more than thirty, noticeably beautiful I might add, and quiet and studious. Speaking always in a calm tone, a professional tone you might call it, she told Bamalford that she is a pharmacist, and that on her own time she does extensive research, cataloging the medical properties of a wide variety of substances and trying out different combinations of them, all in the hope of discovering new and more useful medicines. Something over two years ago there was an astonishing success—she mixed together a selected assortment of resins, extracts, agents and so on, measuring each one according to a set of ratios she had calculated, and the **synthesis** that resulted from this experiment was almost a **panacea**. It had a healing effect on a wide range of illnesses and injuries. She called it by a temporary name—Glinscrimion—and she believed that in five or six years it could be brought to market. Her numerous and bossy relatives, however, believed that in five or six weeks it could be brought to market."

"They had illnesses and injuries?" asked Lumps in an innocent voice.

"What they had was an ache," answered Bezzle, "the ache for cash. In Glinscrimion they saw the restoration, and probably the enlargement, of the family fortune. They had no patience when the woman said that safety required a long battery of testing. They called her the **Fastidious** Pharm—too fussy in her standards. She agreed finally to the manufacture of a small sample in her own lab, saying, however, that commercial quantities would have to wait on a 'clean line,' a production line subject to rigid sanitary controls. They called her the Fastidious Pharm once again, and hounded her until at last she gave in. A hundred barrels of Glinscrimion were produced."

"And if she doesn't want them anymore," said Lumps, "we put them in my garage, for later sale."

> **deleterious**: having a destructive effect, often after being allowed to operate for a time
> **altruistic**: done out of a concern for the welfare of other human beings, without regard for your own gain
> **implacable**: set so firmly in your hostility that nothing can move you to make peace

"No, no," countered Bezzle, "hear the rest of it. The woman told Bamalford that she should have been more stubborn, and that because she was not, her worst fear had come true. During production of the hundred barrels a contaminant had gotten into the mix. It worked gradually but steadily, and under its influence the Glinscrimion in those barrels evolved over a matter of weeks into a destroyer as well as a helper. All the healing effects were still there, but now there was a terribly **deleterious** one as well. Yet what it is, Lumps, I don't know—for this was a quiet woman, and when she told Blodgett about the destructive effect she spoke very low and I could not hear. I missed about thirty seconds worth. When I caught the drift again she was saying that if you swallow the smallest drop of the contaminated Glinscrimion, or breathe its vapors, you run a mortal risk—that much I heard clearly. All of this has been a terrible trial for the woman, and at this point she just wants the one hundred barrels to disappear. The relatives are shattered, but they agree—get rid of the barrels."

"No doubt for **altruistic** motives," Lumps observed.

"My thought exactly," murmured Joannie from the ridge.

"I think it's all pretty commercial for the relatives," said Bezzle. "They don't want a rival getting one of the barrels, cracking the formula, setting up a clean line, going into production and becoming trillionaires. And if you, Lumps, or I were somehow responsible for that happening—a bit of careless speech, that sort of thing—those relatives and their fury, I suspect, would be **implacable**. Just a little item for us to ponder."

345

After a moment's consideration, Bezzle ventured, "The woman's motive, however, in making the barrels vanish has little to do with who becomes a trillionaire. For her, I honestly believe, the concern is to spare humanity a curse. For that matter, to spare Lumps and Bezzle a curse—she grilled Bamalford on the rather interesting question, whether there is any chance that at the moment of incineration the handlers will be exposed to fumes from the barrels, even a whiff."

> **scrupulous**: doing things, or insisting they be done, with detailed carefulness or with complete conformity to moral standards
> **qualification**: a limitation, condition or reservation which restricts some statement or provision from having full effect

"Like Bamalford would worry about such a detail," Joannie muttered.

"Amazingly," continued Bezzle, "Bamalford, or persons smarter than Bamalford, had foreseen the possibility of a **scrupulous** client like this woman—a client insisting, of all things, that the work be done carefully, in an ethical and responsible manner. He was ready for her question. On the spot he pulled out a handsomely bound report—it was from an independent consulting firm. 'They know their chemistry and their chemical engineering,' he told the woman as he handed the report to her and invited her to look through it. It was a technical analysis of … this, what we're doing, this dumping service we're performing. And on the final page of the thing he showed her the major finding, which read roughly as follows: the firm concludes without **qualification** that the burn is complete, that of the original substance, be it what it may, no trace whatsoever—neither particle nor fume—survives the incineration."

> **acquiesce**: to remain silent and raise no objection, and in this manner to let some proposed activity go forward or some statement stand as correct
> **serf**: someone whose place within society is to labor more or less permanently on the land of, and for the interests of, an overlord

"And the beautiful chemistry lady," asked Lumps, "did she buy in?"

"She **acquiesced**. She looked at the report for a long time and then, without raising any objection or pressing Bamalford any further, she handed it back to him. I think she recognized the firm that prepared it, and knew that they were good. But she did set a condition—Bamalford has to be there when the hundred barrels fall. I heard him gasp, but he could scarcely say no. That was the end of the meeting. They set a time to talk again, to work out details, and she was gone."

"So what about the barrel handlers?" asked Lumps. "Do we buy into the complete-burn theory? If it's rigged, if it's wrong, and fumes do come back up the shaft, you and I, after all, are the ones to breathe them, and the ones to run the mortal risk. The barrel handlers are on the line."

"And those who spy on the barrel handlers," said François nervously to her companions.

Lumps was up on his feet now, turning barrel number ninety on its side, ready to send it rolling. "And the tango," asked Bezzle, "where's the little tango? I mean—we don't dance number ninety down to the edge?" There was genuine curiosity in his voice.

The answer was a strange, rambling one, but it did not seem to catch Bezzle by surprise. "I am a **serf** no more," said Lumps. "As we talked now, my poor head was clearing—I wish it would do that more often. I saw that Bamalford does not care the slightest bit about putting me in danger. Take the barrels to the very edge, boy, that's what he said. Even though he knows as well as I do that the very edge slopes and has loose stones and could be undercut and is a place of danger. And now one hundred barrels more coming in, of something bad, and the only protection is some technical report written in old English. I think he sees me now as bound to his service, however dirty or dangerous, as though we of the strong back and lowly birth are meant to slave for lordly types such as he. Well, I won't work for him anymore on those terms! And the tango is history."

> **refractoriness**: a stiff-necked resistance to the attempts of people to guide or govern you
> **elusive**: avoiding capture or detection; always slipping away so as not to be taken or to be seen
> **implausible**: not consistent with known facts and accepted understandings, and for that reason not believable

Even as Joannie was wishing aloud that Calvin would show some of the same **refractoriness** in his relation with Bamalford, Lumps was giving the last barrel a firm push toward the brink. Gathering speed, it took a sudden bounce on the irregular ground, angled sharply to the left, and crossed the rim of the abyss at a point that was easily twenty feet away from the usual launch. Where it crossed there was a small ledge or flange, jutting from the pit wall a few inches below the main surface. It was hidden from the view of Bezzle and Lumps, but to the five watchers, in their more elevated position, it was visible, though barely.

Whether the barrel actually struck against the ledge before plummeting toward the depths was difficult to say. But at that very moment François, with a start, remembered the **elusive** proverb that might be their ticket out of the mountain depths—There's no use crying about spilt milk.

347

She poked Joannie. "I think some liquid spilled out—like the barrel hit a corner of that ledge and got punctured. I didn't see it exactly, but otherwise why would the François brain catch hold of the proverb just then? Something jogged my memory. That's not totally **implausible**, is it?"

"No," Joannie whispered back, "it might work that way. But where are you going with it—you want to collect a sample?"

François thought for a long moment. "I'd like the boys to collect a sample—aren't they good for something?"

When Bezzle had finished the paperwork for barrel number ninety, he climbed in at the driver's side of the bookmobile, and Lumps, after closing the back, took the passenger's seat. With an alarming reverberation, the vehicle sputtered back to life. Fortunately, it climbed at a slow pace, with the wheels often spinning on the sand and stony debris that littered the slope. In this way the watchers had a few seconds to wriggle as far away from the road as they could and flatten themselves inconspicuously in the shadows at the back of the crest. They were not seen, and the heavy van rolled past them and into the long tunnel leading to the doorway

> **reconfigure**: to rearrange the basic structure or organizational plan of something
> **vulnerable**: exposed in some special degree to harm, often for lack of ordinary defenses, but also sometimes because of being positioned squarely in harm's way
> **debunk**: to discredit some belief or claim as exaggerated, fictitious, superstitious or founded mainly on emotion

Even when its rumble had died away, the five companions were silent for a few seconds more, each struggling to **reconfigure** his or her world and make a place in it for the strange things they had seen. Then François gathered the band once more into a circle. Ricky spoke first, a note of sadness in his voice. "I wish Lumps hadn't been here. We all wish Lumps hadn't been here. Bamalford really found his **vulnerable** spot."

He shook himself, and his tone grew brighter. "As far as what we've accomplished on this spy mission of ours, one thing is we've apparently **debunked** that legend about a lake of gold inside the mountain. I knew it was only a wishful tale with a large following, yet in a childlike way I was sort of hoping it was true."

Allen gave a little snort. "You haven't had a look down the abyss yet. Maybe that's where the legend comes true, in a lake of gold at the bottom"

"Or a lake of trash," broke in François. "That's what amazes me—this whole thing is a dumping scheme, not a Mendicant Berry scheme. We've tanked Grandma's theory about Bamalford commercializing the berries, that's what we've done. But then—why that elaborate ad in Ms. Framley's magazine about the gourmet wine Malph?"

guile: the art of clever deceits
caricature: a highly exaggerated portrait or version of something, often provoking amusement and ridicule

"All part of the deceit," volunteered Allen. "It was very cunning. First the fiction about Nameless needing the road, to climb to a mountain retreat and meditate. Then, as that wore thin, another deception was waiting to distract us—the assault on the Mendicant Berries. We are up against a master of **guile** is all I can say."

As he often did in moments of concentration, Allen pushed his fingers quickly through his hair. "Ouch!" he muttered. "What is this?"

"Look at his hair," cried Joannie. "If it was curly before, it has now reached **caricature** status—curl upon curl, and tight as bedsprings. What an exaggeration. Just like ..." She stopped abruptly.

"That's right, Goldilocks," said Ricky, pulling at one of the curls that had formed in Joannie's hair. "Just like Ironbane's, that day he came down from the mountaintop, with the samples of air."

"This looks bad," declared François in a slow, deliberate voice. "Whatever it was that curled Ironbane's hair on top of the mountain—some mist or vapor—it's down here too, curling ours. It starts here, I'll bet, and floats up to the top—because obviously there is some passageway." She looked once more at the dark gaps in the dome which stretched so expansively above them. "You were right, Allen—they probably are chimneys."

extraneous: not belonging to the native material or makeup of something; showing up from the outside
conflagration: a great, all-consuming fire
tacit: not openly communicated through words, and yet somehow understood or agreed on

"Thank you," said Allen, pushing at his hair again, and wincing with the pain. "I knew we were good for something. And let us hope, François, that the curling vapor is a native one, some natural fume that belongs to this place. But what if it's **extraneous**—something trucked in on a bookmobile, just for example?"

Ricky took up the case. "Yeah, that's the scary part. Think—a barrel goes plunging down into the **conflagration**. The metal is incinerated into nothingness, the liquid inside goes up in smoke, the particles in the smoke get burned away—but after all that there still remains a trace, some superheated fume. It doesn't linger at the bottom, it rises from the pit, drifts up Allen's chimneys,

349

and emerges at the mountaintop into open air, all the while mocking the expensive report that Bamalford commissioned."

It was Tedesco who pushed the logic to its conclusion. "Not so big a problem when the fume is from shampoo, from the ninety barrels of shampoo we saw them finish dropping now. But when that quiet lady who talks about mortal risk sends the one hundred barrels down to the fire, and a fume comes up from them—that could be a bad day, huh Ricky?"

READER: Barrel eighty-nine is the "penultimate barrel"—that's nice. But listen to Fulano's example.

AUTHOR: What about our **tacit** agreement that if I get Fulano'd in one chapter, I get spared for the next three or four?

READER: You've gotta hear it. It's from the open road. Listen—"The truck driver choked down the awful sandwich and said, 'That's the first and penultimate mulch burger I ever eat.' Then he choked down another one and said, 'That's the second and last mulch burger I ever eat.' Whereupon he stormed out of the diner and headed west."

AUTHOR: If I had known stuff so beautiful was being written I might have never started this book.

READER: Mumble, mormble.

AUTHOR: I didn't hear that.

Chapter 51: VACILLATION: PART TWO

As François and the others picked their way down the face of Cape Scurrility, well after midnight, they expected crowds. "The search parties will be out in big numbers," Allen had predicted. In fact, the beach was crowded, but not with searchers. The meeting at the stone—which eventually became the meeting on the sand as the tide rose higher—had run very late, and the people were just now heading back to their homes. Some of them were carrying empty and half-empty picnic baskets—council meetings in Dropanchor were quite informal—and the five companions had no trouble in mooching some badly needed bottles of water.

> **thwart**: to block someone effectively from carrying out some plan
> **replete**: filled up or otherwise supplied with a great deal of something
> **tractable**: letting yourself be led, managed or instructed without putting up resistance

The only person who had been looking for them was Meagan. She came running. "The lost sheep—at last I find you, now that the fog has lifted. I looked and looked, but the fog was constantly there **thwarting** me, which I didn't like at all."

François took her friend by the arm and pulled her toward one of the drift logs that lay whitened and huge under the starlight. "Don't be too hard on the fog. You wouldn't have found us anyway. We were far off. We had a night **replete** with adventure, brimming over with it. When you hear our story—well, you had better climb up on this log and take a seat, Meagie, that's all I can say."

François had no doubt that Meagan would be **tractable**, that she would let herself be led to the log, would sit where she was told to sit, and would listen attentively as the long tale unfolded.

It would be a hard tale to ignore. It had become even more hair-raising after the bookmobile motored away from the vast underground chamber. First there had been the collection of the sample—with Tedesco at the very edge of the pit, using his shoe to scoop some of the concentrate that had spilled from barrel number ninety, and with Ricky holding Tedesco's ankles for dear life, and Allen holding Ricky's. Then there was the regrettable matter of the flashlight failing on their return through the inky darkness of the tunnel. Joannie coached François through it, while Ricky swore repeatedly that for the rest of his life he would have spare batteries in his pocket. But it was not pleasant.

> **incantation**: a set of words that is carefully spoken or sung to have a magical effect
>
> **recalcitrant**: stubbornly resisting authority or refusing to go along with plans

And finally, everyone's worst nightmare—the door in the mountainside wouldn't open. François uttered the password as though it were an **incantation**—slowly, solemnly, with each word emphatically pronounced. "No use crying about spilt milk." But the magic they awaited—the appearance of the doorway's grayish rectangle in the surrounding blackness—refused to happen. Improbably, Tedesco was the one who saved them, remembering from his days of learning English proverbs that it was No use crying *over* spilt milk. Then the door slid open and they burst out of the tunnel.

With a story like this to tell, François was confident of a willing audience. But in fact Meagan would not remain quiet, and would not let the story begin. She was so **recalcitrant** that at last she leaped down from her seat on the drift log, crying, "I can't and I won't keep still."

"But—it's a story like none other," protested François.

"That's exactly right," answered Meagan, unable to suppress a growing excitement. "And that's why I have to tell it now. It just can't wait. So you sit up here, François." She almost lifted her friend onto the giant log. "And your four thugs can sit with you. And I will tell you about tonight before I explode."

> **impending**: hanging over you, about to drop or about to happen
>
> **meander**: to follow a casual path, turning this way and that, with no pressing need to get to anywhere in particular
>
> **abridge**: to shorten, especially to shorten a written work by removing less important parts here and there

She herded Ricky, Tedesco, Joannie and Allen onto the enormous log, and with a dramatic sweep of her arm began. "It was there and there, and everywhere, this growing sense that something was about to happen. **Impending**—something was impending. Ms. Jensen felt it too, when I met her on the beach. We were way too early for the meeting about the whale decoy, so we took a **meandering** walk, winding around haystack rocks and tangles of drift, and skirting little cells of fog."

"And dodging sea anemones and looping around sand flea colonies," broke in Joannie. "But, Meags, tell us what it was—the impendy."

Meagan gave a tolerant smile. From her pocket she drew a hairbrush and tossed it up to Joannie. "Work on those outrageous curls. And strap in, girl, because once this story gets moving … Anyway, Ms. Jensen and I shuffled along and little by little through the crash of the waves another sound was emerging—far away, low pitched—and suddenly I grabbed her arm and shouted, 'Is that a quack?'"

Ricky shook himself into full alertness. "I was ready to ask you to **abridge** the story, so we could go home sooner and sleep, but if it's got Harbinger Ducks—I'll take the full-length version."

> **opaque**: blocking light and vision; not able to be seen through
> **brevity**: the quality of taking only a short time (often used of written or spoken expression)
> **ironic**: embodying a pointed, sometimes humorous, conflict between what is literally said and what is intended, or between the beginnings of a situation (the characters involved, opening statements, etc.) and the way it eventually turns out

"Got you," cried Meagan. "It's starting to look like a duck story, is it? Sorry, Ricky, but we saw no Harbinger Ducks. Ms. Jensen stared at the sky, straining to catch a glimpse, but as evening fell the fog above us grew more **opaque**, and you could not have seen a condor through it. Still we waited and waited until she checked her watch and said Whoops, we had seven seconds before the meeting began. We headed back. The tide was turning, runners of froth cut across our path, and by the time we reached the meeting it was already twenty minutes along."

"Let me tell you what you missed," broke in François. "For starters, I'm sure, Povano explained how either we get a plastic whale for a decoy or this could be the first year when no whales come to Whalefest. Then Peter Oakum begged the mayor to keep the shameful business short and to remember that only **brevity** would get them off the rock before the tide got on it. And the mayor remarked how **ironic** it was that a plea for brevity was causing the meeting to drag on. Then Grandma withered them both with some rebuke. So with that the mayor introduced representatives from Companies A, B and C, and each of them explained why his company could make an inflatable whale or a plastic whale that was more beautiful, durable and economic than what the competition could do."

> **surmise** (noun): a careful guess, made when the evidence is too thin to support a firm conclusion
> **relegate**: to put something in an inferior place, often something that for a time has been in a higher place

Meagan was impressed. "Speaking as someone who wasn't there to someone who wasn't there either, I think your description is perfect. It's exactly what you would expect. But by the time Ms. Jensen and I drew near to the assembly stone something unusual was starting to happen. We heard Peter Oakum speaking, and we dimly saw him. We couldn't see who he was talking to because of the fog, but it must have been a stranger—that was our **surmise**, judging from the courteous tone in Peter's voice. And here's a surprise—there was a bit of sunshine in his tone as well."

"Ha," cried Allen from his spot on the log. "He was looking forward to Povano getting salt water in his shoes."

Meagan smiled patiently at this outburst. "No, not quite. Poor old Peter suffers intensely to think about things like huge plastic whales in our bay, right? Well, apparently he had just that very moment heard some glorious news from the stranger—plastic could be **relegated** to second place on the list of necessary materials for the decoy. 'Ceramic!' Peter was saying with emotion. 'A ceramic whale—that could be beautiful. Some plastic, I know, for the internal frame. But mostly ceramic. We are saved from the jaws of death! Now—what about timing? Those Harbinger Ducks could show up any minute—I'll explain that to you later. But suppose the ceramic whale had to be done in three or four days, would that be ... possible?'"

> **jargon**: the vocabulary and turns of phrase particular to some group, as for example the people in some profession
> **crescendo**: (1) a gradual buildup to some high point; (2) the high point itself
> **reminiscence**: the remembrance of some event from your past, often together with some reflection or commentary which that remembrance inspires

"Three or four days!" yelped François. "It could take months."

Meagan raised a single finger in contradiction. "No, no, no, my outspoken childhood friend. That's not the answer which Peter received. I couldn't hear it—the stranger was too far out on the stone—but it was a yes, because look what Peter said next. 'Well, lad, excuse the **jargon** from my corporation days, but that would be pushing the envelope. I'm delighted. And maybe we've got more time than three or four days. It depends on those ducks.'"

A loud yawn escaped from Ricky. "We'll still be listening to this story in three or four days."

"Wrong," countered Meagan. "It builds quickly now to an electrifying **crescendo**. Povano jumped in at this point. Would a ceramic whale float? Would it break? How would it be anchored? Ms Jensen and I were drawing close enough to hear part of the answer to that last one, although only faintly. No anchoring—something about radio control."

"Rats!" François slapped the log. "That's how Merci said it would be done. Can't that girl ever be wrong?"

Meagan pushed straight ahead. "I don't know where Povano got the next question, but he went into this long **reminiscence** about the magical times here

354

in Dropanchor when we would see a mother whale with her calf, and he ended by asking if the ceramic whale could be two whales, a mother with her young."

Ricky started to speak, but François cupped a hand over his mouth. "There's something here. We'd better let Meagan go on."

> **categorical**: stated as something absolute; not tentative in any degree at all
> **pedantic**: overly academic; emphasizing fine points and narrow distinctions of the sort found in scholarly books, sometimes to show off how learned you are
> **dissipate**: gradually to lose mass and density and become thinner and thinner, to the point of vanishing

"We strained to catch the answer," continued Meagan, the tension mounting in her voice. "The words of the stranger were muffled by the fog, sifted by the rising breeze, and I just barely caught them—'I'm sorry, sir, to be **categorical**, but no one does the mother and child bit anymore. No one, nowhere.'

"That much I heard. Did Ms. Jensen hear it as well? I was a few steps ahead of her, and maybe … But by the way her head came up, by the quick draw of breath, I knew she had. 'That's wrong,' she uttered fiercely. 'As wrong as when I said it. Whoever that is, he needs to learn he can't say what he said. I'm going up there and flunk him!'"

Meagan lifted her hands in a gesture of helplessness. "I could not have held her back. The six of us together could not have held her back. She vaulted onto the meeting stone and marched toward its seaward tip, which was still obscured in twists of fog. 'Sir,' she called at a distance, 'you think you're very wise and modern to express that sentiment, but—excuse me for sounding **pedantic**—if Raphael had been nervous about the mother and child bit we would not have the *Madonna of the Chair*. And if Botticelli had shared your view, well—good-by to the amazing beauty of the *Madonna of the Book*.'"

Meagan paused. "I'd better catch my breath now, because it was at this point that Ms. Jensen caught hers, and then, with a little choke in her voice, continued more or less like this. 'I'm not telling you this, sir, to drop a few names from art history. It's much more basic. I made your mistake once about mothers and children in art—only it was poetry then. And … how dearly I paid. I lost the most wonderful … I lost …'"

Meagan was seeing it again. "The fog was **dissipating** now under the breeze, and through its thinning swirls, in the dim radiance of the twilight, the stranger was emerging to view. He was thirty or so, and had a wide, pleasant face and a rugged frame. Ms. Jensen cast one inquiring glance in his direction, and became as stone. Her body locked itself in mid-step and the sentence she had been forming, about the sharpness of her loss, was pent in her throat. All motion and all speech were taken from her for a moment, and when they returned she raised her face slowly toward the stranger and in a trembling voice said, 'I lost ... you.'"

"Martin!" François was rising to her feet, leaping in the air above the huge log. "It was Martin! I felt it!"

> **stoic** (noun): a person who preserves a calm, unemotional bearing even in circumstances of pain and pleasure
> **articulate** (adjective): able to express yourself with clear sentences and well-formed sounds
> **curtail**: to cut down the size or extent of something; to stop something short of the point of completion

"It was Martin," Meagan confirmed in a ringing tone. "When he saw that Ms. Jensen was the one standing before him, and felt the tremble in her voice, it was like ... the fall of a city. Long ago—I think, anyway—soon after the split, he had made his peace with a world that had no Sandy Jensen. But he had to raise a wall. He turned back emotions at the gate. Joy and pain couldn't reach him. He became like a ... **stoic**. Then tonight, as the fog trailed away, he saw once more, and contrary to all his certainties, a world with Sandy Jensen—just surrender the city. And he did. The wall collapsed in the space of a moment, and his voice was as choked as hers and the words were broken— 'Sandy ... I ... I come to this meeting and ... then Sandy ... And she's ... and you ...'"

François seemed determined to fall off the huge log, the way she was hopping about. "He wasn't very **articulate** at this point, was he? Ha—a little problem with vowels and consonants."

"True," laughed Meagan. "But Ms. Jensen was no better off. She couldn't get through a sentence to save her life."

Joannie was on her feet now as well, leaning on Tedesco's shoulder and nearly knocking him off. "We'll send in Tedesco, that's what we'll do, to teach them English!"

"Too late," said Meagan. "Talking was of no use—they saw that. I don't know how this will appear in the minutes of the town council, but Ms. Jensen ran straight through the middle of the meeting, ran to him, and there they stood in this embrace that was way too prolonged for a place called the Non-Dilatory Quadralith. Some early trailers of tide were already lapping at their ankles, warning of worse, but they could have cared less—they had waited too long for this to **curtail** it now, just for fear of being swept out to sea."

Tedesco seemed very happy with the story. "So the town council," he asked, "it just called time-out from its business for this ... this ... matter of the heart?"

> **hierarchy**: (1) the arrangement of persons in an organization on lower and higher levels, according to authority, influence, status, etc.; (2) a similar arrangement of values, goals, etc.
> **disgruntled**: unhappy about something, often with a grumbling, festering unhappiness
> **vacillation**: the condition in which you swing back and forth between alternative choices without being able to decide on one or the other with finality

Meagan smiled. "Maybe our **hierarchy** of values is mixed up, but around here biz is not the absolute top of the pyramid. Still, I have to tell you—there was one very **disgruntled** individual. Your fan, Tedesco—Mr. Bamalford. He doesn't like salt water in his socks, and he was very grumpy about the delay. He has just an awful mouth. You should have heard him when Ms. Jensen ran to Martin. 'Yeah, great. Further **vacillation**. Vacillation: Part Two. First there was dump day, a year ago or whatever, when she put the guy out with the trash. Now her tender heart swings the other way and it looks like she and he are glued together. Tomorrow she'll probably waffle again and tell him she doesn't socialize with the self-employed.'"

Joannie shook her head in wonder. "Bamalford is good at what he does, you have to admit. Almost an artist."

"And when," asked François, "do we meet the real artist?"

"Never," cried Ricky. "I'm sure by now Martin's run away forever with his long lost. That's what I plan to do with Sallie."

> **expatriate**: one who has taken up residence outside of his or her own country
> **nonpartisan**: not said or done to support any particular candidate or party; rising above the conflict of candidates and parties, and seeking the general good
> **avid**: liking something in a wholehearted, enthusiastic way

Meagan pouted. "We're all hurt, Ricky. And after a few days as an **expatriate** you'd come racing back to your native land, I have no doubt. But as for Martin—his mind was on staying, not leaving. After he and Ms. Jensen talked, they came over to Mayor Povano and she told him, 'This man would like to do your whale.' So the mayor answered, 'And do you take this man…excuse me, can we take it for granted that this man, this candidate for the contract, has your **nonpartisan** recommendation, given neither for his special benefit nor yours, but only for the general welfare?' She just laughed and told him that she couldn't even give a partisan recommendation, that she had known Martin the poet, not Martin the sculptor, but that he was very sincere. Then Povano laughed in turn and said we are the last place in the world that still hires on the basis of sincerity, but it had worked with her, so alright—Martin was the whale man."

François and Joannie, already **avid** Martin fans, gave a brisk cheer. "Martin really looks OK," continued Meagan. "He gave this great smile and said that he's still a poet, that if his English language abilities ever fully recover he will write a poem thanking Dropanchor for its kindness to Sandy, and that as for the ceramic whale he will start work tomorrow morning, this morning really, an hour before sunrise, and—oh yeah—that Ms. Jensen says the senior boys should be mobilized."

"Hold everything," groaned Ricky. "This senior boy is too exhausted for any crack-of-dawn action."

Allen echoed the sentiment. And Tedesco held out the shoe in which he had taken the sample of mystery shampoo from barrel number ninety. It was curled into deformity. "Tedesco has this little *sapato* problem, you see ..."

> **indolence**: a distaste for work and an attraction to ease and idleness
> **adjournment**: the closing of a meeting, often with the determination of some later time or day on which it is to be continued

Meagan drew herself up sternly. "Continuing—Povano answered that **indolence** is not in the vocabulary of the senior boys, that hard work is their meat and drink, and that by the crack of dawn they would be assembled on the beach, ready to build a whale."

"Sleep is my meat and drink," mumbled Ricky, sliding off the log and departing for home. The others followed, and the beach lay still, except for the running of the tide and the waddling of some brown birds that had dropped down from the sky.

––––––––––––

READER: Larry thought it was great how Ms. Jensen brought the entire council meeting to a halt.

AUTHOR: Score one for *amóre*.

READER: Someday, he says, the minutes of the UN General Assembly will read: "Deliberations on world peace were suspended when the beautiful dark-eyed simultaneous translator recognized Delegate Larry as her lost love."

AUTHOR: I hope the **adjournment** will be brief. I mean—world peace is important.

READER: The minutes continue: "Highly responsible Delegate Larry soon returned to his seat, knowing the session could not go on without him, inasmuch as he was the principal architect of world peace."

AUTHOR: He thinks of everything.

Chapter 52: UBIQUITOUS FOOTAGE

It was a short night for Ricky. At 3:00 A.M. he sank into his bed, and at 5:00 he was out of it, waiting for François to arrive in her father's Jeep. "Lotta haulin' tomorrow," she had mumbled to him sleepily as they trudged home from the beach, after hearing Meagan's story. "But Dad is a **munificent** man, giving freely, many good causes. He'll help ours too, I'll bet—with his Jeep."

> **munificent**: generous on a grand scale
> **incontrovertible**: true beyond any possibility of being proved otherwise

A shot of coffee, a splash of water on the face—nothing had the slightest effect on Ricky's drowsiness, and his eyes were still glued half shut when he heard the Jeep arrive. He stumbled down the walk and slumped into the passenger seat. François was lost behind a map, so he merely mumbled, "G'morning, François. Pacific Ocean, please," and settled in for a catnap.

No nap was allowed, however. His eyes were scarcely shut when a groaning of brakes came from behind them. He turned in time to see a Jeep pulling up, and François jumping out. "Well, there you are," he said to the person beside him, still screened by the map. "Yep, that's you back there, **incontrovertibly** you. Same crazy curls. Same high-stepping walk. No way to deny it, which does raise a little question …"

There was a bright rippling of laughter, and the map was lowered. Ricky's weariness fell away, as he beheld in person the loveliness which drew him evening after evening to his television. Before the flash of those dark eyes, and the pretty mouth that was parted with laughter, he could only stammer, "Sallie!"

"Sallie Driven," she agreed. "And the name of my passenger might be …?"

Holding up a hand as though to ask for a slight suspension of play, Ricky pulled in two deep breaths. "Whew!" he said at last, "air helps. The name … my name … is … Farbugle Foster."

She laughed again with enjoyment. "You sound like someone filling out an application. And Foster—I believe totally that you are twenty-seven, just as you say. But…never in all my travels have I seen such a young-looking twenty-seven."

> **mendacity**: the art or activity of telling falsehoods
> **reticent**: strongly reluctant to discuss a matter in any detail
> **agrarian**: connected in some way with farming or farmland

Ricky saw that only one path lay open before him—**mendacity**. The lies came swiftly. "Perhaps I do look younger—a payoff, we must suppose, from my ... perpetual youth program. I mention only the legumes—you know, the food group—six small meals a day, of legumes. And my special aerobic routine, both copyrighted and patented, in which I imitate the seven classical forms of mechanical advantage, beginning with the lever. But enough. I'm **reticent** on such topics—trying to keep down the publicity, really don't like it. Normp! Appearances aside, however, true age is twenty-seven. There's my house. Like—I own it. Big investment, you know."

By this time François was approaching the Jeep. Sallie greeted her warmly. "I'm Sallie Driven. Full-time Jeeper. And you?"

Ricky thought it would be safer if he answered. "That's young Miss Dubois," he said, "one of our high school girls. I've hired her to ... to take care of my ... crops. You know, fields and orchards and so forth. She's really very **agrarian**—has farming in her blood."

François greeted Sallie. "I'm young Miss Dubois. I watch your show—when I'm not on the tractor. And—welcome to Dropanchor."

> **transient**: lasting just a little while; making only a short stay
> **imposture**: a deception by which you present yourself as someone you are not
> **unconventional**: departing from the ordinary, established way of thinking or acting

Ricky felt a surge of hope. Maybe the story would hold. Maybe Sallie would buy in. But even as hopes go, this was a very **transient** one. Rachel was the person who promptly sent it packing. She came down the front walk and said in a sleepy voice, "Did you have your breakfast, Ricky? Mom wants to know."

He looked sternly at her. "What are you doing in my house? And why do you address me by a name which I know not?"

"Ricky," said François in her gentlest voice, "I think the game is up, the **imposture** is exposed, and if by any chance Sallie was taken in, she is taken in no longer. And—since you didn't ask—I also think that the maybe, maybe-not quacking sound which Ms. Jensen heard last night with Meagan really was a Harbinger Duck. Which means—whales soon to follow. We need to be on the beach, helping Martin, right away."

Ricky was unperturbed at being labeled a fraud. "A closer look at the birth records will clear all this up. But for now, Sallie, to see Dropanchor at its most **unconventional** we should follow the advice of Ms. Dubois and head for the beach."

360

Sallie started up the Jeep, and Ricky showed the way, through the bending lanes and along the road of timber planking at the top of the beach. The first sunlight was brightening the upper air, the crowing of roosters floated down from the highland farms. Sallie teased her passenger mercilessly. "I note that young Miss Dubois is behind us. Wasn't she supposed to be cutting your alfalfa?"

> **hitherto**: up until the present time
> **blithe**: merry, with a light heart, and putting aside every shadow of care
> **inundation**: the submersion of a place in a flood

Ricky loved it, and said, "**Hitherto**—that's how we talk around here—hitherto you have been a remote star and I have adored you slavishly. Now you're near at hand and approachable and I'll probably ..."

"Begin treating me with contemptuous familiarity," suggested Sallie.

"Probably ... go right on adoring you slavishly, if you wouldn't mind."

"Not a serious problem," she answered **blithely**, "but we can revisit the subject every hundred years or so. And Ricky—if I may call you by your real name—a more important question. Am I supposed to drive through this ... **inundation**?"

They were drawing close now to Cape Scurrility, and they had reached the point where the Bad Pony, free at last of canyons, widened into a racing shallows and came spilling over the rough planking of the road. Ricky spoke with some pride. "I wouldn't stop for photos, ma'am, but you can make it. All of us locals do it no differently."

"The maddened waters took off the tires, deformed the fenders, and so on and so on," Sallie narrated, as she brought the Jeep easily through the shallow flood. "And where to next?"

> **utilitarian**: pursuing usefulness and efficiency on the level of material concerns, often without much regard for spiritual or cultural ideals
> **veritable**: truly possessing the qualities and traits of something to which you are being compared, although you are not literally identical with it

"Park it—that's where."

"Park it!" Sallie was indignant. "I could have parked it on the other side, before shooting the rapids. That would have been far more practical. Is this place not run on **utilitarian** principles or what?"

"Not during Whalefest," laughed Ricky. He motioned along the channel of the stream toward a small group of people, dimly seen in the shadow of Cape Scurrility. "For example, there's Martin and his work gang. They'll sweat today and we'll sweat with them—but not in the name of anything useful. You'll see."

François had parked on the other side of the stream, and she came splashing across to join them. "One thing's obvious," she exclaimed, beckoning towards the distant figure of Martin, "the man is a **veritable** robot. He hasn't slept or eaten, I'm sure. Yet he keeps on working, without rest, assembling and assembling."

What Martin was assembling became clear as they drew closer. It was a framework, a complex structure of ribs and struts, composed of some long silver poles that appeared to be aluminum, and some yellow rods, shorter and more numerous, that were probably plastic.

> **evocation**: an artful representation that calls up before the mind the image of some reality
>
> **belittle**: to convey the message, often in a mean way, that something is of little worth
>
> **preclude**: to shut out the possibility that something will happen or be done

A thought began to trouble Ricky. What if Martin was a Michelangelo? And what if Sallie liked Michelangelos? He found himself hoping, against all his better nature, that Martin's whale would not be a stunning triumph. But with every step across the cool sand, he saw the hope collapsing. Although the sculpture at this point was nothing more than a spindly structure of poles and rods, some genius was in it, and already it was an **evocation** of a mighty whale.

"Oh rats!" said Ricky. "I wanted to make a few **belittling** remarks."

"And your deeply rooted honesty **precludes** them," laughed Sallie. "Eh, Foster?"

> **herald** (noun): one who brings a message or announces news, often by crying it out loud
>
> **pique** (verb): to stir up rather sharply a feeling of irritation or curiosity

Ricky blinked. "For a shameless liar, I'm painfully honest."

The three of them arrived at last at the rude studio which Martin had set up. The place was well chosen: alongside the wide channel of the stream, and only a few yards up from the high tide line, it was a natural launch site for the huge ceramic whale being constructed there. At this early hour the work gang was small, only Martin and Ms. Jensen, Joannie, Tedesco and Meagan. "Allen was with us," explained Ms. Jensen, after introductions were complete, "but he had to be a **herald** and go off bearing some news."

362

That **piqued** Ricky's curiosity at once. "Some news, perchance, about ... some little featherballs that we ...?"

Meagan took his hand and led him to the growing framework of the whale. "Merry Christmas, Ricky. We have visitors."

Four brown birds, plump and comic, were inspecting Martin's work. The appearance of Ricky set off a conversation among them. There was a rather private exchange of little clucks and croons and other clearing noises from within their throats, and then—suddenly—a very public and enthusiastic volley of quacks and quocks.

Meagan laughed and laughed. "You're their man, Ricky."

"Well, they're my birds," he answered. "I love 'em almost as much as the whales." He paused, thoughtful. "So Allen gets to run through the streets, waking citizens from their sleep, crying, 'The Harbinger Ducks! To your stations.' I wonder if there's still time to ..."

> **cacophony**: a jarring sound; often the confused noise that results when several sounds occur together in competition and without harmonization
>
> **sustenance**: (1) food, considered as sustaining life; (2) more generally, whatever supports and nourishes life at any level
>
> **burnished**: rubbed smooth and shiny

His question was answered by a wild **cacophony** coming from the town: auto horns and church bells, fire sirens, dinner chimes and tubas, all were mixing into the single proclamation that the Harbinger Ducks had arrived.

Then after some minutes the noise died away and a strange silence settled in. "So everyone rolls over and goes back to sleep?" asked Sallie.

"Never," answered Ricky. "Everyone goes back indoors and starts grabbing sweatbands, work gloves, water bottles, sunscreen, ropes, waders, buckets and so on. You should be getting your $47,000 video camera ready."

Sallie threw up her hands. "It's with Uncle Reggie. He was behind me in the equipment truck. We saw an all-night waffle house. He radioed me that he desperately needed **sustenance**. He pulled over. I didn't. He could be on his fortieth waffle by this time."

Now the town came alive again, with a clatter of doors slamming, voices calling, boots pounding on the cobblestones. Some minutes later Sallie looked up the gully where the Bad Pony ran, and groaned, "Reggie—I hate you!" The first shafts of sun were glancing there, on water and stone, and the archways of the bridge crossing to the school were traced in the early light. A long column of people was arriving, beginning to cross over. The sun glinted on the pails they carried, and the ropes as well, **burnished** from much handling.

motif: a sentiment, symbol, etc. which is a principal theme in a work and is repeated from time to time in it
solicitous: anxious about the condition of someone or something, and eager to find some way to help

Ricky waved impulsively, then explained, "Those are the harvesters. The harvest hangs down the face of a low bluff. Much of it could be reached with stepladders, but that's too easy. Those maniacs will dangle on ropes from the top of the bluff, bobbing and pitching, plucking the Mendicant Berries—that's the crop, incidentally—as best they can. Doing things the hard way— definitely a **motif** of Whalefest. You'll see it over and over."

"Footage!" cried Sallie. "Beautiful footage, hillside bridges laden with marchers, and Reggie's on a waffle binge."

She pulled a trim pair of binoculars from her pocket. "At the front of the column, a girl all in khaki except for a scarlet glove on one hand."

"That's the invisible hand," came the voice of someone approaching. It was Allen, returning from town. "The girl is Merci, and no one is permitted to see this ridiculous wart on her right hand."

He met Sallie, and told her how Merci was the first lady of Whalefest, and the first to pick a Mendicant Berry.

François asked him, "And was my grandmother with them?"

Allen smiled. "Would she be anywhere else, the way she frets over those berries? She worries Bamalford will bottle them, or they'll be nipped in a late frost. They'd all have padlocks and mittens if she could figure out how to do it."

"She is **solicitous**," admitted François. "Who can blame her? Remember all those briar leaves last autumn, curled and strange—the many little victims of that unknown vapor."

The shadow of something remembered was crossing her face now. "Allen, the mayor, was he with them? We need to talk to him, you know, on that very subject."

"No," answered Allen, after a moment's thought, "not with the berry crowd. I heard him say a couple days ago that this is the year of the kettle. Which means he's probably part of that ... that Labor Day parade starting to form right now, way down there."

Allen was looking southward along the beach, toward some red warehouses that clustered together near the dock. On one of them a pair of enormous doors had swung open. Something bright and metallic, and huge enough almost to fill the doorway, was being dragged out.

"Ho!" cried Martin. "Our decoy is working. Here comes the first whale, made of gold and silver apparently."

> **mundane**: related to ordinary day-to-day, down-to-earth matters
> **paucity**: the condition in which there are only a few of something; scarceness of supply
> **sedentary**: not physically active; sitting a great deal of the time

Joannie laughed. "No—that's way too romantic. It's something quite **mundane**—a cooking pot, a common kettle, cast iron and brass."

"But on the big side."

Tedesco jumped in. "Oh yes—the big side. Ricky has told to me that it takes twenty-five thousand people to drag this kettle."

Squirming under the gaze of François and Megan, Ricky said, "That could be high. I rounded up. But it does take a hundred. And there's no **paucity** of backups either—jillions of people waiting their turn on the rope. You'll see it all, Tedesco, when they come dragging past here, with the kettle making little friction noises in the sand."

"And this is done each day?" asked Sallie innocently. "To get all the Dropanchorites off their couches, so that no one is **sedentary**?"

"No," said Joannie, "it's a once-a-year sort of thing—to boil up a ... a nectar, a sweet cider, from the berries which the harvest gang brings in. The kettle simmers, usually two or three days, until the whales have entered the bay. Then the person who gets to drink first from the cider is—not surprisingly—the first lady."

> **piecemeal** (adjective): done in a disconnected way, now a piece here, now a piece there
> **epic** (adjective): concerned with the grand, historic struggles of heroes, and often with the peoples they represented
> **inertia**: the tendency of an unmoving body to resist efforts to set it in motion

"The girl with the red glove?" asked Sallie.

"With the red glove and the gentle disposition," confirmed François.

Sallie hoped to hear more about Whalefest, and under her skillful questioning the story came out, a **piecemeal** account, everyone telling a part, and all out of order. She listened carefully, commenting at last, "What a beautiful, slightly weird tradition, what a ..." Then she paused abruptly, gazing southward along the beach. "What a rotten piece of luck! For the second time in an hour I see footage like you only see once in a lifetime—and you, Reggie, keeper of my camera, are stuffing your face with waffles."

She was looking at the kettle, and its hundred movers, still far away but emerging into full view from behind a stony outcrop. She saw a struggle on an **epic** scale: a hundred bodies straining heroically, leaning almost to the sand; a hundred shoulders marked with the heavy imprint of the rope; and ranked against their collective energy, the massive **inertia** of the Whalefest kettle. It was huge like Gibraltar, one of those things which if at rest could scarcely be conceived in motion. And yet it was moving, drawn a few inches at a time across the sand.

The kettle held a particular fascination for Martin. He was murmuring to himself, "A giant kettle means a giant fire."

> **redundant**: unnecessarily repetitive
> **clairvoyance**: a gift that lets you see things beyond the perception of most of us, such as the inner thoughts and feelings of others
> **kiln**: a heavy-duty oven where pottery is baked so that it becomes hard

"And you need a giant fire," Joannie blurted on an impulse, her words running ahead of her thoughts, "to bake the clay pieces, the clay ... panels which will form the sides of the whale. And having two giant fires is **redundant**, if one will do. So why not bake the panels in the same fire that heats the kettle?"

Martin gave a low whistle. "Sandy obviously taught a class in **clairvoyance**—it's just what I was thinking—the edge of the kettle fire gets turned into a ring of **kilns**."

> **amenable**: receptive to some plan or opinion, and ready to be won over to it
> **dissuade**: to use argument and persuasion to turn someone away from a choice

Joannie grinned. "All you have to do is talk to the mayor. He micromanages everything during Whalefest, even the kettle fire. I'm sure he'll be **amenable**. You know how badly he wants this ceramic whale."

François said half to herself, "I need to talk to the mayor—about a bigger fire than any of us will ever build."

By midmorning the kettle had inched along the beach to a point just below Martin's work site. The mayor was in the first spot on the rope, closest to the kettle. When he saw François standing near, waiting for a chance to speak with him, he said in little gasps, "We won't take a rest ... until we've dragged this monster ... across the stream. So tell me now. The Mendicant Berries have disappeared ... and Grandma is out of her mind ... I'm sure that's it."

François smiled sweetly. "No, it's worse." Then she described how in the middle of the night, and in the depths of Mount Relief, barrels of waste were plunging into a fiery cauldron; how a sample of the stuff put a tight curl in Tedesco's shoe, like the curl last autumn in the leaves of the Mendicant Briars; and how the future held something much more troubling—one hundred barrels of a very risky product called Glinscrimion.

The news was bitter for Povano. "With every argument," he groaned, "I have tried to **dissuade** Bamalford from this approach of his—looking at Harbinger Ducks, Mendicant Berries, even Mount Relief and seeing only dollars. But he's beyond hope. This much, though, I'll tell you—no more trash is going down the throat of our mountain. Once Whalefest is over—and some able-bodied people are available—we'll seal that spooky door so tight that an earthquake can't open it. Ha—better—we'll take that witch's rock and wedge it in the tunnel. We'll ..."

An indignant cry came from higher up on the beach. "Waffle eater!"

"That's Sallie Driven," explained François. "She's welcoming Uncle Reggie to Dropanchor."

A bulky, cheerful figure was approaching the work site, untroubled by the scolding which Sallie was delivering. "Tourist!" she shouted.

> **pejorative**: carrying an insulting meaning, often one that has evolved from an originally neutral meaning
> **ubiquitous**: being everywhere at once, or in a comparatively short period of time

Uncle Reggie returned a look of amusement. "Tourist? Are you using that in some **pejorative** sense, to criticize me?"

"Pejorative and then some. You poke around like someone on vacation, and I miss the greatest footage ever. **Ubiquitous** Footage, uncle, does that mean anything to you? Everywhere I turn in this town, there's footage to die for. It's on the hillside, it's on the beach, it's everywhere. But it takes a camera, and ..." She stopped in the middle of her sentence, staring south toward the docks. "Oh no—it's happening again."

> **burgeon**: to swell with new growth
> **inadvertence**: (1) a careless failure to pay attention to some matter; (2) a mistake resulting from such a failure

Seaward from the docks, and moving gracefully under the wind, something like a white flower was **burgeoning** before their eyes, blooming, growing fuller each moment. It was *Jack's Equator*, anchor hoisted, sail after sail being unfurled. "It can all be yours!" Ricky told Sallie with great warmth. "My grandfather sails on it, and someday I'll probably inherit the thing, and ..."

"Someday!" answered Sallie, snatching her video camera and gear bag from Uncle Reggie. "It's mine this minute, once I throw in a cassette."

She rifled through the bag: "Battery, spare battery, charger, filter ... several Belgian waffles ... Uncle Reggie!"

Reggie jerked back his hand—he had been reaching out to touch the whale frame—and, with a roll of his head, uttered a long Ooops. Then he marched off toward the truck where he had left the blank cassettes. "Not on purpose, you understand," he explained to no one in particular. "It was a goof, a moment's **inadvertence**."

The bright form of *Jack's Equator* glided north through the bay. The white masts stood out sharply against the pine groves of the long, unnamed island that sheltered most of the bay, and Martin, never pausing in his work, stole what glances he could at the brave sight. "There is a work of art," he said. "Bound for the Orient no doubt, to bring back ginger and other spices."

> **breach** (verb): to break forth from water with a surging leap
> **egalitarian**: with equal treatment for all, regardless of race, gender, etc.
> **utopian**: related to an ideal human society that is blessed with perfect laws, institutions and social structures

Joannie was shaking her head. "No, the ship is part of Whalefest too. It doesn't even put out to open sea—just runs north until it's a little past the protection of the island, and then anchors in the bend of water where Cape Stairstep pushes out. The waves are rougher there, but in some years at least that's where the whales tend the most to **breach**, the most to loiter. The ship is the observation post. Everyone—berry picker, kettle hauler, sailor—has a right to the same amount of time at the rail watching them. It's very **egalitarian**."

"And almost **utopian**," replied Martin, still working steadily at the growing frame. "It's like the perfect society. Each person with an appointed task, and going eagerly to it. And all the tasks orchestrated into one grand expression—Whalefest."

> **discordant**: not in harmony with; conflicting or disagreeing with
> **hypocrisy**: the act of making a show of having some virtue, honoring some rule, etc., when in fact you lack the virtue, behave contrary to the rule, etc.

As though in response, one of the Harbinger Ducks let fly a loud *quakk, quokk*.

Martin was startled. His busy hands dropped to his side for a moment. "That didn't sound like a Right on! It had a **discordant** tone."

Ms. Jensen gave him a nudge. "If it did, mister new boy, then it spoke for all of us, I'm afraid. Dropanchor is not a utopia."

READER: Larry suggests that when the kettle draggers reach their destination and start collapsing on the sand, they should get a call from a guy named Louie back at the red warehouses who says ...

AUTHOR: Tell me Larry is not so mean!

READER: ...who says, "Hey guys, you took the wrong kettle!"

AUTHOR: It would be powerful drama—dragging back the wrong one, dragging out the right one, figuring out who was to blame. But I can't bring a new character—Louie or whomever—on stage this late in the story.

READER: Oh master of **hypocrisy**—you've brought on three in the last two chapters!

AUTHOR: Umm ... true to a point ... Martin, Sallie and Reggie, I suppose. But their case is very different from Louie's.

READER: And the difference, no doubt, is so obvious that ...

AUTHOR: ... that stating it would be stating the obvious, which we don't want to get into.

Chapter 53: PECUNIARY DAYS

Martin felt like the man who picks up a single rock from a hillside and triggers an avalanche. His remark that Dropanchor was a **utopia** set loose a rush of opinion—all of it contrary.

> **utopia**: a human society that is blessed with perfect laws, institutions and social structures
> **virulent**: marked by an intense and forceful hostility
> **misanthrope**: one who hates people in general, and holds them in contempt

First Ms. Jensen told him about the Fram—how she haunted Room 401 from her office in the attic, and how her ownership of the school land let her bully Ironbane and Povano. "Utopia would not have any Ms. Framleys, trust me," she finished.

Then Joannie described Draco, and his frightening arrivals in the purple boat. The Farnum twins, who had now joined the whale builders, imitated the inspector reading from his maroon book and vowing to drag off the children of Dropanchor. "Nice," said Joannie, "but make it even more **virulent**. He does it with so much hostility that it rips into you."

Martin was following the story carefully. "Well, that's a pair of **misanthropes**," he said as he bent an aluminum pole and fitted it into the growing structure of the whale. "The Fram and the Draco—with a poke in the eye for the rest of the human race. But that's not the end of the list, I'll bet. Allen was talking about someone who snitches berries and distresses grandmothers—Bamalford I believe it was."

Joannie and several others started to answer at once and then, hearing the confusion, fell silent. This was why the soft voice of Rachel, who had just arrived to help her brother, stood out clearly. "He's right up there in the sky, everybody." She was looking toward the north, staring at the huge statute of Bamalford, or, more precisely, at the huge head, gleaming in the air. From the shoulders on down the statue was still in shadow, emerging slowly as the sun came rising higher over the eastern ranges.

> **inordinate**: not held in check; breaking past proper limits and proportions
> **beguile**: to pull you into a deception, often by charming you to the point that you stop taking a careful look around

Martin's eyes widened. "That's an impressive piece of work—sculpturewise. Humanwise, too, for that matter—what an unashamed grab for attention! If I had this wild, **inordinate** desire for attention, I hope I would at least be more subtle than standing up on a pedestal and hollering, 'Look at me!' Still, he's your guy, so tell me ..."

So they told him about Bamalford. The story tumbled out, with everyone adding his or her instance—the manhunt for Foster, the threats against the Mendicant Berries, the caging of the duck. Meagan came last, and she described Bamalford's special talent. "He collects people. He finds hurt people, and takes over their lives. He tells each of them the lie they want to hear, and tells it so attractively that they are **beguiled**, and they begin to see in him a protector and friend. And from there it's a small step to cooperating with his schemes."

Ms. Jensen put a hand on Martin's shoulder. "Even you, champ, are not exempt. Bamalford will look you over, to see if you're a promising recruit."

Martin smiled at her. "My allegiances are pretty clear at this point, so Bamalford and his invitations don't scare me. But how about Draco and Ms. Framley? Am I going to light up their screens?"

"Ms. Framley may be a problem for you, and I'll tell you why in a minute," answered Ms. Jensen. She looked to Allen. "But what about Draco?"

> **prow**: the front-most part of a ship; the jutting nose of a ship or boat, formed by the two sides running together
> **impound**: to seize some object, often one involved in some violation of the law, and hold it in the custody of the police or other authority
> **rhetorical**: using devices of language such as dramatic repetition, exaggerated comparison, linkage to famous figures, etc., in an effort to make speech and writing have greater impact

Allen thought for a moment, then turned to Martin and said, "Draco will be interested in you. He apparently dabbles in art. He's got this elaborate carving on the **prow** of his boat, and he buffs it up a lot. So he's going to take notice of your ceramic whale. And if he likes it, who knows—maybe you don't get hassled, but the whale gets **impounded** and winds up in his family room. If he doesn't like it, then brace yourself for the **rhetorical** Draco. He will use all the tricks of English, all the dramatic devices, to put you in the corner where he has put us—the polluters' corner. When he's done with his speeches, things will have a different look: your whale, I'm afraid, will be a form of pollution, and launching it into the public waters will be a pollution episode. That's Draco—we definitely like the guy. Now as for Ms. Framley ..."

"Thank you," Ms. Jensen said to Allen, "but I get to do the Ms. Framley part of this report." She turned to Martin. "You know how all morning you've been muttering about clay and pigment."

"I wouldn't call it muttering," answered the sculptor. "More like calmly mentioning. But yes—clay and pigment—I will need lots of both. To give body and color to the whale. And all this, Sandy, has what to do with Ms. Framley?"

> **provincial**: having the narrow outlook, quaint customs and unsophisticated manners sometimes thought to be associated with out-of-the-way places
> **lore**: a body of specialized knowledge which those who practice some craft or art have gradually built up, and passed along
> **precarious**: especially at the mercy of outside forces, and thus poised on the brink of some change or misfortune which those forces may bring about

"Be patient," said Ms. Jensen with a grin. "We must speak of clay and pigment for a moment. Your pigment is not a big problem. You see—many people here gather plants and shells to make their own dyes. At first that struck me as **provincial**—like, could we open our small-town minds to a new idea called buy it at the store?—but now I'm one of them. They have taught me their **lore**, and I know where to find a plant which yields the blue and black pigment tones you need. So that one we can handle. But clay ... well, that does bring us to Ms. Framley, which really brings us to Mr. Ironbane ..."

Ironbane was there now, having climbed with the harvesters only as far as the school, and then descending. He took the cue. "In all my wanderings around this place, I've come across only one good deposit of clay—and it's on Ms. Framley's land. If you follow the course of the Bad Pony back across the sand and up the ravine, at some point you reach the corner of her property. Unfortunately, the deposit is still farther up, almost to the school, and it's on the north bank of the stream. Which means that it's inside her boundaries. Taking clay from it will be **precarious**. Even if you're there with her permission she may spin into one of her private-property funks and drive you off with falling boulders."

Martin covered his head. "An all-around sweetheart. Is she one of those whom this Bamalford has won over?"

"Oh yes," said Joannie. "Money and power are welcome on his team. And she has some of both."

"So I really am safe after all," laughed Martin, "having neither."

"No, no—there's a place in his schemes for the talents of an artist." Some bitterness crept into Joannie's voice. "He stole a former friend of mine—a boy named Calvin, and a gifted sketcher. Turned him into a fast-track humanoid."

Martin felt the emotion, and he looked at her gently. "Sometimes these things work out, and we humanoids return once more."

> **obdurate**: stubborn and hardened, especially in badness, and pushing aside any grace or influence that might soften you
>
> **premonition**: a feeling, not fully supported by objective evidence, that something is going to happen

"Well ... thanks," she said with a weak smile. "But Calvin has resisted every effort. I mean, how many times have I tried to talk with him, to win him back ... just to what he used to be? But he pushes away very hard. He's so ... **obdurate**!"

Joannie's appraisal of Calvin was a gloomy one, but it was not far off, as became clear from something that happened later that morning. As the sun climbed high over the capes and the long shadows were at last furled, Rachel caught sight of a solitary figure, almost at the top of the beach. He was not directly up from them, but farther north, nearly even with the canyon that separated Cape Scurrility from the enormous trunk of Cape Stairstep. "I think he's painting," she exclaimed. "He's got one of those ... "

"Easels," finished Ricky. "I can't see who it is, though."

"I can't either," said Joannie, "but I have this **premonition** that we aren't going to like it."

Meagan looked sharply at her friend. "You think maybe it's..."

"It's not thinking, really, just this funny feeling that says it's him, he, whatever, and that the whole point of his being there is to set himself against us, and against Whalefest."

"But he's supposed to like Whalefest," protested Rachel, with a stamp of her foot. "Isn't he, Ricky?"

"Rach," answered her brother, "there's not some law ... "

"Well, we should go see!"

"Alright," he laughed, "let's take the indignant one for a walk—see if we can cool her jets."

"Well, bring me along," said Joannie suddenly. "If that's him, and if he's sitting over there like some spoiler, putting a hex ... "

> **resplendent**: glowing, and often glorious, with light
>
> **antediluvian**: belonging to the far distant past; far behind the modern way

It was Calvin, just as Joannie had anticipated. And as she and Rachel and Ricky came closer, they saw that it was a very **resplendent** Calvin. He wore a white tuxedo, which had some linen or silk woven into the fabric, the way it shone in the late morning sun. "Welcome—ambassadors from Dropanchor," he called, as he saw the three approaching.

"So what are you—a foreign country?" asked Joannie disapprovingly.

"Just a little flight of fancy. So you came to see me. Well, then—see me!" He modeled the tuxedo for them. "I got a bonus from Mr. Bamalford for ... a special project. Some of us are getting ahead, you know."

There was some haughtiness in his voice, and it kindled Rachel's temper. Remembering the manner of stern grown-ups, she informed Calvin, "Ricky is here to see your painting, and if it shows what it shouldn't, then he's going to feed it to the sharks."

"Whoopee!" said Calvin with a nonchalant air. "Censorship arrives in Dropanchor. We had hoped it was just an **antediluvian** practice, a tool used long ago and by early forms of government, and totally out of place today. But no such luck it appears."

Rachel blinked, and turned hesitantly to Ricky. He crouched down to be at her level, and said to her quietly, "We don't have to like what he paints, Rach, but we can't feed it to the sharks. He can paint what he wants, you can paint what you want. That's how it works around here. I'll try to explain better, later on, OK."

To Ricky she made no reply. Instead she squared her shoulders and turned back to face Calvin again. "Well, anyway, Calvin..." Then there was a pause, and it lengthened. She couldn't think how to finish. The situation was suddenly too much for her.

> **whimsical**: fanciful, and conceived in the free play of wishes and imagination
> **transmutation**: the change of a thing of one nature into something of a different, sometimes higher, nature
> **pecuniary**: defined in terms of, or otherwise focused on, money

Ricky pulled her gently back a step or two, out of the contest. And Joannie took her hand, saying, "We haven't really seen Calvin's picture yet, so let's have a look. Maybe it's OK, maybe it's about whales and whale journeys, something **whimsical** like that. And maybe I'm the queen of Sheba, and..."

The picture was about whales. Whale journeys, however, were another matter. Something unusual was happening in the painting, but it looked very little like a journey, and more like a **transmutation**. At the far left of the picture was a finely detailed line drawing of a whale. The great creature was all in black, and its head was toward the top of the canvas, while its tail disappeared

374

off the edge. To its right was a second whale, done less with lines, more with blocks and bars of shadow, and exhibiting one marking in color, a vivid green dollar sign just beneath the eye. Moving across the canvas four more whales continued the transformation: each was done in a style more abstract than its predecessor, and in each the green of money was more prominent. It all culminated in a seventh figure, which was nothing more than a depiction of fifty- and hundred-dollar bills, skillfully arranged and rounded to suggest a whale's form.

"Well," said Ricky, lightly touching the dollar sign under the eye of the second figure, "a week of whales. But the interpretation is rather **pecuniary**— whales aren't fish, they're cash, huh?"

Calvin was delighted. "You've got it! Those blubber banks could mean lots of money for Dropanchor. The potential tourist trade ... And I like your word, too. Ha ...!" He grabbed a fine-tip brush and poised his hand at the bottom of the painting. "That's what we will name it—*The Pecuniary Week of Whales.* Or, to keep it shorter, *The Pecuniary Week.* Or even better—*Pecuniary Days.* Thank you, Ricky. There's hope for you yet."

> **revere**: to give a special affection and regard to someone who embodies noble qualities
> **grimace**: a facial expression in which the features pull or twist to show some emotion, such as repugnance or dismay
> **audacious**: boldly and self-assuredly disregarding or challenging some custom, rule or authority figure

"But is there still hope for you, Calvin?" broke in Joannie, shaken and dismayed. "Dropanchor has always ... **revered** the whales. You know, some awe, some affection—silly little emotions like that. But now you put them through this seven-day distortion and at the end they mean nothing—except their cash equivalent. It's so ... monstrous."

A **grimace** of frustration pulled across Calvin's face, then was gone in a moment. "Well—I don't like *your* word. Not monstrous, Joannie. Just **audacious**—the citizens of Dropanchor go out to revere the whales, and Calvin gets in their face with a reminder that the whales are cash cows, nothing more. That's brassy—but it's not monstrous."

With an angry gesture Joannie pointed down the coastline, in the direction from which the whales would arrive. "Those intelligent creatures navigate thousands of miles, exploring the canyons and hollows, singing their lonely songs—and you call them cash cows."

> **flippant**: treating in a light, casual manner something that deserves to be taken more seriously
> **supplant**: to displace something and become its substitute

375

forlorn: sorrowful and without hope, often from a sense of being alone and abandoned

Calvin refused to take her seriously. "I'm not into music," he said **flippantly**. "Visual arts—that's me. And him too, you know."

He beckoned toward the distant figure of Martin, already tying the last rods and poles into the framing of the whale. "What's his school—abstractionist or what? I'm multi-school, if anybody cares to know."

"Multi-school." The phrase caught in Joannie's mind. "Multi-school—that was exactly how Merci described the style of that advertisement—the one that Ms. Framley ..."

The anger had passed from her voice now, **supplanted** by something more **forlorn**. "You did that wine ad, I know you did! That was the special project that earned you a bonus. Oh Calvin—such a short time ago, we were side by side, with our crazy plans for Mercurial Canyon. Research by Joannie, drawings by Calvin. What happened?"

To his credit Calvin saw the pain, and there was no mockery in his answer. But there was no comfort in it either. "What happened? I got older. I looked around and saw the choices. Grandma's world—with its wishful illusions about berries and whales. And Bamalford's—more solid and real, with roots in things that matter. And you know how I chose, Joannie."

remunerative: paying you for your efforts, and often paying rather well
palette: the board where a painter places or mixes a little glob of each color he plans to use

She smiled sadly. "The expensive white tuxedo tells how you chose."

"Well," said Calvin, fingering the coat, "putting my talents to work for Bamalford has been **remunerative**, I won't deny. I'm no volunteer."

"And this," Joannie asked quietly, stretching a hand toward the painting, "how much will you be paid for this?"

Calvin shrugged. "No idea. But Bamalford will like it. And Nameless—well, he's excited about the whales. He's got this idea for virtual harpooning that makes him hear cash register noises. So—he'll love it, especially the little touches, like that dollar sign there under the eye of the ... Hey!"

"Rachel ... whoa!" cried Ricky. "Whoa, girl."

Rachel was at Calvin's **palette**. In her hand was a brush heavy with the darkest paint she could find there. "Ricky," she cried, "just that dollar thing, OK, I hate it and ..."

Ricky gave his sister a smile, even as he took the brush from her. "You hate it, and you want to paint it over. But you don't want to appear in front of Judge Snoozer on criminal charges, do you?"

She sparked like a fine cut gem. "No—but this painting should."

Joannie caught her hand. "C'mon. Grab your big brother. Let's go see what's happening on Martin's whale."

> **dissonant**: sounding a jarring note; out of harmony with; in conflict with
>
> **cavil**: to find trivial problems with something; to bring up picky objections that you should really just pass over

She cast a look at Calvin and then glanced up and down the shoreline, noting all the press and hurry of the Whalefest preparations. "People dragging kettles," she said, "and moving ships, hauling berries, gathering firewood, shaping clay—all saying that Whalefest is worth the trouble. And one lonely figure saying that it's a mistake—one **dissonant** voice. I almost respect you, Calvin, for standing by your conviction. But the conviction itself—that what we have here should be packaged and peddled—that chills me to the bone."

She turned and walked off slowly toward Martin's work site, drawing Rachel after her. Ricky handed the dripping brush to Calvin, and followed.

READER: Larry says that if he lived in Dropanchor and had whales everywhere, he would construct …

AUTHOR: Oh no—is this going to be Larry on ecotourism?

READER: It's more like Larry on love. He would construct a wedding chapel, a floating one, and for a fee you could have a whale as part of your wedding.

AUTHOR: Not to **cavil** or anything, but there is one little difficulty—what possible role could a whale play in a wedding?

READER: Larry sees several.

AUTHOR: Several! To be frank, I can't see any.

READER: The whale as ring bearer, for example, or …

AUTHOR: Ring bearer! Bllbllbllbthwgg—sorry, swallowed another one! But no, no … That's OK. No more questions. I'm sure Larry knows what he's doing.

Chapter 54: ETHAN'S PREDILECTION

On the following day two expeditions went out from Martin's work site. One of them, with Ironbane at its head, pushed up the gully where the Bad Pony ran. It had a single purpose, to mine clay from the deposit located on Ms. Framley's side of the stream. She had consented, but only after a fuss.

> **vitriolic**: using speech that is cutting, acidic and hateful
> **languish**: to fail to be energetic; to be weak, drained and inactive
> **overture**: an approach you make to someone to express an opening offer or to invite discussion

Her first reaction, when Povano had told her no more than an hour earlier that the whale decoy required clay from her property, was **vitriolic**. "You go digging on my estate," she screamed, with the blood rushing to her cheeks, "and you'll be digging your own tomb! Not an ounce, not a gram, of my land, for an old fraud like you."

At almost the same moment, however, Nameless and Bamalford were paying a visit to Martin that would have consequences for Ms. Framley's resistance. Nameless had approached the work site with his usual drooping, could-die-any-moment style. But he put the **languishing** manner aside the minute he had a good look at Martin's whale. Finding a sudden energy, he grabbed Bamalford firmly by the shoulder and declared, "This one we must have. 'Must' in boldface. Must, must, must."

"You want that ceramic whale so bad?" asked Bamalford in a puzzled tone.

"I want that sculptor! There's a future for him in Roxxy's Rekillables—doing life-size figures." He released Bamalford's shoulder and thought for a few moments.

"So what is the Nameless approach? I need an **overture**—some smart little way to kick off discussions with him on this topic. Here—the classic conversation starter." He pulled nine hundred-dollar bills from his wallet, and put them in Bamalford's hand. "Go lash him with these. And if there are any favors we can do for him, find out."

> **adamant**: like the hardest rock; holding an opinion so firmly that you can't be budged or altered
> **palatable**: sufficiently agreeable in taste as to be swallowed without difficulty or dislike
> **avarice**: an intense, active greediness that drives you to store up more and more wealth

Bamalford did as instructed, but Martin pushed away the money and the flattery that came with it. When his cell phone rang he was happy for the opportunity to break off the conversation. The caller was Povano, describing the **adamant** refusals of Ms. Framley. Martin laughed in spite of himself. "So it's no way and never—she's harder than stone. I have to see this lady."

Bamalford soon guessed from Martin's side of the phone call that clay was a problem, and that Ms. Framley might be the answer. This was just what Nameless was looking for—a chance to do Martin a favor. Within moments Bamalford was on his phone with Ms. Framley, softening her resistance with hints that such unfading beauty as hers still belonged on page one of his paper.

She quickly fell into an agony of indecision. "Front-page coverage for my face and body—in return for letting this dirty little mayor carry away buckets of my land. Oh—help me someone. What should I do?"

It was the mayor himself who first saw what was needed to make the deal a **palatable** one for Ms. Framley. "Two for one, my dear woman—that should be to your liking. For every pound of clay we take from your property, we put back two pounds of topsoil."

The glitter of **avarice** awoke in her eyes. "Ooh! I end up with more land—more, more land. You can never have too much."

She accepted the proposal, and Povano telephoned the news to the work site. Within an hour Ironbane and his expedition were at the deposit, and soon the first sack of clay, hoisted on the broad back of Darlingson, was traveling alongside the Bad Pony, down the clean-swept canyon and to the beach.

It was an excellent clay, easily worked. "None better in ancient Athens," said Martin, as he shaped it into curving panels. Joannie and Allen and many others worked with him, straining to achieve the precise rounding and measure which the sculpture demanded.

> **improvisation**: something put together through a creative use of whatever materials happen to be at hand; some arrangement or solution that you come up with on the spot
>
> **foray** (noun): a quick excursion, into an area and out, often a bit like a raid, inasmuch as you go with the hope of bringing back something

"None better in ancient ... ancient ..." he fumbled, as he saw the clay panels glowing with heat. They were baking in his kiln, a rough **improvisation** of stones and concrete blocks which he had pieced together around the kettle fire.

"Ancient ... ancient ..." he mumbled as the panels were attached firmly to the whale frame. "What was that other place?"

"Somewhere in Italy," volunteered Joannie. "And somebody needs sleep."

Throughout the morning, as his clay problems resolved themselves, Martin turned his eyes frequently to Cape Magdalena, the low cape that formed the southern limit of Dropanchor and its harbor. Sandy Jensen was there. By nine she was moving seaward along the crest, through a patchwork of sparse forest and rambling meadow. It was a place she loved. The slopes fell gently, and you could follow them down where you chose, on random **forays** to the beach or valley below.

There was no time now, of course, for any such thing. Ms. Jensen and those with her—Sallie, Ricky, Rachel, François, and Merci with her one red glove—were the pigment expedition. They had come for the plant which gave the bluish-black dyes needed for the coloring of Martin's whale.

> **indigenous**: not imported; occurring naturally in a locality
> **vagrant** (noun): one who drifts from place to place, with no permanent home, and often short on cash and lacking any steady employment

"It's turning out rather homegrown," Ms. Jensen was saying to Sallie. "Except for those poles and rods, he's making this beast from **indigenous** materials. The clay is mined here in Dropanchor. And the coloring will come from plants that are native here. I like that."

Sallie nodded. "Yeah, so do I—very much. Things like that are why I'm a **vagrant**—tramping around the country, eating the waffle scraps left by Uncle Reggie. And, of course, carrying this."

She hefted the video camera which hung from her shoulder, and let her fingers close lightly over the lens cover. As she did so, a quick motion registered at the edge of her vision. It was a flinching, a sudden pulling back. Merci had slipped behind her sister, as though for concealment. Sallie gave her a reassuring smile. "Don't worry. I'm not filming."

> **kin** (noun): (1) the group of persons related to you by blood; (2) something similar to another thing, as though both were descended from a common source
> **longevity**: abundant length of life
> **enhance**: to add to the value, beauty, utility or other positive quality of something

The same thing happened again, however, a few minutes later. Ms. Jensen and her band were drawing near to the only house on the cape, an unusual structure, rounded and narrow and standing very tall, as though it were the cousin or other **kin** of the Pacific lighthouses. The hillside there was carved into seven terraces, dense with squash vines, cauliflower clusters and every other sort of vegetable. Ms. Jensen explained how it was all the work of Peter Oakum. "He wants to make twenty more farming terraces, at least, and he prays for the **longevity** to do it."

380

Sallie was raising her camera to the shooting position. "I can't give him any more years, but I can make his terraces live forever. Just let me ..."

She broke off. Once more out of the corner of her eye—a quick, fugitive motion. Merci had again drawn into the protection of François, and it was François who explained quietly, "Beneath the charming red glove lies the charming wart. And her nightmare fear is to see it—the wart—on national TV, with the image **enhanced** by various editing techniques to be even more vivid, graphic and warty. Just leave the glove on, right? But—for her—when you lift the camera, it's like that nightmare starting to happen."

"Tell her," said Sallie gently, "that the supreme rule for me, my camera, my uncle and my program is that we add to no one's pain."

> **predilection**: the special, sometimes blind, affection you have for someone or something that is your favorite
> **foliage**: leaves on the stem; the cluster of leaves growing on a plant or group of plants
> **serrated**: having an edge formed of small, sharply pointed triangles, like a saw

François put an arm around Merci's shoulder. "I'll tell her."

The place which Ms. Jensen was seeking lay a short distance beyond the farming terraces of Peter Oakum. There was a brushy crown of stone and soil, and just inland from it grew a tangle of vine, with heavy, saw-toothed leaves. "It's called Ethan's **Predilection**," Ms. Jensen said as she knelt down and began cautiously nipping away at the **foliage** and piling what she cut on a wide cloth of burlap. "Ethan was the first editor of the town paper, and he swore, in spite of all the scratches and rashes he got from the **serrated** edges of the leaves, that he loved this plant above all others because of the fine dark ink he made from it. And ... ouch!"

> **exacerbate**: to make a problem or painful situation even worse
> **decorum**: a calm and gracious behavior, founded on courtesy and good taste
> **sinuous**: in the form of a line curving gracefully back and forth

A reddish line appeared along Ms. Jensen's wrist—the first scratch from Ethan's Predilection. As she looked at it, an idea occurred to her, a solution for an awkward situation. Although Ricky and François had joined her in the work, Merci was holding back for fear that Sallie would be filming. And Sallie was holding back from filming for fear of troubling Merci. Now Ms. Jensen called to the girl. "You know—we were worried about scratches, the plant is mildly toxic. And on the hike up here we told Rachel that she is not permitted to get in the patch and do the actual picking. She was upset, and when I said that Ricky would pick his share and hers, that only **exacerbated** the little crisis."

Ricky threw up his hands. "She's afraid I'll get scratched to death, that's what it is. In her eyes I'm helpless—smart, but way beyond helpless—and she needs to be there, protecting. She only gave in this time when François promised to watch over me."

"Anyway," finished Ms. Jensen, with a motion toward a small figure, drifting at some distance along the crest, "now she's gone a-wandering, and someone should probably watch over her as well. And that way, Merci, you would be offscreen, and Sallie could start her filming."

Merci saw the wisdom of it. Her worried face broke suddenly into a smile. "Maybe by senior year I won't be such a problem. Ha—I come from a family that prides itself on **decorum**, but I know my manners this morning haven't been all that great."

She turned to Sallie. "I did hear what you said to François, about no one's pain. That was good. And I wish the only one around here with pain was ... me and this ridiculous wart. But I'm not."

"Someone else ... has a wart?" Sallie inquired cautiously.

Merci smiled and slipped into some deliberation. Then abruptly, with a springing tone, she asked, "Will you come with me—just over there?"

Leading Sallie to the far edge of the clearing, she beckoned down the slope, through a loose screening of pines. The highway ran below, following a **sinuous** course around the folds and bends of Cape Magdalena. The traffic was not remarkable, but it came on steadily, flowing into Dropanchor.

> **chary**: slow and cautious about taking an action; carefully considering the risks associated with it
> **hallowed**: regarded as sacred, and treated with the respect reserved for sacred things
> **de facto**: being something in fact or having some quality in fact, although lacking the official designation that usually establishes that thing or confers that quality

"There's the real pain," said Merci. "Each year the crowd gets bigger—people driving up that highway to see Whalefest. My grandmother is so anxious: don't let our festival become just ... nine letters on a bumper sticker. Our mayor says he's not anxious, only **chary**—cautious and alert to the risks of a tourist boom. Liar! He's anxious too. What gets him most, I think, are the trucks."

"Like trucks bringing in...?"

"Bringing in the snacks," said Merci. "That's the nightmare of the mayor—Whalefest gradually becomes a snacking event, and at the most **hallowed** moments, when the whales are ascending and descending in our waters, the people are dribbling crumbs down their fronts and draining soda cans. I told him once I'll be careful not to dribble, and he laughed, but for him it's a depressing vision. And it rolls in on the trucks. There—look right there."

Below them two trucks were pulled off the road into a level area of grass and stony floor which, although never officially designated a rest area, served **de facto** as just that. One of them, square and white, carried no lettering but only the image of an oversized potato chip hovering protectively above the known universe. The other was longer, heavier, and on its side tangerine letters, all capital, spelled out TEREBINTH.

"That's the beer truck," said Merci. "And—sure enough—the cookies!" A third truck pulled over, painted with the message, Cassowary Cookies.

> **gregarious**: seldom alone; preferring to be with your group; habitually seeking out the company of others
> **proliferate**: to reproduce in large numbers and, often, to spread over a large extent
> **listless**: sluggish and inactive, especially because of a lack of any driving desire

Soon the three drivers were laughing together and trading stories. "They're not all loners," observed Sallie. "I live on the road, and I could write the book. Some of them are quite **gregarious**. Look at those three—time to share a snack on the American Highway."

Each of the three drivers was doing a bit of paperwork and then breaking into his cargo. In just one or two minutes, barbecue chips, packages of cookies, and a keg of beer had been unloaded, and brought up to a natural picnic table—a sturdy slab of granite that projected from the hillside.

"Snack time it is," said Merci. "And I'm afraid that if you do a flashy program about us on TV, the snack trucks will **proliferate**—those three that are parked down there will have fifty or sixty babies each, and Whalefest itself will become one big snack time."

Sallie stared through the scattered pines for a minute. "My story will not do that! Even if I have to hold it off the air. I didn't come here to ruin the festival." Then she noticed something. "But I'm afraid the number of snack trucks is about to go up by one in the very near future. Look how they're waiting."

The three drivers had milled about the granite outcrop, but had not touched the food or drink. Now one of them was hiking out along the flank of Cape Magdalena. Another one, lacking energy for a walk, was picking **listlessly** at some blackberries on a bramble near the outcrop. The third was on his phone.

"Calling another trucker," swore Sallie. "I know that's it. Telling him to hurry up so they can all start together. Better manners than Uncle Reggie."

She looked back across the clearing towards Ms. Jensen, Ricky and François, all bending over the scratchy vine. "I'm the one who'd better hurry. They'll harvest Ethan's Predilection before I ever turn on my camera."

> **skulk**: to shrink from being seen, or to move about in a sneaky manner
> **desist**: to stop doing some action, often before it has come to a natural completion

"And I'd better find that little whirlwind," said Merci to herself. Rachel was not too far off, but catching sight of her took several minutes. She was in the thin stand of pine on the hillside, and she was sneaking from one tree to the next, pressing tightly against the trunks.

"Why the **skulking**?" called Merci, spying her at last. "Are you on the most-wanted list?" But the little girl would not answer, putting a finger across her lips, and then gesturing down toward the granite slab where the picnic had been laid out.

"I'm glad you're on my side, Rachel," murmured Merci, as she found a stone to sit on.

Fifteen minutes went by. Sallie was filming the messy process of gathering Ethan's Predilection. It had left several scratches on François and Ms. Jensen, and more than several on Ricky. Every few moments he was muttering, "The scratch is OK, but what's this rash radiating out from it? I hereby move we **desist**." François was again overruling one of these motions, announcing that the work must continue, and punching him for good measure, when she recognized the voice of her sister. Merci was calling wildly from the distant edge of the meadow. "Fish, large fish!"

> **heedless**: not aware of, or not taking notice of, certain facts, often ones that deserve your attention
> **incoherent**: using speech that is so rambling, fragmented or poorly uttered that you cannot be understood
> **credulous**: believing things too readily and on too little evidence

A moment more and she was tearing towards them, **heedless** of the thistles and burr grass that snatched at her. "It's for real! Major fish. Mobys. Moving in."

François caught her by the shoulders. "Sister—you're **incoherent**. Not even I can follow you. Try using complete sentences."

"Like duh!" cried Merci. "C'mon. One of the drivers—there are three you know—went for a walk out to the end of the cape. Then just four or five minutes ago he starts hollering, 'Thar she blows.'"

"And you believed him at once, without any suspicion that he might be fooling his two friends. You've always been **credulous** like that."

"Wrong, François," answered Merci hotly. "I waited. The other two drivers ran down the path and joined the first one. And after one look southwards along the coastline they also started shouting, 'Thar she blows.' So guess what, François—thar she blows!"

This was vital news. If true, it meant that the whales were early, and that all preparations would have to be accelerated. Ricky knew this, and the first moment he heard Merci's cry, he had dashed along the crest of the cape, out to a little summit that was its most seaward point, to have a look for himself. Already now he was racing back. Pulling to an abrupt stop near Merci, he took her hand—the left hand, the ungloved one—and held it high. "Three drivers and one gremlin cannot be wrong—thar she blows! Still far to the south, but thar she blows!"

> **exigency**: one of the demands or conditions imposed by a particular activity or situation
> **deference**: the practice of allowing someone's wish or opinion to control, sometimes for the reason that you see him as an expert or authority
> **transcend**: to pass beyond some limited condition by rising into a plane of thought and action that is more noble, free, universal, etc.

Ms. Jensen sprang into action, tying up the corners of the burlap sheets where she had piled the crop of Ethan's Predilection. As she rushed about, she said to Sallie, "One of the special **exigencies** of Whalefest is that it requires you to go into fast-forward on a moment's notice."

"It's not a relaxing feast," added François with a laugh. "It makes demands."

They gathered the burlap bundles and, hurrying as well as they could, began the return to the beach. Ricky fetched his sister from her watch post above the highway. The trip to Cape Magdalena had filled her with questions. With unusual **deference** to the wisdom of her older brother she sought and accepted his opinion whether Uncle Reggie could say, "Hang in thar, America," whether Peter Oakum played music for his veggies, and whether terebinth was a kind of angel.

READER: There was a mean anti-snack mood in that chapter.
AUTHOR: Someone has to take a stand. We've become a nation of snackers.
READER: Snacking is in our genes.
AUTHOR: There has to be a moment when we **transcend** eating things.
READER: There is—it's called drinking things.

Chapter 55: COMPLEMENTARY HOG AND FOG

Through broken clouds the moon was shining for the moment. It shimmered on the passage of water between Cape Magdalena and the long forested island, and glinted on the mammoth shapes that circled there.

The whales were arriving, and Rachel was with them in her imagination—wild as they were wild from their journey through the blue hollows, and wary as were they about the calm water that opened before them.

> **vicarious**: experienced indirectly, by linking yourself in your imagination and feelings with the experience of someone else
> **quintessence**: the pure substance of something, without any mix of compromising elements

Ricky was beside her on the beach. He saw how she was living **vicariously** through the huge travelers, and he nodded. For him too that was the **quintessence** of Whalefest, those moments of moving in thought with the journey. Take all the rest, but leave those moments, and the festival was still complete.

> **vigilance**: the state of being watchful and on guard
> **mandate** (noun): an order or directive from a source of high authority, often imposing some continuing responsibility or mission
> **sporadic**: occurring according to an irregular, disconnected, now-and-then sort of pattern
> **breach** (noun): the act of breaking forth from water with a surging leap

The whales were arriving, but they were watchful. As in recent years, some **vigilance** made them pause at the entry into Dropanchor's bay. It had never been more than a pause; always before, they came in eventually. But Povano, who said the true **mandate** of a mayor was to worry about things, felt worried: what if this year the pause became permanent and the whales remained in open sea, bypassing Dropanchor and its festival?

"Will you-know-what be coming up for air soon?" he asked Martin in a troubled voice. "Now would surely be the perfect time."

The two of them were standing on the raised quarterdeck of *Jack's Equator*, which was anchored several hundred yards offshore. Martin had a small electronic panel in his hand, with a screen on one side, and a transmitter and several switches on the other, and at the moment he was working the switches desperately. "I gain control for a minute, I lose control, then after a while I get it back. When it's **sporadic** like that, usually there's an override, something is overriding my signal."

His face brightened suddenly. "OK—now there's a response. Sustained response. Get ready for **breach**!"

The waters near the ship churned for a moment and divided. The immense figure of a whale lifted into the air for half its length, then turned and fell with a rocking splash. The decoy was a work of beauty, sleek and dark, with the head bending gracefully back as though to assure that its calf was safely in tow.

> **entail**: to necessitate the occurrence of something, often in the way a goal necessitates your adoption of the means to reach it, or a cause carries along certain effects in its train
> **indefatigable**: fatigue-proof; not able to be tired out
> **curmudgeon**: a peevish, grouchy, sharp-tongued person, often elderly, and usually a man

It had been launched only two hours before. Its completion in the day and a half since the driver first shouted "Thar she blows!" had **entailed**, as Martin put it, the suspension of several laws of nature. Including the one about not being in two places at once. Martin had been everywhere—at his work site, at the quarry, at the kettle fire where the clay panels were hardened, and at Ms. Jensen's dye-making operation. By now he had been three nights without sleep, and many of those with him had been two. They were becoming known as the **Indefatigables**.

Some of Martin's helpers had been the children, Rachel included. They were the painting team. They were well beyond restless when at last Ms. Jensen and François arrived, carrying several jars of dye, an intensely dark shade between blue and black, laboriously extracted from Ethan's Predilection. A loud cheer went up.

"Bah!" said Ms. Jensen, doing a good imitation of Scrooge and the other great **curmudgeons** of the world. "Bah and good riddance." She showed the scratches on her arms. "Ethan's welcome to his opinion, but this was the most stupid, stubborn, thick-headed plant I've ever worked with."

> **mural**: a large painting done directly on the stone or other material of a wall
> **prodigal**: going through your money or other resource so fast and freely that you risk wasting it or running out

"But it did yield a gorgeous dye," said Martin appreciatively.

He quickly added thickeners, drying agents and sealants, and turned it into a heavy glaze. His painters went eagerly to work. "First some random markings," he instructed, "here and there, until it looks like an abstract **mural**. Then lay on a full coat. And be a little stingy, so we don't run out."

At first it all went according to instruction—random, preliminary markings, applied sparingly, with a single pass of the brush. But the markings stood out dramatically on the bare clay, they were abstract and attractive—art in their own right. Before long the painters forgot stingy and moved on to **prodigal**, spending too much of the glaze to build up the little designs. Not enough remained for the full coat, and in the end the glaze ran out with several areas of the whale still unpainted.

All this escaped Martin's notice. For some time he was completely absorbed in another job, the installation of a remotely-controlled ballast system in the decoy that would let it sink and rise like a real whale. It was maddening work. Even though he had a kit with all the hardware—the valves, pumps, chambers, wires, receptors and so forth—the instructions were almost useless. Progress was only possible because Ricky and Peter Oakum labored with him. They had good instincts for all sorts of gadgetry, and Peter could supply any tool that Martin was lacking.

> **jovial**: inclined to respond with good humor or merriment to whatever turns up
>
> **parsimonious**: tightfisted and stingy; reluctant to reduce your resources whether by using or giving
>
> **apocryphal**: false or inauthentic (often applied to books or manuscripts which are claimed to be ancient or written by someone famous but which in fact are recent and written by someone unknown)

Evening was already deepening when the system was finally functional, and Martin had a moment to spare. When he saw how the painting work had gone and how the glaze had run short, his tone remained **jovial**. "Hmm! A bit shy on the coverage. It was hard to be **parsimonious** with the glaze! I knew it would be. But we can overlook it if the whales can. And with the twilight fading, I bet they will never notice."

That had been just two hours ago. Now the decoy was in service, responding at last to the control panel, riding the low swells of the bay. To Povano's great delight, she was proving to be a distraction. The whales circling and weaving in the passage off Cape Magdalena were becoming intensely curious. Their patterns grew more ragged, as their attention was diverted. At last a stirring ran through the pack, and several of the creatures began to move slowly through the passage in the direction of the decoy.

Povano's face broke into a wide smile and he was turning to Martin, when abruptly a rack of clouds sailed in front of the moon. An innocent thing, but it wiped away the mayor's smile—for as the moon's light was obscured, the whales stopped short.

"Oh, bother," he cried. "I know what this is about. I've seen the book. There's an ancient book in Bezzle's library, by some ... well known naturalist of the seventeenth century, which says that whales born on a clear and moonlit night forever after think the moon is ... well ... you know, a second mother. Grandma says it's **apocryphal**, that the book was probably written in the last five years by a prankster."

"Maybe so," broke in Martin, "but the prankster got it right tonight. Those whales are spooked again."

"We need some help," said Povano simply.

"Oh no!" cried Martin. "We definitely need some help." The decoy had sunk out of sight again, and Martin's frantic operation of his little panel of controls was unable to recall it. By this time Povano was looking around the crowded deck of *Jack's Equator*.

> **physiological**: being part of, or explainable in terms of, the physical systems and processes of a living body
> **prodigious**: awesomely large or powerful or extensive
> **puerile**: silly and childish; lacking the maturity or seriousness that the situation demands

"Who are you trying to see?"

The mayor smiled sadly. "The true answer is—a man who disappeared fifteen years ago, a man named Yuri. He could call the whales, his throat could form their cries. There was a **physiological** basis for it—something unusual in the muscles and cartilages of the larynx. It passes down through the family—Yuri's father did the cries for many years at Whalefest. And he's here, but he's old now and I want him to stay out of this game—the calls are very hard on the windpipe. No, the one I'm really looking for is Yuri's son, Constantin, known to all as Lumps."

"Oh, I know Lumps," broke out Martin. "What a **prodigious** amount of clay he carried down yesterday, he and your friend Darlingson."

"It was a generous service," agreed Povano, "but an even greater one is waiting for him tonight if I can find him. He trained—I think he trained—with his grandfather to learn the calls. And he promised, so far as I know, to be here on the quarterdeck tonight. But ..." Povano was shaking his head, obviously disappointed.

With the clouds thinning for a moment over the moon, Ricky and Rachel, from their position on the shore, could see the mayor looking around the ship for someone. "Wait," cried Rachel, "now it's OK. Isn't that Lumps?"

A figure was crossing the busy main deck, ascending the few steps, and joining Povano at the railing. Peering intently through the moonlight, Ricky declared, "It's not Lumps. I think it's his grandfather. Crazy old man—they say the whale calls tear up your throat, and you should only do them when you're young."

Another voice, in a very different tone from Ricky's, repeated, "Crazy old man, indeed. He's about a thousand, and yet he still does anything for a pat on the head. It's so **puerile**."

Ms. Framley, lounging on a satin cover a few feet behind them, would have said more, but she was interrupted by a strange cry, from the direction of the ship. Slow and faintly musical, it had a force far exceeding its loudness. It carried easily across the water and stirred the whales from their hesitation. They rallied themselves while the cry was still fading, and soon they were once again moving into the bay.

> **expendable**: able to be used up or gotten rid of without any serious inconvenience, either because easily replaced or because not really needed
>
> **exacerbate**: to make a problem or painful situation even worse
>
> **carp**: to complain, often in an indignant or judgmental way, about trivial imperfections

Rachel was at complete attention. "It's kind of beautiful, isn't it," said Ricky. "But I hope he won't repeat it. Too hard on the lungs, of which we have only two, so they're not exactly **expendable**."

Grandpa Lumps, though, raised a second cry, as haunting as the first. He was nearly through it when his voice broke, abruptly and completely, under the strain. Ricky could see the mayor clapping the old man on the shoulder, and pointing out toward the whales, as though to say—you've done enough, they have the momentum, they'll keep coming in.

In fact, however, their momentum failed once more. They stalled again, circling hesitantly. As Povano gestured wildly to them, Grandpa Lumps descended to the crowded main deck and returned a moment later, bringing someone with him.

"He found Lumps," yelled Rachel in Ricky's ear.

"No," said Ricky slowly, "no, too small for Lumps. And too many—look, there's a second one, coming behind the first. I can't quite see who they are— move those clouds, somebody. But ... oh no, no! They look alike, very much alike—which means they have to be the Farnum twins. That will just **exacerbate** the situation, to bring in the Farnums. Everything they touch turns from problem to crisis, from crisis to disaster. Get me out of here!"

Grandpa Lumps stood with the twins, and from the slow lifting and falling of his hands before his chest, it appeared that he was coaching their breathing, getting them to slow down, to draw in more deeply. After a minute of this, he led them toward the railing.

Ricky groaned again. "I know what it is. He suspected Lumps was gonna bail, so in desperation he trained the Farnums also—to do the calls. It can't work."

Even as he spoke, a dreadful sound passed over them, hollow and suggestive of large machines. Henry Farnum had tried to call the whales. "Not to **carp**," Ricky said, "not to be one of those peevy little complainers we hate so much—but at best that sounded like a foghorn. Oh no, now the other one!"

> **repertoire**: the collection of speeches, songs, plays or other theatrical expressions that a person is ready to perform
> **complementary**: going together nicely one with another, in the sense that what is missing in the one is supplied by the other, and vice versa
> **resonance**: the quality of a sound by which it is full, richly toned, echoing, and easily carrying a long way
> **exemplary**: perfect enough to be a model for others to follow

Andrew Farnum advanced to the railing and belted out something very loud, with an irritating amount of squeal in it. Ricky moaned. "That will be of interest up on the farms, at the pens. A foghorn and a hog call—what else is in the **repertoire** of those two maniacs? What ...? No, not that! Not ham and eggs. No!"

Henry and Andrew took a long breath and launched their cries at the same time. The foghorn and the hog call rang out together. To the utter surprise of everyone they were a good match. "**Complementary** Hog and Fog" was the way Allen described it later on in his column. "The mechanical boom of the foghorn," he wrote, "took life from the hog call. And the awful screech of that call drew **resonance** from the foghorn."

The result was not an **exemplary** whale call—according to Ricky, it didn't raise the bar—but it was near enough. The whale pack was in motion once again, working slowly toward *Jack's Equator*.

The Farnums were instant heroes. "We'll name a street after you," said Mayor Povano gratefully.

> **penchant**: a deeply rooted inclination that you have for doing some particular sort of thing
> **magnanimous**: noble in spirit, bearing trials calmly and bravely; rising above jealous squabbles and the need to get even
> **eulogy**: a speech or writing, often formal in tone, in which the character traits or community services of a person are highly praised

391

"Henry and Andrew Avenue," suggested Henry.

"Andrew and Henry Boulevard," corrected his brother.

Martin promised bronze statues. "And I'll do you in gold if you have a call for my decoy. She has this **penchant** for sinking out of sight and—yes—I think she's done it again."

Grandpa Lumps had no voice left to congratulate the twins, so he scribbled them a note. From the shore, gazing through the occasional moonlight, Ricky guessed what he was doing, and said half to himself, half to Rachel, "**Magnanimous** old guy—he's writing a note that will make the Farnums feel like kings, even when he's hurt inside that his own grandson didn't bother to be there."

"Pshaw!" said Ms. Framley loudly from behind them. "Forget the **eulogy**—magnanimous soul, brave spirit. Rot! It's all posturing. He knows that what's-her-name, that television hussy, has been filming out there on the ship, so he wants to look like a star for prime time. But in fact he's still a joker, just like that big ape, no-show grandson of his."

Trying to ignore the woman as best she could, Rachel slid nearer to Ricky and said to him quietly, "I like Lumps. He doesn't do bad stuff on purpose. Maybe he got turned into a whale. Look how they're getting bigger."

The whales were coming in, and their bulk seemed to grow as they drew closer. They were playing now in an endless crossing of dives and breaches. Their progress toward *Jack's Equator* was incidental, almost sideways. But at least, under the light of a fitful moon, they were advancing. Mayor Povano and the people grew still.

READER: Larry says he lives vicariously through the woolly mammoths.

AUTHOR: I just hope he doesn't go vicariously extinct through the woolly mammoths.

READER: He says that when the mammoths trample down the forests so that no more No. 2 pencils can ever be made again, he's there with them, tusk and hoof.

AUTHOR: It's not entirely clear that …

READER: We'd better give him this one.

Chapter 56: GIANT INIMICAL BATS

Each year as the whales drifted into the bay, the people gradually fell silent. It was something instinctive. Grown-ups and children alike let the ancient sounds be heard—the pipe of the gulls, the rushing breakers, the occasional thunder off the mountain. So Ricky was more than surprised when Rachel started whispering in his ear. He would have hushed her, except for the anxious tone in her voice.

> **paragon**: a person in whom some virtue is so perfected that she serves as a model of it
>
> **palliate**: to reduce the severity or intensity of something negative

"Lumps isn't bad, Ricky, like some people say, and ..."

"I know that," he whispered back. "But why ...?"

She dug her fingers into his wrist. "But I am. I did some bad things. I ..."

He tried to ease her nails out of his flesh. "Rach, please. You're ninety-nine percent perfect, you're a **paragon**. Other parents show you to their monsters and say 'Be like her.' But I wish you hadn't said what you did about Lumps—it's making me worry about something. Like why ...?"

It wasn't Rachel's soft voice that interrupted. "Could we shut up, please? This is a sacred moment, right? Who said you little idiots could start jabbering?"

Rachel tried to whisper more quietly, but Ms. Framley was not going to lose her chance. "Oh, sure! A small drop in volume—as though that could take away the beastliness of chatting in these solemn moments, or even **palliate** it. Wrong, chickie!"

Ricky took his sister's hand and led her away toward another part of the beach. Even as they went Ms. Framley was still lashing at them. "Take a lesson from Darlingson, and talk less. Ha!"

When they were far from the scourge, Rachel went on, still in a whisper. "I did two things." She was cutting off the circulation in his wrist again. "Martin only said to make some marks, but I wrote some words on the whale—'Love or Stupid.' Near the eye. We were going to paint it over, it would have been OK, but ... there wasn't enough paint!" The sorrow was still there to be heard in her voice.

"And then," she continued, "there was the second thing that ... that ... Ricky, you aren't hearing a word!"

hypocrite: a person who makes a show of having some virtue, honoring some rule, etc., when in fact he lacks the virtue, behaves contrary to the rule, etc.

denounce: to proclaim in public, often in a fiery and accusing manner, the faults or wrongdoing of another

emanate: to flow out, often quietly and calmly, from a central concentration or other source

Ricky snapped out of some brooding and clasped her firmly by the shoulders. "Sorry! Remember all those sermons you got from me about being a good listener? Looks like I was a **hypocrite**. Because I'm an awful listener right now. Something is really starting to worry me, something you said. And I need to be ... somewhere else. François will be with me—she doesn't know it yet, but she will—and Allen, and some of the others. So I'll be fine, Rach. And now we need to park you. I feel really bad—you should stamp your foot and **denounce** me, as an abandoner of little sisters!"

Rachel didn't get mad. "It's OK, Ricky. At least I told one of the things. You can park me. But Mom and Dad are way at the other end. Maybe—look." She had spotted Merci, standing close by. "She likes taking care of me."

Merci wore a simple white gown, in honor of her role that night as the first to taste the cider made from the Mendicant Berries. Her beauty, remarkable in the scattered moonlight, was made even more complete by her watchful concentration, by the impress it left upon her features as she gazed out over the waters. An air of peace and delight **emanated** from her. Rachel felt its influence, how it called her back into the festival. She took her brother's hand. "I'll stay with Merci. Be back soon, OK." Then she went and stood quietly beside her friend.

Ricky saw that François was nearby. Tapping her shoulder, and sensing that he had been half expected, he led her some ways up the beach where they could talk. "Tell me I've lost it," he began, "send me for a screening. Rachel's to blame. She keeps saying how Lumps is not such a bad person."

"And she's right, of course" said François with a sigh, as though she knew where these innocent beginnings would lead them. "Lumps is not a bad person at all."

"Which raises an awful question."

"Yeah—like why would he let down his own grandfather tonight? Only a major commitment could have kept him away."

"Exactly," Ricky answered. "Like helping Bamalford destroy life as we know it. Because that may be the trip we're on if a hundred barrels of Glinscrimion go down the fire shaft—no matter how much everyone believes in that total-burn theory, that zero-fume theory, whatever, of the consulting firm."

tantamount: fundamentally the same as something else in meaning or impact, although differing in form
loath (adjective): experiencing a strong reluctance to do something

François took a deep breath. "I'm getting angry, you know. Bamalford really is mean. I didn't think he'd do this. It's **tantamount** to declaring war on Dropanchor. I mean—what's the difference? Why doesn't he just hire an army and attack us?"   Ricky reached out and patted her on the head. "It's just a matter of informing the proper authorities, my dear."

"Yeah," muttered François, kicking at the sand. "So let's get started. Where's Tedesco? Where's Allen, Joannie, Meagan?" She looked at the mountain. Its high places were dimly shining in the moonlight. "We need to be up there again, don't we?"

They spied Tedesco in the silent crowd. Ricky felt bad. "I am very, very **loath** to do this. When will he get another Whalefest?"

"It's dirty work," François agreed, as she went and squeezed Tedesco's shoulder, and pulled him away. The three of them dragged off Joannie next, then Allen and Meagan. Ricky explained his worry as the little squad angled back along the beach and entered the dry ravine on the north side of Cape Scurrility. No one responded for a while, as they found the path up the cape and began to climb.

Midway through the ascent they emerged from the ravine's shadow and into the broken moonlight. Then Allen, speaking to anyone who cared to listen, asked, "It's all just a tasteless joke, right?"

refute: to take a statement or claim that someone has put forward and throw it back by showing that it is wrong
scenario: (1) a summary or outline of the plot of a dramatic presentation; (2) one of several alternate sets of events that you suppose to exist in order to help you explain or plan something
aviary: a large cage or other structure where birds are kept, often for show

Ricky winced. "No—but the moment someone **refutes** my theory of why Lumps failed to appear, we can all go back to Whalefest. Like—I don't mind being shown wrong."

"UFO's," said Allen. "Measles. Car failure. Sudden amnesia. Nothing works! The only convincing **scenario** is what you said: Bamalford schedules the big operation for tonight. And Lumps has to be there. If not ..."

"I hate Bamalford," broke in François. "It's really true—he tells you the lie you want to hear." Her voice became mocking. "Like he's monitoring data bases about missing persons, looking for information on Lump's father! Sure—and I'm sprouting wings so I'll feel more at home in the **aviary**."

"I think Lumps sees the frailty of the whole thing," said Ricky. "And we know he's mad. But he's caught by the remote possibility that Bamalford might give him some clue—on the most important issue in his life."

Where the path tucked into the folding granite of the cape, it ran on rather blindly and there was little to see. But where it leaned out toward the ocean it was a long balcony above the passage of the whales up the bay, and the vigil of the people. For the six companions that was hardest of all, the last, vanishing look at the festival. Still, they scrambled up as swiftly as they could, and before long they cleared the brow of the cape and began a rapid march along its crest, in the direction of the school.

> **ilk**: a loosely defined class or group of things
> **parochial**: narrowly focused on the concerns of your own little place, with no interest in or sympathy for what lies beyond

A worry was nagging at Ricky. "We're forgetting something," he muttered. "A key, an ID badge, something of that **ilk**." As the moon broke through the streaming clouds the school building rose before them, silver and blocky. "Four years in that place, getting smarter and smarter, and now I can't ..."

Then it came to him all at once. "Oh yeah—the password. No one gets into the mountain without the password."

He shook Tedesco by the shoulder. "You're always reading the paper, Cabbage, trying to improve your already excellent English. Tell me you remember today's proverb—you know, in that little box, 'Volts from Victoria,' on page one. That's the password, and we'll be needing it."

Tedesco, however, had not looked at the day's paper. Nor had anyone else. Ricky grumped, "No wonder we're so **parochial**—if we don't read the news, how do we ever bust out of local concerns and go global?"

François laughed, refreshed a little by Ricky's odd spin on things. "Global! If Europe sank into the sea Bamalford's paper might print a line."

"Well, whatever. But we need to see today's front page, and the nearest newsstand is at the library."

With Tedesco close behind, he raced off, following a footpath which generations of students had worn into the hillside. It was only a few minutes before the two of them, like ivory stick figures in the moonlight, were hurrying back along the same path.

Ricky's spirits seemed to have lifted. He was waving the newspaper they had bought, and chanting, "Make hay while the sun shines."

> **maxim**: some basic principle or rule, often expressed in the form of a proverb
> **polarize**: to split a group into two camps that line up around sharply opposite positions

> **esoteric**: incomprehensible to all except the members of some inner circle

As he drew near, Joannie grabbed him by the neck. "Would you shut up, problem child! You'll open that mountain door from here."

"But it's a great **maxim**. I may adopt it as a rule of life. Besides—maybe we can go back to Whalefest. Listen to what Tedesco saw."

Tedesco looked at them and said simply, "I saw the bookmobile, parked on the hill behind the library."

Allen lifted his head sharply. "But the bookmo is what carries the ..."

"I knew it could be **polarizing**," broke in Ricky, "with half of us claiming there can't be any barrels hauled tonight if the bookmobile is out of service. And the other half arguing the contrary, that now we definitely have to get up there because ..."

"Because," finished Joannie with a frown, "because of ... what happened with the wooden lizard."

"There you go," continued Ricky, "the wooden ... Hold on, everybody! Wooden lizard, Joannie—that's getting pretty **esoteric**. Like maybe you belong to some special little club that knows what it means, but I sure don't, and ..."

Joannie put a finger to her lips. "Have you heard the story of the second fall of Troy?"

"You mean where the Greeks hid themselves in a huge wooden horse, and the unsuspecting Trojans pulled it inside the city walls, and at night the Greeks came out and ...?"

"No," said Joannie. "That was the first fall of Troy. In the second fall, the Greeks hid in a huge wooden lizard and the Trojans said, 'Nothing to worry about—the Greeks always come in wooden horses,' and they pulled the lizard inside the city walls and ..."

> **ingenuous**: (1) open and unrehearsed in your expressions; (2) so simple and innocent that you fail to grasp the complexity or the evil at work in many situations
> **cogent**: so true or logical or forcefully presented as to push you toward belief and acceptance
> **divergence**: a splitting apart into different paths or opinions

Ricky tried to stuff a sweater in her mouth. "That's not true!"

"Right!" cried Joannie. "It's not true. The Trojans weren't that **ingenuous**. And we shouldn't be either. Classical Greek warriors don't always have to show up in wooden horses. And barrels of unloved chemicals don't always have to show up in bookmobiles. The Glinscrimion may have found another ride."

Ricky stared in admiration. "That is **cogent**. I don't know where I was before, but I'm switching to your side now." In fact everyone switched to Joannie's side, and there was no further **divergence** of opinion. They resumed the climb, pushing themselves along at a quick pace.

They had done it before—the long ascent by the banks of the Bad Pony, the crossing of the tableland, the sweep up the stony shelf alongside Mercurial Canyon—and that made a difference. They slipped through the shadows of the narrow side-canyon and reached the mountain door sooner than they had expected, and with less fatigue. "We're getting better," Ricky murmured, as they paused before the towering face of rock where the door was set.

"Better at getting from down there to up here," said Allen, between gulps of the cool air. "But now that we're here ... people ... what do we hope to do?"

> **paltry**: so small in quantity or value as to be unworthy of attention
> **inimical**: unfriendly; behaving as an enemy toward you

"Make hay while the sun shines, that's what," answered François in a firm voice. The maxim was terribly inappropriate for the dark dead end where they were, where even the moonlight fell only by reflection from the higher flanks of the canyon wall. Yet that **paltry** light was enough to show the empty rectangle opening in the granite cliff before them.

François pushed them through the doorway. "Yes, we have to talk about Allen's question, but on the run. We may be too late already. Oof—it's dark in here!"

"This time is real different than the last," said Ricky as they took their first steps through the blackness. "In some ways better. For example, new batteries." He found the flashlight in his crowded pocket and switched it on. "But in most ways worse. This ..."

"Umm—excuse me everyone." It was Meagan, in a shaken voice. "I am assuming that up ahead there are bats, Giant **Inimical** Bats, who will reject my offer of friendship, and who are waiting to eat my brains by the glow of sulfur fires. Could someone address that?"

> **lurid**: boldly emphasizing gory, grotesque or outrageous details
> **unequivocal**: stated so clearly and definitively that no room is left for doubt, double meanings or confusion

"Nothing so **lurid**," said Joannie in a comforting tone. "And sorry—we sort of forgot it was your first time."

François reached out and took Meagan's hand for a moment. "On the subject of bats—is it conceivable that Bamalford would be here tonight if there were bats? Remember his **unequivocal** little rule governing the relation of humans and beasties—where they go we don't. Not much chance for misinterpretation with that one, and it means he simply wouldn't have come here if ..."

Meagan reacted with surprise. "Bamalford's here? I mean—I'll be OK with the bats, but—Bamalford's here?"

"We think he is," answered Ricky. "That was apparently a condition laid down by the client. Which brings me back to what I was saying—this time is mostly worse. Last time we came here it was only to watch. Now, we have to stop the operation. Last time there was only Bezzle and Lumps to worry about. Tonight, Bamalford weighs in, a big boy in pounds, a big boy in kilos."

They were moving swiftly now through the long tunnel, and it was only with some effort that Allen responded to Ricky's concern. "Remember. Dumping the barrels is a commercial venture. If we show Bamalford that once those barrels drop there's an enormous cost—fines and lawsuits, maybe ruinous medical expenses—well, he's commercial, he'll think twice."

> **purported**: claimed to be of a certain kind or quality, often in circumstances casting some suspicion on that claim
> **indigent**: needy; lacking the basic resources necessary to get beyond mere survival
> **inception**: the beginning of some development or growth process

"Umm—I don't know." Meagan took up the thread. Her voice was firmer now. "The dumping is **purportedly** commercial. Bamalford and Nameless talk about it in commercial terms, I'm sure. But for Bamalford anyway, is it really that? He is so emotionally **indigent** that in everything he does there's a second agenda. Like he's on this wild, unconscious search for the emotional necessities of life—acceptance and esteem and the like. So we need to be on guard when we upset his game."

Tedesco touched her on the arm, as they hurried along. "We must be so much on guard. This poverty in the emotions ... I agree with you, Bamalford is poor like that. But it is only the ... the **inception**, the root. It can become something ... so much darker."

> **obfuscate**: to cover something with darkness or confusion, leaving it difficult to see or comprehend
> **volatile**: changing frequently and abruptly, sometimes with sharp swings back and forth between two extremes
> **engender**: to bring about some effect, often on the plane of human emotion, understanding, interest, etc.

"Just talking to the man is a killer," added Joannie. "You raise a simple matter and when he's done with it, after his murky questions and vague distinctions, it's so **obfuscated** that no one could make sense of it. So even if we can get him to deal with us, this won't be easy."

They hurried along in silence, caught uncomfortably between a walk and a run. A front of sound from the deep furnace began to reach their ears. "The fire must be **volatile** today," suggested Ricky, "flaring and dying, that sort of thing." He said this because the sound had a quality of softening one moment and growing sharply stronger the next.

Allen had the best hearing in the group, and after they had pushed forward another two or three minutes he laughed sadly. "Don't blame the fire, Ricky. Oh boy—I was secretly hoping that he would be somewhere else. Can you hear it?"

Ricky concentrated intensely and perceived how in fact there were two sounds—the roar of the fire itself, cycling through a slow, uneven rhythm between somewhat louder, somewhat softer; and on top of that the sharp rise and fall of a horrible, baying voice, tight with anger. It was the voice he had heard on that evening in September when he called Sallie. He shivered. "Bamalford. He's saying over and over ... I can't catch it ... he's saying ..."

"Ninety-nine," said Allen quietly. "But don't ask me why."

Now at last everyone heard, though no one had an explanation. Every few seconds Bamalford was shrieking out the number ninety-nine.

READER: Larry says the bat part missed a chance to **engender** goodwill in the often troubled man-bat relationship.

AUTHOR: That was an oversight on my part. I'm not anti-bat by any means. In fact, you know that famous bridge where the bats fly out at sunset and ...?

READER: Yeah. So, OK ... you flew out at sunset or something?

AUTHOR: Cute.

READER: Then, you were on it at sunset, feeling the little sonar waves against your forehead?

AUTHOR: Not quite. I drove over it one time, during the day—and turned down the radio.

READER: To not disturb the sleeping bats?

AUTHOR: Correct.

READER: Well, it's a start.

Chapter 57: RAMIFICATIONS, TEN FOR ONE

The barrels were arranged in a rectangle, not a square—that was the first thing to catch Allen's attention as he and the others slowly lifted their heads. They were crouched in the same hiding place as before, the little ribbing of stone at the top of the wide slope. The chamber was lit with the same yellow radiance, pulsing up from the fire shaft and dispersing itself upon the vast ceiling.

The barrels were standing some forty or fifty feet up from the rim of the shaft. Directly above them on the slope was a long, low-riding truck with huge, tangerine letters, all capitals, printed on its side—TEREBINTH. It was a beer truck, the one that Merci and Sallie had seen from Cape Magdalena. And the barrels standing now in neat rows between the truck and the brink were actually beer kegs.

> **allude**: to refer to a person or thing indirectly rather than by name
> **inept**: too clumsy or untrained or slow-witted to perform some task
> **desiccated**: (1) dried out, often to the point of being withered and parched; (2) dry as dust and incapable of stirring interest

"Whoa," whispered Ricky. "To all appearances—a beer dump; several swimming pools of beer."

"It looks like a return to the days of the dry laws," said Allen.

That went right by Tedesco. "**Alluding** to ...?" he asked.

"Oh, sorry. Alluding to the so-called Prohibition Era, a time in this country—the twenties, I think—when all booze was forbidden. There was some cheating, little pockets here and there. Probably in those days Bamalford would have been a rumrunner, instead of doing ... this." Allen pointed down to the strange drama playing out in front of them.

Bezzle and Lumps were moving slowly around the rectangle of kegs, tapping each one lightly, apparently taking a count. Bamalford stood between the kegs and the truck, bellowing. "Ninety-nine! I doubt it. Which one of you two is dumber? Who's more **inept**? You've both staked out a pretty good claim. I can't trust you to do anything right, not even count. Ninety-nine! That's absurd. Look here, OK, just look."

He gestured wildly to the kegs. "Nine rows, eleven kegs in each row, right? So how many kegs—nine times eleven, right? And that, my drubs, is the same as ten times ten. I wasn't like Fearless, just ask Mother Bamalford. He thought math was this **desiccated** thing—dry and shriveled. But I got into it, I internalized it. So I am quite familiar with the commutative property: if ten times ten is one hundred, that answer won't change if you increase one factor and decrease the other by equal amounts. You know—the first ten goes up one to eleven, the second ten goes down one to nine. You multiply 'em, and you still get one hundred. Unless you rookies think ten times ten is ninety-nine to start with."

His voice rose to a shriek on the ninety-nine. "Go on, tell me, is there some reason why ten times ten equals ninety-nine around here?"

> **circuitous**: going somewhere by a bending, looping course
> **inarticulate**: (1) perceptible only as raw sound, but not as individual words and syllables; (2) not able to produce clear, connected speech
> **servile**: putting yourself totally at the service of someone's wishes, in the manner of a slave

When she heard this question François knew she had what she was looking for. It was time to call Bamalford to account, and now she saw how do it, how to get straight to the point without the need for a lot of **circuitous** conversation. Murmuring to Meagan, "I hope you were right about the slumbering courage," she leapt to her feet and waved her arms. Then with all her strength she cried, "Is there some reason why Terebinth Beer equals Glinscrimion around here?"

At that moment, though, the roaring from the pit was in the rising phase of its irregular cycle, and Bamalford failed to hear the individual words that François spoke. What reached his ears was the **inarticulate** sound of a female voice. His head snapped up and his mouth fell open stupidly as he caught sight of a young woman astride the ridge, her hair streaming wildly in the draft from the furnace. To Bezzle and Lumps he stammered, "It's the ... you know ... the ..."

Struggling to regain speech, he addressed the waiting figure. "Pol ... apologies. Millions of apologies. In your realm, of course, ten times ten equals ninety-nine because ... your ancient curse requires it."

He swallowed several times. The dread began slowly to vanish from his words, giving way to the **servile** tone he used when speaking to Nameless. "Bamalford, ma'am, Peerless Bamalford. Your slave, of course. If you have any needs, however small ..."

He stopped short, uttering a loud "Huh?" François said quietly to her companions, "He's starting to see the difference between a François Dubois and a Serquiella. Get ready for some shouting."

> **disparity**: a significant lack of equivalence in power, worth, standing, etc.

402

> **pantheon**: the group or collection of gods that is honored by a particular civilization
>
> **distended**: swollen up or bloated, often beyond normal size or range

"Then we'll shout back," answered Joannie stubbornly.

Ricky gave a little cough. "Yes we will, and the combined volume of the six of us will be less than the volume of Bamalford. There's a major **disparity** here in lung power."

Bamalford's rage struck like a summer storm. "You're not ...! You're just ... You're the sister of that brat who ... And above all you're a trespasser! This is my property, and if you messed up the door..."

Joannie would stay hidden no longer. "Your property!" she yelled. "Who are you—the god of the underworld? That's what you always wanted, isn't it, to join the **pantheon**."

She took her place beside François. The others followed, and in a moment the six of them were standing side by side, gazing down the long slope at Bamalford.

At first he was speechless with fury. Little signs of his wrath were popping out everywhere—distortions around the mouth, whitened knuckles, hissing breath. And these were just the smaller marks. If by any chance they escaped notice, there was no missing what was happening on the grander scale. From the waist up Bamalford's body was becoming **distended**, swelling like a boiler at the point of bursting.

> **rant** (verb): to express rage through loud, uncontrolled speech
>
> **ramification**: some consequence or outcome that develops more or less naturally from a cause, an influence, an original situation, etc.
>
> **propagate**: to cause some belief, method, cultural practice, etc., to be accepted across a wider and wider circle of followers

"I think he's going to let it all out," said Ricky tensely. "I don't especially like ..."

Bamalford exploded. The noise was tremendous, overbearing the timeless rumble of the pit. Much of the **ranting** poured out so rapidly that it was unintelligible. There was one phrase, however, that kept repeating itself, an unpleasant phrase, and Allen finally picked it out: "**Ramifications**, Ten for One."

"Sentence fragment," he said, half to himself. "Bet we won't like the whole thing."

As the sheer blast of rage began to taper off slightly, Bamalford could at last be understood. "Stick your beaks in my business," he was yelling, "a responsible, caring, family-owned service-sector business—and you'll hate the consequences. Give me a bad day, amoeba children, and watch what grows out of it for you—bad years, bad centuries! Because there will be ... ramifications, if you mess with my affairs. Ramifications, Ten for One."

The threats were jarring, but for Joannie, at least, the lies were worse. "Responsible and caring," she muttered. "I hate this art of lying—so much! And you, Bamalford, you **propagate** it, you help it spread by instructing others. You taught Calvin, and taught him well."

She broke from the protection of the little ridge. With fists clenched by her side, she marched to a point halfway down the slope, slipping more than once on the pebbly ground, but never falling. "There's nothing responsible or caring," she cried, "about what you're doing. Those kegs are filled with something toxic and dangerous."

She was close enough that the wind and roar from the deep shaft could not carry off her words before they reached Bamalford. He understood the accusation. "Insect girl," he screamed back, "look—in front of you. Beer truck. Beer kegs. What's inside? Surplus beer. What's happening tonight? Disposal of surplus beer. That's all there is. Questions from Miss Muffet?"

> **duplicity**: a pattern of deception in which you present some object, activity, feeling, etc., under a false description or appearance
> **indiscriminate**: applying in exactly the same way to a variety of objects or persons, without the differences among them being taken into account

Joannie fought back. "The art of **duplicity**, Mr. Bamalford—without a trace of shame. Those kegs of yours, and the stuff inside—you call it beer when you talk to us. But with your client you have another name for it— Glinscrimion. If I'm wrong—drink some."

Bamalford's mouth worked furiously, but for a moment he could find nothing to say.

"And you know," she continued, refusing to relent, "or you should know, that Glinscrimion in the fire pit will eventually become Glinscrimion in the air. And once in the air it will deliver some ... some ramifications, to use your word, including one commonly known as mortal risk. And it will deliver them **indiscriminately**, I might add. Beggar and king, insect girl and editor, everyone who breathes will get their toxic little dose of Glinscrimion."

Bamalford was waving his index finger wildly, back and forth. "Stop there, bug lady. I've got you. Tell the foreign boy I've got him too. I've got you all. My patron, Nameless Entrepreneur, is not an environmental maverick. He did a baseline study—he hired an independent consulting firm, with its own laboratory, to run a model, to see if this thing burns hot enough." He gestured briefly toward the fire shaft.

"In other circumstances," he continued on a mocking note, "I would be more **discursive**. I would take you through the study point by point, showing you how it all ties in. Today, however, if no one objects, let me go at once to the conclusion. The lab gave Nameless a printed report, handsomely bound, and it says this baby is so hot that it will annihilate anything without a trace. The burn is complete! No ashes, no smoke, no fumes. So can we get on with our lives, please?"

Joannie was ready. She had always listened eagerly when Ironbane **propounded** his careful theories on what was happening beneath the mountain. And now she felt sure that on one important point her knowledge was superior to that of the technicians who wrote the "complete burn" report. "There's one piece," she yelled to Bamalford, "that your lab people didn't have. And if they had ..."

He cut her off, infuriated. "I know where you're going, bug woman. You're seconds away from foretelling, on the basis of no physical evidence and in utter defiance of our report, that fumes from the Glinscrimion will get in the atmosphere. What are you, a **soothsayer**? Why don't you predict the next time the stock market will go up ten percent in a day—that at least would be useful."

Joannie did what she could never have done outside that elemental world of fire and stone—she screamed at Bamalford to shut up. "And stay shut until I finish my ... **rebuttal**. You're wrong and I'll prove it. Your technicians, sitting at their computers, were in the dark about one thing. So listen. The front of this mountain pushes out into the sea, OK. That's what Cape Stairstep is, an arm of the mountain. And the cape is **stratified**, you know—a sheet of granite over a layer of sandstone, stacked on a bed of basaltic rock, and ..."

"And then a slice of gorgonzola, and then ... What a joke!"

Joannie pushed on. "At the water line of the cape, by chance, there is a band of softer stone, a sandstone. And it's tunneled out. Over the centuries the waves have cut long corridors into it that pierce through to the hollow parts of the mountain. On almost any tide a strong wave can send a lick of water spilling through one of those corridors and into the depths of the fire shaft there behind you."

"*Fzzz*! Ha. *Fzzz*." Bamalford was dancing about in a grotesque imitation of water meeting fire.

Joannie ignored it. "Repeating—water gets into the pit! Not enough to put out the fires, but—please listen—enough to **abate** them somewhat, to make them less hot than your laboratory assumed. As a result, and contrary to your expensive report, the burn is *not* complete. When you drop your barrels, they incinerate, sure, but not all the way to nothingness. Vapors remain, and vapors escape!"

The case was well argued, but with Bamalford there was no chance. Smirking, he pointed to the pit. "You sound like you've been down there, with your little notebook and meat thermometer. Ha, ha!" He looked to Bezzle and Lumps, a signal that they should join him in the laugh. But they missed the cue and remained silent.

It was hard to keep shouting across the distance, yet Joannie continued with the effort. "No, I haven't been down there. And obviously there's some guesswork and some inference in what I'm saying. But not my guesswork. All that I told you now about the mountain and the invasions by the seawater is from someone who has spent half his life ..."

> **sardonic**: conveying scorn, bitterness or disillusionment, often through words and expressions marked with something of wit or cleverness
>
> **bane**: something which on a regular basis is especially harmful to a particular class of persons or things
>
> **mnemonic** (noun): some trick or device to help your memory keep hold of a name or phrase

"Oh—I bet you mean our good friend Rusty," said Bamalford in a nasty, **sardonic** voice. "Good stuff, alright—threadbare, thumbs-to-spare Rusty. Rust, you know, is the **bane**, of iron. Get it? That's our little **mnemonic**, it helps us remember the jerk's name."

> **peruse**: to read through something, usually in a careful, searching manner; to give something a careful looking through
>
> **oxymoron** (plural: oxymora): a brief phrase in which the sense of one word is contrary to the sense of the other word or words (for example, "a well-organized chaos")

406

He shot a look at Bezzle, and then turned to Joannie again. "Larger-than-life Ironbane! We can't all be like him. We can't all stomp around the mountain the way he does, **perusing** each page in the book of nature until it's half memorized. But at least we can believe him—every last lying word—when he tells us the ocean is draining into the volcano through a spiffy underground aqueduct!"

He paused and moved in closer to the rectangle of barrels. It was an alarming action. "Let me show you just how seriously I take it when Ironbane—speeding-turtle Ironbane, noonday-darkness Ironbane, and other similar **oxymorons**—when he tells me that the independent baseline study commissioned by Nameless Entrepreneur is a piece of junk! I just wanna show you all."

With a savage kick he knocked one of the kegs to its side. Even as François screamed for him to stop, a second kick sent it rolling on a direct line toward the rim of the cauldron.

READER: Larry got into that part where Bamalford swelled up like a boiler explosion.

AUTHOR: It was intellectually satisfying, I agree.

READER: But he thinks that Bamalford's eyes should pop out on thirteen-inch flexible extenders.

AUTHOR: That would push us over the line between the believable and the unbelievable.

READER: Not at all. Just make them very believable thirteen-inch flexible extenders.

Chapter 58: PRELUDE TO 99 YEARS OF INSANITY

Time stopped for François. She was outside of it, looking back at it. "I've stepped off the timeline," she murmured to herself. "And I can see it all."

> **kinetic**: having to do with motion, often motion in the most basic sense of physical objects moving through open space
> **derivative** (noun): an end-product considered as developed or evolved from a given source material

At one end of the line, the closer end, the keg was wobbling and rolling toward the rim of the abyss. It's very **kinetic**, she thought: circular motion, linear motion, back-and-forth motion, all together.

Far off, toward the other end of the line, she saw motion as well: a little girl of two years or so was stumbling at the edge of the dock, starting to tumble over, and a giant figure was running, lunging violently, catching her. Darlingson had gotten horribly scraped up that time, so long ago. "And it's no different now"—François let the words drop indistinctly from her lips—"look how the granite tears at his poor shoulder as ..."

She snapped herself out of it with a furious shake of her head. Darlingson was there, against all probabilities. He was there, and in danger. From somewhere he had come racing on a line that paralleled the rim. To intercept the careening barrel he had thrown himself headlong, catching it in his outstretched hands. Now, before her eyes, he was sliding with it toward the pit.

The line of his slide was a diagonal one, a **derivative** from the descending line of the barrel and the crossing hurl of his approach. He struggled desperately, pressing his shoulder into the granite—anything to stop. The effort succeeded—but by the barest margin. He came to rest no more than fifteen or twenty inches from the rim. He was on his stomach, and his head was pointing toward the deep shaft. The keg itself looked as good as gone, having actually crossed the rim and hanging now with its full weight from his straining fingers, above the fire.

> **adhesion**: the condition of sticking or clinging firmly to something
> **reciprocate**: to respond to an action that someone has performed with respect to you by performing an equivalent action with respect to him
> **pathetic**: so poor or inferior, or suffering from such disadvantage, as to inspire pity or mild repugnance

His frantic attempts to pull it back accomplished nothing. He couldn't get any **adhesion** on the slope. He was digging feet and knees into the granite, trying for a hold, but a scattering of loose stone and sand defeated him over and over. And without some hold there was no chance of drawing in the heavy keg: when he tugged at it, it **reciprocated** and tugged back at him, pulling him closer to the brink.

Bamalford had gasped with fright when the giant figure first charged out from nowhere. But his alarm dissolved quickly when he saw the **pathetic** checkmate into which Darlingson had gone sliding.

> **nullify**: to strip away all effect from something and reduce it to nothing
> **ascendancy**: a commanding influence, often based on some superiority of strength or advantage and not merely on high rank within a power structure
> **defection**: withdrawal from a movement or party that still has a claim to your support, and often because you plan to support a rival

It was a situation to his liking. "Boom box," he gloated, "speak to me. You've been **nullified** as a fighting force—hold up one hand if you agree. Ha! Seriously though, nice job stopping that keg. Too bad there's ninety-nine, or ninety-eight, more of them."

He turned to Lumps. "Up and at 'em. Start herding those doggies over the edge. Whoa—where do you …?"

Lumps was already up, and setting foot on a course that would break Bamalford's **ascendancy** over him forever. He was moving toward Darlingson, picking his way as swiftly as possible over the slope, to help his friend.

Bamalford screamed, "None of that, thick neck. Back at once, or it's over—you can kiss 'em good-by, the data bases and any news they might have about your old man."

Lumps too was in the grip of anger. "This is what you stand for—to leave a person in danger of his life, while you get on with business. My father … my father would never …" He couldn't finish.

Bamalford grew alarmed. He knew the **defection** of Lumps would be a serious setback. He swallowed down his wrath and forced a coaxing note into his voice. "Lumps, there's some stress in the air, I know, but let's regard the matter calmly. Your service has been excellent and, although my plan was to tell you this later, I will tell you now that one of the data bases has been opened to you. I've registered your name, I've set aside a table for you at the paper, with a connection to the net. We'll put out a little bowl of chocolates, and some tokens for the soft-drinks machine. You can come over when you want, bring one of your friends to help out, and do your research."

blandishment: a mix of flattery and attractive promises, delivered in a soft, coaxing manner
irrevocable: coming into effect once and for all, with no possibility of being reversed
benign: kindly and well-wishing; subtly influencing things to turn out well; causing no serious harm

He paused to see if these **blandishments** were having any effect. Not reassured by the gathering scowl on the face of Lumps, he changed tone again, abruptly, and delivered a solemn warning. "But if you go, it is **irrevocable**. You will never return to my service."

Lumps did not hesitate a second. "The service is shameful," he cried, "and you are correct—I will never return!" He had come within reach of Darlingson. Working carefully on the littered surface, he clutched the ankles of his friend and tried to draw him back from the edge. With a spray of loose stone, his foot slipped, and for a moment the two of them were sliding. It was only a few inches, but it was enough to increase their peril.

Bamalford was pure malice now. He was starting to call out a vicious taunt when from the corner of his eye he caught some disturbance, a motion. Tedesco was making his way quickly down the slope, falling, rising, skating over the small debris, going to the aid of Lumps and Darlingson.

"Ha!" Bamalford pounced heavily on one of the kegs and toppled it over on its side. "This goes, foreign boy, this goes!"

Tedesco pulled to a halt, as Bamalford, in a childish fury, let the heavy keg roll again and again, catching it at the edge of his reach and pulling it back. "It's that simple—just lift away my hands. C'mon, foreign boy, give me a reason. You too, bug lady and friends. Lemme make you unhappy. I'm not feeling very **benign** right now—no goodwill toward any of you."

Tedesco looked back to his companions. He was distressed and spoke in a mix of English and Portuguese. "See the Darlingson; his arms are getting more and more *cansado*. He can't hold forever."

idiom: a vocabulary or other set of expressions and verbal structures which is unique to a particular group
posterity: (1) all the people who will be your descendants; (2) all the people down through time who will come after you
check (verb): to bring some motion or action to a halt, often in a sharp, decisive manner

"*Cansado*," screamed Bamalford. "What's that—another piece of teen **idiom**, special teen words that confuse everybody else? It makes me sick!"

"It's Portuguese," Lumps roared back. "That's his language—get it?"

410

Bamalford pulled his hands off the keg, then caught it at the beginning of its roll. "Let me guess, Lumps. You read that somewhere. Ha! With your ninety-ninth percentile reading abilities. Only—get it right next time—the foreign boy isn't from Portugal, jerk. South America, remember—Spanish—all that?"

For a second he caught Bezzle in his gaze. "Look at the two of 'em, Bez—Lumps and Darlingson. One of them can't talk but they're both dumb. Ha! Get it?"

He was glaring at Lumps once again. "Get it, preppie? A joke. You like jokes. C'mon, it's only a bad day if you let it be. Say something quotable for your **posterity**—all those page-turning Lumps and Bumps that are yet to come."

Still securing Darlingson by the ankles, Lumps turned his head to look directly at Bamalford. But as he started to cry out against the tormenter his elbows—the points where he had the most grip against the treacherous ground—slipped, and he and Darlingson were sliding once again, very slowly, toward the edge. Digging in furiously—elbows, knees, toes—Lumps was able to **check** their motion, but several more precious inches had been lost.

> **incongruous**: strikingly inconsistent with, or out of proportion with, something
> **prelude**: an event of relatively minor proportions that introduces and sometimes foreshadows some main event
> **jettison**: to throw out what holds you back; especially, to throw out cargo in order to lighten a ship or plane

François was half faint with the sight. On a trembling note she cried out—"Lumps, in the name of God, don't let the mountain claim for a second time against your family!"

He was steadying himself—physically and emotionally—and in a voice suddenly calm, **incongruously** so for the situation, he called back to her, "Lest the people of Athens sin for a second time against philosophy, is that the idea?"

The phrase was alien to François but, strangely, it had a most powerful effect on Bezzle. His head lifted and his face became intent, as though some riddle were written on the air before him.

"Hold on, Bez," said Bamalford, seeing how the librarian had been jolted. "I'll tell you what it is, a statement out of nowhere like that. It's a … a **Prelude** to Ninety-Nine Years of Insanity. Ha—I like that. Lumps is going bonkers, long-term, and this babble of his about sins is a taste of what to expect. Or—another idea—maybe it's just a different way of saying that Darlingson's arms are *cansado*. That's the news of the hour, isn't it? Well—why doesn't the big oaf **jettison** some cargo—you know, lighten the load?"

"Cabbage!" cried Ricky suddenly, ignoring Bamalford and his ramblings. "It just came to me. Remember when you leaned out over the edge—you know, last time, with your shoe, to get the sample? It was almost the same spot, wasn't it—where Darlingson is now? So that means ..."

Tedesco skipped all the middle steps and raced to the conclusion. "The...the shelf," he called wildly to Darlingson. "Exists a narrow shelf that sticks out from the wall; it stays a little to your right, and it is not too much below you."

> **discrepancy**: an instance in which two statements or reports speak inconsistently on some point
> **avert**: to push aside, and thus avoid, some blow or disaster that is aimed at you
> **vulnerable**: exposed in some special degree to harm, often for lack of ordinary defenses, but also sometimes because of being positioned squarely in harm's way

Ricky was shouting at almost the same time, at the top of his lungs, desperate to be heard. "A perch, a ledge, whatever, Darlingson, jutting out from the wall of the shaft, just inches below the rim and ... on your left."

Darlingson didn't worry about the **discrepancy** in the two messages. All that mattered was the ledge. It might let him **avert** the disaster that was now only moments away. The keg was about to fall. It was slowly tearing itself from his grasp, and he couldn't hold it much longer. With the last of his strength he swung it to the left and then to the right, looking for the ledge.

Bamalford was beginning to mock the futile effort, when the sharp scrape of metal on stone cut him short. Darlingson had found the shelf. It was directly below him, and so close that the keg had almost been touching it. His shoulders were trembling, at the limits of exhaustion, when his burden finally came to rest. Lumps gave a huge sigh of relief for the two of them.

Even now, though, they could not leave their post. The ledge tilted downward slightly, and the keg would have rolled lazily off if Darlingson had not stayed there securing it.

It was a **vulnerable** position, with the ninety-eight other kegs, a large truck and Bamalford all located just up the slope. "The sooner we find some other place for our picnic, the better," said Lumps in a low voice. "Somebody is looking very unhappy."

> **rancor**: a festering hatefulness that you bear toward someone
> **explicit**: expressed so directly and specifically as to leave nothing to suggestion

> **implicit**: not expressed in so many words, but present by suggestion or inference in something

Bamalford was swollen and slightly purple with anger. "I liked it better," he screamed in the direction of François and companions, "when boom box was hanging on to the barrel by his fingertips. You know I cherish a special malice for the guy. When it's bad for him it's great for me." With the back of his hand he wiped savagely at the flecks of spittle collecting on his lower lip. "And that's OK—Mother Bamalford always said **rancor** is human. But you people don't respect where I'm at. You told him about that ledge. You spoiled the game. But don't worry ..."

His voice was rising to a breaking pitch. "Don't worry ..." He still had one hand on a keg, and now with a fierce yank he lined it up so that it would roll on a short line to the yawning shaft.

Only Ricky could think of one last argument. It had to be made at once. "Broken promise!" he shouted. "You gave your word. Now you trample on it."

"Word!" snarled Bamalford. "Promise! Show me my promise!"

Ricky thought fast. "It wasn't **explicit**. You didn't say it in so many words. But a few minutes ago, when you stopped Tedesco in his tracks by shouting 'This goes,' you gave your promise **implicitly**."

> **moratorium**: a period, often established by order or decree, during which some activity or program is shut down or the effect of some law is suspended
> **jurisprudence**: extensive and scholarly knowledge about the law
> **rescind**: to terminate the effectiveness of some promise, permission, governmental measure, etc., before the time at which it would have expired on its own terms

"That was nice of me. And what did I promise?"

"That if Tedesco stayed put, and all of us stayed put, you would quit launching kegs for a time—a **moratorium** on hostile action—so that we could try to talk this out."

"Hoo-eee!" Bamalford was swelling up again. "Your daddy is a judge, and you are a fountain of **jurisprudence**. Well listen, Jack. My brother Fearless is a lawyers' lawyer, and he's taught me more law than you or pops will ever know. If I give my promise to people who are mental infants, then it's not fully binding and I have the right to **rescind** it. Which is what I'm doing now. Zap! My promise is nothing. It's torn up. The moratorium is over, kiddies."

He held up his hands, fingers spread apart clown-style. The keg which he had been restraining was suddenly free. It gave two lumbering revolutions toward the fire shaft and was gaining speed when, abruptly, a sideways lurch threw it against the ninth row of the standing barrels. There it jammed.

413

"Don't anybody laugh," Bamalford screamed. "My man Bezzle will have that keg and all the kegs over the edge in a jiff."

Bezzle was only a few steps from the obstructed barrel, and could easily have freed it. He did nothing, however, made no motion. He was still gazing at the air in front of him, still struggling with the riddle that was apparently written for him there.

> **censure** (verb): to declare against someone, often in a tone of authority and with a punishing sharpness, that he has done wrong
> **reconciliation**: a return to a normal state of communication, cooperation and affection after a period of hostility
> **tenet**: some proposition that is held as true and fundamental by the members of a group

Bamalford sensed new trouble, and his calculating side took over immediately. "Let it be, Bez. Lumps babbled out some madness, but let it be. Who knows what the Athenians did to philosophy anyway, maybe something they shouldn't have, but we don't need to **censure** them. We're not perfect either. So let it be. Stay focused, and remember your little group—you, me, Nameless, Victoria. Don't forget how it supports you, keeps you in touch with your anger, so there will never, never be a humiliating **reconciliation** with you-know-who. Isn't that our basic **tenet**—some wrongs are beyond forgiveness, huh Bez? That's the foundation."

Bamalford made his appeal in a voice that was urgent and compelling, but for Bezzle it was no more than a background noise—the hum of a motor, the droning of insects. And when he finally came out of his thoughts some moments later and gave a reply, it was not to Bamalford that he spoke. "Lumps," he called, with a measure of excitement in his voice, "where did you hear that phrase about sins against philosophy? Who taught it to you anyway?"

READER: Larry says the real contribution of this book may be in the area of time travel.

AUTHOR: I try to help out wherever I can.

READER: When François stepped off the timeline there at the beginning, Larry went wild and started raving about the collapse of time into space, the transformation of before and after into right and left, and so on.

AUTHOR: He's a careful reader, I can see.

READER: He'd like to know if you're planning any time-travel experiments.

AUTHOR: How do you think I got here?

Chapter 59: THE YOUNG BIBLIOPHILES

The last thing Bamalford wanted was a conversation between Bezzle and Lumps. "Bez," he shouted in exasperation. "Who cares where the child got those words about … sinning for the second time? What are they anyway? One little scrap of gossip. Probably came off the soaps."

> **upbraid**: to give someone a sharp scolding
> **bibliophile**: someone who loves books
> **kindred**: significantly alike in structure, character or sympathies

"The soaps!" cried Bezzle, **upbraiding** Bamalford with a new boldness. "Please stop—you have no idea what you're saying! That phrase is a line from a very dramatic moment, a very ancient one, in the history of culture. And for good reasons I need to know who taught it to Lumps."

Lifting his head, but making no further effort to turn about, Lumps called, "I was talking one day, Bez, with Ironbane. He was the one who taught it to me. It stuck in his memory years ago when he read it for the first time."

The impact of this on Bezzle was enormous. He staggered slightly and supported himself on one of the kegs. "Do you realize what this means," he asked in a laboring tone, "that Ironbane was familiar with that phrase? Do I realize what this means?"

A deep growl came from Bamalford. "Bez—not a healthy question. No need to go rethinking Ironbane. We know all we need to know about that pond scum, and the way he knifed you in the ribs. Remember the story, Bez, seventeen years ago, how you came to Dropanchor. The new librarian. High on life, high on literature. You started a club—The Young **Bibliophiles**—people like you who were wild about books. **Kindred** spirits. You had them reading—and not easy stuff either. Remember what you told me—how toward the end there was even that large book about ancient … whatever, ancient Greece I suppose. And one of the bright stars in the club was you-know-who, a punk geology teacher at the high school, named Ironbane."

> **pacifism**: the belief that war is wrong and that wartime military service should be resisted
> **irascibility**: a tendency to lose your temper quickly

As he spoke Bamalford turned another keg on its side and shot a dark glance at Tedesco, Joannie and the others. Then in one of his larger-than-life gestures, he brought the flat of his hand down upon it. A metallic clang shook

415

through the air. "Get mad, Bez! Think battle! No time now for **pacifism**. Remember what he did. For over a year he's a Young Bibliophile, coming to all the meetings, reading the big ones. Your hopes are rising, admit it. Then one day he shows up at the library and requests a book, a manual, on—that's right—log trucks, how to drive a log truck."

Meagan and François exchanged an electric glance, remembering that day at the library when they had run into such a storm of **irascibility** from Bezzle, which had centered—confusingly—around a book about log trucks. What they couldn't see at the moment was that the face of Lumps had also tightened suddenly with the effort of remembering something.

> **refute**: to take a statement or claim that someone has put forward, and throw it back by showing that it is wrong
>
> **recapitulation**: a brief, summarizing review of the key points of a story, report or other narration
>
> **torpid**: barely moving; emptied out of all energy; locked in a state of numbness

"How to drive a log truck," Bamalford repeated. "Why was young Rusty asking for such a book? Dark suspicions came into your mind, dark and legitimate. You wanted, of course, to **refute** them, and as you found the manual and gave it to him you hoped for some explanation that would put the whole affair in a harmless light. But there was none. He took what you offered without a word, and was gone. He missed the session that night, of the Young Bibliophiles, and all sessions thereafter. And there was no longer any doubt about the message you were supposed to read in his behavior, huh Bez? I'm leaving a lot out, but aren't those the highlights? Isn't that a fair **recapitulation**?"

A moment before, Bezzle had been excited, expansive, a man waking into a better day. Now the old story, and Bamalford's grim way of telling it, were once again shutting him down, drawing off his newfound energy.

Lumps could see none of this, turned as he was toward the fire shaft and bending forward to clutch the ankles of Darlingson, but he knew Bezzle well and could feel him slumping, growing **torpid**, losing the capacity for any decisive action. "Bezzle," he shouted, "don't let him control you any more. Be stubborn. You raised a question, now push for the answer. What does it mean that Ironbane knew that phrase about the people of Athens? Try, Bez!"

> **trappings**: the external signs such as as clothing, ceremonies, titles and forms of address, by which a way of life, a code of conduct, etc., expresses itself
>
> **adumbration**: a small token or dim foreshadowing of something to come
>
> **autodidact**: a person who becomes her own teacher, learning things on her own that other people go to school to learn

416

"*Mister* Bezzle to you, ox face," screamed Bamalford. "A clown like you has no right to lay aside the **trappings** of courtesy."

Mister Bezzle or just plain Bezzle, it was beside the point. The appeal of Lumps had struck home. Bezzle shuddered, fought off the heaviness, and lifted his head. In his manner there was again that hint of assertiveness, an **adumbration** of defiance. "Lumps," he called, "it should be answered, I will push for an answer. But before anything—you're so close to the edge. Can you ...?"

"It's OK, as long as I don't move. And Darlingson doesn't move. Don't worry, Bez, just try ..."

"Alright then, listen—those words that Ironbane repeated to you are from near the end of a book about ancient philosophy that we had started reading in the group. He left long before we ever got to that part. In fact, the group broke up before we ever got to it. Which means he found those words on his own, and liked them enough to remember them. He taught himself."

"I knew it," roared Bamalford. "One more tofu-eating **autodidact**. I hate them all—they can't be happy with what they learn in class, so they go off and teach themselves. Whiners and pigs! We should have known that Rusty was one of them."

At this point, Bamalford's words were nonsense for Bezzle. But they gave him a moment to think, to return to the most tangled part of the story. He was struggling fiercely with something. "So the philosophy book was OK," he murmured, staring up at the dome overhead. "He read it on his own, he didn't despise it. I was wrong on that one, fifteen years' worth of wrong. But why"—now his voice was louder, and he was again addressing Lumps—"why under heaven a manual about log trucks? I know you are thinking—what does it matter? Well"—there was a long pause—"because I drove one, OK. I never told you, Lumps, or anyone—but for the seven years before I came here, I was a logger, I drove one of the big trucks. And it's too much of a coincidence that after I became a librarian people start asking for manuals about ..."

> **verify**: to check something out to be sure that it is true or correct
> **fallacious**: leading you to accept what is erroneous, often by presenting false appearances or false reasonings
> **insurmountable**: too much of an obstacle to be gotten around, gotten over or otherwise defeated

Bamalford cut in, trying without success to speak in a voice that only Bezzle would hear. "Bez—there's still time! You can still say it was just a joke—this thing about the log truck. They have no way to **verify** whether you did or didn't. Otherwise they're gonna blueblood you to death. They're all snobs, every one of our visitors tonight, just like Ironbane was. No dirt on their hands, no sweat on their foreheads."

417

Bezzle refused to speak directly with Bamalford, but he seemed to be suffering from exactly the sort of doubt which Bamalford was trying to awaken in him. There was pain in his voice as he said, "I know that human judgment is a **fallacious** thing, Lumps, and that we should be slow to buy its conclusions. But there's only one conclusion I could ever think of for the question why Ironbane wanted a book on log trucks, and even now I can't see any errors in it—his purpose was to express contempt. He found out somehow that I had driven one of them, and in his eyes that was low and common. To show me he knew, and to show his contempt, he requested that book. Why else? He had no connection with logging, no reason to seek out literature on the subject. He was a teacher, not a logger. I know he's your friend, Lumps, but why else?"

Bamalford's big face was expanding with pleasure at the sight of Bezzle's confusion. "Can't get around it, can you, Bez? Can't get over it. It's the one **insurmountable** fact in all that messy history—you spent seven years doing a tough job, hauling timber, and Ironbane despised you for it. I'm sorry, Bez, but in his eyes you were low, unwashed, the riff and the raff."

> **purveyor**: one who obtains a supply of some essential commodity and acts as a distributor of it
> **impute**: to explain something as being the result of some particular cause or influence
> **disdain** (noun): the feeling that someone is far inferior; the scornful manner in which that feeling is expressed

Meagan, silent for so long, could stand no more. Uncertain if she would even be heard, she burst out loudly, "If he prints it in his newspaper, in four-inch letters, it's still a lie, Mr. Bezzle, a filthy, four-inch lie. Ironbane's not a snob! He's as far from that as you can get. He doesn't think he's too good for physical labor. Little known fact: about eighty percent of the plumbing work at the high school is done by—take a guess—Principal Ironbane. It saves money for the District. Besides, Mr. Bezzle, think back on your early days in Dropanchor. Think who you were then—piloting the bookmobile, skidding and bouncing through the crooked lanes, a prince of sorts and a **purveyor** of fine literature, without a single helper, and hardly aware that you were starving on the ridiculous salary—wasn't that you in the early days? How could Ironbane look down on someone like that? I don't know why he asked for a book about log trucks. But please don't **impute** it to any **disdain** for you. That would ..."

She was interrupted by a hoarse cry from Lumps. "I'll tell you, Bez—I know why he asked for that book. I really, really know. I've heard the story."

> **chronological**: organized so as to list or tell events in the order in which they took place
> **torrid**: very hot, often with a dry, baking sort of heat

418

incandescent: brightly shining with the light released by an internal source of heat

There was a pause—Lumps seemed to be readying himself, collecting his powers, finding the strength to stay pressed against the granite a while longer, even as he gave a difficult account. When at last he began he spoke strongly and slowly, in a voice that carried easily to Bezzle and the other listeners. "If I just go **chronologically**, I can probably handle it. So—day one—Lumps is born, hi Lumps. Day two through … whatever, day one thousand—Lumps settles in, gets to know the big people, learns some tricks. Then—day one thousand and one, a **torrid** summer's day. Dropanchor is baking under the August sun. Early afternoon—Yuri, one of the big people and the father of Lumps, goes on the mountain. Late afternoon—the earth is like a hot brick and its heat pulls a storm out of the sky. Over the mountain a mass of cloud presses down; it is **incandescent** with lightning. Yuri does not come home, not for supper, not to sleep. Lumps, at three years, more or less, isn't too worried—the big people always know what they're doing. Yuri's good friend, Ironbane, looks for him all night in pouring rain, but no luck."

derelict (noun): something abandoned for good, such as a ship, and often left at the mercy of the elements
deter: to cause someone to give up an action, often by inspiring his reflection on difficulties or unpleasant consequences associated with it
feasible: within the realm of what you can actually get done; doable

Bezzle shook his head, very slowly, as though he saw what was coming. Lumps went on. "Three or four days go by, but the search has found no sign. The mountain is too big, and there's still a lot of area to cover. A crazy idea gets hold of Ironbane. A vehicle—they have to get a vehicle on the mountain. He thinks first of the bookmobile, Bez, your special beast. It's ugly, it's tough, the ground clearance is good. He can already see it. Just a few modifications and it's ready to go. Maybe with him at the wheel. Or maybe with you—he's sure Povano will take you off that cannot-be-spared list. But the bookmobile is a hard sell, those who know the mountain best shake their heads. And then another vision suddenly catches hold of him. On one of the farms east of town there's an old log truck, at the back of the orchard. But it's not a **derelict**. The farmer, a friend of his, has kept it in running order in case one of his sons ever wanted to go into that line of work. It has a transmission geared so low you could climb a wall. Ironbane is sure the truck is the answer. His plan is to put it on the mountain, to make it part of the search. The total absence of roads does not **deter** him. The little challenges of crossing the Bad Pony and climbing the Steeps do not deter him. To his exhausted, frantic brain the idea is completely **feasible**."

> **imperceptible**: so tiny, or happening so gradually and by such small degrees, as to escape perception
> **polemic** (noun): a speech or other argument assaulting the positions and character of an opponent, and sometimes urging a warlike attitude toward him
> **expurgation**: the process of cleaning up a book, speech, etc. by pulling out any indecent or otherwise offensive material

Lumps paused, looking down, checking that he and Darlingson were not slipping **imperceptibly** closer to the shaft. Bezzle was pale and waiting. He knew where the story must end, but he did not interrupt its telling.

Even Bamalford was keeping quiet at this point, realizing that the account could not be repressed. Rather—to discredit it was the thing, and he appeared to be meditating feverishly on ways to accomplish that.

Lumps resumed, and he seemed to be drawing strength as he went on. "So Ironbane has his plan, and he wastes no time. The first step is to rush to the library. He says he will have to miss the meeting that night of the Young Bibliophiles. Then, remembering stories of multiple gears and complicated braking routines, he asks ... the librarian ... for a book about how to drive a log truck."

Bezzle groaned, bringing a hand to his brow. "And there was the wounding. Mr. Bezzle—not a secure guy—felt an attack. He was badly hurt, his judgment horribly clouded. And for fifteen years he has remained hurt and angry, never understanding until now. Lumps—it wasn't to mock me, it was for your father's sake! Why couldn't I see that?"

Like an injured man he sat down slowly on the keg that Bamalford had rolled, the one that had jammed. "It wasn't that hard to see, it was two plus two, but I was so offended."

He let out such a long sigh that Lumps expected him to crumple. When he spoke again, his voice was drawn and faint. "If you want to throw away your chance for happiness, all you need to do is bear a grudge, nourish a grudge. Watch it suck the joy from your days. And when it starts to weaken, have someone nearby to stir it up again, someone with the gift of **polemic**. Bamalford did that for me in these last few years—countless little speeches portraying Ironbane's conduct as unpardonable, urging me to stay on a wartime footing with him, condemning peace. As for peace, the order of the day was **expurgation**—rip out all mention of it from anything I thought or said or wrote."

"It was all for you, Bez." Bamalford spoke in a purr, deep and hypnotic, as he made his last desperate bid. "We knew what Ironbane is and how he could hurt you. We'd rather have seen you pet a croc than mix with him. That's how we felt—Victoria, Nameless and I. Your little group."

It was too late. Bezzle stood up and faced Bamalford squarely. With a sharp gesture toward the abyss, he declared, "You don't throw any more years of my life down that hole—no more, alright. And no more of these, either." He reached out to the keg on which he had been sitting, and pulled it into its upright position, the stable position in which it would not roll.

> **auxiliary** (noun): someone who is your helper, usually in a role in which he receives orders from you
> **rampant**: (1) raised up in a posture of wild aggression; (2) aggressively active in a given area, and not held in check
> **lassitude**: a heavy, stagnant weariness that makes exertion look irritating or undesirable

Bamalford had now lost two of his most important **auxiliaries**, and in that underground hall there was no one on his side. As he saw this, a horrible cry—with no claim to be human speech—shot out from him. The rage of all lower creatures was there—the rooster in the fighting pit, the boar straining in the trap, the gibbering hyena. Meagan heard the awful sound and knew at once what it meant. Without hesitating she urged her companions, "Up! Up! The talking is through. He's over the edge. I'm sorry—but we treat him like a wild beast now—corner him, pen him. Go!"

They broke from their position, the four of them, Meagan, François, Allen and Ricky. They thrashed across the slope toward the **rampant** figure of Bamalford. They had to contain him before he could send any kegs down the fire shaft. Yet even reaching him was a challenge, for they fell repeatedly on the loose scattering of pebbles and sand that seemed to be everywhere.

For all his rage, Bamalford had not lost his sense of the situation. With a quick glance he took it all in—the four coming at him from above; Bezzle—free at last from the bitterness that had sapped his energy and held him in **lassitude** for many years—charging vigorously up from below; Joannie and Tedesco scrambling to help Darlingson.

There were still a few seconds left, and with the urgent cunning of a hunted animal Bamalford spent them well. Bezzle was the most immediate problem, and Bezzle he took out of the game at once, by toppling two more barrels and rolling them in the librarian's direction.

> **parsimonious**: tightfisted and stingy; reluctant to reduce your resources either by using or by giving
> **travesty**: a twisted, exaggerated imitation or occurrence of something
> **philanthropist**: one who tries to help humanity, often through large gifts to community institutions

Then, with Ricky, François and Meagan still fifty yards off, and Allen even farther, he made a brilliant move. The Terebinth truck was enlisted in the struggle, on his side. Bolting for the front of it, even as the desperate idea was still taking form in his mind, he cried out the strange, bragging words—"Don't call Peerless Bamalford **parsimonious**. He's about to give away everything. He's going to drop it all in the collection basket—all ninety-nine kegs."

Allen saw the play at once, and shouted, "He plans to roll the truck! There won't be a barrel left."

Bamalford was already at the cab of the truck, opening the door, scrambling in. He had gained the advantage. No one would reach him for several moments, and that would be ample time to release the brake, throw the gear into neutral and jump free. He would watch in wild triumph as the heavy vehicle bowled into the kegs and swept them over the rim.

"One other thing. One other thing." He was laughing madly now, leaning out the window on the passenger side. His face was framed there, like some hideous **travesty** of a classical portrait. "Why did I say ninety-nine a second ago, and not one hundred?"

Allen held his breath, trying not to miss a word. The mystery of the one-hundredth barrel was very much on his mind.

"Because," cried Bamalford, answering his own question, "because the donation I'm about to make, of the ninety-nine barrels, that's the second donation tonight. There was an earlier one, ha, yes that's it, an earlier donation. Heh, heg, ha!"

His laughter, loud and cackling, had a touch of hysteria. "I was in my room," he explained, "thinking—how can I help my fellow townspeople today? Surprised, huh? Yes, children, I am a bit of a **philanthropist**. What if, I thought, my fellow townspeople had a single substance, a single elixir, that heals almost everything, a wide range of illnesses and injuries? And what if they had a barrel of it conveniently mixed in with a … beverage they were all going to drink anyway—on this particular night? A beverage which, like fools, they leave unguarded."

"No!" Allen gasped. There was horror in his voice. He stumbled and for a moment could toil no more across the treacherous slope. "Not in the kettle! Every person in Dropanchor …"

"Merci!" screamed François. "She's the first."

"You couldn't!" cried Joannie to Bamalford. "There can't be that much sickness in you."

> **nefarious**: shockingly or wickedly injurious to what is sacred or vital in a community
> **ameliorate**: to cause a situation to get better

autonomous: operating independently; self-regulating; not subject to the direction or control of someone else

He thought that was funny. "Ask shrink lady," he called out, laughing, gesturing toward Meagan. "What's down in the human cellar, shrink lady? What capacity for foul, **nefarious** things? And what sets it loose?"

Meagan had almost reached the truck. She stopped suddenly now, and disregarding her own advice, made a last attempt at talking to the man. Maybe she could get a read on how serious he was. "What sets it loose," she said, breathing hard, "what unlatches the cellar, is oftentimes humiliation. And that was what you suffered, Mr. Bamalford, that night last September on television, and I am honestly sorry about that. But you can't ..."

"But I can!" he broke in. "I can do what I want." His laughter rose up again, hysterical, gabbling. "Because I have freedom of the press. See?" He pulled his yellow press card from his pocket and waved it wildly about.

He was too far gone, the situation was too extreme. Meagan wasted no more time. As she began to run again, however, she slipped awkwardly on the uncertain ground. Bamalford thought even that was funny. "Ooh—you're so close. Clumsy footwork, though—maybe ballet lessons would **ameliorate** things a bit. Think about it, anyway. Ha, Har. Well, excuse me, there's something I need to do. I wonder if it will make those back-up noises—*gnee, gnee, gnee*. That's hilarious—*gnee, gnee* right over the cliff. Ha! Horkk!"

He slid behind the steering wheel to release the brake. His laughter was rising and rising, swelling throughout the vast chamber as he struggled with the lever, swelling up louder and more terrible even as he caught the yellow press card in his teeth to leave both hands free for the work.

That was strange. He paused, frowned, looked vaguely upward, rebuked his own laughter. "When I stop, you stop, do you hear? You're not **autonomous**, you know."

Yet the sound rose higher, reverberating violently from the stony vault. It came on relentlessly, no longer laughter or the echo of laughter, steadily resolving into a furious honking and braying that left Bamalford undone with terror. "That thing!" he cried, as the orangish blare beat against him. "That awful giant duck, which hates me, and ..."

flamboyant: imposing upon your attention, usually through some bold exaggeration in feature, such as a luxurious display of color
recondite: so complex or profound or filled with unusual concepts as to leave most of us baffled and in the dark
clamor (noun): a loud, ongoing outcry or other such noise, often insistent or complaining, and often rising as a confused mix from many sources

Something came back to him. "And hates my yellow card!" With all his force he threw the yellow press card out of the cab. It fluttered in the breeze rising from the pit and was carried onto the windshield, lodging finally under the wiper. In the upper world it would have been a thing unnoticed, a mere scrap. But in the strange color scale of the cavern it stood out with unnatural brightness, and as though that were not enough, it accented and awakened the tangerine lettering of the TEREBINTH, leaving the truck almost **flamboyant**. Bamalford had failed badly in the attempt to become less visible.

The horrible trumpeting grew louder and closer. Bamalford was moaning unintelligibly now, and darting his glance in every direction, seeking rescue. Suddenly he realized that the keys were still in the truck's ignition. His hands fumbled with them madly. They resisted his grasp and he attacked with fury, bending them and almost dislodging the truck's steering column. After a long moment, however, he was able to start the engine.

His only thought now was to escape the approaching creature. He had never been at the wheel of a big truck before, and truck driving for him was one of the **recondite** arts—a deep riddle of gears and instrumentation. But as he finally let off the brake and felt himself rolling backward toward the rim, he learned fast. The huge TEREBINTH, floating like a vision in the air, began moving up the slope. And through a high **clamor** of quacks and quocks and the whine of an over-revving engine the truck passed out of the chamber and into the long tunnel.

READER: Larry tried starting from a dead stop in his uncle's pretzel truck.
AUTHOR: On a flat road, I hope.
READER: No—on a steep upslope in the mountains of northern California.
AUTHOR: And he rolled back a smidge?
READER: More or less into Oregon.
AUTHOR: He's a dramatic figure.

Chapter 60: THE QUIXOTIC SLOW

François started to run, fiercely. She felt a growling inside her, forming in her throat, something she had never felt before. Later she would realize its **vestigial** nature, how it was an echo of savage mechanisms from long ago. But there was no time now for any of that. Only one thing could hold her attention—the need to warn Merci. If the growling meant courage for the race through the tunnel, then it was welcome.

> **vestigial**: carried over, as a trace or remainder, from something that has otherwise disappeared
> **fiasco**: a situation in which everything turns out wrong, often because of massive human error
> **propitiate**: through gifts, sacrifices, etc., to cause a person or divinity to lay aside hostility and be favorable to you

She ran ten steps, twenty, on the rubbled slope leading up from the fire shaft, then slipped and fell hard. At once a strong hand caught her and helped her up. It was Meagan, speaking with haste but looking at her with the hint of a smile. "It will be a **fiasco** if you try to do it by yourself, François. You'll wedge an ankle between two stones, you'll be trapped in a Loser plant. There's the guy you need, to carry the warning."

She pointed toward the rim of the abyss. Darlingson was still there, at the very edge, hanging on to the barrel, and held in turn by Lumps. Joannie, Ricky and Tedesco were straining to pull them back. "C'mon," said Meagan urgently, "that's where we need to be."

They joined the human chain that extended up from the brink and their added strength was enough to make a difference. Inch by inch now Darlingson was dragged back to safety, and the heavy keg after him. "What a relief!" said Meagan, letting out a long sigh. "And it took every one of... Well, almost every one of us. Where's Allen?"

There was the scuff of shoes on the ground behind here, and she turned quickly. "Allen, where have you been?"

He sounded like someone who has held his breath too long. "I buried the card ... my yellow press card. Lots of stones on top. Then put a little snack on the stones ... to **propitiate** the merical."

For a brief moment a look that could arise only from the mothering instinct appeared on Meagan's face. "A snack for the merical!" she cried. "Poor Allen—this has not been an easy night, has it? What you should do ..."

She never finished. Something like a storm front came sweeping up the slope. It was Darlingson, off on a wild race in the hope there was still time to warn Merci about the cider. Lumps was a few steps behind.

> **singular**: out of the ordinary, uncommon to the point of being note-worthy
> **preclude**: to shut out the possibility that something will happen or be done
> **commendable**: deserving to be praised or pointed out with approval

Of the two, Darlingson was faster, though only by a little. He had a **singular** ability to keep his footing—perhaps from his years on the fishing boats—and he ran surely on the loose ground, with no slips or stumbles. Lumps had less grace, falling several times on the scatter of stone and sand, but his determination was so fierce that he did not lag far behind.

Even before the two messengers vanished over the ridge, François was scrambling up the slope, and the others were following in a ragged line. With his jangled nerves Allen should not have been at the end of that line, but the rush of the moment **precluded** any attention to considerations of that sort, and there he was.

Even before the marchers had reached the top of the slope, he was hearing footsteps—behind him. "A product of Allen's fevered, fiction-writer brain, nothing more," he murmured bravely to himself, and continued walking, without turning his head. He reacted with the same **commendable** effort at self-control when he heard a voice softly calling his name, but he was very glad he had cast off the press card. Next, he thought nervously, probably a quack and a quack. And I may not be ready for ...

> **prevalent**: widely encountered; found in many or most cases
> **menagerie**: an assortment of caged or penned animals, often kept for show
> **obsolescence**: the condition of having been left behind by progress and having fallen out of general use

When it came, though, it was not a quack or a quock at all, but the soft, haunting cry of a whale. Meagan, just in front of Allen in the column, swung about and scolded, "You boys are the heroes of the hour, I admit. We'll probably start calling the town after you, and maybe the county. And as for baby names the **prevalent** choice for years to come ... Well, you get the idea. But for all that—leave Allen alone. It's been a rough mission."

Deep within Allen's brain the little calculators responsible for putting two and two together were working busily, and by the time he turned and saw the Farnum twins, he understood. "But not just whales," he said in a recovering tone. "You two aren't just whales, you're like ... an entire **menagerie**."

"A big collection," said Henry with pride, tapping lightly at his throat. "Whales, caribou, howler monkeys, monstrous ducks. We're them."

Allen could only agree, "You're them. And you're my next interview when we get out of here. And maybe you noticed—I left a little snack for you."

With François still in the lead, the column disappeared into the long tunnel. From far ahead, the darkness carried back to them the sound of running feet. Darlingson and Lumps were desperately pounding their way over the rocky course, trying to get out of the mountain. Even as they tore along, constantly overrunning the little circle of light that Darlingson's emergency lamp threw out before them, Lumps was worrying about the password. "I don't know how you got in, but to get out we're going to need a password. There's this voice-activation system—you say a password, and it opens the door to the outside. But Bezzle was always the one…"

A deafening crash pulsed back at them through the tunnel. Lumps was overjoyed. "Ha! Who needs voice activation now? It has just slipped into **obsolescence**! Bamalford has found a more modern way—crash the beer truck through the door, that's my guess."

> **aperture**: an opening or empty space in a wall, panel, etc., usually considered as letting something get through
> **zenith**: the highest point arrived at in some passage, development, evolution, etc.
> **muted**: reduced in loudness; made more quiet

A few minutes more of careening through the darkness, and Lumps saw how right his guess was. The mountain door—one of the lesser known accomplishments of Nameless Entrepreneur—was scrap. Ragged pieces of it were still in place about its edge, but a gaping hole had been smashed in its middle. As he emerged from the tunnel and stepped through this **aperture**, Lumps marveled at the destruction. "The man was in a hurry."

Casting a glance at Darlingson he added, "I know—and so are we."

The two of them picked their way through the litter of torn metal, and broke once again into a run. They were under the towering walls now, in the 40-Watt Defile, and they sprinted toward its entrance, counting its pale light a huge improvement over the inky black of the tunnel. As they emerged into the more generous breadth of Mercurial Canyon, they saw how the moon was near the top of a cloudless sky, and how from this **zenith** she was pouring down a silver tide. It seemed to dampen the sound of things. In its shimmering all the croaks and hoots rising up to them from the busy underbrush were **muted**, and even the grind of the beer truck far below lost some of its harshness.

The truck, easily **discerned** in the moonlight, was almost out of Mercurial Canyon. It was barreling down the shelf of granite that ran the canyon's length.

"That thing's gonna roll," warned Lumps. He and Darlingson were racing along and it was hard to talk, but he couldn't **refrain**. The scene below was too compelling. "When you see one going that fast you just stay back, and cross ..."

It was at that moment he spied the walker. In the high, lonely world of the tableland and the canyon, in the deepening hours of the night, you would have thought a population of one rider and two runners was quite enough. But tonight there was another, a walker.

Bamalford had just made his exit from the canyon and was skittering wildly onto that stretch of Victoria Road that passed in a long curve near the canyon mouth. He was heading for the Steeps. Coming from the opposite direction on the road there was a walker, the lone figure of a man, plainly visible under the high moon. He was marching with long strides over the tableland, as though on a vital errand.

The distance was closing rapidly between him and the truck. There was something alarming in the sight, and Lumps found enough breath to call out an unusual warning. "I'd be a little **paranoid** if I were you, and not so sure that everybody up here is your friend!"

It was a foolish outburst, he knew, for his voice would never reach that far. Yet it was nothing compared to the foolishness, the foolhardiness, of what happened next. Sensing the onrush of the truck, the stranger bent suddenly to the ground and caught hold of something, a long object, a pole, but bigger at one end. Then he stood at attention by the edge of the road, dangerously close, with the pole held upright in front of him and a bit to the side.

"It's my Slow sign," cried Lumps, "the one Calvin laughed at, and Merci hated. Look—the guy is crazy. It's the sort of thing I would do, but it'll never work. Fat chance!"

nemesis: one who habitually opposes you and often succeeds in making your life difficult and painful

The truck came raging on, and the stranger stood against it, stationed like a toy soldier at the edge of the road. He had nothing more than a plywood sign painted with the word SLOW in capital letters. But he held it high and defiant, with the message turned squarely against Bamalford.

"The **Quixotic** Slow," Lumps proclaimed in admiration. "It hasn't got a prayer, but I'll never forget the sight. Just don't crowd in too close. Just keep ... Ahh! Watch out!"

The **vignette** of a moment's encounter, on a high, moonlit plain, between a walker and a speeding truck had taken an ugly turn, and was about to intrude on the story at large. As the truck went shooting past the man, its side mirror caught the edge of the sign he was holding and pushed it violently against him. He went down under the blow.

Lumps gave a loud cry and began to run even faster. Darlingson kept pace, and soon they were through the lower stretches of Mercurial Canyon and drawing near the fallen stranger. The bright radiance of the moon revealed clearly a face that had so often regarded them with contempt. It was their **nemesis** and thorn, Calvin.

"Hold ... on!" struggled Lumps. "Why is he out here ... antagonizing Bamalford and ...?"

tangible: touchable; making an impression directly on your powers of perception; able to be confirmed by immediate observation rather than just by suggestion and inference
prognosis: a forecast of the likely outcome of some illness or injury
opulent: richly done; characterized by a show of abundant wealth and luxury

The struggle was worse for Darlingson. To go on and warn Merci was urgent in the extreme, but now the need of Calvin for help was urgent also. It was maddening, and his frustration was so **tangible** the air seemed to tremble with it. The indecision held him, but only for a moment, and then he broke from it, throwing himself into action, dropping to his knees beside the unconscious figure.

Calvin was still breathing, and deeply enough. He had a pulse, quick but regular. As for wounds, Darlingson found only an angry bruise, without swelling, on the side of the head where the sign had struck a glancing blow. All in all the **prognosis** was good. Calvin should probably be OK once he awoke.

Darlingson leapt up, greatly relieved, and gave Lumps a light push in the general direction of town. That was all the communication they needed—

Lumps would race ahead to warn Merci, Darlingson would remain and help Calvin.

Lumps cast one final look at his classmate, already groaning and starting to stretch a little. There was a deep riddle here. Calvin the fast-track boy, collecting **opulent** rewards from Bamalford, the fur-collared overcoats, the jewel-studded watches; and Calvin the walker, striding over the tableland through the vast simplicity of stone and moonlight. There were two Calvins now, and they were hopelessly at odds.

"Something happened," murmured Lumps to himself as he raced away. "Somebody found Calvin's switch, after most of us gave up thinking that he had one. I hope he's ... as happy as I am."

> **permeate**: to spread, as by flowing or streaming, into every part or corner of something
>
> **retort** (noun): a stinging reply, sometimes throwing back on the original speaker the accusation or insult that was carried by his statement

The truth was—Lumps felt happy as he never had before. The night still had hours to run, yet for him the hour was first morning, and he seemed to feel a quiet welling of sunlight across the mountain spaces. The desperate business of warning Merci still lay ahead, it would probably push him to his limits, and yet a lightheartedness was beginning to **permeate** every part of him. It had worked into his thoughts and emotions—the glorious news that he was free for good from the dark service of Bamalford.

"Laugh at your own jokes from now on!" He hurled the cry after the retreating hulk of the beer truck. It was still there to be seen, far ahead now, maintaining the reckless pace even as it drew near the edge of the tableland and the hairpin stretch of road dropping down the Steeps.

For a moment Lumps thought Bamalford had heard him and was screaming out some bitter **retort**. Through the flood of moonlight a muffled yell came carrying back from the truck. But when it shot out a second time, Lumps realized it was not a response at all. Wild now, and bellowing, it sounded like a single word, "Reptiles!"

> **serpentine**: marked by bends and twisting curves
>
> **preoccupied**: concerned or worried about something, and devoting all your attention to it
>
> **placid**: calm and at peace, often because of being content with your situation

An image formed suddenly before his mind—the sign that Merci had posted above the Steeps, at the side of the newly built road, to advise of "**Serpentine** Conditions." It stood just where Bamalford was passing, and he was

430

apparently reading it in a manner that had nothing to do with twists and turns in the road. But then the outcry came for a third time, and at that moment Lumps saw another reason why Bamalford was suddenly **preoccupied** with reptiles.

On the nameless little summit lifting up from the dry orchard at the base of the Steeps and overlooking the tableland, the great lizard was again on watch, regarding the moon. It was a reptile, though a less threatening one could not be imagined. It appeared completely **placid**, as though the silver sphere overhead met all its wants and left no reason to stir from its place.

> **semblance**: a faint likeness or similarity, often the likeness that something present or achieved only in part bears to what it would be if it were fully present or achieved
> **demolition**: the act of wrecking a structure, usually by knocking it completely to pieces
> **refrain** (noun): a phrase or other string of words that is repeated at regular intervals in a poem, song or speech

Bamalford, though, must have thought the lizard was on the point of attack, because he did the most insane thing possible. At the top of the Steeps, entering the zigzag that led down from the tableland, he accelerated. The result was inevitable. Although he navigated the first switchback by some miracle, there was no chance at the second. He must have perceived this, because he made not even the **semblance** of an attempt to get through the sharp curve. He let the truck go barreling straight off the road and take its own way down the granite face. Almost at once his speed went from excessive to hair-raising. Neither steering nor braking could have done much at the moment except pitch the vehicle into a disastrous tumble.

His luck was the Bad Pony. The truck went sweeping at a long angle toward it, merged into its flow, and dashed with it down the last of the Steeps. Bamalford had found a different highway for his escape from the terrors of the high places.

Sometimes rolling on the stream's hard bed, and sometimes bobbing in its waters, the big truck followed a swift course down the mountain. The upper bridges stood opposed, but it took them out, and the clatter of that **demolition** floated up softly, not only to Lumps, who was now drawing near the Steeps, but farther up and into the puzzled dreams of the waking Calvin.

READER: That was about the nine-millionth time we've had the scene of the lizard gazing at the moon.

AUTHOR: I know—it's getting to be like the **refrain** in a song.

READER: Strangely, though, this time Larry was really blown away, even to the point that …

AUTHOR: That he went out and bought a Gila monster.

READER: No, he went out and started gazing at the moon.

AUTHOR: Uh, oh. So like how was he when he came in?

READER: I don't know—he's still out there.

AUTHOR: This could be serious.

Chapter 61: NON-METEOROLOGICAL THUNDER

One moment Calvin would look around, almost alert, and the next he would slip back into a mumbling fog. He was **fluctuating** between these two states, struggling up toward consciousness, when the crack of breaking timber reached him. The same beer truck that had knocked him unconscious on the high tableland was now plowing through a bridge, somewhere below. His eyes clouded, and he murmured, "Not necessary one bit. Please don't keep stamping like that."

> **fluctuate**: to keep changing back and forth, this way and that, never attaching steadily to one alternative
> **genus**: a broad class or category of things
> **tome**: a big book, often scholarly

Then as he noticed Darlingson, his features cleared a little and he began to explain. "Rachel, you know. She's a stamper. And sort of a pain sometimes— she hated my whale painting, and the whole concept. But mainly she's—well, she's a different **genus** from us altogether. She's an angel, it appears. Sometimes they forget to hide it. Tonight she was watching the whales, holding Merci's hand—and she forgot to hide it. Her face was so intense, she was seeing so much—you could tell. And that was how she made her case. I made mine through the painting, and she made hers just by standing there, watching and seeing, never knowing what she did. And I wasn't ... I didn't ..."

His head nodded, and he fell back into a light sleep. It was obvious that a full recovery was not far off. When he woke again, Darlingson was pointing up Mercurial Canyon, trying to indicate that others would soon appear from that direction. Calvin, though, misunderstood the gesture. "Right. Mercurial Canyon. Many strange bugs and odd creatures. They will be in Joannie's book, a very large book, and very scientific. Joannie's **Tome**, Art by Calvin. That's what we called it, back when ... But where is she? I was on the beach, and someone said they spotted her, and Meagan and the others, climbing Cape Scurrility, maybe coming up here, maybe ... Huh? Looks like you're outta here."

Clutching Calvin by the shoulder for a moment, Darlingson smiled faintly and expressively—as though to say that the new Calvin was quite a different customer—and then bolted away. He had to get down to the beach, to the huge kettle, with the steaming cider from which Merci would be the first to drink.

> **stupendous**: so huge or great as to be astonishing

portent: an object in which you perceive a sign of what is to come
belated: happening only after the right moment or scheduled hour has already passed

He knew that Lumps would arrive first and would give the warning if one could still be given. That didn't matter—Darlingson ran as though the contest were his alone. On a straight and plunging line down the face of the Steeps he flew in great bounds, airborne as often as not. He was already beyond the ancient orchard and tearing in the direction of the upper bridges, when a blast shot through the canyon of the Bad Pony. It was a **stupendous** sound, swelling and definitive, and not even the flood of moonlight could muffle it.

He was jolted but not surprised, for he had felt the **portent** of worse to come when, earlier, the crash and shatter of the bridges themselves had rattled across the tableland. Now with the thunderous report shaking through the canyon, he had no doubt that somewhere farther down the fleeing truck had hurled against a massive object of one sort or another and almost certainly been destroyed. And whether Bamalford had leapt free he could only wonder.

Darlingson sped down the road, slowing only to pick his way across the ruins of the bridge where he and Lumps had set the piling last November. As he swept into the lower elevations of the canyon he expected to see at any moment the wreckage of the truck. None appeared, though, and he began to wonder about the school building—could the truck have made it that far? But that would mean it crossed the East Bridge and ...

A more important question was suddenly pressing for his attention. Should *he* cross East Bridge? The question had arisen **belatedly**—it deserved more than a few seconds of thought, but that was all the time that remained now, because the bridge was already in sight. To cross it, and race down the meadow, by the school and onto the cape, and then drop with the bending path to the beach—that was the land route, the only route, unless—

voluminous: taking up lots of space; having much bulk or mass
haphazard: resulting simply from chance or momentary enthusiasm, desire, etc., rather than from careful planning
embroil: to draw someone or something into a situation of complexity, disorder and strife

Never breaking stride Darlingson left the road, hurtled out onto a spur of stone, and launched himself into the surge of the Bad Pony. That was the water route—direct and swift. And very bruising. Brimming with melt from the high snow, the stream had a **voluminous** supply of water with which to renew its torrents.

Where the flow ran cleanly through channels of stone, with lines of silver combed on the back of the dark current, Darlingson let it carry him. But at many points boulders lay across the bed, scattered in **haphazard** patterns as though dropped around carelessly by the giants of Ricky's dreams. And there the stream became **embroiled** as it went churning through the complex gateways. Darlingson took a hard pounding at these spots, and he escaped more serious injury only by a furious effort, half swimming and half pushing away, to avoid a head-on crack against the rocky hurdles.

> **implore**: to beg somebody, in urgent and desperate terms, to do something
> **intemperate**: not setting any limit on the expression of your emotions or the satisfaction of your desires; going to excess
> **resilience**: the ability to keep bouncing back after troubles and defeats

Throughout all the battering there was a single image before him—he saw Merci scaling the ladder to the rim of the huge kettle, with a pretty cup in her hand. Maybe Lumps was there already, **imploring** her to empty the cup and come back down. If it were anybody else, he thought—giving the warning or receiving it … But those two … Merci would be outraged, her speech would be **intemperate**. And the names she would call poor Lumps, he didn't even …

The stream left no further chance for thought. It was tumbling now through the bends of a channel overhung with branches. The turbulence grew and grew and then suddenly there was no turbulence at all, as the ride simplified into a single motion—falling.

He dropped through the night, wild with despair. A hard smash on the granite below, or whatever lay below, and his race to help Merci would be over. For all his **resilience** he couldn't spring back from that.

Darlingson was a big man, and he hit like a meteor, splattering wet sand in all directions and carving a sizable crater, which at once filled in with water. He was on the beach. Nothing was broken, but he felt dazed and only half conscious. He sat there as the Bad Pony crashed around him and went splashing by.

> **oscillate**: to curve back and forth across a centerline or between contrary positions
> **stupor**: a condition in which shock, drunkenness, pain, etc., so overpower you that you are numb and only half conscious
> **pugnacity**: a disposition to resolve things through a struggle or fight rather than to let them pass quietly

It became a wide stream now, and a shallow one, swinging back and forth in even curves across the sand. Its **oscillating** flow, speckled with moonlight, inspired a sense of well-being, and cast an enchantment. You could sit for a long time and …

Then he heard the taunt, though only in his mind—Boom box! Just as though Bamalford were there, laughing at his helpless **stupor**, and claiming victory.

His jaw set and his hand tightened into a fist. The taunting was premature—Bamalford would not win so easily! Sheer **pugnacity** was at work now, driving Darlingson to rally his scattered powers.

He struggled to his feet. Go to the north, he told himself—the kettle and the people and Merci with her cup are a little ways to the north. He forced himself to begin a rapid march in that direction, but once he had come clear of some huge drift logs and gained an unbroken view, he stopped. Where was everybody?

> **muse** (noun): a divine principle or figure that quietly furnishes inspiration to a poet or artist
> **periphery**: the outer edge or margin of something

The kettle part of Whalefest was the most lighthearted, and there should be dancers, bonfire makers, kite fliers—and the poets, calling on their **muses**, making up their poems. But the beach was empty. He swung about savagely as the realization hit him. He was going the wrong way. The fall had left him disoriented. He had lost time.

His swiftness now was like the charge of a great cat. Sand flew up from his feet, and the breath tore in his throat. In only a minute or two he was overtaking stragglers. Moments more and he reached the **periphery** of a wide throng. In a headlong burst he swept toward its center, pulling up short, however, when he heard the voice of Merci.

A shock of relief passed over him. She was there, perched on the ladder that leaned against the kettle, and obviously unharmed. A closer look, though, showed how everything still hung in the balance. There was a steaming cup in her hand, and she held it before her defiantly.

"Won't I, Lumps?" she was yelling. "I'll drain it, OK, because this is your sickest joke yet! When are you going to work in the wart?"

Lumps was sopping wet, and still wild-eyed from his own bruising ride down the Bad Pony. "It's not a joke," he cried despairingly. "The cider may be poisoned—that's the sort of world we live in! It's not a joke. Please, Merci ..."

> **rend**: to tear something, often in a forceful manner and as the expression of strong emotion
> **transitory**: being in full effect for just a short time, and then vanishing
> **virtuoso**: one who has completely mastered the techniques of an art and who now is capable of brilliant performances in it

She lifted the cup toward her mouth. Lumps shouted "No!" and, scarcely realizing what he did, put both hands to his collar and tore his shirt down the front.

Merci screamed at him. "Right on, Lumps. **Rend** your garments. How theatrical. You're as good as Bamalford, and a wrecker too, a lousy, lousy wrecker. This was my moment—**transitory**, fleeting, I know—but my moment, when I stood here for a few seconds, calm and grown-up, and everybody would say she's not a brat anymore. And now look at me—shrieking like a brat! In fact—a **virtuoso** brat, giving this amazing performance, all because of your sick joke about the cider being poisoned. Well, here's to you. I drink your health, wrecker."

For a moment, as Merci offered the furious toast, the steaming cup was held high. Then its rim was at her lips. And then—after the strange thunder—it lay on the ground, its contents untasted and spilled into the sand.

The thunder of a voice never heard before in Dropanchor had broken suddenly across the scene—"Young lady, put that cup down!" The command was not repeated, but there was such authority in the voice that uttered it, that once was enough. Merci had not hesitated—she had thrown the cup from her hand, murmuring something that might have been "Yes sir!"

A wondering look played on her face. The voice had never been heard before, but it carried qualities of strength and care that were familiar to her since she was little. "Darlingson!" she cried. In a moment she was down the ladder, and dashing through the crowd. "Darlingson—it was you."

> **exalt**: to lift something up into a position of high importance or esteem
>
> **impromptu** (adjective): made up on the spot and for the occasion, without prior preparation or planning
>
> **meteorological**: related to weather and weather patterns, and to the study of them

She knew something extraordinary had happened, and she seized the hand of the giant figure joyously. "Your name ... well, your name will be **exalted**, that's what. It will be written in the skies along with all the other ..."

Someone cut in, breathless, with a trace of amusement. "You sound ... like the people in the Bible." It was François, gasping for air after a tumbling sprint down the mountain and a wild trespass over the Framley estate.

Merci's joy rose even higher, and she surrounded her sister with an **impromptu** dance. "There was thunder, but not ... weather. It was what you would call ... Non-**Meteorological** Thunder, if you must always be so precise. It was him ... he ... Darlingson, don't you see?"

François pulled in several long drafts of air. "Does this dance have a name? Maybe ... Oh, Merci—you came so close! If he hadn't gotten here ... Do you have any idea?"

Merci, however, was not interested in the peril she had avoided. "Look, François," she cried again. "He can speak."

> **elicit**: to call forth some expression or reaction from a person, usually by subjecting him to some stimulus such as an insult, an encouragement, a challenge, etc.
>
> **docility**: a cooperative, unprotesting attitude that makes you an easy person to teach or lead
>
> **deprecate**: to criticize in a mild or roundabout way; to play down the importance of something

François paused and studied something in Darlingson's face. Then she answered very gently to her sister. "I think it's better to say 'He spoke.' You were in the extreme of danger, and that **elicited** a ... a reaction from him, a cry that blew right past the forces normally blocking his speech. Almost like a miracle, but I'm afraid—a one-time miracle."

Merci slowly saw the truth of what François said. "Well," she demanded, "where is Sallie? Did she film it—when he spoke—that one time in his life?"

There was a tugging at her gown, and suddenly Rachel was at her side again, scolding her. "You told Sallie to stay on the ship, remember? You can't blame Sallie, no ma'am."

Darlingson himself shot a Going-crazy? look at Merci, and she had to laugh. "Umm—basically true. I asked her not to film me at the kettle, and she understood and was very nice about it. So she stayed on board *Jack's Equator* for more footage of the whales, and she sent Uncle Reggie here on shore—without a camera—to make some notes. But these are all just details—she should have been here, filming the six words of Darlingson!"

"And filming Merci as she obeyed the six words," added François. "Such **docility**. For once, no lip, huh sister!"

The conversation went on for some time, darting and spirited, and it might have continued until sunrise except for a nasty interruption. A disturbance came pushing through the rings of people around Darlingson and the two sisters. It slowly barged its way to the center, at last stopping squarely before Merci, and materializing as the hulking form of Ms. Framley.

READER: Fulano has a very catchy example of "belatedly."
AUTHOR: Did I use ...? Oh yeah—at the beginning of the chapter.

READER: Just listen, OK. "He dropped off his shirt at the cleaners and then got busy with other things and time passed and spring lengthened into summer and civilizations rose and fell and mountain ranges emerged from the earth's mantle and finally 281 million years later he remembered and he went to the cleaners to pick it up and they said to him, 'Sir, you've come back rather belatedly' and they charged him an extra $0.80 storage fee."

AUTHOR: I know that as a rival author I'm supposed to make some **deprecating** comment—like, not half bad if it had a few more punctuation marks—but actually it's fantastic. It makes you beg for more. Suppose the same guy leaves the water running for a billion years, or forgets the cheese out on the counter, or ...

READER: Shouldn't you be opening the next chapter?

Chapter 62: TRIAL BY POTABILITY

It was clear from her scowl that Ms. Framley wasn't there to congratulate Darlingson on regaining speech, or to **commiserate** with him on losing it again. In her world people like Darlingson had no place talking, and Merci needed to learn that. "A year older, a year dumber, aren't you, goblin girl? You're all gaga about the big ape talking. But he's not meant to talk. We don't want him to talk. It would be obscene."

> **commiserate**: to feel sad about someone's suffering, and to express sympathy for it
> **castigation**: a punishment or affliction someone imposes on you, often in the form of a severe tongue-lashing
> **seditious**: poisoning opinion against the governing authorities, and stirring people to rebellion

Merci was caught off guard by this **castigation**. "But it was beautiful, after so many years of silence. How can you …?"

"Beautiful!" shrieked the unhappy woman. "What would you know about beauty? It was obscene and … **seditious**. Yes—seditious. With six words he inspired disrespect for the law, and disobedience. Six more, and he'll pull down the state."

"Disobedience?" murmured François, uncomprehending.

"Disobedience!" There was an impatient shake of the head, a jangling of ornaments. The golden spoon swung like a tiny pendulum from Ms. Framley's ear. "Your sister had a duty to drink that cider. She was the first lady, and under the law of Dropanchor the duty of the first lady is to drink from the kettle—first. But did she? Tell me that!"

> **condolence**: a word or sign by which you extend sympathy to someone
> **maltreatment**: treatment that is harmful or abusive
> **pomposity**: the exaggerated use of formalities, high speech, ceremonies and show, often to inflate your own importance

Merci and François were so thunderstruck that it was Lumps who finally gave an answer. "Not joking at all, Ms. Framley, but that was really sick. I mean—we think the kettle may have been poisoned. Does that matter, just a little? I mean—if you're that sick, I'm going to send a sympathy card. I'm gonna…"

"I could care less for your **condolences**! And you couldn't read the card anyway, clod."

Merci's anger found a tongue. "You leave Lumps alone! I've already acted like a witch toward him tonight. And if he can't read the card he sure read you, and you spell sick, just like he said!"

The sight of Merci regretting her **maltreatment** of Lumps, and then dishing out the same to Ms. Framley, was too much for Darlingson. He broke into a wide smile, and shook his head in wonder. It was the worst possible thing he could have done.

Ms. Framley was provoked beyond tolerance. "Baboon!" she screamed. "First the wart girl won't drink the cider. And now this ... this primate starts grinning at me. There's a growing lack of respect around here. Perhaps we are forgetting what is owed by the lower ranks to the higher. Perhaps a reminder would help."

With a heavy finger she pointed at Mayor Povano, standing some ways off, and ordered, "Bring the pudgy one here, and let him spread his outer garments before me, that I may trample upon them."

"That would be **pomposity**, Victoria, and it could never bring you a particle of happiness." The answer was from Grandma Dubois, who was at Merci's side. Her voice was restrained, with little of its usual sharpness.

> **hedonism**: a way of life that treats pleasure as the supreme good
> **balm**: an ointment that comforts and heals; something that gives relief, comfort and healing to body or spirit
> **patronize**: to treat someone with an insulting degree of gentleness or helpfulness, as though he is a child who will be at a loss without your guidance

"And then," continued Ms. Framley, ignoring the advice, "take the goblin child and the baboon, and this old sorceress besides, and make them drink of the cider. They're afraid it might not be as pleasant as they expected, as though all that matters in life is pleasure. That is what we call **hedonism**, isn't it, class? And Abner warned against it long ago, when he wrote this."

From a pocket on her hip she pulled a yellowing document—the Dogmatic Lease. She was paging through it, and would have read from it, but there was another interruption. Povano came hurrying forward, with his jacket in his hands. "If I thought, Victoria, that spreading this on the ground could bring you some peace, I would do it. But the real answer, for someone ... in your situation, doesn't lie in humiliating the mayor. It lies—I believe more and more—in Whalefest itself. This festival has so much **balm** for ... for wounded souls that ..."

441

"That's what you think of me!" screamed Ms. Framley, with a violent up-sweep of her arms. A crackling came from the brittle pages of the lease. "I'm a human shipwreck, and you're this we-care type with all the answers, who's going to show me the way, as a favor. Well, I won't be **patronized**. I ... I'm furious, I'm so furious!"

> **parity**: a rough equivalence, as between two prices, two sets of resources, two social positions, etc.
> **medium**: a substance or material in which a message is expressed or through which it passes
> **slight** (noun): the insult that consists of being ignored or treated as someone of trivial worth

She swung her arms again, pounding her fists down against some imaginary tabletop. Again the aging paper in her hand gave off its dry crackle. And this time it caught her attention. "I was going to read from this. But now"—her lip curled, and her voice flatted to a snarl—"I'm going to tear it up! On national TV! I may be outnumbered here, a million to one, but there will soon be **parity**. I'll have my million also—intelligent viewers, cheering as I rip this baby up and take back the high school. So where is that Sallie hussy and her television camera? Where?"

She wheeled around, looking here and there, and her dark frown as much as said, "Where have you fools hidden that television woman?" The ship caught her eye, and she paused, remembering, and then bellowed, "So that's where you are! Forget those stupid fish and get back in here—the action now is me, ripping up this lease. And in the morning the action will be me—when I take a hammer to the high school, 'cause that thing is coming down. Haargh!"

There was no chance of Ms. Framley's shout reaching its destination. The ship lay out a good distance from shore, and a ways to the north. And the air, thick with the endless rumble of the surf, was a poor **medium**. Yet when there was no answer, she took it personally. "It's a **slight**," she fumed. "Sallie's giving me the shoulder, trying to ignore me. That girl needs to know who runs it! And she will."

> **dory**: a boat that is sharply upturned at the front, fit for passing through breaking waves without swamping
> **sate**: to satisfy an appetite to the point of weariness and disgust
> **epithet**: (1) a bad name you call someone; (2) a short descriptive "label" that you use in place of someone's name

For a moment Ms. Framley fell silent, staring expectantly at Mayor Povano. When he did nothing, she snapped, "The **dory**, fool! Have the dory ready. Everybody gets one turn, right, to row the dory out to the ship and then—like someone on a pastry binge—to feast on the sight of whales until

442

sated. Isn't that right? Now it's my turn, and if I skip the whale nonsense and go directly to my business with Sallie—seeing to it once and for all that she learns her place—no one should complain. And when that's taken care of, then she can film while I rip up this."

She was walking now, angling northward toward the point where the dory was beached. Her indignation was still at an extreme pitch, and she was muttering as she went along. The goblin, the baboon, the fat mayor—her speech was a stream of **epithets**. Again and again she lifted her head, as though appealing to a high judge or panel of judges with authority to convict the dreadful people around her. That was why she did not see the water, until it was up to her ankles and pouring into her boots.

"A tide pool," she shrieked. "Where is Povano? Why do we even have a mayor if he can't keep our beaches dry?" She splashed on to the other side.

> **nebulous**: not sharply defined; fuzzy, indistinct, fogged over
> **decipher**: to make a coded message comprehensible, usually by restating it in ordinary language

The mayor in fact was not far off. There was a small crowd coming along behind Ms. Framley, also going to the dory, and Povano was in the lead. François was there, and Allen and Ricky and all those who had come racing down from the mountain, including the Farnums and Bezzle. Even Calvin had appeared at the last moment, tottering, and mumbling **nebulous** remarks about the recent past, the distant past, things to be erased and things to be restored. Joannie was at his side, supporting him, trying to **decipher** what he was saying.

As Ms. Framley bent to squeeze water from her boots, she caught sight of the group coming behind her. "Stop following me! Stop staring, stop wondering what it's like to have the perfect body."

The mayor tried to calm her down. "It's nothing like that, Victoria. Most of the young people with me have been on a very difficult mission tonight, on the mountain, and now they just wanted their turn to see a whale and ..."

> **clemency**: the disposition to deal gently with wrongdoers, either granting pardon or lightening punishment
> **amphibian** (noun): a creature that routinely passes part of its time in water and part on land
> **abstruse**: dealing with a complex or remote subject matter, often in technical or otherwise hard-to-follow terms

"And here I am!" gasped Ms. Framley with indignation. "That is unpardonable. You may go down on your knees and beg, but there will be no **clemency**. You'll pay in full for that remark!"

443

She stamped off in the direction of the dory, but after a minute she swung round again. "And we can skip the little conversations. You look like a bunch of babbling **amphibians**."

The mayor and his band were wading through the water now. Bezzle and Peter Oakum were at Povano's side, Bezzle with a book in his hand, and the three of them were talking in low voices. Darlingson was at the edge of this little group, listening intently.

On hearing the taunt about the babbling amphibians, Peter looked up sharply. "Oh yes—we're babbling here, the three of us. In English, by the way. And look—François and Merci doing the same, though maybe in French. And there's Ricky babbling with his little sister, perhaps using the Portuguese that Tedesco taught them. Which does raise a question, Victoria. Tell me, do you see any babbler here babbling in a universal language? Don't be alarmed. Just a riddle, to entertain you."

Ms. Framley would have nothing to do with an **abstruse** question like that. She glared furiously at Oakum. "Old fools may play at their puzzles, but I have better things to do."

Peter remained silent, but Darlingson, whose very existence was an affliction to the woman, chose this moment for an odd little ritual that was a further puzzle in its own right. He halted near the middle point in the crossing of the water. In his hand was a ceramic cup, the one that Merci had thrown down. Now he gave it the most thorough washing it had ever received, scrubbing it repeatedly in the water at his ankles, scouring it with sand, rinsing it over and over. Finally, he dipped it one more time, filling it up. Then he looked to Peter, who said simply, "Wait."

> **whet**: to sharpen the insistence of an appetite or desire for satisfaction
> **prow**: the front-most part of a ship; the jutting nose of a ship, formed by the two sides running together
> **wright** (usually used in compounds such as "boatwright," "wagonwright," etc.): a skilled maker of some class of objects, especially objects in wood, such as ships, wagons, etc.

"No doubt you think that **whets** my curiosity," barked Ms. Framley. "Well—forget it. I could care less why the big ape is drawing a cup of water. He can draw another one for all I care. He has his business—idiotic though it be—and I have mine." She waved the Dogmatic Lease at them, and stormed off toward the dory, grumbling as she went.

The dory was a good-sized wooden boat, whose high sides and upswept **prow** made it ideal for shuttling people across the line of waves between *Jack's Equator* and the shore. For all its virtues, however, Ms. Framley detested it because of its close tie with Grandma Dubois. It had been built locally, after Grandma had put up the money for it, explaining, "Now the young people can stay around here and become boat**wrights**."

"Nosy old fool," growled Ms. Framley, as she hauled herself on board and settled onto a wooden bench. "Let them drift away to the big cities and become nameless cogs. Am I supposed to care?"

She spied the boat keeper, waiting at a little distance down the beach. He had just brought the dory in from a run, and was resting in the crook of a stone. "Up, tramp!" she called. "Come aboard and row me out to the ship. Oh—it's squeakface."

The boat keeper was Squeaky, the timid freshman. He swallowed hard twice and then, to the amazement of Ms. Framley, responded in an impressively deep voice, not much above a bass. "During Whalefest, ma'am, the rule is that I can't go until all the benches are full."

> **evanescent**: having only a fragile hold on existence; vanishing away like smoke
> **circumvent**: to frustrate a law by finding some clever way around it

"Not again," she moaned, on the edge of despair. "First the baboon, now you. He wasn't meant to talk at all, and you're supposed to squeak, the way nature intends, not rumble like a rockcrusher. But I'm sure your little victory is **evanescent**—once this Whalefest insanity is over, you'll squeak again."

On every bench she was placing an item—a scarf, a hat, a handbag. "All the benches are full. Row me to the ship."

"Ma'am," answered Squeaky, hitting one high, fluting note before settling back into the lower registers, "we will not **circumvent** the rule like that. The benches must be full of people. And anyway ..."

Mayor Povano and his troop were arriving, and surrounding the dory. Half of them clambered on at once, seizing oars, and half, waiting for the next high wave, shoved the boat down the beach and into the surf. The tide was rising, and the breakers leaned against them, pushing them back toward the sand.

"Row, ye sons and daughters," called Squeaky, his voice still rich and deep.

Meagan could not resist—she left her oar, slipped forward in the pitching boat and gave him a warm embrace, declaring, "My captain and my love."

> **dally**: to let time slip by while you amuse yourself or chat idly
> **consign**: to put something in the possession of another person, often on the condition that he use it, care for it or dispose of it in some specified manner
> **extemporaneous**: (1) made up or pieced together on the spot, without advance preparation or rehearsal; (2) spoken in spontaneous fashion

> **trite**: (used mostly to describe words and expressions) stale, unin-
> spired; worn down from too much use, and now lacking impact and
> appeal

It was glorious and overwhelming, and for a moment Squeaky was like someone picking up spilled packages—grabbing his wits, grabbing his memory. But very soon he had put it all together again and was sending Meagan back to her bench. "Gladly would I **dally** with thee, maid, but duty has **consigned** into my care this vessel and all who go upon it."

Peter Oakum laughed out loud. "They do babble don't they, Victoria?"

"And the pot calls the kettle black, doesn't it, old man?" She paused, and there was a little swivel of her head, as though something had just caught her attention. "Ha! Another one! Another great proverb. I can't help it. They come crowding into my mind. I invent them on the spot—**extemporaneous**, you know. That one will go in the paper."

Even as the dory tossed in the waves Peter Oakum held his gaze steadily on her. "You know you didn't make it up, Victoria. The pot calling the kettle black is already **trite**, it's been around so long and used so much. But I did make something up tonight—a riddle that you didn't like. Listen again—which babbler babbles in a universal language?"

> **imbue**: to soak into the material of something and mark it, in the way
> that dye soaks into and colors a fabric
> **potability**: the fitness of water or other fluids to be drunk without
> harm
> **spartan**: practicing a self-discipline in which you accept simple,
> harsh living conditions, and put up with pain or danger bravely and
> without fuss

She cast him a chilling look, and said nothing.

Peter pressed on. "I'll give you a clue. I'll give you the answer!" He was on one of the oars and the labor broke up his speech, yet his tone was **imbued** with a deep sense of assurance. "A brook! A brook babbles in a universal language, understood by everyone. I thought of that back there on the beach when we were wading through that ... brook."

Sensing, although vaguely, some challenge to her empire, Ms. Framley snarled back, "That was no brook. It was salt water—a tide pool, some such stupid thing."

Peter was still looking steadily at her, and now he shook his head. "Wrong, I'm afraid. That was a flowing stream of fresh water, a babbling brook."

She exploded with irritation. "Then drink, old man! Go ashore, take a drink. I'll believe it is fresh water when somebody drinks it. And if no one does, the verdict is simple—you're not just a fool, but a liar besides."

446

"Trial by **Potability** it shall be," answered Peter, very calmly. He gave a slight nod, and Darlingson, resting on his oar, took up the ceramic cup from its place on the rowing bench. It still contained the water that he had dipped from the shallows they waded through. He had taken great care in the last few minutes, as they came tossing on the surf, to prevent the cup from being overturned.

READER: You know the part where Squeaky has a voice like a rockcrusher.

AUTHOR: Yeah, I like that part.

READER: Larry says that's what the ancient Greeks would do, to become better speakers—they would put rocks in their mouth and crush 'em.

AUTHOR: Er—that could hurt. I think they just tried to speak with a stone in their mouth, but didn't go crushing anything.

READER: No—Larry says the ancient Greeks were a lot more **spartan** than we are.

AUTHOR: Well, some of them, of course, actually ... No, that's OK, let's move on.

Chapter 63: CHICANERY CREEK

Darlingson held the ceramic cup on display for a moment, like an object of evidence in a trial, and then drank down the water it contained, easily and without any show of discomfort. When he finished he set the cup gently on the bench once again and returned to his rowing.

> **superfluous**: in excess; over and above the amount you need or can put to use
> **chicanery**: a clever deception, often involving some fake logic or misapplication of the law, by which you gain some advantage
> **vacuous**: empty of intellectual or cultural content; blank, and without sign of insight or understanding

In Peter's view, that was enough proof. "More would be **superfluous**," he said to Ms. Framley. "We go wading through some water, Darlingson draws a cup of it, now he drinks that cup without any trace of difficulty. That's enough to make it pretty obvious ..."

"Pretty obvious," cried Ms. Framley, struggling to rise to her feet, "that something terribly cute is going on." The dory dropped down the back of a wave, and she lost her balance, sitting heavily. "Pretty obvious," she persisted, "that there's some **chicanery** here. You've taught your orangutan how to drink salt water, in order to fool me, to make me think a tide pool is a freshwater stream. It's a dirty game. You're after what is mine, I'm sure of it."

A huge comber passed under the dory and lifted it high. "Look!" It was the voice of Merci. She was gazing back toward the beach. For a moment, riding the crest of the wave, all of them—even Ms. Framley—saw it. The water where Darlingson had dipped his cup was part of a moonlit stream, flowing out from the once dry gully between Cape Scurrility and Ms. Framley's mountain slope, and running in easy curves over the sand.

For an instant Ms. Framley was at a complete loss. Her face collapsed into a **vacuous** gape, and her head rolled dumbly to one side. Yet before the boat came sliding into the trough behind the giant comber, she was already recovering. "So ... so Dropanchor has a new stream. Well ... we can call it Chicanery Creek. I know trickery and deception are the forces which put it there. I just don't know how. Anyway—let's give it a name and move on."

> **pedagogical**: oriented toward helping people learn; more generally, having to do with the art of teaching

lucidity: the excellence by which something written or spoken is especially clear and laid open for the mind to comprehend
incessant: going on and on, without stopping or pausing

"It has a name," said Peter sternly. "It's called the Bad Pony."

He looked around at the others in the dory. There was confusion on many of the faces, and it stirred what he sometimes called his **pedagogical** instinct. He had never been a teacher, but he liked to give explanations, to bring people to comprehension.

"A major event," he began, "took place on the mountain tonight." He was still working his oar as he spoke. "Joannie is my source for much of this, and she tells me that the huge reddish pillar of granite by East Bridge—the Giuseppe Stone—was struck by a runaway beer truck, just a couple of hours ago. The truck was almost certainly destroyed. The driver was … Bamalford, and we have no idea what happened to him. Ironbane is up there now looking for him—with two paramedics just in case. And the stone pillar—much more delicately balanced than we ever suspected—was knocked from its place. And that has let the Bad Pony …"

"Escape from its channel?" asked Squeaky, following the story closely even as he struggled at the rudder to hold the boat on line.

"Escape from its channel, and return to its channel," answered Peter.

He saw the questioning looks. "OK, I know, not a model of **lucidity**. Here—let's say it's all about two gullies, running up from the beach, and merging—almost—at East Bridge. The front gully, lying in front of the school, has carried the Bad Pony for as long as we can remember. The back one, cutting along behind the school, has been dry. So far, very elementary, I know. Now if you follow the back gully all the way up, starting at the beach, coming past Cape Scurrility, the school, the long grassland, you ultimately bump into the Giuseppe Stone, the seaward side of it. And, of course, as you're bumping into the seaward side of the stone the Bad Pony is hurling against the opposite side, bouncing away, passing under East Bridge and flowing down the front gully. But—did anyone notice?—in my description I don't say *incessantly* hurling against the stone, *incessantly* bouncing away, and so forth."

"I noticed," said Mayor Povano helpfully.

"Thank you, Marion. I don't say it because I cannot—those familiar activities have ceased, and when I describe the hurling against and the bouncing away I am describing what no longer exists. The Giuseppe Stone has been knocked from its place. It was a plug, and the plug has now been pulled—the back gully is open. And the Bad Pony has jumped—for the last two hours, and maybe for all time to come, it is pouring down that gully, flowing behind the school."

terse: expressed in (or expressing oneself in) phrases that are short, compact and well constructed
immutable: fixed and unchanging; resistant to any variation

As Ms. Framley listened, her eyes grew narrow, and she looked set to pounce, like some overgrown leopard. "I will be **terse**," she snarled. "I will compress my words like vacuum-packed coffee. All this talk is about my boundary, isn't it? Well, the boundary of my property is the Bad Pony—as it flowed on the day of the grant, not today!"

A tense silence followed, until at last she exploded, "Duh! Alright, dunces, here's the expanded version. When your beloved Captain Farnum granted land to Abner, the southern boundary was 'the leaping brook,' and that meant the Bad Pony, as it flowed at that time. Got it? As it flowed, where it flowed *at that time*—which by the way was over there." She pointed vaguely through the moonlit night toward what Peter had called the front gully, the one that ran along the south of Cape Scurrility, passing in front of the school. It was, of course, the gully that for as long as anyone remembered had been the channel of the Bad Pony.

Glaring fiercely at Peter Oakum, she continued. "That's my property line, old pest. Yes, it includes the school. And yes, it is **immutable**. Once it's fixed, it's fixed. So the school is still on my property. At least for now. After I tear this up"—she waved the lease again—"the school won't be on anybody's property, because it's coming down, brick by brick. And ... and that's very nice of you to wave back, Mr. Bezzle, but frankly you look like an idiot."

The dory was past the breakers and closing steadily on *Jack's Equator*. Bezzle had risen to his feet, holding out before him an old book with leather binding and yellowing pages. He started to speak, Peter Oakum started to speak, and Povano, clearing his throat, quietly overrode them both.

phenomena (plural; the singular is phenomenon): the raw data of reality (the images and appearances, the motions and occurrences, etc.) which present themselves to our perception prior to any interpretation or theoretical analysis
ethereal: (1) made or appearing to be made from the most immaterial elements such as light and air; (2) related to the upper realms of the sky

"This is for the mayor, I'm afraid. The old book, Victoria, which Maurice Bezzle is holding, which he pulled from the library only an hour ago—it's the ship's log that Captain Jack kept. It's full of weather observations. I think the captain had this thing with weather. He didn't know much about its theory, but he recorded its **phenomena** with the greatest care, from the pounding squalls to those **ethereal** designs of lace that the winds draw in the highest clouds.

450

One entry, from one of the later voyages, is especially fascinating; and to the point, Victoria, to the point."

> **gargantuan**: impressively enormous; huge to an exaggerated degree
> **augmentation**: the process of causing something to become bigger, more numerous or more complete; the growth or increase resulting from that process

Povano took the book carefully from the hands of Bezzle. Holding it wide open under the moonlight, and bending over it closely, he was able to make out the text. "Listen to what old Jack writes.

> September 2, 1817. Nature at her fiercest today. During the early morning a storm of lightning fell upon the mountain. From a single roost of cloud three rays struck ferociously, one following the other, against a rounded summit, and pried out half of it, a **gargantuan** piece of reddish stone that at once began a crashing descent.
> In moments it plunged down the slope of which it had been the crown, and came tumbling onto the tableland. There it met obstacles that I thought would stop it—channels cut by the stream, boulders from prior storms. It dashed against them, and they stood in its way, tearing off pieces, sculpting the huge mass, slowing its speed, but ultimately failing to halt the onrush.
> In only a few seconds the fearsome stone was across the plateau and onto the steep granite faces that drop from there. Now it struck fire again and again, and the **augmentation** in its speed was terrible. As it flew into the upper end of the canyon where the stream runs, I lost sight of it, but I knew that if it emerged from the lower end there was nothing to prevent it from driving all the way and destroying the settlement."

"Go stone," growled Ms. Framley.

"Victoria—you don't have to react that way. To wish ill on others is to do far worse harm to yourself."

> **sententious**: overly inclined to deliver little sermons and other gems of moral wisdom
> **ricochet** (noun): the bouncing away of an object from a surface after striking it at an angle
> **interdict**: (1) to forbid further use, access or contact; (2) forcibly to block or cut off some channel of supply or communication

"I don't have to, but maybe I want to—old, **sententious** mayor!"

Povano sighed, finding his place in the journal again. "By this point Captain Jack was in great anxiety—

> I prayed not to see the stone again. Let the canyon smother it somehow. But even as I began to hope that it might be, the missile came shooting from the canyon's mouth, no longer rolling but tumbling madly, end over end. An awful moment, and yet only one moment later—we were

saved! It was most improbable, it was because of the little stream. You see—where the stream bends around the foot of the hillside that was granted to Abner Framley last year, its channel pinches in and runs narrow and deep. That was our luck. The stone—revolving through the air on one of its long **ricochets**—struck down in the stream, wedged violently but perfectly into the pinch—and never escaped. The hillside shook, the walls of the streambed were fractured, almost shattered, and the stone, I think, was very close to smashing through. But in the end its force was spent and it came to rest, standing upright now, a massive pillar rising from the water. The channel was blocked at once, and the flow of the brook was **interdicted** completely.

"Now," said the mayor, waving the old book at Ms. Framley, "what happens when a stream is interdicted, as Captain Jack puts it? It has to go somewhere, doesn't it, Victoria?"

"I wish you had to go somewhere!" shot back Ms. Framley. "I have never been so blabbered at! Why don't you swim the rest of the way, old mayor? It's not far to the ship now, and you could show us that you're fit for something. And I could have some peace."

> **deluge** (noun): a flood, typically one that is vast or overpowering
> **premise**: a statement taken as established and serving as a starting point from which you reason your way to conclusions

Povano shrugged off the bad humor. "It is almost over, Victoria. Listen to how Jack finishes the story.

> The currents poured against the reddish pillar and, finding no way by it, have been pooling higher and higher all this stormy day, until just an hour ago they broke through an earthen ridge that was helping to hold them back. There could easily have been a **deluge**, washing into the settlement, but again we have been fortunate. The stream found a new channel, another gully, along the south side of that ridge where Nathan insists the school should go, and there it is flowing at this moment. As for the gully along the north side—the stream's channel until this morning—it will be dry in two or three days once there is sun."

Povano returned the book to Bezzle, all the while holding Ms. Framley steadily in his gaze. "We accept your **premise**, Victoria. The boundary of your property is the leaping brook—as it flowed on the day when the property was granted to Abner."

> **implication**: something which has not been said in so many words but which can be understood from what actually has been said
> **depraved**: given over to evil habits; morally fallen, in the sense that one's tastes and preferences are oriented toward what is mean and evil

> **subsistence**: an economic condition in which you manage to stay alive but have little beyond the basic necessities

"And on that day," declared Ms. Framley, without the slightest regard for the **implications** of what the mayor had just read, "it flowed on the south side of the school ridge, right where it has flowed all our lives until tonight when some **depraved** teenagers ..."

"No," said Povano firmly. "I'm sorry, but it never flowed on the south side of the ridge before the day described by Captain Jack—the day of the stone. At all times before that, including the day of Abner's grant, it flowed where it's flowing now—at the foot of your hillside, between your hillside and the school ridge. All Abner got by that grant, and all you got, Victoria, was the hillside. Not the ridge, not the school."

The dory was easing alongside *Jack's Equator*, and Squeaky was making ready to tie up. Povano wanted to end on a gracious note. "It's Whalefest, Victoria, not a time for being enemies. There might still be a place for you at the school—in the library, maybe the kitchen. The pay wouldn't be much, barely more than **subsistence**, but that's irrelevant for someone with the investments I'm sure you have. And working that way you'd still be part of the scene ... it could be a new beginning, a ..."

> **seminal**: having an influence or effect which, like a seed, grows and grows over time, and eventually becomes very significant
> **convoluted**: complicated and hard to follow because of being all twisted about, wound around, folded in and out, etc.
> **vanguard**: the group of persons who are at the front, leading some movement or trend forward

"The kitchen!" screamed Ms. Framley. She was standing now, unsteadily, and panting with rage. "Chopping broccoli for the mini-quiches. The library! Writing call numbers on little teen romances. And for opportunities like these I should be paralyzed with gratitude. I should take this moment and frame it and call it the most **seminal** in my life. Yes, boys and girls, out of that moment of kindness there emerged a new and better existence for Victoria Framley. Well, everyone, I can't stand it anymore. This is a show of disrespect that has gone too far. Dreadfully sorry, old joke of a civil servant, but I am declining your offer of a place in the school, because when I'm done there will be no school to have a place in!"

She was holding the Dogmatic Lease in front of her, and now she finally did what for so many years she had threatened. She tore it in two, tore it again into fourths, and then in a frenzy reduced it to shreds. Half of these she hurled at Povano, and the rest at Bezzle.

Most of the pieces flew wide of their mark and landed in the water. "I hope Draco sees them!" she shrieked. "I hope he carts all your watery-eyed, mouth-breathing babies off to that Melanie's enforcement school. Ha—that's my curse on you. Curse number one, more to follow—many, many more. Big ones, small ones, simple ones, **convoluted** ones."

Povano's eyes were widening at this talk, and Peter Oakum laid a comfort-ing hand on the shoulder of his friend.

Ms. Framley barged on. She was swelling in her fury. "Yes, pudgy mayor, more to follow. I'm going up to the stone where that Serquiella babe used to write her gems, and I'm calling down more dooms on this pig hole than you can count."

Peter spoke quietly to the mayor. "There's nothing you can do to help her right now, Marion. And nothing she can do to hurt us. Let's get up the ladder and see a whale before they're gone."

READER: Larry says that all of a sudden the first six million pages were worth it when he came to that blinding climax about Ms. Framley ripping up the lease.

AUTHOR: That was raw action alright. Younger readers strongly cautioned!

READER: And then there was that stunning revelation that Captain Farnum was a weather freak.

AUTHOR: In the field of action writing I'm so far out in front that I'm in the **vanguard** of the vanguard.

READER: I just hope you can keep up the blistering pace.

AUTHOR: Strap in is all I can say.

Chapter 64: THE REALM OF TURPITUDE

Sallie was filming parts of her program on board *Jack's Equator*, and was near the end, when Mayor Povano and the others started coming over the rail.

"Invasion!" she exclaimed. "Pirates, revenue agents, thrill seekers—maybe all three. What a pity—my crew is signaling that we're almost out of time here on *The Last of the Unconventionals*. I'm supposed to start the closing routine—that is, if I could just find my unc … Oh!" She looked relieved. "There's the face loved by millions."

At that moment Ms. Framley came swinging on board in a special chair. She struggled out of it and lurched toward Sallie, muttering, "Billions, to be more precise."

> **malinger**: to fake a sickness so that you may be excused from school or work
> **hidebound**: rigidly and unbendingly attached to your customs and beliefs

A figure stepped around her to take a position in front of the camera. It was Uncle Reggie, his cape billowing on the late night breeze, his hat pulled down to keep it from blowing away. He waited as Sallie worked through the introduction. "Oh, **malingering** uncle—coming to work at last. He was loafing on shore, everyone, he had a story about an upset stomach. Too many waffles, maybe? But now he's here and … honestly, Uncle, why a waffle eater should be loved by millions is beyond me."

"It's the dignified manner," cried Henry Farnum. He had no second thoughts about breaking in—Uncle Reggie was fair game at all times.

"It's the totally undignified manner," called out Andrew Farnum.

Joannie was a loyal fan, and she yelled. "It's the stylish cape."

"No," shouted Meagan, "it's the highly original sign-off."

Sallie groaned. "Highly original sign-off! He does the same thing, show after show. I beg him for some variations, a little flexibility, but **hidebound** is hidebound, even when it's your uncle. Apparently any bending would break the man in two."

Uncle Reggie gave his cape a twirl.

"I know," laughed Sallie. "For once there's nothing you can say. Well, do the sign-off, and we'll close out one of the greatest episodes ever filmed."

With another twirl of his cape, and a short cough to clear his throat, Reggie boomed out the farewell. "Hang tough, America."

Rachel tugged on Ricky's arm and asked him, "Hang in where?" She was grinning broadly. "Get it? It's a joke, my old joke, Ricky. It's ... Wha ...? He didn't say ..."

A stir of confusion was running across the deck. "He didn't say ..."

Even Sallie was at a loss. "You didn't say ... 'Hang in there, America.' I know I asked you, uncle, to try a variation, but somehow ... And don't stretch your mouth like that, it ..."

> **inarticulate**: (1) not able to produce clear, connected speech; (2) perceptible only as raw sound, but not as individual words and syllables
> **noxious**: (1) inspiring disgust; foul; (2) having a destructive impact on body or spirit
> **equitable**: satisfying our sense of fairness

François, suddenly **inarticulate** with panic, screamed out what syllables she could. "He's going to ... He's ... Fire!"

They all saw it now—the spurt of flame from Uncle Reggie's hand. With a violent quickness the big man leapt to the rigging that hung in long sweeps from the foremast. He held the torch—an oversized lighter with a huge flame—high in one hand. "So—what about my Statue of Liberty imitation? It's even better than my Uncle Reggie one! Ha!"

Ms. Framley broke forth with savage delight, "It's you! You're here! So now it's their turn. Fry them, Mr. Bamalford! Burn their rotting ship—this **noxious** heap of stinking lumber."

It was becoming horribly clear. Fighting against the shock, Sallie cried, "So, where is my uncle, Mr. Bamalford? How did you get his cape? And why are you doing this?"

Her questions were fierce and rushing, but Bamalford was unimpressed. With the flame just inches under the rigging, the situation belonged to him. "That roundish thing out there," he said with a lazy gesture toward the moon, hanging now in the west, "means that it is night. And at night people get sleepy, and don't hold on to their capes very well."

"Well said!" Ms. Framley raised a triumphant fist to the sky. "Scorch them, Mr. Bamalford. Turn their ship into toast. It is so good to have you here. They took my property, so now you torch theirs. And when they collect the insurance they can give it to me, to pay for what I lost. That would be fair or—as your brother would say—it would be **equitable**. And once the ..."

> **voluble**: talking in an easy, flowing manner; rolling on in your speech
> **metaphorical**: spoken or written in a form that claims an improbable identity (for example, "his mind is a butterfly net"), but on the understanding that what is really asserted is a similarity ("the way his mind grasps ideas is similar to the way a net catches butterflies")

456

> **antipodes** (plural, but often used in a singular sense): (1) two points as far away from one another as possible on the surface of a globe; (2) the point on the other side of the Earth that is exactly opposite the point where you are

She seemed ready to go on at some length, but Bamalford broke in. "My dear Seismo, the very sight of you is inspiring, but we must not be ... be **voluble** on an occasion such as this. Immediate action is what we need. Never fear, their ship will be torched ... after one last voyage."

With the lighter still raised to the rigging, Bamalford turned to Povano. "Weigh anchor. Run up the sails. Let's go—I'm not talking about a **metaphorical** voyage, life's journey and all that. This is for real. We're bound for the **antipodes**—I want the whole globe between me and this Dropanchor hole, and if I could ..."

He paused suddenly, alert, listening to something. A throbbing sound of uncertain origin, still very low, was making itself felt. He held perfectly still, but it didn't go away. "It's that terrible duck," he bleated at last, staring anxiously in the direction of Mount Relief. "Load all cannons!"

> **spectrum**: a range or scale defined by two contrary extremes (such as conservative-liberal or comic-tragic) and containing all the values that lie in between those extremes
>
> **salutation**: a greeting, often expressed with a bit of ceremony or with some words that fit the occasion

The sound grew steadily, losing its duck-like qualities, becoming the pulse of an approaching motor. You could tell now that it came from seaward, from the south entry of the bay. Bamalford's anxiety vanished, and as he peered across the water his mood took a violent swing for the better. There was a wild gloating in his voice as he said, "This is just too nice! Oh little amoebas of Dropanchor, I can already hear you crying, 'Help us, help us.' And you will cry in vain! So sweet! Guess where I am, everyone, on the emotional **spectrum**. Way down at the positive end, past contentment, past delight."

There was more sense to Bamalford's ramblings than at first appeared. The descending moon cast a fairway of light across the bay, and a boat came speeding down it, swelling quickly into a sizable vessel. "And dark," said Meagan apprehensively, "with a color that by day could easily be purple."

"Not that!" groaned Povano, pronouncing the dreaded word. "Draco!"

"Looks that way, doesn't it?" crowed Bamalford. "Good luck, my amoeba friends. You're on your own. Maybe when he roars up, you should begin with a **salutation** like—Greetings to Draco, uncaged dragon, unmuzzled hound. Get it?" His tone grew harsher. "I was the cage and the muzzle. But not anymore."

veneer: a thin layer forming the surface of something and often disguising the true nature of what lies at the core
quarry: the object of a hunt or pursuit
camouflage (noun): the cover-ups, false resemblances and disguises that you use to make something escape notice

Povano must have thought no salutation was appropriate, for he remained silent, staring intently as the purple boat drew alongside. Draco was there, stern and unsmiling, with the moonlight glinting on his wide forehead. He returned Povano's gaze for a moment and then called in a loud voice, "Mayor, by the authority of this badge"—he opened his wallet and held it up to view—"I must order you to relax! And to blink, and to take a breath. And—please—to listen. This will be hard to believe, but the regrettable nastiness I've displayed on our former visits is a **veneer**—crack through the surface and there's a decent guy inside, Decent Guy Draco, a family man, a lover of fine art. I had to be tough with you, to keep the real **quarry** off guard. It's an ancient strategy."

Povano was so caught by surprise that he could only stammer, "But the Terebinth Beer ..."

"I know, I was a creep about the bottle in your harbor, but I had no options."

"Your threats," answered Povano, in the voice of one trying to comprehend, "your threats to take our children and twist their minds, pursuant to that horrible Title 51, were not ... not ...?"

"Not what they seemed," confirmed Draco, almost sympathetically. "They were part of the **camouflage**. There is no Title 51. There's no law—I guarantee it—that would let a Bureau of Ecology inspector start snatching your kids. And we weren't after your children. You have fine children. We were chasing a serious offender, a big-league polluter. And a major fat mouth, I might add."

> **tactile**: impacting or registering on the sense of touch; getting information through the sense of touch; in general, having to do with the sense of touch
> **forestall**: to take steps ahead of time and by those steps to prevent something from happening or reaching its conclusion
> **turpitude**: moral ruin, ready to express itself in low, unprincipled actions

Bamalford had been paying the closest attention to this exchange, and it was easy to see in the yellow glare of his torch that he was no longer at the positive end of the emotional spectrum. When he heard the mention of a "big-league polluter," he screamed, "You have no evidence. And I have fire. If you don't believe me, stick your bowling-alley forehead up over the rail and have a look. Or if you need to touch the fire before you believe it—maybe you're the

458

tactile sort—just stay where you are. Because when this ship goes up there'll be a storm, with burning canvas and burning timber falling everywhere."

Ignoring everything on the theme of arson, Draco yelled back, "No evidence! How does ninety-nine barrels of evidence sound? Or is it one hundred? We had that beer truck loaded with cameras, mikes, transmitters, you name it—it was like a Hollywood shoot."

That was devastating news for Bamalford. Something raving and unstable was working into his voice. "At first it was very, very bad—" he gnashed, "the big duck, the really big stone, swimming—I don't like swimming. Then it was getting better, the torch guy was earning respect. But now—just like that— zilch revisited! This little ogre boats in and starts **forestalling** everything in sight—he forestalls me, he forestalls my plans. I'm so frustrated. I'm within a trillionth of an inch of just flaming this old scow."

The inspector gave a short laugh. "Maybe you lack what it takes."

François, who was at the railing, shook her head and called down, "If you mean he lacks the sheer rottenness of character, you should have been with us tonight."

Draco didn't argue. "You are undoubtedly right, young lady—in the Realm of **Turpitude** Bamalford towers above us all. But I meant something else— what he lacks is the utter stupidity to start a fire. He's dense, but even he can grasp that on a burning ship there are no favorites. He goes overboard with everybody else—and I'll fish him out and haul him off wringing wet."

That took some of the fight out of Bamalford. "Let me think," he cried peevishly. "My arm is so tired. Let me think."

> **comportment**: behavior, especially behavior considered as following (or not following) social rules, the norms of courtesy, the demands of honor, etc.
> **moot**: no longer a "live" question, and therefore no longer requiring attention and argument
> **ostentatious**: favoring a style which is showy and eye-catching

"Think about this," called Draco, in complete control. "Here's a deal, the only one I'm offering. I need to see some model **comportment** from you. You behave, put out your fire and get down here on my purple boat, in three minutes, not one second more, and maybe I won't need to add resisting arrest to the charges. That could be worth seven to ten."

"Seven to ten what, huh widescreen man?" roared Bamalford, with a final show of defiance.

"I'm timing," said Draco calmly. "Two minutes and forty-seven seconds left. Do you accept my deal?"

At that point Bamalford's resistance was over. There was a final outcry—"I hate you, I accept!"—and then he capped the lighter and bounded heavily for the railing. Grandma Dubois snapped at him as he lumbered by, "I saw it—you were out of fuel anyway."

"Lady," he shrieked without breaking stride, "you go talk to my brother Fearless the lawyer, OK, and he will tell you that it is now a **moot** question whether my lighter has fuel. The only question now is whether I beat the three minutes—that's what the deal says. Fuel or no fuel doesn't make any difference any more, old bat, old beak lady!"

He was on the ladder now, descending, muttering feverishly. "Send that old woman to law school, huh Fearless. She doesn't know a moot from a smoot. Put her in Moot 101 and they'll moot her smoots and smoot her moots, they'll ..."

Draco called up from below, "Stop raving at everybody and get down here. And no tricks. Because I have some hardware, if you know what I mean. It may be out of sight—I'm not **ostentatious** about that sort of thing—but it's here."

Bamalford was more than halfway down the ladder. "I vote," he growled, "that we take some of that hardware and blow away your purple tub, and then we blow away this old embarrassment of a sailing ship, and ..."

> **recluse**: a person who habitually avoids social contacts and seeks to be alone
> **malaise**: a vague discontent; an uneasy sense that your health is in a poor state or, more generally, that things are not right
> **reprobate** (noun): a person firmly established in habits of evil and rascally conduct

"You are unfit for human society," declared Draco loudly. "Maybe in the big house you'll do everybody a favor and turn into a **recluse**. But anyway, I vote no—none of that awful stuff you're talking about."

"So it's a tie vote." Bamalford was near the bottom of the ladder.

"Which means I win." Draco was enjoying himself, drawing out his words. "The captain breaks a tie ... in the absence, of course, of any additional person entitled to cast a vote."

Lumps was looking at Darlingson now, and saw the cocked head, the slight expression of **malaise**.

At the first sound of velvet both were up, leaping to the rail, trying to pull in the ladder before Bamalford was off it. But they were too late. He was landing heavily on the deck of the *Purple Omniscience*, as the velvet continued. "Well, I cast my vote with Bamalford. We shouldn't leave that hardware unused."

460

A weary figure emerged from the boat's cabin—Nameless Entrepreneur—and Bamalford dropped to one knee. "Sir, it wasn't my fault! The moose went over, the librarian went over. Two **reprobates**, sir, moral scum, foul abandoners. And then a giant duck ..."

Rachel was tugging at the sleeve of Merci's white gown. "Look—there are two prisoners."

"Or three rats," answered Merci, trying like everyone on *Jack's Equator* to make sense of the confusing scene.

"When you have two prisoners," continued Rachel in a knowing tone, "you need to show them who's boss. That's why Draco is ..."

"Yes, ma'am," said Merci, drawing the little girl to her for a moment. "That's why Draco is going down on his knees just like Bamalford. Oh, Rach, what is this?"

> **fulminate**: to shoot off fiery condemnations and criticisms
> **candid**: making a full and honest disclosure, even of personal sentiments and delicate information
> **emolument** (often used in plural): the fee or other compensation that is paid to you for performing a service or holding some official position

Draco was on his knees, and there was a tremble in his voice. "Sir, Nameless sir, I've seen you like this before—mellow outside, but white hot inside, and then you hit the flash point all of a sudden and begin **fulminating**, and everyone is scrambling for cover."

"Tut," answered Nameless, half pleased with the description. "Fulminating and all that. You and Bamalford are clowns, but at least you show the proper respect. In fact, the two of you may rise."

"But as for the rest of you"—he was turning toward *Jack's Equator*, and lifting his gaze to the railing—"you little swine of Dropanchor, I will be **candid**. You shall know my feelings, just as they are, without any filtering. Basically, I hate you. I hope bad things happen to you. Don't even try to imagine the anger—beneath the professional exterior I am, as Captain Draco puts it, white hot, and the settling of accounts is on my mind."

He paused, letting the silence mount for a few moments, perhaps waiting for an apology, and then went on. "I build, you tear down. I create, you trash. Slowly and carefully I assemble the perfect project, and you spoil it. Because it was perfect—barrel after barrel of toxics and contaminants falling into a fire pit inside a mountain and burning by a complete burn into non-existence. Yes—non-existence, we have a guarantee on that point. And the evil result of all this evil activity? Well—the world is cleaner, my clients sleep better, and for me and to a lesser extent for my jolly companions there are modest

emoluments—some cash, maybe some stock options. A perfect project—until these little wreckers you call your children wrecked it, just a couple of hours ..."

> **derision**: the expression of contempt through a mean humor or ridicule
> **effigy**: a likeness of someone, usually done as a sculpture, carving or engraving
> **exploit**: to use something to get as much advantage—often commercial advantage—as you can from it, sometimes in a manner that ignores environmental or humanitarian concerns

He stopped abruptly, with obvious annoyance. "Pardon me, little mayor, but I'm not quite finished, you know. Yoo-hoo, chubs, Mayor Chubs ..." A mean **derision** came into his speech. "You're trying to be cute, that's it, trying to lighten the somber mood everyone is in—and should be in."

Mayor Povano, standing at the railing close to where it met the ship's ladder, had simply hauled off and started talking—to Bamalford. "I don't count it against you, Bamalford, that you tried to make the Giuseppe Stone your **effigy**—everyone wants attention. And as for your reaction to what Foster Farbugle said about you on TV, I don't count that against you either—a lot of people would have gone into a funk. But to take advantage of our simplicity as you did, to **exploit** our trust and play on our fears—that I hold against you. You have played a game with us, Bamalford, played us for fools! And Draco too—he has played a game. And so has that Nameless fellow."

> **collaborative**: dependent on the coordinated efforts of two or more persons, each participating more or less as an equal
> **colleague**: a companion in a profession or line of work
> **minion**: someone who has a position in your service, and will do as you command, often in a slavish manner

Grandma added her own outburst. "And it's all been the same game, hasn't it? Three players, but one **collaborative** effort. One dirty project, carried on by Bamalford and **colleagues**, or Draco and colleagues, or whatever."

"Actually," said Nameless, obviously interested in this last point, "it's Nameless and colleagues or, more precisely, Nameless and slaves. These two do as I say. Back on your knees, toads."

Astonishingly, Draco and Bamalford again fell to their knees, and waited. Nameless smiled up to Grandma and the others at the railing. "You see, it's not majority rule on this boat."

He walked slowly around his **minions**, as though making an inspection of troops, and then lifted his face again to those on the ship. "But there are a couple of things on this boat that require a majority." With a flick of his wrist, he

462

ordered the kneeling figures to rise. "Up lads—we mustn't grovel. Let's show them what I have in mind."

They knew what he had in mind from the nod he gave toward the foredeck of the *Purple Omniscience*. Two tarps were lashed down there, side by side. One was of a dark-colored canvas, and one of light, and each covered an object that was long and comparatively low. Scurrying forward, Bamalford and Draco began to undo the cords that held the light-colored tarp in place.

> **aesthetic**: related to the beauty or lack of beauty that is in the things we see
>
> **contraband** (adjective): being imported, exported, offered for sale, etc., in violation of restrictions or bans imposed by one or more governments
>
> **indulge**: to answer the demand of a desire or passion by furnishing it the object that it craves

They were working within easy reach of the agate dragon, the reddish-orange figurehead that Draco always made a fuss over. It wound like a scroll along the bow rail, and as Bamalford, laboring at the tarp, pulled free the first of the cords, he draped it unceremoniously over the neck of the creature. Draco was not happy with that. The dragon was for him an **aesthetic** object first to last, a moment of beauty, and not some towel bar to hang things on. He was reaching over to lift the cord away when Nameless with a soft "Ahem" called him back to his task.

The cords were soon loosened, and the canvas was folded back. What appeared was a horn, extraordinarily long, tapering gracefully, casting off sparks of moonlight. "No solos on this horn," Nameless called up to the watchers on the ship. "It's just too big. Bamalford pumps the air, and Draco works the stops. But for all that it's an exceptional object of art. I wish you could see it in the daylight—half gold, half ivory."

He paused, sensing disapproval. "But not **contraband** ivory, so tell the old lady to stop her clucking. This thing was made long before there were any bans on the ivory trade. It's very old, and very expensive. It was part of Draco's signing bonus."

"Along with the dragon, I suppose," shouted Peter from *Jack's Equator*.

"Excellent guess, old man," answered Nameless. "Draco has a passion for things of beauty, but never had the cash to **indulge** it. We've helped him with that little problem, and in return he's helped us with some of our little projects." He gave a dry laugh. "Good thing he goes for art and not music, because when you hear this old beauty a few minutes from now, you'll call it anything but musical."

prolongation: an extending of the time during which something will last or within which it is to be accomplished

synchronize: to cause the timing of one series of movements to be lined up with the timing of another series of movements; to set to the same time

spurious: false or forged, in spite of appearing—often by reason of deliberate effort—to be true or authentic

"You're planning a serenade?" asked Peter.

"Exactly—but not for you." He beckoned toward the northern passages of the bay, where the whales were moving lazily out to sea, on a weaving line toward the falling moon. "What happens is—we motor out beyond them a bit, we play them something beastly on the horn, they move away of course, and before long we've herded them back in here. A little **prolongation** of Whalefest."

"Thanks, but no!" snapped Grandma Dubois. "They don't need an interruption like that in their journey. And we don't need the sight of your goons tripping over each other as they try to play that thing."

"Hey lady!" cried Bamalford. "Easy on the abuse. Draco and I have trained. We're more **synchronized** than a marching band. Those blubber banks will love it."

A new voice rang out, pure and high. "Why do you have to bother them?" It was Rachel, standing on tiptoe to peer over the railing.

Nameless caught her in his gaze, and she fell back, afraid. "I'll tell you why, little girl." A short spasm of laughter escaped from him, and his voice was harsh, stripped of even that **spurious** good humor that often accented his mockery. "We need an opportunity to show all of you what's under the second tarp."

Rachel looked around for help. Merci was standing nearby, and the little girl grabbed her hand, saying, "He scares me. But it's not anything bad is it, Merci, under there?"

Merci gave her a hug, but could think of nothing to say. Both of them were trembling.

decimate: to kill or remove every tenth member of a group; more generally, to slaughter or get rid of a large portion of a group

din: a loud confusion of sound, as for example from a crowd in which everyone is talking or yelling

Everyone on *Jack's Equator* felt it now—some evil course was begun. A wave of dread swept across them. Grandma clutched at the arm of Mayor Povano. "The whales—they could be **decimated**. They haven't been hunted for years. They've lost most of their distrust."

The mayor was slower to anger than almost anyone, but it came welling up now. He drew in a very long breath, and another, and his jaw set in a stubborn line. The people saw this and began to take heart from him, and with their dread giving way to a deep indignation, they cried out. A wild, momentary confusion rose up from the deck, yet with a shout that lifted over it all—the **din** and the fury—Povano made himself heard. "There will be no slaughter, I don't care what's under the second tarp."

He was looking around, looking for someone. "Lumps," he called after a long moment, "where are you? This one is yours. They have to be warned. The Farnums brought 'em in, but I think it's up to you to get 'em out."

Lumps was there, across the deck, but as he shouted back there was a note of shame in his voice. "Here, sir—only I don't know the calls."

Povano saw no reason for a public conversation, so he hurried over to where Lumps was standing. "To be honest, your grandfather is the only one in Dropanchor who knows the calls, but tonight they were too much for him. He broke his voice."

Lumps shook his head slowly, as though in pain. "He tried to teach them to me, but I was ... scared. If I talk with whales, people will start to think it's just too strange—I'm an odd sort of person already, you know—and they'll tell me to go away, to be my own company!"

> **ostracize**: to force someone to leave your group or social circle and remain outside it, enjoying no further interaction with it
> **stern** (noun): the back of a ship; the trailing end of a ship

Povano frowned, as though to say he was not convinced. "Your father called the whales, son, and in all honesty he was a pretty unique sort of guy too, but around here he was never **ostracized**, never lonely. Far from it. And the same goes for your old grandfather over there, except ... I think tonight he did feel sort of alone."

Lumps waited no longer. He headed off quickly to join his grandfather, who was at the **stern** rail of *Jack's Equator*. The ship had swung about on its anchor, and from his position the old man was looking directly toward the northern entry of the bay, where the whale pack was slowly drifting. He was straining to call out a warning that would drive off the great creatures. But there was no sound. Even as Lumps drew closer he could hear no sound except a thin piping. The voice of his grandfather was truly broken, and the only result of all the effort was to provoke an ugly burst of laughter from the *Purple Omniscience*.

> **ossify**: to lose all flexibility and set gradually into a hard, unyielding condition, like bone

goading (noun): the act of jabbing someone, often with sharp words, to drive him into some action or reaction
legacy: something passing down from one generation to the next, often within a family

"Hey, pops," shouted Bamalford. "Problem with the cords?"

"These aging cowboys," Draco explained in a mocking tone, "they **ossify**. Everything turns to bone, including the vocal cords. The brain too, in most cases."

"Don't leave out the attitudes," said Nameless. "They harden as well, and pitching a new idea to one of these old guys is like talking to a pile of bricks. A new idea, just for example, about a more recreational approach"—he patted the second tarp affectionately—"to the whales."

"Pardon, sir," said Bamalford, "but he's not understanding a word, I bet. English is like a second language for that old fossil ... and there isn't any first one."

The old man let the **goading** pass over, but Lumps, who by this time was at the stern rail, could not. "Only a boatload of punks," he roared, "lost and clueless punks, giggling at each other's jokes ... "

Then he broke off, seeing how fruitless it was, and he drew his grandfather away from the railing. They had a couple of minutes, at best. In a scratchy whisper—all he could manage—Grandpa Lumps tried to describe the call of warning. He showed how the chin should be tilted, and the tongue pressed down against the air rushing up from the larynx. Lumps had never concentrated so intensely. The raw sounds of whale speech were already in his throat—that was the **legacy** passing from father to son in his family line—but forming calls from those sounds was an art of immense subtlety.

> **marginal**: barely good enough; just on the good side of the line dividing the acceptable from the unacceptable
> **condone**: to tolerate and make excuses for something that may in fact deserve to be criticized or condemned

Bamalford knew enough about the strange potential which Lumps possessed to guess what was happening. "If you can't learn to read in eighteen years," he shouted, "how will you learn the whale calls in three minutes? It's more than freaky tonsils, you know. Brains perhaps—just the point where your equipment is **marginal** at best."

Draco added his own touch of humor, calling, "If you have a message for the whales, send it with us, we'll be seeing them soon."

"Better yet," joined in Nameless, raking all on board *Jack's Equator* with his boyish smile, "you can give it to them yourselves, because in a few minutes we're bringing them back here—to demo the more recreational approach I happened to mention above. And to teach you villagers to keep your paws off my projects! Ha! So let's go, thugs."

At lower speeds the *Purple Omniscience* was a very quiet boat. Draco throttled it gently, and it pulled away toward the whale pack without a sound.

READER: Larry had this dream the other night that he could do the whale calls.

AUTHOR: He might be the type.

READER: It started in Europe. The only place in the world you could still find trees was in the hills of Europe, and some of them were cut and loaded on three ships that sailed to America, where the wood was desperately needed for …

AUTHOR: You aren't going to say No. 2 pencils, I hope.

READER: None other! But it didn't happen. Larry did these calls and the whales came and formed like a wall of ruffians in front of the three ships and made rude and uncooperative noises, and the ships turned back rather than provoke an international incident. There were no No. 2 pencils in the world, and the SAT had to be canceled.

AUTHOR: Obviously in my position I can't **condone** Larry canceling the SAT for the entire nation. But it's hard not to admire his persistence.

Chapter 65: THE TWENTY-FIRST-CENTURY ICONOCLASTS

It could have all turned out for the better. Lumps could have mastered the calls and sent the whales safely off to sea. The *Purple Omniscience* could have run out of fuel, the horn could have frozen up or the horn blowers could have flubbed, the secret of the second tarp might have been a telescope, a floodlight, something **innocuous** and not made for harm.

> **innocuous**: not designed or equipped to cause harm; harmless
> **engulf**: to catch something up in an oncoming force, such as a tidal wave or an outburst of political turmoil
> **tepid**: (1) somewhat warm; (2) neither hot nor cold, and therefore not forceful or dramatic enough to stir strong reactions

In fact, though, at every turn hope was dashed, and the bad news piled up. After a frantic lesson with his grandfather, Lumps sent out a long cry of warning. It was in the whale speech, and the whales hesitated when they heard it. But it was like a word said too indistinctly, you don't catch what it is. The whales were uncertain what Lumps had cried, and instead of taking flight they circled about in confusion. In this circumstance the *Purple Omniscience* had no trouble gaining a position between them and the northern entry of the bay.

For their part Bamalford and Draco didn't botch the horn. They were competent enough to squeeze a dreadful noise from it, a heavy droning that exploded slowly outward. The whales were **engulfed** by the sound, and they hated it. It was like the negation of everything that mattered. They were creatures of endless spaces, and it spoke of cages and confinement. They swam through seas that were chilly and blue, and it gave the awful feeling of **tepid** brown water. So they churned about in anxious circles until at last, to escape from the blare, they turned back on their course and headed again toward the inner reaches of the bay, where the ship lay anchored. Just as Nameless had planned.

That left only the wild hope that whatever lay under the second tarp was something innocent—a hope that vanished minutes later, as Nameless continued pushing the spectacle toward a deadly conclusion.

Once the *Purple Omniscience* had herded the whales into the water just seaward from *Jack's Equator*, it cut the horn and quietly slipped around them, taking a position midway between them and the ship. Like a circus master with the crowd before him and the ring of animals at his back, Nameless called up

468

to Povano and the others at the railing. "I think you will like the show. Great cast."

> **acme**: the highest peak; often, the peak of perfection or fullness at which some growth process arrives
> **wherewithal**: the stuff you need (money, materials, skills, etc.) to get a job done

He beckoned behind him, toward the nearby whales. "One of them will reach the **acme** of its career tonight. Never before, such a stunning performance, and—I guarantee it—never again. Great performers—like I said, Mama. And great props. Doing this trick takes expensive gear, and the bucks to pay for it. But we've got it, the **wherewithal** to bring you class entertainment."

He motioned to Bamalford and Draco. "Boys, show them the ... wherewithal." Like actors on cue, they drew back the second tarp, revealing a long shaft of metal, wickedly pointed and barbed at one end, and flared at the other with three fins. "Little Wanda," cried Nameless with delight. "You're lookin' good."

Rachel may have been the only one who had not already guessed, and now she wailed in despair, calling to her brother, "A harpoon, Ricky! It could ... it could ... It's so unfair!"

> **vogue**: the latest way of dressing, speaking, acting, etc., which you must adopt if you want to be "in"
> **defunct**: having passed from life; having ceased to be in effect; dead
> **meticulous**: thoroughly attentive to every detail; sometimes excessively so

"Unfair!" barked Nameless. There was indignation in the usually tired voice. "That's the **vogue** these days, isn't it—all the beautiful people whining that the animals aren't being treated fair. Well—if you think Little Wanda is unfair you should have seen Little Rhoda. Rhoda was a real harpoon—she had radar. Just pull the trigger and she does a lock on the target, and you've got yourself one dead—excuse me, let's use the sanitary term—one **defunct** whale. But we wanted to keep an element of sport in this, so we left Rhoda on the shelf and bought Little Wanda."

"If I'm right about what your goons are strapping onto Little Wanda this very moment," shouted Peter Oakum in an angry voice, "then she's anything but sporting!"

Draco and Bamalford were crouching beside the harpoon, attaching a slender packet. Their motions were slow and careful, and every detail of their work received maximum attention. As they felt the gaze of their overlord upon them, Draco explained, "We're being rather **meticulous**, sir." And Bamalford added, "Better than a premature launch, sir."

Nameless looked up again to the railing. "You're right, Mr. Oakum. My goons are attaching a fuel pack. A delicate job, I might add. But Wanda has no radar, which means that I could simply ... miss. And that's sporting."

"No one misses at fifty feet," roared Oakum, with not a shred remaining of his usual calm. "This isn't sport. It's power-tripping. And bloodlust. And a terrible blindness."

> **obstreperous**: noisy in a rude, ungovernable sort of way, often with the effect of expressing disrespect or protest
> **retrospection**: the act of looking back over what is past, often to learn its lessons or note its significant moments
> **eon** (also spelled aeon): a vast period of time, not precisely defined as to beginning or end

"Old man," returned Nameless, with the beginning of a sneer in his lazy voice, "you are getting **obstreperous**, aren't you? When I'm finished here today, you'll still have ninety-five percent, ninety-six percent, whatever, of your whale pack left. So what's the problem?"

"Can't you see—or is Peter right about your blindness?" Merci had suddenly left Rachel and shot to the railing. The white of her gown was emphatic and sharp against the dark sky. She drew a long breath and cried again, "Can't you see? You don't just kill five percent of the pack, you kill an individual creature, all one hundred percent of it, with its own features and character and—around here anyway—maybe its own name."

The remark touched a nerve, and the drooping body of Nameless gave a jerk, as though snapping itself to attention. "There! A perfect example of what I call the death of **retrospection**. You are the voice of the present, young lady, but you have no sense of history. Look back across the **eons** and you will find that there has always been a rule. For millions of years a rule—don't give names to the animals. Don't see the individual face in the flock. That way you won't form silly attachments, and when you get a chance like I've got tonight, you can be wholehearted about it."

This was one of the most astonishing statements Merci had ever heard. "So the wonderful differences," she asked, "and peculiarities, from one beast to the next, mean nothing for you?"

> **fungibility**: the quality of being so much the same in every part or unit that any part or unit can be used, sold, delivered, etc., in place of any other (for example, rice, sugar and molasses are all fungible goods)
> **complacent**: marked by an untroubled satisfaction with your situation, often to the point of overlooking problems and shortcomings
> **lugubrious**: showing grief in an overdone or theatrical way

"From one beast to the next!" returned Nameless with a snort. "How about from one human to the next? Even among the humans, the only interesting difference is that some of them have money, and some don't. Beyond that, a carton of 'em here is worth a carton of 'em there. **Fungibility**—that's my approach."

"But you miss what life is all about," cried Merci. "It's the little differences ..."

Nameless broke in, observing **complacently**, "There's very little need to sermonize me on what life is all about. Look at what is mine—there are people who go on their knees when I say so, there are revenue streams I can't keep up with, there are amusements fit for a king. Nameless is content, my little guilt merchants. And if life *is* all about something, Nameless is not letting it slip through his fingers. Now stop the pestering. I'm preparing for an amusement, as you can see."

He was fiddling with a dark, metallic item in his hand, a firing button, and was checking a wire that ran from it to a jack on the harpoon. After a minute he lifted his head again toward Merci. "Action time here on the bay, finally. But you can't feel it, can you? Because you had to give cute little names to the whales, so that now when one of them, in a few minutes, goes night-night, you'll probably get all **lugubrious** and splash quarter-pound tears on your gown and ..."

He stopped in mid-sentence, still staring up at the ship. His mouth slowly opened in mock terror. "Look there, boys—white on white. Have we got trouble or what?"

> **windlass**: a lifting device, usually a frame supporting a barrel with one or more handles, for winding in or letting out the rope to which some heavy object is attached
> **berserk**: in a frenzy; maddened, crazy, throwing yourself into wild and sometimes destructive activities
> **talisman**: a small object, often distinctive in shape or markings, that is possessed of a magic adequate to bring about some result or range of results

Merci's white dress was no longer contrasted against the dark sky. A huge expanse of canvas was unfurling behind her, as the Inveterate Seadogs and all on board made a desperate attempt to rush *Jack's Equator* into action. Ricky and Tedesco and the Farnums were high in the rigging. Darlingson and a small crew were straining at the **windlass**, trying to reel in the anchor. "Everybody," cried François, who was at his side, "more bodies! Help!"

Nameless shook his head, as though in the presence of embarrassing foolishness. "Little people of Dropanchor, it would be comical, really, if it weren't so ... sick. I mean—what is this with you and the whales? For them you go **berserk**—this mad rush. Come on. What are they? It's like you've turned them into **talismans**—but very, very jumbo—or twenty-ton good luck charms. I mean, do they make your crops grow or something?"

> **icon**: an image or item which in the cultural or religious life of a people has become an object of its devotion and a representation of its ideals
>
> **iconoclast**: one who smashes the images, or tears apart the beliefs, to which people are devoted
>
> **sagacious**: sharply perceptive in human affairs, and possessing wise judgment

"I have lived in this community now, sir, for several years," said Bamalford, with the tone of a schoolboy hoping for a sticker. "I saw at once when I moved here that this is a primitive people, desperately in need of a central **icon**, some image to which they can give their complete loyalty, and in which they can find the symbol of their ideals and longings, such as they may be. I volunteered. Never counting the cost, and overcoming great personal shyness, I made my image widely available—both on the front page, almost daily, and in the bronze statue of myself atop the Dome. But the fools, as I came to see, already had their icon after all—they had the whale. In their imaginations, above their doorways, and—once a year—all along the length of their bay, it is the hulking figure of the whale that holds their juvenile attention. It's all rather ... revolting."

"Supremo!" A cry went up from Ms. Framley, harsh and exuberant. "Oh thank you, Mr. Bamalford, for saying it so well. These horrible people and their whale icons! You—Mr. Bamalford, and you Mr. Nameless and Mr. Draco—you must smash their icons, you must be the Twenty-First-Century **Iconoclasts**. It is a vital work, and I anoint you for it."

She removed the little jar of vitamin elixir from her purse and shook out its remaining contents in the general direction of the three heroes. The breeze caught most of the sticky spray and blew it back on her dress, but that did not lessen her satisfaction in the grand gesture.

Nameless was laughing. "But not at you, dear Ms. Framley. You are quite a **sagacious** young woman, I can see, with a shrewd understanding of the small town mentality, and its diseases. I am laughing at that ridiculous ship. It's trying to ram us! *Phweeet*! Ramming speed!"

With its anchor stowed and sails lifted, *Jack's Equator* had come about sharply on the breeze and was bearing in the general direction of Draco's boat. But ramming was not its mission, and it went gliding cleanly past, and on toward the whale pack.

472

Nameless could not take it seriously. "Ram the whales, then, whatever works for you."

He might have been more worried if he had seen Lumps and his grandfather advancing toward the bow of the ship. The old man was going to try it again, a call of warning to the pack, but this time at close hand where his broken voice might be heard. He waited until the ship had drawn into the midst of the whales, where the sea was welling and bubbly from their movement. Then with his head lifted he forced out a faint and wavering cry.

> **underling**: one whose role is to take orders and be bossed around
> **perpetrate**: to bring something bad to accomplishment, such as crime or fraud
> **privation**: the painful lack of something basic to your existence

Draco had lightly throttled the *Purple Omniscience*, and it was stalking behind the sailing ship. The interval between the two vessels was now too far to speak across, so Nameless had his **underlings** dial Ms. Framley on the cell phone. "Please tell that old fossil," he said to her, "that he's **perpetrating** an ancient fraud. He wants us to believe that humans can talk with beasts. That's one of the oldest lies, one ..."

The whales were disappearing. As Grandpa Lumps continued his eerie chant, they were slipping below the surface until at last there was nothing to see but the moon glinting on the water that closed over them.

"My whales!" cried Nameless, in the outraged voice of a child.

Bamalford sprang to the aid of his master. "Enough!" he roared in the general direction of the ship. "This man has endured every **privation** to be here with us tonight. He missed his supper, he's lost his sleep, he's chilled to the bone, and now ..."

"My whales!" cried Nameless again, this time into the telephone. "Tell them, Victoria, that now it's two for one. I'm lining up two whales and taking them both out with the same shot. It won't be pretty, and it won't be easy, but I'm not the sort to run from a challenge."

> **anecdotal**: based on or otherwise having to do with the little stories people tell about what they've seen or heard
> **hybrid** (noun): something that unites in itself distinct elements from two or more sources
> **unkempt**: rough and sloppy in appearance due to a lack of care and grooming

After a pause to catch his breath, he continued, in a nasty, mocking tone, "And tell them about that story going around, how whales are not fish. It's just **anecdotal** evidence, I know, and not hard science, but personally I find it convincing. And then there's the related story that whales can't meet their oxygen requirement from water. Isn't that very interesting? It seems to say—they'll be back, coming up for air with little bull's-eyes on their chubby flanks! Oh yes, Victoria, say all that."

Miss Framley passed on the message with obvious pleasure. When she spoke again to Nameless it was a strange **hybrid** of a telephone call and a face-to-face conversation. Although she had the phone to her mouth, she could see his figure clearly in the moonlight. And for her, with her industrial-strength voice, to see someone, no matter how far off, was to have him within shouting distance. So she was bellowing, but into the speaker, when she exclaimed, "This is so historic ..."

"Ow!" Nameless cried, grabbing at his ear.

"Excuse me, sir," she apologized, "but this is so historic. And it's all being recorded because ..."

Nameless forgot his ear and brightened into a sudden happiness. "Yes! Of course—we're being recorded. Because that oddball woman who travels around filming other oddballs is up there with her camera running. Thugs! Thugs!" He had turned to Bamalford and Draco now. "Your combs, your brushes. Spruce up. We're going to be on TV. But she might not film us if we're **unkempt**."

Ms. Framley was enjoying herself, and she relayed these remarks of Nameless on to Sallie in a cheerful tone. The effect was instantaneous. Sallie grabbed the phone from the older woman and shouted into it, "I'm OK with unkempt, but not with unholy! If you spoilers want to be on TV, that's enough reason to stop right now. Can you hear the click? Just turning off the camera we'll be using not to film you with, OK, you and your vandal games."

> **tirade**: a long, angry speech, often marked by shouting and the exaggerated statement of grievances and criticisms
> **encompassed**: included within the sphere of activities and topics that belong to some profession, program, undertaking, etc.

Wincing again, Nameless held the phone far from his ear. This let Bamalford hear Sallie's **tirade**, and he roared back at her. "You dishonor our profession. I'm a reporter, you're a reporter. What do you think is **encompassed** by that—just covering the stories that suit your taste? You have a sacred duty to cover all the news, even ..."

> **bellwether**: one who is first to do something and whose example is then followed by others
> **fallow**: (1) (said of farmland) left unplanted with crops for a time, often to restore fertility; (2) (generally) lying unused or at rest, but with the clear potential to blossom or otherwise find fruitful expression

Nameless was breaking in, his voice rising with excitement. "Boys, boys—we have a sacred duty to *be* the news, do you get me, to *be* the news, right now. Look there!"

One of the whales had come up, out at the far edge of the turbulence of water that lay over the pack. It was a large adult—and apparently a **bellwether**, for others were following. Once again the sea was like pasture—everywhere you looked there was flock.

Draco leapt to the controls of the *Purple Omniscience*, awaiting instructions. Bamalford knelt close to the harpoon, also waiting on orders. And Nameless, with the firing button in his hand, surveyed the scene before him, the circling whales, the unresisting sea.

READER: Larry went Boing! when he read the words "a sacred duty."

AUTHOR: Even as spoken by the likes of Bamalford and Nameless?

READER: Even so, Larry went Boing!

AUTHOR: Lemme guess ...

READER: He's got these fantastic talents, but they're lying **fallow**, and ...

AUTHOR: And a sacred duty might call them to life.

READER: Something like that.

AUTHOR: I for one think they're out there—the sacred duties. But beware of manipulators—like Bamalford, like me.

READER: A crumb of explanation, please.

AUTHOR: Suppose I convinced you and Larry that you have a sacred duty to burn all known copies of Fulano's book. That would ...

READER: That would take a ton of matches. He's sold like crazy. They print his book night and day. He's in fifty-three countries. He gets his own display rack. He ...

AUTHOR: OK, OK, it was just an example.

Chapter 66: THE DIDACTIC BEASTS

For Nameless it didn't get much better than this, a chance to take down the mightiest of creatures, to bag the trophy of a lifetime—all through a daring night attack. One thing, though, was chiseling away at his happiness. "I wanted to **savor** the moment," he said indignantly, "to draw it out, but they keep rushing me."

> **savor** (verb): to enjoy the taste of; to take a slow, deliberate delight in something
> **prow**: the front-most part of a ship; the jutting nose of a ship, formed by the two sides running together

There was no missing his reference. *Jack's Equator*, under full sail, was swinging about for another run through the whales. Lumps and his grandfather were at the **prow**, and the old man was ready again—as best he could—to call a warning. Others on board were mobilizing as well. Darlingson looked like a buccaneer—over the railing, half down the ladder, as though daring Draco to make a close pass by the ship. And the Farnums, from somewhere, had found a length of fishing net and were rehearsing the casts by which to lay it down in the path of the *Purple Omniscience*.

> **translucent**: (1) imperfectly transparent; letting through enough light to become glowing and sometimes to show indistinctly what is on the other side; (2) transparent
> **proletarian**: related to the common working people, especially those struggling to make ends meet
> **automaton**: any sort of robot-like creature capable of carrying out tasks and commands in a mechanical, unreflecting way

Nameless gestured toward the ship, just as it went gliding across the circle of the setting moon. Against that silver backlight, the straining sails grew **translucent**.

"Spooky!" said Bamalford.

"Spooky is not the problem," answered Nameless with his usual sureness. "These people have a nasty **proletarian** cleverness, the sort you often find in the working class, and that's the problem. They're trickier than I thought, and they're rushing me. Well—let's show them what else they're rushing."

The *Purple Omniscience* came sliding down the back of a lazy comber, into an expanse of still water. Nameless saw conditions turning favorable for his shot, and a tension came into the effortless voice as he began to issue the necessary orders. "Draco—that big one, farthest out, close on it until there's about seventy yards of distance. And be very quiet about it."

He turned to Bamalford. "Now is the time—yank it." Bamalford pulled a retaining pin from the base of Little Wanda, leaving the harpoon and its cradle free to swivel. Then he dropped into a crouch, alongside some gearing that would let him control the line and tilt at which the missile would launch.

"That's good," said Nameless approvingly. "But remember—it's my kill. You are the **automaton**. I say rotate five degrees left or tilt seven downward and zip, you go five left or seven down. I'm the gunner, you are merely part of the gun."

> **complicity**: the condition of being part of a guilty activity and, often, of cooperating with others in it
> **agility**: a quick and graceful sureness in your movements
> **diminutive**: small; scaled down to a size below normal

Conditions were almost perfect now. The sea was momentarily calm, as though in **complicity** with the hunters. There was a tinge of amber and rose in the surrounding air, the first suggestion of the morning light, and already enough to compensate for the vanishing moon. Most importantly, *Jack's Equator*, for all its **agility**, was still too far off to cause any trouble for the next two or three minutes.

As instructed, Draco piloted his boat quietly, slowly out toward the whale that Nameless had indicated, and took up position about sixty or seventy yards from it. The bad time was not far off.

"Why do we have to watch this?" said François in a sad voice. She was by herself at the railing. She looked small and frail. Slumping from exhaustion and with a dread pressing heavily on her, she was for the moment a **diminutive** figure.

Her face lifted toward the sky, and she asked quietly, "Why can't we just watch that?" High above her the first stream of sunlight had cleared the peaks and was threshing itself across the rays of the setting moon. At this moment the bay was still deep in shadow. The realm of light on which François gazed was distant and hopeful.

"There is even music," she whispered, "as the gold runs across the silver. Maybe if I just stay ..."

She brought her fist down on the railing. "No ma'am! Back to earth! You can't just abandon Merci. She's too young, she's the one who mustn't watch." Then she struck her fist against the railing again, and this second blow was as strange as the first, delivered in a curious, floating way.

> **expurgation**: the process of cleaning up a book, speech, etc., by pulling out any indecent or otherwise offensive material

Merci was some distance off, with Rachel, and when François caught sight of her she called in a voice that was scarcely a murmur, "You don't watch, Merci—we'll do the **expurgation** thing, OK? I'll watch, I'll tell you what's happening, but the really ugly things get screened out, OK? Like when we were kids and there was that nest on the ground."

At the base of the railing someone had forgotten a telescope, and François took it and trained it on the hunters. "Please, Merci," she begged softly, "I'm covering it now, OK? I'll tell it to you. Bamalford is making these tiny corrections on the aim, and Draco's doing something on the throttle to hold the boat steady. And Nameless, dear inhuman Nameless ... Oh Merci, please don't look at that face. It's got this little smile and it's **devoid** of any pity, any ... Ahh! Ahh!"

It was a cry of pain. She had seen the hands of Nameless twitch and squeeze against the firing button which they held. The harpoon had launched. With a soft kick against its cradle it had shot out toward the whale, riding a small streak of flame. François instinctively closed her eyes. The intense fatigue reached for her, grasped at her, but she pushed it back. When she looked again, she saw in the wide circle of the telescope how ... she had misjudged the situation completely. Things were not as they had seemed.

"Can you believe it, Merci?" There was a note of relief now in her murmuring voice. "The whole thing ... it's an art event. Because, look. The circle I see—that's the world. And though I hadn't noticed before, the world is a **collage**—clips and photos, images, graphics. There are watercolors of the sun and the moon, pinned up near the top. There's a cutout of this schoolgirl with red hair—I'm sure that's Little Wanda. And off to the side I see sketches of animals—the basic big ones. Now, sister—Wanda combs her red hair, and sets out. She's going across the world—toward the animals. But that's OK, you know, because ..."

An outcry was rising up from the ship. It hung like a high plume, trembling in the air, and for François it was the fear and grief of Merci.

"It really is OK," she went on gently. "Wanda needs to walk across the world because ... she's a schoolgirl. The world is the school. And the big animals—maybe you guessed, Merci—they are the books. See—the rhino is math—numbers and signs all over his flanks. The giraffe has a very long sentence on his neck—I think he's grammar. And so forth, and so forth. Wanda reads them, she calls them her **Didactic** Beasts. And another thing—what a fast walker she is—she has almost crossed the world now. She's getting very close to ... a whale, but just to read it, Merci, just to read its lesson. It has a little poem written on it, just one line, maybe just the title, 'Love or Stupid,' and ..."

The morning calm was shattered with a horrible sound. "Love or Stupid! They painted on my whale! It's a flawed trophy!" The choking, furious voice, with nothing of velvet in it, was that of Nameless. And even before he had flung his binoculars to the deck in rage, another sound was telling the rest of the story. It was like a little bar of music, bright and **skittering**—a million notes struck all at once on a hard, melodious surface. It was the sound of metal on ceramic.

The harpoon had been brilliantly shot, catching the whale just behind the eye. That was the point where its body started to curve in a deep arc, and was also the point where this whale—unlike most whales—bore the handwritten message Love or Stupid. It was a brilliant shot, but in the hard, receding ceramic there was no entry, even for Little Wanda's razor tip. The harpoon was conducted glancing and chattering into the graceful arc, the perfect half-circle around which Martin had formed the whale's body—and was conducted out again. Now it was hurtling in exactly the reverse direction of that along which Nameless had fired it.

To his credit, he saw the danger at once, and shrieked to Draco, "Gun it, fool, gun this tub." Draco, however, was running an instant behind. He had always been something of an **aesthete**, and now, realizing that the whale was a giant sculpture, he had lost himself for the briefest moment in the contemplation of its artistic claims. It was only a moment, but it was all he had, and when he did hear Nameless screaming the warning for a second time and did slam the throttle, the result was disastrous. The boat lurched forward squarely into the path of the returning harpoon, and what would have been a slanting shot to the bow, possibly glancing away, now became a direct hit at midship. There the angles were square and deadly, and in the gleaming hull of the *Purple Omniscience*, two or three feet above the waterline, Little Wanda ripped a gaping hole.

> **flaccid**: limp and slumping; too weak to maintain standard firmness
> **lachrymose**: disposed to shed tears; easily weeping

sever: to cut clean through an object, dividing it into separate pieces or separating a part from the main mass

The boat rocked wildly under the impact. The three hunters were thrown to the deck, as the whaling horn gave one short honk and fell silent again. After a moment of confusion Bamalford and Draco struggled awkwardly to their feet, but Nameless lay like a rag doll, a **flaccid** heap, with one arm bent under his back. A large coil of rope was across his chest. "You're so selfish," he screamed at Bamalford. "Help yourself up, and don't even think of anyone else. Do you suppose I can get this rope off by myself?"

Bamalford had barely stretched out a hand to his master, when Draco demanded their attention. He was looking over the side. "See what they've done to my boat—a big hole, a very ugly hole." There was a sob in his voice, suggesting that tears would soon follow.

"Like we've got all day to be **lachrymose**," shouted Nameless. "On the throttle now, crybaby, and get us to shore before the big hole lets in the big water!"

"The throttle," said Draco with another sob, "is now an ornament, nothing more. Because—look what else they did to my boat." He walked to the other side and pointed. Little Wanda was sticking out. The tip and part of the shaft had pierced through the hull, from the inside out, before Wanda's force was spent. Even worse, the harpoon was draped with a mass of torn wires.

"She **severed** most of the wiring," groaned Draco. "Just like a knife. Nothing works. There's no ignition. We're a big purple rowboat."

"Then start rowing!" commanded Nameless in a high shriek. "You and Bamalford. If we're going to sink, let's sink on shore and not get wet!"

plebeian: not sophisticated or upper-class; commonplace and often rather rough and basic
exhortation: speech which tries to stir you up and encourage you to do something, but which does not command you
succor: help or relief that is administered in response to an emergency or other distress

Draco was pushing his fists into his forehead. He was still at the point of tears. "Sir—don't be angry. But when you are a very sophisticated enforcement vessel, with gear most boats can only dream of, you don't carry something so **plebeian** as ... oars."

Nameless bent and picked up his binoculars from the deck—solely to smash them down again. "We have exactly one thing left on this wreck that works—that stupid horn. So you and Bamalford get back on that thing and belt out an international distress signal. Because I am in distress."

"Sir, if you wouldn't mind," began Draco apologetically, but he got no further. In a withering tone Nameless made clear that his request was more than mere **exhortation**. "It's not like I'm just urging you clowns to blow that horn. I'm ordering you! Now!"

The horn was independent of the boat's electrical system, and was still working. Bamalford scrambled to pressurize the air chamber, and Draco began pulling desperately on the stops. Something between a quack and a bleat, and more complicated than either, came wavering out. It failed to bring rescue or **succor** of any sort, but it wasn't totally without effect. The whales found it intriguing, and much more agreeable than the earlier blaring to which they had been subjected. A stir of curiosity ran through them. They had been circling around Martin's ceramic masterwork, but now they abandoned it and began to move toward the strange sound. Bamalford and Draco played on: their orders were to play the horn, and that is what they did, even as the whales drew ever closer.

> **desist**: to stop doing some action, often before it has come to a natural completion
> **contort**: to twist or jerk something into an unnatural form

Nameless, for his part, was no longer thinking straight. He was staring out to sea with glassy eyes, still searching the horizon for a rescuer. It was only when he noted an immense whale forehead pushing toward him through the water, and not far off by any means, that he screamed frantically to Bamalford and Draco, trying again and again to make himself heard by them above the strange music of the horn. "Stop! We're going ... Stop, you idiots, we're going to get ... Stop and **desist**, we're going to get a huge tidal ..."

The two of them, staring dumbly, failed to grasp the point even when they caught the words. Draco stammered, "Tidal as in tidal wave, is that it, sir? Something on the weather station, I'll bet, or ..."

Nameless was becoming too mad to speak. His anger wound him up like a watch spring. Without warning, his body **contorted** itself in a weird hop, and for a split second he was airborne as his knees jerked up, pulling his feet several inches off the ground. Then, snapping out straight again, he stamped savagely against the deck. "Look there!" He spit out the words with great effort, pointing toward the whales.

> **inconsequential**: of small significance; not making much of a difference
> **aggregate** (noun): the total mass or quantity that results from pooling together all the distinct instances or occurrences of something
> **concert**: the deliberate coordination of actions to achieve some unified effect

The beasts had begun plowing heavily and repeatedly through the waters around the *Purple Omniscience,* and waves were starting to slide at the boat from every direction. They weren't the tidal waves Nameless had feared, but they were tall enough that their caps came spilling into the gash which Wanda had torn in the hull. The amount of water poured in by any single wave was **inconsequential**. In the **aggregate**, though, the effect was ruinous—the hold of the *Purple Omniscience* was slowly flooding, and the distance between her deck line and the surface of the sea was shrinking toward zero.

The proud boat was going down, and her proud crew was no longer working in perfect **concert**. Nameless was yanking cards out of his wallet and mumbling about "the roadside assistance number." Draco kept flapping his arms, as he tried to shoo off the whales. And every few seconds Bamalford roared up at Povano and those with him, "You amoebas are responsible for your pets. We'll see you in court."

Sallie and her team filmed it all, the *Purple Omniscience* slowly disappearing, and the three smaller boats moving out from *Jack's Equator* on their difficult mission, one for Nameless, one for Draco, and one for Bamalford.

The whales were curious for a while, as though this were the spectacle to which the horn had summoned them. They escorted the three boats, and when the mission was done, part rescue, part capture, they stayed and swam spirals around the *Purple Omniscience* as it drifted to the bottom of the clean, shallow canyon that held the waters of the bay.

> **file** (noun): a line of objects or persons, often in motion, with one following behind another
> **nomadic**: traveling around most of the time, with occasional stays here and there, but without a fixed place to live
> **spangled**: covered with a scattering of shiny, reflective bits or spots

Beyond that nothing could have kept them longer. Morning lay vast upon the ocean. The gathering light and the vanishing dark together traced out long sea roads, and the need to travel them was calling to the great creatures.

Merci watched as they passed in a stretching **file** through the northern straits and on to the open sea. Her face was intent with such obvious longing that François hugged her and asked, "**Nomadic** thoughts, Miss Dubois?" And Rachel caught her wrist with surprising strength and added, "I would go with you, Merci, and we could wander forever... except that Ricky needs me around."

The three of them fell silent, and some while went by as they gazed out to sea. Eventually a flurry of fire seemed to move above the whales. It was a brown bird, high enough in the air to brighten with the early sun. The whales themselves were still in the mountain's shadow. But as they angled northward and farther from shore—drawn on by the bird, or so it appeared—they too passed into the returning day, and the waters streaming from their backs were **spangled** with light.

READER: Larry sent this chapter to his local school board.

AUTHOR: Like, maybe it was the excessive violence?

READER: No, no—it was the Didactic Beasts. If beasts and T-shirts and bumpers and tablecloths all had little bits of learning written on them, Larry says we could close the schools.

AUTHOR: But then we would sacrifice the socializing effect.

READER: Umm …

AUTHOR: I mean, take Larry's social skills, for example. He's …

READER: Umm … you don't really wanna go there.

Chapter 67: THE HOUR OF MAGENTA

"Well," said Meagan brightly, "we're not dead."

Allen lifted his head sharply. "I was noticing the same thing, exactly the same thing."

> **impugn**: to challenge or otherwise put in question the integrity, truthfulness, competence, etc., of someone
>
> **redoubtable**: so strong, brave-spirited, resourceful, full of accomplishments, etc., as to stir respect, awe or fear

"Not to **impugn** Mr. Bamalford's honesty," added Ricky, "but maybe it was a lie when he told us that the hundredth barrel of Glinscrimion was poured into the cider. All of us were near the kettle, all of us breathed in the steam from the cider, and yet here we are—in the pink."

It was a week after Whalefest, in the late afternoon, and they were hiking to a picnic on the tableland. They could already see the smoke from the barbecue fires. Lumps and Darlingson and Bezzle had come early and built the fires in a clearing not far from the long bluff where the Mendicant Briars grew. The picnic was Tedesco's farewell—his departure to Brazil was the following day—and all those who knew him were making the climb up Victoria Road to the stony meadow.

Grandma Dubois was at the back of the column, with the mayor and Peter Oakum. To cross the meadow the three of them left the road and threaded their way through the complex tracery of rushing water that the Bad Pony made there. "Awesome old lady," whistled Peter as they finished their trek and entered the clearing.

"**Redoubtable** old gentleman farmer," she said, repaying the compliment.

They turned to Mayor Povano, to bring him into the nonsense, but his expression said that something was not well. "Mayor P," cried Peter, "what a vacant, unhappy look. And here in this place that you love, with an enchanted twilight soon to descend and the Bad Pony running in its many streams. Where have you gone?"

Grandma stepped lightly on the mayor's toes. "The new witch, eh Marion? It was a bit of a shock."

> **genre**: a particular form of literary expression (for example, love sonnets, space novels)
>
> **malediction**: the act of calling down evil on someone; a curse

484

On the ascent, approaching the footbridge—the first of the fallen bridges to be repaired—they had passed Ms. Framley leaning against the very rock where long ago Serquiella had written her strange curses. "New and nasty," the big lady had screeched at them, waving a tablet. "I have found my **genre**, the perfect literary form—curses, fresh curses on all of you!"

Now Grandma stepped a little harder on Povano's toes. "Old mayor man—do you really think our sun will be darkened with new curses? When did Victoria ever come up with anything new? Her output will just recycle Serquiella's—you know, faulty clocks instead of inaccurate weights, some grief with nine times nine instead of ten times ten. Nothing we haven't already dealt with, fundamentally."

Povano smiled weakly. "Why a grown man should be rattled by some silly **maledictions**—the ancient ones of Serquiella or the modern ones of Victoria—is beyond me. It's rather humbling. But I'm better now, Grandma, thank you."

"Then come along. The children are having an **animated** conversation about death. I'm sure we can crash it."

The conversation of the "children"—which in fact was about the one-hundredth barrel of Glinscrimion and whether Bamalford had really poured it into the Whalefest cider—had turned electric. Rachel was now the center of it. Ricky was staring at her with astonishment. "So that was the second thing. I only got to hear your first thing that night, and this was what I missed. Rach—you are like a ... a no-coupons-accepted thriller."

"I would call that news," cried Allen. "Barrel number one hundred gets rolled, into a gorseberry bush, a lechuguilla cactus, whatever. That's definitely news."

Ms. Jensen grabbed Martin by his collar. "Did you hear that, Michelangelo? Bamalford lied. Barrel number one hundred wasn't poured into the cider. It just rolled off the scene. I was there that day—we were gathering the plant for your blue dye, on Cape Magdalena. There were two food trucks that stopped on the road below, and a beer truck. The drivers took samples from

485

their cargoes—don't call it **pilfering**, there was some paperwork—and they threw a picnic. They had cookies and chips, salami, olives and so on. And they had a small keg of beer—or at least that's what they thought. But this darling child Rachel—and may I never be on her list—was upset. For her, the trucks were a plague, infesting Dropanchor, loading it with drinks and munchies. This would eventually **subvert** the festival—I think that is what she felt— subvert it and undercut its spirit. So ..."

"So our little **vigilante** took the law into her own hands." Merci caught up the thread of the story. "I was there too that day, and it all makes sense now. She spied on the drivers setting up their picnic, and when they went to see the whales she crept down the slope and rolled their keg into the brambles. And probably saved their young lives—because that was no keg of beer. And neither was any of the other ninety-nine kegs riding on that truck."

> **bureaucratic**: (said of organizations, government agencies, etc.) characterized by a complex structure of departments and chiefs, and by procedures that are rigid and overly complicated
> **magenta**: a color which appears to blend in itself purple and red
> **revelry**: loud, high-spirited partying or celebration

With a wide smile she knelt down by Rachel and made the girl's braids stand up like two horns. "Little monster—if you thought those trucks were a threat to Whalefest, then your duty was to come to city hall, fill out a twelve-page form, get it notarized, submit it to nine different departments, and then wait several years for some action to be taken. That is the correct **bureaucratic** way in these matters, young lady."

Rachel gave one of her exaggerated blinks, and began to swirl a little knot in Merci's hair. "I feel a lot better," she said. "I finally told Ricky the second thing."

Ricky gave her a long look. "I hate to ask this, but is there a third thing?"

Rachel seemed not to hear the question, and then suddenly she laughed and blurted, "Look what I did to the sun."

By this hour the sun was sinking swiftly behind a ridge to the west. It had grown swollen and plum-colored, and the warm flame of its light penetrated everywhere, calling out the reds and purples in the stony mountain flanks. "The Hour of **Magenta**," murmured Povano.

"Sir!" responded Peter Oakum briskly. "You said something?"

"The Hour of Magenta," repeated Povano in a firmer voice. "Or at least that's what I call it, Peter, and let me have my way on this one. This twilight is tinted like the wine we had on our trip—do you remember, many years back— to the fishing villages in Portugal. It is a twilight in which everything appears so ... so ... Oh, blast it, what is that word?"

While the mayor struggled to recall the word, everyone observed a respect-ful pause, even though you could see Peter Oakum working to hold a grin safely under control.

Povano tried again. "It makes everything appear so ... so ... well ... so big!"

There was a general groan. "Marion," said Grandma severely, "the **revelry** was interrupted, the party creatures were silenced, for a full minute to let you hunt for the forgotten word. And it turns out to be that extremely challenging specimen—'big'?"

"Big like ... grand ... heroic," he struggled. "Like any moment a band of heroes might appear, to begin a vast labor of ... of ... Oh, blast it, what is that word?"

This time no one waited. "Mayor," laughed Meagan, "they sound like the giants that Ricky is always dreaming about."

Povano laughed in turn. "With all due respect to Ricky and his dreams ..."

"Wow, I had one last night!" exclaimed Ricky, jumping up.

"Who is this boy?" cried Grandma.

"He's a case," said Meagan. "To cope with the school year ending, he has mentally reconstructed reality—the universe is now an extension of Room 401. That's where he felt safe, where he could blurt when he wanted to blurt, and tell his giant dreams when he chose." She gave the explanation with a shrug, as though to say—there is little we can do.

> **mediate**: to go between two opposed persons or groups, working to bring them closer together
> **unfathomable**: too deep or complex to be understood
> **euphoric**: experiencing a profound contentment or sense that all is well

"Thank you, Meags," said Ricky graciously, "for **mediating** between my **unfathomable** weirdness and the world of normal people. Anyway, it starts off with Mr. Ironbane. I dreamed he had a mission—to put a railing along the edge of the fire shaft, to ..."

Ironbane had been cutting a watermelon into oversized slices, but at the sound of his name he turned and said, "Highly honored, of course, by the star-ring role. And highly **euphoric** if in fact we could put a railing by the caul-dron. I've been up there now, and it's a dramatic place—with surprisingly good air, at least when barrels aren't going over the edge. With that long slope, I think it wants to be a theater, a very simple, minimal theater. But the slope is scary too, and the first thing would have to be a railing. If we could pull that off, I for one would beam with contentment. So how did I do it in the dream, Ricky?"

amnesty: a government program that pardons a group of people, sometimes on the condition that they now perform an action (such as paying a tax) that they failed to perform when they should have
stratagem: a clever and deceitful scheme you follow, or tactic you use, to gain some objective
postulate (noun): a basic proposition or rule which you take as true and beyond question, and which is the foundation of some science, code of conduct, etc.

"First, sir, you tried to finance it yourself. Your approach was quite clever. To begin with, you noted that Mr. Bezzle had declared a general **amnesty** on library fines."

"Ha!" cried Bezzle, who was manning one of the barbecue pits. "So you think the new Maurice is soft on crime!"

"Gormph!" said Ricky, continuing. "After some scrounging, Mr. Ironbane, you found that indeed you had an aging overdue—*The Million-Mile Logger*."

"Where angels fear to tread!" groaned Meagan, glancing over at Bezzle.

It appeared, however, that the new Maurice was still OK, so Ricky went on. "You went to the library, sir, and Mr. Bezzle confirmed that the fine owing on your book had risen to $57,000, and in keeping with the amnesty, sir, he canceled that amount. But when you held out your hand to receive the money, he looked amused and asked if you were the Million-Mile Con Man."

"A brilliant maneuver, nonetheless," exclaimed Ironbane, with his own look of amusement. "If that **stratagem** had worked ... Oh well—so what did I do next to get a railing by the fire shaft?"

"Suddenly there was a suggestion box," said Ricky, "and you hiked up to it and dropped one in. And the big lizard did the review. 'Only if,' he kept muttering in a lizardy manner, 'it's consistent with the **postulates**.' I think he meant postulates of mountain management—if there are such things—some unquestioned principles. Anyway, he sat with your suggestion, sir, for a long while in the moonlight, and at last grumbled, 'Very well—minimum disturbance, maximum incorporation of natural features, and so on and so forth. The postulates will be alright. Let him have his railing.' And he puffed out his throat like bubble gum. This was a signal, telling the giants to go ahead and put a man on the job."

indiscreet: barging right ahead in speech or action without being alert to the sensitivities of others or the delicacies of the situation
tenacity: the act or habit of holding tightly and stubbornly to some position or value
cranny: a crack, notch, or other small fault that interrupts a smooth surface

"Hey," broke in Lumps, "lob the fat one, why don't you? You mean to put a giant on the job, don't you think?"

"Funny you mention that," answered Ricky slowly. "It was a giant that eventually came striding up with a long steel bar. A giant of sorts, I should say—it was you, Lumps! And the steel bar, which of course was intended for service as a railing, came from ... from ... Well, maybe I'm being **indiscreet** by getting onto that. If you ..."

"That's OK," murmured Lumps. "It's not like some state secret. And Tedesco was there too, he was part of it."

"Speaking of whom," said Ricky, "where is the Cabbage? He went for a last climb on the bluff, to see the briars, and ..."

"And was carried off by gobblings, to marry the princess," called a voice. It was Tedesco himself, hiking alongside one of the crooked streams of the Bad Pony. "When I return to Dropanchor, Ricky," he went on, "I'm coming at once to see these briars. There's so much ... **tenacity**. They won't give up. They grow in the little cuts and pockets in the rock ... how do you say?"

"**Crannies**," said Ricky. "Definitely crannies."

"Then they grow in crannies, so stubborn. It is a good skill. But what is going on here?"

"Cabbage," said Ricky, "we were saying what a perfect husband you would be for a goblin princess. Besides that I was telling this dream about Lumps. A very strange dream. He was carrying a long steel bar which had not always been ..."

Tedesco lifted his head in surprise. "This steel bar is not just a thing of your dreams, Ricky. There is a very nice story ... except ..."

Sensing the hesitation, and glancing for a moment toward Lumps, Ricky broke in. "A very nice story, and fortunately for us the hero of it has already cleared it for release."

So Tedesco began. "On that morning you know—I was in the boat that picked up Mr. Bamalford. Of the three boats, it was the smallest, and after it came back to the ship and Bamalford was taken out, I was looking at it for a minute, and thinking. Then Lumps was there—all of a sudden he is telling me, very quietly, 'You can't handle this boat alone, and you probably can't open the cage alone. I will come with you.'"

> **surmise** (noun): a careful guess, made when the evidence is too thin to support a firm conclusion
> **clairvoyant**: able to see things beyond the perception of most of us, such as the inner thoughts and feelings of others
> **inadvertence**: (1) a careless failure to pay attention to some matter; (2) a mistake resulting from such a failure

People fell silent. The story had been guessed at, but now there was no further need for **surmise**, as Tedesco continued. "I am—you know—astonished. Lumps is **clairvoyant**. Maybe he does not read books, but he has read perfectly what I am thinking. And he is right—by myself I cannot do it. So we take the boat, the two of us, and row it in through the surf. That is not easy, and pulling it onto the beach is not so simple either. We get pretty wet. We are shivering, because the bay is still in shadow. But on the top of Cape Stairstep the sun is up, warming up everything, and that is where we arrive in just a few more minutes. The doors into the Dome are open—this is very good luck. The rays of the sun are shining into that corridor, do you remember, the one that makes that long curve. From the outside you cannot see the cage, but we run like crazy people and soon we are beside it—and the brown duck."

He was interrupted by a soft Whoops! Bezzle was so caught in the story that he had forgotten the barbecue and it had started to blaze up. Smiling sheepishly, and making little finger signs to guarantee there would be no more **inadvertence**, he sprinkled back the flame.

> **inaudible**: not able to be heard; outside the range of hearing
> **parameters**: the limits and ranges within which some organism, system, program, etc., performs or is expected to perform
> **apex**: a peak; high point, crowning point; as, for example, the crowning point arrived at in the growth or development of something

Tedesco went on. "You remember the cage—how they made it with a single rod of steel, very thick, like from a railroad track. OK, maybe that is an exaggeration—but the steel is very thick, and the cage is very locked. And I cannot find the key. I am going crazy, but it does not appear. So I am searching all around for it, and then I start to hear this sound. Very low, almost **inaudible**, but with great power—like when the locomotive, it is first straining to pull the cars."

He saw the smile forming on Meagan's face, and had to smile in return. "I do like trains, yes—they are in all of my comparisons. Anyway—it is Lumps, pulling on one of the bars of the cage. Pulling like nothing I have ever seen. His arms are like cables of wire. The sweat is running from his forehead. He is the bull, the *touro*. He is far beyond the normal human limits, way outside the human ... human ..."

"**Parameters**," volunteered Ricky. "Go on, Cabbage."

"At that moment," resumed Tedesco, "I am standing where the corridor opens into the big hall, where the sun is reflected down so strangely by those pyramids of glass ... in blocks, in pillars. And that is where I stay. Even when there is another groan, a very deep one, I do not go and help. It is a great and private struggle. He finds more strength somewhere, he pulls against the

490

bar...and now it is bending. I swear by all my family whom I see very soon—it is bending. With some shaking in the arms, he bends it all the way down. And then he looks toward where I am standing. But it is not me that he is seeing—this I can tell, I don't know how. And he finds some peace. And after that nothing can stop him. When the third bar, maybe the fourth one, is bending down, the duck comes out."

There was a little pause. The story had risen to its **apex**, the solemn moment that closed out the tale of the imprisoned duck in a better way than anyone had dared hope. Yet something in Tedesco's look said it is hard to remain solemn for long when there's a duck in the story. "It waddles out," he resumed, "it flaps out, I don't know, it is such a funny thing. But it comes out and it stares at Lumps a bit. Then it jumps on his wrist, still looking at him, although sideways. He tells it softly, 'No more cages, my friend.' It gives a loud honk and bites his wrist, a little bite, a kiss, something. He cannot help laughing for a second, and he says to the bird, 'You had better talk with Uncle Tedesco, and tell him we don't need the key.'"

Tedesco was laughing now too. "So then the duck is on my wrist, also doing the bite that is a kiss. It is a beautiful creature. After a long time I say to it very gently that it must get a life, but it stays on my arm."

> **parasite**: an organism fixing itself permanently to some other living thing and drawing nutrition from it
> **vocational**: related to the professions, trades or other fields of work for which you can prepare yourself
> **novice**: one who is just beginning to learn some profession or way of life

"If it's still there," declared Allen, "we're going to do an article—Duck Turns into **Parasite**, Complicates Return Flight of Exchange Student."

Tedesco checked his arm. "No—because I told Lumps that he should do the whale sounds, to remind the bird of its occupation, always flying ahead of the whales."

Allen still thought there was a story. "Boy Offers **Vocational** Guidance to Duck. That'll sell."

"Anyway," Tedesco went on, "Lumps is very shy about this. He thinks his whale calls never work. But I encourage him. I say that it is always tough in the beginning, when you are still a **novice**, and I tell him that he is improving quickly. So at last he does a call, a beautiful one. The duck raises its head, looking around. You can see in its eyes, something is awakening. I am waiting, it is waiting, then there is this pain in my wrist—it is saying good-by. It goes with a loud honk, flying into the main hall and following the sunlight up through an opening high in the dome."

Merci interrupted. "And Lumps freaked with joy, I bet, because his whale calls work—at least on ducks."

> **ecstatic**: feeling a joy so intense that it lifts you above ordinary worries and concerns
> **propensity**: a compelling tendency (often part of your basic makeup) toward some particular activity

Lumps caught the faint smile, and knew that this was as close as Merci could get to saying let's end hostilities. He called back to her, "I was **ecstatic**, you got that one. And another thing, wart girl, now that the lines of communication are open—I'm learning to read. All of a sudden I'm old enough."

She laughed. "I can help if you want, really. Reading is important around here—even the animals have stuff written on 'em."

"The giraffes and their sentences!" It was Tedesco, in a tone of admiration. "I will miss this place of dreamers. Ricky dreams by night and Allen dreams by day. And François—you are the most incredible because you have the dream about the beasts and the words, and you are not even sleeping."

"That is a charitable spin," said François, smiling warmly, "on what is really an alarming **propensity** to tune out every time there's trouble. I'll be seeking professional help from Meags, that's what I'll be doing. But you, Tedesco, you should finish your story. What happened next after the Harbinger Duck flew away?"

> **industrious**: working steadily, resourcefully, and with much energy
> **melancholy** (adjective): marked by a depression or sadness that is often brooding and given over to thought
> **uxorious**: (usually said of husbands) attending with excessive care to each little wish and command of one's wife

Tedesco smiled. "What happened next—Lumps went to sleep, right on the floor, by the ruined cage. I thought he would sleep all day, but after five minutes he jumped and said, 'We need Darlingson. He's not a napper, he's the most **industrious** guy in existence, and he won't rest until the work is done.' We found Darlingson at the docks—the ship was in by this time, and secured—and he came with us at once, carrying some hammers and safety things, back to the Dome. Once they started, the two giants, the noise was like … well"—he glanced apologetically at Meagan—"many locomotives, of course. They worked a long time, four or five hours, but when they finished, the cage was not there anymore, there was only a piece of steel, a long, straight bar."

"And now Ricky has dreamed what it's for," declared Lumps. "And we'll even install it there at the fire shaft—Darlingson and I—unless we could leave it at your door, Ricky, while you're sleeping, and in the next dream you get someone to do the job."

Ricky gave a **melancholy** smile. "Don't know if Sallie does installations. Because my next dream will probably be a Sallie dream. I really miss that girl—perhaps you noted my melancholy smile. I sent her away, and that was the right thing, but ... but it tears at a man."

"Ricky!" cried Joannie sternly. "Of all the brass. You sent her away! Hah! She has a career—she has to move on to other places. She ..."

"Five years," broke in Ricky, with a lazy waggle of his finger. "I told her we need a cooling-down period of five years or so."

Joannie was nearly speechless. "Like ... like she was already pricing gowns!"

Ricky went on calmly. "I told her that life is really big and I need to ride the wave for a while. Once we're married, though, that won't happen, because then she will get every last ounce of my attention, I promise. That's just how I will be, the most **uxorious** husband ever, bringing her little crackers with imported cheese, polishing the little hologram thing on her credit cards, and so on. So before that begins I need five years. I have some big ideas."

Joannie saw the risk. "Ricky, please understand, I'm not asking about your big ideas. I have another question, but it's not about the big ideas, OK? Just tell me—what happens after five years?"

> **hinterland**: an isolated, undeveloped area, far from the centers of political and cultural activity, and usually inland from the coast
> **unprecedented**: bearing no similarity to anything that has gone before; occurring on a scale or magnitude not encountered before
> **ancillary**: performing some activity not for its own sake, but in a supporting role to help some other activity succeed

Ricky drew in a long, easy breath. "Thank you, Joannie. One of my favorite ideas has to do with energy transfer. At fitness centers everywhere the workout machines would be hooked to little generators. When you did your whatevers, twelve reps at a time, you would be driving the generators, which in turn would charge super-high-capacity batteries. And these would be supplied to scientific outposts in remote **hinterlands**, to serve as the power source for the parabolic telescopes and the biphasic emulsifiers and"—Ricky was starting to feel a new claim on his attention—"and the solar ovens and geothermal grills and those special pizza maker things and ..."

The theme of magenta, so conspicuous in the early twilight airs, was mixed now with an increasing portion of dusk, and the night breezes were lifting off the warm stones of the meadow, carrying rich smells from the cooking fires. There was a bubbling chili, a smoking chowder with pepper grains caught in butter slicks, a rack of enormous burgers, and even a steaming hot cheese bread baked from a recipe sent by Tedesco's mother.

493

Joannie fixed a burger and held it just out of Ricky's reach. "None for you, idea man, until my question is answered—what happens after the five-year cooling-down period?"

"That," answered Ricky, raising a hand to block his sight of the distracting burger, "is where you come in. And Calvin. And all of you. There has to be enough weird stuff accumulated in the next five years, new weird stuff—OK, so that Sallie and Uncle Reggie will take the absolutely **unprecedented** step of returning to a place they've already filmed."

"You could win your own ball game, Ricky," broke in Calvin, laughing. "I mean the way you're raving about 'biphasic emulsifiers' and so on, you could win your own game."

"I'm good, no question." Ricky had grabbed the elusive burger and was eating the bun separately. "But everyone's got to help—widespread weirdness, OK? Even you, Calvin. Think of that great argument you have with Joannie— whether your drawings are **ancillary** to her text, or her text to your drawings. It's got potential—a small civil war in the Mercurial Canyon book. Dueling titles, peevish and competing prefaces. That would be modestly strange. Uncle Reggie will call it subtle, but Sallie will like it."

> **lapse** (verb): to slip or slide, often in the sense of slipping down or back into a condition, activity, etc., that was to be avoided
> **constituents**: the persons who are represented by an elected official and to whom that official is answerable on election day
> **commensurate**: on the same scale as something else; of similar proportion or measure; roughly as small or great in degree as something else

Turning now to the Farnum twins, as though in search of yet odder stuff, Ricky made a vague, circular gesture toward the western sky, where a scatter of stars was appearing in the faint suspension of scarlet and purple that lingered there. "We know very well, do we not, my *sparnling glernths*—oh, excuse, excuse, I **lapse** now and then into the home speech—we know very well that it was not one but two commercial reps who came out from the home planet. Take note, then—the time for concealment is over. Begin to show your wares, and the stranger the better."

"*Terlone!*" said Henry Farnum, with a smart salute.

"*Terloon!*" echoed Andrew, also with a salute.

"Eee!" said Ms. Jensen, "they're gonna be in my class ..."

Ricky turned his attention now to Mayor Povano. "And you, sir, if you could assure that the civic and political life of Dropanchor remains sufficiently abnormal, I know Sallie will be grateful."

Povano gazed about with affection on his **constituents**, young and old, and then replied, "We're well staffed for that, young man. It shouldn't be a problem."

READER: Larry saw a documentary that said they're running out of hard words for the SAT.

AUTHOR: I hope they've got a back-up plan.

READER: One idea is to make up some new words. Or change the meanings of old ones. But the option finally adopted, according to Larry, is to start using words from Mars.

AUTHOR: I'm sure they thought it over carefully.

READER: They say the attention they gave the matter was **commensurate** with its gravity.

AUTHOR: That works for me.

READER: So Lare says it was a stroke of genius to put some Martian vocabulary in this chapter.

AUTHOR: Please tell him that his compliment is appreciated. And tell him also that it's been real, OK, these last sixty-seven chapters, and the same goes for you.

READER: Well—we want you to know we've both decided to keep this book after all.

AUTHOR: Harrumph—I am touched by the gesture.

READER: I mean with only twenty-seven copies in print it may get caught up by collector mania and be worth some major bucks one day.

AUTHOR: I know we'll blast by the thirty mark before long. There has to be a lot of pent-up demand. But anyway, for now, the best to all twenty-seven of you.

THE END

495